Travaux
d'Humanisme et Renaissance

N° CCXLVI

Stephen Kolsky

MARIO EQUICOLA
The real courtier

LIBRAIRIE DROZ S.A.
11, rue Massot
GENÈVE
1991

In memory of my mother
who will always be remembered

Contents

Critical premise   13

I.   Education of a secretary   17

II. Declarations of intent   61

III. In the service of Isabella d'Este 103

IV. A secretary for two masters 171

V.   The courtier's progress 227

Appendix: Notary documents concerning Mario Equicola 273

Abbreviations 289

A note on the transcription of Italian and Latin documents 290

Bibliography:

A. The letters of Mario Equicola 291

B. Equicola's manuscript works 318

C. Equicola's printed works 319

D. Works of doubtful or uncertain attribution 322

Select Bibliography 323

Index 337

Acknowledgements

My first debt of gratitude must go to Conor Fahy who put me on to Mario Equicola as a post-graduate student in the University of London. The original thesis was read by John Woodhouse, Giovanni Aquilecchia, Christopher Cairns and Cecil Clough, all of whom made valuable comments about ways to improve the text. John Gatt-Rutter made useful criticisms which enabled me to make certain points clearer. I owe a debt of profound gratitude to Dennis Rhodes who shared with me his precious bibliographical information on Equicola. Denise Ryan has been of invaluable assistance in the preparation of the book — her linguistic and bibliographical skills have been of great service to me.

My work on Equicola would not have been possible without the generous assistance of the staff of the Archivio di Stato in Mantua. I wish to thank, in particular, Anna Maria Lorenzoni, whose patience and scholarship prevented me from making many errors in the transcriptions of Equicola's letters. I received advice from Giancarlo Schizzerotto, Director of the Biblioteca Comunale in Mantua which was of great assistance to me. Other libraries and archives, namely the British Library, the John Rylands Library in Manchester, the Biblioteca Apostolica Vaticana, the Biblioteca Nazionale in Rome, the Marciana in Venice, the Biblioteca Nazionale Universitaria in Turin, the Archivio di Stato and the Biblioteca Estense in Modena, provided essential support.

The book could not have been completed without additional research involving further visits to Italy. My gratitude is due to the British Academy which awarded me a small research grant in 1981; and to the generosity of the Faculty of Arts of the University of Melbourne in financially supporting my research. I further wish to thank the Comunità Israelitica in Mantua for its warm hospitality during my various stays there.

Finally, I owe a great debt to the efficient and painstaking work of Ingrid Barker who prepared the manuscript for publication.

Needless to say, all errors are my own.

Melbourne, May 1988   S.D.K.

Critical premise

Mario Equicola has generally had a bad press from the critics when he has not been ignored altogether. The last twenty years of the nineteenth century saw a notable growth of interest in the Mantuan court in the age of Isabella d'Este. Foremost amongst those who studied the period were A. Luzio and R. Renier whose literary interests ensured that Equicola was not neglected. Their opinion of Equicola was extremely negative:

> La fisionomia dell'Equicola, qual ci appare nelle due medaglie che di lui si conoscono, non è molto simpatica, si direbbe di riconoscervi i tratti del servilismo. E infatti egli fu eminentemente un Cortegiano: ma nella pratica della cortigianeria, se anche non portava la *nobiltà* del Castiglione, sapeva farsi apprezzare e ben volere.[1]

---

[1] A. Luzio, R. Renier, *La coltura e le relazioni letterarie di Isabella d'Este Gonzaga*, Turin, 1903, for the impressive array of information concerning those humanists and writers who had contacts with Isabella d'Este.

Equicola had not been entirely neglected by earlier scholarship. Tiraboschi, for example, includes him as one of the intellectuals associated with the Gonzagas (*Storia della letteratura italiana*, VII, iii, Florence, 1812, pp. 967-69). Svevo, surprisingly, has Equicola as one of the characters in his first literary work *Ariosto governatore* (for which see S. Kolsky, «Italo Svevo and Mario Equicola: A strange encounter», *MLN*, 102 (1987) 128-40).

For a rather superficial survey of contemporary views of Equicola consult S.C. Vial, «Mario Equicola in the opinion of his contemporaries», *Italica*, 34 (1957) 202-21. Equicola's high standing as an intellectual, particularly in the learned circles of Mantua and Ferrara, is further emphasized in works not mentioned by Vial. A Ferrarese contemporary of Equicola's, for example, names him in a poem immediately after Dante and Petrarch:

> Per Equicola Mario si riserba
> Qual pel suo lume di virtù (che extingue
> ogni altro) è asceso a sì sublime grado
> Dove parer fa ciascun dotto ellingue

(Lelio Manfredi, *Poema in terza rima*, Biblioteca Trivulziana, Milan, cod. 908 L. 43, fs.40^v-41^r; on Manfredi see C. Zilli, «Notizia di Lelio Manfredi, letterato di corte», *Studi e Problemi di Critica Testuale*, 27 (1983) 39-54).

Although Manfredi was undoubtedly trying to influence Equicola, perhaps with the idea of his acting as an intermediary with the Gonzagas, nevertheless, there does seem to be a clear recognition of Equicola's abilities. The latter is mentioned again in another Ferrarese work composed by Celio Calcagnini, *Dialogi quorum titulus Equitatio ad Herculem Secundum Estensem Ducem Ferrariae Quartum* (in *Opera Aliquot*, edited by A.M. Brasavola, Basle: H. Frobenius and N. Episcopius, 1544):

> Accivi ergo ad me Marium Aequicolum virum et manu strenuum et lingua desertum et ingenio clarissimum. (p. 558)

For further details on this work see G. Savarese, *Il «Furioso» e la cultura del Rinascimento*, Rome, 1984, pp. 15-37.

It can be postulated from this that Equicola found favour with Isabella d'Este because of his courtiership skills rather than for his usefulness to her, or for any innate qualities he may have possessed. Isabella's relationship with Castiglione was quite another matter: it was nothing less than a marriage of soul-mates. [2]

At other times Luzio is even harsher in his judgement of Equicola, especially when the latter appears to be contravening his own code of moral conduct. Luzio works up a moral fury against Equicola for his role in the love-affair between the Marquis of Pescara and the otherwise unknown Delia:

> il quale [Equicola] sembra non riputasse disdicevole al suo ufficio anche l'incarico di mezzano.

Equicola's sin is all the greater because it forces the Marquis and Vittoria Colonna even further apart by driving a terrible wedge between them. [3]

Luzio wished to depict a particular society — the Mantuan court at the time of Isabella d'Este — which would serve as a reminder of Italy's glorious past. This society is peopled with heroes and heroines — an Isabella d'Este or a Castiglione — to demonstrate the virtues of the old nobility. Moreover, Isabella's court represents an indirect condemnation of the Austrian barbarian domination of northern Italy: Luzio and his generation believed that the Austrians had destroyed the foundations of Italian society. [4] Through the medium of culture, Isabella d'Este succeeds in rendering the principle of monarchical government acceptable and even inviting. Isabella represents the achievements of Italian culture at its most glorious. She and her noble servants serve as a source of inspiration to the new Italian monarchy which presides over Luzio's early studies of the Marchesana.

Luzio's view of Equicola and Isabella d'Este is one that still receives a good deal of support. Yet, paradoxically, Equicola's presence and eventual success at court renders Luzio's interpretation unlikely. The success of Equicola (and others like him) should lead to a reconsideration of the mechanisms by which the courts functioned. Luzio's blinkered vision of the Mantuan court does not take into account the point of view of an outsider whose very

---

    [2]   «Un nobilissimo spirito com'era quello di Baldassare non poteva che nutrir simpatia per la più eletta fra le gentildonne del tempo suo.» (*La coltura*, pp. 134-5).

    [3]   A. Luzio, «Vittoria Colonna», *Rivista Storica Mantovana*, vol. 1, fasc. 1-2 (1885), 1-52; the quote is to be found on p. 3 and the letters of the Marquis of Pescara to Equicola on pp. 3-8.

    [4]   This point is discussed by M. Aretta, «Lavorando con Alessandro Luzio» in M. Bianchedi (ed.), *La figura e l'opera di Alessandro Luzio*, San Severino Marche, 1957.

presence unbalances the idealized picture of court life and casts doubt on the motives of the other protagonists.

To date, only one significant attempt has been made to rehabilitate the figure of Mario Equicola in his biographical context. The monograph, written by Domenico Santoro, was intended to serve in Equicola's defence against Luzio's attacks, with the express purpose of salvaging Equicola's reputation. Santoro, from Equicola's own region, indirectly fires a shot for the *Mezzogiorno* by illustrating the debt northern Italian culture owes to a southern Italian.[5] Indeed, Santoro defends Equicola to a fault, often distorting the reality of a particular situation in his subject's favour. In spite of this, the book is still useful, especially in its attempt to throw some light on Equicola's early years before he was forced to move northwards. Other periods of his life are dealt with in a much less satisfactory manner. The information concerning his later years needed to be augmented with material from various archives in northern Italy, especially from Mantua, a place Santoro did not visit. However, the biography's gravest defect, evident in the title, lies in the strict division that Santoro makes between life and works, a defect not uncommon in this kind of writing. This division leads Santoro to neglect almost completely the intellectual side of Equicola's character and, when he does examine the works, they are seen in isolation, bereft of their context from which a large part of their significance derives. For want of anything specific to say about Equicola's works, Santoro is at times compelled to make absurd comments about them. At one point, albeit a little hesitatingly, he refers to Equicola as being a predecessor of Galileo.[6] Such a procedure is particularly inapt in Equicola's case since the majority of his works were written in response to a given historical situation or through direct commission.

When referring to Equicola's most important work, Santoro can only repeat the traditional criticisms that are directed against the *Libro de natura de amore*: its unpolished style and the overabundance of references to other works. He falls into the error of following too closely what other nineteenth-century critics had already said: twentieth-century critics fall into the same trap.[7]

---

[5]   The work is *Della vita e delle opere di Mario Equicola*, Chieti, 1906.

[6]   Santoro writes (p. 179): «Non voglio esagerare l'importanza di questo passo, ma, fatta ragion dei tempi, mi torna in mente la magnanima lotta che, in nome di quel principio stesso, sosteneva un secolo più tardi il Galilei.»

[7]   Santoro, p. 179. For example, L. Savino calls the *Libro* an 'arido trattato', suffocating to death beneath mountains of erudition (see *Di alcuni trattati e trattatisti d'amore italiani della prima metà del secolo XVI*, *Studi di letteratura italiana*, vol. X, Naples, 1914, pp. 1-101; p. 2).

Santoro's biography is the last full-scale attempt at a general study of Equicola. Although it was lacking anything approaching a satisfactory conclusion, later scholars have simply gone on adding their own footnotes instead of placing Equicola more firmly in his social and biographical context. They have preferred to concentrate on ever more specialized aspects of his sources or particular facets of his literary production. Equicola's vast erudition can be easily broken down into neat, little compartments, or in other words, into ready-made articles.[8]

One of the primary aims of a new biography of Mario Equicola should be to integrate his life and works in order to form an overall impression of the man. In Equicola's case the results of such a synthesis should be particularly fruitful since at every stage of his career his erudition played some part in the functions he was called upon to perform, either as a secretary or a tutor. This biographical study provides a detailed analysis of the actual conditions under which a court humanist functioned. The interest of such a study is increased because it will permit a close comparison with Equicola's exact contemporary, Baldassar Castiglione. Their intellectual attitudes towards the situations in which they found themselves will provide an interesting point of departure for discussion. Courtier-writers were not of necessity a homogeneous group even if they served the same master and seemed to perform the same duties. The analysis of a single courtier's career puts into a slightly different focus the other courtiers with whom *our man* came into contact. Instead of a Castiglione dwarfing his colleagues, who are then often treated in an unworthy fashion, we are faced with the opposite. A so-called minor figure casts judgement on his elders, albeit indirectly. It will be necessary to examine the cultural influences which shaped Equicola's intellectual outlook and the ways in which he had to adapt his learning to the situation he found at court. For, above all, Equicola was a courtier and it is very difficult to imagine such a person existing outside the court environment. In fact, the court is the most important influence on Equicola's character, which becomes a reflection of the predicament facing the humanist courtier.

This study aims to rectify what the present author considers the, by now, traditional picture of Equicola, using the results of detailed biographical research.

---

[8]   Studies of Equicola's source material abound but perhaps for this kind of article the chief culprit is C.P. Merlino who literally plundered the *Libro* to obtain quick results (see the bibliography for a list of his publications). It must be stated, however, that nothing like a systematic appraisal of the sources used in the *Libro* has been undertaken.

CHAPTER I

Education of a secretary

Although the early years of Equicola's life are shrouded in obscurity, it is possible to ascertain, to a certain extent, his movements and cultural contacts during his first thirty years. For these years hardly any contemporary documentation exists; we depend mainly upon what Equicola himself says about his early life in his own works, and upon chance references which occur in documents datable to his later years in Mantua. Indeed, it was from a letter found in the Archivio di Stato at Mantua that Renier was able to deduce that Equicola must have been born in or around 1470. This date is confirmed by another document which allows us to remove any doubt about 1470 being the year of Equicola's birth. [1]

The years around 1470 saw the birth of a number of the figures who were to have a decisive influence on the culture of the early sixteenth century: Machiavelli was born in 1469, Bembo in 1470 and a little later, in 1474,

---

[1]   A. Luzio, R. Renier, *La coltura*, Turin, 1903, p. 77. Another document provides confirmation of Equicola's age. It is a letter written by Equicola to Castiglione, Mantuan ambassador in Rome, in which he urges the latter to press his case in the matter of certain church benefices. The letter written from Marmirolo on 1 May 1524 expresses Equicola's ecclesiastical ambitions: «Et sia certa Sua Santità che passati lo decimo anno del suo pontificato che io harò LXIII anni...vorrò essere vescovo» (BAV, Vat.lat. 8211, f.291ʳ). If Equicola was born in 1470 he would be sixty-three in 1533, the tenth year of Clement VII's pontificate.

Earlier accounts of Equicola's life are full of inaccuracies and at times completely wrong. C. Minieri Riccio, *Biografie degli Accademici Alfonsini detti poi Pontaniani dal 1442 al 1543*, Naples, 1881 [reprinted Bologna, 1969], pp. 104-105, gets nearly every fact about Equicola's biography wrong. Other works are less noteworthy for their errors: N. Toppi, *Biblioteca napoletana et apparato a gli huomini illustri in lettere di Napoli e del regno*, Naples: Antonio Bulifon, 1678. Fol., p. 206 and L. Nicodemo, *Addizioni copiose alla biblioteca napoletana del dottor Niccolò Toppi*, Naples: Salvator Castaldo, 1683. Fol. *Ad vocem.*

E. Faccioli writing in *Mantova. Le lettere*, II, Mantua, 1962, perpetuates factual errors in Equicola's biography. In particular, he claims, without clearly indicating his evidence, that Equicola was a law student at Naples and later became Margherita Cantelmo's secretary. No evidence exists, as far as I know, that Equicola ever studied law (he is not mentioned, for example, in C. De Frede, *Studenti e uomini di leggi a Napoli nel Rinascimento. Contributo alla storia della borghesia intellettuale nel mezzogiorno*, Naples, 1957). Furthermore, Faccioli is wrong in asserting that Equicola was Margherita Cantelmo's secretary. In fact, he was her husband's secretary.

Ariosto and Isabella d'Este were born. All these figures had reached maturity when the Italian states were suffering their worst political crisis. In many ways the careers, and more particularly, the writings of these outstanding personalities were a response to the prevailing political turmoil. They all had first-hand experience of the impotence of the Italian states in the face of superior forces. It was this shared outlook that brought together the diverse reactions of intellectuals and rulers alike.

Unlike the above-mentioned figures Equicola's family background is notable for its obscurity. Compared with a Castiglione who could boast of an impressive family history, Equicola found himself on the lower rungs of the social ladder, preferring to remain silent about his family background and ambiguously taking advantage of his «connections» with a powerful baronial family in the *Regno*. However, he often mentioned his birth-place, Alvito, so much so that «di Alveto» is frequently added to his name. The last book published in his lifetime bearing his name carried this extra detail in the title of the first book: «di Mario Equicola di Alveto nel primo libro de natura de amore» (f.1^r). Towards the conclusion of the *Libro* he mentions the region in which his birth-place is to be found as part of a discussion on the language, thus indicating that it still held a place in his memory and was a continual source of pride for him:

> Et io in quel paese mi trovo haver la patria che Q. Vectio Marso, L. Papirio Fregellano, Q. Valerio Sorano et M. Tullio di Arpine produsse (*Libro*, f.239^r and Santoro, p. 13).

Thus, he implies that his region has not stopped producing noteworthy men since he himself is a native of the area. He characterizes the district in terms of its contribution to the civilization of Ancient Rome rather than in terms of any personal or family ties that bind him to the place. The obscurity of his family origins is counterbalanced by the renown that has been given to Alvito and its environs through the birth there of celebrated Romans.

The fact that Equicola frequently refers to his native village but not to his family has given rise to speculation about his origins. It has been argued that Equicola's silence over the name of his father could imply that his relationship with the Cantelmos was much closer than that of someone merely in their employ. Indeed, it has been suggested that Equicola was no less than the illegitimate son of Pietro Giampaolo Cantelmo, at one time the most powerful member of his family.[2] Furthermore, it has been alleged that Castrucci, the seventeenth-century commentator on Alvito, does not mention the name of Equicola's father because he is acting out of respect for an illustrious fellow-

---

[2]   Santoro, pp. 17-21; P. Rajna, «Per chi studia l'Equicola», *GSLI*, 67 (1916) 360-75; in particular pp. 372-73.

citizen and the families concerned.[3] All kinds of hypotheses could be thought up in order to explain the difficulty in identifying and locating Equicola's father. They would have to account for the absence of the father. One such hypothesis could run as follows: Equicola's father died when his son was very young and his mother entrusted him to the Cantelmos for whom he became almost an adopted son. Another and perhaps more sinister proposal would be to suggest that Giampaolo Cantelmo made Equicola's mother pregnant while she was still married to her husband and the matter was hushed up out of respect for the latter. Given the lack of documentation it seems unlikely that the truth will be discovered.

To strengthen the view that Equicola was related to various noble families through the Cantelmo connection, Ferdinando d'Avalos, Marquis of Pescara has been suggested as a possible relative. In this case, the argument carries a large degree of persuasion. The evidence consists of a number of letters written by the Marquis to Equicola whom he addresses as his «parente più che caro». However, it is interesting to note that the Marquis of Pescara only called Equicola «parente» in those letters which referred to Delia, one of Isabella d'Este's ladies-in-waiting, with whom the Marquis was in love. On all other occasions, as far as can be judged from the letters in the *Archivio Gonzaga* (that is, when the subject-matter was political or military), the Marquis addressed him as «Magnifico Signor Maryo».[4] This peculiarity provided Luzio with the opportunity to explain away the family ties between the two, by asserting that Delia was Equicola's relative and not the Marquis'. Luzio refused to believe that his «unworthy» Equicola could be related in any way to his «noble but misguided» Marquis. Santoro, on the other hand, focussed attention on the Marquis' own statement which indicates that they shared a common parentage:

> Caro parente, se la conformità de lo animo, lo istinto naturale tanto conforme in servire Delya, el sangue da una origine procedente, jovaranno in farve conoscere li affetti del animo myo, certa speranza tengo essere da vuy meglio conoscyuto che da me... (Luzio, «Vittoria Colonna», p. 4).

---

[3]   Santoro, p. 18; G.P.M. Castrucci, *Descrittione del Ducato d'Alvito nel Regno di Napoli in Campagna Felice*, Naples, C. Cavallo, 1686, 8°. In this work, Castrucci gives a very brief summary of Equicola's achievements: «Mario Equicola d'Alvito che lungo dimorò con Francesco Gonzaga, Marchese di Mantova, e scrisse con molto elegante stile, in lingua volgare, le vite de' Signori Gonzaghi, l'Historie di Mantova, di Natura d'amore e altre dottissime opere, molto honorato da tutti i Prencipi del suo tempo e dalla Republica Venetiana, da quali riportò molte scritture e lettere de quelli conservati dalla Famiglia Prudentii, successori di quello per parte di Donna» (pp. 41-42). Apart from Castrucci's vagueness about Equicola's life, he is also inaccurate: he makes no mention of Isabella d'Este, the person with whom he was most closely associated before Federico Gonzaga, and Castrucci is muddled about Equicola's works.

[4]   A. Luzio, «Vittoria Colonna», p. 7 n. 1. Here the two types of letter are neatly juxtaposed.

Notwithstanding the Marquis' convoluted syntax, there is little doubt that he was acknowledging Equicola as a blood relative. However, the vagueness of the Marquis' assertion, together with the difficulty of finding corroborative evidence, means that any attempt to be more precise about how they were related can only be speculation for the present.[5]

Santoro tried his utmost to raise Equicola's status so that he would not be at a disadvantage in the most elect circles. It would be easy to accept Santoro's genealogical tree if it were not for certain awkward factors which must be considered. This particular game of genealogical gymnastics depends on one essential fact, namely that Equicola himself was a member of the Cantelmo family, perhaps even an illegitimate son of Pietro Giampaolo.[6] The argument becomes yet more complicated if, as has been suggested, Equicola's real surname was not Cantelmo but something quite different. Caccialupi is the suggestion which carries the most weight.[7] In fact, there exists a document of a fairly early date which supports this theory. It is an oath of loyalty to the French king sworn by various Neapolitan barons in 1496. Amongst the conspirators should have been Pietro Giampaolo Cantelmo but, being unable to attend, he sent in his stead his two sons, Ferrante and Sigismondo, with a statement of his loyalty to the conspiracy: «Ho facto fare la presente a *Mario de Cacalupis de Albeto*, mio secretario, sottoscripta de mia propria mano, signata col sugello pizolo elquale uso in cose mie importante.»[8] There can be no doubt whatsoever that Pietro Giampaolo's secretary was Mario Equicola. The importance of the document (it is an oath of allegiance) meant that there was no room for the nicety of a Latin, academic name. It may be argued that the secretary had not yet assumed the name by which he would later be known, but as will be shown later in this study, it seems highly probable that he was already using the name Equicola. Moreover, the document serves to elucidate Equicola's position with the Cantelmo family: he is referred to not as Pietro Giampaolo's son but as his secretary, already in that position he will hold with various employers for the greater part of his life. The question to

---

[5] It seems that Ludovico da Canossa is obscurely referring to Equicola's parentage in terms which appear to indicate Canossa's aristocratic disdain for the secretary's recent success: «Havendo assai maggior speranza in la importunità de le lettere mie di quello che io m'habbi nel nuovo parentado trovato per messer Mario...» (ASMN, AG, b. 1895, 25 August 1519, Ludovico da Canossa to Isabella d'Este, f. 218ʳ).

[6] Santoro, pp. 17-18; R. Feola, «Pietro Giampaolo Cantelmo», in *DBI*, 18, Rome, 1975, pp. 272-74. One should also consult P. Litta, *Famiglie celebri italiane*, fasc. 6, Cantelmi.

[7] Santoro, p. 11.

[8] Quoted in R. Filangieri, «Una congiura di baroni nel castello d'Isola in vista di una seconda spedizione di Carlo VIII (5 Agosto 1496)», *ASPN*, n.s., anno 28, 1945; pp. 109-33; p. 130. The emphasis in the text is my own.

ask here is whether a father would employ his son as secretary, and the answer must be that it would be most unlikely for him to do so.

It is true that there appears to have been a close relationship between Equicola and Pietro Giampaolo. In what amounts to a declaration of good faith on the part of his family towards Equicola, Sigismondo Cantelmo, Pietro Giampaolo's son, recalls the affection that his father had for Equicola:

> Oltra le virtù che in voi sono et infiniti rispetti che mi moveno, lo amor grande che la bona memoria del Signor mio patre vi portava me legha de sorte che sempre serò dispositissimo altrotanto fare nelle occorrentie vostre quanto nelle mie.[9]

It could be suggested that Sigismondo is subtly hinting at the precise nature of the relationship between his father and Equicola. In this case, one of the «infiniti rispetti» would be that Sigismondo was Equicola's half-brother. However, the vagueness of Sigismondo's statement does not bear the weight of such an assertion, given that no other evidence has yet been found. On the contrary, fragmentary pieces of information suggest that Equicola did have some family in what was formerly Cantelmo territory, but members of the Cantelmo clan drew a clear distinction between the two families. Sigismondo's brother, Giulio Cesare, wrote from Popoli in 1502 to Equicola that «tucti li vostri stanno bene e Madonna Lavinia l'altro dì me requese che li volesse fare dare lo grano della roccha e per havere inteso che voi lo havite dato ad prudentia lo soprasecluto fine alla venuta vostra.»[10] Unfortunately, not much can be gleaned from so short a statement and Giulio Cesare could easily be referring to Equicola's mother and his relations on her side of the family. She was a member of the Prudenzi family which, according to Castrucci, was one of the leading families in Alvito.[11] So, at least on his mother's side, Equicola could claim membership of a not-totally obscure family, one which would have been wealthy enough to ensure that Equicola achieved a certain position in society even though it was only that of a secretary, completely dependent on the favour of his employers. This situation perhaps reflected the position of the Prudenzi in respect to the Cantelmos.

Evidence concerning his father's surname may be found in a number of legal documents drawn up at Mantua in the latter part of Equicola's life. As these documents are of a late date, it is perhaps surprising that the name

---

[9] ASMN, AG, b. 1107, Florence, 24 September 1519, «Tuus Cantelmus» to «Magnifico messer Mario charo». On Sigismondo Cantelmo, see the entry by T. Ascari in *DBI*, 18, Rome, 1975, pp. 277-79.

[10] ASMN, AG, b. 283, 26 February 1502, Giulio Cesare Cantelmo to Equicola.

[11] Castrucci places the Prudenzi family amongst the «fameglie nobili e principali» of Alvito (p. 45). The name of the Cantelmo family appears in the same list. Castrucci is very vague about the Prudenzi: «Vi è anco la famiglia Prudentii molto antica, e descendente da quell'insigne scrittore Mario Equicola d'Alvito per parte di donna» (p. 47).

Caccialupi appears rather than the more obvious name of Equicola. On at least one occasion Equicola is referred to as «Marium Equicolam Cazalupum» although there appears to be no real necessity for this extra detail.[12] Nor is the use of Caccialupi exceptional in the *Registrazioni Notarili*; it is rather the rule. Undoubtedly, most people at the Mantuan court were not aware of his real name, yet Equicola made a point of it in these official, legal documents. In the same *Registrazioni* other people still refer to him as Equicola without the addition of his patronymic.[13] It is as if the moment Equicola left the closed circles of humanist gatherings and its writings he felt compelled to drop his humanist disguise before another power which called him to account. At court, matters were greatly simplified since he was commonly addressed as «messer Mario» which, as well as indicating a degree of familiarity with his superiors, also indicated his lack of a noble name. He was a man seeking his identity through the medium of the court.

However, people from his own region still persisted in calling him by his original name, «Mario Caccialupo».[14] Legally, he was the son of «Baptiste Cazaluppi de Albeto»[15] but, unfortunately, it has so far been impossible to add any other information to his name. Additionally, research into the Caccialupi family has not yielded any positive results.[16] What is known is that for reasons not fully understood Equicola decided to abandon the use of his patronymic, except in special circumstances, in favour of a name of humanist inspiration.

[12]   ASMN, AG, Libri dei Mandati, registro no. 23 (formerly FF), b. 9, f. 95r. Perhaps the only reason would have been to ensure observance of legal requirements.

[13]   ASMN, Archivio degli Instrumenti, Registrazioni Notarili: «Emptio domini Marii Cazalupi a Vincentio de Arabustis» (the year 1521, f. 620). An example of the second case where other people do not use his patronymic is the «Prorogatio locationis facte per spectabilem dominum Marium Equicolam Iohanni Francisco Scopulo et Iohanni Iacobo de Calzonis» (1522, f. 1014).

[14]   ASMN, AG, b. 283, Naples, 7 March 1502, «Paris De Bonitatibus de Pectorano» to «domino Mario Caccialupo». Equicola's superiors also referred to men of noble birth as «messer» including Castiglione on occasion. But whereas with Equicola there was no choice, Castiglione could be referred to as «Conte».

[15]   ASMN, Archivio degli Instrumenti, Registrazioni Notarili, 1521, f. 620.

[16]   B. Pecci refers to a certain Angelo de' Caccialupi, Bishop of Veroli, a town not very far from Sora (*L'Umanesimo e la «Cioceria»* Trani, 1912, pp. 30, 69-70). However, both Gams and Eubel give a different version of the bishop's name. The former's version is dismissed by Pecci as erroneous while Eubel's bears only the slightest resemblance to Caccialupi: «Angelus Mancini de Cavis, legum doctor» (*Hierarchia Catholica Medii Aevi*, II, Monasterii, 1901, p. 291). Unfortunately, Pecci does not reveal the source of his information but it does not seem to be trustworthy in any case.

The entries under Caccialupi or Caccialupo in *DBI*, 15, Rome, 1972, pp. 790-99, do not throw any light on the family of Equicola's father.

The name he chose was Equicola. The commonly accepted view is that Caccialupi became Equicola as a result of his membership of the *Accademia Pontaniana*. This does not seem likely for reasons to be discussed later. In the author's opinion, it is reasonable to say that he assumed the name Equicola at the Academy of Pomponio Leto in Rome where there existed a close precedent for choosing such a name; another member of the Academy had assumed the name Volscus which referred to the Volsci tribe, in the same way as Equicola's name referred to the Equi. [17] By adopting the name Equicola, he asserted his membership of an ancient tribe closely associated with his native region, the principal feature of which was its savage and warlike nature to which Virgil alludes. [18] However, according to Livy, in spite of its warlike nature, the Equi tribe introduced a certain formality into its declarations of war which the Romans themselves copied. [19] We can, perhaps, discern more personal reasons as to why Caccialupi chose Equicola for his new name. He would have known that the members of the Equi tribe had been engaged in a seemingly never-ending war against the Romans which they were doomed to lose; when the Romans finally subjugated them they were granted citizenship, but without the right to vote. One can perhaps draw a parallel with the recent history of the Cantelmos: they had been one of the most powerful families in the *Regno* before Pietro Giampaolo lost the greater part of his possessions and was forced into exile, powerless in the face of much stronger forces. Firstly, the Aragonese monarchy had asserted itself to the cost of the Cantelmos whose own sense of impotence had been compounded by various clashes with the national monarchies of France and Spain. The name Equicola carried with it the meaning of exile, the sense of being dispossessed, and the hope that he might assimilate into the culture and social world of the conquerors at some future time.

This feeling of disorientation is emphasized by the uncertainty of Equicola (and many other people) as to the correct spelling of his new name. [20] For many years our humanist found it impossible to decide whether his name was Equicolo or Equicola or some other variation. As well as reflecting the general uncertainty about orthography prevalent in the period, this problem

---

[17]   See A. Della Torre, *Paolo Marsi da Pescina. Contributo alla storia dell'Accademia Pomponiana*, Rocca S. Casciano, 1903, pp. 7, 103.

[18]   Cf. *Enciclopedia Italiana*, vol. 14, p. 142, Equi. The reference to Virgil is *Aeneid*, VII 746-47:
> Horrida praecipue cui gens adsuetaque multo
> Venatu nemorum, duris Aequicula glaebis.

[19]   Livy, Book I, XXXII, 5: «a se bellicae caerimoniae proderentur nec gererentur solum sed etiam indicerentur bella aliquo ritu, vis ab antiqua gente Aequicolis.»

[20]   See Rajna, pp. 360-72.

also had its roots in the precariousness of Equicola's position which is revealed in his constant changing back and forth from Equicolo to Equicola. Around 1521 his use of Equicolo became increasingly rare until it seems to disappear altogether. This particular year coincided with the publication of the *Chronica di Mantua* and the preparation of the *Libro de natura de amore* for the press. Thus, in a short space of time, he had expended a major effort on two works in the vernacular which would have undoubtedly compelled him to crystallize his views on orthography. Moreover, the last years of Equicola's life saw him in a position of importance, with his future completely assured. Even when he had decided to spell his name Equicola he was still not satisfied and felt the need to add «di Alveto» or a variant of it as we have already seen. Proud of his region, he wished to call attention to the fact that he still saw himself as an Alvitan and not a Mantuan. In 1521 the «Comunità de Alvito» wanted their newly-built church to be taken under the protection of the Carmelite order. To further their cause they wrote to the Marquis of Mantua who agreed to lend his support to the request, prompted no doubt by Equicola who was described as «mosso da medemo desiderio come persona amorevole alla patria sua».[21] In spite of the fact that in 1519 he had been granted Mantuan citizenship it is quite clear that for Equicola Alvito was more than just an obscure reminder of a distant past. It was a fixed point in a relatively restless existence. His memories of Alvito were probably made all the more poignant by the realization of how little of his life was actually spent there.

It should not be thought that Equicola's circumstances were exceptional, that he represents a unique case. On the contrary, it might be argued that his situation was typical of a number of southern intellectuals, subject to the vagaries of fortune and politics. So often dismissed as minor figures, of little interest to the history of ideas, these humanists have been relegated to a fate worse than that of «minor» writers. Yet their importance cannot be denied especially in the light of the political upheavals in the Kingdom of Naples subsequent to the French invasion. Significant numbers of southern intellectuals, still often connected with their employers, found themselves snatched out of their habitat. The usual solution imposed by political forces was to head north. How far north was dependent on individual situations. Not that there was no movement or circulation of intellectuals before the French expedition of 1494 but the latter event certainly caused much greater migrations than there had been previously. Thus, if scholars have spoken of «rootlessness» in connection with humanists in general, here, it might be better to speak of «transplants» which involve the creation of new networks or the revival of old

---

    [21] ASMN, AG, b. 2927, Copialettere, Federico Gonzaga, libro 268, 27 April 1521, to «Giovanbattista di Milano», f. 92ʳ.

systems of interrelations in a different soil. Mantua, Equicola's future home, is a good example of the way in which northern courts could offer refuge to the dispossessed Neapolitan nobility. Antonia del Balzo, sister of the former Queen of Naples, had already set up court in the *Mantovano*. Hence, it is not difficult to see her acting as a magnet for other southerners.[22] Old relationships could be re-established; a pertinent example would be that between Equicola and Sannazaro who seem to have first made their acquaintance in Sora but later renewed contact in France.[23] Thus, Equicola was estranged from the south only to a degree: he was still employed by a baronial family until 1508 and had numerous contacts with southern intellectuals.

*

Equicola himself informs us that he received his earliest education from Pietro Giampaolo Cantelmo, describing himself as his «alumnus».[24] We are immediately faced with the problem of why Equicola's father did not supervise his education. Once more we are in the realm of pure hypothesis. Suggestions which can be advanced but not substantiated could include: Equicola's father was already dead or that he and/or his family were not concerned with their son's education. Another possible solution might be that Equicola's parents decided to entrust him to the care of the leading family of the region in order to assure his future and cement their own relationship with the Cantelmos. Hence Equicola can be regarded as Pietro Giampaolo's «creato» in that he was educated in his household while, at the same time, winning Pietro

---

[22] Castiglione in the *Seconda Redazione* is well aware of the Neapolitan presence in the more important northern courts. He names first of all Eleonora d'Aragona, Duchess of Ferrara, who along with her husband, Ercole I, not only gave refuge to dispossessed Neapolitan royalty (the ex-Queen of Naples) but actively favoured former *baroni*, giving them preference over the local nobility. Perhaps the most notable instance of the latter are the privileges accorded to the Cantelmos by the Duke of Ferrara (*Seconda Redazione*, pp. 257-58). Antonia del Balzo is also singled out by Castiglione «la qual per le sue virtù merita esser celebratissima» (p. 258). It could be argued that a network was already in place before the French invasions of 1494 and consequently it served to attract other Neapolitans in search of refuge.

[23] It is hard to judge how far political allegiances entered into their relationship; Equicola and Sannazaro were on opposite sides in France — the latter remaining loyal to the deposed King of Naples and the former, on behalf of his masters, attempting to gain concessions from the French King. However, political considerations may have been outweighed by intellectual affinities. The evidence suggests that there was little time for literature during their stays in France because of these urgent political matters. However, at a much later date, Sannazaro was to paint a positive picture of Equicola's achievements (for which see Luzio-Renier, *La coltura*, p. 414 n. 2).

[24] Santoro, p. 22.

Giampaolo's confidence and affection as if he were his son.[25] In a dedicatory letter addressed to Giulio Cesare Cantelmo, Equicola makes a passing reference to his special relationship with the family: «jure quasi hereditario sum tuus». The «quasi» is all-important here. For those who still wish to view Equicola as an illegitimate son of Pietro Giampaolo it provides a piece of ambiguous ammunition, but for those who reject that assumption the phrase merely reiterates the fact of Equicola's intimacy with the Cantelmos.[26] As a «creato», Equicola resembles a family heirloom which is passed down from father to son. Consequently his life was gravely affected by the serious misfortunes that befell the Cantelmo family. Their decline directly resulted in Equicola having to leave his *patria* at a relatively early age. The King of Naples' campaign to destroy a too-powerful Pietro Giampaolo forced the latter to abandon Alvito, his last possession in the *Regno*, in 1487 and to seek refuge in Rome.[27]

---

[25]   On the Spanish equivalent, the «criado», see R. Boase, *The Troubadour Revival*, London and Boston, 1978, p. 61. For a brief discussion of the term «creature» in the Florentine context see F.W. Kent with P. Simons, «Renaissance patronage: An introductory essay» in *Patronage, Art, and Society in Renaissance Italy*, edited by F.W. Kent and P. Simons with J.C. Eade, Oxford, 1987, pp. 1-21; 14-15.
The question poses itself here of Equicola's relations with the other branch of the Cantelmo family headed by Pier Giampaolo's brother, Giovanni and then by his son Restaino. It is difficult to gauge with any precision the possibilities of cultural exchange between the two branches. However, it cannot be ruled out altogether that Equicola had access to the library of Antonio Cantelmo. It was not a humanistic library by any means but concentrated on vernacular poetry with some prose works, particularly chronicles. An interesting item in view of Equicola's connection with a Latin translation of Plutarch's *Lives* is «Le *Vite* di Plutarcho in vulgare ad stampa coperto de coyro» (quoted in N.F. Faraglia, «La casa dei conti Cantelmo in Popoli e il suo arredamento secondo un inventario del 1494», *Rassegna Abruzzese di Storia ed Arte*, 4 (1900) 3-33; 20. The emphasis on vernacular poetry, particularly the lyric, might have encouraged Equicola in his studies of early lyric poetry to which the *Libro* bears witness. The dedication of a collection of Neapolitan verse to Giovanni Cantelmo confirms the impression of a person extremely interested in this form of literature. On this figure see M. Santagata, *La lirica aragonese. Studi sulla poesia napoletana del secondo Quattrocento*, Padua, 1979, pp. 377-86. See also C. De Frede, «Biblioteche e cultura dei signori napoletani del '400», *Bibliothèque d'Humanisme et Renaissance*, 25 (1963) 187-97.

[26]   Santoro, pp. 11-21.

[27]   *DBI*, 18, p. 273. Proof of Pietro Giampaolo's removal to Rome is provided by his son Sigismondo (ASMN, AG, b. 1231, Ferrara, 15 March 1487, Sigismondo Cantelmo to Francesco Gonzaga f. 560r):

> A dì passati la Maestà del Signor Re [of Naples], havendo messe graveze inseportabile a mio padre e ne le terre sue, lui condolsene e tal parole perveneno al'orecchie a Sua Maestà. Per il che ordinò guardie per il paese de mio patre che non potesse andare fora. Et essendo dicto mio patre avisato per cierti suoi amici come la Maestà del Signor Re lo voleva far pigliare, per il che ciò sentito, *lui se partì et esse riduto a Roma*, lui insieme con Ferrante, mio fratel menore. (my italics)

Sigismondo had been in Ferrara from at least 1485 as can be shown from letters to Mantua which seem to begin in this year (ASMN, AG, b. 1231, Ferrara, 4 March 1485, Idem. f. 465r). Other letters in the same *busta*, all addressed to the Marquis, include the following:

Under such circumstances it is highly improbable that any person closely connected with Pietro Giampaolo, as Equicola undoubtedly was, would consider going to Naples. It is not known whether Equicola accompanied his master to Rome in 1487 or whether he had already taken up residence there earlier. In any case, it appears from a variety of evidence that Equicola made Rome his home. This hypothesis is confirmed by a letter which throws some important light on Equicola's social situation in these years. In spite of the fact that the letter was written long after the period in question and that some of its details are not confirmed elsewhere, it indicates that Equicola was in contact with the leading Roman intellectuals of the day. The letter concentrates on Equicola's relationship with Bernardino Capella who had a reputation in Roman circles as an orator and a Latin poet.[28] Equicola was still vividly remembered in the Capella household according to the letter he received from the Archdeacon of Mantua, Alessandro Gabbioneta:

> Poeta mio, lege carmen del tuo padrezolo Capella cuius ubera suxisti, existimato tanto quanto che'l merita. El me ha dicto che se tu li fusse apresso, che faria asai meglio. L'altro giorno me fece parlare con Madona Iuliana, tanto vechia che in quello corpo non è restato se non la loquella vivida. Essa, parlando di te, disse: «Volesse Dio che lo vedesse anti che mi mora. Me lo haio alevato ben nove anni quello figlio.» Aut, disse XI, si recte memini. Capella repplicò: «Madona li

---

17 October 1485, f. 489^r; 5 December 1485, f. 489^r, concerning a legal dispute in which his wife's family, the Moloselli, was involved; 12 December 1485, f. 495^r; 16 May 1485, f. 518^r; 15 July 1486, f. 532^r; 7 February 1487, f. 548^r; 10 March 1487, f. 557^r. Sigismondo's permanent base was Ferrara which did not change even after his father's establishment in Rome. Other letters can be used as evidence: Ferrara, 11 May 1488, f. 621^r; 15 October 1488, f. 638^r; 10 November 1488, f. 643^r; 4 April 1489, f. 691^r; 31 August 1489, f. 715^r. This is confirmed by Bernardino Zambotti, *Diario ferrarese [dall'anno 1476 sino al 1504]*, a cura di G. Pardi, *Rerum Italicorum Scriptorum*, XXIV:7, pp. 52, 95, 216, 218, 282, 339. A number of letters (for example, 10 November 1488 and 4 April 1489) provide evidence of Sigismondo Cantelmo's interest in the theatre. This is confirmed by his letter of 13 February 1501 to the Duke of Ferrara, Ercole d'Este which contains a long, detailed description of the theatre and its decoration used in the Mantuan carnival that year. It has not been noted that the handwriting in this particular letter is Equicola's so it is possible he may have had a part in its composition. The letter may be read in A. D'Ancona, *Origini del teatro italiano*, II, Rome, 1966 (Ed. anastatica secondo l'edizione Loescher, 1891), pp. 381-83.

Pietro Giampaolo did come to Ferrara, presumably to enlist the support of the Duke for his cause and for the same reason he wrote from Ferrara to the Marquis of Mantua (b. 1231, 27 January 1490, f. 850^r).

Not all members of the Cantelmo clan were unhappy at Pietro Giampaolo's expulsion. His brother, Restaino, for example, had been expelled from his feud by Pietro Giampaolo. The former's aim was to recover his own territories and add those of his brother and cousin, Sigismondo. He thus aligned himself, first with the Aragonese monarchy and then with the Spanish. Even if Cantelmo feuds remained in the family there was little love lost between its members. In any case, when Restaino was assassinated in 1514, the Cantelmo feuds passed into other hands (see Litta, fasc. 6, Cantelmi, and R. Feola, «Restaino Cantelmo» in *DBI*, 18, pp. 275-76).

[28]   G. Ballistreri, «Capella, Bernardino» in *DBI*, 18, Rome 1975, pp. 468-70 and F. Ubaldini, *Vita di Mons. Angelo Colocci*, a cura di V. Fanelli, Città del Vaticano, 1969, pp. 68-69 n. 111.

voleva bene come a mi, non tanto per rispetto che suo patre era l'anima di suo fratello, la quale lei amava più cha l'anima sua, ma perché Mario sempre li stava intorno, laudandola et dicendo Madona da bene et Madona savia et chara et similia, de modo che la non se l'è mai scordato et lo voria veddere et io tochare la mane.» El me pare che Capella facia con sua matre quello se fa con li puti picoli, semper in blandiciis, et non credere perhò che mai dica messer Bernardino, ma Bernardino mio, figliolo mio, et adhuc noscit se esse matrem. La me disse che la si ricordava de Papa Martino. Io non credo che sia la più vechia dona a Roma de lei et anchor va alla pace a missa.[29]

This letter provides an indication of the length of time Equicola spent in Rome which is in itself an indication of the familiarity he enjoyed with Capella and his mother. It transpires from the letter (bearing in mind the Archdeacon's obscure use of the vernacular) that Equicola's family already had contacts in Rome, particularly with Capella's mother. Equicola's arrival in Rome allowed «Madona Iuliana» to lavish her affection upon him as if he were her own son. In a slightly different way, perhaps with a touch of irony, the Archdeacon refers to Capella as Equicola's «padrezolo». As far as we know, Capella was born between 1460 and 1461, making him Equicola's senior by approximately ten years.[30] He would have been old enough to act as Equicola's guide to Rome and advise him on how best to pursue his education. The Archdeacon's use of the word «padrezolo» may have other shades of meaning not apparent at first sight. It was possibly an innuendo about Capella's homosexuality — the Archdeacon himself was not free from accusations of this kind.[31] Indeed, the Roman Academy had gained a certain

---

[29]   ASMN, AG, b. 864, 24 April 1520, the Archdeacon to Equicola. Luzio knew of this letter's existence and indeed paraphrases it (in «Isabella d'Este ne' primordi del papato di Leone X», *ASL*, 6 [1906] 456 n. 1). However, Luzio misses the significance of the «ben nove anni» in Rome in the context of Equicola's biography.

[30]   *DBI*, 18, p. 468.

[31]   M. Bandello, *Tutte le opere*, a cura di F. Flora, Verona, 1952, vol. 1, *Le novelle*, I, 30; pp. 387-89. The Archdeacon, in the letter referred to in note 34 (ASMN, AG, b. 864), does not disguise the feelings he has for his own sex. At a banquet to celebrate the victory over Longueil, he writes: «Ge era una infinità de gioveni docti et alcuni formosi». He must have been able to write to Equicola in this tone, knowing that the latter would not disapprove of his comments and salacious stories. The Archdeacon recounts an anecdote which involves Capella: «Ita che Capella disse, el dì sequente che quando la sera fu compagnato a casa da molti de questi gioveni, el macellaro, suo vicino, ge disse, 'Messere, vi foteti uva questi citelli cum quessa 'cademia.' Del qual ditto assai se risò et fu parlato fin in Vaticano.»

Even though the exact meaning of the butcher's obscene comment is difficult to grasp, Cian found it comprehensible enough to cut the offending part.

It should also be stated that Capella was named as one of Imperia's lovers (or perhaps admirers). For this sixteenth-century Roman courtesan see P. Pecchiai, *Donne del Rinascimento in Roma. Imperia, Lucrezia figlia d'Imperia, la misteriosa Fiammetta*, Padua, 1958, pp. 18, 22; G.L. Moncallero, *Imperia de Paris nella Roma del Cinquecento e i suoi cantori funebri*, Rome, 1962, p. 137 n. 4, and G. Masson, *Courtesans of the Italian Renaissance*, London, 1975, in particular pp. 44-45. The evidence, however, is rather scanty for Capella's «involvement» with Imperia and he may have just been playing a game along with some of the other Roman humanists.

notoriety in this respect with one of the charges against Pomponio Leto in 1468 being that of homosexuality.[32] Equicola's experience of this side of Roman life seems to have led him to a wholly negative response to homosexuality although, arguably, there was no other way of approaching so dangerous a subject. His treatment of it in the *Libro* leaves the reader in no doubt about his point of view: «Ogni aversa Venere dal nostro libro volemo lontana» (f. 121ᵛ). I do not wish to appear an amateur psychoanalyst, but one has the feeling that in these pages Equicola was cleansing himself of guilt and establishing his distance from this form of sexual activity. He is particularly harsh against boys becoming involved in «questo vitio horrendo», and urges that «exterminemo puerili coiti ove il paziente ha in odio l'agente». He repeatedly emphasizes the utter powerlessness of a boy caught in «Venere mascula», stressing that «quello amore esser tyranno che a gioveni li amanti per intemperantia portano è certo» (*Libro*, f. 120ʳ). To Equicola, who placed great importance on individual liberty, sexual relations of this type were all the more abominable because they enslaved the people involved. He could not share the Roman Academy's attitude towards sexuality, against which he put forward the ideal of the court lady (*Libro*, f. 119ʳ).

Nonetheless, the period he spent in Rome did have a positive influence on his intellectual development. He went to Rome in the years around 1482-1484 and left about 1492-1494 (these dates only indicate approximately the broad period of his stay in Rome). These ten years or so saw Equicola grow from boyhood to manhood. His stay in Rome was to be a double-edged experience: on the one hand it represented a long period of relative stability, and on the other it marked the beginning of his permanent exile from his native region. He was fortunate though to have found a second mother, «Madona Iuliana», who seems to have cherished him like her own son and a «padrezolo», Capella, whose affection for Equicola continued right to the end of his life.

On the intellectual horizon a third figure stood out in relief: Pomponio Leto. Equicola, the grateful pupil, openly acknowledges his debt to the leader of the Roman Academy in a number of his published works.[33] Leto is the only member of the Academy he mentions, and even Capella's presence is passed over in silence. Again, it is the Archdeacon of Mantua who confirms Equicola's association with Pomponio Leto, if confirmation be necessary. In the extract from the following letter the Archdeacon refers to the uproar caused by Longueil's address to the Roman Academy in 1519, recalling to

---

[32] See I. Carini, «La difesa di Pomponio Leto» in *Nozze Cian-Sappa-Flandinet*, Bergamo, 1894, pp. 151-93.

[33] Santoro, p. 25.

Capella's mind the time when Equicola was part of the circle that formed the Academy.[34] In 1519 Capella still regarded Equicola as possessing those qualities of an Academician which were necessary to combat the pernicious doctrines of Longueil:

> [messer Bernardino Capella] mi venne a ritrovare et me disse se creddeva che vui fustovi per venir in qua se lui mandasse per vui. Io ge disse che no, per l'officio novamente hauto, referendoli ogne cosa, la resposta fu: «oh, segurato mi, non poterò più haver Mario mio! Tutto el dì ho gente in casa a manzar el mio, la sera se parteno e Bernardino resta solo e Madona sta male.» Io lo consolai assai et più che puoti. Creddo che la fantasia era di farvi venir qua per opponervi a questo Longonio perché dice Capella che vui eravati qua cum lui quando Pomponio impetrò li privilegii de la accademia et che vui seti membro de la accademia.[35]

Ironically, at this late stage in Equicola's career (he had just been appointed Isabella d'Este's secretary) the gap between him and the Roman Academy could not have been wider. He was now an actor on the public stage and far removed, both physically and mentally, from the closed circles of academic debate.

Now that Equicola's association with Pomponio Leto has been established, it remains to be seen what kind of influence the leader of the Roman Academy might have exerted over the young Equicola. Teaching was perhaps the key to Leto's identity, both formally as a professor of rhetoric at the University of Rome, and more informally at the Roman Academy.[36] Leto's editing of classical texts should also be seen in the light of his teaching ideals, that is, as an extension of his classroom activities. In this context, Leto saw himself in the role of a latter-day Valerius Probus:

> Unice vetustatis amator cum animadvertisset veteres negligi et gloria fraudari, contracta multa exemplaria emendare, distinguere et annotare curavit... Ego tanti

---

[34] On Longueil see D. Gnoli, *Un giudizio di lesa romanità sotto Leone X*, Rome, 1891; T. Simar, *Christophe de Longueil, humaniste, 1488-1522*, Louvain, 1911; P.A. Becker, *Christophe de Longueil. Sein Leben und sein Briefwechsel*, Bonn and Leipzig, 1924.

[35] Quoted in V. Cian, «Recensione a D. Gnoli, *Un giudizio di lesa romanità*», GSLI, 19 (1892) 151-58; the relevant document is quoted on pages 155-56.

It is unclear to which specific occasion Capella is alluding when he speaks of Pomponio Leto obtaining the privileges of the Academy. It may perhaps refer to the year 1484 in which Pomponio had been granted the right, by the Emperor, to confer the title of poet laureate and that year saw the first ceremony.

G. Tournoy-Thoen, «La laurea poetica del 1484 all'accademia romana», *Bulletin de l'Institut Historique Belge de Rome*, 42 (1972) 211-35. The following studies are still useful, G. Tiraboschi, *Storia della letteratura italiana*, t. VI, i, Florence, 1807, pp. 107-113 and M. Maylender, *Storia delle accademie d'Italia*, IV, Bologna, 1929, pp. 320-27.

[36] See V. Zabughin, «L'insegnamento universitario di Pomponio Leto», *Rivista d'Italia*, 9 (1906) 215-44 and by the same writer, *Giulio Pomponio Leto. Saggio critico*, 3 vols, Rome, 1909-1912.

viri exemplo impar licet doctrina et ingenii dotibus id ipsum aliqua ex parte facere conatus sum.[37]

Leto's tendency to worship the world of Ancient Rome and to follow in the footsteps of the Romans led him to immerse himself completely in all things related to that culture. Consequently, critical and comparative elements are almost entirely absent from his scheme of things. The editing of a Latin text became the perfect vehicle for his world-vision, for this exercise allowed him to restore a part of classical antiquity: «Emendavimus nihil addendo, detraximus non pauca fide vetustatis admonente.» (*Vita*, f. n3[r]) It also allowed him to develop «scientific» principles which were based on a need for accuracy and the desire to produce the best possible text. In order to edit a Latin text correctly a knowledge of grammar and philology were indispensable. In fact, he devoted his later years to the study of Latin grammar. He perceived it as the foundation on which all else must be built; it was particularly necessary for young men beginning their studies, as Equicola would have been: «Grammaticae est ars necessaria pueris, iocunda senibus et dulcis secretorum comes.»[38] Although the study of grammar is useful at all stages of human development, Pomponio Leto placed especial emphasis on the education of the young since this was an essential part of his professional duties as a teacher:

> Pomponius studiose iuventuti:
>
> Noscere Romanae qui vis primordia linguae,
> Huc fuge polliceor me duce doctis eris,
> Prima rudimenta et puerili etate calores
> Ostendo... (*Grammatica rudimenta*, f. 1[r])

Leto was the editor-teacher whose task it was to clarify, simplify and tabulate, making lists and indexes. He defined grammar as the science of «recte loquendi et verba interpretandi».[39] His chief concern was with the meanings of individual words which involved an interest in etymology. This is one of the reasons why Leto was interested in extending the range of Latin authors available for grammatical study. In this way he could locate unusual and rare words which would provide additional material for his studies. Hence etymology provided a safe outlet for his thirst for knowledge. It was the acquisition of curiosities or rarities which attracted his attention more than establishing a clear and

---

[37] See *Francisci Philelphi elegantes et familiares epistolae, Pomponii Laeti ad amicos epistolae aliquot tersissimae, eiusdem vita Sabellico autore* [1520?] 4°.

[38] *Grammatica rudimenta Pomponi Letii Togatorum in lingua latina facile principis*, Paris [1505?] 4°.

[39] Leto's definition of grammar differs slightly from Quintilian's. They both agree on the first part, that it is the «recte loquendi scientiam» but, for Quintilian, the second part entails the «poetarum enarrationem». In this respect, Leto is more «scientific».

precise ideological framework for his work, even if this in itself constituted a choice as to his place and objectives in the social structure. He seemed to have been blind to the wider implications of his work, or perhaps he saw his method as a way of avoiding the certain difficulties of a more critical approach. It may have been a reaction to the over-audacious researches of Lorenzo Valla, an attempt not to become embroiled in religious matters especially. That Rome became the centre of a humanism rooted in archaeology under Leto's influence is not only due to the influence of the ruins of the ancient city but also to the fact that it was easier and safer to collect and catalogue exotic material than to pass critical judgements on classical antiquity.

The authors Leto chose to edit betray the same concern with grammar: Nonius Marcellus and Varro were themselves students of Latin. Even Leto's interest in Plautus does not appear to have been, at least initially, an interest in him as a playwright but as a source of interesting vocabulary, indicated to the humanist by his study of the Latin grammarians. Similarly, Leto's studies of Roman history bear the stamp of a grammarian. His principal concern in this field was to study the institutions of Ancient Rome, including the legal and religious structures of the Roman state. This kind of study may be regarded as an application of his grammatical method to the history of institutions. Grammar and law both act as important organizational factors in their respective fields. Leto's «compendiosa doctrina» serves the purpose of providing a copious material which can be re-ordered into a logical pattern. In this way, he sought to avoid in his later life, especially after the «conspiracy» of 1468, any discussion which may have led to controversy: he wished to sit safely behind his reconstructions of the ways in which Ancient Rome was governed. However, it should be said that these studies may be regarded as an indirect criticism of the organization of papal Rome, though in this case we would have to imagine a much more politically aware Pomponio Leto.[40] The distinc-

---

[40] For example Pomponio Leto, *De Romanorum magistratibus, sacerdotiis, iurisperitis, et legibus ad M. Pantagathum libellus* [1490 ?] 4°, provides a clear example of Leto's interest in the institutions of Ancient Rome.

Whether he wanted to or not Leto found himself in political hot water. The most notorious instance was his imprisonment in 1468 by Paul II for what could have been political reasons. It would seem impossible for a fifteenth-century humanist working in Rome to remain politically «unaware». The picture of Leto as an unworldly scholar, uninterested in the contemporary world who *happened* to get on the wrong side of the Pope through no fault of his own needs revision. Leto has been noted as an anti-cleric but this has not been taken any further. The humanist's arrest in 1468 was also due in part to suspicions that Leto was involved in a Republican conspiracy against the Pope in Rome. Support for this view of Pomponio Leto comes from a later writer, Marco Antonio Altieri, who composed his principal work *Li nuptiali* in the first years of the sixteenth century. Altieri presents a Leto, aware of the political traditions of Rome, and who shows allegiance to the ideals of republicanism. For a detailed account of

Altieri see my «Culture and politics in Renaissance Rome: Marco Antonio Altieri's Roman weddings», *Renaissance Quarterly*, 40 (1987) 49-90.

It is interesting to note that Altieri proclaims Pomponio Leto as his teacher («lo un [Leto] preceptore» [p. 30]), something that Equicola himself does. This is not to suggest that Equicola had republican sympathies — his entire career denies it, rather to suggest that both Equicola and Altieri shared a common intellectual heritage, though used for radically different purposes. Altieri's major work *Li Nuptiali* and Equicola's *Libro de natura de amore* present similarities in their methodologies which can be traced to their common source in Leto. Both Equicola and Altieri place considerable emphasis on the use of examples to prove their case as well as an active interest in etymologies. The frequent citation of classical authors to bolster their opinions, to give their writings the authority of classical antiquity is another regular occurrence: «Per gran soccurso de quello che della mea sì debil fede dubitete, redducome alla memoria colle vigilie de Festo Pompeio» (*Li Nuptiali*, edited by E. Narducci, Rome, 1873, p. 88) writes Altieri. The Roman writer in another instance adduces classical *exempla*, piling one on top of the other, in a manner that has much in common with Equicola: «El che ben demostrose per la sententia de Marco Valerio et de Iunio Censori con asperrimo decreto promulgata... Alla quale opinione conformosece la lege promulgata dal Numidico Metello... Nè meno atroce selle demostrorono et Camillo et Postumio... Notose fussiro della medesma opinione quelli immortali et gran latori de lege Lygurgo, anche Solone...»(*Li Nuptiali*, p. 89). In Altieri the desire to go back to one's origins has an express political purpose: to renew the values of his class. The interest in Roman *exempla* is not for him merely academic — he is citing the greatness of his ancestors to inspire his contemporaries. For Equicola this particular political strategy is not present. His large numbers of examples suggest the concept of knowledge as power, a desire to overwhelm people with his learning. It is more of a personal politics than a practice developed for the purpose of defending class interests.

The language used by Altieri also has particular political significance. It is a language which is learned in the extreme, consciously Latinate so as to emphasize the origins of his class. The refusal to write in Latin was perhaps a response to the political position of the Papacy in Rome which was threatening the existence of the patriciate. Altieri did not wish to use the language of the Church but to develop his own which combined erudition with the vernacular culture of Rome. What is remarkable is that Equicola's own vernacular bears more than a family resemblance to the Roman writer's. First of all, the decision to write their most important treatise in the vernacular instead of Latin was a bold move; and then to use a Latinate variety of the vernacular seems to be more than a coincidence. If the two writers were poles apart politically speaking, in linguistic terms they are half-brothers. It could be that the influence of Pomponio Leto made itself felt on both their attitudes towards writing in the vernacular. Even when other pressures made it imperative for them to write in some kind of Italian, they could not forget their Latin heritage. It was also a way of increasing the prestige of their chosen language. In Equicola's case, the necessity of creating an aulic language, partly along the lines suggested by Calmeta, must have been a factor taken into consideration. Whether Altieri would have been open to such influences, given his attitude to the *Curia*, is doubtful but cannot be altogether excluded.

Another intellectual feature held in common brings the two writers together: their admiration of Plato. Equicola's knowledge of and devotion to the Greek philosopher is well documented in his writings, culminating in the *Libro de natura de amore*. Altieri frequently refers to Plato in *Li Nuptiali* in glowing terms, for example, «ce sopragiunse la auctorità de quel divino auctore sì spesso da noi comemorato» (p. 82). It was well known that Leto did not read Greek and that his humanist interests were limited to the Roman world. Where would have Altieri gained such a passion for the Greek writer? There may have been left in Rome a residue of Greek learning even after Bessarion's departure. Florentines could have well brought a renewed interest in Neoplatonism to Rome during stays in the city. It also depends on who knew whom well enough to gain access to circles which had even a little interest in Plato. From this point of view, the culture of the cardinals residing in Rome would be of significance. Equicola's friendship with Francesco Soderini might prove a fruitful starting-point since the latter did have associations with Marsilio Ficino which will be discussed in their appropriate place.

tion Pascal draws between the «esprit de géométrie» and the «esprit de finesse» seems to apply to Pomponio Leto's case.

Indeed, this distinction was not missed by some of Leto's contemporaries. Paolo Cortese, for example, made an attempt to explain what he considered the surprising friendship that sprang up between Pomponio Leto and Ermolao Barbaro by suggesting that this was a friendship of opposites:

> Quidam etiam amicitiam contrariorum genere servari ut si dicamus Hermolaum Barbarum, hominem quotidie natura meditantem et suaptebilis affectione tristem, libenter delectari Iulii Pomponii familiaritate solitum proptereaque is maxime esset faceta iucunditate letus...[41]

Cortese was implying that Barbaro was a much more serious scholar than Leto and he was not alone in this view.[42] Raffaele Maffei also attacked Leto's

---

[41]   P. Cortese, *De Cardinalatu*, in Castro Cortesio, 1510, fol., f. 60[r].

[42]   Bembo also uses the friendship between Leto and Barbaro in his Latin dialogue *De Virgilii Culice et Terentii fabulis Liber*, Venice, 1530. He describes the circumstances of their relationship: «Dum ille apud Innocentium Pontificum Maximum a nostra Republica Romam missus legati munere fungeretur, posteaque ab eo in sacerdotium adscitus, legatione renuntiata, in urbe remansisset, ad quem (ut ipse aiebat) a Pomponio Laeto cuius erat sector, saepissime deducebatur. Magnam enim inter illos viros benivolentiam conflaverat artium studiorumque similitudo.» (f. a2[r]) Bembo seems to be falsifying Barbaro's situation — he did not resign his office of his own free will, but was forced to do so (E. Bigi. «Barbaro, Ermolao» in *DBI*, 6, pp. 97-99). He is perhaps using Barbaro as an example of another Venetian humanist who renounced public office in favour of the more private pursuit of knowledge. To Barbaro's numerous areas of expertise is added his knowledge of Greek: 'Hermolaus autem ad humaniores illas doctrinas et cultum litterarum in quibus excellere Pomponius existimabatur, cum iuris civilis scientiam quam quidem admodum adolescens fuerat consequutus. Tum vel maxime philosophiae studia in qua semper multum operae insumebat, adiunxerat easque omnes artes Graecarum litterarum luminibus illustrabat quarum esse peritissimus credebatur.» (f. a2[v]) Bembo himself would, of course, go farther than Barbaro and actually write in Greek, an experiment that was in keeping with the more «open-minded» attitude he had early on in his career towards linguistic variety and choice. In this he came closer to Equicola's position than one might have imagined. Such a shifting perspective on language helps to explain, at least in part, the antagonisms that were unleashed in the period 1512-1513 (pp. 137-41), once Bembo had gone a long way towards establishing a single, coherent theory. His suggestive coupling of Leto and Barbaro in the *De Virgilii Culice* may indicate a certain superiority on Bembo's part by glossing works which are of especial significance in a new linguistic/literary theory. Yet, at the same time, it indicates a certain adherence to the tastes, methods and tendencies of Roman antiquarian humanism. Bembo's decision to find a more rigid linguistic schema, to discover a secure sense of direction meant his abandonment of the freer standards of some Quattrocento humanism. On this see P. Floriani, «La giovinezza umanistica di Pietro Bembo fino al periodo ferrarese», *GSLI*, 143 (1966) 27-71. Although Floriani discusses Barbaro he makes no mention of Leto. Neglect of the latter does not allow for a proper appreciation of his influence nor of the strength of the eclectic, antiquarian brand of humanism. Bembo's reaction against this more «open» scholarship can be counterbalanced by Equicola's preservation of what would be considered in the sixteenth century, an old, out-moded style of erudition. Equicola's almost anarchic fullness and love of the (obscure) reference is replaced by a systemic approach to language and literature, permitting less freedom to the writer but making him more respectable and accessible to power.

particular kind of humanism as being defective because of his ignorance of the Greek language.[43] Cortese may also have been implying that Leto had a detrimental influence on Barbaro. The Venetian humanist originally went to Rome in his capacity as a diplomat but, owing to political pressures, was forced to resign his office. It was probably only at this point that he could find enough time to devote himself, once again, to his studies. Stimulated, in part, by Leto and the environment of the Roman Academy, Barbaro was able to produce some of his most important work, involving the correction of Latin texts, including an edition of Plautus which only appeared posthumously.[44] Barbaro's greatest humanistic achievement was accomplished in Rome, namely his *Castigationes Plinianae et in Pomponium Melam*.[45] Barbaro's return to the purely humanist exercise of editing a text may have been a form of refuge from the turbulence of political life. It followed his treatise *De Officio Legati* which represents the application of a humanist-diplomat's experience of contemporary Italian politics to the Latin treatise form, written immediately before his arrival in Rome. In this treatise Barbaro adapted the models of classicism to the situation in which humanists were to increasingly find themselves, acting as diplomats instead of teachers.[46] Thus he moved his humanism out of the class-room into the wider spaces of contemporary politics. However, the humanists were still uncertain of which course to take. Barbaro is a case in point. The last two years of his life probably made him more acceptable to certain members of the Academy as he could devote himself entirely to study — a kind of study readily appreciated by the Academicians and especially by its leader. Cortese, on the other hand, was very much in favour of a more dynamic role for humanists, even if it entailed the sacrifice of a certain amount of intellectual independence.

Cortese's dialogue, the *De Hominibus Doctis*, registers these different currents within humanism[47]. The chief interlocutor is Antonius whom we

---

[43]   See C. Dionisotti, *Gli umanisti e il volgare*, Florence, 1968, p. 48.

[44]   *Plautus cum correctione et interpretatione Hermolai, Merulae, Politiani et Beroaldi* [1500?] Fol. Such a commentary written by Barbaro represents a concrete example of the influence of the Roman Academy. Plautus was of great interest to Leto because of his lexical interests and to other Academicians who were interested in the theatre.

[45]   The work is edited by G. Pozzi, 2 vols, Padua, 1973-74. It is interesting to note that Barbaro emphasizes his own relations with Pontano and the latter's with the Roman Academy («Ioviani Pontani mei», see *Introduzione* to the edition of the *Castigationes*, pp. CXIX-CXXI, CXXXVII-CXL). This case makes more explicit connections that existed between the Roman and Neapolitan Academies.

[46]   E. Barbaro, *De Coelibatu, De Officio Legati*, a cura di V. Branca, Florence, 1969.

[47]   There are two modern editions of the dialogue, the first in chronological order is less rigorous than the second. Hence, all references will be to Ferraù's edition. P. Cortese, *De Hominibus Doctis Dialogus*, a cura di M.T. Graziosi, Rome, 1973; Pauli Cortesii, *De*

presume to be Antonio Augusto Baldo; Paulus corresponding to the author, and Alexander (Farnese) are the two other people involved in the dialogue. Antonius regards letters as a separate discipline which should be independent of all attempts at adulation: the pen is not a mercenary instrument like the sword. For Antonius, a humanist of an earlier generation, a Filelfo is the worst type of humanist imaginable: «sed erat vendibilis sane scriptor, et is qui opes, quam scribendi laudem consequi malebat» (*De Hominibus Doctis*, p. 150). Antonius wishes to urge the humanist to remain within the confines of certain activities, such as the editing of texts, which he himself can control, instead of placing himself completely at the command of his social superiors and perverting his art. The younger Alexander disagrees with Antonius, for precisely the same reason that the latter was attacking Filelfo: «Mihi vero ille (patrem dico) hoc facto sapiens videtur, qui ex litteris divitias quaesierit» (p. 151). The example of Filelfo gains in import when it is realized that he had held a Chair of Rhetoric at the University of Rome in 1474.[48] Cortese's dialogue, composed in about 1490, lays bare the contradictions of contemporary humanism and warmly approves of humanists becoming involved in affairs of state.

Not all the members of the Roman Academy would have disapproved of the notion of humanists becoming more involved in political affairs. A number of them already held offices in the papal administration and regarded the Academy as a refuge from their more worldly cares.[49] Literature and scholarship were for them separate from their everyday business. However, there were those inside the Academy who realized the advantages of Filelfo's position. As a university teacher he did not wish to isolate himself from the sources of wealth and power which would be beneficial to him.[50] Filelfo did not hesitate to serve the Italian despots in a way which was advantageous both to himself and the prince.

Hominibus Doctis, a cura di G. Ferraù, Palermo, 1979. If Cortese accepts the reality of and need for princely patronage he cannot avoid the contradiction that this position implies. In other words, the comfortable position of certain intellectuals able to devote themselves completely to study depends upon adequate patronage which usually meant pressures of one kind or another to produce particular types of writing. Cf. Ferraù, pp. 25-26, 37-38 who, however, does not note the compromises that Cortese realized had to be made in order to become a court intellectual.

[48] Consult D.S. Chambers, «Studium urbis and gabella studii: The University of Rome in the fifteenth century» in *Cultural Aspects of the Italian Renaissance*, ed. by C.H. Clough, Manchester, 1976, pp. 77, 80 and E. Lee, «Humanists and the 'Studium Urbis', 1473-1484» in *Umanesimo a Roma nel Quattrocento. Atti del Convegno, New York 1-4 dicembre 1981*, a cura di P. Brezzi e M. de Panizza Lorch, Città di Castello, 1984, pp. 127-46.

[49] See E. Lee, *Sixtus IV and Men of Letters*, Rome, 1978, pp. 203-204.

[50] A. Luzio, R. Renier, «I Filelfo e l'umanismo alla corte dei Gonzaga», *GSLI* 16 (1890) 119-217; on Francesco Filelfo see pp. 161-72.

It is important to note that the Roman Academy was not united in its attitude to patronage and various positions existed within its ranks. Cf. C. Dionisotti, «'Lavinia venit litora'. Polemica virgiliana di M. Filetico», *IMU* 1 (1958) 283-315; 286, 302.

Giovanni Sulpizio Verulano, a teacher of rhetoric at the University of Rome and a member of the Academy, felt the need to take full advantage of the unique situation to be found in Rome where patronage was readily available from cardinals and other high-ranking church officials with an interest in cultural pursuits.[51] As a university teacher of rhetoric, Sulpizio did not neglect to write works of a traditional character, in the same vein as Pomponio Leto and other humanists, and indeed, these works formed the bulk of his output. We can perhaps point to one work which represents an awareness of a changing situation, the *De componendis et ornandis epistolis*[52] although superficially it may not seem to represent any advance over the rest of academic literature. The question this humanist seems to be asking is whether rhetoric and grammar serve any purpose beyond the confines of the academy and the university. Although these subjects have always been regarded as useful, Sulpizio evidently felt that they needed to be adapted to contemporary demands. He did not then depart from tradition when he emphasized the usefulness of his book:

> Quare maiorem in modum tibi est enitendum ut praeter utilitatem tuam et gloriam que mihi tecum communis est, eius expectationem et spem quam de te et de me concepit egregiam non frusteris. Scis, si doctus evaseris, qui honores et quanta tibi praemia proponantur...[53]

Thus the work does not represent a clear break with the academic tradition, only a tentative adaptation. Sulpizio merely transfers the rules for writing an *oratio* (a word he employs when he forgets that he is talking about the *epistola*) to the art of letter-writing. In fact, here may be seen the first hesitant step towards a rapprochement between the academy (including the university) and the outside world. Cristoforo Landino had earlier recognized both the importance of style in the ambience of the Chancellery, and the contribution humanists had made to the development of this notion.[54] Sulpizio demonstrated his awareness of the increasing importance of correctly addressing a highly-placed personage by providing a list of adjectives, including «munificus» and «splendidus», to be used according to the person's position.

The difference between Sulpizio and Pomponio Leto becomes even clearer when we examine their respective attitudes towards the theatre. For Leto, theatre was fundamentally a grammatical exercise transferred to the stage (even if

---

[51]   B. Pecci, *L'umanesimo e la «Cioceria»*, pp. 29-111.

[52]   G. Sulpizio, *De Componendis et Ornandis Epistolis ad Philippum Gentilem Pallavicinum Patritium Genuensem Opusculum*, Venice (?), 1488 (?), 4°.

[53]   See previous note. The passage quoted occurs in the dedicatory letter.

[54]   C. Landino, *Formulario de Epistole Vulgare Missive e Responsive e Altri Fiori de Ornati Parlamenti*, Bologna, 1485, 4°.

it appears that he directed productions) whereas, I would argue, Sulpizio had a deeper interest in the theatre: as well as being an editor of Vitruvius, he supervised performances of classical drama. He dedicated his edition of Vitruvius to Raffaele Riario to whom he writes in the preface:

> A te, quoque, theatrum novum, tota urbs, magnis votis, expectat. Accinge te ocyus ad hanc beneficentiam alacriter exhibendam. Quid enim popularius, quid gloriosius ista tua actione facere possis?[55]

Sulpizio, then, understood the potential of the theatre as a popular entertainment on a large scale and as a way of increasing the prestige of the individual patron. He saw it as part of the «court system» in which intellectuals had an important role to play.

Equicola would have had the opportunity of studying these two trends at first hand and admits to the influence that Leto had upon his future development. It seems likely that he would have known Sulpizio since there exists a clear indication that Capella was in contact with him.[56] Further, Capella would have been an ideal person to gain Equicola entry to various Roman circles which signifies that Equicola would not have been unaware of the antagonisms and jealousies which tore Roman intellectual society. It was against this background, in my opinion, that he formed his own cultural response to the situation.

Another essential factor in Equicola's development would have been his exposure to Roman social life, particularly to ecclesiastical circles. Again, Capella would have been useful to him since the former was in receipt of church benefices through his contact with various high-ranking curial officials.[57] Equicola himself is known to have been on friendly terms with Cardinal Francesco Soderini whom he probably met during his stay in Rome. Their friendship endured right to the end of Equicola's life. Thus it may be said with some certainty that Equicola had access to the highest echelons of Roman society. Lack of documentation renders it difficult to determine the part played by Pietro Giampaolo Cantelmo in promoting his *protégé* in Roman society. In any case, it appears that Equicola was free from financial

---

[55] See B. Pecci, *L'umanesimo e la «Cioceria»*, p. 52. My interpretation of the role of theatre in the Roman Academy differs significantly from that offered by A. Grafton and L. Jardine, *From Humanism to the Humanities. Education and the Liberal Arts in Fifteenth- and Sixteenth-Century Europe*, London, 1986, pp. 89-91. In my view, the authors evade the central question of any political implications of theatre in Renaissance Rome. The statement that Leto's and Sulpizio's productions were possible «thanks to the support of a generous patron, Cardinal Raffaele Riario» (p. 89) fails to acknowledge that theatre was, above all, a political event which reflected on the patron.

[56] See R. Weiss, «In obitu Ursini Lanfredini. A footnote to the literary history of Rome under Pope Innocent VIII», *IMU*, 2 (1959) 353-66.

[57] Consult *DBI*, 18, pp. 468-70.

problems. He even owned a house in Rome, though we do not know exactly how or when he acquired it.[58] All in all, his time in Rome appears to have been well spent; according to one of his correspondents he even managed to secure a certain reputation for himself:

> De voi multo s'è parlato con uno dotto putto, et ultra le lettere è formuso de corpo et bellissimo de vulto, d'età de 16 anni. Ve conosce per fama in Roma. È creato de Fedra [Tomaso Inghirami], se chiama Ioan Francesco, è scripto al numero delli altri servitori. Quando serrete venuto, ve piacerà sua pratica.[59]

Equicola recognized the first place that Rome held in his intellectual development. From all the possible influences that could have affected him, he chose the one which emanated from Pomponio Leto. It appears rather strange that a humanist whose career was so different from Leto's did not find it contradictory to declare that he owed so much to the Roman humanist. Altogether, Equicola lived in a different world from that of his teacher. If he had praised Raffaele Maffei it would have been rather less surprising.[60] As it is, Equicola decided to single out Leto for praise in three of his works: the *De Mulieribus*, the *Chronica de Mantua* and the *Genealogia de li Signori da Este*.[61] The last two mentioned works are both historical, a field into which Leto had also ventured. These works may be seen as a transposition of Leto's method from the strictly limited area of the institutions of Ancient Rome to a study of the institutions of the northern Italian states — to put it simply, the ruling families. Just as Pomponio Leto had studied the structure of power in Roman society in his work *De Magistratibus*, Equicola studied the sole source of power in the Ferrarese domains, namely the Estensi. The same may be said for the *Chronica* which is a history of the Gonzaga princes. Leto had studied the history of the Roman Emperors whereas Equicola was only concerned with the history of the families which employed him. Equicola did not completely neglect Roman history: he used it, in the same way as many other humanists in the service of despots, to add a further dimension to his praise of the ruling families.

The *De Mulieribus* presents a more difficult problem, as it raises the question as to why Equicola should lavish praise on Leto in a work alien to the spirit of the Roman Academy where, with the exception of Pomponio Leto's

---

[58] For reference to this house see Luzio, «ne' primordi», p. 456 n. 1; Luzio-Renier, *La coltura*, p. 75 n. 2.

[59] ASMN, AG, b. 283, 26 April 1502, «Nicolaus Athyas» to Equicola. This letter is important in that it provides relatively early evidence of Equicola's stay in Rome. It also indirectly points to his connections with the Roman Academy because «Fedra», Tomaso Inghirami, was a well-known member.

[60] See Dionisotti, *Gli umanisti*, pp. 41-43.

[61] Cf. Santoro, p. 25.

daughter, women played hardly any part at all. From the moment Equicola addresses Leto as «Pythagoras meus» doubt is aroused, and when he claims that «divus ille Pomponius Laetus» was responsible for directing him towards the study of Plato, disbelief sets in. Leto was no Greek scholar and it is unlikely that he would have advised anyone to study Plato. A possible explanation is that Equicola was attempting to repay a debt of profound gratitude to his old teacher who had stimulated his interest in Latin culture. He was probably trying to restore confidence in Leto's abilities as an accomplished humanist, given the low opinion humanists outside the University of Rome had of him. The *De Mulieribus* was the first work that Equicola wrote in Ferrara and it is likely that he wished to establish both his own credentials and those of his mentors. Finally, in this work Equicola again discusses the northern Italian courts in terms of their institutions, but in this instance he directs his attention to the court Lady — he had understood Leto's method of studying Ancient Rome through its various institutions and applied it to the study of the court.

Equicola followed his master in one other respect: Leto was an archaeologist who took great pleasure not only in discovering the physical remnants of Rome's glorious past but also in the recovery of the rarest Latin texts. Likewise, Equicola was seduced, to a point, by the possibility of exhibiting his knowledge of the most esoteric subjects and the rarest texts, often to the detriment of a more organized approach to his material. Pomponio Leto in particular, and Roman humanists in general, may be said to have conditioned his response to the other intellectual currents that he would meet in the future. Leto remained for Equicola a symbol of intellectual purity which had moved out of his reach because of his decision to employ his humanism in the service of princes. Equicola's method and style express a certain nostalgia for a life devoted to study. His fondness for etymology and the study of the origins and history of institutions are an essential part of his scholarship, inherited from the Roman tradition of humanism.

Although Equicola was to remain basically «Roman» in his intellectual outlook, his actual stay in the city of Rome was of a limited duration. It is probable that he had left Rome by 1494, although so far no evidence has been discovered to support such a hypothesis. Yet from what we know of Equicola's intellectual formation and his relations with the Cantelmo family, 1494 or the period immediately preceding would be the most likely date for his departure. Thus, after a relatively long period of stability, he set out on a journey which was to lead him through some of the major cultural centres of the Italian Renaissance.

*

The period from about 1490 to 1498 is distinguished by an almost total lack of documentation about Equicola, with the documentation that we do have (especially for the early part of this decade) often being of a much later date than the events described. Such is the case with the letters of the Archdeacon of Mantua, written almost thirty years later, which inform us that Equicola spent nine or eleven years in Rome. Other later evidence also seems to support the theory of a long stay in Rome: the fact that Equicola owned a house there and that Bernardino Capella, towards the end of his life, intended to give up church benefices in Equicola's favour.

It may be possible that Equicola spent a short time in Cesena where Giulio Cesare Cantelmo was governor in 1490-92.[62] The evidence is only indirect and ambiguous. The fact that Francesco Uberti, a Cesenate humanist, addresses an epigram to Equicola could merely be an acknowledgement of the latter's fame, perhaps made more pertinent through the Bishop's sojourn in the city. It is also possible that Equicola and Uberti met independently at some later date. The Cesena connection is strengthened with the appearance of the *Epithome Plutarchi*, the work of another Cesenate humanist, Dario Tiberti.

---

[62] Equicola always seemed to be having trouble with his affairs in Rome. On occasion, Isabella d'Este intervened in his favour:

> La pregamo voglia interponere sua auctorità che'l signor Troilo Savello non dia in inpacio alle cose de ditto Mario né voglia inpedire le sue ragioni.

(ASMN, AG, b. 2997, libro 33, Mantua, 28 May 1516, Isabella d'Este to Pietro Margano. Isabella wrote in similar terms on the same day to Ettore Romano.)

Information on Capella is to be found in P.L. Galletti, *Canonici Lateranenses 1475-1519*, BAV, Vat.lat. 8037). He adds a number of details which he discovered as a result of his archival researches. According to Galletti Capella was elected secretary of the Chapter for the year 1497 (he had taken possession of the canonicate in 1494, p. 33). Galletti notes that Capella undertook a journey to France with Giordano Ursini in 1498 (p. 33). In August 1508 Capella resigned because he had been elected canon of St Peter's: «ed a 19 di ottobre restituì al Capitolo Lateranense vari libri di letteratura che aveane ricevuto per suo uso d'onde si scorge che vi era biblioteca. Ne fu fatto il seguente decreto:

> MDVIII. XIII Octob.

> D. Bernardini Capella consignavit in Capitulo certos libros quos ipse tenebat ab ecclesia, videlicet, Iuvenalem, Fastos, Decretali, Gratianum, Donatum super Terentium, Priscianum et quandam bullam qualiter Antoniani est voster, videlicet, Capituli et Ecclesiae. k. ix. 22. (p. 33)

Uberti's *Epigrammaton Libellus* can be found in the Biblioteca Malatestiana, Cesena, S XXIX 21 (an inaccurate 18th-century copy is in the Biblioteca Comunale Ariostea, Ferrara, MSS., classe II n. 305B). The poem to Equicola is on f. 4 :

> Ad Marium Equicolum

> Docte Mari infestum potes o tibi credere Syllam
> Me puer? Ergo ad me quae rogo causa fugae?

Equicola's letter has been published with brief notes by G. Resta, *Le epitomi di Plutarco nel Quattrocento*, Padua, 1962, pp. 77-79. For details of Giulio Cesare's governorship of Cesena consult G. Fantaguzzi, *Caos. Cronache cesenati del sec. XV*, a cura di D. Bazzocchi, Cesena, 1915, p. 37, for the year 1491.

The preface bears the date 30 April 1492. The first dedicatory letter is from Equicola to Giulio Cesare Cantelmo. Certainly it does not mean Equicola was with the Bishop in Cesena but the possibility cannot be dismissed.

Closer in time to the period in question is the reference to Pomponio Leto in the *De Mulieribus*. If, indeed, Equicola did spend about ten years in Rome, as seems likely, and taking into account the time he spent in Alvito under the tutelage of Pietro Giampaolo Cantelmo before 1487, the date of the latter's expulsion from Alvito and his flight to Rome, serious consideration must be given to the hypothesis that Equicola left Rome in 1494, or even later, to go and fight in the *Regno* by the side of his feudal lord.[63] If, on the other hand, we do not completely accept the testimony of a very ancient and perhaps senile lady we are still left with the other evidence concerning Equicola's Roman connections which presupposes a stay of some length in the city. The number of years actually spent there may be open to question but that they add up to a substantial amount seems a reasonable assumption given the nature of the evidence.

This hypothesis has important implications for the intellectual biography of Equicola as it has often been asserted that during this period he stayed in Florence long enough to acquire an interest in Neoplatonism.[64] There is no doubt that Equicola visited Florence but the question is when. His documented visits to that city all occurred later in his career, at a time when he was already in the employment of Isabella d'Este. Although Florence would have constituted an important stopping-off place on the way from Mantua to Rome,[65] the urgency of Equicola's diplomatic missions would not have allowed him sufficient time to attend to his cultural interests. Before entering Isabella's service, as will be shown, he may have had opportunities for contact with the leading figures of the Neoplatonic movement, yet, once again, he would only have been passing through either en route for the *Regno* or on the return journey north to Ferrara. The problem of any connections with Florence is rendered all the more acute by the early date of the first draft of the *Libro de natura de amore*, begun in about 1495.[66] It would appear that Equicola's absorption of Neoplatonism must have been at a relatively early date in order to provide him with the necessary stimulus to write the *Libro*.

[63]   R. Feola, «Cantelmo, Pietro Giampaolo», *DBI*, 18, pp. 272-74.

[64]   Cf. L. Savino, *Di alcuni trattati e trattatisti d'amore italiani*, p. 10 n. 6.

[65]   Consult M. Catalano, *Vita di Ludovico Ariosto*, vol. 2, Geneva, 1931, pp. 130-31. Equicola writes in the letter quoted by Catalano that he was staying in Giuliano de' Medici's palace in Florence and that he had supper with Lodovico Ariosto (21 March 1513).

[66]   See R. Renier, «Per la cronologia», pp. 220-21; L. Savino, pp. 2-3.

However, since this first draft is not extant it is impossible to state with any degree of certainty how imbued it was with Neoplatonic philosophy. Further, by this date it was no longer necessary for a person interested in Neoplatonism to travel to Florence: he could just as easily have read the Latin translations and commentaries of Ficino. The second generation Neoplatonist no longer needed the pioneering spirit which characterized Ficino and his circle.

On the other hand, it must be said that Equicola does not seem to have been entirely isolated from the centre of the Neoplatonic movement. Years after the period in question, Sigismondo Cantelmo, still in pursuit of his lost duchy, found his way to Florence where he gave Equicola's greetings to various people:

> Ho fatto le vostre ricommandationi ad messer Francesco Iaceto col quale molto ho praticato. Tutto dice esser vostro et vi referisse gratie che teniate de lui memoria. Il simile fa messer Ioanne et Palla Rucelaio.[67]

«Francesco Iaceto» was no other than Francesco Diacceto, the Neoplatonic philosopher and the leading figure of that movement in Florence after Ficino's death.[68] This discovery is not as conclusive as at first sight appears. For in common with a number of Equicola's early acquaintances, we cannot tell exactly when and where he first met him. In this case, friendship with Diacceto would militate against the theory of Equicola having been to Florence in the early 1490s. It must be remembered that Ficino was alive throughout the decade, only dying in 1499.[69] Also, in the last years of Ficino's life Diacceto became one of his closest companions as well as his most outstanding pupil. Equicola always speaks of Ficino as if the only contact with him had been through the medium of the printed word. Moreover, Equicola places particular emphasis on one aspect of his work, affirming that he is one of those «preclari ingegni» who have made their contribution to makind «con fatigarse per commune utilità in interpretare li nobili scritti di altra lingua in la sua».[70] This and similar statements do not speak well for Equicola's

---

[67]   ASMN, AG, b. 1107, Florence, 27 August 1519, Sigismondo Cantelmo to Equicola.

[68]   The fundamental essay on this philosopher is P.O. Kristeller, «Francesco da Diacceto and Florentine Platonism in the sixteenth century» in *Studies in Renaissance Thought and Letters*, Rome, 1956, pp. 287-336. Cf. Francisci Catanei Diacetii, *De Pulchro Libri III*, edited by S. Matton, Pisa, 1986, pp. 366, 379-83.

[69]   For Ficino's biography see R. Marcel, *Marsile Ficino (1433-1499)*, Paris, 1958.

[70]   *Libro*, f. 20r.

intimacy with Ficino nor his knowledge of Greek. There is not the slightest hint that Equicola ever knew him personally.[71] In the printed edition of the *Libro de natura de amore* Equicola, in his review of modern writers on love, discusses Diacceto after Ficino:

> Francesco Cattani Diaceto da Fiorenza, di Marsilio Ficino creato et amato discipulo, homo da ogni ambitione alieno, di mediocrità contento, del suo lieto, fu philosopho platonico (*Libro*, f. 24ʳ).

These details, entirely absent from his treatment of Ficino, though they may be nothing more than a common-place description of a philosopher's temperament, could indicate that Equicola may have had personal contact with Diacceto. He regarded Diacceto as a living example of a Platonist philosopher whereas Ficino is a mere translator. However, a search of the autograph manuscript for the section on Diacceto reveals no mention of him although there is a section on Ficino.[72] It must thus be argued with some conviction that, because Diacceto is a later addition, Equicola had not yet met him or, alternatively, had not been sufficiently influenced by him to warrant including him in his review of writers on love. It is much more probable that Equicola's relationship with Diacceto was a product of the first or second decade of the sixteenth century when Equicola was at Mantua. The former's missions to Rome may have provided the opportunity for brief discussions[73].

If Florence did not have a direct influence on Equicola's decision to write the *Libro*, it is necessary to ask whether there would have been any stimulus in Rome itself? However, Equicola's own personality as an intellectual must also be taken into account. He may have been drawn to Neoplatonism because he saw it as a convenient vehicle for his thought. It is important to emphasize

---

[71] During his discussion of Giovan Francesco Pico, Equicola does not omit to mention that he saw him once in an activity that had little to do with the philosophy of love: «Ne li primi giovenili soi anni il vidi conduttero di molte gendarme di Alphonso secondo, Re di Napoli et quelle governare con molta prudentia» (*Libro*, f. 22ᵛ).

[72] In the autograph manuscript the section on Ficino is preceded by that on Boccaccio (as in the printed version) and followed by that on Battista Fregoso, whereas in the printed version it is followed by the section on Giovanni Pico. In the manuscript the section on Ficino comes much nearer to the beginning of the «rassegna». See also M. Pozzi, «Mario Equicola e la cultura cortigiana: appunti sulla redazione manoscritta del *Libro de natura de amore*, *Lettere Italiane*, 32 (1980) 147-171; 158.

[73] Equicola was certainly aware of Diacceto's translations into the vernacular of the latter's work while it was still circulating in only manuscript form. The vernacular versions of his writings on the philosophy of love would only be printed after Equicola's death:

> Et scrisse tre libri in lingua latina di amore, redutti da lui medesmo in idioma fiorentino patrio, solamente per far intendere a questi toscanezanti che non bene scriveno né bene parlano la lingua tosca, laqual se credeno benissimo haver appressa et essere in quella docti doctori et maestri (*Libro*, f. 24ʳ).

Diacceto's *Panegirico* was published in Rome in 1526, and *I tre libri d'amore* in Venice in 1561.

that Equicola approached Neoplatonism as someone schooled in the traditions of Roman humanism, not as a pure philosopher. But a concrete link with Florentine culture might be provided in the figure of Francesco Soderini who, in the years to come, was to demonstrate the intimacy of his relationship with Equicola. Soderini was personally acquainted with Ficino and was highly praised by Paolo Cortese as a man of considerable learning with an active interest in culture, indicated by his large collection of books.[74] Through his friendship with Soderini Equicola could have been initiated into the mysteries of Neoplatonism in an environment which showed little enthusiasm for this philosophy.

*

[74] For example, Ficino includes a letter entitled *De Perseverantia* addressed to Soderini in his *Liber epistolarum* (*Opera omnia*, Basle: *Ex officina Henrici Petrina*, 1576, p. 672, bk.I of the letters); *The letters of Marsilio Ficino*, I, London, 1975, pp. 194-95, 232, but see K. Lowe, *Francesco Soderini (1453-1524), Florentine Patrician and Cardinal*, Ph.D., Warburg Institute, University of London, 1985, p. 258, where it is argued that because Ficino wrote letters to all of the Soderini brothers there would have been political motives present rather than praise of just one of them.

Cortese mentions Soderini a number of times in the *De Cardinalatu*, nearly always to praise his learning:

> Quo magis (in audiendo et consulendo) Franciscus Soderinus senator in hoc genere laudari potest qui quamquam vehementer scientiarum cupiditate flagret quotidieque magnorum negociorum assiduitate occupetur in lucubratorium, tamen, admittere postulantes solet quo abeuntibus salutatoribus facilis ei detur ad studia inchoata reditus, partitaque vicissitudine semper in actione rerum et doctrinae cognitione sit in quo est hominum vita beata sita.
>
> (*De Card.*, f. 83ʳ; see also f. 67ʳ)

Cortese, right from the beginning of the work, wishes to lay considerable emphasis on Soderini's commitment to learning:

> Ex quo Francescus Soderinus senator, homo rerum usu limatus et magnarum artium scientia dissimulanter doctus, saepe dicit celerrime hominum quotidiana colloquia solere sine disciplinarum cognitione consumi.   (*De Card.*, f. 13ᵛ)

Independent evidence for the size of Soderini's library can be found in Archivio di Stato, Rome, Notari dell'Archivio Capitolino, Jo. Jacobus Apocellus (1523), 410ʳ, 126ᵛ: «In studorio dicti domini Cardinalis fuerunt plures libri diversarum facultatum et diversorum autorum, quorum numerum non notavi.» The *De Cardinalatu* represents an important attempt at creating a theoretical structure which will accommodate changes in the way cardinals should behave and act. However, Cortese did not theorize in a vacuum and he drew heavily upon his memories and experiences of Roman society, often in a polemical fashion (see J.F. D'Amico, *Renaissance Humanism in Papal Rome*, Baltimore and London, 1983, pp. 78-80, 227-37). The quarrels that split Roman society are never far absent from the work. Cortese, as well as praising his friends, is not slow to pour scorn on those people who do not meet his standards, such as Pomponio Leto. Even Bernardino Capella is bitterly attacked in the chapter «De simonia»:

> Velut si in altero affirmemus Bernardinum Capellam poetam lateranense flaminium permutare cum sacerdotio vaticano velle, nullo modo dicamus eum

Equicola's departure from Rome probably coincided with that of Pietro Giampaolo's who sought to regain his possessions in the *Regno* with the help of the French. The invasion of 1494 also caught up Equicola in its whirlwind of hopes and actual change. He came into contact with Neapolitan culture for an extended period of time after his exile in Rome. Although it would have been possible for Equicola to have visited Naples while in Rome it seems unlikely, especially considering the political climate. Moreover, an extended stay in Naples would have been rendered difficult, partly through Equicola's close association with the Cantelmos and partly for financial reasons: the family's fall from grace resulted in the necessity to transfer the remainder of their wealth to other places in the peninsula, to Rome and Ferrara in particular. However, Equicola would not have lost all contact with the *Regno* since Rome acted as a magnet for the Neapolitan humanists.[75] In spite of the furious military activity, Equicola would have come into contact with various Neapolitan intellectuals. The shock of this sudden change could have induced him to crystallize his ideas on the philosophies of love and begin the composition of the *Libro*. Throughout this period in the *Regno*, Equicola was employed as Pietro Giampaolo's secretary, perhaps the same position he held in Rome during the former duke's exile there.

At first, nothing seemed to stand in the way of Pietro Giampaolo's return and the successful reconquest of his dominions. As long as the French remained in control the Cantelmo family fortunes were high.[76] The climax of the French success was the entry of Charles VIII into Naples on 22 February 1495: «e fu accompagnato da gran numero de signori e baroni napolitani».[77] Amongst these, there must have been members of the Cantelmo clan loyal to the French, if not Pietro Giampaolo himself. Equicola would not have lacked an opportunity to make contract with the centre of humanism in southern

---

debere postulari ambitus etiam si sacerdotium vaticanum possit dimidio aestimari pluri.

(*De Card.*, f. 195ᵛ)

This bitter rivalry between various groups of intellectuals does not appear to have prevented Equicola from forming a friendly relationship with Soderini. It is impossible to determine, in the present state of our knowledge, how well, if at all, Equicola was acquainted with Cortese. Since Equicola was closely connected with both Leto and Capella he may not have been able to overcome the stigma attached by Cortese to his association with them.

[75]   For example, Calmeta, in his life of Serafino Aquilano, names the Neapolitan Pietro Gravina as a member of Cortese's academy (V. Calmeta, *Prose e lettere edite e inedite*, a cura di C. Grayson, Bologna, 1959, p. 63). See also B. Croce, «Un umanista gaudente: Pietro Gravina», in *Scritti di storia letteraria e politica*, vol. 20 (*Uomini e cose della vecchia Italia*), Bari 1927, pp. 13-26.

[76]   See V. Lazari, «Della zecca di Sora e delle monete di Piergiampaolo Cantelmi», *ASI*, n.s., 3 (1856), dispensa seconda, pp. 221-25.

[77]   G.A. Summonte, *Dell'historia della città e regno di Napoli*, III, Naples, 1640, p. 515.

Italy.[78] But time was running out for the French. The Cantelmos were quickly losing the possessions they had just won. In the last days of the French occupation Equicola took on an active, military role in the desperate attempts to save his lord's territories. In charge of the fortress of Sora, Equicola refused to surrender until Pietro Giampaolo himself arrived and handed over the fortress to Spanish troops.[79] Equicola's loyalty had its origins not only in his

---

[78]   In this connection some of his relations with fellow southerners have yet to be explored: such is the case with Ambrosius Flandinus. This Neapolitan cleric was later to become suffragan bishop of Mantua (perhaps as a «punishment» for some of his views on theological matters he was posted to a minor provincial city). It is difficult to know when Flandinus and Equicola first met since the former's early biography is so obscure but it is likely that they only made their first acquaintance in Mantua (on him see C. Minieri Riccio, *Memorie storiche degli scrittori nati nel Regno di Napoli*, Naples, 1844, p. 130). Equicola is briefly mentioned in the preface of Flandinus' *De Animorum Immortalitate* (on which see D.E. Rhodes, «A bibliography of Mantua, II, 1507-1521», *La bibliofilia*, Anno 58, 1956, p. 166 n. 12; on Flandinus' ability as a thinker see R. Lemay, «The fly against the elephant: Flandinus against Pomponazzi on fate» in *Philosophy and Humanism*, ed. by E.P. Mahoney, Leiden, 1976, pp. 70-99). Equicola seems to have been involved as an intellectual go-between in the dispute, though Flandinus still retains a high opinion of him: «Mario Aequicolo viro et litteris et ingenio praestantissimo» (*De Animorum Immortalitate*, f. uA2). Flandinus is the author of a number of commentaries on various works by Plato. It is probable that there was a fruitful exchange of ideas on the Greek philosopher as well as on topics of religious significance. Equicola also provides a preface to Flandinus' *Quadragesimalium Concionum Liber*, published in Venice in 1523 («Marius Equicola amplissimo patri et Illustrissimo domino Sigismundo Gonzaga Mantuano Cardinali. Salutem», [f. 664ᵛ]). The preface is interesting in that Equicola does not fail to mention Jacques Lefèvre («Ecce Jacobus Faber preceptor meus optimus et eruditissimus» [f. 664ᵛ]). Such a mention of someone with clear heretical tendencies places both Equicola and Flandinus in a possibly difficult situation vis-à-vis the established Church. Other intellectuals are mentioned who are seen as being influential on the secretary:

> Veneramur Egidios, Picos, Erasmos, Georgium Franciscum, Franciscum ferrariensem. (f. 664ᵛ)

As in all else Equicola demonstrates in the matter of religion an eclectic culture, mentioning in a single breath Egidio da Viterbo, Giovanni Pico, Erasmus, Francesco Giorgio (on whom see C. Vasoli, «Intorno a Francesco Giorgio Veneto e all''armonia del mondo'» in *Profezia e ragione: studi sulla cultura del Cinquecento e del Seicento*, Naples, 1974, pp. 129-403) and Francesco Silvestri. The purpose of this list is to show what distinguished company Flandinus keeps: «Inter hos noster Ambrosius Neapolitanus fulget» (f. 664ᵛ). For further details on him see S. Seidel Menchi, «La discussione su Erasmo nell'Italia del Rinascimento. Ambrogio Flandino vescovo a Mantova, Ambrogio Quistelli teologo padovano e Alberto Pio principe di Carpi» in *Società, politica e cultura a Carpi ai tempi di Alberto III Pio. Atti del convegno internazionale (Carpi, 19-21 maggio 1978)*, 2 vols, Padua, 1981, pp. 291-381.

[79]   Et contò (Sannazaro) come lui si trovò presente quando tenivate (Equicola) lo castello di Sora, et benché lo Re ce fusse accampo et lo figlio primogenito del Duca di Sora venesse con lettere del patre che rendisse lo castello, non lo voliste mai rendere insino che 'l Duca non venne dentro lo castello et lui lo rese (quoted in Luzio-Renier, *La coltura*, p. 414 n. 2; ASMN, AG, b. 809).

Sannazaro is here recalling events that happened over twenty years previously. Yet there is no doubt that Equicola's action remained fixed in his mind: that Sannazaro is able to recall the event in some detail is evidence of this.

service to the Cantelmos but also in the realization that once the family
returned into exile, he would lose his predetermined place in society. The year
after Charles VIII's entry into Naples, the Cantelmos had lost nearly
everything. Their last possession, Alvito, surrendered to King Federico, in
January 1497. Here, their humiliation was complete when they swore
allegiance to the king.[80] Pietro Giampaolo could not long endure the thought
of once more being exiled from his lands, and he died in February of that year.

Pietro Giampaolo's sons had a decision to make: either they could continue their father's pro-French policy or attempt a reconciliation with the
Aragonese king in the hope of being reinstated in their feuds. Those who had
remained loyal to Pietro Giampaolo now found themselves divided.
Sigismondo never seems to have had the slightest doubt about the French being in a position to restore the family to their duchy. Thus, for him, the best
way to help their cause was to return north to Ferrara where he would be
assured of a warm welcome from Ercole d'Este who was still obstinately pursuing a pro-French policy. Pietro Giampaolo's eldest son, Ferrante, seems to
have been much more of a realist and saw the improbability of another French
conquest of the *Regno*. Thus, for his part, Ferrante reversed the direction of
his father's politics and sought a rapprochement with the Aragonese dynasty
as being the only way of recovering his lands.

Almost by law of succession, Equicola found himself in the employment
of Ferrante Cantelmo, probably as his secretary. Both Ferrante and Equicola
are mentioned in a poem which describes the progress of Isabella del Balzo,
wife of Federico d'Aragona, through the Kingdom of Naples until her arrival
in Naples itself (15 October 1497). The poem ends with the king and queen
reunited in Naples (13 February 1498). The importance of this narrative poem
lies in its accurate historical portrayal of Isabella del Balzo's court, written
shortly after the event. In spite of its clear encomiastic intent, Rogeri de
Piacenza's *Lo Balzino* does not lose sight of historical reality.[81] It seems probable that Ferrante Cantelmo stayed with the Queen of Naples for most of her
journey to Naples, only leaving her to fight the Prince of Salerno, one of the
last remaining rebels to the crown.[92] It is during the Queen's long stay at

---

[80] See R. Feola, p. 273.

[81] Rogeri de Piacenza di Nardò, *Opere (cod. per. F27)*, a cura di M. Marti, Lecce, 1977.

[82] Ferrante does not seem to have been with the Queen from the start of her journey. He
joined the Queen at Andria and stayed at her court throughout her stay in Barletta. At some
time, he left her court in order to fight for the king, though he may have entered Naples with
her on 15 October 1497. The poet describes the meeting between Ferrante and the Queen at Andria:

Barletta that Equicola makes his appearance in the poem. We see him playing his part in an attempt to win the Queen's favour. He places his learning at the disposal of his master in the form of a Latin poem lauding the virtues of Isabella del Balzo to the skies:

> Stava in Barletta col signor Ferrante,
> figlio al Duca de Soro, un poeta,
> iovene dotto, con manere sante,
> chiamato misser Mario De Albeta.
> Un giorno, ne la sala ognun llà stante
> con accorta eloquencia e discreta
> parlò e basò la mano a la regina
> e dideli sti versi in gran dottrina. *(Lo Balzino, VI, ll. 935-42, p. 215)*

Rogeri de Piacenza quotes Equicola's poem in full, a not unusual procedure in the context of *Lo Balzino*, used perhaps to enhance the rough vernacular of the rest of the narrative. Equicola's poem locates the Queen in the world of classical mythology where she becomes its brightest star.[83] The poem represents the extent of Equicola's contribution to the cause of Ferrante Cantelmo: he did not need many lessons on how to conduct himself at court.

The choice of Isabella del Balzo's court had by no means been fortuitous. Ferrante would have been able to hold a place of some distinction there since he was related to Isabella through his mother, Caterina del Balzo, who was her aunt.[84] This would explain the reason behind the name of Pietro Giampaolo's eldest son: it was supposed to represent an act of submission and loyalty to his feudal lord, King Ferrante. However, after the events of 1494 which served to emphasize Pietro Giampaolo's disloyalty, the fact of being a relative of the Queen was not sufficient to wipe the slate clean. He had to prove himself loyal by his actions. For this reason Ferrante decided to fight for Federico d'Aragona against the Prince of Salerno, but his show of loyalty

---

> In questo, venne lo illustro Don Ferrante
> primo figliolo del Duca de Soro.
> Un manto de broccato avea in bando
> fatto a la franciosa in bel lavoro. *(Lo Balzino, VI, ll. 81-84, p. 191)*

The poet brings out with remarkable simplicity the difficulties of Ferrante's position. Rogeri de Piacenza is discreetly alluding to the French defeat («fatto a la franciosa») and Ferrante's kissing the Queen's hand was the act of submission of a rebellious subject.

[83] Equicola's poem fills lines 943 to 980 (pp. 215-16). The poem is in the form of a dialogue between a disgruntled Apollo and Jupiter. Apollo is angry because of Isabella del Balzo:

> Baucia (quis ferat hoc) en nostris emula flammis

(Lo Balzino, VI, l. 949, p. 215)

Jupiter calms him down and launches into praise of the Duke of Calabria:

> Regius ex ista puer inclitus ille resurget,
> dux Calabrum, egregios qui superabit avos.

(Lo Balzino, VI, ll. 963-64, p. 215)

[84] See Santoro, p. 19.

cost him his life on the battlefield early in 1498.[85] After Ferrante's death,
Equicola would have had to make a choice of his own: to try his fortune in
the *Regno* without the support of Ferrante, or go to Ferrara where Sigismondo
Cantelmo would welcome the family secretary with open arms, especially
because he had remained loyal to the family in its most difficult moments.
Equicola chose the second course of action, preferring a known protector to
the struggles which would face him in Naples. Thus the poem to Isabella del
Balzo represents an isolated incident, ended by the necessity of having to
assume a pro-French attitude at Ferrara. Sigismondo was to be intransigent
in his support for the French whether it produced results or not. Equicola, in
the future, was to see himself solely as an ally of the French; Ferrante was to
be forgotten.

*

Equicola was not permitted to remain long in Ferrara. Almost immediately the surviving Cantelmo brothers enlisted his aid in their efforts to retain the
goodwill of the ruling dynasty at Ferrara. Assuming that Equicola did not
depart from the *Regno* until after the death of Ferrante, his presence in Milan
at the beginning of March 1498 indicates the swiftness of his journey. The reason for his visit was the official installation of Ippolito d'Este as Archbishop
of Milan. It was no doubt part of his duties to the Cantelmos that he found
himself in Milan because Giulio Cesare Cantelmo was called upon to accompany Ippolito d'Este[86]. The exact length of Equicola's stay there is not known,

---

[85]   Rogeri de Piacenza is not at all niggardly with his praise of Ferrante's exploits on the
battlefield:
> Questo quel giorno fece como Orlando   (*Lo Balzino*, VIII, l. 517, p. 264)

His «cruda sorte» leads him to his death, the news of which greatly saddens the Queen:
> Venne la nova a la Signora Regina
> de la morte acerba de sto iovenetto
> (e) così a maddamma Vittoria mischina
> ch'era sorella de quel poveretto.   (*Lo Balzino*, VIII, ll. 529-32, p. 264)

[86]   A letter from Giulio Cesare Cantelmo to the Duke of Ferrara, dated Milan, 6 March
1498, is without doubt written in Equicola's hand (ASM, ASE, C, Ambasciatori: Milano,
b. 16). The text of the letter reads:
> Solum me basta fare parte de mio debito dandoli notitia como sabato III del
> presente alla Excellentia del' Illustrissimo Signor Duca piacque Monsignor
> predecto intrasse in lo burgo de la porta senese. Hogi VI de questo ad XIII hore
> da tucto 'l clero parato in processione socto 'l baldachino, et dal'Illustrissimo
> Signor Duca et tucta sua corte, imbasciatori et nobile è stato accompagnato (lo
> Illustrissimo Signor mio lo Signor Cardinale per tucta la provincia subdita alla
> metropolitana eclesia de Milan) al Domo sollennemente, con grandissimo con-
> curso del populo, dove con admiratione di ciascheuno, laudato da ogni homo ha
> facte tucte cerimonie.

but it might have been for quite some time. Even if he had stayed in Milan for only a couple of months he would have had sufficient time to meet with various humanists, one example being Battista Pio, who shared a similar outlook as far as Latin was concerned, though Pio himself was much more of an extremist than Equicola.[87] Equicola seems to have been in contact with the University of Pavia since two of his works from this period are in the form of orations delivered there.[88] Moreover, Ippolito d'Este's immediate circle provided Equicola with figures who had more than a passing interest in humanism.[89] For the most part the output of Equicola's Milanese period takes up the theme of religion as being the most appropriate subject-matter, considering the reason for Ippolito d'Este's visit and the fact that Equicola was in the entourage of Giulio Cesare Cantelmo.

The two works of this period that deal directly with a religious theme or the phenomenon of religion itself, as is the case with the *De Religione Libellus*, both have a double dedication. Both works commence with a dedication to either the cardinal or the Duke of Milan by Giulio Cesare Cantelmo who was himself frequently involved in the administration of Ippolito d'Este's ecclesiastical interests in Milan. The second dedication is from Equicola to the

---

[87]   According to both editions of the *Oratio De Passione Domini* the oration contained in the book was delivered on 29 March 1499. If this is not a misprint or a mistake it means that Equicola spent over a year in Milan. He would have had time to renew or make initial contact with Francesco Soderini who was in Milan on a diplomatic mission from 24 December 1498 to 13 September 1499 (I thank Kate Lowe for the information concerning Soderini). On Pio see E. Raimondi, *Codro e l'umanesimo a Bologna*, Bologna, 1950, pp. 108-113; Idem, «Il primo commento umanistico a Lucrezio» in *Politica e commedia. Dal Beroaldo al Machiavelli*, Bologna, 1972, pp. 101-40; C. Dionisotti, *Gli umanisti*, p. 114 n. 1.

It is not impossible that Equicola may have made Castiglione's acquaintance during his stay in Milan, especially because of the former's connection with Ferrarese interests. Cf. BAV, Vat. Lat. 8213 «Jo. Stephanus de Castiliono» to «Cristophoro de Castiliono», Milan, 2 February 1499, f. 7 (quoted by V. Cian, *Nel mondo di Baldassarre Castiglione. Documenti illustrati* [Estr. dall'*ASL*, Anno VII, Fasc. 1-4, 1942], MIlan, 1942, pp. 28-29):

> «Ceterum facio intendere ala Vostra Magnificenza como messer Baldessaro suo figliolo sta bene et è molto ben visto dal nostro Illustrissimo Signore e universalmente da tuti e meritamente perché in vero non poria essere né più gentile né più virtuoso quanto è. La Vostra Magnificenza ha a fare pensiero di accompagnarlo qui a Milano e fare qualche parentado honorevole e serà a consolatione de la Vostra Magnificenza e de tuti li suoi parenti».

[88]   For a typographical description of Equicola's works of this period see *Gesamtkatalog der Wiegendrucke*, Band 8, Stuttgart, Berlin and New York, 1978, *ad vocem*, columns 71-73.

For a list of teachers employed at the University of Pavia see G. Porro, «Pianta delle spese per l'università di Pavia nel 1498», *ASL*, ser. 1, 5 (1878) 505-16.

[89]   The Ferrarese edition of the *De Passione Domini* ends with reference to two humanists in Estense employment: Luca Ripa (for whom see M.E. Cosenza, *Dictionary*, IV, pp. 3061-62) and Pescennius Franciscus Niger (for whom see G. Mercati, *Ultimi contributi alla storia degli umanisti*, Fascicolo II, Città del Vaticano, 1939, particularly pages 69-82).

same Giulio Cesare.[90] These dedications reflect the hierarchical order of precedence adopted in the court: Equicola at this point was not in a position to
address the prince, Cardinal Ippolito d'Este, directly and was totally dependent on the intercession of Giulio Cesare. However, with the passing of time,
he was able to impress upon the cardinal his personal worth and his usefulness
to him.

The *De Passione Domini Oratio* deals with a common enough theme of
medieval religious literature, yet Equicola managed to insert a number of
ideas which he was to develop in later works. Indeed, his description of the
Passion fills less space than discussion of other topics and seems to serve only
as a base on which to practise his erudition and rhetoric. Equicola claims that
Giulio Cesare was responsible for removing certain infelicities of style and, in
general, making various corrections:

> Ab omni animi et corporis purgatus contagione, ex tuis sacratissimis manibus sus-
> cepturus Eucharistiae salutare sacramentum, Theologicae me tradidi lectioni. Et
> qua ursinum quodammodo foetum peperi que tu postea eruditissimus in formam
> figuramque redegisti. (Quoted in Santoro, p. 121 n. 1.)

The oration is substantially a revised version of an earlier attempt at a Latin
oration for a specific religious purpose, whereas the present work is made to
demonstrate the fruits of Equicola's humanist training. It is difficult to ascertain the extent of Giulio Cesare's influence on Equicola because of an almost
total lack of information on the former's intellectual interests although, from
the brief reference here, they appear to have been of a theological nature.
Thus, not only Pietro Giampaolo, but his sons as well were able to encourage
Equicola's interest in learning.

This brief work mentions in passing the chief events of Christ's life, but
never forgets that it is an oration. One of Equicola's stylistic devices is the rhetorical question. It allows him to vary his passion for listing things, although
one feels that he is excessive in its use. At times, Equicola is encouraged by
the subject-matter to discuss such topics as number-symbolism or the utter
uselessness of magical practices, themes that will recur in the *Libro*. The *De
Passione Domini*, however, pales beside the much more complex *De Religione
Libellus*, both published in the period 1498-1499. One thing they do seem to
have in common is that they both have their roots in an earlier period of Equicola's life, and Milan provided the opportunity to make them public.

The *De Religione* is of particular interest in the development of Equicola's
thought. The work seems to fit in neatly with the Roman tradition of humanism. It was not however free from controversy as can be seen from the fact

---

[90]   The *De Passione Domini* has as its most important dedicatee the Duke of Milan, Ludovico Sforza, while Giulio Cesare Cantelmo, in the *De Religione* addresses Ippolito d'Este.

that Battista Spagnuoli makes the work the subject of a poem written to defend Equicola from his detractors. Although the poem was composed quite a while after the publication of the *De Religione* (but not later than 1513), it is not unlikely that Spagnuoli could have obtained his information first-hand, from Equicola himself.[91] Spagnuoli asserts that Equicola produced the work in Rome:

> Dum iuvenis Roma florentes degeret annos,
> Lascivum ediderit laesa gravitate libellum.
>
> *(Pro Mario*, ll. 2-3, f. 189ᵛ)

Spagnuoli gives a faithful resumé of the entire work towards the end of his poem in order to prove that it is not at all an anti-Christian pamphlet:

> Legimus illius de religione libellum
> Multa fruge gravem: natos ab origine ritus
> Subiicientem oculis, per regna externa vagantem,
> Per populos omnes, per sacra antiqua deorum.
> Et demum nostras, velut ad tutissima quaedam
> Littora tranquillosque sinus se sistit ad aras,
> Vociferans Christum pleno ore deumque triformem.
>
> *(Pro Mario*, ll. 64-70, f. 190ᵛ)

Such a description does not distort Equicola's methodology in the *De Religione* which is a careful chronological study of the development of religion. Equicola begins his work by affirming that the need to believe in a supra-human force is a universal phenomenon. Thus, the basis of all religions is the same.[92] The gods of differing pagan religions may have different names, yet they all express the same concept. Equicola pays particular attention to the religion of ancient Egypt, especially to their gods. So far, Equicola's interest has been that of an antiquarian who knows the clear superiority of his own religion, but nevertheless feels the early pagan religions represent something interesting in their own right. However, when he reaches the Roman religion there is a difficulty because the Romans are the object of a new faith, the humanist faith. Equicola attempts to find a way out of his predicament:

> Romanos idolatriae deditos non negamus. Sed non temere affirmamus unum siquidem deum sine dubio credebant.
>
> *(De Religione*, f. a7ʳ)

The Romans, according to Equicola, did not believe in the physical reality of their gods but only in the abstract virtues they represented. This does not

---

[91] *Pro Mario Olivetano ad Ptolemaeum Fratrem* in B. Spagnuoli, *Opera Poetica*, Paris: Praelo Ascensiano, 1513. Fol., (3 vols), III, f. 189ᵛ-190ᵛ.

[92] Nulla tam feris moribus gens ab omnique humanitate aliena extitit, quae cum ignis acutam celeritatem, aeris amplitudinem, maris diffusionem, terrae soliditatem, temperiem et faecunditatem rerum animadverterit, non crediderit haec non esse fortuita sed esse numen aliquod prestantissimae mentis cuius nutu et ratione mirabili talia eveniant et regantur.
    (De Religione, f. a2ʳ-a2ᵛ.)

prevent Equicola from describing the priestly institutions in early Rome as he had done for ancient Egypt. Using this method Equicola is gradually approaching the true monotheistic religions:

> Liceat mihi hoc in loco non ab re, antequam ad Hebraeos nostrosque deveniam, per Arabis Mahumeti digredi ineptias.   (*De Religione*, f. b1ʳ)

The digression is in the form of a fairly detailed account of the Islamic faith. But, finally, he is able to begin his discussion of the Jewish faith, something which places less strain on the beliefs of a Christian:

> Inchoatam non perfectam veritatem cognoscerent, unum deum mente sola intelligunt.   (*De Religione*, f. b3ʳ)

From Moses to Jesus the path is now easy and Equicola is able to discuss the coming of Christ:

> Atque ut Moses tribum Levi ad dei cultum destinavit, sic forsan Iesus ex duodeci discipulis ad Israel filiorum similitudinem electis.   (*De Religione*, f. b5ʳ)

As he did with the previous religions he discussed, Equicola examines the institutions of the new Church. Christianity differs from the more «primitive» religions in that it aspires to be a universal religion. He traces its earliest beginnings:

> Petrus (ut caeteros missos faciam) cum Antiochenam fundasset ecclesiam, ubi primum christianum nomen exortum est, et alias provincias legibus evangelicae praedicationis implesset, imperante Claudio, ut nostra religio ab ipso capite per totum mundi corpus diffunderetur.   (*De Religione*, f. b7ʳ)

Once Equicola has established the basic characteristics of the Christian religion he takes a historical approach to the development of the new religion which, in his view, means the history of the papacy. Equicola is very much aware of the method he has employed throughout the *De Religione*, that of an eclectic:

> Ex vocum dissimilitudine redditur concentus. Apes varios flores in suavissimum redigunt sapore. Ego ex diversis corpus confeci.[93]

Some of Equicola's sources may have been novel but his overall method, which bears a close resemblance to that used by Flavio Biondo, is certainly not. This humanist treated the theme of religion extensively in the first book of his *Roma Triumphans*.[94] Biondo begins his discussion by quoting various

---

[93]   Quoted in Santoro, p. 118 n. 1. Poliziano had used a similar image. Cf. E. Bigi, «La cultura del Poliziano» in his *La cultura del Poliziano e altri studi umanistici*, Pisa, 1967, pp. 67-101; 98.

[94]   F. Biondo, *Roma Triumphans*, Brescia: per Bartholomaeum Vercellensem, 1482. Fol. On Biondo see R. Fubini, «Biondo, Flavio», *DBI*, 10, Rome, 1968, pp. 536-60; R. Weiss, «Lineamenti per una storia degli studi antiquari in Italia dal XII secolo al sacco di Roma nel 1527», *Rinascimento*, 9 (1958) 141-201.

classical authorities on the fundamental meaning of religion. This conscientious procedure of always mentioning one's source was to become one of the corner-stones of Equicola's own intellectual system. Biondo quotes Cicero on the nature of religion:

> Nullam enim gentem esse dicit neque tam immansuetam necque tam feram quae etiam ignoret qualiter habere deum deceat.   (*Roma Triumphans*, f. a3ʳ)

Biondo does not omit the Neoplatonists' view of religion but he takes only a scholarly interest in their theories; he is far from being a Neoplatonic philosopher. Equicola may have found these brief references enough to spur his interest and make him explore further. Biondo is concerned with writing a «religionis historiam» and his starting-point is the Egyptian religion:

> Eruntque primi Aegyptii quos constat omnium primos cum in caelum oculos sustulissent motum ordinem et quantitatem caelestium admiratos solem et lunam deos putasse.   (*Roma Triumphans*, f. a3ᵛ)

Biondo deals with the Phoenician and Greek religions in a dismissive manner.[95] He does so in order to place the Roman religion, the principal object of his enquiries in this case, in a better light:

> Et nonnullos ex Graecis sensisse videmus Romanos in deorum susceptione multas Aegyptiorum Phoenicumque et Graecorum ineptias impietateque omisisse sed, praeter deos deasque, alia nequaquam meliora a gentibus barbaris ad Romanos reducta fuisse videmus.   (*Roma Triumphans*, f. a6ʳ)

Equicola adds to all this a Neoplatonic sub-structure which lends a certain validity to the ancient religions.[96] He is always interested in tracing traditions and in discovering links between disparate schools of thought. He always tries to make sense of the vast mass of material which faces him by imposing order on it, often of a chronological kind. What was so conspicuously lacking in his everyday life, the sense of continuity, is remedied in his writings.

Bound in the same volume as the *De Religione* is another work by Equicola, an *Oratio dicta Papiae 1498*, which seems to be directed at an audience of «adolescentes» who, in all probability, would have been attending the university. If these students had just started out on the road of learning, Equicola wished it to be known that he had already travelled a long way; Equicola no longer regarded himself as a student but as someone who had reached

---

[95]   «Vana vero atque ridicula Phoenicum theologia fuisse» (*Roma Triumphans*, f. a5ʳ).

[96]   Ficino's view of religion does not take into account its historical development, he is solely interested in the philosophical content of religion. The pre-Christian religions interest him only in so far as they, in some way, predict the coming of Christ.

maturity,[97] and it was probably that feeling which urged him to make public
certain of his opinions. Indeed, Equicola himself states that the thoughts
expressed in the *Oratio* are the result of «non repentino quodam calore aedita
sed longo elaborata studio» (*Oratio*, f. c6ᵛ). The publication of three works
in quick succession points to Equicola's intention of making a name for himself with the help of the contacts he had made through Giulio Cesare Cantelmo. The fact that so undistinguished a work as the *De Passione Domini
Oratio* was honoured with two editions underlines the favour Equicola
enjoyed.

The *Oratio dicta Papiae* is almost a mirror image of the *De Religione* in
that the same methodology is used in both works and, as far as the subject-
matter is concerned, the *Oratio* seeks to demonstrate that the acquisition of
knowledge is a godly activity. As a general introduction to his subject, Equicola states that those men who have advanced the human race in some way
are to be praised above all others:

> Nam cibi caerealis artificium, agricultura, domorum constructio utilia quidem et
> necessaria sint. Artesque caeteras (quas moechanicas vocant) humano afferre
> auxilium generi non negabimus.   (*Oratio*, f. c6ʳ)

The above occupations may be essential to the well-being of mankind, but
they have no place in the world of the intellectual who wishes to make his
career at the court. Equicola wished to loan his mind to the rulers, not his
hands. The pursuit of learning was a means of breaking away from one's own
class and attaching oneself to those in power, as well as creating a deeper sense
of self-awareness:

> Tamen quia humi serpunt nec quicquid aliud terrena curant plebi et ignobilioribus
> relinquendas censuere maiores, disciplinarum vero eruditionem praestanti et
> excellenti ingenio viris demandarunt. Litterarum siquidem cognitio ex mortalibus
> immortales et ut caeteris animantibus praestemus effecit docuitque. Tum, res
> omnis, tum quod difficillimum est ut nosmet ipsos cognosceremus cuius precepti
> magna est vis.   (*Oratio*, f. c6ᵛ)

In addition to having a religious significance, knowledge is essential to the
running of a well-ordered state. In this way, Equicola is expressing his desire
to become part of some ruler's governmental machinery. The man of learning
has his place both metaphysically and socially in the system of things:

---

[97]   Right at the end of the oration Equicola urges his young audience to pursue their studies:

> Agite, igitur, (ut facitis), adolescentes atque in id studium, in quo estis, incubite
> ut vobis honori, amicis utilitati et patriae emolumento esse positis. Invigilate his
> studiis.   (*Oratio*, f. e5ᵛ)

> Cumque se ad civilem societatem natum senserit, eo diriget consilia qua regat populos ratione qua castiget improbos, tueatur bonos qua hortari ad decus.[98]

The history of literary culture follows the same course as the history of religion had done in the *De Religione Libellus*. Learning is elevated to the rank of a religion in its own right: the authority of religion, the ultimate power controlling people's lives, needs to express itself. Equicola traces the development of literary culture from Hermes Trismegistus through to Roman times. The Israelites passed on their understanding of letters to the Phoenicians:

> A Phoenicibus Cadmus in Graeciam transtulit unde eas per Nicostratam, Evandri matrem, Latium recepit ante urbis Romae natalem annos septingentos quinquaginta.
>
> *(Oratio, f. c8ʳ)*

Flavio Biondo does not give so detailed an analysis of the spread of written culture. Most of his efforts in the *Roma Triumphans* go towards describing the Roman achievement, and he does not feel it necessary in this particular case to offer the same kind of analysis for the history of letters as he had done for religion.[99]

Letters, like religion, ought to express clearly the writer's orthodoxy, thus it is not out of place in the *Oratio* for Equicola to list the basic tenets of

---

[98]   *Oratio*, f. c6ᵛ. It is interesting to note that both Biondo and Equicola are authors of works urging the necessity of a crusade. Their encyclopaedist tendencies, especially as related to the study of non-Christian religions, seem to force them to make a clear statement about their orthodoxy without carrying out an exhaustive examination of their own beliefs. A crusade represents a single event, outside the normal sphere of religious activity. (Biondo's work *Ad Alphonsum Aragonensem Serenissimum Regem de Expeditione in Turchos* is to be found in B. Nogara, *Scritti inediti e rari di Biondo Flavio*, Rome, 1927, pp. 31-58.)

[99]   Biondo's digression on learning is very limited in scope. He mainly concentrates on the Greek sources of Roman literature:

> Fuerunt autem diu ante apud Graecos literae scriptoresque maximo in honore. Nam multi tradidere et Aulus Gellius enucleate colligit.
>
> *(Roma Triumphans, f. K4ᵛ)*

Biondo does have knowledge of earlier literatures but does not present his findings in a systematic way:

> Vetustior tamen praedictis notitia literarum fuisse videtur in libris Hetruscorum quos rituales appellatos...   *(Roma Triumphans, f. 4Kᵛ)*.

The Etruscans stand isolated because of Biondo's attempt to be stricter in his approach to the sources.

Learning is not as fundamental to human behaviour as religion, so, in Biondo's view, would not have merited such extended treatment:

> Ego multos homines excellenti animo ac virtute sine doctrina naturae ipsius habitu prope divino per seipsos et moderatos et graves extitisse fateor. Etiam illud adiungo saepius ad laudem atque virtutem naturam sine doctrina quam sine natura valuisse doctrinam.   *(Roma Triumphans, f. K3ᵛ)*

Such an attitude would find little sympathy with Equicola who placed his «faith» in the efficacy of learning.

Christianity.[100] The religious theme forms a basic subject for a number of disciplines:

> Cum nihil maius, nihil excellentius dici possitque quod de deo ut nomine patet est fermo. Haec de theologia quam potui breviter sectatus sum. Nunc a philosophia petimus fluentem fontibus medicinam persequamur.   (*Oratio*, f. d4^v)

Equicola's treatment of philosophy includes a historical study of the main figures of Greek thought, including Plato:

> Semideus Plato inter Pyttagoram et Socratem medius, alterius sublimitatem ad humilitatem, alterius vero humile ad gravitatem excellentiamque deduxit. Et disiecta atque confusa philosophiae membra in unum corpus animalque integrum reduxit.   (*Oratio*, f. d1^v)

Equicola also deals with the diverse schools of classical philosophy.[101] This chronological approach to all matters, tracing something from its inception onwards, can be said to be one of the hall-marks of Equicola's methodology. It also allows him to draw up long lists which physically show off a superficial knowledge of many different objects of inquiry.

After dealing with the abstract spaces of theology and philosophy Equicola turns his attention to the application of knowledge in the practical sphere, particularly to medicine and law. Equicola had no time for the controversies about whether law or medicine was the nobler science. He was an encyclopaedist through and through, and was more concerned about the extent of knowledge than its quality. Thus medicine receives high praise as a «saluberrimum studium».[102] If medicine is essential for the well-being of the body, then law is the foundation of a well-ordered society.[103] Here again, Equicola takes up his historical comparative method in order to demonstrate that laws vary from place to place and from century to century. He illustrates his assertion with reference to Roman and Christian laws on homosexuality and to the legal position of the wife in different societies.[104]

---

[100]   Rectam et salutiferam orthodoxae fidei semitam et simplicitatem capessemus. Mundum a Christo Iesu redemptum non dubitamus.   (*Oratio*, f. d4^r)

[101]   Equicola examines the doctrines of the various schools as briefly and as clearly as possible. For example:

> Epicuraei duas partes philosophiae pronuntiarunt: naturalem et moralem. Rationalem vero removerunt.   (*Oratio*, f. d2^r)

[102]   *Oratio*, f. d6^v. On these controversies see E. Garin, *La disputa delle arti nel Quattrocento*, Florence, 1947.

[103]   Sic nec domus ulla, nec civitas, nec gens, nec hominum universum genus stare nec ipse mundus posset. Legibus enim nihil praestantius, nihil accomodatius nec hominum vite necessarium magis excogitatum est.   (*Oratio*, f. d7^v)

[104]   Puerorum ibi (Romae) esse amatores lex nulla prohibebat... At nostrae leges armari iura et gladio ultore puniri mandant.   (*Oratio*, f. e1^v-e2^r)

In the last section of the speech Equicola directly addresses his audience on the subject of composing an oration. He is particularly interested in the language one should use:

> Satis erit si verba erunt non rudia et si non Ciceronis saeculum redolebunt, Ulpiani, Augustini et Celsi facite sapiant etatem.[105]

Such an attitude could be partially explained by his more than casual acquaintanceship with Battista Pio (bearing in mind that Equicola wanted a language that matched his encyclopaedic content). Proof of such a relationship can be found in the fact that an anonymous satirist links their names and attitudes towards Latin in a dialogue intended to discredit their views.[106]

The works of Equicola produced in this period show him as having reached intellectual maturity and ready to be compared with the leading humanists of Mantua and Ferrara. The *De Religione* had ended with a call to «semideum Paridem Caesareum» («mihi patronum cupio»). Paride da Ceresara was, at that time, the humanist most in favour with Isabella d'Este.[107] Likewise, the Ferrarese edition of the *De Passione Domini* ends with a reference to Pandolfo Collenuccio «nostra tempestate litteratorum litteratissimus». This particular humanist may be said to represent the ideal that Equicola had set himself. Collenuccio, who was not a Ferrarese citizen by birth, had managed to combine a career as one of Ercole I's most trusted ambassadors with the pursuit of his humanist and literary interests.[108] Equicola further adds the names of Battista Spagnuoli, Luca Ripa and Pescennius Niger, whom he appoints as the «censores» of the work. However, due to the extreme difficulty involved in changing his employer, he must have realized that he would have to remain for some considerable time with the Cantelmos. The member

---

[105]   *Oratio*, f. e4v.

Sit vostra oratio candida et quadrata, necessaria non quaesita, natura non fucata. Apud vostros auctores usitatis vocabulis loquimini opifices sua artificia tueri non possent nisi vocabula retinerent propria... Nam si ad antiquorum illam elegantiam vostra redundabit oratio nemo doctus mirabitur. Era illa illis prima lingua et etiam nolentibus se se sponte offerebat. Nobis vero elaboratum est quid illis est innatum... Satis erit si verba erunt non rudia et si non Ciceronis saeculum redolebunt.

[106]   See C. Dionisotti, *Gli umanisti*, pp. 111-16.

[107]   See Luzio-Renier, *La coltura*, pp. 148-52.

[108]   On Collenuccio see A. Saviotti, *Pandolfo Collenuccio, umanista pesarese del secolo XV*, Pisa, 1888; P. Negri, «Le missioni di Pandolfo Collenuccio a Papa Alessandro VI (1494-1498)», *Archivio della Reale Società Romana di Storia Patria*, 33 (1910) 333-439. Any acquaintanceship on a personal level that Equicola may have had with Collenuccio would have been superficial. Equicola is rather taking him as a model and a hopeful protector for the future. The same may be said at this time for Paride da Ceresara, though, in this case, Equicola may have had closer contacts because of Margherita Cantelmo's friendship with Isabella d'Este.

for whom Equicola had the most affection was Ercole Cantelmo (though he did not forget Ercole's father, Sigismondo) mainly because of his interest in classical learning.[109] The period in Milan permitted Equicola to launch a campaign which had as its aim his acceptance as a humanist in Ferrarese intellectual circles. Equicola gave a display of his credentials to the circle of Ippolito d'Este as well as to the Mantuan intellectual circles which fell within range of Cantelmo interests through Sigismondo's wife, Margherita. Equicola wished to demonstrate the extent of his knowledge in the hope of winning the favour of possible protectors.

On his return to Ferrara, most probably in 1499, Equicola must have been optimistic about the prospect of pursuing his humanist interests in a suitable environment.

---

[109]   Equicola mentions Ercole's tutor Dominico Gaza as evidence of Ercole's commitment to learning on the last page of the Ferrarese edition of the *De Passione Domini*.

CHAPTER II

Declarations of intent

No less than the first French incursion into the Italian peninsula did the second leave its mark. In the same way as Equicola suffered from the effects of the first onslaught, so the second was to disturb his life-style once again. After his sojourn in Milan he naturally felt that Ferrara, the city where Sigismondo Cantelmo had remained throughout the period of his father's decline in power, was to be his new home. Again it is difficult to say exactly when Equicola made his first visit to Ferrara. Certainly it is possible that in between fighting in the *Regno* and proving himself humanistically in Milan he made an occasional visit to Ferrara. The earliest evidence so far discovered reveals that Equicola was in Ferrara during the months of October and November 1497. He seems to have been acting as both Sigismondo's and Giulio Cesare Cantelmo's secretary since letters signed by them are clearly written in Equicola's hand. According to the date of an extant letter written in his hand, Equicola returned to Ferrara in September 1499 where he resumed his work as scribe. It is likely that he held this position throughout the following year, as his presence in Ferrara in the autumn of 1500 is attested to by his presence at a degree ceremony held on 7 September 1500.[1] However, his stay in Ferrara

[1] ASMN, AG, b. 1235, Ferrara, 25 October 1497, Sigismondo Cantelmo to Isabella d'Este, f. 282^r. Other letters of the same period, also written in Equicola's hand, are dated 31 October 1497 (f. 284^r) and a letter from Giulio Cesare Cantelmo to Isabella d'Este, 11 November 1497 (f. 292^r).

For 1499 there is a letter, again in Equicola's hand, from Sigismondo Cantelmo to his wife who was away in Mantua (ASMN, AG, b. 1235, Ferrara, 28 September 1499, f. 749^r). For the year 1500 there are a number of letters written in Equicola's hand, usually in the name of Sigismondo Cantelmo: ASMN, AG, b. 1236, 14 January, 8 May, 20 May, 29 June, all written in Ferrara to Enea Gonzaga. The letter dated 20 May 1500 is addressed to the rulers of Mantua congratulating them on the birth of their first son. A letter in the name of Margherita Cantelmo (Ferrara, 16 September 1500) written in Equicola's hand, is also addressed to Enea Gonzaga. The reference to Equicola's presence at the degree ceremony is to be found in G. Pardi, *Titoli dottorali conferiti dallo studio di Ferrara nei secoli XV e XVI*, Lucca, 1900, p. 107. There is a more doubtful reference, exactly three months earlier, in a letter from Margherita Cantelmo to «mio charissimo misser Sebastian, canzeliero del magnifico Cavalier [Enea Gonzaga]»:

was destined to be cut short because of certain events affecting the Cantelmos. Indeed, Equicola spent the greater part of the eight years preceding his removal to Mantua away from Ferrara.

After his disappointment at the first French expedition's failure to maintain control of the *Regno*, Sigismondo Cantelmo would have been much more hopeful at the way Louis XII's expedition was now proceeding. The French king had captured Milan, taken its Duke prisoner, and, more importantly for Sigismondo Cantelmo in November 1500, he had signed the Treaty of Granada which allowed for the division of the Kingdom of Naples between France and Spain.[2] Granted a second chance, Pietro Giampaolo's son was not slow to seize it. He appears to have left Ferrara immediately after the signing of the treaty and travelled to the French court in order to present his case personally to Louis XII and his officials. There is no doubt that Equicola accompanied him since, in mid-February 1501, Francesco Soderini wrote from Paris to the humanist, who had returned to Ferrara, to inform him of the latest developments in the situation since Equicola's departure from France.[3] It has previously been thought that Equicola's first visit to France was datable to the autumn of 1504 and lasted until January 1506.[4] Although his first stay in France seems to have been of limited duration, it appears likely that his

---

Havendo in casa un zoven in ogni liberale litteratura eruditissimo, desiderosa in mia complacentia componesse qualche cosa poetica, non ho trovato più degna materia che le laude del signor mio fiolo, sufficiente excitare ogni infimo e basso ingegno a sublimarlo. E per esser il cumulo de quelle immenso, se non satisfarò, non se debe imputare a la mia voluntà né a la litteratura del predito zovene, ma a la magnitudine de le virtù del predito signor mio fiolo, le quale afatigariano greci et latini poeti e li occupariano. Così, ha dato principio cum questo intercluso tetrastico e farò dispensarà in tale exercitio tempo assai, postponendo li soi peculiari studii philosophici e theologici.

(ASMN, AG, b. 1236, 7 June 1500, Ferrara)

The description of the «zovene» corresponds, in its general lines, to what we know of Equicola's interests. Even if the person in question is not Equicola, the letter throws light on Margherita Cantelmo's literary patronage. Thus it seems that her interest in literature was not an invention on the part of Equicola and Trissino. The son who is to be honoured by a poem would be her eldest, Ercole.

[2] Consult C.M. Ady, «The invasions of Italy» in *The New Cambridge Modern History*, vol. 1, ed. G.R. Potter, Cambridge, 1957, pp. 343-67.

[3] ASMN, AG, b. 283, Paris, 18 February 1501, Francesco Soderini («Tuus F. Vult.») to Equicola («Al mio carissimo messer Mario Equicolo de Oliveto col signor Gismondo Cantelmo in Ferrara):

Questa è la terza vi ho scripta *poiché partisti* et non è possibile che a questa hora non le habbiate ritrovate in Ferrara. (My italics)

Thus, it is likely that Equicola arrived in France late in 1500.

[4] This is the conclusion of F. Simone, «Fonti e testimonianze mantovane sulla civiltà francese del Rinascimento», *GSLI*, 154 (1977) 1-44, who did not use the evidence in the Mantuan archives.

contacts with French humanism began at this date, and hence his exposure to French culture as a whole would have been greater than has previously been supposed. Equally important, Equicola would have had the opportunity of making contact with other Italian humanists, such as Sannazaro, whom he may have already met in Italy. He would also have been able to form new friendships with the many Italians who found themselves at the French court for one reason or another. There is evidence to show that Equicola became acquainted with Fra Giocondo during his various stays in France.[5] Sigismondo Cantelmo would have felt the need for a secretary to aid him in the intricate negotiations necessary to regain his duchy, and Equicola, with his experience as secretary to the Cantelmos and the wide range of his humanist contacts, was the natural choice. Equicola's friendship with Francesco Soderini meant that the Cantelmos had an agent who would act in their interests whenever they were absent from the French court.[6] The Greek humanist, Janus Lascaris, was also able to use his influence with the French king in Sigismondo Cantelmo's favour, undoubtedly because of his friendship with Equicola.[7] Soderini seemed confident that it would only be a matter of time before Equicola obtained the royal privileges necessary to ensure the legitimate return of Sigismondo Cantelmo to his possessions:

> Le cose del Regno sono ne' medesimi termini lasciasti et più presto meglio per li amici del Re.
> (Letter cited at note 3)

If Sigismondo were to obtain the restitution of his territories, Equicola would be able to recover his own possessions in Alvito. However, that dream was rapidly receding into the gloom of European politics.

---

[5]   R. Brenzoni, *Fra Giovanni Giocondo Veronese, Verona 1435 - Roma 1515*, Florence 1960; on his relations with Equicola see p. 27; L.A. Ciapponi, «Appunti per una biografia di Giovanni Giocondo da Verona», *IMU*, 4 (1961) 131-58. It is always possible that Equicola had made Fra Giocondo's acquaintance in Rome where the latter's strong interest in epigraphy drew him into Pomponio Leto's circle. In Naples, around 1493, Giocondo was on friendly terms with Pontano and Sannazaro (Ciapponi, pp. 141-50).

It should be borne in mind, however, that political allegiances would have been a strong divisive factor. The Cantelmos were seeking to take advantage of the discomfiture of the Aragonese monarchy whilst the supporters of the latter were striving to come to a different sort of arrangement with the French King.

[6]   The letter cited at note 3 continues:

> El vostro oratore vi harà scripto circa le altre cose. A me haveva decto che quel secretario voleva dieci ducati, et avanti et domandavami consiglio. Io li dixi non consiglerei, se non intendessi il bisogno o la vogl[i]a vostra, ma che non mancherei di pagare il danaio nelle cose vostre quando lui mi dicessi che io pagassi, ma che da me non lo farei.

[7]   Letter cited at note 3:

> Come harete inteso per altre mie, noi partimo da Bles et per diligentia che si facessi con maestro Ianni, non si potetto non havere quelle lettere.

In spite of the fact that the French were still in a strong position, by March 1501 Sigismondo and his brother Giulio Cesare were becoming uneasy as their goal continued to elude them. It is easy to imagine that they felt time was running out for them to achieve their long-cherished ambition of restoring their rule to Sora and the other territories. In order to press their case with the French they decided that Giulio Cesare should go to Milan accompanied by Mario Equicola, much to the latter's consternation (he had only recently returned from France):

> Mi maraveglio sia più humore in mi, solo pensando alla grande disgratia mia. Non ho parole le quali possano in minima parte correspondere al dolore nel qual sto et so certo starrò finché la stancha anima lassarà questo infelice corpo. Subito ioncto, inteso lo andare de Monsignor Cantelmo in Milano, restai morto, presago del mio mal. Lo signor messer Sigismundo alla prima melli donò, concedè et exhortò mi andasse. Et così, fra loro doi è fixo et fermamente concluso, vada. Guardate voi mia infelicità. Quando crederando l'uno, serrà l'altro. Mi ho ancor concluso quel ho da fare et stabilito. Prego Vostra Signoria mi aiute che possa mia servitù discoscire, non stracciare. Scriva lei, de sua mano, ad messer Sigismundo como per soe lettere havete inteso che mi lassa andare in Milano et che cognoscete il servitio de Monsignore et utile recerchare questo et è honesto. Ma che'l pregate che voglia pregare il vescovo mi lasse cqui fine in tanto che se trove un maistro bono ad messer Hercule et in ciò non domandate tempo se non un mese et dite che mastro Sebastiano ne ha uno bono per le mano, che è il vero. Et che poi, non solamente mi, ma Vostra Signoria in persona andaria ad servirla.[8]

Equicola was not merely content to take orders from the two Cantelmo brothers: he seemed to regard his position in the Cantelmo household as superior to that of an ordinary servant. He even appeared to be offended when he was not consulted on matters that affected his work. Sigismondo Cantelmo still acted as though he were Duke of Sora more than in name alone. The Neapolitan baron did not see the need to consult his secretary, whereas Equicola, who played an important part in furthering Sigismondo's case, understood the weakness of his master's position and did not wish to become a victim of his short-sightedness.

Instead of openly protesting to the head of the family, Equicola preferred to enter a kind of conspiracy with the one person who was likely to take his side: Margherita Cantelmo. She, too, was excluded from the decision-making structure of the family and had other concerns besides those which obsessed her husband. Equicola played on Margherita's sense of duty as a mother whose task it was to ensure that her eldest son received a good education. It is not surprising that Equicola took an interest in the upbringing of the eldest son, since it was a role that had become traditional for a humanist in a noble household and certainly would have been a more pleasant prospect to Equi-

---

[8]   ASMN, AG, b. 283, Ferrara, 11 March 1501, Equicola to Margherita Cantelmo.

cola than that of immediately recommencing his travels. The secretary seems
to have been already well-versed in the methods of persuasion and in the
subtleties of deception necessary to achieve his end.

For the most part, Equicola revealed his troubled state of mind only to the
mistress of the house-hold, with whom he built up a special relationship. In
many ways it resembled the relationship that he was to form later with Isabella
d'Este with one major difference: Isabella d'Este was not as amenable to
Equicola's suggestions as Margherita Cantelmo seems to have been. Isabella's
aggressive nature did not allow Equicola the same freedom as he enjoyed with
Margherita Cantelmo. Both relationships were composed of a mixture of
elements which alternated between an exaggerated adoration of the Lady and
the love of a teacher for an intelligent pupil. Whether Equicola's attitude
towards these women was hypocritical, merely a ploy to win their favour, is
difficult to assess. Certainly, there could well be an element of knowing how
to ingratiate oneself into the favour of important court ladies. The question
of sincerity is not really relevant because the pressure on the humanist to produce what his audience wanted was impossible to remove. The humanist was
there to celebrate the powerful which in theory provided a reciprocal arrangement because the grateful «prince» would reward him who sang his praises
loudest and most effectively.

Margherita appears to have offered the solution to Equicola's dilemma:

> Invocato il nome de Vostra Signoria et da la ambiguità retornato in certeza, la
> quale è non volere, sensa mandato expresso, uscire de vita, pensando alla verità,
> quella divinità de la quale ho il vivere, non ha più ad fare meco che ja doi anni
> poco manco fa...[9]

---

[9]   ASMN, AG, b. 283, Ferrara, 15 March 1501, Equicola to Margherita Cantelmo. Equicola, perhaps in a half-joking fashion, bombarded Margherita with all sorts of information
about the classical world. In a letter of 13 March 1501, from Ferrara, the humanist demonstrates
a wide-ranging knowledge of Neoplatonic philosophy, attempting to «popularize» for his
audience some of its esoteric aspects. Hence, one of Equicola's roles was to render difficult philosophy palatable to circles often presided over by the ladies of the court. These court ladies
who were struggling to find their intellectual identity would have appreciated the help of
someone who was only too willing to share his knowledge. In time, Equicola did not need to
surrender entirely his intellectual aspirations since he had found an outlet for them in court
society. His letters to Margherita Cantelmo are crammed full of learned references and consequently assume the appearance of short treatises. A letter written in Ferrara on 13 March 1501
(b. 283) seems an excerpt from a longer meditation on prophecy, a theme he will come back
to in later works. There is no lack of proper nouns to lend authority to his arguments, names
that would have probably been new to Margherita and may have been intended to dazzle her:

> Donde Madama mia, commoto da la auctorità de sì preclarissimi scriptori et pro-
> moto dalla experientia, credo indubioso alli sonni, le spetie delli quali se fanno
> cinque.

The erudition functions as a framework for his narrative of a prophetic dream: «Tutto lo ho
visto verissimo et mi è uscito ad vero per la qual cosa mi reputo et tengo un altro Joseph.» The
self-deprecating joke co-exists with rather arcane knowledge, to the detriment of the latter. Any
attempt at philosophical discourse in a letter becomes ambiguous and is usually employed to
lend a particular tone to an everyday event or a «happening» at court.

*

Following Equicola's arrival in Ferrara and his subsequent visits to France, he had had to relearn his humanism, to remould it in such a way that it would render him valuable service in the difficult conditions of the court, especially that of the French king where he expended a great deal of energy in the employ of Sigismondo Cantelmo. He had learnt that underhand means were often the most successful in trying to secure an advantage over one's rivals. Thus he had realized the importance of bribery in court circles. Under such conditions, the art of courtiership would have been quickly learnt and usefully applied. To reach the desired goal it was necessary to resort to any means which might prove successful but, as a consequence, a tension was set up between «verità», an absolute, a humanist ideal and the reality of court life. This tension was the first of a series which were to become more apparent the longer Equicola stayed in a court environment. The tensions were caused by the fact that the courts with which Equicola came into contact wished to exist as separate institutions, without interference from traditional value systems. For example, on a moral plane this attempt at liberation from encroaching value systems led the humanist-courtier to make a choice between the conflicting values of pleasure and Christian asceticism. Our humanist could not hope to resolve these contradictions; the best he could hope for was to find a way of living with them. Initially he had been quite unable to cope with them but had found a way out of his intellectual impasse, as we have seen in part, by swearing allegiance to Margherita Cantelmo who was elevated to the level of a goddess. As a consequence, Equicola's own status was implicitly elevated and his profession gained in sanctity; it also meant that his conscious intellectualizing of every kind of phenomenon was not an end in itself but sought social validation:

> Mi moretti et resi il debito alla natura et ad Dio qual mi haveva concesso. Poi, per gratia, clementia, benignità, humanità et purità di Vostra Signoria foi retornato in vita et così vivo de Vostra Signoria sola, non de altri. Lei è dio, Lei è genio, Lei è natura. Lei opera in mi quel in li altri mortali operano li elementi. Et se la opinione pyctagorica è vera poi la mia secunda morte mi deventarò Perlina [Margherita Cantelmo's pet dog] per posser esserli propinqua. Se è vera la platonica che poi la longa erratione purgata un'altra volta l'anima tome in questo Emisperis, questa anima li serrà più dedita che non adesso, se cosa alcuna se pò adiungere; se è vera la opinione de chaballisti mi sempre serrò ad Vostra Signoria quel Mario deditissimo so adesso. (See note 9)

Further, this attitude denoted a refusal to be a mere tool in the hands of his masters, it represented a step along what was perhaps the only path left open to someone who had been dispossessed both of his property and of his «natural» position in society. If Sigismondo Cantelmo still insisted on acting in the manner of a feudal lord when he was no more than a dependant of Ercole I,

Equicola felt at liberty to change allegiance intellectually, if not physically. From this point on, as long as he was still employed by the Cantelmos, Equicola was to ally himself with Margherita Cantelmo, the daughter of a wealthy Mantuan notary and an intimate friend of Isabella d'Este. Equicola managed to create a mystique out of his servile position in that his knowledge served to obliterate external reality and the «real» nature of his social relations. It was all part of an elaborate game to entertain others and at the same time carve out a place for himself in that area of court society which was centred on women.

*

By 1501 he had already written the «contract» between himself and the aspiring court lady: the work entitled *De Mulieribus* or the *Perigynaecon*.[10] Whatever the personal reasons which led Margherita Cantelmo to commission two works in defence of women (the other being Agostino Strozzi's *Defensio Mulierum*), these works form part of a wider cultural discussion which was taking place in these years. Nevertheless, we should bear in mind that Equicola's treatise was undoubtedly written during this critical period of Cantelmo family history and it would not be an outrageous conjecture that Equicola himself suggested the idea. Isabella d'Este would not have been ignorant of the venture, especially considering the close relationship between the two women. Further, it seems likely that Equicola and the two ladies would have been aware of the Ferrarese tradition that had produced a number of treatises in defence of women. Amongst the authors of such works can be included Antonio Cornazzano who was on the Estense pay-roll for a time, Bartolomeo Gogio, a Ferrarese notary, and Sabadino degli Arienti, also employed by the Estensi for a while. We may add the name of Jacopo Filippo Foresti whose treatise *De Plurimis Claris Selectisque Mulieribus* was published in Ferrara.[11] Even if all these works were not specifically dedicated to Eleonora d'Aragona, Isabella d'Este's mother, the writers always mentioned her in their

---

[10]   On this work see C.F. Fahy, «Three early Renaissance treatises on women», *Italian Studies* 11 (1956) 31-55; J.R. Woodhouse, *Baldesar Castiglione. A Reassessment of «The Courtier»*, Edinburgh, 1978, pp. 115-16.

[11]   For Cornazzano see C.F. Fahy, «The *De Mulieribus Admirandis* of Antonio Cornazzano», *La Bibliofilia*, 62 (1960) 144-74; for Gogio see Fahy, «Three early Renaissance treatises», pp. 30-36 and W.L. Gundersheimer, «Bartolommeo Goggio: A feminist in Renaissance Ferrara», *Renaissance Quarterly*, 33 (1980) 175-200, who makes exaggerated claims for the work's «feminism» which could have been avoided by careful comparative analysis with other similar texts; for Sabadino degli Arienti see the entry by G. Ghinassi in *DBI*, IV, Rome, 1962, pp. 154-56; for Foresti see V. Zaccaria, «La fortuna del *De Mulieribus Claris* del Boccaccio nel secolo XV: Giovanni Sabadino degli Arienti, Iacopo Filippo Foresti e le loro biografie femminili (1490-1497)» in *Il Boccaccio nelle culture e letterature nazionali*, a cura di F. Mazzoni, Florence, 1978, pp. 519-45.

lists of famous contemporary women. She was regarded as an important example of a woman taking the reins of power firmly in her hands and controlling the administration of the Ferrarese state. In this respect she was unlike her
contemporary the Marchioness of Mantua, Barbara of Brandenburg, who
was the junior partner, forced into a secondary role by her husband, Ludovico
Gonzaga. In his absence, she was obliged to consult him before taking action
in any matter which could affect the Mantuan state; on occasion she did take
minor decisions, such as ordering that the alarm be raised on the escape of
certain prisoners.[12] Her restricted power could no doubt be attributed, in part,
to her being a foreign princess, and consequently, unable to form the same
political alliances as would have been possible for an Italian-born princess.
Eleonora, on the other hand, faced with her husband's incompetence, particularly as an administrator, had no choice but to carry the burden of the administrative duties herself.[13] It is perhaps significant that Diomede Carafa
dedicated his *Memoriale sui doveri del principe* to her.[14] Isabella d'Este's
character seems to closely follow her mother's in so far as they were both able
administrators and both took an interest in the cultural developments of their
time. Isabella, however, had a more extreme character than her mother and
carried her interests to the point of obsession.

*

It may be that Equicola had already decided to enter Isabella's service at
some future date. In any case, we can go so far as to say that Equicola's career
was mapped out here, at least along its broad lines of development. Equicola
saw that his humanist learning would be far more acceptable to Isabella d'Este
than to her husband, Francesco Gonzaga. Indeed, by attempting to
demonstrate the equality of women in society, Equicola was at the same time
defining his own position as someone in the avant-garde of court culture who
was willing to produce new modes of behaviour for this society. As the women
at court tried to find new avenues into which they could direct their energies,
eager also to present a new image of themselves, so Equicola became their
agent, expressing the aspirations of this group of women to change their traditional position in society.

---

[12]   See E. Ward Swain, « »My excellent and most singular lord»: marriage in a noble family of fifteenth-century Italy», *Journal of Medieval and Renaissance Studies*, 16 (1986) 171-95;
L. Chiappini, *Eleonora d'Aragona, prima Duchessa di Ferrara*, Rovigo, 1956.

[13]   See L. Chiappini, *Eleonora d'Aragona*, pp. 34-43.

[14]   Cf. E. Mayer, *Un opusculo dedicato a Beatrice d'Aragona regina d'Ungheria*, Rome,
1937; F. Petrucci, «Per un'edizione critica dei memoriali di Diomede Carafa. Problemi e
metodo», *ASPN*, Quarta serie, Anno XV (XCIV dell'intera collezione), 1977, pp. 213-34.

In order to be useful to these women Equicola had substantially to revise the humanist education he had received from Pomponio Leto. Equicola's training would have only partially prepared him for the conditions he was to meet in the northern Italian courts and, in some respects, it would have been something of a hindrance in that although Rome may have had its princes (and even a king) women could play no official role in court society. The taint of something illegitimate and ultimately evil would always be attached to them at the court of Rome. Equicola took a firm stand against this kind of attitude prevalent in a male-dominated, academic society. Equicola's great distance from the views of the Academy is illustrated by an incident which occurred after his return from his second visit to France. Equicola's description of the incident provides concrete evidence of the split between Academy and court (excluding the court of Rome). His letter to Margherita Cantelmo (5 May 1502) is of the same period as the *De Mulieribus* and expresses the same sentiments. The document in question formed part of a controversy which arose in the aftermath of Lucrezia Borgia's wedding celebrations at Ferrara. The debate centred upon the behaviour of certain guests, in particular Isabella d'Este. [15] The letter also serves as an indication of the intimacy Equicola enjoyed with certain members of the Mantuan court. He seems to have been on particularly close terms with a fellow southerner, Jacopo d'Atri, Francesco Gonzaga's secretary (the letter provides the briefest indication of a network serving the interests of dispossessed *meridionali*):

---

[15] Maria Bellonci gives a brief discussion of the circumstances surrounding the controversy in *Lucrezia Borgia*, pp. 355-59. The letter is partially quoted in W. F. Prizer, «Isabella d'Este and Lucrezia Borgia as patrons of music: The frottola at Mantua and Ferrara», *Journal of the American Musicological Society*, 38 (1985) 1-33; 6. It is difficult to determine the exact source of the letter sent to Elisabetta Gonzaga and Isabella d'Este. The reference to «quella inclita Academia romana» might possibly be to Paolo Cortese's Academy especially if the «Carmeta» of Equicola's letter becomes Vincenzo Calmeta who may have been airing a personal grudge against Francesco Gonzaga by insulting his wife and sister (however see V. Calmeta, *Prose e lettere inedite e rare*, ed. C. Grayson, Bologna, 1959, where the editor quotes approvingly Calmeta's own self-defence on another occasion: «non fu mai mia natura de lacerare altri» [pp. XXV, 89]. Yet another letter does show that he was capable of writing defamatory epistles, «M. Vincenzo più atto a dir male che non sono io [Bembo]», [p. XXIV] and more convincingly, «mi dice che m. Vincenzo appo l'una e l'altra l'ha infamato con le sue lettere» [p. XXV]). Although a case can be made for Calmeta's authorship of the letter it is far from certain since Equicola himself comes to a different conclusion, asserting that it was the work of Mario Bonaventura, associated with the Roman Accademy. The grounds for this identification are not given and so leaves room for ambiguity and doubt.

The substance of the letter, as reported by Equicola, throws interesting light on Isabella d'Este's behaviour, seen from an unusual viewpoint. The image of her as a patroness of the arts is replaced by that of a greedy, slovenly, *boy*. Certainly, such an image would have been most unwelcome, alluding to an intemperance of behaviour by Isabella d'Este and demonstrating a complete lack of respect. No wonder «la Marchesana è in su le furie»!

Ho vista messa in Santo Andrea. So' andato in castello dove ho trovato il Conte de Pianella, il quale mi ha date le ordinationi delle cose de Pianella, poi le domande de Vostra Signoria et desyderio se conducesse cqui. Mi ha ancor referito de una lettera, la quale vene da quella inclita Academia romana (directa alla Signora Marchesana et Duchessa de Orbino). La continentia et tenore de dicta lettera è che reprende tucti vitii et mancamenti delle donde lombarde in le noze de Ferrara et dice, fra le altre, della Signora Marchesana, che non era ben conza, che magnava nella festa et multe altre cose, che voleva parere pucto. Et così delle altre. Solo lauda Constantia de Rozon et un'altra la quale non nomina. Et questo è arte che sempre possa dire lo auctore della epistola ad ciascheduna llì non nominata: «Tu sei quella». Messer Jacopo d'Atri ha havuta la cura de respondere et ha resposto assai bene qualche cosa che mend'ha ragionato. La lettera dice va in nome de Carmeta. Credo sia stata farina et invento de messer Mario Bonaventura. Predicto messer Iacopo, respondendo ad quella parte de quella che non nomina, vole che quella sia la Brugna [one of Isabella d'Este's ladies-in-waiting] et la Marchesana è in su le furie...[16]

Once Equicola had examined the original letter he found it of no value whatsoever, devoid of anything that would allow him to call it a «bella cosa»; in contrast to the worthlessness of the attack Jacopo d'Atri's reply is «multo elegante et bella».[17] In 1502, Equicola could still look at the affairs of Isabella d'Este somewhat dispassionately, without being caught up in the intricacies of her personal politics. He still viewed Mantua from afar, through the eyes of Margherita Cantelmo, as a visitor not an inhabitant.

Margherita's decision to commission two works in defence of women may indicate the urge felt by court ladies to assert themselves in a male-dominated world. But, despite the commission originating from the same source, she does not appear to have dictated the «angle of approach» the two writers were to take. For there are marked differences between the two, especially in how far each of them is prepared to go in his advocacy of the female cause. It amounts to the difference between a pure defence and a more «advanced» attitude which involves a recognition of the essential equality of women with regard to men. It is now proposed to examine some of these differences in order to clarify Equicola's point of view.

First of all, the *De Mulieribus* is much more erudite than Strozzi's work; it is more obviously the work of a humanist who seeks his authority from classical writings, using, for example, Plutarch, a source absent in Strozzi.[18] What differentiates the two works, probably more than anything else, are the

---

[16]   ASMN, AG, b. 283, 5 May 1502, Equicola to Margherita Cantelmo.

[17]   ASMN, AG, b. 283, 5 May 1502, «hora 4 noctis», Equicola to Margherita Cantelmo.

[18]   Strozzi's treatise is published as *La defensione delle donne d'autore anonimo. Scrittura del secolo XV, ora pubblicata a cura di Francesco Zambrini*, Bologna, 1876; it was identified

varying degrees of conviction to be found in the treatises. Equicola seems to be utterly convinced of the basic equality between men and women:

> Qua re eandem originem idemque habere principium viri feminaeque animam et corpus non video posse dubitari.   (*De Mulieribus*, f. a2ᵛ)

The other author aims for a more limited objective in writing his treatise:

> Mi apparecchio pigliare la defensione delle donne contra li loro invidi e maledici detrattori.   (*Defensione*, p. 5)

Moreover, it would be mistaken to think that Strozzi places men and women on the same level of equality. His work is still rooted in the idea of male superiority:

> E certamente, quando si vuole provare che per la imperfezione del corpo feminile sia ancora più debile in loro la capacitade di mente e di ingegno che nelli uomini, se ben non possiamo noi contraddirli (imperò che assai per ragioni si prova e per esperienzia è manifesto), nondimeno, non è da credere né può provarsi che siano di sì poco ingegno, di tanto poco e debile vigore di mente quanto li maledici e malivoli loro colunniatori si sforzano di provare sì come tutte insipienti, pazze e vanisssime fusseno da connumerare tra le brutte bestie irrazionali...
>
> (*Defensione*, pp. 36-37)

Strozzi is closely following the Boccaccian tradition, not only in his selection of *exempla*, but also in his ambivalent attitude towards women, unwilling to relinquish, once and for all, the male domination of society. In theory, at least, Equicola has no doubts about his own position: he does his utmost to fight the usual arguments against women on their own ground. Strozzi, however, finds difficulty grappling with some of the traditional arguments, such as the relative bodily vigour of men and women:

---

as being the work of Strozzi by C.F. Fahy, «Three early Renaissance treatises», pp. 40-47. On Plutarch's women see P.A. Stadter, *Plutarch's Historical Methods : An Analysis of the «Mulierum Virtutes»*, Cambridge Mass., 1965.

Mario Equicola's *De Mulieribus* was probably published in Ferrara after 8 May 1501. The work seems to have been in the last stages of completion by April 1501:

> Ho havute lettere da messer Paris, il quale mi dice laudò la mia apollogea alla Signora Marchesana et alla Donna Cecilia. Sia con Dio. Per lo Bailo mandarò alla Signoria Vostra tutto quel scrivo de la predicta Signora Marchesana. Se lli piacerà, bene, se non, mute quel li piace, leve et adiunga.

(ASMN, AG, b. 283, 6 April 1501, Equicola to Margherita Cantelmo).

This letter demonstrates an intellectual rapport between Equicola and Paride da Ceresara who acts as the former's go-between. The extent of Equicola's encomiastic intent seems most extreme. Intellectual integrity is a thing of the past. What matters is Isabella d'Este's reception of the passage that directly concerns her. That part of the work exists only on a propagandistic level and no other. She is given the right to change anything that does not satisfy her. The awareness of the right of intervention on the part of the court could not be more clearly expressed.

> Ma il robusto vigore della complessione dell'uomo, più abundante di callido e di
> secco, molto meno si dilunga dalla mediocritade media dell'ottimo temperamento
> che la affluente umidità delle donne, e per tanto, molto più alla temperanzia e
> perfezione si appropinqua.   (*Defensione*, pp. 34-35)

In contrast to Strozzi's unequivocal opinion on this matter, Equicola is more impressed by the diversity of ideas. In the end, he decides it is impossible to know absolutely the secrets of the natural universe. In the midst of all this uncertainty, Equicola remains convinced that men and women go through the same process of life and death: «Eodem enim femine corpus nascitur, alitur, crescit, senescit, moritur» (*De Mulieribus*, f. a5^v).

For Equicola, the traditional arguments against women concerning their physical weakness are not so harmful as those which aim to limit the role they play in society. Equicola realized that as soon as a woman entered society the inequalities became evident. However, none of these considerations are taken up by Strozzi who simply follows the traditional ahistorical, «unsociological» view that since women are the weaker sex they themselves have permitted men to take the leading role:

> essendo loro contente di avere ceduto alli uomini la cura delle cose grandi con
> tutta la gloria che glie ne può seguire.   (*Defensione*, p. 42)

Women have their proper place assigned to them by men and Strozzi is very clear about what he considers to be woman's role in society:

> stabilita la fama di uomini con tutta la domestica gloria e splendore di sua fami-
> glia.   (*Defensione*, p. 43)

In spite of Strozzi's unwillingness to go beyond the traditional framework which had been constructed precisely with the aim of praising women for those qualities that help to maintain the male domination of society, he must be commended for even broaching the subject of women. As an abbot, he would have been expected to hold traditional views on the position of women in society and, in any case, Strozzi probably did not need a female patron. He would have gained experience of court society through his relative, Margherita Cantelmo but, nevertheless, he was a cleric who was only living on the fringes of that society of which Equicola was already a part. Moreover, Strozzi proved himself to be more Florentine than Mantuan, inheriting the ethic of a business-orientated society which saw the woman solely as a homemaker whilst the man conducted all activities that fell outside the boundaries of the home. The court offered women of noble birth or high social standing the opportunity, if they wanted to take it, of becoming involved in affairs of state, as well as of being able to develop more fully their own interests.

If a woman was unfortunate enough to live outside the court environment, she found herself isolated and unable to change her mode of existence (in this respect, some Florentine women were exceptional in wielding considerable power, for example, Alfonsina de' Medici, whose influence over her son, Lorenzo de' Medici, the Duke of Urbino, was great. However, these women lived in a milieu which, for all intents and purposes, can be termed courtly. Equicola was appalled by the waste of human life involved for a woman condemned to sit at home and weave. Domesticity, he found, is equivalent to life imprisonment.[19] Traditionally, to justify the misuse (or rather non-use) of women in society, they have to be seen as inferior to men and emphasis must be placed on those virtues which imprison them more. The «poverelle» are allowed to excel men in the exercise of chastity. Abstract virtues did not have the same importance for the historically-minded Equicola who was also inferring that this difference of emphasis in upbringing between men and women causes great damage to the chances that a woman may have in competing against men. In other societies women have played a fuller role:

> Apud Aegyptios feminae negociantur...Apud Gallos, Thraces et Scythas virorum mulierumque communis est utilitas.
> (*De Mulieribus*, f. a8^r)

We can see that, unlike Strozzi, Equicola does not restrict his choice of *exempla* to those already used by Boccaccio and to those found in the Bible. Throughout the *De Mulieribus* frequent reference is made to Plato and Aristotle and Equicola shows himself to be aware of the traditions emanating from Hermes Trismegistus. Moses, the first person mentioned in the work, is not, as it would have been in Strozzi's case, a simple reference to the biblical figure; here «Moses sapientissimus» is part of the *pia philosophia* which, in turn, constituted an element of the Neoplatonic corpus.[20]

Further, Equicola's attitude towards certain of the stock examples is the exact opposite of the feelings voiced by Strozzi: Pope Joan is a case in point. Strozzi takes the view we would expect from a cleric:

> Detestabile fu certo la audacia di cotal donna impudentissima, con quale ebbe ardire di aspirare a tanta altezza con sua profana temeritade.

However, he does try and tone down his indignation:

> ma, nondimeno, fu ammirabile la virtù e solerzia sua, per la quale potesse parere degna del sommo pontificato.
> (*Defensione*, pp. 156-57)

Strozzi's praise of her depends on the fact that no one knew Joan was a woman. Pope Joan is the last of Equicola's *exempla* and there is no hint of

---

[19] Cf. Woodhouse, *Baldesar Castiglione*, p. 115.

[20] See D. P. Walker, *The Ancient Theology*, London, 1972; F. A. Yates, *Giordano Bruno and the Hermetic Tradition*, London, 1977; C. B. Schmitt, «*Prisca Theologia e Philosophia Perennis*: due temi del Rinascimento italiano e la loro fortuna» in *Il pensiero italiano del Rinascimento e il tempo nostro*, ed. G. Tarugi, Florence, 1970, pp. 211-36. Cf. Fahy, «Three early Renaissance treatises», pp. 38-39.

any of the stains against her character mentioned by Strozzi. She is praised
because she was a woman who attained to the highest rank Christendom has
to offer:

> Quid de Ioanne septimo dicam? Quam ad pontificatum, summam in republica
> christiana dignitatem, feminam ascendisse manifestum est. Divina (ut arbitror)
> providentia nequid mulieres quod viri possent desparent.[21]

Besides a philosophical framework and the traditional *exempla* Equicola does
not omit reference to three contemporary women, all of whom he knew personally. The limited nature of this «digression» corresponds to the writer's aspirations and at the same time to the reality of his relations with important
women.

Isabella d'Este is given pride of place and the most extensive treatment.
Equicola has skilfully prepared the reader to receive the description of Isabella, in all its classical suggestiveness, by referring to a number of classical
women who excelled in the arts.[22] Isabella d'Este is seen as the presiding deity,
the patron who watches over the artists to ensure they produce an acceptable
work. She is elevated to a level beyond the human to become «Venerem sed
pudicissimam». (*De Mulieribus*, f. b2ʳ) To be sure, Equicola was well aware
of the compliment he was paying Isabella, his definition of the «Venere
celeste» being the «anima universale del mondo». And, as we have already
seen, her future secretary was hoping to enter a world which was dominated
by women.

Equicola wished to impress upon the reader that this woman was not just
a fanciful invention on his part, a goddess of classical mythology beyond the
reach of his own age. He therefore invests her with her own physical reality,
even more than he does with Margherita Cantelmo, to establish her ultimate
duality in the manner of Petrarch's treatment of Laura:

> Totiusque corporis habitudo profecto longe late que supra mortalem ostentant.
> Si mores sanctissimas actionesque inspicias divinam iudicabis.[23]

As a whole, Isabella's physical form is praised for its classical proportions, its
«mediocritas»: «Quam corpus quadratum neque gracile neque obesum» (*De
Mulieribus*, f. b2ᵛ). Apart from her ornamental beauty, what role would such
a woman perform in society? Equicola's answer is that she will prefer to act

---

[21] *De Mulieribus*, f. b7ʳ. Equicola claims that he cannot provide details about female
saints and martyrs because he has no space. This attitude could be taken for a demonstration
of his adherence to the secular and to court society. Later on in his career he will be involved
in the «courtization» of a saint.

[22] Cf. Fahy, «Three early Renaissance treatises», pp. 39-40.

[23] *De Mulieribus*, f. b2ᵛ; cf. A. Luzio, *La Galleria dei Gonzaga venduta all'Inghilterra
nel 1627-1628*, Milan, 1913, p. 231.

in the political sphere and he manages to portray, with a few, incisive strokes, Isabella's hard, no nonsense approach to politics:

> Nemo pensius cogitat, agit consultius, maturius expedit. Cives suos, circumspecta providentia, protegit et defendit.
>
> *(De Mulieribus,* f. b2ᵛ)

This figure of a woman, hovering between the exemplary and the real, is distinguished for three particular qualities: her beauty, political ability and culture. The last-mentioned quality is characterized by Isabella's gift for music, especially her skill at playing the lyre:

> Siquid autem ab oeconomicis politicisque resipiscit negotiis citharam sumit.
>
> *(De Mulieribus,* f. b2ᵛ)

On one level, her cultural activities are seen as a well-earned respite from the difficulties of political life; in this way, the prince returns to being a princess. On another level, we can perhaps see wider implications. First of all, there is a clear biblical allusion to the soothing effect of music, subtly suggesting David playing the lyre to Saul. Secondly, and more importantly, Equicola is alluding to the significance of music within Neoplatonic philosophy.[24] It is known that Ficino was adept at playing the lyre, an exercise which not only helped him to relax but also enabled him to contemplate God more freely than normally possible. Equicola is attempting to see in Isabella a new Apollo, god of medicine whose name is connected with the lyre. He may be suggesting that Isabella, in her Neoplatonic guise, is the woman chosen to restore harmony to a broken social system and to the Italian peninsula as a whole. It is as if Isabella is presented as the new David who will bring about the downfall of the giant Goliath.[25]

Equicola's two remaining women seem to have less imposing tasks. Cornelia Cantelmo does not possess any distinguishing traits or really any marks of personality at all. It could very easily be argued (and convincingly) that her only reason for being included is that she is a relative of Margherita Cantelmo.[26] However, this lack of reference to any personal traits allows Equicola to describe the type of woman who will later be termed «donna di palazzo» by Castiglione, perhaps as an antidote to what could be called the «donna

---

[24] See P.O. Kristeller, «Music and learning in the early Italian Renaissance» in *Studies in Renaissance Thought and Letters,* Rome, 1956, pp. 451-70; E. Moutsopoulos, *La musique dans l'oeuvre de Platon,* Paris, 1959; L. Spitzer, *Classical and Christian Ideas of World Harmony,* Baltimore, 1963; D.P. Walker, *Studies in Musical Science in the Late Renaissance,* Leiden, 1978.

[25] M. Ficino, «De Musica» *(Epistolarum Liber* I) in *Opera Omnia,* Turin, 1962, pp. 650-51 (vol. I), (Monumenta politica et philosophica rariora ex optimis editionibus phototypice expressa, curante Luigi Firpo, series I, numerus 7-8, *Opera Omnia,* Basilea 1576).

[26] See Santoro, p. 278.

di casa». Indeed, Cornelia Cantelmo is described almost solely in terms of her social graces:

> Cuius ut taceam suavissimae vocis leporem et formosissimi vultus decentiam quam mira gestuum dignitas convenustat. Sermo nunquam inanis, grata semper urbanitas, temperata severitas, maximum in verbis pondus et sine superstitione religio, cui non sunt admirationi?
> (*De Mulieribus*, f. b3^r)

The writer places particular emphasis on the social skills of communication as if to make it clear that his lady will not be locked away and condemned to live in solitude. Conversation is the chief requirement of a woman at court where she will have to learn to use it correctly.

Margherita Cantelmo has a little more space devoted to her since she is treated along the same lines as Isabella d'Este with, of course, due regard to her less exalted position.[27] Although the differences in stature and power are easily discernible, the three women are linked together by their common interest in representing a new and dynamic picture of women. Isabella may be the leader of these women but the other two are prototypes of the lady who will receive her final theoretical clarification from Castiglione. At this relatively early date Equicola has already formulated the principles that will be needed by later theorists:

> Redeat igitur unde digressa est oratio et, si fieri potest, enitamur totis viribus ostendere muliebrem sexum per omnes virtutes cum laude cucurrisse. Ad quas exequendas ita ut fieri solet in magnis domibus et ipsa regia cuius interiorem luxum ornataque penetralia vestibulum deauratum et marmoribus facies incrustata declarat.[28]

*

---

[27]   «Lauderem Margarita (ut iure possem) tui quoque oris gratiam et venustatem tuosque imprimis glaucos illos oculos acrius intuenti, nescio quid divini vigoris (ut de C. Octavio Augusto legitur) prae se ferentes, si te Deus et natura ipsa corporis tum dotibus beasset. Nec te ad sanctimoniam, frugalitatem, continentiam, gratitudinem, constantiam et prudentiam. Ad omnes denique virtutes effinxissent magnam atque excelsam. Ad quam quidem eximiam et illustrem naturam quia ratio, bonarum artium studia et consumatio doctrinae adcessit, Pepere in te nescio quid praeclarum et singulare. Plura dixi quam locus ipse requireret et plurima de vestris laudibus reticui.»
                                                                    (*De Mulieribus*, f. b3^r)

[28]   *De Mulieribus*, fs. b3^r-b3^v. Castiglione recognized the importance of Equicola as a writer on women in an early draft of the *Cortegiano* (dropped in the *Seconda redazione* proper):

> «o almen dui che sono precipuamente affecionati alle donne perché so che mi dariano soccorso non piccolo.» «E quali son questi?» disse la signora regina. Soggionse Messer Camillo: «Messer Zoan Francesco Vallerio e Messer Mario Equicola, l'uno per un cunto, l'altro per un altro, ma tutti dui però per servizio e laude de le donne e confutazione de la sentenza vostra e minor mia fatica.»

In the *Seconda redazione* proper the reference to Equicola is removed and only that to Valerio remains. The reasons behind this deletion still need to be clarified (*La seconda redazione del «Cortegiano» di Baldassare Castiglione*, edizione critica per cura di Ghino Ghinassi, Florence,

If, in theory, women at court had found their abode, Equicola had certainly not. At first, the new «partnership» with Margherita Cantelmo did not meet with great success. However much Equicola may have boasted about the strength of this new alliance, even going so far as to sign himself, «Mario di Madonna, il quale non andarà in Milano», the matter at the heart of the dispute, the two Cantelmo brothers were set on sending him to that city. [29] Equicola, for his part, did not think there was any real need to go there, and this time, more sure of himself, openly objected to the waste of time, effort and money involved:

> Messer Sigismundo pare habia deliberato andare in Milano con Monsignore [Giulio Cesare Cantelmo]. Ad mi non pare al proposito, che non so vedere ad che effecto, se non forsi che ha denari soperchi. Li ho facto intendere il mio parere multo caldamente. Vostra Signoria faccia quel li pare... perché costoro tengono per certo et indubitamente che questo Maio serrando in Reame. Per questo, facilmente, Vostra Signoria mi farrà una singular gratia de fare et operare che messer Sigismundo prege Monsignore mi lasse per omni modo restare per messer Hercule [Cantelmo], havendo tanto poco tempo ad impararlo che poi se va in Reame. So certo Monsignore il farrà perché ancor lui cognosce mia voluntà. [30]

It can be said that Equicola only obtained a delay in his departure for Milan, but now Milan had become the first stage of a journey to the French court. By the end of September 1501 Sigismondo Cantelmo and Equicola were in Milan and Giulio Cesare had been despatched to Popoli, a former family possession. [31]

Try as he might, he was ineffective in his pleas to remain where he was and by October 1501 he was back in France. [32] The journey was fraught with

---

1968, p. 181). Castiglione is implicitly recognizing the help he received from his study of the *De Mulieribus* as well as from the lost work of Valerio. The passage just quoted from the *De Mulieribus* may have given Castiglione the idea for his term «donna di palazzo» because Equicola makes it clear that the lady he is discussing will be attached to the court («in magnis domibus et ipsa regia»).

[29] ASMN, AG, b. 283, undated but evidently written in March 1501, Equicola to Margherita Cantelmo. Another letter dated 15 March 1501, from Sigismondo to his wife is written in Equicola's hand from Ferrara. If more explicit proof were needed of this change of attitude towards his feudal lord, Equicola himself writes to Margherita:

> Ad mi non più signore ma semplice messer Sigismundo, consorte di Vostra Signoria.

[30] ASMN, AG, b. 283, Ferrara, 25 March 1501, Equicola to Margherita Cantelmo.

[31] ASMN, AG, b. 283, Milan, 27 September 1501, Sigismondo Cantelmo to his wife, written in Equicola's hand.
ASMN, AG, b. 283, Popoli, 14 October 1501, Giulio Cesare Cantelmo to Margherita Cantelmo.

[32] ASMN, AG, b. 283, Lyons, 17 October 1501, Sigismondo Cantelmo to his wife (in Equicola's hand):

> Arrivai qui in Lione alli XIII del presente dove trovai la Maestà del Signor Re. Et lo jove poi lo disnare de quella li basai la mano et exposili la causa della mia venuta et quanto da lei domandava. Con grandissima et bona cera mi accolse e

difficulties from the start. It seems that Sigismondo Cantelmo fell seriously
ill on the way, but such was his determination to reach France that he tried
to disguise the fact and insisted on continuing the journey.[33] Under these conditions, Equicola's disposition towards his master would not have changed
very much. On the contrary, a sense of desperation and with it anger assailed
Equicola:

> Crepo de rabia, moro de dolore, il quale non passarà sensa mia grandissima
> adversità, se passarà mai più. Ogn'hora più il cel mi molesta, deveria bastare ad
> dio et lo diavolo, alla fortuna et mio mal genio molestarme in un modo, non in
> mille et tucti, varii et miserabili. Mi cognosco essere ioco de sorte... In mi non
> serrà mai altro che patientia con perseverantia, Amor con fede... Al presente, mi
> trovo in Purgatorio, in le pene eminentissime et grandissime. Non so se serrò man-
> dato a l'Inferno ad eterno supplicio, che ne dubito, o vero se serrò remesso in
> Paradiso che vorria.[34]

Equicola realized his impotence before events over which he had no control
and found that perhaps the best way of facing the situation was to assume an
attitude of submission towards the circumstances which were engulfing him.
At other times, as can be seen from his theoretical writings, he assumed a
more aggressive stance with regard to *fortuna*, holding the view that people
must create their own destiny, an opinion well suited to the philosophy of a
self-made man. However, in 1501, he was not his own man; he was still the
feudal vassal of the Cantelmo family. That relationship severely restricted his
freedom of action and caused him a great deal of anguish.[35] Although there

---

> fandome careze assai voler me in tucte mei domande satisfare con dire che
> domandava cose iuste e le quali mai se potriano denegare.
> Et la spesa l'ho facta grande per la mia malatia la quale è stata gravissima,
> al presente mi trovo sano e per seguire la corte [to Blois] ho facto prestare al Ves-
> covo de Vulterra [Francesco Soderini] cinquanta scudi li quali mi darrà hogi.

Equicola's first surviving letter from Lyons is also dated 17 October.

[33]   ASMN, AG, b. 283, Lyons, 17 October 1501, Equicola to Margherita Cantelmo:

> Quanto sia stato lo affando et angustia mia de mente Vostra Signoria credo il
> consydera. Retrovandoci in la Savoia, paese tristissimo et sterelissimo, et lo
> signore malato de sorte che qualche volta dubitai della vita et non posser in cosa
> alcuna demostrare mia servitù se non in dolere che medici non havevamo né per-
> sona la qual ci consegliasse il meglio. La febre era grandissima et ardentissima et
> tersana duppia et il mio parere è che mai ne fosse necto. Questo male comensò
> ad discoprirse un poco in Pavia et lui non disse niente et cavalcò colla febre fine
> in Asti dove fo constrecto ad dire, «Mi sento male». La sera non cenò, ma perché
> soleva delle altre volte non magnare la sera, non ne pigliai multa admiratione.
> Cavalcammo la matina, et per fugire terre ammorbate che tucto'l paese ne era
> pieno, fonmo constructi fare quaranta miglia, che so' cinquanta de italiane.

[34]   ASMN, AG, b. 283, Pavia, 1 October 1501, Equicola to Margherita Cantelmo.

[35]   This anguish is not only mental: Sigismondo's journey to France put severe strains on
the family's finances:

> Cqui se spende assai et li cento ducati devevamo havere in Bologna ci so' stati
> remessi in Lione. Llì li haveremo.
> (ASMN, AG, b. 283, «Lunelli», Equicola to Margherita, 24 September 1501)

were moments of rebellion, usually taking the form of outbursts most often to Margherita Cantelmo, Equicola's protests seem to have gone unheeded, perhaps increasing his resentment and his resolve to become more closely involved with Isabella d'Este and her court. His letters make clear his unhappiness at the situation in which he finds himself; he will try to change the ground-rules but most often he writes to Margherita Cantelmo in such a way as to render his misery more bearable.

From his isolation in France his only source of comfort was again Margherita Cantelmo «la quale mi è patria, patre, matre, sorelle, fratelli, roba, reputatione, fama, honore, lettere et vita et questo è più certo che non è la certeza».[36] Equicola was engaged in an endless search for the appropriate stylistic register to express his feelings in a way which would be acceptable to her. He sought to convey an impression of the torment he was suffering and had frequent recourse to the metaphors of Hell and Purgatory.[37] The monotony of his sentiments is barely relieved by the stylistic effort to convey such feelings. He became obsessed by the thought of returning to Ferrara and to his Lady:

---

[36]   ASMN, AG, b. 283, Pavia, 1 October 1501, Equicola to Margherita Cantelmo.

[37]   ASMN, AG, b. 283, Lyons, 18 October 1501, Equicola to Margherita Cantelmo:

> Se la continua meditatione pò alcuna cosa appresso la mente nostra, io non so' più Mario, ma tucto pensieri, nel quale sensa intermissione mi resolvo lo animo et core è fixo con chiodo cupidineo inextrahibile in Italia. Il corpo sensa anima è in Franza il quale pure alcune volte repiglia vigore per expedire et posser tornare alla viva Divinità presentialmente. Et perché della expeditione bene exequita spero merito et beneficio dala prefata divinità de men mala voglia patisco l'absentia. Il mio vivere cqui è morte manifesta sensa dubio. Ma fo stima de esser in Purgatorio dove dicono theologi che la pena grande è llì non è altro che'l non possere fruire et vedere il conspecto de Dio. Uscerò, spero presto, et serrò in Paradiso. Questa speransa de questa futura amenità patientemente mi fa supportare fochi, sulphuri, incendii et mille varie generatione de misere morte nelle quali mi retrovo. ... In mi non è altra mano che quella che scrive quanto mi persuado sia cosa grata ad vostra divinità... Il mio nome è romano et il nome troiano mi deve, se non vencere, farme dubitare della victoria...

The over-rhetorical use of anaphora, the personalized use of Hell and Purgatory imagery are meant to create sympathy in Margherita Cantelmo's mind. But, for the modern reader, one cannot help but note the over-use of these galant conceits which reduce language to a game played for a particular purpose.

Equicola also needed to express his loyalty to the family, yet at the same time, gave vent to his resentment in regard to Sigismondo's irresponsible behaviour. The humanist implied that his employer had no idea of his secretary's status nor of the value of his judgements:

> Basta dire so' de casa Cantelma: quel nome è più potente che non è lo adonai nelle cose sacre. Io non posso non dolerme per vedere le cose sensa misura. Noi stentamo cqui como asini. Et dove llì se deveria sparamiare la roba per possere supplire alle spese venerando necessarie et honoreveli se butta...
>
> (ASMN, AG, b. 283bis, Blois, 25 November [1501?], Equicola to Margherita Cantelmo).

> Sopra omni desyderato desyderio, desydero Italia, la quale tene et sustene il mio
> desyderio et summo voto. [38]

Equicola's letters of this period vacillate between the hyperbolic and rare moments of unadorned despair. Most of the time, however, he had to resort to certain rigid formulae to express his thoughts, repetition being one of his principal devices, as we have seen above. At times Equicola falls into the comic in his efforts to convey his willingness to serve. He becomes a rather ridiculous figure with no notion of self-restraint. The humanist ideal of the «mean» is alien to him because it imposes limitations on his self-effacement. It is the utter servility of his statements that tend to raise the suspicion of their acceptability, of their «morality».

Sigismondo had not lost any of his optimism and, once again, his expectations were high. The French king had received him very favourably, but had promised nothing concrete. [39] While Sigismondo was being impressed by the ceremony of the French court, Equicola was involved in dealings which would give his master the opportunity of continuing his negotiations. Money was the most pressing problem and Equicola used his friendship with Francesco Soderini to obtain a loan from him. [40] Matters seem to have made no progress since Sigismondo's last visit to France and Equicola's position remained exactly the same; firm in the assertion of his personal worth and in his refusal to be sent off wherever his master pleased:

> Benché de andare in Reame habia concluso de non, per nesciun modo, non volendo mettere mia purità in man de mostruosi muli et muli li quali dominano et so' signori essendo como so' li veri signori de la sorte sonno. Per il che ad Reame ho dicto et dico «Vale». Lo signore sta sano et io del corpo, ma non malato de la mente, ma morto. (See note 40)

---

[38]   ASMN, AG, b. 283, Blois, 16 November 1501, Equicola to Margherita Cantelmo.
[39]   ASMN, AG, b. 283, Lyons, 17 October 1501, Equicola to Margherita Cantelmo, concerns the French king's reception of her husband:

> Jove poi lo suo disnare visitò et li basciò la mano et felli intendere il tucto con bona cera et con gran careze et tanto più che lui è stato lo primo barone del regno... De denari stamo male. Ho facto lo vescovo de Vulterra [Francesco Soderini] ci presta cinquanta scudi... Del dare ad secretari et cancellieri farremo con multo manco io non credeva, havendo la voluntà del signor re et favore de la corte. Ma la spesa grande seria per il vivere andando adpresso la corte et tanto più che ci sforsaremo sempre havere allogiamento vicino al signor re per possere omni dì il signore cortegiar Sua Maestà colla quale, quando serremo ad Bles [Blois], andarà ad caccia de falconi.

The use of the verb «cortegiar» is interesting here: it implies that Sigismondo's lack of real power leaves him no alternative except to employ those arts and skills which may win him the king's favour. The term seems to be employed as a matter of course to express the means by which the gap can be narrowed between the French monarch and a dispossessed Neapolitan baron.
[40]   Cf. note 39. Also see, ASMN, AG, b. 283, Blois, 6 November 1501, Sigismondo Cantelmo to his wife: «In denari non sto troppo bene, ansi malissimo et la spesa è grande.»

This time Equicola employed humour to cast doubt upon Sigismondo's judgement in wanting to send his secretary to Naples. Equicola did not refrain from passing comment on Sigismondo's conduct in financial matters:

> Ma io de spendere denari non parlarò ad Signor Sigismundo, essendo lui como li putti che de quel tengono in mano non dando, ma nel resto sonno prodigi. Che quando caccia una corona per il vivere pare li escano li occhi, pense Vostra Signoria che farrà nelle altre cose; ma in donare castelle è liberalissimo. (See note 40)

Sigismondo's quixotic behaviour found a harsh judge in Equicola who had to suffer its effects.

November passed without anything being achieved and even with the arrival of December Sigismondo was as determined as ever not to leave France empty-handed:

> Io so cqui et non partirò sensa resolutione per omni modo et vederò la mia venuta in Fransa non sia stata in vano.[41]

Christmas still found him in Blois:

> Al presente so' le feste et per questo non posso altro fare che expectare che passino. Poi, serrò subito expedito et volarò in Italia.[42]

This time Sigismondo was not deluding himself and he wrote to his wife on 7 January 1502 that he had finally obtained the necessary privileges:

> Con qualche spesa et tribulatione de cancellieri ho havuta expeditione che in Napuli messe facciano li privilegii de quanto ha posseduto Casa Cantelma per cinquanta anni et più.[43]

Shortly afterwards, Sigismondo Cantelmo must have left on his return journey to Ferrara, for Equicola wrote a letter from that city towards the end of February. In Ferrara, Equicola now had to set in order Sigismondo's affairs which had been neglected because of the various visits to France:

> Per esserme stato necessario fare rescrivere il instrumento delle robe [che] donò il Signor Duca de Ferrara al Signor Sigismundo non lo ho ancor expedito. Questa matina lo haverò per ogni modo... Ho data la supplicatione ad messer Thebaldo dela fossa drieto al'horto. Mi ha promesso expedirme; non cessarò de sollicitare. Ho parlato con Gentile de' Sardi che mi leve lo instrumento de quel poco terreno discontro alla nostra stalla che questi Calcagnini pare che brontono. Levato harò lo Iusto ordinarò al factore ci faccia un palmo de muro ad ciò sia nostro sensa

---

[41] ASMN, AG, b. 283, Blois, 10 December 1501, Sigismondo Cantelmo to his wife.

[42] ASMN, AG, b. 283, Blois, 23 December 1501, Sigismondo Cantelmo to his wife. From this point on the correspondence becomes increasingly concerned with the prospect of completing the business in hand and returning to Italy:

> Ad mi resta dire che lo signor re con tutta la corte facti tre dì poi natale va in Parisi et noi seguirò in la bona ora dove spero seremo subito expediti.

(ASMN, AG, b. 283, Blois, 23 December 1501, Equicola to Margherita Cantelmo).

[43] ASMN, AG, b. 283, Blois, 7 January 1502, Sigismondo Cantelmo to his wife.

disturbo. Farrò ancora lo signor Sigismundo sia facto della Casa d'Este. Metterò
in ordine la causa del 'erno [?] che haveremo la sententia per noi et presto. Como
vene don Alfonso vederò havere la tracta del frumento et expedirò le lettere al
papa et ad lo prencipe de Squillaci per obviare ad li errori se fanno da quelle
bande. Madonna mia, queste so' le cause che mi fanno restare... Maxime essendo
ogni cosa in ordine et in procinto de farse non mi è parso lassare tante cose im-
perfecte, essendo bene state comenzate per doi dì. Maxime che in quesse parti
adesso non fo niente in suo servitio, in mio fo assaissimo.[44]

It does not appear that these administrative duties were to keep him very long
in Ferrara because he was already talking of leaving (he uses the verb
«volare») to join Margherita Cantelmo in Mantua.[45] Equicola was free to go
to Mantua owing to the fact that it was Giulio Cesare Cantelmo who had to
go to Naples. Sigismondo's brother was also caught up in the euphoria following the successful conclusion of the negotiations in France. He felt that the
French were taking a firm hold of the *Regno* and that their own troubles were
over:

Spero che serrà fine d'ogni male nel quale la nostra barcha è stata longo tempo
agitata. La lettera del Signor Re et li dui privilegii ho receputo. Et per essere dicta
lettera et uno privilegio in francioso, non li ho possuto legere.[46]

Little did he know that a storm was brewing which was to capsize their
boat. Even if he was struggling against the tide, Giulio Cesare showed himself
to be relentless in his pursuit of the restitution of the Cantelmo possessions,
through the legal processes.[47] However, as the year progressed things were
becoming increasingly difficult:

Me erano cognite le cose gallice essere prolixe et defficile, et tanto più per li Rago-
nisi essere decorati et muniti de illustro titolo de riccheze.[48]

To make matters worse, Giulio Cesare lacked the authority of his brother, and
he desperately needed his presence in Naples. Sigismondo did not share his

---

[44]   ASMN, AG, b. 283, Ferrara, 22 February 1502, Equicola to Margherita Cantelmo.
[45]   The letter quoted at note 44 continues:
Io serrò hogi et domani cqui in Ferrara, et poi volando in Mantua, como quel che
summamente desydera servire Madama, et ad questo se pò cognoscere che resto
in Ferrara, che non voglio mi reprendate como del partire de Bles.
[46]   ASMN, AG, b. 283, Popoli, 26 February 1502, Giulio Cesare Cantelmo to his brother,
Sigismondo.
[47]   Various servants of the Cantelmo family were dispatched to find witnesses to support
the family's claims:
Gionto heri qui in Popoli da Sulmona, dove era stato cinque giorni per lo examino
se fa della rebellione del signor Antonio [Cantelmo, who had taken possession of
Sigismondo's territories], ho produtti circha quarantacinque testimonii, tucti
schiavi de questi nostri signori.
(ASMN, AG, b. 283, Popoli, 26 February 1502, «Nicolaus Athyas» to Equicola).
[48]   ASMN, AG, b. 283, Popoli, 26 February 1502, Giulio Cesare Cantelmo to Equicola.

opinion and believed that more could be achieved by yet another journey to the French court. Nothing could induce him to change his mind, especially since he had been given the honour of accompanying Alfonso d'Este to France.[49]

However, even before the company reached Lyons they heard the news that Spain and France were quarrelling over Capitanata and that Louis XII was preparing to enter the Italian peninsula, «sensa dubio, serrà guerra in Italia et presto et questo» was Equicola's comment on the situation (Carmignola, 15 May 1502). Equicola adds sardonically: «Il facto nostro che come se comenza guerra taceno le legge et chi sta in possessione se tiene». What, a few days earlier, had seemed within Sigismondo Cantelmo's grasp, was now as far away as ever. Everything had once again moved out of his control; the European powers («questa machina» as Equicola called them) did not have to take into account the position of a dispossessed Neapolitan baron. In spite of these setbacks, Equicola managed to retain some of his optimism:

> Dove sperava quiete et mi imaginava omni generatione de piaceri, al presente vedo guerre et turbulentie et quantunca non dubite della victoria, pure non serrà sensa dubio et incommodità grandissima *et maxime mia*, che mi serrà necessario per commandamento de Vostra Signoria andare sempre in volta. Ogni cosa supportarò per la mia Enzelechia la quale è et seria mia vita. (My italics)[50]

It seems that whenever the possibility arose of there being some obstacle placed in his path Sigismondo fell sick, as if paralysed by the thought of not achieving his goal.[51] In spite of the fact that the fate of the Cantelmo possessions was to be decided by the force of arms, Equicola spared no effort to obtain all the privileges necessary to recover their lands:

---

[49] Even his wife could not make him change his mind:

> Non sença mio grandissimo dolore ve fo la presente lettera, co[n]siderando il termene ve lassai con lacrime e pianti et se io ve dicesse aver facto il simile, voglio me'l credate. E zuro a Dio che mai me partì da vui che più me recressese che questa volta. Ma de questo non voglio i[n]colpare né Dio né Fortuna, ma solo il Fato mio che non vole mai abia cosa ch'io desidero a conpimento.

(ASMN, AG, b. 283, Mantua, 5 May 1502, Sigismondo Cantelmo to his wife). The journey to France would have certainly improved Equicola's acquaintance with the next Duke of Ferrara, something that would be extremely useful later on in his career.

[50] On their way to France Equicola and company had stopped over at Mantua:

> So' in quest'hora arrivato in Mantua tutto bagnato dal capo al piè che da pelagallo mai me ha lassato aqua, tempesta et grandine. Allogio in casa de messer Ludovico.

(ASMN, AG, b. 283, Mantua, 4 May 1502, Equicola to Margherita Cantelmo).

[51] ASMN, AG, b. 283, Lyons, 1 June 1502, Equicola to Margherita Cantelmo:

> Lo signora ha pigliati, per conseglio del nostro predecto medico, sciroppi et la medicina et sta multo sano et bello.

Subito subito fo la corte cqui tentai de expedire li privilegii de donatione et confir-
matione. Et così, Dio gratia, la ho havuta de tucto quel tenemo in Abruzo. Sappia
quella che solo io ho parlato con omni persona et mai ho voluto signor Sigismundo sia stato pur visto per demostrare se sa fare quando se vole. Intertanto il
privilegio se expediva. Io non perdeva tempo, ma andava investigando che voleva
fare questo re Federico per il conte de Populi et trovai che li have facto fare lo indulto et una lettera se ha iustitia li sia facta. Subito, personalmente, andai in
cancellaria ad fare como pazo, che'l Signor Re de Franza era tradito, che la
cancellaria haveva expedito cose assai in favore de chi se retrova colli Spagnoli...[52]

Through Equicola's efforts, Sigismondo Cantelmo's position appears to have
become more secure and he therefore considered it possible to leave the French
court before the end of June 1502.[53] Alfonso d'Este also left at the same time
after completing his successful visit.[54]

---

[52]   ASMN, AG, b. 283, Lyons, 20 June 1502, Equicola to Margherita Cantelmo. Equicola's resentment at Sigismondo's ineptitude grew in proportion to the humanist's hard work
for his employer:

> Quanto errore ne succeda da uno solo, quanto inconvenienti ne genere uno solo
> facilmente nelle cose nostre se vede. Et se fosse restato in Franza quando il biso-
> gno il recerchava et io continuo il diceva haveremo havuti li nostri privilegii auten-
> tichi et in optima forma, haveremo facti restare li nostri adversarii de tucti loro
> pensieri et l'uno non haveria havuta speranza et l'altro non ne haveria obtenuta
> scripta del conseglio de essere restituto in possessione. Non haveremo spesi li
> docento ducati invano. Non serria stato necessario havere più molestia de tornare
> in queste parti et io non serria absente con chi sta continuo lo animo sensa inter-
> missione de tempo. Mi sforsarò con omni possibilità se recupere il mal facto per-
> ché ho in animo far forzi circa ciò farrò poche parole.
>
>   Casa del Marchese de Peschara ha havuti li privilegii; Casa Carrapha, Casa
> de Altavilla le quale so' sempre state Aragonese. De francese non intendo alcuna
> per vero se non fredamente.

(ASMN, AG, b. 283, Lyons, 27 May 1502, Equicola to Margherita Cantelmo).

[53]   ASMN, AG, b. 283, Lyons, 21 June 1502, Sigismondo Cantelmo to his wife:

> Hogi, XXI del mese, il signor Don Alfonso è partito da Lione verso Italia
> appresso la corte. Io partirò domani et ad bon iornate serrò presto da voi.

Equicola, however, has doubts about the French king's ability to defeat the Spanish as well
as the weakness of their own position:

> Monsignore nostro mi persuado che l'intenda et faccia provisioni necessarie, sì
> alle rocche de victuarie, sì alli populi, che havendo inimici fore non se sta così
> securi della volubilità de vulgo...Credo li nostri adversari siano ben informati de
> questi futuri moti et però con maior instantia cercarando le possessioni. Noi
> havemo ad tenere in tempo finché se principia de rompere che bene se differisce
> in questi casi. Subito che guerra se principia non dubito haveremo quel et del'
> altro... Questa guerra serrà multo ambigua et dubiosa et non così facilmente se
> pò iudicare ad chi se habia ad adtribuire la victoria. Re de Spagna et sua consorte
> sonno prudenti et potenti et hanno Sicilia donde securamente pò dare omni suc-
> curso alli soi. Li Spagnoli so' de sorte che sanno accarezareli populi. Re Christia-
> nissimo è prudente et potente et ha Milano et Genua donde pò dare aiuto alli soi.
> Li populi non amano francesi. Et essendo de cqua et dellà ragioni probabili,

In the short term, Equicola's stay had been fairly fruitful and was made less soul-destroying by his meeting with some of his old acquaintances. He had the opportunity to renew his friendship with Bernardino Capella who was on his second visit to France, on behalf of certain cardinals, probably of the Orsini clan. Equicola's attitude towards him was not one we would expect from someone who had been so close to him; with one deft stroke Equicola succeeded in turning Capella into a figure of fun:

> Ho trovato cqui il mio Capella, quel che ha il volto che pare una trippa revoltata, che vene da Roma per parte de alcuni cardinali. (See note 55)

The affectionate «il mio Capella» is undermined by the suggestion of cruelty that informs Equicola's words. If this were not enough, Equicola states that he was going to use Capella for his own ends without regard for their long relationship. In other words, Equicola had the tendency to place expediency above personal and private values.[55]

There can be no doubt that Equicola left the French court with Sigismondo Cantelmo but, unfortunately, from this point on there is a large gap in the Cantelmo papers which stretches from June 1502 until 1511 by which date Equicola was no longer in the employment of the family. It is most probable that Equicola returned directly to Ferrara, but it is difficult to determine the length of his stay there. According to Equicola himself, he was at his master's side at the battle of the Garigliano.[56] As the date of his return to Ferrara

---

> io non so che iudicare, se non che so li Franciosi valere colle arme in mano più che Hispagnoli et Spagnoli valere più de ingegno et astutie.
>
> (ASMN, AG, b. 283, 22 May 1502, Equicola to Margherita Cantelmo).

[54] ASMN, AG, b. 283, Lyons, 14 June 1502, Equicola to Margherita Cantelmo:

> Dismontato che fo lo signor Don Alphonso, la Christianissima Maestà li fece omni demostratione de careze possibile ad deverse desyderare, menandolo con si sempre, et in camera volse fosse al suo dispogliarse. Poi dalla regina la quale basciò similmente fo adcarezato et da Monsignor de Roana.

Equicola must have felt pleased at the reception he received from the future Duke of Ferrara: «Lo signor Don Alphonso mi fa multi favori» (ASMN, AG, b. 283, Lyons, 2 June 1502, «Mario più che deditissimo» to Margherita Cantelmo).

[55] «Usarò lui...in nostro favore» (Lyons, 14 June 1502. See first letter in previous note).

[56] Santoro quotes the relevant passage from the *Pro Gallis Apologia* on pp. 45-46, n. 2:

> Re male ad Lyrim gesta, cum nostros ex hibernis pulsos esset renuntiatum, multique supramodum Gallis detraherent, officio me defuturum existimabam si qui manu rem gallicam, Sigismundi Cantelmi Ducis Sorae auspiciis, pro viribus tutatus sum, dignitatem voce non defenderem et qui avitis bonis privari me passus fueram cur verba continerem ratio nulla videbatur. Respondi, nil dissimulans, id non diuturnitate belli defatigatis Gallis sed specie pacis accidisse; quaestorum et qui militum equitumque stipendiis praeerant avaritia, ducum imbecillitate ne dixerim negligentia aliorumque quorum summa erat auctoritas, rei militaris inscitia omne incommodum esse acceptum. Fugatos igitur nostros potissimum contendebamus quod Duces praestantissimi, quos prudenter tantae provinciae Rex praefecerat, adversa valetudine loco interesse non potuerint.

is unknown, it is a matter of conjecture whether or not he took part in the
rearguard action against the Spanish following the French defeat at the
Garigliano. It is certain that Sigismondo Cantelmo decided to fight to the last
and, as it turned out, this was nearly the case. [57] The illusions that Sigismondo
still nurtured about becoming Duke of Sora more than in name alone would
not permit him to abandon a now hopeless enterprise. Equicola may have
followed his master into battle in order to decide the fate of the *Regno* but,
once it was clear that there was nothing to be gained from continuing the
struggle, he felt that the time had come to return to Ferrara, where we find
him in the middle of May. [58]

*

After the recent events, it seems that Equicola was determined more than
ever, to break free from Sigismondo Cantelmo. It might be said that Equicola
was contemplating nothing less than a betrayal of his master at a time when
he needed him most. Although this point of view is not without justification,
it should be taken into account that Sigismondo placed a heavy burden on
Equicola's shoulders, and that his merits went unnoticed and unrewarded.
Equicola probably decided that he had had enough of his master's childish
behaviour and would seek employment elsewhere. It is true that he did not
formally leave Cantelmo service until 1508 although in the years following
1503 he became increasingly involved in the affairs of Ippolito d'Este and
Isabella, his sister. Immediately upon his return to Ferrara, he seized an opportunity of furthering his cause with Isabella d'Este. At first sight the pretext
seems trivial — the sending of a birthday greeting to the Marchioness. [59] The
whole exercise was part of Equicola's demonstration of his loyalty to the *Marchesana* and he used it as a means of heaping praise on her, with the authority
of classical antiquity. Equicola implied, by his greeting, a connection between
Isabella's first day in the world and his first day as her newest and most loyal
servant:

---

[57]   ASMN, AG, b. 1239, Ferrara, 24 May 1503, Bernardo Mazono to Isabella d'Este:
Significo a Vostra Signoria che heri ali XXIII del presente quie in Ferrara giunse
uno fante a piede, qual si ritrovò nel conflicto in Puglia facto tra Galli et
Spagnoli... mi ha detto che apresso una terra di Puglia chiamata Chanossa si
ritrovoron lo exercito gallico et hispano... Furon prima li Franzosi ch'andoron ad
assaltare li Spagnoli et prima dice che fu la squadra di messer Sigismundo
Cantelmo che li assalì, da la qual non campò se non epso cum dui de li soi; tutto
il resto furon ucisi.

[58]   Cf. ASMN, AG, b. 1239, Ferrara, 17 May 1503, Equicola to Isabella d'Este.

[59]   Margherita Cantelmo also sent Isabella d'Este a birthday greeting. She excused herself
for not being able to come to Mantua in person but, nonetheless «non fatigha, non incommodo
me'l fa pretermettere, ma solo il non volere parere adulatrice, il quale vitio sempre serrà da mi
alienissimo» (ASMN, AG, b. 1239, Ferrara, 17 May 1503, Margherita Cantelmo to Isabella
d'Este).

Essendo hogi quel memorabile et sacratissimo iorno, causa et principio de vital luce ad Vostra Excellentia, da mi con ogni veneratione se deve observare et secundo l'antiqua consuetudine celebrare. La quale era bene imprecare et augurare felice anno con mandar doni. Il che non voglio pretermettere con quella. Et così, primo, li do il bon dì, bon natale, ad ciò, dal principio sia fortunato tucto'l resto. Li dono, qual se sia, mio animo, mente, imaginatione, rascione, intellecto et intelligentia, spogliandome del proprio libero arbitrio et sensi corporali. Solo la supplico ad acceptare tal dono et disponere de mi como de monete se sole, le quali de oro, argento et rame se usano. Non mi cognosco né reputo degno del primo né secundo metallo. Spendame per rame, che summa gratia mi serrà et ad ciò sia certa de mia voluntà, li mando li infrascripti capituli in testimonio de fede, li quali mi obligo finché vivo inviolabilmente, sensa reserva, observare sempre:

Amare, servire, obedire, reverire et adorare la Illustrissima Isabella estense;
Sprezare ogni altra cosa presente et futura per lei;
Esser con quella, se non col corpo, col'animo de continuo;
Amare omni cosa ad lei pertinente;
Desyderare sue laude et non patere il contrario;
Credere in lei omni virtù et fare opera ciascheuno il creda;
Desyderare patere incommodo per suo servitio;
Amare, servire, adorare lei unica né pensare mai de premio o mercede.[60]

The gift Equicola is offering Isabella d'Este is his loyal service. In rebellion against his feudal lord, Equicola compares himself to the very thing that had made Sigismondo Cantelmo's position so precarious, namely, money (or in his case, the lack of it). A coin does not have a fixed place, it is spent at will and in Equicola's case, it represents his decision to enter a different kind of service from that to which he is accustomed. In fact, the language of the *capituli* recalls to mind the expressions used to declare the devotion of the troubadour poet to his lady and it is easy to believe that Equicola is aspiring to this ideal. For him, this ideal is no longer transposed to the realm of poetry, it can now be realized in a concrete situation. The expressions of adoration do not seem, in Equicola's mind, to be in contradiction with the form of the document, which is a contract. Thus Equicola is seen to be preferring a relationship which will be based on his usefulness to the lady. Equicola was offering himself as Isabella d'Este's ideologue: he will be responsible for «putting over» her public image in the most effective way possible. Instead of seeking a position of power and responsibility he preferred to be a tool in the hands of an ambitious woman. All this is crystallized in the *capituli*, the programme he set himself. In this programme Equicola lays especial emphasis on the words «amare» and «servire», closely linked in Equicola's mind. The humanist is attempting to define this relationship, not solely in monetary terms which

---

[60] ASMN, AG, b. 1239, Ferrara, 17 May 1503, Equicola to Isabella d'Este.
B. Dovizi, *Epistolario*, ed. G.L. Moncallero, 2 vols, Florence, 1955-65, I, pp. 252-53 offers a slightly different version from mine without revealing the source. For him the document represents a series of «regole d'amore» to which he does not attach any great significance.

would be objectionable to Isabella d'Este and which would not provide
Equicola with a firm foundation on which to build his future career, but in
terms of courtly love, with its tendency to idealize something earthly. Equicola
was offering his services to Isabella as the «perfect» propagandist: his own
personality will fade into nothingness by an act of his will. He claimed he was
there only to be spent and his value was in the «goods» he provided: humanist
works of praise for those who employed him. Despite the pedestrian manner
of expression and the hollowness of certain sentiments («né pensare mai de
premio o mercede»), the document represents an important turning-point in
the way Equicola viewed his career, not that it is really a surprise following
Sigismondo's treatment of him.

Castiglione realized, very early on, the choice Equicola had made:

> Eccovi che messer Mario Equicola nostro ha scritto infinite cose e di diverse
> materie, ma tutte però per compiacere la excelsa signora Isabella, Marchesana di
> Mantua, dalla quale come da uno Apolline ha preso vigore e forza allo ingegno
> suo.[61]

This is not just a simple compliment; it correctly evaluates the influence that
Isabella d'Este had on Equicola (though it is precisely because of Equicola's
work that Castiglione regards Isabella as an «Apolline»). She had given Equicola a new sense of direction and indeed, a new lease of life.

*

Equicola did not focus his attention solely on the *Marchesana*; he opened
a correspondence with the Marquis, Francesco Gonzaga, the following month
(June 1503). Equicola's intentions were clearly to make himself useful to the
Marquis and, hopefully, to be remembered by him at a future date. To Isabella, he had declared that his service was comparable to that of a lover's, the
proof of which has already been seen in the *De Mulieribus*, a powerful piece
of «propaganda» in itself. To Francesco, evidence of his willingness to serve
was offered through supplying the Marquis with useful information which
Equicola had probably received, ironically enough, from Sigismondo Cantelmo. Equicola wished to impress the Marquis with the fact that he had reliable sources of information. Further, he wished to demonstrate his capacity for
unravelling the complexities of the rapidly changing political situation by putting to good use his humanist training, especially the study of classical texts
and all the skills such an exercise involves. Francesco Gonzaga accepted Equicola's new role as a political informant with equal enthusiasm.[62] The quality

---

[61]   *La seconda redazione*, pp. 277-78.

[62]   ASMN, AG, b. 2911, libro 177. The Marquis' first letter to Equicola was from Gonzaga
in the *Mantovano* and dated 12 June 1503:

of Equicola's information was not as important as the fact that Equicola was informing the Marquis of anything at all. Equicola wanted to indicate that he could be as well used as Iacopo d'Atri, Francesco's secretary, who had also come north from southern Italy.[63]

In view of the fluidity of the political situation which for some of the Cantelmos had meant the loss of their feuds, Equicola preached one doctrine, relevant both for himself and the Marquis, that of opportunism. In order to survive the onslaught from powers with much greater resources than he himself could raise, the Marquis had to resort to any and every means possible to retain control of his state. Hence, Equicola's discussion of the subject would not have fallen on deaf ears:

> Dicono li poeti essere una donna alata et tucti li capelli sonno voltati denanti al vulto per non essere cognosciuta et ad ciò fugendo, non possa per capelli essere

---

> Messer Mario. La copia de le tre vostre littere ni è stata grata da leggere et in questo l'officio vostro ni è tanto più accepto quanto che l'è spontaneo et irre-quisito. Ma se non vi gravarà la fatica nel perseverare, ni accumulareti il piacere in summo gradu et benevalete.

A second letter (Mantua, 1 July 1503) thanked the still busy Equicola:

> Messer Mario. In una hora medesima havemo recepute quatro vostre littere a noi grate e de le quale vi ringratiamo assai, cognoscendo in esse il vostro animo of-ficioso et amorevole verso noi. E perché sapemo vi serrà grato che per noi vi sia imposta qualche cosa, vi imponemo non vi gravi proseguire questo vostro incepto. E per declararvi lo animo nostro, qual coniecturamo in esse vostre desyderati in-tendere qual sia, dicemovi che expectamo di hora in hora dinari da la Chris-tianissima Maestà, li quali recevuti, seremo apparecchiati venire cum monsignore Tramoglia a patir ogni sudore, fatica e periculo in servitio di la prefata Maestà, como quel bono servitor che li siamo et in questo meggio non cessamo di prepararni al meglio che possemo per ritrovarni in ordine a tempo.

A third letter (21 July 1503) illustrated the extent of Equicola's commitment:

> Messer Mario. El ni è di tanto piacere legere le littere vostre che non si vederessimo mai strachi, né mai ni potresti fastidire cum esse, se ben ogni dì ne havessimo due o tre. Unde havemo lecto quella de XIII instantis copiosa de avisi, la qual ni è stata sopramodo grata e vi ne ringratiamo pur assai.
>
> Per esserni sopravenuto in Parma uno pocho di male e poi per haverni scritto la Maestà Christianissima che vole servirsi di noi in Lombardia per secureza de le cose sue ad ogni caso che potesse sopravenire, seremo forzati restar a casa, cosa che ni doleria molto, se non fusse cha havemo perpetuo proposito de sempre ser-vire la Maestà sua a modo suo. Siamo ali piaceri vostri apparecchiati.

It is obvious that the Marquis was not being totally frank with Equicola. His excuses ring com-ically hollow, since, as usual, Francesco Gonzaga was performing a delicate balancing act so that his state would not be compromised. In these letters he is expressing the official reasons for his non-participation. There is also the possibility that Equicola might have been prompted by the Cantelmos to correspond with the Marquis as an ally of the French. However, one cannot exclude the personal implications of such a move for Equicola.

[63] See G. Coniglio, «La politica di Francesco Gonzaga nell'opera di un immigrato meri-dionale: Iacopo Probo d'Atri», *ASL*, serie nona, I, (Anno 88), 1961, pp. 131-67.

revocata. Socto'l piè dextro tene una palla per demostratione de instabilità. Drieto
ad costei sempre va la penitentia. Questa donna prefata è quel che vulgari
chiamano «pigliar il Tempo», che chi 'l lassa preterire, piglia quella compagna
che è il pentirse non haver pigliata la occasione et oportunità. So certissimo la Excellentia Vostra harà pigliata questa donna per capelli et cavalcarà alli danni de
Spagnoli. De questo non dubito, essendo prudentissima et magnanima, et
dell'una et l'altra virtù fatta manifesta prova...non men operando la prudentia
che la fortitudine: del che, essendo priva la natione francese, omni honore, omni
gloria, omni fama se darrà meritamente al Signor Marchese... Non è piccola laude
che fra tanti signori francesi, fra tanti italiani, fra tanti barbari, solo il Signor
Marchese sia rechiesto, pregato et supplicato ad recuperare il regno ad re de Franza. In lui solo è omni speranza de victoria.[64]

This theme of «oportunità» is reiterated throughout the course of Equicola's
career, so much so that one of his works has as its title, *De Opportunitate.*[65]

The fortunes of Sigismondo Cantelmo seemed at this point to have dropped even lower, partly because of the death of his brother, Giulio Cesare. One
of Isabella d'Este's correspondents reported his death to her, adding the comment that it is an «exempio al mondo delle humane cose».[66] To some extent,
the gap left by Giulio Cesare was filled by Equicola. The dead bishop had
been active in the affairs of Ippolito d'Este and Equicola was to continue that
role. It provided him with the opportunity of being less dependent on Sigismondo Cantelmo while, at the same time, obviating the necessity of breaking
off dramatically his relations with him. It is likely that he spent the rest of 1503
and most of 1504 (until he left for France) either as a member of Ippolito
d'Este's court or accompanying Margherita Cantelmo on her frequent visits
to Mantua. The regularity of her visits to Mantua are attested to by her
request to Ippolito d'Este to be granted a particular favour:

Desyderando io summamente fabricarmi una stantia da Ferrara in qua dove possi
reposare quando vado in anti et in dreto. Et intendendo che la Signoria Vostra
Excellentissima, ne l'assagio ha facto fare de li terreni di Felonicha, ha ritrovato
sopravanzarli bona quantità da allivellare, me pare per questa via possi conse-
quire il desyderio mio.[67]

However, in the autumn of 1504 Equicola was in France again, once more
in the company of Sigismondo Cantelmo, though this time the latter was
acting in the capacity of special representative for Ercole I Duke of Ferrara
as well as pursuing his own affairs. In the same way, Mario Equicola was
acting on behalf of Ippolito d'Este, principally in the role of an informant,

---

[64]   ASMN, AG, b. 1239, Ferrara, 12 June 1503, Equicola to the Marquis of Mantua.

[65]   Marius Aequicolus, *De Opportunitate*, Naples: Ioannes Antonius de Caneto, 1507, 4°.

[66]   ASMN, AG, b. 1239, Ferrara, 24 July 1503, «Iano Pincharo» to Isabella d'Este.

[67]   ASMO, Particolari: Cantelmo. Mantua, 29 October 1504, Margherita Cantelmo to
Ippolito d'Este.

though he did not neglect the cardinal's interests in the matter of obtaining certain benefices for him.[68] He found himself on opposite sides to Francesco Gonzaga over the blinding of Don Giulio d'Este in which the cardinal was involved.[69] Equicola did not hesitate to defend and even justify Ippolito d'Este's action. At this moment Equicola paid no attention to the consequences that his willingness to serve were to have on his reputation or on his own moral code.

At the French court Equicola was still expected to act on behalf of Sigismondo Cantelmo, even in the now hopeless situation as far as the latter's territories were concerned. He was referred to as «Mario de messer Sigismundo» in an *instructio* from the Duke of Ferrara since, by this time, Sigismondo had been given specific duties to carry out in the absence of the resident Ferrarese ambassador.[70] In spite of his temporary duties Sigismondo did not leave off the negotiations over his feuds, the possession of which was his only ambition.

*

Equicola, meanwhile, was able to pursue his literary interests. He had connections with the circle led by Jacques Lefèvre d'Etaples.[71] His relations with

---

[68]   For the relevant letters consult Santoro, pp. 45-53; 229-30.

[69]   Santoro, pp. 242-45; for a detailed account of the events surrounding the conspiracy see R. Bacchelli, *La congiura di Don Giulio d'Este*, 2 vols, Milan, 1931.

[70]   ASMO, ASE, C, Ambasciatori: Francia, b. 4, Ferrara, 15 October 1505, the Duke of Ferrara to Francesco Rangone:

> Nondimeno, dicemovi che siamo contenti che potiati ritornare a casa quando messer Sigismundo Cantelmo possa pervenire ale occurentie nostre sino a tanto che el serà gionto lie messer Manfredo di Manfredi quale mandamo in loco vostro.

There follows another letter on the same matter of 29 October:

> Et quando per caso fusti già partito da la corte remettereti questa nostra a messer Sigismundo Cantelmo, dicendoli che lo exequisca quanto in epsa se contene et cum presteza, instruendolo bene de la continentia... Et veramente se maravigliamo che dicte lettere non siano sta' mandate, poiché furno promesso come ni scrivesti et che a questo effecto fu mandato Mario de messer Sigismundo inseme col cancellero vostro ala corte, non potendoli andare vui per la indispositione vostra. Se che per Dio fati ogni [sforzo] perché dicte lettere se habino ad ciò che potiamo terminare quanto siamo per fare per assetto de queste cose de Cento et de la Pieve.

[71]   See E.F. Rice Jr.(ed.), *The Prefatory Epistles of Jacques Lefèvre d'Etaples and Related Texts*, New York and London 1972, pp. 126-28, 130-31; Idem, «The humanist idea of Christian Antiquity: Lefèvre d'Etaples and his circle» in *French Humanism 1470-1600*, ed. by W. L. Gundersheimer, London, 1969, pp. 162-80; Idem, «Humanist Aristotelianism in France. Jacques Lefèvre d'Etaples and his circle» in *Humanism in France at the End of the Middle Ages and in the Early Renaissance*, ed. by A.H.T. Levi, Manchester and New York, 1970, pp. 132-49; G. Bedouelle, *Lefèvre d'Etaples et l'intelligence des Ecritures*, Geneva, 1976, p. 33.

the leader of the circle must have been of a certain intimacy since Equicola was the author of a prefatory epistle to an edition of Aristotle, annotated by Lefèvre d'Etaples. Awkward problems may be seen to have arisen from Equicola's friendship with the French humanist: if, as is stated almost everywhere, Equicola is classed as a Neoplatonic philosopher, what can be made of his friendship with this most fervent of Aristotelians? It is true that Equicola did not see irreconcilable differences between Plato and Aristotle, but his manner of approach to certain aspects of Platonic doctrine will need to be re-examined. For him, both Giovanni Pico and Ficino are remembered for excelling «in remotioribus scientiis». Ficino's achievement as a Neoplatonist is practically passed over in silence. In the prefatory epistle, he also praises Ermolao Barbaro and Janus Lascaris (the last-mentioned is the only humanist out of six to be referred to as «nostrum»). These two humanists both excelled «in multiplici rerum cognitione» and the latter in particular can be said to have served as a model for Equicola who could see him as a successful humanist with editions of classical texts to his credit, while at the same time managing to combine this with a great deal of diplomatic activity. Further, both were exiles: Barbaro was sent from one Italian state to another while Lascaris found his way across a variety of countries.[72] A line from the verses which conclude the epistle shows, however generically, Equicola's rejection of an unsuitable life-style (inextricably linked with Sigismondo Cantelmo):

Vita in continuo labore mors est.

The search continued for a way to decrease the amount of energy spent on diplomatic activity and to increase the amount of time spent on other activities of a more tranquil nature.

*

As well as allowing Equicola the opportunity of mixing in humanist circles, his extended stay in France gave him time to take up the pen on his own account. His compositions were intimately connected with his personal insecurity in the Cantelmo household. There can be no doubt that Equicola was seeking fresh sources of patronage from those poeple who recognized his value as a man of learning. It has already been seen that Equicola showed himself to be tireless in promoting the interests of Cardinal Ippolito d'Este.[73]

---

[72]   See B. Knos, *Janus Lascaris. Un ambassadeur de l'Hellénisme*, Upsala, 1945.
[73]   We may add the following of Equicola's letters addressed to the Cardinal Ippolito as an example of his efforts in this area:

Lo indulto è venuto et le lettere al Papa. Alle cose del secretario se attende et maxime che Monsignor il legato predecto me ha dicto vole habbia la ecclesia

Ippolito was not the only person to whom he made approaches; he continued to play on Isabella d'Este's pretensions to learning. His birthday presents to her were becoming more involved and increasingly ambitious. A couple of years before a few lines had been sufficient to celebrate the occasion, whereas he now felt compelled to dedicate an entire book to her. Equicola announced the completion of the *Nec Spe Nec Metu* towards the end of November 1505 from Blois.[74] However, Isabella only acknowledged receipt of the work in May 1506.[75] The reason for the delay may have been that Equicola was waiting for the work to be printed before he sent it to the *Marchesana*. But, to date, no copy of a 1506 edition has been found to confirm this hypothesis.[76] Equicola's work did not receive as warm a welcome as he perhaps expected from Isabella d'Este. Her praise of the work, when addressed to Equicola, sounds conventional and rather hollow:

> La littera vostra et lo libro che ni ha mandato Madama Margaritta, composto da vui sopra la declaratione dil motto nostro «Nec spe, nec metu», ni sono stati senza dubio più grati in memoria dil n[a]talicio nostro che non seria dono di oro né di alcun'altra preciosa cosa, essendo in nostro honore alzata tanto et sublimata la picola impresa nostra.[77]

Isabella's reply contains an ambiguous mixture of self-satisfaction and disbelief at the result of Equicola's tortuous erudition. She expressed her thoughts much more clearly to Margherita Cantelmo:

> perché da la alteza dil ingegno suo serrà sublevato un motto che da noy cum tanti misterii non fu facto cum quanti luy gli atribuisse. Et perché non manco lo reconoscimo da vui cha da egli, ne meritati summa comendatione et molte gratie vi ne refferimo[78]

---

raudense. Non se ometterà cosa alcuna né in quello né nelle altre cose de Vostra Signoria.

    Ho scricto più volte ad quella de tucte occurrentie della corte. Lo indulto fo expedito et dato in mano del conte Francesco alli VII Iulio, le lettere alli V de octobre. Subito hebi soe lettere me levai per quella expeditione in modo che mai più ho havuto male ad la gamma.

    (Biblioteca Estense, Modena, ms. Alpha G, 1, 16 (It. 834) b. 9, lettere autografe).

[74]   See C. D'Arco, «Notizie di Isabella estense», *ASI*, Appendice II, 1845, document 78, pp. 313-14; Luzio-Renier *La coltura*, p. 50 n. 5 and p. 66.

[75]   See Luzio-Renier, *La coltura*, p. 66 where the relevant letter is partially quoted.

[76]   Moreover, no trace has so far been discovered of any of Equicola's compositions on the other devices mentioned in the letter. It seems most likely that the work was only printed much later and therefore Isabella read the text in manuscript in 1506.

[77]   ASMN, AG, b. 2994, libro 18, Sachetta, 18 May 1506, Isabella d'Este to Equicola, but see note 74.

[78]   ASMN, AG, b. 2994, libro 18, Sachetta, 18 May 1506, Isabella d'Este to Margherita Cantelmo.

It seems that Isabella d'Este was trying to spare Equicola's feelings as she did not tell him directly that, in her opinion, he had gone too far. In this particular instance it was Isabella's judgement that Equicola had misapplied his learning to a subject which did not need so much energy expended on it. She might have preferred her motto to have remained enigmatic instead of being subjected to a full-scale interpretation. Isabella said about her motto that «siamo state la inventrice et habiamola facta nostra impresa peculiare» (quoted in Luzio-Renier, *La coltura*, p. 50 n. 4). Isabella considered, in no uncertain terms, that the motto was the distillation of her own wisdom rather than forming part of a long, classical tradition and thought up by other people.

In any analysis of the *Nec Spe Nec Metu* it must be borne in mind that the sole edition known to us is datable to 1513, the year of a vicious polemic with Tebaldeo. Thus, in the absence of the alleged first edition or any manuscript evidence, it is practically impossible to assess the extent of any changes Equicola wrought in the text. On the other hand, given the circumstances and the importance of publishing something quickly, it seems unlikely that the book underwent a complete transformation (the addition of a polemical preface and a few minor alterations could be the sum total of the changes in the text). Along general lines the work corresponds to Equicola's description of 1505. [79] But, for example, there is no way of telling whether Equicola replaced any or all of the interlocutors from the original dialogue. [80]

The dialogue is remarkable for the single-mindedness with which its author approached his chosen theme. Its starting point is of course Isabella d'Este and her motto. But as the dialogue progresses one loses sight of the point of departure amidst the wealth of quotations and erudition in general. At the beginning of the work Isabella d'Este is considered a source of inspiration, in fact:

> Cum mea presens Diva mihi sit Isabella estensis quae in omni actione et iam in humanitatis studiis falli nescit cui ben scribendo supra fidem studio placere.
>
> (*Nec Spe Nec Metu*, f. A4ᵛ)

Though at first sight the connection between literary themes and patronage seems very close Equicola's insistence on classical reference tends to reduce

---

[79] The letter quoted by D'Arco, see note 74, leaves no doubt that the 1513 edition has exactly the same purpose as the original in the main body of the text: «si discorre per poetica philosophia, et nostra et antiqua theologia, appropriando 'nec spe nec metu' ad tucte, laudandola supra altre sententie mai dicte.» For the polemic see pp. 137-41.

[80] The interlocutors are listed by Equicola in his introduction with some details of their professional activities:

> Io. Iac. Calandra et Statius Gadius Fed. F. ambo huius magnanimi principis Mantuae Marchionis; alter etiam arcis custos. Iter hos salutatum cum irent Baptistam ter maximum Spaniolum qui Carmelita inter Carmelitas principem dignitatis gradum obtinet...
>
> (*Nec Spe Nec Metu*, f. A4ᵛ)

this element and emphasizes instead the writer's skill at academic display. The dialogue proceeds by way of a debate between two of the interlocutors, namely Calandra and Gadius. The latter supports the motto while the former opposes it. They both martial an awesome series of classical *exempla* to back up their contrasting views. At times it is difficult indeed to pick out the principal lines of argument. It is no surprise then to find Calandra talking about the «meandrios dialecticae giros» and the «spiras cathegoricas» (*Nec Spe Nec Metu*, f. A8^r). A number of related themes are discussed, such as the happy life with abundant references to classical sources. Happiness, virtue, the greatest good are all treated in relation to the main theme. Often the discussions do not follow a logical pattern, or if they do, it is only for a part of the debate. The analysis of *Fortuna* is foreclosed by Gadius with a simple assertion, even taking into account Socratic irony: «Profiteor 'nec spe nec metu' nihil dici potuisse praeclarius quae nam ait» (*Nec Spe Nec Metu*, f. B7^v).

The discussion then turns to an analysis of Fate. This part of the debate is only brought to an end by the timely intervention of Battista Spagnuoli who makes an authoritative pronouncement in his capacity as a humanist, Latin poet, and as a proponent of Christianity, head of the Carmelite order. It is in the combination of these two qualities that resides Spagnuoli's superiority over the other interlocutors.

Spagnuoli's declarations are meant to clear up ambiguities. He asserts:

> In presentia sat nobis erit ostendere ad faelicitatem nec conferre plurimum. Indocti doctique omnes faelicitatem summum bonum consentiunt quae autem sit faelicitas.
> (*Nec Spe Nec Metu*, f. B4^r)

Even Spagnuoli cannot refrain from listing classical authorities. He states, «inter ipsos dissentio est» (f. B4^r) and then proceeds to enumerate the different views of a fair number of ancient writers on the subject. The pattern repeats itself when Spagnuoli sits in judgement over the term *fatum*. There is yet another disquisition on this topic: «De quo duas fuisse veterum sententias legimus» (f. C1^v). However he does finally come to a conclusion:

> Hic volo nos spe et metu liberos. Satis liquet nos ratione duci. Consultatio nostri iuris est que electionem praecedit. Electio a ratione progreditur.
> (*Nec Spe Nec Metu*, fs. C2^v-C3^r)

When Gadius seems to deviate from the correct interpretation Spagnuoli is forced to intervene and correct the errors made by the Secretary: «Praeponenda mihi quaedam sunt quasi monentia quae nos magis ad cognitionem intelligentiam que convertant» (f. C4^r). On other occasions Gadius presents his point of view forcibly and without contradictions. *Prudentia* acts as an antidote to fear and hope. As fear and hope are generally considered in the context of the dialogue as being unreasonable then *prudentia* has the benefit of being a humanistic virtue:

Agendi vim illam cum recta ratione boni malique scientiam prudentiam dicimus.
Prudentes vero eos nominamus qui privatim et publice bene utiliterque consulunt.
Haec caeteris virtutibus prestantior et facere et pati fortia edocet.

(*Nec Spe Nec Metu*, fs. D1ᵛ-D2ʳ)

Thus the philosophy that Gadius proposes is deeply fixed in the public
domain: it is a philosophy particularly suited to life at court. It places emphasis on reason, moderation and work in the public sphere, all qualities needed
to succeed at court. It does not seem out of place to point out that Gadius
is representative of Mantuan court culture, himself being a chancery secretary.
Prudentia thus has a political purpose: «Prudentia est civilis facultas quae
civium curat utilitatem. Boni et mali cognitio illi opportuna est qui gubernata
ad finem optimum parat perducere» (f. D2ᵛ). Now Calandra, another court
official, chimes in supporting Gadius. The attitude conveyed by the term *prudentia* is considered essential in strengthening other qualities that are connected with court life:

Neque virtutes sine prudentia sunt: in liberalitate, temperantia, magnificentia,
magnanimitate, modestia, mansuetudine, affabilitate, veritate, comitate, iustitia
et amicitia non est quid speremus aut metuamus. (*Nec Spe Nec Metu*, f. D2ᵛ)

Although these virtues are commonplace, Equicola will repeat them in his discussions of the courtier in the *Libro de natura de amore*. The implicit courtly
theme is extended by the introduction of a comparison between *prudentia* and
adulation. It appears that Equicola is attempting a theoretical exercise in
which career-minded courtiers (although they are never mentioned explicitly)
receive some rather unflattering descriptions. Equicola seems to be showing
a different path to courtiers, using the motto «nec spe nec metu» as his excuse.
In spite of the fact that the entire argument is constituted so as to fit in with
the theme, nonetheless one can perceive the intellectual effort of creating in
these pages a figure that remains unmoved by base emotions and has a certain
nobility of his own. Thus, hope is considered the cause of vile adulation:

Adulatores spes excitat, adulator nanque dum omnia extollit facitque verbis
maiora. Thesauros fodit. Stupescet admirabundus ad singula, suam in re nulla
proferet sententiam nisi illius cui adulatur cognita. Ubi presenserit cum eo pariter
sentiet (consensus voluntatum dator est benivolentiae); id laudabit in quo eius
studium inesse noverit, pugnabit, cedet. (*Nec Spe Nec Metu*, f. E2ᵛ)

The term «benevolentia» firmly places the context of these comments in
court society. Equicola will use the same terminology in the vernacular when
he discusses the courtier-lover in the *Libro de natura de amore*. The writer is
careful to present relationships in a way that minimizes any dependence on
power and any sense of self-seeking gratification that might have endangered
this notion of the noble philosopher (-courtier). The fact that the bulk of the
argumentation is in the hands of two court functionaries, Jacopo Calandra

and Stazio Gadio, future colleagues (in 1506) of Equicola, gives an aura of prestige and humanistic seriousness to court life. Battista Spagnuoli, as presented by Equicola, has bestowed upon him the authority of a judge. Yet it is interesting to note that he adheres to the Equicolian methodology in his attempts to end the dispute in favour of Isabella d'Este's motto. Battista is quite openly eclectic, putting his faith in numerous proper nouns rather than in a more coherent discussion of the theme. Almost every sentence introduces a new philosopher and a new set of ideas without being overly concerned with logical development:

> Mihi reliquus cursus orationis perfacilis ostenditur. Rogo vos me paucis differentem ita audiatis ut non ad unum veluti ad cynosuram qua fidunt Phenicum naves, sed ad clarissimos quosque tanquam ad helicen et septemtriones orationem dirigere, existimetis eoque fiet ut me magnum opinatorem cognoscatis.
> (*Nec Spe Nec Metu*, f. E3^v, but this is an error in the original and should read E4^v)

The work thus ends if not on a note of confusion, certainly with a plethora of quotations from classical sources that lend the text an obvious veneer of erudition. The conclusion is obvious and returns finally to Isabella d'Este:

> Cal[andra]: Fortunae domitrix, salve Isabella. Sitque aeternum et immortale Nec spe nec metu.
> (*Nec Spe Nec Metu*, E7^v-E8^r)

*

Formed from the same root but directed to a different branch, the *De Opportunitate* represents another aspect of court ideology. The immediate stimulus for its composition is to be found in Equicola's visit to Naples, not long after his return from France.[81] His journey there was occasioned by the arrival of Ferdinand the Catholic in the capital of the *Regno*. More specifically, Equicola was sent by the Cardinal Ippolito d'Este to establish rights to certain benefices that fell under the king's jurisdiction.[82] Again, Equicola proved Ippolito's judgement correct about his willingness to serve the cardinal's interests. The *De Opportunitate* is written to reinforce that impression and to link its author ever more securely to the cardinal's patronage. The work illustrates one of the cardinal's devices, as the *Nec Spe Nec Metu* illustrated one of Isabella d'Este's. In both cases the device is rich in personal connections and, at the same time, offers Equicola a chance to use his learning. Equicola's term

---

[81]   Cf. Santoro, pp. 246-56.

[82]   Spero senza dubio obteneremo Castel ad mare per non ci essere interesse del Signor Re. Ma, de Silva longa il mio parere è stato non ne parlemo adesso perché è interesse del Signor Re.
(Quoted in Santoro, p. 250).

for a device is «privatum signum» (*De Opportunitate*, f. a2^r) which indicates the non-official role he intends to play, in the hope of entering into a special relationship with the prince.

The dialogue celebrates Equicola's connections with the remnants of Pontano's academy and with the *Regno* in general. It is dedicated to Agostino Nifo as someone who will give authority to the work because of his fame as a man of learning.[83] Equicola would have been in no doubt about the academic value of the exercise and he wished to emphasize, in this way, that even the trifles of rulers were worthy of attention by intellectuals. The cardinal's device of a falcon perched on a clock invited Equicola not so much to explain it as to write a gloss on it which would demonstrate the ingenuity of both Ippolito and Equicola.

The fact that the work is dedicated to Agostino Nifo is of some significance for the way Equicola wished his text to be read. Nifo was, above all, a professional philosopher and dedicating the work to him, might allow Equicola to avoid charges of adulation towards Ippolito d'Este. His writing then was aspiring to a different level of sophistication, placing the emphasis on abstract argumentation rather than a non-systematic approach to the subject-matter which would be characteristic of a *dilettante*. It seems that Equicola was anxious to «elevate» his chosen topic in order to make it appear less utilitarian and more «noble». The precise subject of the discourse, however, could hardly be more courtly, a device of a prince of the Church, a device which will test the ingenuity of the writer since on Mauro's admission it seems self-explanatory:

> id quidem tale est quod, nullis additis litteris, quicquid acturi sumus, captato tempore agendum quasi viva voce pronunciat et opportunitatem tempestivitatemque a nobis non omittendam sapientissime docet.   (*De Opportunitate*, f. A2^v)

Equicola however immediately introduces rather exotic antecedents for the device in order to stress both Ippolito d'Este's inventiveness and the writer's own knowledge. He traces the origins of the device in general back to Egyp-

---

[83]   Equicola probably met Nifo on one of his visits to Naples. For this philosopher, whom Equicola addressed as «Niphe eminentissime», see G. Monarca, *Agostino Nifo*, Latina, 1975. On the interlocutors see on Paetus, M.E. Cosenza, *Dictionary of the Italian Humanists*, III, p. 2537. On Carbone in particular see R. Pastore, «Carbone, Girolamo», *DBI*, 19, 1976, pp. 695-97 and P. de Montera, *L'humaniste napolitain Girolamo Carbone et ses poésies inédites*, Naples, 1935. A brief discussion of the *De Opportunitate* appears on p. LXXII. The copy that de Montera saw was intended as a gift for Filippo Beroaldo junior. Equicola probably made his acquaintance in Rome or perhaps in Bologna (E. Paratore, «Beroaldo, Filippo, junior», *DBI*, 9, 1967, pp. 384-88). The significance of a relationship between Beroaldo and Equicola lies in the fact that they both cultivated eclectic tendencies in the writing of Latin. It has not been possible to identify Citrarius who has been linked to Equicola himself; Cesare Mauro was a Ferrarese court intellectual.

tian practice so that he can emphasize the cardinal's originality: «Hippolytus vero aliter suam mentem expressit nobilissima sententia» (*De Opportunitate*, f. A3ᵛ). Equicola attempts to explain the use of devices by laying the emphasis on the pleasure they produce whilst enunciating a particular truth, in accordance with classical precepts: «oportet prodesse et delectare ut veritas sensim obrepat» (*De Opportunitate*, f. A3ʳ). Such an explanation fits in fully with the ethos of court society which stresses the importance of pleasurable activities and the need to impress («memorandam sententiam», f. B1ʳ); the use here of the term «voluptas» is not fortuitous. As is normal in Equicola this discourse is not developed and is indeed lost in a historical review of animals used in devices in classical antiquity. This discussion is eventually interrupted:

> CITRARIUS. Fortasse, sed omittamus et ad rem redeamus. Ille ipse qui nobis opportunitatem cognoscendam proposuit, temporis habet ne rationem. Nam si temporis habet, habet et loci et personarum habere necesse est.
>
> (*De Opportunitate*, f. B4ʳ)

This passage marks the transition from a historical, court-centred discourse to an attempt at abstract philosophical thought. What follows is a summary compiled by Equicola from classical sources of the notion of time:

> Quia tempus varium fortitur significatum satius est aliqua prius de tempore percurrere.
>
> (*De Opportunitate*, f. B4ʳ)

Such discussion is justified by the courtly agenda: time and philosophical treatises on it are useful as background but the essential point is that the real subject is «opportunitas» and «occasio». This is not to say that the philosophical disquisition is merely decoration or display, though certainly it has this role in part, rather it is subordinate to other practical considerations such as behaviour at court. «Opportunitas» is associated with the subaltern function of the courtier who depends upon the ruler's favour:

> CAE. Hinc morale illud elicitur quod petitur: aliquid a regibus observent tempora quibus laeti sint.
>
> (*De Opportunitate*, f. B4ᵛ)

Citrarius' question, «quid tempus definitum est?» (f. C1ʳ) allows the dialogue to become almost a treatise on time based on a number of classical writers including Aristotle, Cicero, Varro and so on. The complexity of the scholastic style of argumentation may have been intended to enhance Equicola's reputation as a man of learning. Abstruse thought lends authority to the discussion and underlines the complex nature of time as it is philosophically defined:

> CIT. Non recte Aristotelem temporis invenisse finitionem Galenus clara voce testatur, tempus per tempus definitum monstrans. Quid rogo est illud numeratum prioris et posterioris in motu? In quo motu an videlicet quid hoc preterit? (*De Opportunitate*, f. C4ʳ)

This passage illustrates the level at which the discussion operates: an unoriginal compilation which chooses its readers by dint of the way in which the material is treated.[84] As a work meant for Ippolito d'Este it invested meanings and authority in his emblem which could only serve to emphasize his social status. It requires many pages before the dialogue returns to the theme of «opportunitas»:

> [CIT.] Inter tot opinionum scopulos mens mea naufraga agitatur; satisque mihi erit si tabulam comprehendebo qua ad litus tute prevehar.
>
> (*De Opportunitate*, f. D2^r)

«Opportunitas» is presented as a general category which has applications for the human race as a whole. In this way Equicola can justify its particular use amongst the courtier-caste: «Ad omni generis ordinis conditionis dignatisque viros hoc spectat et respicit» (f. D3^r). The extended example of the farmer who has to work in harmony with nature in order to produce crops suggests that the courtier too is not acting in a reprehensible manner when he seeks the right moment for certain actions. Indeed, the right moment is considered more important than the traditional virtues on certain occasions:

> At occasio ut rei militaris scriptores testantur plusquam virtus ipsa iuvare solet fortunamque superat.
>
> (*De Opportunitate*, f. E1^r)

Through a relentless rush of examples Equicola builds his case for «opportunitas» as the prime consideration in the conduct of business of any kind to reach the obvious and much-reiterated conclusion:

> Sic in negociis arduis nihil fructuosius quam tempus eligere, nihil dannosum magis quam intempestive agere.
>
> (*De Opportunitate*, f. E2^r)

In comparison to *Nec Spe Nec Metu De Opportunitate* is more coherently organized, especially with regard to the encomium of the ruler. In the former text this theme remains surprisingly undeveloped whereas in the latter it takes up the last third of the book. A reason for this could be that Equicola was in closer contact with Ippolito d'Este and expected more concrete signs of appreciation from the cardinal than from his sister. Equicola does not hesitate to spell out his own hopes by presenting Ippolito d'Este as an enlightened patron:

---

[84]   In the dialogue the problem of Equicola's competence in Greek is indirectly raised by Citrarius: «verba Platonis, inquam, latine loquentis apud nos beneficio M. Tulli Ciceronis qui ex Timaeo ea huic nostro sermoni congruentia latina fecit» (f. D^v). It is probable that Equicola only read Greek with effort and that he himself read Plato in Ficino's translations. It is true he quotes passages in Greek in the *Nec Spe Nec Metu* but they seem to have an ornamental value more than anything else, rather like the emblems he describes.

> sibi elegerit preclarissimumque in omni virtutum genere eminentissimos viros ad
> se undique vocaverit quibus (audeo dicere) nullibi neque prestantiores esse neque
> eruditiores.
> *(De Opportunitate*, f. E3ᵛ)

Equicola makes extensive use of classical sources in order to draw out comparisons with the cardinal, such as Augustus Caesar. Then, the writer makes the link, even if somewhat tenuous with the subject of the work: «quia illud observat suum insigne» (f. F1ʳ), that is, his political skills are a result of following the doctrine of «opportunitas». It is interesting to note that the cardinal's military prowess receives pride of place in recognition of his particular rôle in the Estense hierarchy:

> CIT. Et ego plusquam dici potest hominem laudibus summis dignum duco qui
> contra Christi hostes se et bonum imperatorem et militem optimum potest osten-
> dere.
> *(De Opportunitas*, f. F3ʳ)

The presentation of Ippolito d'Este is the culminating point of the text where the philosophical discussion gives way to an illustrious *exemplum*. The work itself is a clear example of how Equicola combines erudition and eulogy for the consumption of court society. This assertion is borne out by the statement Equicola makes concerning his willingness to incorporate any of Ippolito d'Este's *imprese* into his writings:

> Ho inteso dal mio messer Hercule Vostra Signoria Illustrissima havere facte
> alcune imprese belle et sententiose et dove qualche uno se porria fare honore per-
> ché in una mia operecta mende potria farsi de qualche una prevalermene. Sup-
> plico Vostra Signoria sia contenta col suo nome et auctorità de quella illustre li
> mei scripti in una carta... simplicissimamente. Quella non me repute prosump-
> tuoso che voglia sapere sue imprese che non voglio li significati sui. Se non le
> applicarò bene secundo il mio ingegno quella me punirà como li parerà benché
> da mi non serrà publicata cosa alcuna se primo non la farrò intendere ad essa Vos-
> tra Signoria alla quale me recomando.
>
> (ASMO, ASE, C, Ambasciatori: Mantova, b. 1, 18 July 1508, Capriana, Equicola
> to Ippolito d'Este)

Equicola's enthusiasm for *imprese*, compounded by the recent publication of his *De Opportunitate*, may have been due to a pressing need to become personally close to Isabella and Ippolito d'Este. The letter stresses the fact that Equicola will write only with the cardinal's permission and will not reveal anything that his patron wishes to remain secret. Such a system emphasizes the public duty of the court writer to respect the patron even to the extent of allowing his writing to be utterly shaped by these constraints.

At this stage of his career the cardinal surely appeared as his most likely employer of the future. In any case, Ippolito seems to have used him as if he were already in his employ. In May 1507, Equicola was in Milan where he probably carried out some business for the cardinal who was archbishop of Milan, as well as trying to assist the Cantelmo cause, for he was still formally in the employment of Sigismondo. Indeed, there is some indication that

Equicola still acted as Sigismondo's secretary since at least one letter exists written by Equicola in the name of his feudal lord.[85] His relationship with Margherita Cantelmo does not seem to have undergone any radical changes: he accompanied her to Gazzuolo in 1507 to pay their respects to Antonia del Balzo who was related to the Cantelmos and a centre of attraction for fellow southerners as the sister of Isabella, the former Queen of Naples.[86] It was probably through maintaining his relationship with Margherita Cantelmo, as well as through his own efforts, that he was often brought to Isabella d'Este's attention more frequently than he would have been. It was not long before the opportunity came for Equicola to leave Ferrara and change his employer.

---

[85]   For Equicola's visit to Milan see Santoro, pp. 256-57. The letter in question is to be found in ASMN, AG, b. 2468, San Matteo, 31 March 1506, Sigismondo Cantelmo to Francesco Gonzaga.

Apart from his diplomatic duties for Ippolito Equicola acted as a book agent and a translator of Latin texts into the vernacular (G. Bertoni, «Nota su Mario Equicolo bibliofilo et cortigiano», *GSLI*, 66 (1915) 281-83).

[86]   ASMN, AG, b. 1813, Gazzuolo, 15 November 1507, Margherita Cantelmo to Isabella d'Este, written in Equicola's hand:

> Basiando la mano de Vostra Excellentia, ad quella me recommando, pregandola che se digne admectere una scusa se ho tenuti li cavalli de la carrecta più che'l devere non recercava. Ad Madonna Antonia questo se pò imputare, la quale me ha sforzata ad stare una sera in Gazolo ad vedere la comedia de Monsignore Reverendissimo [bishop Ludovico Gonzaga]. Al presente li mando. La supplico non me repute né prosumptuosa né temeraria, che, havendo ad retrovarme fra tanti Napolitani, fui constructa tenerli.

See also U. Rossi, «Commedie classiche in Gazzuolo nel 1501-1507», *GSLI*, 13 (1889) 305-15. The scholar publishes another letter of 15 November, from Margherita Cantelmo to Isabella d'Este, in which there is also mentioned the fact that, in Gazzuolo, at that particular moment, «tanti Napolitani» were present (p. 314). This is indicative of Gazzuolo's function as an obligatory stopping-off place for southern Italians in general. Antonia del Balzo's sister, Isabella, the former queen of Naples seems to have been a frequent visitor (see ASMN, AG, b. 1813, Gazzuolo, 16 April 1507, 11 August 1508, Antonia del Balzo to Isabella d'Este, fs. 100ʳ, 163ʳ).

CHAPTER III

In the service of Isabella d'Este

Early in 1508 Isabella d'Este finally decided to employ Equicola on her own account. This decision was the fruit of a relationship that had been growing ever since Equicola's arrival in Ferrara. To this end she created a special post for him as her tutor. It might be thought strange that a thirty-four year old woman felt the need to employ someone for the express purpose of educating her in the field of classical culture, especially when she already had a reputation as a woman of learning. Indeed, the post was unique amongst the consorts of Italy's rulers and she must have thought that it would be prestigious to have her own personal tutor, unlike any other woman in her position. The creation of such a post bears witness to her seriousness and willingness to learn. But, in spite of all her enthusiasm for the classical world, she had never managed to master its linguistic expression, that is to say Latin, essential for anyone who wished to have more than a superficial knowledge of classical antiquity. Her inability to read Latin texts was the great stumbling-block in her attempts to be treated as an equal by contemporary men of learning. She herself made no secret of this unfortunate gap in her knowledge: when Francesco Silvestri da Ferrara sent her his life of the Beata Osanna Andreasi in 1505 she urged him to translate it, as her studies were not so far advanced that «compitamente senza preceptor lo intendessimo».[1] Thus, she would have a twofold need for a preceptor: someone who would be able to translate Latin texts into the vernacular and who, at the same time, would undertake to improve her own standard of reading Latin.

The choice of Equicola was by no means fortuitous. Apart from Equicola's willingness to serve, Isabella d'Este was herself attracted by the kind of classical erudition that he had to offer. One of her former tutors had been Bat-

---

[1] ASMN, AG, b. 2994, libro 18, f. 59ᵛ. Quoted in G. Zarri, «Pietà e profezia alle corti padane: le pie consigliere dei principi» in *Il Rinascimento nelle corti padane* (con una premessa di Paolo Rossi), Bari, 1977, p. 230 n. 98. Zarri quotes the passage to illustrate her own particular theme without making any reference to the state of Isabella's knowledge of Latin. Cf. S. Kolsky, «Images of Isabella d'Este», *Italian Studies*, 39 (1984) 47-62; 59-60.

tista Pio, admittedly only employed for a short while, probably because he was more suited to a university career than as a tutor to a princess. [2] Ercole Strozzi recommended him to Isabella in the first place because he was «molto erudito» and «doctissimo» and not because of his outstanding ability as a teacher. These qualities are the same as those for which Equicola is and was often praised. [3] Both are eclectic in their approach to the question of style and vocabulary, though Pio must be judged the more extravagant of the two: perhaps that is one of the reasons why Isabella d'Este found him unsatisfactory. A contemporary satirist linked their names together in an attack on the language they used, the «gergo mariopioneo». [4] Isabella's choice of tutors who both, more or less openly, rejected the restricting force of Ciceronianism in favour of a less rigid and more open system was not without significance. Comparable to this search for effect through the rarity and *bizarrerie* of vocabulary was Isabella's passion for collecting medals, antiquities, and *objets d'art* to name but a few items. In this way, she could surround herself with the tangible evidence of the classical world. Books, at times, meant more to her as rare and precious objects than as instruments used for the transmission

---

[2]   A. Luzio, *I precettori d'Isabella d'Este*, Ancona, 1887, p. 27. That the period of Pio's employment by Isabella was not so short as to be completely passed over by contemporaries is indicated by the fact that Diomede Guidalotti wrote a poem addressed to «Giovanni Baptista Pio de la Illustrissima Isabella» in his *Tyrocinio de le cose vulgari*, C. di Bazaleri: Bologna, 1504, 4° (f. S5r):

> Fu di virtù compagna allhor natura
> Quando creò nel mondo altra phenice.
> E Vener dimandò per sua nutrice
> Che diligentia haveste al parto e cura.
> Socia gli dette pudicitia pura,
> E fece leggiadria ministratrice,
> E le tre gratie sempiterne amice.
> De pianeti benigna ogni figura,
> Chiese a Giove prudentia. A Phebo il canto.
> A Mercurio dolcezza de favella.
> Volse de l'arti de Minerva il vanto.
> Amor gli donò l'arco e le quadrella,
> E questo è che in honore ha il mondo tanto
> La Illustre excelsa tua diva Isabella.

[3]   Luzio-Renier, *La coltura*, p. 70.

[4]   See R. Sabbadini, «Una satira contro Battista Pio», *GSLI*, 27 (1896) 185-86; C. Dionisotti, *Gli umanisti e il volgare fra quattro e cinquecento*, Florence, 1960, pp. 111-16. The most recent study of Renaissance Apuleianism is J.F. D'Amico, «The progress of Renaissance Latin prose: The case of Apuleianism», *Renaissance Quarterly*, 37 (1984) 349-92; discussion of Battista Pio is on pp. 362-63 where he is described as being «especially adventuresome in his investigations of archaic or archaizing writers» (p. 362) and of Equicola on pp. 377-78 where the writer properly states that «Equicola did not subscribe to Pio's type of Apuleianism» (p. 378).

of culture.[5] Rarity of an object was a key factor since it was an undeniable advantage to have something other people did not have, especially if they coveted it for themselves. She was willing to lend Don Cesare d'Aragona her precious copy of Eustathius only on certain conditions:

> et fare che non capiti in mano di troppo persone perché, essendo cosa rara, è da tener caro né lassarlo vedere a molti per non diminuirli la reputatione.[6]

Apuleianism, which aimed for special effects in the context of an extravagant vocabulary, corresponded to Isabella's taste for the acquisition of *objets d'art*. Hence, Equicola's encyclopaedic turn of mind, his never-ending search for classical references to put in his works to add to their rarity and *preciosité*, were well appreciated by Isabella. It is necessary to be very careful when speaking of Isabella's interest in classical antiquity. Spurred on by her enthusiasm for the classical world, she flirted, though very seriously, with the possibilities of ancient culture, not in the way a professional humanist would approach his subject through the study of grammar and philology, but by harnessing classical culture to her own designs. At the time of the sack of Rome she affirmed that she had always had certain principles or policies which she followed throughout her life. All had the intention «reportarni benevolentia et laude».[7] It was one of her desires to be praised as a learned lady.[8] She had gradually been evolving a long-term cultural strategy, plainly seen at work in the paintings of her *studiolo*. By means of the *studiolo* and *grotta* Isabella was able to pursue her policy of creating a cultural identity for herself over which she would have great control.[9] It is not unlikely that Equicola played a part in their development. Equicola's name has been linked with a number of paintings found in the *studiolo* as the person responsible for the *invenzioni*.[10] In particular, Costa's *Comus* and the *Coronation of a Lady*, because

---

[5]   On collectors and collections in a later period see W.E. Houghton Jr., «The English virtuoso in the seventeenth century», *Journal of the History of Ideas*, 3 (1942) 51-73; 190-219.

[6]   See Luzio-Renier, *La coltura*, p. 25 and cf. S. Kolsky, «Images», pp. 51-52.

[7]   From a letter dated 27 October 1527, quoted in A. Luzio, *Isabella d'Este e il sacco di Roma*, Milan, 1908, p. 96.

[8]   See S. Kolsky, «Images», p. 59.

[9]   See E. Verheyen, *The Paintings in the Studiolo of Isabella d'Este at Mantua*, New York, 1971; C.M. Brown, «»Lo insaciabile desiderio nostro de cose antique»: New documents on Isabella d'Este's collection of antiquities» in *Cultural Aspects of the Italian Renaissance*, ed. by C.H. Clough, Manchester and New York, 1976, pp. 324-53. On the more general features of her patronage see A. Martindale, «The patronage of Isabella d'Este at Mantua», *Apollo* 79 (March 1964) 183-91.

[10]   R. Lightbown, *Mantegna*, Oxford, 1986, convincingly argues that Equicola was not consulted about the *invenzione* for Mantegna's *Parnassus* which hung in the *studiolo* (pp. 192-93). This is not to say that he was not involved in the *invenzione* of the *Comus*, begun by

of their intricacy and complexity, make one think of Equicola with his taste
for the rare and obscure reference. We might add that this was precisely
Isabella d'Este's intention so that she alone would be able to explain their
meaning down to the last detail. Hence Equicola would have been regarded
as suitable for this kind of enterprise. It is true that, as far as the *grotta* is concerned, Equicola would not yet have been in the employment of Isabella when
she first decided to use the term in 1498. However, that does not mean the
grotta did not undergo substantial revision after its original conception. The
grotta may have begun life simply as a kind of secret retreat without too much
emphasis given to its classical derivation. But, around 1507, it seems that the
grotta had become an important part of Isabella d'Este's cultural strategy.[11]
In a letter to Isabella, Margherita Cantelmo, or rather Equicola, since the letter is written in his handwriting and in his style, refers to the *grotta* in terms
befitting the description of an inner sanctum where Equicola sees himself in
the role of the high priest worshipping in the divine presence (an example of
Equicola's tendency to exaggerate the importance of the enterprises in which
he was involved):

> Non per questo ad me se leva il desyderio de essere nella sacra grocta, nel conspec-
> to venerando de la diva imagine de quella, la quale in terra meritamente adoro.[12]

The following day Equicola wrote to Isabella in his own name, enclosing an
elegy:

> Et sappia quella che ho composto per la Grocta et spero bene.[13]

Thus it can be seen that the *grotta*, in Equicola's view, should be a reflection
of Isabella d'Este's cultural interests, both literary and artistic, in such a way
that it created the impression of a superhuman intelligence at work. In the
world of the *studiolo* and *grotta* Isabella was the centre of attention; she was
able to explain the mysteries of the decoration, if she so desired, or simply to
be admired for her taste and erudition.

Mantegna and completed by Lorenzo Costa. The litterariness of the painting, its links with the
cultural life of Isabella d'Este's court strongly suggest the influence of Equicola (cf. Lightbown, pp. 202-209). It should be stated, however, that Equicola seems to have been periodically
involved in drawing up *invenzioni* for patrons who included Alfonso d'Este (see pp. 235-36)
and Federico Gonzaga (see L. Martines, *Power and Imagination*, London, 1980, pp. 319-20).
It would appear that in Mantuan circles at least, intellectuals associated with the court were
expected to be versatile in their lending of knowledge to the rulers.

[11]   On the *grotta* see C.M. Brown with the collaboration of A.M. Lorenzoni, «The Grotta
of Isabella d'Este», *Gazette des Beaux-Arts*, 89 (1977) 155-71 and part II, 91 (1978) 71-82.

[12]   ASMN, AG, b. 1813, Gazzuolo, 15 November 1507, Margherita Cantelmo to Isabella
d'Este.

[13]   ASMN, AG, b. 1813, Gazzuolo, 16 November 1507, Equicola to Isabella d'Este.

Isabella's character was not such as to allow her to take the back-seat in any matter in which she was engaged. Her domineering personality saw culture as a means of asserting herself and increasing the sense of her personal worth. The verve and energy with which she negotiated for *objets d'art* and paintings are reminiscent of the manner in which she conducted affairs of state. However, the overall impression gained is that her fervour for collecting reflected the instability of her position in the government of the state. There were periods when she alone was at the head of the Mantuan state during which she paid very little attention to cultural matters which were relegated to the bottom of her list of priorities. At other times, when she appears to have been excluded from the political apparatus, she focused a great deal of her attention on artistic and literary concerns. Sometimes Isabella managed to combine the cultural and the political, as in her first visit to Rome. Perhaps the most important link between her two passions was that formed by Mario Equicola: though employed in the first place as her tutor, he acted for her, on many occasions, in political matters. Equicola's appearance on the Mantuan literary scene was of no small significance given the limited nature of local resources. It would not have gone unnoticed by anyone who had intellectual pretensions. Equicola already had a number of publications to his credit and his reputation was such that Isabella felt secure in employing him in so far as his intellectual abilities were concerned. Not long after his arrival it would appear that Equicola was asked to compose a learned letter which would serve as a postface to Tolomeo Spagnuoli's defence of his brother's poetry (the letter is dated «quarto Idus Novembris MDVIII»).[14]

At the beginning of 1508, Equicola was called to Mantua in order to take up his new position at court. But it seems that no sooner had he left Ferrara than Sigismondo Cantelmo needed his presence back in that city, much to Isabella's annoyance:

---

[14] Equicola's letter appears in a miscellaneous volume of Battista Spagnuoli's poetry which also contains his brother's defence: *Ptolomei Spagnuoli Apologia contra detrahentes operibus fratris Baptistae Mantuani* etc., Lyons: *in officina Bernardi Lescuyer*, 1516, 8°, fs. Cc3r-Cc3v.

The letter is addressed to Joan. Jacobo Bardellone, a rather obscure intellectual associated with Isabella d'Este's circle. Equicola naturally supports Tolomeo Spanguoli's venture:

> Quibus inter caetera certiorem me reddis Ptolemeum Gonzagam iam ultimam manum imponere *Apologiae* quam pro germano Carmelita Baptista ter maximo contra litteratores suscepit. Laudo officium. (f. Cc3r)

As we have already seen, Battista Spagnuoli had defended Equicola over the *De Religione* and the latter had employed him as the most authoritative interlocutor in *Nec Spe Nec Metu*. Hence, Equicola was part of a well-established network of intellectuals who had obtained important posts not only in the Gonzaga administration but outside it as well.

> Segnore Sigismundo, havendo inteso da Mario che Vostra Signoria lo ha
> chiamato a Ferrara per volerlo operare in alcune sue facende et perché el ni ha
> principiato ad legere, malvoluntieri lo vederessimo adesso partire.[15]

Sigismondo evidently regarded his business as being more important than
teaching Latin to a middle-aged princess; Equicola, it appears, was still available for Cantelmo family business, notwithstanding his change of employer.
In order to placate him, Isabella alleged that Equicola was not merely teaching her Latin but was also acting on Margherita Cantelmo's behalf:

> Et non essendo più cha necessaria la persona sua, non voglia darni questo incom-
> modo, che ad un medemo tracto servirà se stessa et noy, perché molto è al propo-
> sito vostro che'l se trovi qua tractandosi lo assetto de le cose de Madama, vostra
> consorte, cum l'opera et solicitudine sua.[16]

Isabella thus showed her determination to become proficient in Latin by
enthusiastically prohibiting the departure of Equicola. However, she did not
refuse permission for him to return to Ferrara in the August of the same year.
From here, he reported to her on the literary activities of the Estense court,
particularly on the efforts of Lucrezia Borgia to make herself a serious rival
to the *Marchesana*. Equicola exposed her as a shameless imposter and revelled
in her duplicity, indirectly strengthening Isabella's position as a woman of
learning. He took up Isabella's cause with a vengeance and tried his utmost
to «unmask» Lucrezia Borgia:

> Io ho deliberato scoprire tanta ambitione et far cognoscere che le scimmie, con
> reverentia de Vostra Signoria, quanto più se alzano più monstrano le parti pudi-
> bonde, per non havere naturalmente con che le coprire.[17]

At this early point in his employment with Isabella d'Este, Equicola wished to give concrete evidence of his loyalty: what better way of doing so than
by demolishing one of her most serious rivals?

At Ferrara, he was in contact with the *Unico Aretino*, a poet much favoured by the Duchesses of Urbino and Ferrara as well as by the Marchioness of
Mantua:

> Dice volere venire in Mantua. Il che subito che io sappia, verrò ad succurrere Vos-
> tra Signoria, che so con lo Unico haverà bisogno de laudative parole.[18]

Part of Equicola's job as tutor included making contact with poets and scholars and drawing them into Isabella d'Este's circle of admirers. Once they had

---

[15]   Quoted in V. Cian, «Una baruffa letteraria alla corte di Mantova. L'Equicola e il
Tebaldeo», *GSLI*, 8 (1886) 387-98; 389 n. 3 and in A. Luzio, *I precettori*, p. 41.

[16]   ASMN, AG, b. 2994, libro 21, Mantua, 16 March 1508, Isabella d'Este to Sigismondo
Cantelmo. See also note 15.

[17]   Quoted in A. Luzio, *Isabella d'Este e I Borgia*, Milan, 1915, pp. 152-3.

[18]   ASMN, AG, b. 1242, Ferrara, 11 August 1508, Equicola to Isabella d'Este.

been enticed, it was up to Equicola to ensure that Isabella lived up to her reputation by advising her on how to behave in the literary games of the court. In spite of all this activity, Equicola promised that «Mario de Alvito serrà con la sua ornatissima discipula per omni modo al principio de septembre» (see note 18).

In Ferrara Equicola had clearly proclaimed his attachment to Isabella d'Este, particularly on the literary front. At this point he composed a work, the *Pro Gallis Apologia*, which may be construed as a fruit of the alliance between himself and the *Marchesana* on the political front. It has been suggested that the work in question was written at Isabella's instigation to confirm her francophile loyalties and to debase the Venetians after their defeat at Agnadello.[19] This view tends to minimize Equicola's own role in the formulation of the book's theme. Isabella's tutor would have found by himself more than one good reason for writing such a work. The battle of Agnadello would have provided the stimulus needed to write it, though Isabella would not have failed to encourage him in his task:

> Nunc vero cum Ludovicus duodecimus non per prefectos aut legatos sed per se ipsum Venetos magno praelis fuderit et paratae servire Italice iugum subtraxerit.[20]

Although the battle would have provided the immediate stimulus to write the *Pro Gallis Apologia*, Equicola's support for the French cause went as far back as his connection with Pietro Giampaolo Cantelmo. His son, Sigismondo, continued the French alliance and, as we have seen, Equicola accompanied him on a number of visits to the French court. Thus, it is not surprising that he stressed the personal element in the work: the idea to write the book came first of all from the circumstances surrounding the French defeat at the Garigliano in 1503.[21] He emphasizes his personal commitment to the French cause (*Apologia*, fs.A1v-A2r). Equicola's reason for actually residing in Mantua was due in large part to Sigismondo Cantelmo's obstinate loyalty to the French. Thus it is misleading to assert that Isabella was the prime mover in the composition of this book; indeed, from the point of view of chronology, it was Equicola's own idea influenced by other attempts in the genre. Moreover, Equicola did not dedicate the *Apologia* to Isabella d'Este as one might have perhaps expected, instead he dedicated it to Janus Lascaris (Santoro, p. 26). He dedicated the work to Lascaris not only in recognition of the intellectual debt that he owed him, as we shall see later, but also because of their meeting in France bringing together two exiles in the refuge of a temporary

---

19 Cf. Santoro, pp. 126-28; F. Simone, «Fonti e testimonianze», pp. 7-41.

20 *Apologia pro Gallis*, fs. A2r-A2v.

21 See Santoro, pp. 43-46.

patria. The work ends on a note of triumph, not sounded at a victory in the Italian peninsula but at the possibility of a crusade to recapture the holy places. Equicola urges Lascaris to speak to the French king on this matter.[22] In this way the *Apologia* assumes a much wider significance than simply a work in praise of France and the French. Equicola adds his voice to the cry that this nation should not use its strength to subjugate the Italian peninsula but should concentrate its forces on a more worthy object. For Lascaris, the crusade would mean a chance to return home. For Equicola it would signify the possibility of putting aside his problems by allowing himself to be carried along the well-known path of single-minded religious fervour, instead of charting his own course in a northern Italian court. The theme of the crusade reoccurs in Equicola's work and to it he devotes an entire work, the *De Bello Turcis inferendo Suasoriae.*

*

The delight at the French victory was short-lived in Mantua: news reached the city on the 8 August 1509 that the Marquis had been taken prisoner by the Venetians. Although Isabella was first shocked by the news, she quickly gathered her senses together in order to seize the opportunity of becoming the effective ruler of Mantua:

---

[22] In a speech to Charles V (Biblioteca Apostolica Vaticana, Città del Vaticano, Vat. Lat. 3890, *Discorso fato per el Signor Joanne Laschari ad la Cesarea Maestà de Carlo Quinto in Mandivile de l'anno 1526*, fs.1-10) Lascaris recounts the efforts he has made to convince the Christian rulers to embark on a crusade, without any success.

These efforts are the result of the Turkish occupation of his homeland and are thus rooted in a personal view of history, not necessarily the same as one motivated by purely Christian principles: «trovandomi expulso dali Infedeli dala mia patria sempre ho pensato se ci fosse modo de potere ritornare in essa libera» (f. 1ʳ). The speech traces a life-time of commitment to the idea of a crusade, from the time of Lorenzo de' Medici to the present. Lascaris emphasizes the fact that he did not fail in his duty to speak in favour of the cause, but those who had the power to do something always prevaricated:

> Doppoi certo tempo passò Re Carlo in Italia [Charles VIII of France in 1494] con bello exercito a pede et a cavallo, parlai anchora a lui, informandolo et per che el prometeva, tornando in Franza et fatto che havesse magior apparato atendere alle cose de Turchia. Io lo seguitai. Essendo manchato anchora lui, parlai più fiate con Re Luigi [XII]. Lui mi mandò a Venetia dove steti molti anni per suo ambassatore e parlai molte volte con quelli signori (f. 2ʳ).

The list of important people with whom he pressed his case is long and impressive; it includes most popes and several powerful rulers. It is clear then that Equicola knew that Lascaris would not rest until a crusade had taken place and that the latter's pro-French position neatly coincided with the theme of the *Apologia*. This view is supported by the number of manuscripts (in Latin, Greek, and Italian) which contain texts pertinent to the launching of a crusade. For a list of such manuscripts consult F. Ubaldini, *Vita di Mons. Angelo Colocci*, a cura di V. Fanelli, Città del Vaticano, 1969, n. 145, pp. 79-82.

> Imagini quanto noi restamo consternate et accorate per questo caso, non semo perhò cossì perse de animo che non deliberamo de conservare questo stato illeso per quanto serà possibile.[23]

She acted immediately to assure the support of the leading families.[24] In another state a similar disaster would have been the signal for the dissident elements to rise up in revolt. Her brother's state, Ferrara, illustrates the effects of a divided ruling family and an ambitious nobility. The most recent conspiracy from within the family itself had been led by Giulio d'Este in 1506. Much to Isabella's relief she experienced the exact opposite, winning the co-operation of the majority of the population, including the most powerful families.[25]

It is self-evident that the priorities of the *Marchesana* in this time of crisis had to be drastically altered: the activities which occupied her so greatly during more tranquil times no longer had the same importance.[26] Clearly, Equicola's role as preceptor in such circumstances would have been greatly reduced and probably he was not called upon to exercise this function during the time of Isabella's regency. For the conduct of state affairs, Isabella depended upon the men already in positions of power and upon her own agents of long-standing reputation. We should also bear in mind that Equicola was a

---

[23]   ASMN, AG, b. 2995, libro 21, 8 August 1509, Isabella d'Este to Pietro da Novellara. See also A. Luzio, *La reggenza di Isabella d'Este durante la prigionia del marito (1509-10)*, Milan, 1910.

[24]   Isabella d'Este recalled to Mantua any citizen or «gentiluomo» who for any reason was in the *Mantovano* «perché havimo ad servirsi dil consiglio et opera di cadauno, secundo che serano apti al bisogno dil stato nostro». (ASMN, AG, b. 2916, libro 206, Mantua, 8 August 1509, Isabella d'Este to all *potestà* and other local officials).

[25]   Ogn'hora più conoscemo la fede de quelli nostri amorevoli subditi per le demonstrationi che ni fano et maximamente per questa spontanea et tanto prompta oblatione de gli cento ducati che ni scrivi essi volerci donare per questo bisogno di mandare la duchessa a marito, che ni è sta' gratissima et tanto più acepta quanto che l'hanno facto senza sprono alcuno ma da sì spontaneamente: indicio de gran bontà de quelli nostri fideli homini.
(ASMN, AG, b. 2917, libro 209, 30 October 1509, Isabella d'Este to Francesco Malatesta).
Such generosity could be interpreted in a more cynical vein as an attempt to anticipate any heavier taxation the *Marchesana* may have thought to impose.

[26]   The noble occupations of her absent husband were also neglected, for example, the breeding of falcons. She declared that it was at present impossible to send falcons to the King of France or any other gifts of a similar kind «perché non era che ni havesse cura et noi havevamo et havemo altro che pensare. Noi ne assicuramo che sarremo excusate... se in questo non seguemo la liberalità del signor nostro, perché lo attendere ad falconi non è cura de donne et maxime sconsolate como semo noi» (ASMN, AG, b. 2995, libro 23, Mantua, 16 December 1509, Isabella d'Este to Jacopo d'Atri).

«new man» who did not enjoy the favour of important Mantuan families.[27]

Although Isabella d'Este was too occupied with political matters to employ Equicola fully in his capacity of tutor, she would not have wished to see him idle. Equicola would have been one of the courtiers who entertained her in the rare moments of relaxation that she could allow herself. Perhaps it was in this period that Equicola first assisted in the up bringing of the future Marquis of Mantua, Federico Gonzaga, either as a temporary tutor or simply as a courtier whose duty it was to entertain him. At the same time, throughout 1509, Equicola was working on a major revision of the *Libro de natura de amore,* an effort which produced a manuscript written in the vernacular nearly the same length as the final text of the printed edition. There is no reason to suppose that he would have stopped working on it altogether because of the Marquis' capture.[28] However, it would be wrong to create the impression that Equicola concerned himself only with literary matters or affairs that did not have much bearing on the political situation in Mantua. Isabella d'Este recognized the potential of a servant whose sole hope of advancement was through loyal service to her. Thus, he was sufficiently identified with the interests of the *Marchesana* to be chosen to represent her in political matters. His first recorded diplomatic mission on behalf of Isabella indicates the particular nature of this aspect of his career. It was a mission to Isabella's brother, Ippolito, concerning the matter of some benefices:

> Da li primi dì che messer Mario venne qua a me, mandato da Vostra Excellentia, li dedi expeditione secundo il debito mio. Et se prima che adesso non è retornato a lei, è stato causato che, per delectarmi la sua pratica, ho voluto mi faccia compagnia insino a qui.
> Circha li beneficii recerchati per Vostra Signoria Illustrissima, ho facto cum honestate et cum dishonestate quello che ho possuto, secundo che epsa intenderà da epso messer Mario, al quale in tutto et per tutto me remetto per non essere tedioso a Vostra Excellentia.[29]

---

[27]   An anonymous letter written to Isabella (quoted by Luzio in *La reggenza,* p. 99) directed her in the reforming of the Mantuan state and one of the pre-conditions for such a reform was that «la corte vostra sia honorata de zentilhomini de la terra: li fioli de misser Zuan Piero da Gonzaga, el fiolo de Madonna Alovisa (i.e. Baldassare Castiglione), el fiolo de Zuan Batista Bardelono, li Strozi...» These, especially, would be the most suitable companions for the future Marquis, Federico Gonzaga.

[28]   On the composition of the *Libro de natura de amore* see R. Renier, «Per la cronologia e la composizione del *Libro de natura de amore* di Mario Equicola», *GSLI,* 14 (1889) 212-33; I. Rocchi, «Per una nuova cronologia e valutazione del *Libro de natura de amore* di Mario Equicola» *GSLI,* 153 (1976) 566-85; G. Castagno, «L'autografo del *Libro de natura de amore* di Mario Equicola», *Lingua Nostra,* 23 (1962) 74-77; Eadem, «L'autografo del *Libro de natura de amore* di Mario Equicola» in *Arte, pensiero e cultura a Mantova nel primo Rinascimento in rapporto con la Toscana e con il Veneto,* Florence, 1965, pp. 133-43; M. Pozzi, «Mario Equicola e la cultura cortigiana: appunti sulla redazione manoscritta del *Libro de natura de amore»,* *Lettere Italiane,* 32 (1980) 149-71.

[29]   ASMN, AG, b. 1192, 4 March 1510, Ippolito d'Este to Isabella.

Equicola's former position as Sigismondo Cantelmo's secretary had allowed him some acquaintance with certain members of the Estense family, notably Ippolito who seems to have particularly appreciated his company. As Isabella's personal agent, Equicola could lay claim to an intimacy with the *Marchesana* that few enjoyed and she would have been aware of the reception he received from her brothers. It is somewhat ironic that Equicola, who was cut off from his native region and family, should become an important element in Isabella d'Este's dynastic politics. His position as her personal agent enabled Equicola to cast off the remaining vestiges of his own personality and political outlook in order to devote himself more completely to the ideals represented by Isabella d'Este.

The dynastic ideal was one that was particularly dear to her. In the first place, dynastic politics meant, in Isabella's eyes, an interest in the well-being of the Estense family; to be more precise, the Duke of Ferrara and the Cardinal Ippolito. The welfare of the Estensi was of at least equal (if not more, at times) importance to her as that of the Gonzagas into whom she had married. The labels which were often attached to the kind of political strategies adopted by Isabella were usually made with reference to some foreign power; even her father called her a «bona Francese» and at one point the Emperor thought her a «bona Imperiale».[30] Behind the label can be detected her sense of dynasty (to include most of the leading families of Italy) which survived the French invasion and to which she clung as far as was possible or practicable in the belief that such a policy was the last remaining hope against the total subjugation of Italy to those forces that intended the destruction of the Italian dynastic system. Although her brothers always came first in this strategy, as a member of the Estense family she could boast connections with various important Italian families, the Bentivoglios, Sforzas and the House of Aragon, and as a Gonzaga by marriage she was connected with the rulers of Urbino and French and German noble families. For her, dynastic politics represented

---

[30]   The Archdeacon of Mantua reported to Isabella the esteem in which the Emperor held her: «oltra al respetto de la persona sua Lei è tenuta bona imperiale» (20 March 1516; quoted in A. Luzio, *Isabella d'Este e Leone X dal congresso di Bologna alla presa di Milano (1515-1521)*, Florence, 1907, p. 47). Isabella's father had no doubts as to where her loyalties lay:

> Potrite dire ala Signoria de la Marchesana come pare che la Maestà Christianissima sia sta' facta in passione che Soa Signora non la ami et in questo gionto che serite a la corte farite molto ben chiara [a] la predetta Maestà che la Signoria de la Marchesana come nostra bona figliola sempre è stata et è ben conforme a la voluntà et opinione nostra, et perhò è bona francese et se il signore marchese havesse seguito il parere suo haveria asai più satisfacto ala Christianissima Maestà che forsi non ha.
>
> (ASM, ASE, C. Ambasciatori, Francia, b. 4, «Instructio Illustrissimi Domini Ducis data III D. Alphonso in Galliam ad Christianissimum regem proficiscenti»).

an opportunity to spread her political wings, to have an appointed place in a time-honoured system which would serve to increase her authority and put her on an equal footing with other members of the dynasty. The breakdown of this system meant a great reduction in power for many Italian families, and for some it signalled the end as ruling dynasties. Isabella d'Este had witnessed the expulsion of the Bentivoglios from Bologna without being able to lend much assistance.[31] On their restoration in 1511, Isabella felt it necessary to apologize to Annibale Bentivoglio for not having been able to help him more during his exile «per defecto di maiore auctorità et facultà». She saw the political significance of the event in terms of the effect it was to have on her brother:

> De la ritornata de Vostra Signoria et fratelli in Bologna ni pigliassimo quello piacere et contento che facessimo de la secureza del stato del'Illustrissimo Signor Duca, nostro fratello, concoscendo che l'una cosa depende da l'altra, ultra il rispecto et amore che sempre havemo havuto alla Illustrissima Madama Lucretia [d'Este], nostra sorella.

The Bentivoglio episode is a good illustration of Isabella's limitations in trying to maintain a seriously weakened dynastic structure to rule the Italian peninsula.

Isabella's husband, Francesco Gonzaga, often found himself voicing opposition to his wife's policies, especially in situations when his state would suffer the consequences of her determination to have her own way. On other

---

[31]   Mi congratulo cum la Excellentia Vostra de questa prospera expeditione, ma mi doleo de la ruina di Bentivolii, exemplo veramente di fortuna et de la varietà de l'humana vita. Se alcuno de loro capitarà qua, serrà da me amorevolmente raccolto.
(ASMN, AG, b. 2994, libro 19, Mantua, 3 November 1506, Isabella d'Este to her husband).
The «expeditione» in question was precisely the capture of Bologna by the papal forces in which Francesco Gonzaga took part. Isabella was placed in a difficult position because of her husband's role in the fall of the Bentivoglio dynasty. She did not have the power to change this *fait accompli* so she took the only opening left to her: the offer of Mantua as a refuge for members of the Bentivoglio family. Her loyalty was not without its price because the Pope placed Mantua under interdict which strained Isabella's inventive mind to the extreme when trying to liberate the city from the weight of excommunication. Even her brother Alfonso tried to preach moderation to the Marquis:
> Ni sono dispiaciuti summamente li termini usati verso la Excellentia Vostra per li agenti per la Santità de Nostro Signore in presentarli quello interdicto per il caso de li Bentivoglii, li quali non potemo ni volemo credere siano de voluntà de la predetta Santità né de sua commissione speciale, ma solo procedere da li ministri soi... Et perhò ni pare de ricordare a Vostra Signoria di novo che, come prudentissima et circumspectissima, così per beneficio de li Bentivoglii come per satisfactione de la predetta Santità, se voglii accommodare a gratificare a la predetta Santità cum qualche bona resolutione come stimiamo habia mo facto.
(ASMN, AG, b. 1190, Ferrara, 8 March 1507, Alfonso d'Este to Francesco Gonzaga).

occasions, the Marquis lent his support to dynastic policies, as, for example, when he encouraged co-operation between Bologna and Ferrara, with the admonition that «la catena vole essere de bon ferro».[32] Thus, it is an over-simplification to state that Isabella was pro-French and Francesco in favour of the Emperor.[33] Francesco saw for himself the effects of the French invasions, the physical ruin and desolation of Italy in which he played his part. On occasion, he allowed himself the luxury of recalling nostalgically a time when the concept of the balance of power was the byword:

> Et non solamente un Duca di Milano, ma voressimo possere vedere un re di Napoli et tanti signori in Italia quanti solevano essere, se ben ogni città n'havesse uno perché serria molto meglio per noi et seressimo più estimati che non siamo.[34]

The Marquis understood the inherent weakness of his state, and realized that in order to retain control over it he would have to resort to trickery and subterfuge. It was with sadness that Francesco Gonzaga accepted a position which, in his own estimation, offended his dignity as a prince. In the eyes of the nation-states as well as in his own, he was little more than a courtier, using all his arts to avoid being conquered.[35] Francesco Gonzaga was continually forced to destroy any remaining self-esteem he may have had for himself as a ruler or a prince. He placed one objective before anything else: the safety of his state. To achieve this end, he used whatever means were necessary. The Marquis realized that to pursue a particular policy energetically would have exposed his state to all kinds of dangers; caution and lack of speed in any matter were essential to survival.

Isabella's energy is often compared to her husband's lack of it in affairs of state. Ultimately, however, it was the Marquis who carried the responsibility for his state while Isabella, in her position of relative freedom, could afford to be energetic. At times their policies did coincide perhaps more often than is generally believed: Francesco supported Ferrara on occasion and a pro-French line; at other times, Isabella needed to follow a more eclectic policy. But on numerous other occasions there was a clash of policy brought about by

---

[32] This and the previous two passages are quoted in A. Luzio, *Isabella d'Este di fronte a Giulio II negli ultimi tre anni del suo pontificato*, Milan, 1912, p. 66.

[33] F. Simone, «Fonti e testimonianze», pp. 9-10.

[34] ASMN, AG, b. 2919, Mantua, 14 August 1512, libro 223, Francesco Gonzaga to Folenghino.

[35] See the following letter in which we can glimpse the Marquis' bitterness and frustration (ASMN, AG, b. 2914, libro 197, Asti, 19 April 1507, Francesco Gonzaga to his wife):

> Siamo doventato bon cortegiano che alli volte ni è accaduto star sette hore continue in piedi alla presentia dil re.

this fundamental difference of approach: for Francesco, dynastic policies may have had a role, although whatever that role may have been, it was subordinate to a political strategy dictated by more powerful neighbours. This clash found interesting expression in the argument which ensued over the naming of their second son:

> Ni rincresce ben che la Signoria Vostra perseveri in voler al suo poter mutar il suo diricto nome a Loysi, nostro figliol, a cui elegessimo quello nome per reverentia dil re di Franza et a cui volemo per ogni modo el corri. Perhò, cessi Vostra Signoria di nominarlo altramenti aciò che'l non si pensassi che l'andassi cercando nove cause di noiarni...[36]

After her husband's death Isabella no longer felt obliged to call her son «Loysi» and returned to calling him Ercole, in memory of her father, the name by which he is known to history. We find here in embryo the conflict which often arose between Francesco and his wife as a result of her loyalty to her family, though it may perhaps be unwise to suggest that they never worked together or that they were always on opposite sides.[37]

Equicola may be described as having entered the Mantuan diplomatic machinery by the side door; unlike Castiglione he was not a career diplomat. Equicola cannot be said to have aspired to the rank of ambassador, which for a *residente* would have meant being employed by the Marquis under whose control the diplomatic apparatus fell.[38] Marked very much as Isabella d'Este's own man, Equicola had a different set of priorities from those of Francesco Gonzaga, partly because of his attachment to Ferrara and partly because of the politics of the Marchioness. If Equicola's diplomatic activity is not viewed in this light, a personal agent involved in the personal politics of Isabella d'Este, his political missions will appear trivial and devoid of much significance. The distinguishing characteristic of his diplomacy is that he acted as a go-between amongst members of the same family, and sometimes for their friends. Only very rarely was he sent on a mission involving negotiations

---

[36]   ASMN, AG, b. 2914, libro 193, 1 October 1506, Francesco Gonzaga to his wife.

[37]   M. Bellonci, «Isabella d'Este a cinquecento anni dalla sua nascita» in *Mantova e I Gonzaga*, p. 52 and S. Kolsky, «Images», pp. 47-62; 55-58.
  Tolomeo Spagnuoli managed to exclude Isabella from power almost completely during the later years of her husband's life: «Noi tenne sì bassa che dove in li teneri anni havevamo qualche auctorità in questo stato, adesso ne eramo in tutto privata... Spendessemo nove mesi fuora de casa... vergognandoci star così abiecta in Mantua» (Quoted in A. Luzio, *I Borgia*, p. 169 n. 1 from ASMN, AG, b. 2997, libro 37). Her attitude to political exclusion also meant taking an interest in the affairs of other states to compensate for her humiliation in Mantua, thus, suggesting other reasons for her constant travelling.

[38]   On Mantuan diplomacy see R. Quazza, *La diplomazia gonzaghesca*, Milan, 1942 and S. Kolsky, «Castiglione's biography: The courtier and the Italian princes», *Spunti e Ricerche*, I (1985) 1-34.

which had nothing to do with Estense family interests. He did not possess the authority nor, perhaps, the diplomatic skill essential for success in a wider-ranging diplomacy.

*

After Francesco Gonzaga's release, Mantua was again placed in a difficult position because one of the conditions of his freedom had been that he accept appointment as Captain of the Church. In conjunction with Venice he was supposed to aid the Pope against the French and their allies the Estensi. Shortly after his return to Mantua the Marquis had to leave again to go to Bologna and Venice to finalize the conditions of his release from captivity. Isabella, worried by the length of his absence from Mantua and needing to inform her husband of certain developments that had taken place while he was away, possibly to defend her actions during his imprisonment, thought it best to send someone to look for him. The choice fell upon Mario Equicola who found himself in the role of mediator between Francesco and Isabella, a slight variation of his normal diplomatic function:

> Madonna mia et signora illustrissima. Da Sermete arrivai dal signor providetore, magnifico messer Andrea Gritti, in Montagnana per essere certificato dove se retrovasse lo nostro illustrissimo signore. Non ne havendo Sua Magnificentia cosa certa, me condusci in Padua dove dal Gobbo, cavallaro, intensi predicto signor nostro aspectarse in Venetia. Così, subito montai in barca et iunsi in Venetia nanti l'alba. Trovai messer Ioan Francesco Valeri et messer Baptista Scalona. Parlai con messer Carlo Valeri, colla Magnificentia del quale fui ad longi ragionamenti de Vostra Signoria... Per più certeza exhortò messer Baptista ad volere intendere dalla Serenissima Signoria del principe la verità del signor nostro. Andò messer Baptista, et ben visto et accarezato, portò una lettera alli magnifici messer Francesco Cappello et messer Andrea Trivisano, savii de terraferma, li quali erano in Chiozia per recevere et honorare prefato signore... So dunque qui in Chioza con prefati messer Ioan Francesco et messer Baptista. Montaremo in galea et trovaremo il signor.[39]

At one point, the search for the Marquis seemed to have degenerated to the level of a vaudeville turn as Isabella dispatched one messenger after

---

[39]   ASMN, AG, b. 1444, Chioggia, 13 October 1510, Equicola to Isabella d'Este. Equicola's acquaintanceship with Giovan Francesco Valerio finds correspondence in the way Castiglione links their names together as writers of treatises on women (*La seconda redazione*, p. 181). Battista Scalona confirms the situation with a letter of the same day, emphasizing the more pleasurable side of their mission:

> Semo qui una bella brigata: messer Zoan Francesco Valier, messer Mario, qual ni ritrovò a Venetia, il Buse che gionsi qui in prestezza et io et così andaremo di compagnia. Prima che adesso non ho possuto dare aviso alcun certo dil signore nostro a Vostra Excellentia.

It should not be forgotten that Valerio played a crucial role in the linguistic revisions of the final version of the *Cortegiano*, for which see G. Ghinassi, «L'ultimo revisore del *Cortegiano*», *Studi di filologia italiana*, 21 (1963) 217-64. These two letters confirm Valerio's close connections with court society.

another, none of them being able to find him. Once it was realized, shortly afterwards, that the Marquis had come by a different route, the situation was rectified,[40] and the first person to speak to him was not, as one might have expected, Benedetto Capilupi (Isabella's secretary and a member of an old and well-established Mantuan family) but Mario Equicola.[40] Her tutor had been her immediate choice and it was only with his failure that Isabella was obliged to send the others. When the Marquis was finally found one would have expected Capilupi to be given precedence over the newcomer Equicola, yet the reverse happened: the secretary spoke to Francesco only after Equicola made the first approach. It is true that after their individual addresses to the Marquis they both combined forces to put Isabella's case. This prominence of Equicola in Isabella d'Este's affairs after so short a period in her service may be explained by a number of reasons (which were due to some extent to the conditions for his employment Equicola himself set down and the *Marchesana's* approbation of his views). Because he was concerned with the projection of her image in the select circles of the court, he was the perfect choice to implement the extension of that image into the realm of political affairs; and Isabella knew that Equicola would be acceptable to her husband as her trusted agent:

> Heri, primo che'l signor Aloisi [Gonzaga] et primo che messer Ludovico [da Fermo], parlai doi hore col signor illustrissimo. Ogni cosa sta ad nostro voto, le cose vanno como è il devere et como noi desideramo... So de la tavola del signore et in favore, pure tornarò da Vostra Signoria presto.[42]

---

[40] ASMN, AG, b. 2996, libro 28, 21 October 1510, Isabella d'Este to Giovanni Gonzaga:

> Sapendo che la Signoria Vostra desidera intendere como siano successe le cose nostre cum lo Illustrissimo signor nostro consorte, gli significamo como Mario non ritrovò Sua Excellentia et cossì il Scalona fin che'l non fu gionto a Sermede per la diversione che la fece da Ravenna. Ma noi anchora gli mandassimo el Codelupo, il quale, doppo Mario, parlò a Sua Excellentia et adaptorono inseme la cosa tanto bene et tanto rimase quieto et satisfacto el signore quanto havessimo saputo desiderare...confirmandone magior auctorità che non havevimo in le cose del stato, como quella che ha cognoscuta la fede nostra.

The Marquis had decided to visit the Venetian *terraferma* on the way home from Bologna where he had paid homage to the Pope and negotiated the terms of his *condotta*. The Venetians had approached the Marquis, but he refused their offer:

> Et pareani che la servitù che portamo a quella Illustrissima Signoria et la grandeza de la presente impresa ricercasse che fossemo conducti più honorevolmente. Imperhò che non solo non se accresce, in questi capituli, la conditione che havevamo putti et inexperti circa la summa dil soldo, ma la vedemo molto diminuta. Havendo noi a fare el mestiere de le arme più per honore che per altro respecto non ni è parso de volere firmare essi capituli perché seria contra l'honore nostro. Mandamo alla Illustrissima Signoria una forma de capituli assai honesta et acceptabile. (ASMN, AG, b. 2917, libro 212, Mantua, 7 September 1510, Francesco Gonzaga to the «provisores generales» of Venice).

[41] On Benedetto Capilupi see the entry by T. Ascari in *DBI*, 18, Rome, 1975, pp. 528-30.

[42] ASMN, AG, b. 2480, Sermede, 18 October 1510, Equicola to Isabella d'Este.

He had skilfully won the Marquis' favour, but with no intention of changing his allegiance, identifying himself completely with Isabella's cause. He had stayed with the Marquis in order to inform interested parties in Mantua of the military preparations of both Isabella's husband and brother. Here, too, he acted in the capacity of a go-between; the Marquis having no desire to fight was prepared to use Equicola to act on his behalf, to prevent the further deterioriation of relations between Mantua and Ferrara. The Pope was so intent on capturing Ferrara that the Marquis needed to make clear his position, at least in words. He went so far as to refer to Alfonso d'Este as «il già Duca» whom he will betray should he ever flee to Mantua:

> Il che faremo tanto più volentieri, anchor che'l ci sia congiunto come l'è, quanto che speramo la serrà iudicata gran cosa.[43]

The text appears to us to be a piece of pure theatrical bravura, in the hope of impressing the reader with the seriousness of his threats. This interpretation gains in credence because of Francesco Gonzaga's reluctance to commit himself to mount any sort of attack against Ferrara. For the moment the problem of Alfonso d'Este remained in the flights of fancy since the Duke decisively defeated the intending conquerors. However, Equicola's contact with the Duke and his brother remained uninterrupted. Isabella sent him to Ferrara to seek a solution to a minor problem concerning some of the Marquis' officials. Unfortunately, it proved to be a wasted journey for Equicola since Alfonso d'Este had already acted on Isabella's letter before the former's arrival.[44]

---

[43] ASMN, AG, b. 2918, 20 January 1511, Francesco Gonzaga to the Archdeacon of Mantua and Ludovico Brognolo. Equicola plays an active part in the complicated manoeuvres:
> Io credo che retornarò in Ferrara perché 'l signor Duca ha deliberato non fare facto d'arme se'l signor marchese li è in persona per multi bon respecti et optimi che dirrò ad Vostra Signoria... Parlai sera col signore in lecto circa doi hore et per ordinatione di Sua Signoria resto hogi et credo andare in Ferrara.
> (ASMN, AG, b. 2480, 28 October 1510, Equicola to Isabella d'Este).

[44] ASMN, AG, b. 1192, Ferrara, 27 November 1510, the Duke of Ferrara to Isabella d'Este:
> Se siamo maravigliati quando havemo visto venire qui messer Mario per la causa di quello officiale del sale, quale se sia monstrato a lo Illustrissimo Signor suo consorte essere stato retenuto che non vadi al camino suo de Cervia che, come havemo dicto ad epso messer Mario, havuto la lettera de Vostra Excellentia da lo Illustrissimo Don Sigismondo, nostro fratello, quale ne la remisse, subito gli scrivessimo che lo facesse expedire al factore et cussì per lui gli fue dato quello spazo che'l seppe dimandar et sempre, dove potremo, siamo per satisfare a quanto ni recercarà.

Isabella had written to her brother, the Duke, informing him of Equicola's imminent arrival to resolve the matter:
> Lo Illustrissimo signore mio havea mandato suoi officiali per levare certa quantità de sale che l'ha a Cervia, parte guadagnato col corso de suoi barbari, parte pagato già molti mesi. Quali officiali intendo essere stati retenuti lì per gli officiali de

Isabella was not always pleased with Equicola's advice; his judgement in certain matters was not too dependable:

> La difficultà che me fece Mario del mandare li dinari a Ferrara, credendo a lui per havere frequentato il viagio et anche per li richiami venuti de li viandanti retenuti per quelli de Figarolo mi fece stare suspesa ad inviarli subito como doppo ho compreheso se haveria potuto fare.[45]

Isabella was to prefer to use Equicola solely as a messenger and as an informant rather than someone who would take an active part in decision-making. The kind of mission he was expected to carry out was illustrated by his next visit to Ferrara in January 1511:

> Il signor Duca nostro fratello è, per Dio gratia, megliorato assai de la ferita et spero non haverà male. Mi è parso advisarne la Excellentia Vostra, quantunque da messer Mario l'haverà inteso questo medesimo, perché scio che quella voria non che ogni giorno ma ogni hora intendere del star suo.[46]

*

Not all of Equicola's time was spent on diplomatic missions. In the midst of these political and military struggles the court at Mantua strove more than ever to live its own life. When in 1511 Isabella d'Este was excluded, temporarily, from Mantuan politics, she made a determined effort to enjoy herself, and considered the death of the bishop Ludovico Gonzaga an untimely interruption of her plans.[47] Equicola joined in the activities at court, especially those which called for some erudition, such as the *sortes virgilianae* combining a pretence of learning with the need to apply this learning to present amuse-

---

Vostra Signoria che non gli ha voluti lassare, dicendo che ne dovemo fornire de sale da Vostra Excellentia et non altrove. Et perché la importantia de fornire questa terra adesso de sale è grande et molto instante, mi è parso mandare Mario mio a posta a lei, el quale la pregarà in mio nome a essere contenta de permettere che gli decti officiali vadino de longo a Cervia et gli facci relaxare subito, che la mi farà grandissimo piacere. Se hora si havesse voluto levare sale per questo bisogno con exborsatione de dinari, se serria mandato a levare de quello de Vostra Signoria, ma era in proposito a levare quello là, che già è pagato e guadagnato, come la intenderà anche a boca dal predetto Mario.
(ASMN, AG, b. 2996, libro 28, Mantua, 26 November 1510, Isabella to Alfonso d'Este and also to Benedetto Brugia).

[45]   ASM, ASE, C, Ambasciatori, Mantova, b. 16, 5 December 1510, Isabella to Ippolite d'Este.

[46]   ASMN, AG, b. 1193, Ferrara, 22 January 1511, Ippolito to Isabella d'Este.

[47]   ASMN, AG, b. 2996, libro 29, 21 January 1511, Isabella d'Este to Sigismondo Gonzaga:

> Io era in tante collera de la morte de Monsignor Vescovo nostro barba per rispecto che ne havesse impedito un bel carnevale cum maschare et feste principiato che non scio come mi havesse potuto remettere se non succedeva la bona nova de succession de Vostra Signoria Reverendissima in dicto vescovato, la quale ad me et a tutti li altri farà... tollerare la privatione de li piaceri carnevaleschi...perché, facti li officii, iudico ni serrà licito secretamente fare allegreza di quello.

ment.[48] It is probable that Equicola had become, by this time, the centre of a group which included learned court officials, Calandra, for example, and the ladies of the court.[49] Equicola would have undoubtedly been present at certain court gatherings as at the ceremony to mark the occasion of Isabella's daughter Ippolita taking the veil. When another «tragedy» struck the Mantuan court (the death of Isabella's favourite dog Aura) it may have been Equicola's suggestion to turn the dog's death into a literary event, to which a number of humanists contributed verses.[50] Apart from these courtly activities Isabella planned to extend Equicola's role as tutor to include the teaching of her son, Federico, after the latter's return from Rome:

> Perché quando Nostro Signor Dio gli prestarà gratia che'l ritorni a casa, haverà qui maestro Francesco [Vigilio] o Mario che non gli mancarano de bona doctrina.[51].

In the event, it was Francesco Vigilio who was appointed official tutor to Federico Gonzaga. This does not, however, exclude the possibility that Equicola stood in for the tutor whenever the need arose. In any case, a close relationship was to develop between Federico and Equicola in the course of the next few years.

Equicola was not long allowed to enjoy the routine of court life. The April of 1511 found him in Bologna, sent on a diplomatic mission by Isabella, probably with orders to try and discover the direction of papal policies insofar as they would affect the Duke of Ferrara.[52]. At the end of the same year Equicola was again in Ferrara on unspecified business with the Duke. Alfonso d'Este had realized by this time that Equicola could be used other than as a messenger: he could, for instance, be employed more profitably at Ferrara in a capacity where his erudition could be drawn on more fully.

[48] ASMN, AG, b. 2482, Mantua, 5 January 1511, Calandra to Federico Gonzaga:
> Mando a Vostra Signoria il suo bolettino levato in camera dil signore vostro patre et quello che levò la signora Donna Hippolita et uno levato in le sorte virgiliane in casa di messer Mario [Equicola]. Se più mi ne veranno a mani, gli mandarò a Vostra Signoria.

Cf. Luzio-Renier, *La coltura*, pp. 447-69.

[49] See Luzio-Renier, *La coltura*, pp. 84-97, 110-59.

[50] ASMN, AG, b. 2482, Mantua, 6 October 1511, Calandra to Federico Gonzaga:
> Et non heri l'altro, che fu il dì di San Francesco, Sua Excellentia et la Excellentissima Madamma con tutta la corte andonno a farle vestire l'habito de quel ordine.

On the death of Aura see Luzio-Renier, *La coltura*, pp. 44-47.

[51] ASMN, AG, b. 2996, libro 29, Mantua, 21 April 1511, Isabella d'Este to Matteo di Ippolitis.

[52] ASMN, AG, b. 1147, Bologna, 26 April 1511, Equicola to Isabella d'Este:
> Bella horrida, bella et cetera. La pace è disconclusa fine in mo. Pure è opinione de alcuni che habia ad sequire per ciò che pare che Franza habia più voglia de pace

Al signor Duca piace che reste qui otto dì. La causa è la pictura di una camera
nella quale vanno sei fabule o vero historie. La le ho trovate et datele in scritto.[53]

It seems likely that Equicola was already experienced in furnishing *invenzioni* for Isabella d'Este at Mantua and that Alfonso was simply drawing on
his skill in this field. This would not be difficult since the two patrons were
almost of one mind and in using the same humanist, particularly one in Equicola's position, recognized the same underlying ideologies which would serve
to buttress their political alliance at an important period. Nevertheless, Isabella, though willing to allow Alfonso to employ her preceptor, was loathe to
see him away too long.[54]

---

che d'altro et quante volte habia salvo il Duca di Ferrara, del resto non si cura.
Il Papa non è per lassare Venetiani, anzi vole che la chiesa li piglie in protectione
che mai habiano ad perdere quel che hanno al presente né pata che più se augu-
mentono in Italia. Maximiliano voleva che lassassero terra ferma. Questa è stata
la discordia principale. Gurensis [Matthew Lang] partì heri ad XVIII hore accompagnato da messer Pier Margano romano, capo dela guardia del papa, ad cavallo.
Il Papa cavalcò heri ad San Mattheo. Hogi è cappella vederò la corte tucta et poi
montarò ad cavallo per Mantua.
Cqui è fama certa che Spagna è con lo Imperio né creda Vostra Signoria che scriva
ad quella cosa che non l'habia da bonloco et più li dico che le gente del Signor
Fabritio Colonna è qui in Bologna per iustificare le sue cose et le imputationi che
li son date, et presto se partirà con sue gente. Donde se tene per certo che'l Papa
faria pace tanto più che Franza ne ha voglia. Ad Vostra Signoria me recomando.
Portarò lo sonecto del signor Unico. Bebiena se recomanda et questa è scricta in
sua camera.

Cf. the letter of Bibbiena from Bologna dated 3 January 1511 addressed to Isabella d'Este in
which Mario Equicola is mentioned, in the *Epistolario di Bernardo Dovizi da Bibbiena*, vol.
I (1490-1513), letter no. LXXXV, pp. 249-51. It is not an unlikely hypothesis that Isabella sent
Equicola to report on her son when the Papal court moved to Bologna. The same letter of 3
January 1511 reveals further links between Giovan Francesco Valier and Equicola through Bibbiena. As is often the case Equicola is portrayed as a somewhat extravagant character particularly in the matter of religion. Valier is also shown to have contacts with Isabella d'Este since
he will be bringing the letter to her: «se il p.to gentilissimo Valerio vi conferissi un suo madria-
letto che ha composto da pochi dì in qua, molto buono, et m. Mario volessi farlo renegare Dio,
gli dica che l'ho composto io et che molti giorni sono il mandai lì, et echovelo incluso. Etiam
ne' travagli è prudentia talhora far coveletta da ridere» (p. 251).

[53] Quoted and discussed in G. Robertson, *Giovanni Bellini*, Oxford, 1968, pp. 134 and
141.

Alfonso d'Este put forward other reasons as to why he needed to extend Equicola's stay in
Ferrara:

Ma la serà contenta lassarnelo per sei on octo dì per satisfactione del Cantelmo
et per nostra recreatione per essere la più parte de la nostra famiglia infirma.
(ASMN, AG, b. 1193, Ferrara, 10 October 1511, Alfonso to Isabella d'Este).

[54] Isabella wrote to the Duke saying that he could keep Equicola for a week:

La Signoria Vostra non deve fare scusa meco di havere retenuto lì Mario per sei
o octo dì per satisfactione sua et dil Cantelmo, perché la sa ben che la può disponere di mei servitori come di suoi proprii et comandarli como io istessa.
(ASMN, AG, b. 2996, libro 29, Mantua, 14 October 1511, Isabella to Alfonso
d'Este).

It was not long before Equicola returned to Ferrara; the reason for this visit was perhaps more important than that of the last. Isabella sent him there so that he could keep her informed of the progress of the Duke's illness. Illness would be a cause of anxiety in any ruling house but given the significance of Alfonso's role in Isabella's personal politics, it is easy to understand her concern and why she dispatched Equicola. Apart from the grief the Duke's death would undoubtedly have caused her, his loss would be a grave blow to her political status in the Italian peninsula. The alliance forged between Isabella and her brothers depended heavily upon the health of its members, and a visit of this semi-political kind must not therefore be considered something trivial. [55]

To Equicola she wrote that she would prefer his quick return:

> L'è ben vero che haveressimo havuto piacere de la vostra presta venuta de là: tutta via semo contente che restate lì a piacere et voluntà de la Excellentia del Signor Duca, nostro fratello honorando. El quale volemo vi possi commandare non altramente che noi proprie, mentre sereti alli servitii nostri, con quella libertà che ha Sua Signoria de disponere de nostri servitori come di suoi proprii; sì che restate pur lì quanto piace a Sua Signoria, maximamente per il spacio che Sua Signoria predetta ni scrive, cioè, per sei giorni o octo, che così la ni scrive, standone con l'animo reposato che'l serà con nostra satisfactione. Racomandatine al predetto signore nostro fratello honorando, salutando in nome nostro il signore Sigismondo Cantelmo.
> (ASMN, AG, b. 2996, libro 29, Mantua, 14 October 1511 [same date as letter quoted above], Isabella d'Este to Equicola).

[55] Equicola tersely stated the one reason for his journey and its urgency: «So arrivato et visitato lo Illustrissimo Signor Duca il quale sta allo obscuro» (ASMN, AG, b. 1244, 19 January 1512, Equicola to Isabella d'Este).

On his return to Mantua Equicola acted as Ippolito d'Este's *oratore* to the Marquis:

> Madama mia Illustrissima se recomanda ad Vostra Signoria tucta alegra, tucta iucunda del ben stare di quella et che'l Signor Duca sia fora di ogni periculo. Al Signor Illustrissimo Signor Marchese feci le recommandationi et offerte di Vostra Signoria Illustrissima et con apte et pensate parole me sforzai farli intendere quanto quella haveva caro gratificarla. Non si potria dire con quanta allegreza se reofferse al simile, Vostra Signoria è il figlio benedecto, magnanimo et prudente et ad mi summamente piace che resulta bene per noi.
> (ASM, ASE, C, Ambasciatori: Mantova, b. 1, 24 January 1512, Equicola to Ippolito d'Este).

If the Marquis wished to convey information to Ferrara Equicola was seen as the person most suited to the task, particularly when he wished to make a point of something. He probably used Equicola in this way and not for confidential missions, realizing the pivotal role the tutor played between Mantua and Ferrara due to Isabella d'Este:

> Heri, il Signor Marchese mi monstrò una lettera del Signor Re Christianissimo ne la quale Sua Maestà multo commenda Sua Signoria et multo se ne lauda con farli multe offerte per havere inteso diportarse bene nelle cose sue et lo exhorta ad perseverare... Ogni dì scriverò ad Vostra Signoria Reverendissima simile ciancie, se la fastidio habiami per scuso che in qualche modo ho deliberato tenere viva la memoria di me appresso Vostra Illustrissima Signoria alla quale so et morirò suo.
> (ASM, ASE, C, Ambasciatori: Mantova, b. 1, 10 February 1512, Equicola to Ippolito d'Este).

Barely three months later (April 1512), Equicola, in the manner of a shut-tlecock, found himself back in Ferrara for exactly the same reason: Alfonso was sick again. Although he appeared to make a speedy recovery he refused Equicola permission to return until he, Alfonso, was fully restored to health:

> Lo Illustrissimo Signor Duca, tre dì sono, ha havuto un gran fluxo di corpo in modo che Vostra Excellentia non crederia mai che così presto lo havesse tal male extenuato e il fluxo comenzato ad cessare... Io voleva partire, ma primo il signor Duca non vole et io so restato volentieri per portare bone nove ad Vostra Signoria della sua sanità.[56]

His stay seems to have dragged on interminably. There may have been rea-sons for this other than the Duke's health: one being the growing intimacy between himself and the Duke who seems to have been drawn towards this learned courtier. Again, we find Isabella ambiguous in the expression of con-sent to Equicola's request for the extension of his stay in Ferrara. Ferrara was a convenient listening-post in the critical period after the battle of Ravenna. On the one hand, there is solicitude for her brother and, on the other, a desire for the tutor's presence, with the pleasures and counsels his company provi-ded.[57] Meanwhile, she was busily preparing a plan, the purpose of which was

---

Equicola did indeed keep his promise, for the same day he wrote to the cardinal, informing him of a meeting he had had with the Marquis:

> Ultra questo mi fece fare [the Marquis] imbasciata alla Signora Marchesana che quando li piaceva li voleva fare festa in San Sebastiano et che non li seria interve-nuto se non chi paresse ad lei et che tanto l'amava quanto si pò amare persona, che desiderava gratificarla più che mai et mille altre bone et belle parole le quali ad Madama sono state gratissime et ne ha havuto gran piacere in modo che semo in gran favore et stamo assai di bona voglia.. Il mio parere seria che per ogni modo ad questo Signor [the Marquis]se mandasse qualche falcone.

[56]   ASMN, AG, b. 1244, 12 April 1512, Equicola to Isabella d'Este.

[57]   Mario. Per gli avisi che per le prime et secunde vostre ni haveti dati del stare del signor Duca restamo molto satisfacte, piacendone che siati andato in tempo che cum le vostre zanze habiati tenuto in spasso Sua Excellentia, cum la qual restareti fin che uscischi di casa quando così sii cum bona satisfactione et volere suo. (ASMN, AG, b. 2996, libro 30, 25 April 1512, Isabella to Equicola).

But three days later (28 April 1512), Isabella d'Este wrote to Bernardino Prosperi in Ferrara:

> Mario fa bene a sollicitare il ritorno perché noi anchora patimo sinistro de l'absentia sua.

Isabella explained the reasons why she especially favoured Fabrizio Colonna in the complex intrigue which followed the battle of Ravenna. The latter was a prisoner of Alfonso d'Este and according to Isabella's calculations might prove useful in any negotiations with Julius II, hos-tile to Ferrara:

> Nui sempre havemo amata Sua Signoria per l'amicitia et parentela che fra casa sua et questa è stata, ma molto più per essersi portato discretamente in la impresa di la guerra contra Ferrara (for the reference, see first letter quoted in this note).

Equicola perhaps was secretly charged with the task of broaching the matter with the Duke and with opening negotiations.

to bring about a rapprochement between the Duke and the Pope with the help
of such people as Fabrizio Colonna.[58] It was a plan in which Equicola would
play a part, but for the time being he was called upon only to report on the
health of the Duke and others:

> Il signore cardinale, anchor lui, non è stato questa nocte bene. De la Duchessa
> non ho domandato.
> (ASMN, AG, b. 1244, Ferrara, 22 April 1512, Equicola to Isabella d'Este).

His telling remark about Lucrezia Borgia reveals just how serious he considered the rivalry between her and Isabella d'Este to be.

Equicola's expectations of a speedy return home were dashed when the
Duke suffered a relapse, forcing him to postpone his departure yet again.[59]
Equicola sent daily reports on the progress of the Duke's illness to Isabella.[60]
He also proudly announced to her his privileged position at the Ferrarese
court: «nesciuno cortesiano lo ha visto, se non io.» Yet, in spite of this especial favour shown to him by the Duke, Equicola was unwavering in his loyalty
to Isabella and Mantua: «pure, voria essere ad casa che in nesciun loco sto
meglio.»[61]

Isabella's plan to reconcile her brother with the Pope in the changed political situation after the battle of Ravenna gradually gained momentum. The
way was facilitated through the intercession of Isabella's various «friends»
who repaid their debt to her by using their influence in favour of the Duke.
Apart from Fabrizio Colonna, Isabella asked Giuliano de' Medici to plead her
brother's case before the Pope. But, in order to pave the way for a settlement,
Alfonso would first have to go to Rome, something which was not possible
until the Pope granted him safe-conduct (since he was still an enemy against
whom the Pope was fighting); a suitable person was therefore needed to

---

[58]   It seems that the Duke had become well enough by 25 April for Equicola to return to
Mantua but Isabella now had other plans:

> Quando fusti partito, volemo che ritorniati indreto a far questo officio, facendo
> poi intendere al Signor Fabritio [Colonna] la resposta havereti, visitandolo da
> parte nostra et offerendone se in altro potemo gratificare Sua Signoria che siamo
> sempre per farlo voluntieri, alla quale ne racomandareti (see note 57, first letter
> quoted).

[59]   For example, see the following letter concerning the Duke's continuing illness:

> Tornò [Alfonso d'Este] tardi a casa, ragionò meco et io cognobi che era indis-
> posto. Cenammo; Sua Signoria cenò poco et bevè assai acqua.
> (ASMN, AG, b. 1244, Ferrara, 25 April 1512, Equicola to Isabella).

And the following day Equicola again wrote to her:

> Heri che fu domenica, il signor Duca fo sempre in lecto con qualche febre et multo
> lasso.

[60]   See A. Luzio, *Isabella d'Este di fronte a Giulio II*, pp. 132 and 135.
[61]   ASMN, AG, b. 1244, Ferrara, 26 April 1512, Equicola to Isabella.

precede him, to acquire the safe-conduct from the Pope and to bring it to Ferrara. The person chosen was not unnaturally the much-travelled Mario Equicola, who could be trusted by both sides, the Pope, Isabella and Alfonso. His return from Rome was eagerly awaited by all concerned, by Isabella most of all:[62]

> Adesso adesso è gionto Mario. Non ho anchor ben parlato seco. Vado a San Sebastiano a parlar con lui al signor mio.[63]

The Marquis, although interested in the outcome of this affair, had something else on his mind: the ill-fated negotiations in Rome by which he hoped to bring about the marriage of his illegitimate daughter Margherita, to Agostino Chigi.[64] He had expected Equicola to bring news of the progress of the talks. Disappointed Francesco Gonzaga now realized where Equicola's loyalties lay:

> Alla parte di quello che ni doveva dire Mario da parte tua circa le cose di Augustin Ghisi, dicemo che Mario non ni ha ditto questo. Ma quando el venne era cussì stanco, per haver corso la posta, che non ci pottè fare la piena relatione di ogni cosa et anche andò presto via andando a Ferrara colla Illustrissima Madama, nostra consorte. Et lui reputava di tanto momento la cosa dil signor Duca, che era la principal sua impresa, che'l non reputò di gran importantia quella di esso Augustino.[65]

---

[62] A. Luzio, *op. cit.*, p. 135. Equicola returned also bearing a letter from Federico Gonzaga:

Ritorna a Vostra Excellentia messer Mario et da lui la intenderà quanto si è operato nel caso dil Signor Duca.
(ASMN, AG, b. 2119, Rome, 11 June 1512, Federico Gonzaga to his father).

[63] A. Luzio, *op. cit.*, p. 135.

[64] Cf. A.M. Lorenzoni, «La vita e le vicende matrimoniali di Margherita Gonzaga, figlia naturale del marchese Francesco II», *Civiltà Mantovana*, Quaderno 63-4, 1977, pp. 173-219; in particular, pp. 175-76.

[65] ASMN, AG, b. 2919, libro 223, 30 June 1512, Francesco Gonzaga to Folenghino.
Isabella wrote to her son Federico in Rome that he should do everything he possibly could to help the Duke of Ferrara and to this end she was sending her own man, Mario Equicola:

> Il Signore remanda il Folenghino et noi Mario alla Santità de Nostro Signore per la causa che intenderai da loro. Volemo che tu gli presti fede a quanto te diranno e che tu faci ogni opera possibile perché se induchi la Santità Sua alla resolutione et bona. Però che, retirandosi lo assetto del Signore tuo cio, col mezo tuo acquistaresti una gloria perpetua et a noi se daria quel magiore contento che a questo mondo potessimo havere, ma bisogna governare la cosa dextramente et cum grande secreteza.
> (ASMN, AG, b. 2119, Mantua, 5 June 1512, Isabella d'Este [«toa matre che te ama quanto sé»] to Federico Gonzaga)

Folenghino, the Marquis' representative in Rome, reported on Equicola's visit there:

> Subito che Sua Santità hebbe fatto legere il breve che portò Mario in presentia de li ambassatori le basai il piede in nome di Vostra Excellentia... La Santità di Nostro Signore mi disse in presentia di Mario che dovesse posar qualche dì che dopoi volea andar a Civita castellana ove il Signor Federico andaria seco di compagnia. Poi volea darli licentia et ch'io el menassi a Mantua a Vostra Excellentia.

The passage indicates his scorn and regret that Equicola should place Isabella's business above his own, and he emphasized that it was the former's poor understanding of the situation which led him to neglect the Marquis's interests.

On Equicola's return to Mantua, Isabella, unable to contain her excitement, aware of the need for prompt action, immediately set off for Ferrara:

> Io gionsi qui ale decenove hore. Prima trovato el signor mio fratello a la Stellata, col quale così sucintamente dissi el reporto de Mario et holo trovato disp[o]sitissimo de andare ali piedi de Nostro Signore et obedirla in tutto quello li comandarà et relaxare el signor Fabricio et altri pregioni. [66]

*

By the end of June, the Duke of Ferrara had begun his journey to Rome, taking the route which passed through Pesaro and Urbino. At Pesaro, Equicola (on his second visit to Rome within a month) described their progress through the Marches to Isabella:

> Il signor Duca sta sano et alegramente sequitamo il nostro viagio per le terre de la Chiesa. Havemo havuti mille honori, presenti et careze. Messer Baldasar Castiglione hieri matina, verso Arimini, trovò il signore, invitandolo per omni modo in Urbino dove il Signore [Alfonso d'Este] et signor Fabritio [Colonna] non volsero andare et così andò via per honorarci in Cagli et Fossa Imbruna. Questo Signore in Pesaro fa tanta demostratione che più non si potria dire. Hogi che è domenica ha voluto per omni modo ne fermemo qui et così se fa. Il signor Duca se recomanda alla Vostra Signoria et io li bascio le mano. [67]

> Mandai ad dir a quella per Mario che la volessi avisar dil camino che l'havesse ad far et mandar dinari aciò che si possesse venir a casa...
> Avisai anchor per Mario ciò che havea fatto messer Augustino Ghisi ma non ho havuto altra risposta.
> (ASMN, AG, b. 860, Rome, 24 June 1512, Folenghino to the Marquis).

As did Magdalena Taiapreda to Isabella d'Este on 18 June 1512 (b. 860):

> Illustrissima madama mia observandissima: essendo stato qua messer Mario nostro, et lui parlando come lo Illustrissimo Signor Federico del venire nostro a Mantua. El predetto Signor Federico dise a messer Mario che quando lui sarà a Mantua se'l ge vorà insignare gramaticha. Presto messer Mario respose et dise che lui non voleva tore questa impresa de insignarge quando la Excellencia del Signor Marchese et la Vostra Excellentia non havese fatto provisione de alcuno maestro venendo Sua Signoria a Mantua. Madama mia, al presente ge insigna uno maestro Fabio da Revena, homo de età de anni 50, manza solum una volta al giorno et mai non beve vino et è homo tanto exemplare che non pottria dire a Vostra Excellentia de littre in latino docto, in grecho doctissimo, et al presente traduce uno libro grecho de medicina in latino dove sarà di grandissima utilità alli medici: et è multo al proposito del Signor Federico quando alla Excellencia del signor Marchese et di Vostra Excellencia piacese.

[66]   ASMN, AG, b. 2119, Ferrara, 16 June 1512, Isabella to her husband.

[67]   ASMN, AG, b. 860, Pesaro, 27 June 1512, Equicola to Isabella. The following day Equicola wrote again:

> Illustrissima Signoria Mia: Grandissimo honore è facto all'Illustrissimo Signor Duca per tucto il stato del'Illustrissimo Signor Duca di Urbino. Gran tapezaria con le arme del dicto Signor Duca nostro per tucto senza quelle del signor Fabri-

The journey had by now assumed the character of a carnival which was brought to an end only by the serious business in Rome. Equicola went ahead of the main party to make preparations:

> Ad meza nocte partì io per le poste et intrai in Roma, domenica 4 del presente, all'alba. Subito andai dal bellissimo signor Federico.[68]

As well as ascertaining the state of affairs from Federico Gonzaga Equicola needed to know whether Fabrizio Colonna had kept his part of the bargain with Isabella d'Este and turned for this purpose to the Cardinal d'Aragona. At the court of Rome Equicola made use of his various connections both with the cardinals and the humanists who formed part of the papal bureaucracy.[69]

> tio. In tanta copia il magnar, che è cosa fora di modo. Il Signore sta sano et letamente sequimo nostro viagio. Io me recomando a Vostra Excellentia. Il signor Fabritio spesso ragiona meco di Vostra Signoria. Li è multo affectionato et servitore. Il signor Duca selli recomanda.
> (ASMN, AG, b. 1077, Fossombrone, 28 June 1512, Equicola to Isabella d'Este, f. 363).

[68]   ASMN, AG, b. 860, Rome, 5 July 1512, Equicola to Isabella. Equicola's arrival was also noted by Folenghino:

> Dominica matina il signor Fabricio Colonna giunse da Nostro Signore, qual fu ben visto et accarezato da Sua Santità. In quella hora arrivorno in Roma messer Girardo dal Saresino et messer Mario con una quantità de servitori dil signor Duca.
> (ASMN, AG, b. 860, Rome, 6 July 1512, «servo indigno ma fidel Folenghino» to the Marquis).

Some people wished to check Equicola's progress at court and put an end to his relationship with Federico Gonzaga. Consequently, before Equicola arrived in Rome, Federico had been warned that certain of the courtier's political opinions were suspect. Federico's informant, Amico Maria della Torre, seemed to be suggesting that the young prince should show more loyalty and favour to his father's servants and policies than to those of his mother:

> La Signoria Vostra di presenti ha presso sé una persona che continuamente ha tenuto più la parte francese che non fanno li baroni proprii di Franza, nominato Mario Equicola, quale la Signoria Vostra fa grande male ad honorarlo et farli careze. Nondimeno, accadendo che'l sia venuto lì per farsi absolvere de li errori suoi, quella sempre serà laudata ad perdonarli et donarli la sua gratia.
> (ASMN, AG, b. 2485, 22 June 1512, Amico Maria della Torre to Federico Gonzaga).

The letter is also a further indication of how intense rivalries at court could be. The substance of the denunciation seems to correspond to Equicola's early allegiance to the French through his connections with the Cantelmi. If Equicola had not changed his political views this would have been in part due to the new stimulus offered by Isabella d'Este. This letter can be seen as part of the reverberations which were caused by the publication of the *Pro Gallis Apologia*, probably in 1510, and seem to have marked Equicola out as being particularly dangerous in his political views and allegiances. It is interesting that Amico della Torre's advice was overruled as can be seen from Equicola's close association with the future Marquis of Mantua.

[69]   See, for example, A. Luzio, «Isabella d'Este ne' primordi del papato di Leone X e il suo viaggio a Roma nel 1514-1515» («Primordi»), *ASL*, Ser. quarta, 6 (1906), p. 458.

That he seemed not to be deluding himself about the influence he may
have hoped to wield with the cardinals was demonstrated by the following
report which Stazio Gadio, a secretary attached to Federico Gonzaga, sent to
the *Marchesana* from Rome:

> Io non scriverò altramente le cose a Vostra Excellentia perché messer Mario non
> è meno diligente in scriverli il tutto quanto el sia in agitar le cose dil signor Duca
> con questi signori cardinali. E veramente il signor Duca monstra restar molto
> satisfatto di la diligentia et dextreza sua. Et molto ben visto è lui da alcuni car-
> dinali. Perhò mi remetto al scriver suo.[70]

Equicola himself did not belittle his role in this affair; on the contrary, he
was glad to have the opportunity to prove his worth in so delicate a matter.
He was well aware of the influence humanists now had in the Curia, and how
this influence (combined with his own official position in the Duke of Ferrara's company) increased his effectiveness: «Non è loco in palazo che, o
como homo di Vostra Signoria o como homo intincto di lettere, non penetre.»
But at the very moment when everything seemed settled a new storm broke.
Equicola was taken completely by surprise at the new turn of events. Up to
this moment he had been concerned solely with reporting court gossip to the
Marchesana.[72] The Pope insisted on certain conditions which were unaccepta-
ble to the Duke:

> Questa matina li signori cardinali ellecti hanno fatto intendere al signor Duca che
> Nostro Signore, non si fidando di Sua Excellentia, vole Ferrara et che la si piglii
> contracambio di qual città la vole, che ascenda al valore di XXV o XXX millia
> ducati, et che si liberi Don Ferante et Don Iulio. Il signor Duca li ha fatto rispon-
> dere di non voler far cosa alcuna di queste et che da messer Mario, da messer

---

[70] ASMN, AG, b. 860, 6 July 1512, Stazio Gadio to Isabella d'Este.

[71] A. Luzio, *Isabella d'Este di fronte a Giulio II*, p. 140; see also pp. 139, 141. Equicola
emphasized his own industriousness: «Vostra Signoria [Isabella d'Este] intenderà quanto farà
Mario et quanto opera la lingua che più posso io che altri, che fo in nome di Vostra Signoria»
(quoted by Luzio, *op. cit.*, p. 140).

[72] An example of this kind of letter is the following:
> Da poi la arrivata nostra in Roma ho avisata Vostra Signoria da dì in dì quanto
> se è facto et dicto. Mi persuado che quella reputarà le lettere mei tucte chiazangole
> piene di ciancie senza effecto, che cosa certa non li ho possuto scrivere. Ma mi
> confido che li gran caldi essa Vostra Signoria li potrà in gran parte passare in
> legere quelle longhe philastocche.
> (ASMN, AG, b. 860, Roma, 13 July 1512, Equicola to Isabella d'Este).

«Ciancie» were the property of the court, the result of its compressed atmosphere and the endless scheming. In this case, the notion of «ciancie» contrasts with the more formal concept of
negotiations between rulers (or their representatives), which Equicola could not put into practice for the moment because it was not in his power to do so. The word «ciancie» refers to the
frivolous and insubstantial side of court life. Equicola used the word to classify the offers of
help given by the «Unico Aretino» to Alfonso d'Este which are «tali che sono altre che ciancie
et sonecti» (A. Luzio, *Isabella d'Este di fronte a Giulio II*, p. 140). In this way Equicola made
a clear distinction between events that transcended the limited arena of court pleasures and
those activities which had no other purpose than to entertain the members of the court.

Folenghino et dal'orator di Spagna li fu fatto intendere che di Ferrara non si havea
da parlare. Dimane, li prefati cardinali ellecti referiranno a Nostro Signore la
risposta dil signor Duca. Da quanto seguirà circa ciò Vostra Excellentia ni serrà
avisata.[73]

In such circumstances, there was no doubt that the Duke's personal safety was
at risk; so he and his party managed to flee from the immediate presence of
the Pope before Julius II decided to imprison him.[74]

Attention was now focussed on Mantua which became the scene for a diet
held in the August of 1512. While Francesco Gonzaga was notable for his
absence from most of the diet's sessions, Isabella d'Este was concerned to
make her presence felt.[75] She had two objectives in mind: to prevent any decisions that might be harmful to Ferrara and to achieve the installation of Massimiliano Sforza as Duke of Milan. Equicola would be part of her strategy,
his courtly graces and friendship with a number of the people involved in the
diet exploited. He dedicated his *Nec Spe Nec Metu* to Giuliano de' Medici no
doubt partly in recognition of his support in the discussions.[76] Isabella,

---

[73]   ASMN, AG, b. 860, Rome, 15 July 1512, Stazio Gadio to the Marquis. In the postscript
of the same letter Stazio Gadio refers to óne of the suggestions being made as to which state
Alfonso d'Este be appointed ruler:

Intendo che l'è sta proposto a Nostro Signore che'l dia il Stato di Urbino al signor
Duca di Ferrara et al Duca di Urbino Ferrara, che melio si potrà fidare, al che non
consentiria mai il signor Duca di Ferrara.

[74]   See A. Luzio, *Isabella d'Este di fronte a Giulio II*, p. 224. Equicola arrived back in
Mantua in the night of the 23 July. The Marquis of Mantua attempted to smooth over the situation by sending a special envoy, though by now the damage had been done:

Instructione de Federico Cataneo mandato a Roma in nome del'Illustrissimo
signor nostro.
Federico, gionto che serai a Roma, vederai di parlare al'Illustrissimo Federico
nostro figliolo, al Folenghino et Mario, prima che la Santità di Nostro Signore
sapi la gionta tua, communicandoli la causa de l'andata tua, facendo che li ditti
Folenghino et Mario vadino a trovare el signor Duca et cardinale de Aragona, da
quali toranno instructione de quanto haverai a dire alla Santità de Nostro Signore
in nome nostro... Poi col ditto Federico et Folenghino andarai a basare il pede in
nostro nome a Sua Santità.
(ASMN, AG, b. 831, 20 July 1512).

Although the Marquis instructed Equicola to visit Alfonso d'Este on his behalf, he did not
allow him to become part of *his* diplomatic service since Equicola's name was omitted from
the list of those who would make the official representations to the Pope.

[75]   Cf. L. Mazzoldi, *Mantova: La storia*, II, Verona, 1961, p. 223; Giuliano de' Medici,
Duca di Nemours, *Poesie*, a cura e con uno studio di G. Fatini, Florence, 1939, pp. XXXIII-IV.

[76]   D. E. Rhodes, «A bibliography of Mantua (II 1507-21)', *La Bibliofilia*, Anno 58, dis-
pensa 3, 1956, pp. 161-75; for the *Nec Spe Nec Metu* see p. 164 no. 6.
There seems to have been a solid rapport between Isabella d'Este and Giuliano de' Medici with
Equicola the recognized intermediary. The latter paid his respects to Giuliano on his way to
Rome to congratulate Giovanni de' Medici being created Pope: «Non potria dir como mi vide
volontieri et con quanto romore mi abracio et accarezzò» (Luzio, «Primordi», p. 456).

however, only achieved half of her objectives: it was decided to treat Alfonso d'Este as an enemy. The installation of Massimiliano Sforza in Milan gave new substance to Isabella's ideal of dynastic politics. Milan ruled by the eldest son of her sister Beatrice, seemed to present, to Isabella and others, the oppor-

---

Another letter (ASMN, AG, b. 1106, Prato, 31 August 1512, Giuliano de' Medici to Isabella d'Este, f. 149r) refers directly to the Diet of Mantua and its principal result, namely, the return of Medici rule to Florence:

> Io so bene che Vostra Excellentia se allegrerrà d'ogni commodo et bene mio come di vero signore suo. Et però la aviso come con satisfactione et contento di tucta la città di Firenze, Monsignor reverendissimo, patrone et fratello mio, et io, domani cene tornamo in patria et in casa nostra. Et a questo effecto son venuti più mandati da quelli magnifici et excelsi signori, tre oratori, infiniti cittadini son venuti qui a congratularsi con noi di tanto bene nostro. Del quale son certissimo Vostra Excellentia devere pigliare piacere grande insieme con lo Illustrissimo Signore suo consorte. Et però li mando a posta el presente homo mio, informato delle particularità di queste cose nostre. Però non dirò altro a quella se non che quanto più posso meli offero et raccomando, ricordandoli che di tanto più potrà Vostra Excellentia valersi et servirsi quanto io più potrò in casa mia che nel lungo exilio. Alla mia Madonna Alda et al mio Equicola me racomando inseme con tucta la sua virtuosissima corte. Et così fa el Moccicone vero servo di Vostra Excellentia.

Moccicone (Bernardo Bibbiena) had always had close relations with Isabella's court, including her ladies-in-waiting; Giuliano de' Medici seems to have had a liking for Alda Boiardo, perhaps at Isabella's instigation during the negotiations at Mantua. Another beneficiary of the agreements reached at Mantua was Massimiliano Sforza who would become Duke of Milan as his father once was. It appears that special arrangements needed to be made between the Gonzagas and the son of Ludovico Sforza and that Equicola was chosen as the representative of Mantuan interests:

> Con grandissimo piacer mio ho letto le lettere de la Signoria Vostra e inteso quanto a bocca a nome suo me ha significato Mario Equicola, servitor d'essa. Donde grandemente la regratiamo del materno offitio usato verso de mi. Acceptando apresso la optima dispositione de quella tanto quanto se ne vedesse lo effecto. E perché del mio animo verso de la Signoria Vostra ho parlato plenamente col prefato servitore de Quella. Remettendosi a la relation d'esso, non li dirò altro cha pregarla che a quanto li dirà da parte nostra volia dar indubitata fede. A Quella con filial amor recommandandome.
>
> (ASMN, AG, b. 1616, Trent, 19 September 1512, Massimiliano Sforza to Isabella d'Este).

Massimiliano Sforza wrote in the same tone to the Marquis clarifying the role of Equicola as both Francesco's and Isabella's representative whose mission had repercussions for the entire Mantuan state, particularly for marchional politics:

> Illustrissime Domine affinis tanquam pater optime. L'officio fatto per Mario Equicola, servitor de la Signoria Vostra in nome de Quella ...e dirme quelle amorevole parole quale me ha referto. Non poria esserme stato più grato per provenir da persona a mi conzonta in quella strettezza de affinità che è et qual me ama como optimo patre. Però la regratio d'esso quanto più posso lassando el carico al prefato servitor de la Signoria Vostra de exprimerle lo animo servo verso d'essa per havergelo io dechiarato secundo che da lui intenderà, al qual in questo prestarà fede indubitata et io a Quella como bon fiolo de continuo me recommando.
>
> (ASMN, AG, b. 1616, Trent, 19 September 1512, Massimiliano Sforza to the Marquis of Mantua).

tunity of rebuilding Italy on previous lines, that is, according to a system of
related dynastic orders. The restoration of the Medici was another step in this
direction. Her prolonged stay in Milan at the beginning of 1513 marked a
decisive break with what had been a purely domestic form of dynastic politics.
Her absence from Mantua indicated both the great importance she attached
to helping Massimiliano Sforza in the first days of his new regime, and the fact
that she was by no means indispensable to the government of Mantua. For
political reasons of his own Francesco Gonzaga had been only too willing to
give his blessing to the Milan visit. He was of the opinion that Isabella's
absence from Mantua would provide her with less opportunity to think about
Ferrara and would also prevent her from being labelled a pro-French sup-
porter.[77]

However, there may have been more to Francesco Gonzaga's position than
his own rather obvious explanations. He could not have failed to note that
Milan was not really so far away from Ferrara and that she could easily keep
in contact with her brother if she wanted. In spite of Francesco distancing
himself from the Diet of Mantua on the surface, he was in reality acquiescing
to its conclusions, perhaps in unison with his wife. It can be claimed with
some justice that the Marquis was tacitly lending his support to Isabella
d'Este during the realignment of the Italian states after Ravenna.

Early in January 1513, Isabella had set off for Milan but without Mario
Equicola who had probably been left behind to keep her informed of developments concerning the affairs of Alfonso d'Este, and any other news which
could prove useful to her.[78] However, events took another turn: Julius II died
on 21 February 1513. Until a new Pope was elected Isabella saw no need to

---

[77]   The Marquis wrote to the Archdeacon of Mantua, then Mantuan ambassador in Rome
probably to clear himself of any accusations that might be made against him in papal circles:

> Lo Illustrissimo Signore Duca de Milano, fin dapoi che'l fu in questa terra, non
> ha mai cessato di pregarni che vogliamo lassare andare la Illustrissima Madonna
> nostra consorte a godere con la presentia sua del piacere di questo suo felice suc-
> cesso... Poi havemo pensato che nostra mogliere fin hora ha havuto nota di essere
> di animo francese et non ci è spiaciuto questa occasione di levarsi questa machia
> perché senza dubio l'andata sua a Milano vien de diretto contra quello che
> voriano Francesi. Appresso consideramo che, andando lei a Milano, la se lon-
> tanarà pur alquanto da le cose di Ferrara perché, come più volte vi havemo
> significato, non stemo securi che lla non tenghi intelligentia con suo fratello stan-
> do qui, et senza dubio sì come la se ne lontanarà col corpo, così la alienarà molto
> l'animo da le passioni de le cose di Ferrara.
> (ASMN, AG, b. 2920, libro 225, 1 January 1513, Francesco Gonzaga to Alessan-
> dro Gabbioneta).

[78]   At the beginning of her journey Isabella's party consisted of her *donzelle* and two
gentlemen:

> Per compagno solo vi è messer Cesare da Gonzaga. Per secretario il Tridapale per
> la non troppo buona dispositione de messer Benedicto Capilupo.
> (ASMN, AG, b. 2487, 9 January 1513, Amico della Torre to Federico Gonzaga).

return to Mantua. [79] Indeed, her presence at the capture of Piacenza by the Duke of Milan brought out a theatrical reaction from Francesco who feigned despair at his wife's behaviour. The obvious and traditional interpretation of Francesco's hysterics was that he realized his mistake in encouraging Isabella to go to Milan because far from removing her from the centre of northern Italian politics, it had only made her carry further her own strategies. Such an interpretation depends on reducing the Marquis to the level of a dullard and does not take into account that Isabella might have been working to *both* their advantages in a tense situation. Isabella's *liberty* was perhaps what was needed by the besieged Marquis. However, the taking of Piacenza went further than he perhaps intended because of Isabella's too close connection with an anti-papal action («ma molto più per essersi ritrovata nostra mogliere col Duca di Milano alla dedicione di quella città» quoted by Luzio, «Primordi», p. 109). And Isabella herself was on the defensive in her reply to these accusations. She notes that political harmony between them was a terribly difficult thing to achieve: «mi doglio de la mia mala sorte che sempre indusse Vostra Signoria a despiacerli ogni mia actione per bona che sia». A case could be made here for Isabella exaggerating the tensions in their relationship in order to clear herself of blame in this particular matter. She appears to be also arguing that she should not be so facilely dismissed and is answering her husband's main objection to her: «A noi dole et horamai havemo vergogna di havere per nostra sorte una mogliere di quella sorte che sempre vol fare a suo modo e di suo cervello» («Primordi», p. 109). It is a taxing task attempting to untangle the web of subterfuge necessary for survival in a rapidly changing political situation. I would attempt to argue here that Francesco had reasons other than those he stated for «sending» Isabella to Milan, though after Piacenza he appears to have regretted his initial decision. [80]

---

[79] The Marquis asked Isabella to return to Mantua in February 1513. He claimed that he needed her to govern Mantua in his absence from the city. It is more likely that Francesco Gonzaga wanted Isabella back in Mantua because he felt he was losing control of the situation and did not want her to go any further. His offer was probably intended to be the bait designed to draw her home:

> A noi conviene andare fori ad exercitarci per consiglio di medici... Serrà necessaria la Signoria Vostra a Mantua al governo de le cose nostre.
> (ASMN, AG, b. 2920, libro 225, Mantua, 9 February 1513, Francesco Gonzaga to Isabella).

[80] Quoted in A. Luzio, «Isabella d'Este e la corte sforzesca», *ASL*, ser. terza, 15 (1901) 145-76; 164. Luzio's discussion of Francesco Gonzaga is blinded by prejudice and preconception and refuses to see anything positive in him. Thus, Luzio's assertion that Francesco's politics were at times guided by personal jealousy fails to consider the Marquis' undoubted political skills («Primordi», pp. 109-10). There needs to be a full-scale re-evaluation of Francesco Gonzaga, particularly of his cultural patronage which many scholars, under Luzio's influence, fail to recognize or refuse to believe that it could exist.

As soon as the election of Leo X was announced Isabella ordered Equicola to leave for Rome.[81] The speed with which he was sent was indicative of Isabella's excitement over the event. A Medici pope would, it was thought, provide support for the Italians' desire to be free from the «barbarians». Equicola succeeded in obtaining an audience with the Pope and to offer his congratulations on Isabella's behalf. During the course of the meeting he recited some Latin verses, indicating how important the new pope considered humanists to be («Primordi», pp. 454-56). Equicola's other duties in Rome were to analyse the changes in the college of cardinals and to test the Duke of Ferrara's popularity. Last of all, he was to discover the pope's opinion of the Marquis («Primordi», pp. 456).

Equicola's memories of Rome as the place where he commenced his humanist apprenticeship (at a time of relative stability) inspired him to prolong his stay. It would give him the chance to «godermi li amici» (a pleasure often denied him by the pressing nature of his many duties), and at the same time the opportunity to keep a watchful eye on Alfonso d'Este's affairs.[82] He stressed the fact that although he had no place in the decision-making machinery of the Curia he did enjoy some influence: «Io fo poche facende, ma chi me vede correre mo' ad questo mo' ad quello cardinale pare che io governi la corte, da Vulterra [Francesco Soderini] et Ragona [Cardinal d'Aragona] et altri publicamente favorito» («Primordi», p. 458). Equicola was content for the time being with the pretence of power, relishing being on show in Roman ecclesiastical society and in a position which yielded positive results. However, it seems reasonable to ask why, if he enjoyed the patronage of a number of cardinals, did he not take advantage of it and seek advancement through the church? It is likely that his income was not very great (even though he was one of Isabella d'Este's most trusted agents); and his other sources of revenue were uncertain, as, for example, the rent he received from his house in Rome:

> Messer Accursio, olim favorito di Iulio secundo, pare sia stato prohibito che non si parta di Roma. Io ho da comenzare una lite con lui di trecento ducati quali me era debitore un messer Iulian Spinula de ficti de casa et di altre mei facende et dicto Accursio tene la casa che fu de dicto messer Iuliano...[83]

---

[81]   Consult A. Luzio, «Primordi», p. 116. (Another letter quoted by Moncallero, *Epistolario*, I, p. 515, from Francesco Gonzaga to Bibbiena: «Mario Equicola mandato a basare il piede a Nostro Signor»).

[82]   A. Luzio, «Primordi», p. 456. Apart from his Roman friends, Janus Lascaris and Giovanni Rucellai arrived during his stay («Primordi», p. 461). Sigismondo Cantelmo was also in Rome. Bibbiena, Bembo and Sadoleto are singled out for mention by Equicola («Primordi», pp. 457-58).

[83]   ASMN, AG, b. 861, Rome, 27 March 1513, Equicola to Isabella d'Este.

Perhaps, he had decided to link his fortunes to those of Isabella d'Este and her brother Alfonso. He may well have thought that his present intimacy with the leading members of the Este family would yield benefits in the years to come.

Part of Equicola's mission in Rome had been to prepare the way for another visit by the Duke of Ferrara who hoped to reach a settlement with the new Pope. Isabella and her family were altogether optimistic about the outcome of these negotiations.[84] On the Duke's arrival in Rome in the April of 1513 Equicola changed his role slightly: he now assumed the title of «oratore de Vostra Signoria», Isabella d'Este. His decision to extend his stay in Rome he had thought to be a good one: he had worked to prevent a repetition of the fiasco of the year before, and was now honoured by the Duke as his sister's personal representative: «Cenammo in gran festa et io come oratore accanto a Sua Signoria nel loco più honorato» («Primordi», p. 460). As far as their personal relationship was concerned, Equicola in his letters to Isabella frequently drew attention to the intimacy that had grown up between himself and the Duke.[85] Isabella had again acted outside the Marquis' diplomatic system, appointing her own man so as not to be dependent on her husband's interpretation of events. Equicola was again the perfect choice since he had totally identified himself with the Estense cause, for example, using the plural «our» in talking about the restitution of Reggio to Alfonso d'Este. The pope's treasurer approved of Equicola's conduct in the affair: «Scrivi alla Signora Marchesana che ha in corte appresso il Papa un bon servitore.»[86]

*

---

[84]   Isabella d'Este wrote to Massimiliano Sforza concerning her brother Ippolito's income from the archbishopric of Milan:

> Però che se al tempo che viveva Papa Julio la era disposta a gratificare il cardinale tanto più hora che havemo uno Pontefice iustissimo et amico de casa nostra alli pedi dil quale presto si trovarà il cardinale e forsi il Signor Duca... Questi beneficii gli furono dati col favore et consentimento de la felice memoria de lo Illustrissimo Signore vostro patre a fine de conservare Sua Signoria Reverendissima et lo Signor Duca uniti al stato suo. Che quanto importi questo, maxime in li tempi presenti Vostra Excellentia lo deve considerare. (Archivio di Stato, Milan, Archivio Ducale Sforzesco, Potenze Estere: Mantova, cartella 1014, «Il iovedì santo MDXIII in Mantua», Isabella d'Este [«Desiderosa servire et vedere Vostra Signoria, la Marchesana de Mantoa, de mano propria»] to Massimiliano Sforza.)

[85]   A. Luzio, «Primordi», p. 460, publishes other letters in which Equicola commented on his particularly favourable position: «Io, benché oratore de Vostra Signoria, non mi dedignai cavarli li stivali et feci poi officio di camerieri». Equicola carried out the same kind of duties that were his lot when Alfonso d'Este was ill. Isabella's tutor was proud of these special favours: «pensa Vostra Signoria che'l Signor Duca et io soli stamo in finestra ad veder chi passa.»

[86]   A. Luzio, «Primordi», p. 461. The treasurer is Bibbiena, appointed on the very day of Leo X's accession (*Epistolario*, I, p. 518).

When Equicola returned to Mantua he applied himself to Isabella's other political preoccupation, Milan. It is probable that at her instigation he wrote the *Epistola* (addressed to Massimiliano Sforza).[87] To judge by the number of copies that survive in libraries the work seems to have been widely diffused. Although the Duke of Milan is taken as the point of departure, Equicola broadened his perspective so that Massimiliano Sforza was made the focus of all hopes for the deliverance of Italy from the foreign invader. The historical thus gave way to the ideal, as Equicola developed his notion of a princely saviour, in much the same way as Machiavelli did in *Il Principe*. The work undoubtedly had a wide appeal because of its call for an «Italian» revival seen as a reality. And the election of a Medici pope, the restoration of the Medicis in Florence and the Sforzas in Milan were impressive proof of the new vitality. The *Epistola* presented the Duke of Milan as the perfect prince, powerful and magnanimous and strong enough to take the reins of Italy in his hands:

> In te siquidem prudens magnanimitas, clemens animus et humanitas non vulgaris. Illaque praecipue quae ad res gerendas maximas, maxime est necessaria: Liberalitas amabilis.
>
> (*Epistola*, f. Z19ᵛ)

The praise heaped upon the Duke by Equicola reveals just how much was expected of him:

> Felix regnes. Fortunam loci superasti, tuis adversam felix vincas. Pater Patriae, hostium domitor, libertatis assertor, publicae letitiae restitutor, felix valeas. Salutis dator, quietis auctor, superi te servent quos ego supplicibus rogo votis.
>
> (*Epistola*, f. Z20ʳ)

The particular choice of a Sforza and not a Medici reflected Isabella's sense of commitment to her family, and the *Epistola* can be regarded as the translation of that sentiment into an acceptable work of Latin prose.

In October 1513 Equicola once again became Isabella's *oratore* because of his special relations with the Viceroy of Naples, Raimondo Cardona (a result of the latter's infatuation with one of Isabella's ladies-in-waiting, La Brognina). Equicola was best placed to fuel the flames of Cardona's love, for political advantage:

> Col signor imbasciadore mantuano, circa meza hora di nocte, me presentai al signor Vecere, datali la lettera di Vostra Signoria et quella da Sua Signoria lecta, quanto me accarezasse, quanto me abracciasse, con quanta familiarità et domesticheza ragionasse meco di Vostra Signoria infinite sue laudi, perché non potria se non diminuire il vero non voglio altramente scriverlo, reservandome questo ad viva voce se la memoria sino ad quel hora me servirà. Questo solamente non

---

[87]   *Ad Invictissimum Principem D. Maximilianum Sforciam Ducum Mediolani M. Equicola Viri Doctissimi De Liberatione Italie Epistola*, Rome, 1513, 4°. In the British Library copy the folios are numbered by hand: Z18, Z19, Z20.

> voglio tacere per haverlo Sua Signoria più volte replicatolo con mille iuramenti
> che da la persona del Signor Re suo in fora non è persona al mundo che più volon-
> tieri vedesse et servisse che Vostra Signoria et cum questo fo dicto assai. Fo poi
> ragionato de la signora Brognina multo amorosamente. Le careze et favori che
> havesse dal signor Prospero [Colonna] non se potria dire. Lo credo andarà mo
> mo in campo. Ad quella me recomando. [88]

*

In the period 1512-13 literature and politics became entangled in a way
detrimental to Equicola who had so far successfully combined the two. The
episode in question concerned a literary attack on Equicola's use of the vernacular. [89] The *contesa* had been going on for over a year and although Francesco
Gonzaga had at first enjoyed the literary dispute (surprising the critics who
generally picture him as an uncultured soldier), the debate had become very
bitter, especially on the attackers' side:

> Ma troviamo essersi tanto exacerbata dal canto vostro (Antonio Tebaldeo), che
> non haveti havuto rispetto ad prorumpere in ogni ville persecutione contra esso
> Mario sino ad haver fatto stampare libelli famosi et attacare sonetti in diversi loci
> di questa nostra città in vergogna et carico suo. [90]

---

[88]   ASMN, AG, b. 1447, Verona, 14 October 1513, Equicola to Isabella d'Este, plus another letter of the same day.
   The whole episode involving «La Brognina» is recounted with relish by R. Castagna in
her *Un viceré per Eleonora Brognina alla corte di Isabella d'Este Gonzaga*, Mantua, 1982.
   Isabella also instructed Equicola to carry out some business for the Marquis and the tutor
reported on the matter in a letter to her of the same day:

> Messer Rozon, quale me ionse in Villafranca, me dixe da parte di Vostra Signoria
> che devesse far un certo bono officio col Signor Vecere per servitio del Signor
> Marchese Illustrissimo, circa certo pagamento di denari. Sia certa che Vostra
> Signoria che con gran dextreza et bel modo il feci et con gran satisfactione del
> Signor Vecere, di sorte che spero harà facto fructo.

[89]   Consult C. Dionisotti, *Gli umanisti*, pp. 116-30; V. Cian, «Una baruffa letteraria» for
the relevant documents.
[90]   ASMN, AG, b. 2921, libro 231, 5 November 1513, Francesco Gonzaga to Antonio
Tebaldeo.
   The «sonetti» to which the Marquis of Mantua refers have, so far, not come to light; the
«libelli famosi» would seem to refer not only to the *Epistola in Sex Linguis* but to the *Dialogus
in Lingua Mariopionea sive Piomariana Carmentalis Pulcherrimus* (for which see the brief
note by R. Sabbadini, «Una satira contro Battista Pio», *GSLI*, 27 (1896) 185-86). The linguistic
complexity of the *Dialogus* and the clarity of its position on the basic issue of Latin style would
seem to militate against attributing the text (solely) to Tebaldeo. Bembo was capable at this date
of analysing Latin style in these terms but whether he could draw on a satirical vein in such
trenchant fashion is open for discussion. The message of the text is clear enough and is even
explained at the end of the dialogue proper:

> Tu, vero studiose lector ut tandem serio tecum loquar. Fuge tanquam scopulum
> ridiculum et putidum atque ut ita dixerim rusticum hoc dicendi genus et imitare
> bonos (Biblioteca Ambrosiana, Milan, D 465 inf., *Dialogus*, f. 154v).

The statement clearly directs the reader to imitate Cicero in preference to the more recondite
Latin authors. The *Nec Spe Nec Metu* in its introduction reproduces the poem which is satirized
in the *Dialogus*. The presentation of a poem which was the butt of much derision indicates that

One of these «libelli famosi» referred to what must be the *Epistola in Sex Linguis* in which Equicola was made to condemn himself by his own words. Although it was the Marquis' considered opinion that Tebaldeo himself was the author of these satires, one must take into account the possibility that the original idea about the form of the attacks came from more informed humanist sources.[91] It is interesting to note that the Marquis considered that Tebaldeo, in order to cover his trail, cunningly allowed the blame for the episode to fall on Bembo. For Bembo and Equicola to publicly express their opposing views on the vernacular (Equicola represented as the leader of one school and Bembo of another), was to indicate the ferocity of the debate.[92] The Marquis could not believe that Bembo would have stooped to such vile behaviour, «conoscendo la modestia et dolce natura di essa Vostra Signoria» (letter of 5 November 1513). The reason for the Marquis' intervention did not, in the final analysis, have much to do with the *questione della lingua* but rather with the defence of one of his wife's ladies-in-waiting, Isabella Lavagnola. He wrote to Tebaldeo:

> Non havemo possuto fare che non entramo in quello sdegno contra vui che si conviene ad una tanta offesa. Et poi che in questo caso haveti voluto più presto satisfare a l'odio, invidia et malignità vostra che tenere conto del rispetto nostro, del honore di la giovine et de la benivolentia che meritavamo da voi per le amorevoli demostrationi et gran beneficii che di continuo haveti recevuti da noi et da la predetta Madama nostra consorte, dovi ben demostrati la ingrata natura vostra, volemo siati certo che mai siamo per scordarni questa iniuria (Letter of 5 November 1513; see above).

Equicola was determined to make a firm stand against his detractors (the poem is in the *Dialogus*, fs. 149r-150r and in *Nec Spe Nec Metu*, fs. A1r-A2r). The author(s) of the *Dialogus* is merciless in his criticisms of the stylistic defects of the «pentecontametron». The criticism extends to Equicola's most important Latin prose works (*De Opportunitate*, the manuscript version of *Nec Spe Nec Metu* and the *De Religione*). Equicola in the printed edition of the *Nec Spe Nec Metu* asserts his Latin can be compared with the best writers and is based on a thorough knowledge of the language.

The *Dialogus* alludes to the other satirical work, the *Epistola* which was originally a letter written to Giovanni Muzzarelli (on whom see the short biographical note and bibliography in G. Muzzarelli, *Rime*, edizione critica a cura di G. Hannüss Palazzini, Mantua, 1983, pp. 7-18).

It should also be noted that Sabbadini was correct in asserting that the two manuscripts of the *Dialogus* were copied from a printed text, a copy of which is to be found in the Bibl. Universitaria, Barcelona, *Dialogus in Lingua Mariopionea*. It is followed by *Macharonea* printed in Pesaro [8°]. It is unclear, however, whether the latter work is part of the same book or they just happen to be bound together because of their linguistic similarities. The date seems to be around 1511.

[91] See C. Dionisotti, *Gli umanisti*, pp. 112, 115, 117-21, 127. It may not be too far-fetched to see Bembo and Tebaldeo working together here.

[92] See P. Floriani, «La «questione della lingua» e il «dialogo» di P. Valeriano» now in his *I gentiluomini letterati*, Naples, 1981, pp. 68-91.

The bitterness of Tebaldeo's attack first on Equicola and then, openly, on Isabella d'Este, was perhaps due to the bad treatment he had received when employed by the Marquis contrary to Francesco Gonzaga's assertion that he had treated Tebaldeo very well.[93]

The Marquis was right about Equicola's readiness to defend himself. At the end of November 1513 Equicola's dialogue *Nec Spe Nec Metu*, written before he had officially entered Isabella d'Este's service, was published in Mantua. The *Marchesana* had already accepted the work, in manuscript form, as a gift.[94] Why, then, did Equicola decide to have it published? The answer must lie in the fact that Equicola believed that the *Nec Spe Nec Metu* provided a confutation of Tebaldeo's accusations. Indeed, the subject of the work is the search for the meaning of moral equilibrium, of «mediocritas»; and it stresses the benefits to be obtained from a balanced way of life. The author seems to imply that anyone approving such a balance could not make exaggerated claims about his achievements as a writer in the vernacular. It would appear that the introductory pages at least have been re-written to provide a suitable vehicle for Equicola's polemic. He referred to the recent affair in specific terms:

> Quid maxime excellat non est omnibus facilis explicatio: eos tantum id posse contendimus qui plura observarint, scripserint plurima quod quidem dant anni et multa lectio. Horum igitur qui in litteris parum versati sunt maledicentia et iudicio nostra non infringitur spes ut nec eorum invidia nostra languescit industria. Qui insolentissimo mendacio arrogantiae mihi notam inurere impudenter tentarunt dum in calce epistolae quae materna italica lingua de in curia agentibus circumfertur, me gloriante falsa additione finxere, his minime commoveor qui nihil aedendum putant.
>
> *(Nec Spe Nec Metu*, fs.A2ᵛ-A3ʳ)

In order to add weight to his argument, Equicola cast doubt on Cicero's suitability as a model in whom all one's trust could be placed. Equicola delighted in pointing out the contradictions and uncertainties of Cicero's own position, especially when Cicero himself admitted this:

> Multa redundantia, quaedam etiam paulo hilariora, sicut adolescentis in oratione pro Sexto Roscio fatetur. At pro habito, pro Cornelio compluribusque aliis eam inesse gloriatur quam ipse probavit varietatem. *(Nec Spe Nec Metu*, f. A3ʳ)

According to Equicola, the Ciceronians had an impossible task: not only would they have had to take into account Cicero's own uncertainty about

---

[93] The Marquis had in the past employed Tebaldeo for his literary skills. Tebaldeo's precise task had been to compose poetry which the Marquis then passed off as his own. Francesco had been forced to practise this deceit because his betrothed Isabella d'Este had first written poetry to him. The Marquis was sufficiently aware of cultural values to realize that it would elevate him in Isabella's esteem if he replied to her poems in a similar vein. Unfortunately, Francesco was slow to reward Tebaldeo for his services, much to the latter's anger. The bitterness of Tebaldeo's attack on Equicola and the Gonzagas should be seen principally in this light.

For the Marquis' «attempts» at poetry see A. Luzio, *Isabella verseggiatrice e le velleità poetiche del marito* (appendix to *I precettori*, pp. 51-68).

[94] Luzio-Renier, *La coltura*, pp. 50-52 and pp. 93-97 of this volume.

his position but his followers lived under completely different conditions from those experienced by their master:

> Nos vero eorum perversa subtilitas non deterreat qui ad Antiquorum incorruptam linguae latinae puritatem omnia referunt. Nam si quod illis erat innatum, nobis elaboratum est. Si eos tantum recte locutos arbitratur M. Tullius qui extra urbem non vixerant et quos barbaries aliqua indomestica non infuscaverat, si illa tempestate expurgandum omnem sermonem admonet et latine loquendum, si C. Caesar de ratione loquendi ad Ciceronem scripsit et consuetudinem vitiosam atque corruptam, pura et incorrupta consuetudine emandavit, qui fieri potest ut nos quibus a lacte fere nutricis (ad eo lingua immutata est) error inesse videtur ad illorum numerosam elegantiam in simplicibus seu maius in compositis verbis sine lapsu nos ipsos possimus effingere.   (*Nec Spe Nec Metu*, f. A3ᵛ)

Change and adaptability to circumstances should mark the writer's approach to the language he uses. For Equicola, inflexible rules served only to exclude him since they became the property of an élite to which his membership was in doubt. He preferred not to be shackled by hard and fast rules and limited to a single writer:

> Magna ea putemus quae ab optimis non longe absunt. Id facilius consequemur si bonos tantum legerimus auctores. Bonos autem eos maxime puto qui a Terentio ad P. Ovidii floruerunt aetatem. Illa enim aetas mihi aurea esto quae subsequitur ad Theodosii usque tempora argenteam mihi facio.
>
> (*Nec Spe Nec Metu*, f. A4ʳ)

Equicola wished to allow himself a reasonable space in which to manoeuvre.[95] Were he to limit his discussion to the vernacular, he would have had to use the same arguments. In this area also, he emphasized the importance of freedom of choice within a loose but recognizable framework.[96]

It is obvious that Equicola belongs to a tradition of linguistic eclecticism which perhaps found its most forceful expression in Poliziano's refutation of Cortese's Ciceronianism. Both Poliziano and Equicola offer similar defences of their linguistic choices. The latter emphasizes the role of personal inclination in style which is based on a quantitative analysis of written language («qui plura observarint, scripserint plurima, quod quidem dant anni et multa lectio» [*Nec Spe Nec Metu*, f. A2ᵛ]) and not a qualitative appreciation of few texts. Equicola uses Cicero in order to add weight to his own position as an eclectic; he implies that even the Latin writer was aware that texts were constituted by many other texts, and rightly so («studiorum praeterea fructus est scriptio» [*Nec Spe Nec Metu*, f. A3ʳ]). He does, however, set limits perhaps

---

[95]   He writes: «Quos autem ego mihi terminos certosque fines statuam quos non egrediar ex hoc libello cognosci poterit» (*Nec Spe Nec Metu*, f. A4ʳ).

[96]   On Equicola's position in the *questione della lingua* see, for example, B. Migliorini, *The Italian Language*, abridged and recast by T. Gwynfor Griffith, London, 1966, p. 217; M. Vitale, *La questione della lingua*, Palermo, 1971, pp. 25, 37-38; P. Floriani, «La «questione della lingua»», pp. 72, 80.

because the influence of Ciceronianism was already making some kinds of language-use appear excessive and ridiculous.

*

Not all of Equicola's literary activities were conducted in an atmosphere of fierce polemic. Isabella d'Este regarded him as her foremost literary adviser: when verses were sent to her she claimed on occasion that she did not have any competence in judging poetry:

> Quali (versi), per il poco iudicio che ne havemo et per quello di tutti quelli che ne fanno professione, che è molto più, et maximamente di Mario nostro precettore, sono dottissimi et elegantissimi et mostrano ben d'essere fatti in una bona officina et per mano d'un bon maestro.
> (ASMN, AG, b. 2996, libro 30, Mantua, 3 January 1513, Isabella d'Este to the Bishop of Comacchio, Tommaso Foschi).

On another occasion he had suggested to both Isabella and Federico Gonzaga that they should try and have Pandolfo Collenuccio's work on the history of Naples published.[97] When an opportunity arrived to examine the *raccolta aragonese* Isabella seized it, no doubt urged on by Equicola. Her reasons for wanting to see the manuscript were partly intellectual, partly political: she thought she would gain in prestige by having seen such a rare collection of Italian poetry. Equicola's interest was unequivocally more scholarly and the use he made of his special knowledge of the *raccolta* can be seen in the *Libro de natura de amore*.[98]

*

The time not spent in study or instruction was often passed, as far as we can tell, in the company of the *donzelle*, usually with the *Marchesana* presiding (the connection made by Tebaldeo between Equicola and the *donzelle* — one in particular — was not, it would seem, fortuitous). Isabella herself had known of the «affair» and had approved. She had written in defence of Equicola, declaring that he had been led into the affair «più presto per suggetto di scrivere che per affecto».[99] In this closed female society, where men intruded only with Isabella's permission, the privileged Equicola played a game with the *donzelle*. His playfulness may have stemmed from a simple wish to entertain; or from the desire to explore the nature of a love-relationship in its social context, and to test the range of his own emotions (perhaps with the

---

[97]   See A. Bertolotti, «Varietà archivistiche e bibliografiche», *Il bibliofilo*, 9 (1888) 35-38, document no. CCLXXXV.

[98]   On this see D. de Robertis, «La composizione del *De natura de amore* e i canzonieri antichi maneggiati da Mario Equicola», *Studi di Filologia Italiana*, 17 (1959), 189-220; 218-20 for the episode in question.

[99]   Quoted in V. Cian, «Una baruffa letteraria», p. 397.

intention of verifying the theories he described in the *Libro*). The unsatisfactory, «inauthentic» nature of social relationships may have led Equicola to cultivate an «artificial» relationship, that is to say, one based on a fiction; this was for him the medium of communication, and the substitute for more profound friendships. His incapacity for «real» affection was indicated by his endless search for a doctrine which would adequately define his attitude to society and the world.

In March 1514, Isabella went to lake Garda for reasons both personal and political. [100] To add to her enjoyment of the trip she took with her some of the *donzelle*, and Mario Equicola. Once there, she delighted in the beauties of nature and immersed herself in contemplation of the past. [101] While she was thus occupied, the *donzelle* were lamenting their absence from Federico Gonzaga who had become a central figure in their love-games. It was Isabella Lavagnola (the woman calumniated by Tebaldeo) who took the lead in these games, with Equicola's help (scribe to all the *donzelle*): he wrote most of her letters to Federico as the handwriting shows. Equicola wrote to Federico in his own right keeping him informed of the latest news concerning his mother and the ladies-in-waiting. He graphically describes, in one letter, the kind of role he played, and was expected to play, at Isabella's court:

> Gran romore era per casa: Isabella gridava, «Dove è Mario? Dove è costui? Che'l diavol il porte. Mo che ne ho bisogno non compare, sempre mi è fastidioso, sempre me sta negli occhi, mo che'l voglio non lo trovo». Queste et simile parole io ascoltava di nascosto che ella le dicea con la Tortorina, Isabetta et Livia. Mandò uno, poi un altro. Al fine uscì io fora et ella come mai mi havesse dicto male, «O mio Mario, presto, presto, presto! Carta et calamaro che voglio respondere al mio signore, al mio dio. O Maria, acconcia la tavaloza. Iannetto, damme lume. Iannectin, accendi questa candela. Lucia, levame questa camorra.» Deile carta et calamaro. Et appena entrata in camera, mi rechiamò, dicendome, «Basame la mano, che così commanda chi il tucto commandarme mi pò». Di questo, signore mio, rengratio Vostra Signoria solo che di tanto et tal favore non so mai per dimenticarme, et como se sole con Dio più presto ne la mente che con parole, li renderò gratie di tanto dono et rendo al presente, supplicandola persevere in farme far qualche gratia extraordinaria et io in recompenza de ciò, non potendo altro fare, li darò aviso di quanto si fa tra noi. [102]

The vivacity of the narration is a far cry from what we expect of Equicola's style, and demonstrates Equicola's ability to adapt it to the age and character of the letter's recipient: Equicola's chief aim was to entertain the young prince, but at the same time he sought to remind Federico of his importance to the life of Isabella's court.

---

[100]   See A. Pedrazzoli, «La Marchesa Isabella d'Este Gonzaga a diporto sul lago di Garda colla sua corte», *ASL*, ser. seconda, 17 (1890) 866-78.

[101]   A. Pedrazzoli, *art. cit.*, pp. 873-76.

[102]   ASMN, AG, b. 1449, Lonato, 19 March 1514, Equicola («servo di Isabella et incatenato di Vostra Signoria») to Federico Gonzaga.

But the light-hearted frolics were disturbed by serious matters of state. Isabella had important political reasons for her journey. She had planned at the request of her husband to visit various towns of the region which were part of Mantuan territory and under threat of Venetian expansion. It was thought that a state visit by Isabella would help him maintain his rule. Equicola meanwhile had his own allotted tasks. Isabella d'Este again sent him to Raimondo Cardona, probably to encourage the latter's «love» for one of her ladies-in-waiting but also to assess the political situation. [103]

Later on in the year, Cardinal Francesco Soderini was to «borrow» Equicola for some business which would be facilitated because of his acquaintanceship with the viceroy. The Archdeacon of Mantua, Alessandro Gabbioneta, informed the *Marchesana* of Soderini's desire:

> Prega cordialissimamente quella che voglia essere contenta di concederli messer Mario per XV giorni, per andare a tore la posessione del suo vescovato de Vicentia, quale a questi dì ha hauto in permutatione. La persona de messer Mario è stata electa da Sua Reverendissima Signoria como di persona dalla quale sa essere reamato et che lo servirà volontiera, ultra che in messer Mario concureno delle altre qualità tanto in proposito che Sua Reverendissima Signoria non se ne haveria potuto inmaginar più. La Excellentia Vostra, in questo caso, non solum gratificarà el prefato Reverendissimo Monsignor, ma serà causa di fare havere bene a qualche atinente de messer Mario. [104]

Far from being delighted at this expression of confidence in Equicola, Isabella seemed reluctant to let him go (there may be an element of cunning in her reply):

> Noi gli havemo volentieri dato licentia che'l vadi, non havendo respetto alcuno al bisogno continuo che havemo di lui. [105]

---

[103]   Equicola informs Federico that he has been sent to Cardona by Isabella d'Este, but in the letter he dwells on his playful relationship with Isabella Lavagnola as being a subject more appropriate to the young prince's interests:

> Io me allontano dal magior mio bene [Isabella Lavagnola], mandandome questa mia signora al Signor Vecere. Et perché so che persona al mundo né nata né ad nascere alla bella et humana Isabella è più chara, più pretiosa, di più stima, di più amore che li è Vostra Signoria, ad quella, benché presumptuoso forse, ricorro, supplicandola che se digne per mio amore et per farmi gratia basarla quindici volte per supplire al numero delli giorni che semo stati absenti da essa Vostra Signoria. Et questo non dubite che ad mi serà gratia singular quanta merita tal piacer che ad mi per uno non potria esser il magior. Et io como suo servo in tucto se non tanto quanto di me vole Isabella, me li recomando.
> (ASMN, AG, b. 1449, Sermione, 28 March 1514, Equicola to Federico Gonzaga).

[104]   ASMN, AG, b. 862, Rome, 16 June 1514, Alessandro Gabbioneta to Isabella d'Este. The episode is analysed by K. Lowe, *Francesco Soderini (1453-1524), Florentine Patrician and Cardinal*, unpublished Ph.D. thesis, Warburg Institute, University of London, 1985, pp. 212-13.

[105]   ASMN, AG, b. 2996, libro 31, Pavia, 25 June 1514, Isabella d'Este to Alessandro Gabbioneta.

The terms that Isabella employed to describe the intimacy of her relationship with Equicola suggest a regard which went far beyond that of a pupil's affection for her teacher. He was an essential element in the fabric of her life: a constant companion, a trusted servant and a humanist whose exalted task was to create for her an image in works of a literary nature. With Isabella's blessing, Equicola brought the affair to a successful conclusion. [106]

At the time Equicola was engaged in the negotiations on Francesco Soderini's behalf, Isabella d'Este and some of her *donzelle* were on their way to Milan. Apart from the favour done for Soderini, Equicola was in a position to report to Isabella on the military situation in the area. He did not return directly to Isabella but first paid a short visit to Mantua to see Federico (who appears to have been ill) rather than to make a special report to the Marquis. [107] Federico now considered himself old enough to assert his political independence: to this end, he commissioned Equicola to act as his *oratore* to Massimiliano Sforza. This is the first sign of Equicola's movement away from Isabella towards the future Marquis of Mantua although obviously too much weight should not be attributed to it at this stage. [108] The commission coincid-

---

[106]   According to G. Mantese, *Memorie storiche della chiesa vicentina*, III ii, Vicenza, 1964, pp. 178-79, Francesco Soderini arranged to transfer from the bishopric of Volterra to that of Vicenza. Equicola was therefore thought trustworthy enough by Soderini to act on his behalf in these negotiations.
    Cf. Eubel, *Hierarchia Catholica*, III, p. 353, where the date of the transfer is given as 12 June 1514.

[107]   ASMN, AG, b. 2920, libro 229, Mantua, 11 July 1514, Federico Gonzaga to his mother:

> Venendo messer Mario a Vostra Excellentia non la fastidirò altramente con mie longe littere volendole rendere conto del star et actione mie, perché esso messer Mario vien informatissimo dil tutto et di la causa impulsiva ad farmi sicopare.

Francesco Gonzaga also wrote to Isabella:

> Qua non havimo cosa degna di sua noticia se non che l'exercito spagnolo et veneto sono redutti alle confini di Paduana et tanto propinqui che non potemo credere non siino per fare qualche cosa rellevata, secundo che anchor da Mario, che se lì è ritrovato personalmente, Vostra Signoria potrà haverni meliore informatione. (ASMN, AG, b. 2921, libro 233, Mantua, 11 July 1514, Francesco Gonzaga to Isabella d'Este).

and another letter giving evidence of his role as Isabella's personal intermediary:

> Illustrissima et Excellentia Domina mater et Domina mia honorandissima: Messer Mario che ritorna adesso a Vostra Signoria le referirà in nome mio pienamente il nostro ben stare. (ASMN, AG, b. 1894, «Filii et servitores Loysius, Ferdinandus de Gonzaga», Mantua, 11 July 1514, to Isabella).

[108]   Dal'eloquentissimo messer Mario Equicolo, preceptor de la Illustrissima Signora mia matre, ho inteso, con grandissimo mio piacere et contento, Vostra Excellentia dimandar et parlar di me, suo servitor, molto amorevolmente... Stando in continuo desiderio di poterla servire personalmente come esso messer Mario referirà a Vostra Excellentia. (ASMN, AG, b. 2920, libro 229, Mantua, 11 July 1514, Federico Gonzaga to the Duke of Milan).

ed with Isabella's plan to oversee the final stages of her programme to install Massimiliano Sforza in Milan (that is, to arrange his triumphal entry into that city). By her presence at such a ceremony Isabella gave her seal of approval to the Duke's succession. But Equicola cast doubt on the viability of her policy because he had seen that the Duke was militarily impotent, being utterly dependent on foreign, «barbarian» arms. Equicola had occasion to describe the life of the Milanese court which he saw had made a concerted effort to extricate itself from a desperate situation:

> La vita che hora vivemo è questa: levamo ad hore XIII; ad XVI si desna; dormese, dase odientia, cenase, vase ad spasso o per il giardino verso le Gratie o per la cità, poi si balla sino alle cinque et sei hore. Madama sta ad vedere et più delle volte, mo con questo, mo con quel, ragiona.[109]

The Duke's situation was becoming intolerable and Equicola remarked on the gravity of Massimiliano Sforza's predicament in a noteworthy manner: «Lo signor Duca non fece le careze solite alle nostre donzelle, donde credo che le cose non vadano multo a pelo» (Santoro, p. 270). However, most of Equicola's time was spent in the company of the *donzelle* whose delights he shared with Federico Gonzaga in writing. In his dealings with Equicola and the *donzelle*, the young prince avidly enjoyed the pleasures afforded him by his privileged position. He intervened in disputes that arose between Equicola and certain of the ladies-in-waiting.[110] He even commanded Isabella Lavagnola to treat Equicola as his merits deserved:

---

[109]   Santoro, p. 259. Santoro published letters from Equicola to Ippolito d'Este of the same period, particularly pp. 263-67, which illustrate Equicola's awareness of the Duke's predicament: «se lo Signor Duca consente alle inhoneste domande di Squizari serà subdito, et in man di barbari ponerà suo stato» (p. 266). The letter ends with a quotation from Petrarch which reveals the pain Equicola felt at the Duke's humiliating position:

> Nel primo cerchio del castello sono Squizari, nel resto, fanti italiani in modo che io soglio dire spesso quel di Petrarcha: «hor dentro una gabbia — fere selvagge et mansueto gregge — s'annidan sì che sempre il miglior geme.»

[110]   An example of this playful dispute, no doubt in part meant to titillate the young Federico is the following letter:

> Isabella mia, ho presentito che messer Mario è accorreciato con Catherina et Tortorina. La causa non credo possi essere de molta importantia perché l'una et l'altra è pur da bene et discrete et mi dispiace che quelle persone ch'io amo, come facio messer Mario et lor due, tengano insieme rancore. Però, sapendo quanto posseti disponere di messer Mario, anchor che vi fussero cause di grandissima importantia, vi prego vogliati constringere il vostro messer Mario ad fare la pace con lor damigelle et haverle chare come prima per amore vostro, che mi fareti gran piacere.
> (ASMN, AG, b. 2920, libro 229, Mantua, 16 August 1514, Federico Gonzaga to «Isabella ballarina» i.e. Lavagnola).

L'amor et obsequentia, che vi porta messer Mario incredibile, ricercano che voi l'habiati per supremo amico et più grato amator che si possi ritrovar.[111]

All this could not have taken place without Isabella d'Este's approbation since she regarded the *donzelle* as her property. She certainly approved of Equicola's and her ladies' behaviour towards Federico.[112] Federico was brought into the activities of the group as the master with Isabella remaining a shadowy figure in the proceedings; but there can be no doubt that she was in control, since the activities were to her liking and perhaps suggested by her. «Darsi piacere» was an essential factor in Isabella's view of life and she was to encourage such a notion in Federico.[113] The sense of power Federico now enjoyed and the sanction he received to realize that power was to reap dire consequences for Mantua and Isabella d'Este. In later years, the latter expended much energy in trying to find a suitable bride for Federico, so that she could break Isabella Boschetti's hold over her son. She was made to repent her eagerness to so quickly make a man of Federico and (for the Gonzaga dynasty) so disastrously.[114]

At the present time, there was no evident danger. Equicola, as Isabella d'Este's lieutenant, was a prime mover in the games with the *donzelle*, making no attempt to curb the future marquis who lacked any sense of restraint, *mediocritas*; on the contrary, Equicola encouraged him to think of the *donzelle* in terms of their physical beauty, a beauty which Federico would one day be able to possess:

Isabella se recommanda et desidera la sua bocca forse più o non meno che altri la sua.[115]

Equicola provided a theoretical basis for his actions in the fifth book of the *Libro de natura de amore*. In it he stated that «la virtù de la urbanità» must be regarded as a key to the court's social structure within which limits the courtier would operate (in Equicola's terminology the courtier is always the «cortegiano-amante»). He defined this virtue in the following way:

---

[111]   ASMN, AG, b. 2920, libro 229, Mantua, 11 July 1514, Federico Gonzaga to Isabella Lavagnola.

[112]   This can be seen from the following letter:

Piacque l'altri heri di far prova di Francesca. Così ella dictava in presentia de le nostre donzelle et io scriveva, donde nacque la inclusa. Madama Illustrissima ne hebe piacer.

(ASMN, AG, b. 1640, Milan, 31 July 1514, Equicola to Federico Gonzaga).

[113]   Cf. S. Kolsky, «Images», p. 61. The fact that Isabella equated marriage with the privation of one's personal freedom may reflect both her own experience of marriage and the cultivation of the *donzelle* to provide pleasure outside a strict moral framework.

[114]   Isabella's frenzied efforts to find Federico a suitable wife are documented in S. Davari, *Federico Gonzaga e la famiglia Paleologa del Monferrato*, Genoa, 1891.

[115]   ASMN, AG, b. 1640, Milan, 18 June 1514, Equicola to Federico Gonzaga.

> Giocosamente ragionare senza offendere altri, senza latrare et senza mordere.
>
> (*Libro*, f. 168ᵛ)

In Equicola's opinion the courtier had also to entertain and not criticize. It was essential for him to adapt to the circumstances in which he found himself; and if need be, even change himself. The courtier should also aim to provide relief from the problems of everyday life by creating for the court another set of social values which would unite its members in a way which distinguished them from the people who lived outside it. He should have the total «annihilation» of the outside world, that is to say of all its worries, troubles and dangers as his principal object:

> Quello non extimarò io alli homini grato che con honestà sa et pò altri ad riso incitare, et in letitia la mestitia convertere et ogni turbido pensiero dalla mente removere.
>
> (*Libro*, f. 168ᵛ)

It was beyond the scope of the courtier envisaged by Equicola to seriously advise the prince, particularly in matters of state policy. When Equicola's courtier appears, weighty and solemn affairs are banished: «Amor, facetie et giochi bisognano» (*Libro*, f. 168ᵛ). Equicola's point of view was always that of a person at a relative financial and social disadvantage compared to a member of the landed nobility. His courtier had to win favour from his masters, «conciliare benivolentia», without expecting any special treatment because of his rank. Equicola was himself aware that sacrifices were necessary if one was to achieve the goal:

> Così noi poniamo cura in comprendere qual è l'amata, et secondo a quella potemo piacere, componere nostri costumi et noi stessi che privata et publica benivolentia ne acquistemo.
>
> (*Libro*, f. 169ʳ)

Equicola would have liked us to believe that it was a simple matter to shrug aside one's own personality and re-construct another from a blank. In his view the courtier could act freely only if unhampered by ethics and a conscience. It was a question of creating a «new» man, fashioned in the image of his environment. Once the object of one's attention had been chosen, in Equicola's opinion, the rewards were high enough to justify this moral suicide, or so he thought (the relationship between Federico and Equicola should be considered in this light). Equicola was to be given greater opportunities for advancement with Federico than he could have hoped to find with Isabella.

*

Equicola left Milan in Isabella's company under the impression that they were heading towards Mantua probably arriving according to his calculations, by 10 September. Equicola was mistaken about Isabella's intentions: she kept extending her journey until finally she decided to visit Rome. Many factors contributed to this decision, not least the desire to win the firm support of the pope for Ferrara and Milan, since it was rumoured that he was preparing to carve a state out of central Italy for Giuliano de' Medici (Urbino was also a target for papal expansion). Another reason would have been her wish to prepare the process of canonization for Osanna Andreasi. Then there was the fact that she had never seen Rome, the Mecca of humanists: especially those interested in the tangible remains of classical civilization.[116]

As soon as Francesco Gonzaga learnt of Isabella's intention to continue her journey to Rome he was not content merely to approve but appointed the Archdeacon of Mantua as his representative in Rome with instructions to keep him informed of her progress.[117] The Marquis wanted both to exploit the possible political advantages of Isabella's visit and to curb her tendency to embarrass him as she had done in the past; hence the Archdeacon of Mantua. His task was two-fold: to act as her guide in Rome and to inform her of the Marquis' wishes:

> Piaceni che Sua Signoria habbi ritrovato pasto conveniente al'ingegno suo in contemplare quelle antiquità, cosa di che sempre la s'è delettata molto. Voi tenetila allegra più che sia possibile et procurati di ricondurla presto a casa.[118]

Isabella's political mission ended in utter failure when the pope bought Modena, a former Estense possession, from the Emperor for the sum of forty thousand ducats. This was a slap in the face for Isabella since the deal was concluded during her stay in Rome. Francesco Gonzaga now considered that as her ineffectiveness in her brother's affairs had been amply demonstrated, she would put more effort into his own business, and he no longer insisted that she return to Mantua.[119] Isabella had other ideas: rather than suffer the

---

[116]   On the pope's territorial ambitions see F. Nitti, *Leone X e la sua politica*, Florence, 1892, particularly pp. 20-21.

Isabella's trip to lake Garda may have whetted her appetite to see the ruins of ancient Rome because on that excursion she was impressed by what Roman remains she had seen (A. Pedrazzoli, *art. cit.*, p. 873).

[117]   Essendo lo Archidiacono nostro quel bon servitore che l'è, non meno alla Signoria Vostra che a noi, c'è parso mandarglilo in questo viagio che la fa alla via di Roma acciò che la introduchi e guidi a vedere le cose notabile di la corte e di la città e le facci recognoscere le amicitie nostre.
(ASMN, AG, b. 2921, libro 234, 11 October 1514, Francesco Gonzaga to Isabella d'Este).

[118]   ASMN, AG, b. 2921, libro 234, Mantua, 3 November 1514, Francesco Gonzaga to Alessandro Gabbioneta.

[119]   Haveressimo ben noi voluto oltra il desiderio di vedere la prefata Madama per qualche nostro dissegno che la fosse ritornata a Mantua. Nondimeno non reputamo che sia fori di proposito alle cose nostre che Sua Signoria se ritrovi in Roma a questi tempi... perché l'habbi veduto non havere giovato la presentia sua né quella del Reverendissimo cardinale, suo fratello, che non se sia acquistato Modena contra li dissegni de la casa da Este.
(ASMN, AG, b. 2922, libro 236, Mantua, 22 November 1514, Francesco Gonzaga to Alessandro Gabbioneta).

humiliation by staying in Rome, she decided to leave for Naples where she would be made much more welcome. Equicola described her triumphal entry into Naples: «La strada di Capuana era piena como se fosse congregata tucta la città per vedere una Imperatrice.»[120] For Equicola too, the visit to Naples was a return «home» in triumph.[121] There was also some serious business for Isabella to attend to, a matter not unrelated to her other affairs in Milan and Rome, namely, the negotiations which she hoped would lead to the marriage of Giovanna d'Aragona and Massimiliano Sforza.[122] After a brief stay, Isabella felt that she could honourably return to Rome.

At about the same time, the correspondence between the *donzelle* in Rome and Federico Gonzaga in Mantua resumed after the visit to Naples.[123] The *donzelle* lament the length of time they have been absent from their prince:

> Signor mio, me sa mille ani de venire a Mantua per poser vedere el mio signor bello et poserlo bassare et poserli contare el viagio.[124]

Equicola persisted in his «affair» with Isabella Lavagnola, «se Isabella vole sacrificii Mario vole essere adorato.»[124]

There may be a hint of self-satisfaction in Francesco Gonzaga's «non havere giovato la presentia sua» at his wife's discomfiture, pleased that she has become aware of the limitations of her personal politics. It is this failure that prompts the Marquis not to insist on Isabella's return as if now she will be less of a liability for his state diplomacy.

[120]   Santoro, p. 280. Santoro includes in his appendix a number of Equicola's letters written to Ippolito d'Este which describe the reception he received in Naples (pp. 277-83), and the letters concerning the journey there.

[121]   See Santoro, p. 281.

[122]   See L. Mazzoldi, *Mantova: La storia*, II, pp. 227-28.

[123]   Isabella Lavagnola resumes her correspondence with Federico with the assistance of Equicola. Adjectives like «macilenta» seem to be taken straight out of the *Hypnerotomachia Poliphili*:

> Per le continue fatighe che sostengo per lo servitio in servir mia Illustrissima Signora et per le vigliate nocti, so diventata tale che appena la macilenta pelle copre le extenuate ossa. Donde la prego me habia scusata se in Napoli non ho continuato in far il debito del mio officio in scriverli.
> (ASMN, AG, b. 862, Rome, Isabella Lavagnola to Federico Gonzaga, 24 December 1514).

[124]   ASMN, AG, b. 863, Rome, 8 February 1515, Isabella Lavagnola to Federico Gonzaga.

[125]   ASMN, AG, b. 863, Rome, 8 February 1515, Equicola to Federico Gonzaga. The letter opens with a few general remarks about love:

> Amor rege suo imperio senza spada. Volesse Dio che amor se potesse commandare o per forza li homini se potessero fare mutuamente reamare, che non seria Cupido chiamato dio et dio tale et tanto.

By the time Equicola reached the end of the letter theoretical considerations gave way to matters of a more practical nature:

> La Delia li basa lo labro di socto, la Tortorina quel di sopra. La Livia la man dextra, la Lucia la sinistra. Isabella vole la lingua.

With the aid of a papal brief Isabella managed to stay in Rome for the carnival, much to her husband's disappointment, since he had arranged various festivities to celebrate her return.[126] Isabella finally returned to Mantua in the March of 1515 and her court now seemed to her to lack the refinement of Rome. In terms of numbers Equicola was a poor substitute for the throngs of humanists that surrounded her in the papal city. Her court at Mantua had become for her a «loco tanto alieno da quella divina Conversatione». Equicola himself did not have much time to lament his departure from Rome. His presence was required in Ferrara because Alfonso d'Este had fallen ill yet again, and Equicola returned relatively easily to his normal routine, providing Isabella with the usual progress reports on the Duke's illness.[128]

*

His visit to Ferrara interrupted the composition of his oration to honour Osanna Andreasi in anticipation of her canonization. He first thought he would be able to finish it while in Ferrara, but found himself in constant attendance on Alfonso:

> Mi dole che non ho finita di rescrivere la oratione della Beata Osanna che, intertanto sto qui, l'haveria fatta vedere a docti. Pur fo voto a la prefata, se presto serò in casa, di finirla bene quanto posso.[129]

---

[126]   Noi aspettavamo con grandissimo desiderio Vostra Signoria a Mantua a questo carnevale prossimo et preparavamo di riceverla con piacevoli feste et apparati di comedie et con ogni altra demostratione de l'amore che le portamo.
(ASMN, AG, b. 2922, libro 236, Mantua, 19 January 1515, Francesco Gonzaga to Isabella d'Este).

This letter was followed by another of 27 January 1515. This time to Alessandro Gabbioneta:

Havevamo deliberato, venendo la Illustrissima Madama nostra consorte, di fare un carnevale allegro, ma, poiché la non viene, pensamo di passarlo senza molte feste.

These letters must make one reconsider the personal ties that bound Francesco and Isabella as husband and wife. Although it cannot be denied that tensions as well as open antagonisms existed between the two, it is possible to argue that they have been exaggerated by traditional historiography. It is true that in the years before Francesco Gonzaga's death relations were more strained than they had been in the past but this does not mean that the marriage was a complete failure nor that there was no affection between husband and wife.

[127]   Quoted from a letter of Isabella d'Este to Marino Caracciolo (ASMN, AG, b. 2996, libro 31, Mantua, 4 May 1515).

[128]   He was able to report that the Duke «questa nocte è stato men male» (ASMN, AG, b. 1245, Ferrara, 21 April 1515, Equicola to Isabella d'Este).

[129]   ASMN, AG, b. 1245, Ferrara, 26 April 1515, Equicola to Isabella d'Este. The precise meaning of «rescrivere» is unclear. It seems to imply an elaboration of a draft already in existence.

There had been no diminution in the favour shown to Equicola by the Duke since their last meeting:

Io so in summo favore, cameriero di nocte, di iorno compagno del signore. Ad tucte l'hore et in omni tempo servidore et affectionatissimo como ad Vostra Signoria schiavo et deditissimo.
(ASMN, AG, b. 1245, Ferrara, 30 April 1515, Equicola to Isabella d'Este).

The successful canonization of Osanna Andreasi was a personal victory for Isabella d'Este, and it was fitting that the person most involved with her, both politically and culturally, should write an oration for the occasion. Having promoted the secular image of Isabella d'Este, Equicola turned to the religious aspect of court life, now also annexed by the *Marchesana*. Francesco Silvestri, who had argued Osanna Andreasi's case at Rome, saw the canonization in terms of a personal triumph for Isabella:

> Se la canonizatione haverà effecto, como spero, Vostra Signoria acquistarà grandissima laude e perpetua benivolentia et aricordatione da la città di Mantua, como quella che ogni altra marchesana, in farli beneficio, haverà superato. [130]

Silvestri said exactly what Isabella wanted to hear, that she had outdone her predecessors in procuring for herself the prestige of a saint. She treated the religious in precisely the same way as she treated any of her other interests, that is to say, all her actions were guided by a desire for «laude» and «benivolentia». Equicola also did his erudite best to outdo the other writers on the subject of the Beata Osanna.

Equicola's treatment of the saint, as has been pointed out, was radically different from that of earlier writers. [131] This difference was partly due to Equicola's humanist perspective and his rigorous historicism which led him to treat even the institutions of Christianity from a historical point of view. For Hieronymus Monteolivetanus, on the other hand, there was no question of setting the background in this way: he took it for granted that everyone knew what a saint was and merely wanted to describe the saintliness of the Beata Osanna. He presented her in the familiar context of the cell and engaged in spiritual conversation:

> Desideroso et anxio di sempre ritrovare doctrina spirituale, havendo più volte cum la virgine parlato et domesticamente longo tempo cum spirituali coloquii converzato. [132]

Although Hieronymus Monteolivetanus realized that the Beata Osanna was not a member of a closed order, he did not specify where she carried out her work. [133] Equicola, on the other hand, made it quite clear that her place was

---

[130]   ASMN, AG, b. 1641, Milan, 11 August 1515, Frate Francesco Silvestri to Isabella d'Este. Cf. Zarri, «Pietà e profezia», p. 226. On Silvestri, see Luzio-Renier, *La coltura*, pp. 213-20.

[131]   Zarri writes in «Pietà e profezia» that «non si può fare a meno di notare nell'orazione dell'Equicola uno scarto profondo fra l'elegante profilo della monaca tracciato dal cortigiano e l'affettuoso ritratto che il Silvestri e il Monteolivetano ne avevano fornito quasi un decennio prima» (p. 233).

[132]   I am using the translation *Libretto della vita et transito della beata Osanna*, Bologna, 1524; f. 22r-22v.

[133]   Io ti ho electa ad questo per salute de le anime et per questo non ho mai voluto che tu sia intracta nel monasterio. (*Libretto della vita*, f. 33r).

in the court, she was considered almost a member of the Gonzaga clan, and
that she was particularly dear to Isabella d'Este who often had need of her
counsel. Indeed the work ends in praise of various court figures who had par-
ticipated in the canonization process, for example: «prudentissime Alixandro
Gabloneta huius patriae civi et archidiacono id curante.»[134]

However, the Beata Osanna posed a dilemma for Equicola, precisely
because she was a court figure. Osanna Andreasi provided a yardstick with
which one could measure the other ideal of the court, in Castiglione's phrase,
the «donna di palazzo». She did indeed possess some of those qualities which
would not be out of place in a court lady:

> Nullum in vultu superbiae vestigium sed divini decoris gravitatem hilaritatemque
> praeferens ostendebat. Nulla armata simulatione, nuda et innocua simplicitate,
> ad amicorum leniendos dolores, nullam operam, nullum consilium in miserorum
> levamen abnuebat. Nulla nunque, te o diva Osanna, aut ambitio aut inanis gloria
> a recta deiecit.
> (*Oratio*, f. B5^v)

Osanna also rejected the refinements of court life in accordance with the asce-
tic tradition of Christianity:

> Dum oculorum solat a aurium delinimenta, oblectamenta odorum omnium con-
> tenta quo vis obvio cibo fugit, vitavit, respuit. Humi cubare, antelucanis horis sur-
> gere illi locus ludusque.
> (*Oratio*, f. B1^r)

The Beata Osanna was paradoxically both the symbol of the rejection of
the ideals of court society and at the same time the ideal which the «donna
di palazzo» should try and reach. The Christian life of the saint contrasted
with the life led by Isabella d'Este's *donzelle*. Equicola expressly emphasizes
Osanna's qualities as a modest virgin: «vultu demissa, oculos deiecta modes-
tos» (*Oratio*, f. B3^v). At one point, the Beata Osanna Andreasi acts as a cor-
rective to the author of the work, Equicola himself, when he states that her
example leads to «pietatem et religionem non docta sed facta, non instituta
sed imbuta recte intuentibus videbatur qua humilitate, qua constantia, humanitate et facilitate homines sibi probos devinxerit» (*Oratio*, f. B1^r). Within the
ambience of the court Equicola wavered between two poles: the *donzelle*, the
unchaste ladies of Isabella d'Este and the virgin saint, Osanna Andreasi.

The composition of the *Oratio* could not be allowed to prevent him from
performing the duties that were required of him. The «moral crisis» had to
be pushed back into the realms of an unresolved intellectual debate since he
did not dare to contemplate the consequences of his actions on his moral
self, in any case, there was little he could do to change the situation.

---

[134]   *Marii Equicoli in Conservatione [sic] Divae Osanne Andreasiae Mantuanae Oratio
ad D. Isabellam Estensem Mantuae Principem*, c.1515, f. C7^r. See D.E. Rhodes, «A bibliography of Mantua», II, p. 165 no. 9.

For the moment, more immediate problems faced Equicola: he was accused of passing off certain poems of Sannazaro as his own. Only a little over eighteen months had gone by since the end of the scandal caused by Tebaldeo and it is probable that there was a connection between the two episodes.[135]

Federico Gonzaga, who was hostage at the court of the king of France, needed to be kept informed about the latest antics of the *donzelle*, so Equicola again took up this task, perhaps with renewed zest:

> In corte quel se fa è che le nostre donzelle hanno havuto un gran spasso nel ammazar di porci. Multo se sono affatigate in quel mestieri et con piacer.

Sometimes Equicola took his role to the point of absurdity:

> Io vo in scoffiocto di zennale negro con la berrecta roscia che me par di essere proprio un dio di amore.[136]

It might be said that at this point Equicola embodied the prevailing ethos of Isabella's court. There were other moments when Equicola attempted to reverse the education that Federico had so far received, by sounding a more moral and Christian note:

> Imita la Signoria Vostra proprio Dio al qual, sopra omni stato, humiltate exaltare sempre li piacque. Che altro è in noi doi se non simplicità (che costoro hanno tanto in abominatione questo nome)... Signor mio, le anime subito se seccano, l'arte presto si scopre, la simulatione longamente non pò durare.[137]

It was not long, however, before Equicola returned to the themes of «letitia» and love which were to be the ruling passions of the young prince.[138] Equicola assured Federico that love is necessary to a person's well-being but unfortunately he had been unable to follow his own advice. He was forced to interrupt his normal practices involving «lo amor», perhaps because he felt he was too old, or because he regretted his sins, or because he was influenced by

---

[135]   See Luzio-Renier, *La coltura*, pp. 411-12.

[136]   ASMN, AG, b. 2491, Mantua, 6 December 1515, Equicola to Federico Gonzaga.

[137]   ASMN, AG, b. 2491, Mantua, 12 December 1515, Equicola to Federico Gonzaga.

[138]   ASMN, AG, b. 2494, Mantua, 3 January 1516, Equicola to Federico Gonzaga:

> Piaccia a chi si voglia lo andar di Vostra Signoria in Francia, a mi me è et serà sempre molestissima l'absentia di quella perciò che in essa hormai in tutto depende la letitia de la corte... Prego et exhorto Vostra Signoria ad andare lietamente.

And in a letter dated 29 January 1516 he wrote:

> Et perché io non so medico et de la sanità non so dar precepti se non quelli che la experientia me ha insegnati, dico ad Vostra Signoria non esser magior medicina né più efficace medela ad far l'homo star sano et lieto che lo amor, perciò che il sangue sta unito et non pate corruptione et la mente, pensando alla amata, concepe letitia in sé, benché sempre li amati siano queruli.
> (ASMN, AG, b. 2494, Mantua, Equicola to Federico Gonzaga)

his own work on the Beata Osanna. By treading this new path Equicola did not find the desired happiness; he realized instead how much court life meant to him in spite of all the problems associated with it:

> Se io non havesse interlassato lo amor questa estate passata, so certissimo che non me seria malato. Ma, lassato il solito viagio, me trovai fora di strada in modo che anchora non so ben reducto alla publica et maestra.[139]

At this time, the activities which formed the substance of Equicola's life were largely fixed; one of his regular duties, the health of the Duke of Ferrara, took him outside Mantua. In February 1516 he was required to make this journey to report to Isabella d'Este on the Duke's illness.[140] Other duties took him farther afield: on the death of Ferdinand the Catholic, Isabella decided to send her own *oratore* to commiserate with the sister of the late king as part of her family duty. There were other matters Equicola would have to deal with during his stay in Naples (though of secondary importance in comparison to his principal task). Don Ferrante d'Aragona wished to obtain for one of his clients a post at the University of Pavia through Isabella's intercession.[141] As one might expect, Equicola was glad to find old friends and learned company. Without Isabella d'Este he became the centre of attention which left him in a state of rapture. He was someone recognized by lords and other humanists for his own talents:

> Se Vostra Signoria potesse imaginarse quel che hora io vedo, essa conosceria che cosa è essere adorata. Molta nobilità, molta magnanimità, multo valere et multa

---

[139]   ASMN, AG, b. 2494, Mantua, 29 January 1516, Equicola to Federico Gonzaga; cf. second letter quoted in n. 138.

[140]   Equicola simply gives his judgement on the present state of the Duke's health:

> Non bisogna più parlar né pensar di mandare medico alcuno.

(ASMN, AG, b. 1246, Ferrara, 2 February 1516, Equicola to Isabella d'Este).

[141]   Ho visto quanto Vostra Signoria mi scrive per una sua de 26 del passato in commendatione del Reverendo Maestro Apolonio, suo patre spirituale, perche 'l sii promosso in regente del studio di quello convento... In caso che quelli frati (prefato Maestro Apolonio è molto odiato da li altri frati di quello convento) non si potessino acquietare gli offerisce la lettura de Pavia vacata per la morte di Maestro Beda... Mandando Mario, mio preceptore, a condolermi con la Maestà Reginale de la morte del Re Catholico, gli ho commesso visiti Vostra Signoria in mio nome et circa il negotio de Maestro Appolonio, facci quanto la Signoria Vostra gli ordinarà con il Reverendo Vicario Generale, ultra quello che io gli scrivo. (Santoro, p. 81. See also ASMN, AG, b. 2996, libro 31, Mantua, 29 February 1516, Isabella d'Este to Don Ferrante d'Aragona).

On his way to Naples Equicola passed through Ferrara from where he wrote (b. 1246) to Isabella on 6 March 1516:

> Signora mia, sto a riva di Po ferrarese dove intendo gran cose di Tedeschi. Lo Signor Duca sta sano. Io arrivarò questa sera in Ravenna o vero lì vicino. Domani al mio viagio. Basoli le mani.

> excellentia in arme et consiglio è qui presente. Scrivendo io, tucti racomandano
> con loro parole et mia scrictura lo Signor Loys, presente portatore.[142]

The discomfort of an illness was not sufficient to depress Equicola in so buoyant a mood, indeed, it became almost a pleasurable experience due to the attentions that were showered upon him:

> Heri che fu sabato hebi poca febre, hogi so stato bene senza noia alcuna. Quel
> favore et careze che me son facte da tucti signori et gentilhomini io non potria
> scriverlo.[143]

His illness could not have been very serious since he intended to leave Naples on 1 April to undertake the rigours of the long journey back to Mantua. Once back in Mantua he did not stay there very long before he left once again to see the Duke of Ferrara, although this time the Duke was enjoying good health. For Equicola the visit was in the nature of a convalescence because Alfonso d'Este was not at Ferrara but taking pleasure in the countryside:

> Lo Illustrissimo Signor Duca sta sano et tutti stamo in tanti piaceri quanti se sono
> desiderati in queste parti, satisfaremo al'effecto per il quale semo in Marina. Pes-
> camo con delecto, ragionamo assai et di cose iocose, magnamo quanto basta,
> sempre aspectando la fame, dormino [sic] quelle hore che non si pò il corpo et
> l'animo nostro exercitarse in altro et tanto è il somno quanto lo mantenerci sani
> recercha. Cqui è una libertà degna di decembre antiquo, omni un dice quel vole,
> omni uno ascolta quel che vole. Ad suo arbitrio ciascun magna et beve, dorme
> et veglia, se affatiga et sta in ocio. Trovai lo Signor Illustrissimo ad Pomposa.
> Hogi, 13 del presente, semo in Magnavacca dove si starà tre o quactro dì. Poi tor-
> naremo in Ferrara.[144]

This must have made a welcome change from the pressures of travelling and diplomacy:

> Stamo qui in piaceri et io lietamente vivo, bene accarrezato; parlo, dico, ciarlo,
> ciancio.[145]

In that year, Equicola remained at Ferrara for an unusually long time. The Duke was reported to be seriously ill in the August of the same year and it was Equicola who from Ferrara alerted the Marchesa to the gravity of his condition: «in vero lo signore non sta bene et li medici murmurano.»[146] At Ferrara, Equicola played two roles, that of Isabella d'Este's official envoy to her brother and that of personal companion to the Duke. The intermingling of

---

[142]   ASMN, AG, b. 809, «In Napoli in tavola del Signor Marchese di Pescara XVII di Marzo 1516», Equicola to Isabella d'Este.

[143]   ASMN, AG, b. 809, Naples, 31 March 1516, Equicola to Isabella d'Este.

[144]   ASMN, AG, b. 1246, Magnavacca, 13 May 1516, Equicola to Isabella d'Este.

[145]   ASMN, AG, b. 1246, Magnavacca, 15 May 1516, Equicola to Isabella d'Este.

[146]   ASMN, AG, b. 1246, Ferrara, 3 August 1516, Equicola to Isabella d'Este.

these was essential to Equicola's effectiveness. It may be said that Equicola's
gifts, both social and courtly, were used to pursue Isabella's dynastic policies
where the personal became the political. So it is very difficult to determine at
what point «friendship» began and political design ended. In any case, it is
clear that Equicola took pride in both his roles; yet, there is a suggestion that
he was hankering after public recognition for his talents and that to be the
companion of princes was all very well as long as this role offered rewards on
a scale comparable to that offered by a more official position. To entertain
the prince was of crucial importance if one was to win his favour but it was
not so dignified a function as that carried out by high-ranking court officials.
Equicola is his own commentator on the dual position he held at the Ferrarese
court:

> Signora mia Illustrissima, martedì che furono xx del presente al Signor Duca si
> scoperse una febre, nectose il mecore, giove la hebe grandissima, venere stette così,
> sabato ne hebbe poca, domenica fo aggravato molto forte con febre grandissima
> et con inquietudine grande con somno excessivo in modo che fece qual che prima
> mai se è poi nectato sino alla venuta mia. Heri ad xx hore il medico lo trovò
> totalmente senza febre. Cenò da sano et alegramente. Questa nocte l'ha havuta
> quieta, se resvegliò alle sei hore, bevé un poco d'aqua et sino ad quest'hora che
> sono XI dorme benissimo. Et multo reposato me so levato et uscito di camera.
> Non me ha sentito et pense Vostra Signoria che dextro ocellino sono! Questo è
> il stato in che se trova prefato signore donde non si pò nè deve sperare altro che
> bene... Havendo fallita et lasciata la febre, retrovandose qui messer Antonio
> Pallavicino in sala grande di socto lo predecto signore si fece un bel pasto... Ad
> mi fo dato il capo de la tavola, come oratore di Vostra Signoria fui molto onorato
> con pacto che lassasse lo acto di cotanto officio subito finita la cena et fosse
> Mario simplice. Così mi levai di tavola alla torta per proveder al Signore de le cose
> necessarie alla nocte.[147]

---

[147] ASMN, AG, b. 1246, Ferrara, 29 August 1516, Equicola to Isabella d'Este. During his
stay in Ferrara Equicola did not forget his own interests, particularly his fishing for church
benefices through contacts in Rome:

> Signora mia unica, baso le mani ad Vostra Signoria de la gratia et favore che
> quella se è dignata farme con Sancta Maria in Portico [Bibbiena]. La certifico se
> di questo negocio mi svoluppo che mai più *spem emam pretio.*
> (ASMN, AG, b. 1246, 30 August 1516, Equicola to Isabella d'Este).

For the most part his letters from Ferrara are in the form of minute analyses of the Duke's
progress. He managed to maintain a steady stream of reports back to Mantua emphasizing his
efforts to cheer up the Duke. On the 30th of August he portrays himself as a court clown whose
aim is to divert the Duke and his brother:

> Lo Signor Cardinale è stato circa tre hore con Sua Signoria in varii et iocosi ragio-
> namenti; ha pur riso de alcune mie pazie. In Camera Marchesana dove dorme,
> poche persone vi entrano, che non li piace turba. Ma tucto'l mundo vene a diman-
> dare como sta et como è stato. Io spero per quanto me iudica lo animo et la sua
> cera bona che questa nocte non verrà cosa alcuna.

It would seem that the Duke was suffering continual relapses:

> Dio sa l'afflictione ho quando il vedo così. Sforzome di farlo star più leto che si
> pò et ciarlando diverterlo dal qualche melancolico pensiero.
> (ASMN, AG, b. 1246, 1 September 1516)

Equicola's ability to be funny and provoke laughter is of prime importance in any consideration of his character, particularly in the circumstances in which he found himself at Ferrara, having to keep the ailing Alfonso d'Este entertained:

> Da quel'hora (hogi alle XVII hore) in qua è stato bene et ha facto quel che mai havemo potuto da Sua Signoria impetrare, cioè che stia alegro. È stato alegro, ha tanto riso, ha tanto burlato meco che li altri induceva ad ridere.

All his time and energy were spent in this occupation except for the very occasional visit outside:

> La mia vita è questa: qualche volta disno col Signor Cardinale, la Signoria del quale me fa pur troppo careze. Il resto del dì et fino ad sei, septe et octo hore in camera del signor Duca ad dire parole, contare historie, fabule et ciancie. Quando Sua Signoria vole dormire, vo ad visitare, correndo, Signor Sigismundo [Cantelmo]. Et questo è raro, che non vi son stato se non doi volte.[148]

Equicola was himself the subject of a standing joke about his intention to return to Mantua, a joke likened to the Emperor's intention to come to Italy.[149] But Isabella did not think it so amusing. Throughout September she exhorted him to hurry back:

The extent of Isabella's commitment to her brother's health is demonstrated by Equicola's acknowledgement of the frequency of reports that will satisfy her:

> Illustrissima Madama mia. Ogni dì doi volte ho scricto et scriverò ad Vostra Signoria secundo 'l stare del'Illustrissimo Signor Duca. Non so se quella ha mie lettere.
> (ASMN, AG, b. 1246, 2 September 1516).

There are however moments of «intellectual confession» in the form of a reiteration of his links with Roman humanism:

> In Roma Phedra [Inghirami] è morto. Fo sepellito alli 5 di questo con gran mio dolore. So certo dole a Vostra Signoria che li era bon servidore et laudatore delle singulari vertù di quella.
> (ASMN, AG, b. 1246, Ferrara, 10 September 1516, Idem).

[148]   ASMN, AG, b. 1246, Ferrara, 3 September 1516, Equicola to Isabella d'Este and ASMN, AG, b. 1246, Ferrara, 16 September 1516, Equicola to Isabella d'Este.

[149]   Gran riso è stato in camera del Signor Illustrissimo de la comparatione facta del mio ritorno in Mantua con la venuta cesarea in Italia; furovi decte di belle sententie.
> (ASMN, AG, b. 1246, Ferrara, 17 September 1516, Equicola to Isabella d'Este).

There had been uncertainty about Equicola's departure going on for days:

> Del mio venire io non so che dire. Vorria che così me pare il devere et lo Signor Cardinale me consiglia che aspectasse finché si vede questa nova febre del Signor Duca como termina. Signora mia, creda Vostra Signoria che sto volentieri dove quella sta par ogni respecto et sappia che qui sto como Dio vole, bene del resto, ma mai mi parto del camera del Signore.

This letter of 11 September to Isabella was followed by another on the 13th:

> Aspecto resoluta resposta del mio venire che io non voria errare como feci già septe anni fa quando Vostra Signoria mi mandò a Bressello ad aspectare lo Signor Cardinale che tornava da Francia: Io aspectai tre dì et non venendo me ne venni in Mantua. Poi il Cardinale si trovò lì. Vostra Signoria me disse che devea aspectare. Aviseme dunque, di gratia, quando vole Vostra Signoria che me parta.

> Circa el venire vostro quanto più presto fosse tanto più ni seria caro, expettandovi
> con desiderio per ritrovarni qui, si pò dir, solitarie et stiamo como disperse senza
> voi.[150]

The sense of direction that Equicola imparted to Isabella's multifarious
activities rendered him indispensable to her. He seems to have become something like the *Marchesana's* other self. So it is not surprising that she did not
directly interfere with Equicola's business in Ferrara, at one point even assist-
ing him by providing a book that the Duke wished to read.[151] But Isabella's
impatience finally got the better of her:

> Vedemo che con queste vostre lettere ce andati allongando la venuta vostra
> d'hoggi in dimane, et siamo certe questa nostra vi atrovarà anchora a Ferrara, ma
> stati sicuro che noi, in questo mezo, non studiremo in altro se non in ritrovare
> qualche cosa per farvi o componere o studiare, tanto, poi che sereti ritornato, che
> vi ne crepareti.[152]

Equicola was also occupied in writing another book which had close connections with Isabella d'Este and her family: the *Genealogia de li Signori da
Este*, written in the last months of 1516. The frequency of his visits to the Duke
of Ferrara, especially in the August and September of 1516, must have strongly
influenced Equicola in his decision to write such a work. The *Genealogia* is
the literary monument which commemorates his service and loyalty to the
Estensi as well as being a work which would win recognition from the mem-

---

[150]   ASMN, AG, b. 2997, libro 33, Mantua, 3 September 1516, Isabella d'Este to Equicola.

[151]   Equicola wrote to Isabella d'Este:

> Semo stati hogi in varii ragionamenti con Sua Signoria, il medico et io, tra quali
> se è parlato di geomantia. Vorria che me fusse qui un libro per poter passar in
> quella pazie qualche hora. Così, per il Signor Illustrissimo, il medico et io pre-
> gamo Vostra Signoria che ne voglia gratia di imprestar il suo libro, che è in la
> grotta, di questa scientia, che serà sicuro et rehaveralo securamente.
> (ASMN, AG, b. 1246, Ferrara, 17 September 1516).

To which Isabella replied:

> Mario. Per servire el Signor Duca Illustrissimo et compiacere il medico et voi, vi
> mandiamo el nostro libro de geomantia.
> (ASMN, AG, b. 2997, libro 33, 22 September 1516).

[152]   Quoted in A. Luzio, *I precettori*, p. 44. Equicola finally returned to Mantua towards
the end of September:

> Illustrissima et Excellentissima Signora mia observandissima, essendo partito
> messer Mario al quale lassarà la cura del advisare la Excellentia Vostra del stare
> del Signor Duca. Per mio debito li significo Sua Excellentia andare de bene in
> meglio. Già sono octo dì che è senza febre.
> (ASMN, AG, b. 1246, Ferrara, 26 September 1516, Jo. Francesco Calcaneo to Isa-
> bella d'Este).

bers of the family with whom he was in closest contact.[153] The work is distinguished by its careful adherence to historical evidence in an attempt to prove the greatness of the Este without having recourse to legends and other similar types of material. He sets out to describe the achievements of each Estense ruler. Ercole I is the last Estense prince he treats in detail, listing his various noteworthy undertakings:

> Lo magnanimo principe applicando lo animo ad ampliare sua città, et religiosissimo, di religiosi templi ornarla. Excicò paludi et valli infertili da sterili redusse. Revocò l'uso de le antiche scene comice...   (*Genealogia*, p. 53)

*

[153] Cf. Santoro, pp. 152-55. Equicola writes in the *Genealogia* that he will not discuss Alfonso since he has already done so in another work: «non ne parlaremo havendo nel quarto libro di nostri *Comentarii* di lui et Hippolito, suo fratello Cardinale da Este, largamente ragionato». These *Comentarii* are not to be confused with the sections of the same name into which the *Chronica de Mantua* is divided. The *Comentarii* are also not to be identified with the *Annali* which are tightly chronological and do not allow room for an extended study of the Duke of Ferrara. In any case, the *Annali* go far beyond the year of Equicola's death so that one could never really be sure that our writer was the person who began the entries. The form of the *Annali* also militates against our acceptance of Equicola as their author: the strict sequence and the small amount of space allotted to each year would seem too disciplined for Equicola who preferred the looser structure provided by the *Comentarii* (cf. Santoro, pp. 164-67).

Different manuscripts of the *Genealogia* end at different dates because some copies have received quite long additions to the original text. For details see pp. 318-19.

(1)   Alpha F. 3. 11 (Ital. 162)
             Genealogia delli Signori da Este composta da Mario Equicola di Alveto nelli 1516 del mese di octobre (p. 1)

Notwithstanding the title this manuscript is continued in the same hand right up to the death of Alfonso d'Este and indeed beyond (there is a reference to the death of Alfonsino 18 August 1547).

(2)   Alpha W. 6. 28 (Ital. 265)
             Genealogia de Signori da Este
             «Finisce lo Estense composto da Mario Equicola et scritto da mi Fra' Paulo de Clerici Veronese Carmelitano de osservantia a dì XXII di febraro MDXXXVIII».
             No additions are made to Equicola's text.

(3)   Alpha G. 8. 29
             Idem, «Scritto in due dì nella medesima mala maniera di ortographia in che era scritto per non partirsi dalla antiquità. Fu cominciato a scrivere adì 26 di Iuglio. Fu finito adì 28 a hore sei 1554» (p. 432 old hand, ink; f. 53ʳ pencil).
             No additions.

(4)   Alpha P. 4. 19 (Ital. 482)
             Genealogia delli signori estensi, prencipi in Ferrara con breve trattato de loro preclari gesti composta da Mario Equicolo de Alveto dell'anno MDXVI (f. 1ʳ).

The manuscript ends with the section on Alfonso d'Este at the battle of Ravenna. Note also

> *Compendio di Mario Equicola in ord. alla Casa da Este, originale dell'autore e dal med. dedicato ad Isabella d'Este... li 6 Genn° 1513* (Archivio di Stato, Modena, Cancelleria ducale, Archivio per materie, Letterati, Equicola b.18.)
> Two other manuscripts of the work are to be found in the archive, one incomplete and the other copied in 1598).

Although Equicola boasted his connections with the Estensi he must have
felt disappointed that after eight years in Isabella's service he had not substantially improved his financial position. He may have envied Tolomeo
Spagnuoli, Francesco Gonzaga's first secretary, honoured with the name of
Gonzaga along with much wealth. For a person in Equicola's position, there
was a simple solution to this problem: the Church. This path would have been
facilitated by the fact that Equicola was not unknown to high-ranking papal
officials, including a number of cardinals. In order to press his claim more
forcefully Equicola enlisted the aid of the Marquis in his search for preferment. The Marquis wrote to Bibbiena to urge his continued support for his
wife's tutor:

> Messer Mario Equicolo, preceptore de la Illustrissima Madama mia consorte,
> m'ha fatto vedere una lettera che Vostra Signoria Reverendissima li scrive per la
> quale gli avisa come la Santità di Nostro Signore, per sua benignità, ha promesso
> di fargli dare lo primo officio che vacharà da VIII cento ducati in giù. De la quale
> cosa me sono allegrato summamente per lo amore grande che porto ad esso
> messer Mario et ne ringratio infinitamente la prefata Vostra Signoria Reveren-
> dissima, cognoscendo l'opera di quella essersi giovata in ciò molto. Et perché so
> esso messer Mario havere saviamente reposto ogni sua speranza in Vostra Signoria
> et so che la me ama et voluntieri me fa piacer, per il desiderio che ho del contento
> et utilità di messer Mario la prego quanto posso che la voglia tenire modo che la
> promessa di Nostro Signore habbi loco. Et se le paresse di cavare qualche ferma
> secureza, ne haverei piacere secondo che ne la ricercha anche la prefata Il-
> lustrissima Madama mia consorte. In suma di ciò che Vostra Signoria farà per
> beneficio del prefato messer Mario, la certifico che le restarò supremamente
> obligato. Et a lei me raccomando di core.[154]

The Marquis could no longer be disregarded as someone who had no bearing on Equicola's life if the latter wished to climb the social ladder: and the

---

[154]   ASMN, AG, b. 2924, libro 247, Mantua, 14 September 1516, Francesco Gonzaga to
Bibbiena. Bibbiena mentioned the matter in a letter of 7 February 1516 to Isabella d'Este (in
Epistolario, II, p. 64, letter 201: «Le cose di messer Mario mi sono alla memoria et Vostra
Excellentia ne lasci a me la cura che le condurrò al fine che egli desidera. Non rescrivo a lui,
per ciò che havendo desiderio di servirlo non ho voluto darli prima parole che effetti.»)
The Marquis had first approached Bibbiena in the January of the same year:

> Se pare che forsi troppo licentiosamente use la benignità de Sua Beatitudine et
> più che'l dover non recerca affatighe la humanità di Vostra Signoria, scusemi in
> questo lo piacere che ho in fare omni opera che Mario Equicolo, preceptore de
> la mia Illustrissima consorte, senta il mio favore esserli stato proficuo appresso
> Vostra Signoria ultra la sua servitù con quella. Et così la prego che in nelle cose
> de lo officio di esso Mario interpona sua auctorità con la Santità di Nostro
> Signore che sia satisfatto di quanto Vostra Signoria è pienamente informata. Et
> come fu principio et mezo in favorirlo con Sua Beatitudine, così sia lieto fine in
> farli conseguire la gratia li fu concessa, con ampliarla presto che diminuirla.
> (ASMN, AG, b. 2923, libro 242, Mantua, 15 January 1516, Francesco Gonzaga
> to Bibbiena).

tutor's need to improve his financial position made it imperative for him to reach some kind of understanding with the Marquis. It is no coincidence that at about this time Equicola began work on the *Chronica di Mantua* which he considered as a part-repayment of the debt he owed to the Gonzagas.

Equicola was still employed by Isabella d'Este and when she undertook a pilgrimage to Provence he naturally accompanied her. His knowledge and experience of France would have been seen as very useful on such a journey. Although the declared reason for the journey was Isabella's desire to fulfil a vow, there were undoubtedly other factors involved: her husband wanted her removed from the arena of Italian politics for a while (Milan had not been distant enough). Isabella herself, always eager to see the new, would not turn down the opportunity of such an interesting visit. Equicola's presence would furnish entertainment, erudition and a correspondent to provide Federico Gonzaga with news of the trip.[155] The last-mentioned task was by now a routine part of his duties; he knew precisely the kind of subject-matter that appealed to the future marquis and did not hesitate to use it whenever a suitable occasion arose.[156]

---

[155]   When the party was still in Mantuan territory Equicola wrote to Federico Gonzaga:

> Madama Illustrissima sta bene et la cavalcatura la porta benissimo. Li ragionamenti di questa matina sono stati in laude di Vostra Signoria.
> (ASMN, AG, b. 2496, Redondesco, 22 April 1517).

[156]   Equicola's skill as a letter-writer and his ability to know what pleases are recognized by the young Federico:

> Messer Mario mio, le lettere vostre giocose et piacevole mi hanno continuamente aportato gran piacere legendole. Perhò ve ne ringratio assai et l'officio che haveti fatto in scrivermi il viaggio mi è stato gratissimo et resto summamente gratificato da voi, di sorte che voglio essere debitor di farvi ogni gran piacere et pagarò anche il debito se'l mi accade l'occasione che vi possa fare piacere. A voi me offero tutto. Raccomandatime alla bona gratia di Madamma et salutati quelle donne et quelli gentilhomini.
> (ASMN, AG, b. 2924, libro 251, Mantua, 18 June 1517, Federico Gonzaga to Equicola).

The letters that Equicola wrote during the trip are indeed full of anecdotes and stress the pleasurable side of the journey. The humanist emphasized his roles as a joker, an entertainer, creating a particularly carefree atmosphere amongst members of the party: «io di tutto mi ioco et burlo, et da tutti so burlato» (quoted in Santoro, *Il viaggio*, p. 26). Equicola refers to himself as «allegro Mario» (*ibid.*, p. 28) in another letter to the future Marquis of Mantua. If Isabella's tutor was involved in creating a holiday mood and, at the same time, making himself acceptable to his companions, he nevertheless seems to have been aware of the possible political implications of the «pilgrimage»:

> Madama Illustrissima, mansueta et discreta, de li honori fattile tacitamente tra sè si gode, et più goderia se l'absenzia di Mantua et di Vostra Signoria (Federico Gonzaga) et del Signore Illustrissimo lo animo in queste parti non revocasse»
> (*ibid.*, p. 26).

The suggestion is that Isabella was worried about her absence from the sources of power, both present and future, and that honours did not fully compensate for her exclusion from Mantuan affairs.

Another important reason for the pilgrimage is that it allowed the *Marchesana* to break the journey at Casale where she was able to «inspect» her son Federico's future spouse. Isabella was pleased with Maria Paleologa and Equicola saw it as his task to portray her in a more attractive light than the *donzelle*, emphasizing qualities that would persuade Federico of the suitability of this girl as the future Marchioness of Mantua:

> La sposa di Vostra Signoria Illustrissima è molto arguta et viva di ingegno et spirito. Ha molto ben toccato alcuna di nostre donzelle.[157]

Equicola was free to absorb all the pleasures of their *gita* which appeared to be untroubled by serious political concerns:

> La matina a bona hora a cavallo; disnase un poco cioè Madama, noi altri assai. Poi si dorme sino alle XX hore, li altri dormeno, io sonnacchio. Alle XXI hore ciascun si trova in corte. Madama esce fuora, io ciarlo et dico parole per dieci ciaratani. Li altri iocano ad scacchi. Le donzelle si fan parte di lor frecare le carni crevate, parte cerca vedere li amanti, tra quali è primo messer Vicenzo de' Preti che ama Catherina di Ferrara et serve la Innocentia.[158]

Equicola did have one important task to perform after the return to Mantua: to compose the official history of the pilgrimage.[159] For him, the reason why Isabella undertook the journey is quite clear:

> Isabella Estensis in quam superi congessere tot naturae decora atque fortunae ornamenta ut morum integritate et animi altitudine est illustris sic clarissima in sanctitate atque religione excellit.[160]

---

[157]   ASMN, AG, b. 746, Casale, 2 May 1517, Equicola to Federico Gonzaga. Equicola described to him Isabella d'Este's meeting with the «bella sposina»:

> Madama la pigliò con tanto amore, con tanta tenereza, con tanta allegreza che ne li occhi et nel vulto si dimostrava la letitia evidentemente. (ASMN, AG, b. 746, 28 April 1517)

[158]   ASMN, AG, b. 746, Casale, 2 May 1517, Equicola to Federico Gonzaga. The letter is reproduced in the appendix to D. Santoro, *Il viaggio*, p. 25.

[159]   The only printed edition of this text so far located is to be found in Bergamo and is incomplete. See L. Chiodi, *Le cinquecentine della Biblioteca Civica «A. Mai» di Bergamo*, Bergamo, 1973, p. 129. There also exists a nineteenth-century copy made from the printed text which, since that time, has gone missing (Biblioteca Comunale, Mantua, mss Negri 1252). There is in neither case any indication of the printer or the date of publication. However, we can deduce from a letter (see below p. 194) that the work was probably printed in 1520 at the latest. See also S.D. Kolsky, «Further corrections and additions», pp. 311-12.

Santoro had originally intended to produce an edition of the work, basing it on the printed text but the poor state of the version he saw persuaded him against such an enterprise. The extremely low quality of the printing leads one to suspect that it was the same printer who was responsible for the *Chronica di Mantua* or for *Nec Spe Nec Metu*, since the same features can be noted in both texts: «è purtroppo da lamentarne la scorrezione: a prescindere dall'interpunzione, trasandata o cervellotica, dalle iniziali maiuscole messe lì a casaccio, da qualche sbaglio grossolano che salta subito agli occhi, s'incontrano a volta passi o periodi, di cui, se si afferra il senso, non è facile la esatta restituzione sintattica» (D. Santoro, *Il viaggio*, p. 7). Faced with these difficulties Santoro decided to produce a paraphrase which omitted most of Equicola's learned digressions.

[160]   *D. Isabellae Estensis Mantue Principis Iter in Narbonensem Galliam per Marium Aequicolam*, f. A1ᵛ. The work is dedicated to Ferrante Gonzaga, one of Isabella's sons.

We are asked to consider Isabella only as a devout and humble Christian; nothing else is allowed to interfere with this view of her. The visit to Casale is mentioned because it shows Isabella in a Christian light, welcoming her future daughter-in-law into the family.[161] But Equicola preferred to discuss the disputed locations of the places mentioned by classical authors. It was only in such debates in which Raffaele Maffei and Flavio Biondo had made their opinions known that Equicola could demonstrate his intellectual prowess.[162] For Equicola writing brought into play a number of elements that were increasingly difficult to accommodate in the round of his court activities. His learned digressions recalled a time entirely devoted to study, when scholarship needed no justification. Now, he had to try and reach a compromise between his thirst for knowledge for its own sake and the demand for the practical (in this case, the task of describing Isabella's pilgrimage in an ideologically acceptable way). At the same time, he needed to be tactful in his portrayal of the *Marchesana*: she had to be depicted as the empress she would liked to have been in reality. It is in such terms that Equicola described her triumphal entry into Marseilles, and her other successes.[163] Part of this por-

---

[161]   Isabella Mariam toto amplexata pectore mentem explere nequit tuendo... (Negri ms. p. 16)

The specific Christian connotations of the pilgrimage do not prevent Equicola from briefly mentioning other religions, as he had already done in the *De Religione*.

[162]   For example:

    Raphael Volaterranus vel nihi ab ipso Raymundo dissentit nisi Graias, Cottias et Poeninas putat easdem quibus Annibal et Hercules transmisere easque existimat montem Cinesium (*Iter*, f. C1^r).

Numerous other intellectuals are mentioned by Equicola, something that was perhaps intended to indicate his grasp of the subject including the «latest» discussions. Such figures as «Hermolaus Barbarus doctissimus» (f. Cz3^r), Filippo Beroaldo (f. D2^r) find their way into his pages.

    Equicola also mentions Lefèvre d'Etaples as having a special place in his intellectual formation:

    Legi que meus in mathematiciis et physiciis olim Lutetie Parisiorum praeceptor scripserit Jacobus Faber (*Iter*, B1^v).

There is occasionally an attempt at conveying the difficulties and excitement of the journey:

    Nos, igitur, ex Taurinis, ex Segusione per alpias accolas difficili itinere rudibus saxorum, molibus viam intersecantibus obsequitabamus (*Iter*, D1^v).

The «tourist» aspect of the trip is emphasized as when, for example, the group went to see the «musicum ingens organum» (f. HZz1^r) at Marseilles.

[163]   Equum conscendit Isabella. Nam sol tam altissimus, comitabatur universa civitas, nobilissimi ante ambulant. Rogabat hos Isabella ne dum ipsi honorandi excaederent modum, ipsa superbia notaretur... clamore nautico, tubarum clangore salutaret et fenestris pulcherrimarum aediumque novalia supra sunt cariophilorum atque aliorum bene olentium florum nymbus in Estensem discendebat... (*Iter*, Fz2^r-Fz2^v).

trayal included surrounding Isabella in an aura of learning, as if to indicate
that his pupil had received the full benefit of his instruction. Equicola's pride
in his erudition denotes a certain self-respect; he did not want to be totally
enslaved by the circumstances of his employment: and for him scholarship
provided a means of escape, and of relaxation. He was fortunate in being
allowed to concentrate his attention on literary matters almost without interruption in the year preceding Francesco Gonzaga's death.

It seems that Isabella d'Este had by this time been completely excluded
from the government of Mantua, as can be seen from an examination of her
copialettere for the year 1518 (where the pages are almost entirely filled with
letters relating to the acquisition of *objets d'art*). Equicola would not therefore
have had to spend a great deal of time on diplomatic missions. As far as we
can tell, he was called upon to act as Isabella's *oratore* on very few occasions
in 1518. On one occasion, he acted as Federico's and Isabella's intermediary
for the purpose of asking the Marquis to supply his eldest son with more
money. Unfortunately, the opportunity of speaking to Francesco Gonzaga
did not arise and he returned to Isabella without seeing him.[164] Another mission required Equicola to go to Gazzuolo on some unspecified business for
the Marchesa, and previous to that journey he had gone to Ferrara for reasons
that are not clear.[165] So he probably had the time to spare to work on various

---

[164]   Havendo nui mandato questa sera Mario nostro a Marmirolo per parlare al'Illustrissimo Signore, tuo patre, è ritornato hora, che sono 24 hore, et dice non gli
havere potuto parlare perché Sua Excellentia non si senteva bene. Et per quanto
dice Mario havere inteso da quelli de la corte sua, la notte passata et tutto hozi
è stato travagliato et molto lamentatosi de dolori de corpo.
(ASMN, AG, b. 2123, Porto, 21 May 1518, Isabella to Federico Gonzaga).

[165] ASMN, AG, b. 1813, Gazzuolo, 5 August 1518, Equicola to Isabella d'Este:
Ho havuta la informatione Vostra Signoria vederà per la allegata di bocca et di
stato del Signor Federico (da Bozzolo).

Equicola also narrates a journey to Ferrara in two letters to the *Marchesana*:

(i)   Signoria mia: Montai in barca carca di Thodeschi con doi marcelli de vino. Fui
sempre Signore; a mio arbitrio il tucto si disponea. Uscì fuora di barca verso
Follonica per servitio necessario. Subito hebi quattro alabardieri alla guardia
della persona. Domenica matina al far del dì smontai al boschecto, ivi factone far
da disnare. Stetti tucto il dì con gran piacere facendo del loco come se fosse stato
il Duca. Alli XXI hore pasate il Signor Duca venne et da la barca receputome con
voce et ni fui visto volentieri et con tanto riso di Sua Signoria quanto meritava
vedermi in cambisa et essere stato tucto 'l dì lì.
Sua Signoria sta bene. Menome in Ferrara et volendome Sua Signoria menare al
paro seco io repugnava perché non era imbasciatore pur fu facto quel honore al'
honore passato. Ho havuta la torre in mia potestà et tucte le scriture; questa nocte
ho dormito in camera di Sua Signoria [nel] boschecto et ho havuta bona licentia
di non compare ogni dì sino alle XX hore ché la matina voglio legere, el dì revedere
il legiuto. Heri visitai li signori, la signora regina et figliole et lo signor Infante,
la Signora Duchessa, madama Diana, madama Gratiosa et fui al mio signor

literary projects including the *Chronica di Mantua*. His most ambitious work, composed in this period, was perhaps the exhortation to Christian princes to make preparations for a crusade against the Turks. It consists of three *Suasoriae*, all of which urged the same thing: the recovery of the Christian holy places.

The work was to gain him access to the highest echelons of the ecclesiastical hierarchy. *Suasoria prima* is addressed to the Pope, Leo X, and to the Christian princes according to a second sub-heading. [166] The date that appears at the end of *Suasoria tertia*, «MDXIX Mense Iunio», coincides with the Pope's call for a general war against the Infidel which, in reality, was motivated by the political situation rather than by religious reasons. [167] The discourses can therefore be placed within the framework of a particular political strategy, though not completely, because the exhortation to a crusade had long been part of humanistic culture, from the early fifteenth century in

Sigismundo Cantelmo, il quale sta, Dio gratia, assai bene. Tucti se recomandano ad Vostra Signoria.

Lo Signor Duca manda a visitar lo Signor Marchese Illustrissimo et invitar qui. Ad Vostra Signoria me recomando.
(ASMN, AG, b. 1246, 15 June 1518).

(ii)   Illustrissima Signora: Ogni sera ho dormito col Signor Illustrissimo al boschecto. Heri sera tornai in Ferrara per essere ad bona hora al comminciato lavoro. Era l'alba quando il Signor Duca mi mandò a dimandare che subito mi trovasse al boschecto per la gionta dell'Illustrissimo signor Federico. Andai, trovai che erano socto la logia verso Ferrara. Subito el Signor Duca, poi facte le debite reverentie al mio Signore, mi chiamò et con tanta allegreza mi narrò il piacere havea havuto di questa venuta et né esso exprimerla né io saperemo. Tucto era gioia. Creda Vostra Signoria che quel modo di honorare che si può fare a Signore l'ha facto et fa. Arrivato in Ferrara lo ha allogiato in castello del modo et ornato che Vostra Signoria pò considerare sumptuosamente. Eravi parata la collatione con lecti bianchi che invitavano ad dormire chi non dormì mai. Poi si partì il Signor Duca, io restai, et dormendo li soi, Sua Signoria et io sempre ragionammo de diverse cose. Mai dormì né fece segno di voler dormire. Sonarno in questo le XI hore; queti queti, per no excitare li altri, andammo al Signor Duca, acto domestico. Il Signor Duca ci mostrò picture et ogni altra cosa pertinente ad piacere. Ordinammo la vita de hogi, la quale serà questa. Dirò prima quella parte che ne è stata adimpita. Desnamme bene et... poi vinnero li signori et visitarono lo signor Federico. Andammo ad dormire. Sua Signoria dorme, io scrivo et sono hore XVI. Alle XVIII andaremo da la duchessa. Alle XXI dalla regina et signor don Sigismundo [Este], alle XXII al boschecto dove se cenarà. Il Signor Duca ha facte mettere in ordine banche che vole commodamente Sua Signoria sia in revere ad desnare con cavalli che farà tirare. La sera che serà domani venere dice volere essere in Mantua. Io ci serò marte, che lune o marte mi partirò.
(17 June 1518, Ferrara. Equicola to Isabella d'Este).

[166]   The second *Suasoria* was dedicated to the Cardinal Egidio da Viterbo who was to be asked to lend his assistance to Equicola's attempts to gain an income from the Church. The title of the first *Suasoria* reads: «Leoni X. Pont. Opt. Max. Marius Aequicola» [f. A1ᵛ] and «Marii Aequicolae ad Leonem X Pont. Opt. Max. et Christianos principes suasoria in Turcas» [f. A2ʳ] are the recipients of the dedicatory letter and the exhortation respectively.

fact. And Equicola was composing his tracts within an identifiable tradition
which included many noteworthy practitioners such as Flavio Biondo.[168] It
cannot be denied that personal motives were probably not absent (church
benefices) in Equicola's decision to write the *Suasoriae*.

Equicola applies the philosophy of «opportunitas» to the crusade, stating
overtly that the right moment had come to launch such an enterprise.[169] The
qualities of leadership and the nature of the war to be undertaken are set out
in the clearest terms:

> Cum his enim non de vectigalibus sed de patria, non pro finibus sed pro dignitate
> Imperii, non pro sociis sed pro gloria, non pro libertate modo atque salute sed
> pro religione quae rebus omnibus anteponenda est et pro deo quo quod maius dici
> potest? Certamen ad quod non iure belli porta premia sed divina iniuria invitat,
> propellit, incitat.
> *(Suasoria prima*, f. A2ᵛ)

The theme of the crusade as an antidote to present anti-Christian tendencies
in Europe had been used by Equicola before in the *Apologia Pro Gallis*. It is
one of the poles to which the humanist was periodically attracted in his search
for a basic philosophy which would guide his existence.

Faced with the threat of the encroaching Turkish Empire, Leo X was transformed (in Equicola's imagination) into an energetic military leader and
popes of the preceding century were unfavourably compared with him:

> Sixtus IIII Tuscos Venetosque vexavit. Innocentius VIII contra Aragonios in
> Campania reges populos excitavit. Alexandrum Sextum suorum amor immodicus
> in rabiem dominandi vertit.
> *(Suasoria prima*, f. B3ᵛ).

This statement reinforces the general theme of returning to a Christian way
of life, representing a move towards harmony and peace away from discord
and internal strife, a message endlessly repeated in this period of extreme political disintegration. Leo X seemed a most unlikely candidate for the role: he
pursued the same political aims of papal aggrandizement as his predecessors
and was deeply interested in humanistic culture. Equicola nevertheless, single-
mindedly praises the Pope for thinking of launching a crusade, drawing parallels between Leo and other great leaders:

---

[168]   Kristeller writes in «Lay religious traditions and Florentine Platonism» (*Studies in
Renaissance Thought and Letters*, p. 112 n. 51) that «compositions in prose and verse against
the Turks represent a considerable body of literary production in the fifteenth and sixteenth
centuries that has never been listed, let alone studied. This is usually dismissed as empty rhetoric. Yet the defense against the Turks was a very real problem in that period...» Apart from the
threat posed by the Turks to trade and the political integrity of Christian Europe, in Equicola's
case, serious moral questions are raised in the *exhortationes*.

[169]   Quare, Pontifex optime, nihil magis hoc tempore convenire arbitror quam ea
dicendo prosequi quae tantae letitiae votoque tuo propria sunt. Testor quo in te,
iam, sentimus numen (*Suasoria prima*, f. A2ʳ).

> Tu, alter Josue, in sacrosanctam terram christianos deducturus more maiorum deum ante omnia placari manda supplicationes indixisti. Ieiunia imperasti ut victoriam non casuram neque interituram unquam consequamur. Tu Cyrus exulibus restitues Palestinam.
>
> (*Suasoria prima*, f. C4ʳ)

Not only is the pope urged to act, but the Italian princes are also told in no uncertain terms to re-think their priorities.[170] The expertise and readiness of the Italian states to participate is expressed by Equicola in the form of a list, made as impressive as possible for the occasion. Equicola points to princes who would make effective leaders of the expedition:

> In Italia aristocratia Venetorum que suis viribus suaque molestat exteris parere non dignabitur. Florentinorum democratia, Senensium et Lucensium tua estis. Alfonsus Estensis, Ferrariae Dux, sapientissimus magnanimitate re militaris scientia et consilio nulli inferior tuo volens se subiicet imperio. Francisco Gonzagae, Mantuae principi quis se audebit conferre? Qui non solum nostram memoriam virtute bellica superavit sed ter Italicae libertatis assertor antiquitati est quam proximus. Hic apostolice militie vexillifer (Confalonerius vulgo dicitur) arma omnium regeret ex dignitate si per valitudinem liceret. At filius nostri saeculi delitiae Federicus per patris vestigia tua sequetur auspicia sint hae induciae loco pacis firmissime tantisper.
>
> (*Suasoria prima*, f. D4ᵛ)

Suasoria prima ends on a note of exaltation, confusing Biblical and classical *exempla* to achieve an effect of emotional euphoria at the possibility of victory.[171] The second tract traces the rise of Islam and its propagation into the Christian world. The same themes reappear, treated in more depth: the struggles between Christian princes and the change in world-views brought about by a concern for personal luxury and wealth instead of truly Christian principles.[172] These criticisms were or were to be made by various writers who

---

[170]   Vosque, christiani principes, in quorum manu respublica nostra est a calamitatis huiusmodi formidine, vestra virtute liberate. Si res, iam atrox, non permovet, si iniuria quam insignem accaepimus, non tangit, excitet atque impellat religionis honor et christiani nomini dignitas (*Suasoria prima*, fs. C4ᵛ-D1ʳ).

[171]   Omnis illa ora summorum ingeniorum semper parens quae Platonas, Homeros, Aristoteles et Demosthenes genuit, quae Epaminundas, Pyrrhos, Alexandros, Themistocles peperit quae Christiani dogmatis lumina extulit. Et te nostro saeculo maxime Iane Lascaris si tantillum affulserit retinendae libertatis spei trucidatis hostibus e vinculo servitutis se eximet. Demergebatur Pharaon orabat Moses tuba canere sacerdotes iube, Iesus nave, nuit Hiericus. Gedeon cum misteriis ocurrit hosti, dedit ille religioni terga. Ezechias pro scuto et thorace induitur cilicio non galea caput ornat sed diras caesaque sunt Assyriorum octoginta milia (*Suasoria prima*, fs. E5ʳ-E5ᵛ).

[172]   Non hostis ullus rempublicam christianam perfundat sed illecebre, non Turca nobis sed delitiae minantur ruinam. Ocium quod prius beatas perdidit urbes Asiam nobis abstulit. Pro labore enim desidia, pro studio negligentia, pro continentia libido omnia immutarunt. In parandis avidius divitiis virile ingenium nobis effeminavit avaritia. In profundendis prodigalitas decus infamiamque iuxta habere docuit. Ad usus siquidem proprios immoderatosque sumptus plerique omnes illas trahunt, vexant, perdunt (*Suasoria secunda*, f. Bz2ʳ).

had set themselves the task of trying to explain why the Italian states succumb-
ed so easily to the French invasion of 1494.[173] In the *Suasoria prima* Equicola
had been principally concerned with the Italian princes, now he turns his attention to foreign rulers: François I, Henry VIII, Charles V, Manuel of Portugal, the kings of Hungary and Poland, praise of whom fills the greater part
of the *Suasoria secunda*.[174] The *Suasoria tertia* was dedicated to Ercole Gonzaga and it was addressed to the clergy in general. At this time Equicola was
interested in writing the history of the genre. It was to help place him in the
humanist tradition and associate him with established names. This tract, more
than the other two, perhaps reveals Equicola's intentions in writing the
Suasoriae. Although they should not be dismissed as mere exercises in the
writing of the *oratio* (one of Equicola's concerns was to outdo previous attempts in the genre by extending arguments and forms used before). Employing
this method, Equicola constructed what he considered a respectable literary
work.[175] But the whole of the text should not be dismissed because it appears
to be an excessively rhetorical exercise. It has other features which are worth
mentioning. The composition of such a work allowed him to take an un-
complicated stand on the problems confronting Europe. The call to a crusade
enabled him to leave the politics of a divided Christendom behind him; the
crusade was the cure for an ailing institution: «Egrotat christiana respublica
corpus morbo corruptum languet» (*Suasoria secunda*, f. Cz2r). Consequently, after using every rhetorical device he knew to make his point, Equicola had
to face the question as to why a crusade was needed in the first place.[176] He did

---

[173]   For example, Machiavelli in *Il Principe* (*Il Principe e Discorsi*, edited by S. Bertelli,
Milan, 1973, p. 62): «quando e' principi hanno pensato più alle delicatezze che alle arme, hanno perso lo stato loro.»

[174]   Tibi, EMANUEL Lusitanorum, rex inclyte, veniat in mentem tuos preclara in
Saracenos gesisse. Alphonsumque primum qui tui generis auctor est. Quinque
Saracenorum reges uno praelio superasse unde tibi quinque in scuto scutorum in-
signia refulgent. Succuratque Alphonsus avus tuus in Aphrica urbes expugnavit.
Non ignobiles satius sanctiusque atque laudabile magis ducimus iminenti succur-
rere periculo quam novum orbem conquireretur. Malo tua classis nostro coelo
Palestinae quatiat littora quam atlantico insultans mari tuus nauta extra equinoc-
tialem plagam naviget (*Suasoria secunda*, fs. Ez1r-Ez1v).

[175]   Frustra, igitur, (mea quidem sententia) ea videntur omnia quibus rhetorici libri
referti sunt. Nisi verba sensibus mentibusque hominum accommodentur talisque
sit ipse orator ut vitae dignitas rerumque usus et ipsa commendet Prudentia. Nec
Demosthenes semper voti compos et ali quando non persuasit Cicero. Mihi vero
cum eorum nihil adsit quae persuadendi fiduciam praestare possunt praeter
causam. Novum orationis genus de bello Turcis inferendo vobis afferre non ab re
visum est. Inusitata rei facies nihil vos perturbet (*Suasoria tertia*, f. A1r).

[176]   An imperatorum regum ve an pontificum clerique culpa acceptum sit, nec scio
nec si sciam ausim dicere (*Suasoria secunda*, f. B1v).

not avoid the problem and suggested a number of reasons, claiming, for instance, that the Christian nations had lost their fighting spirit (*Suasoria secunda*, f. Bz2r).

Equicola is specific in his charges against his contemporaries:

> Non est tantum, crede mihi, ab hostibus armatis, aetati nostrae, periculum quantum a circumfisis undique voluptatibus.   (*Suasoria secunda*, f. Bz2v)

Although this was written with a conviction that was seemingly heartfelt, Equicola must have been aware of the irony of his words. «Voluptas» was the philosophy by which the Mantuan court lived; and he himself was very much involved in those activities which went to make up the acceptable definition of pleasure. Equicola's attitude in the *Suasoriae* toward «voluptas» was conditioned by the fact that he had discovered another «philosophy» which can be opposed to it in the context of a call to arms. To the life of pleasure he opposes the soldier's life, giving the classical examples of Alexander the Great and Hannibal:

> Maluit (Alexander) tamen cunctis gentibus aperire quas natura longe summoverat terras periculoque suo atque incommodo terrarum orbem peragrare victoriis quam domi tutus vivere inglorius.   (*Suasoria secundus*, f. Cz1r-Cz1v).

It is interesting to note that when Equicola was called upon to go to the battlefield he responded with the greatest reluctance and found excuses, chiefly his age and condition to delay his departure. But he saw that there was a long way to go before the Italian states would take part in a crusade. The *Suasoriae* may be seen as the expression of Equicola's uneasy conscience (he had been seduced by the ideals of court society but remained dissatisfied). In an attempt to push this feeling aside he took up the call to a crusade with all the vigour his rhetorical skills allowed him.

After the death of Francesco Gonzaga Equicola's horizons were of necessity to shrink: he was to become increasingly involved in the day-to-day running of the Mantuan state and these universal questions may have had less importance for him. The Marquis' death set Equicola's career on a different course and he entered this new phase of his life with the greatest eagerness.

A secretary for two masters

By the time of the Marquis' death in 1519 Equicola had already completed the greater part of his *Chronica di Mantua*, a fact that seems to have been generally known, since a number of eminent writers and scholars asked to borrow it in order to have a factual base for their own works in praise of the dead Marquis:

> Marino Bezichemo, historico in l'una et l'altra litteratura eruditissimo, habia instantemente cercato haver il presente libro, como l'hebe per el mezo de Io. Iacovo Calandra, tuo secretario et de la tua Mantua castellano fidelissimo. Né men meco tacitamente mi glorio et godo che sì me inalze lo eminentissimo iudicio di F. Mattheo Bandello, il quale in la funebre oratione del tuo illustrissimo genitore non se è dedignato de la presente opera servirse in le paterne lodi.[1]

Equicola was evidently satisfied at the success of his *Chronica* even before its publication. Part of Equicola's satisfaction may have derived from the fact that the book was to be useful to a variety of people in the public sphere and was not merely a work of humanist erudition without any general application. The emphasis on the public nature of the *Chronica* becomes particularly apparent in the second preface to the work or, as Equicola prefers to call it, the «prohemio» to the fourth book of the «commentarii mantuani» into which the *Chronica* is divided (there are five altogether). The fourth book was the first to be dedicated to Federico Gonzaga and indeed it marks a break with what has gone before. The first preface was allowed to remain, dedicated as

---

[1] *Chronica*, f. T7ʳ-T7ᵛ. For the *Chronica see G.B. Intra, «Degli storici e dei cronisti mantovani», ASL*, 5 (1878) 409-10; D.E. Rhodes, «Mario Equicola's *Chronica di Mantua», Gutenberg Jahrbuch*, 1957, pp. 137-41, now in his *Studies in Early Italian Printing*, London, 1982, pp. 153-57; G. Pillinini, «La *Chronica di Mantua* di Mario Equicola e la sua posizione nella storiografia rinascimentale» in *Mantova e I Gonzaga*, pp. 145-50.

On Marino Becichemo see the entry by C.H. Clough in *DBI*, 7, Rome, 1965, pp. 511-15.

Castiglione was suitably impressed by the *Chronica*: «Pregovi facciate al Jovio, a messer Hieronimo da Vicenza [Girolamo Verità] et a messer Mario nostro la *Cronica Mantuana* del quale già ho cominciato a legere con molto piacere e quando l'haverò fornito scriverovi poi tutto il mio parere. Forsi che questa rottura di gamba sarà causa di farli fare qualche altro bel libro» (ASMN, Archivio Castiglioni, b. 23, Rome, 27 November 1521, Castiglione to Jacobo Calandra, f. 59ᵛ).

it was to the late Marquis.[2] The first three books, which form about two-thirds of the total work, are entirely devoted to events that took place before Francesco Gonzaga's birth and before Equicola's arrival in Mantua. Up to this point, the work can be described as a genuine attempt at historical reconstruction. Equicola had carefully examined the various histories of Mantua, compared them in order to discover any differences or errors and then arrived at his own conclusions.[3]

Although Equicola's study of the late Francesco Gonzaga may have started out with the best intentions, it would have been impossible for him to apply the same criteria and the same methods as he had done for the earlier Gonzagas. In any case, it would have been dangerous to criticize a ruling prince under any circumstances — a dead prince could not retaliate. To write a study of Francesco Gonzaga in a vein other than encomiastic would have been almost impossible, but in the shift of emphasis occasioned by the death of the Marquis, the «truthful» elements of his praise now took second place to the elements that glorify Francesco (obviously necessary since he was the father of Federico):

> Et benché la vera laude non possa star nascosta per haver naturale splendor sempre fulgido tra mortali. Pur noi con guida di docti, di lui così cominciaremo.
>
> (*Chronica*, f. T7ᵛ)

In the first preface to the work Equicola insisted on quite another point, though he did not by any means neglect the theme of «gloria». Equicola wanted to impress upon his reader something of the nature of history and historical writing and that (as Pliny had dictated) «la historia non dever passar li termini de la Verità»; in other words, the historian must not glorify his masters at the expense of historical «truth», nor be a mere tool in the hands of the ruler.[4] The sentiment is an excellent one, in theory, but put into practice

---

[2]   *Chronica*, f. A2ʳ-A4ᵛ (first preface); f. T6ʳ-T7ᵛ (second preface).

[3]   Pillinini, pp. 147-48. Equicola explains his method:

> Questa speranza me havea dato animo et ardire di congregare insieme quanto de la tua Mantua et de toi magiori mi soccorrea haver lecti in auctori probati (f. T7ʳ).

However, Equicola omits to mention the use he has made of chancellery documents which provide some of the original material to be found in the *Chronica*.

Interesting points are made by S. Jacomuzzi, «Un modello del principe rinascimentale: Francesco II Gonzaga nella *Chronica di Mantua* dell'Equicola» in *Miscellanea di studi in onore di Vittore Branca*, vol. III, tome II, Florence, 1983, pp. 701-15.

[4]   *Chronica*, A4ʳ. An earlier example of history in the form of «commentarii» and also having explicit ideological concerns is analysed by G. Ianziti, «The *Commentaries* of Giovanni Simonetta: History and propaganda in Sforza Milan (1450-1490)» in *Altro Polo. A Volume of Italian Renaissance Studies*, ed. by C. Condren and R. Pesman Cooper, University of Sydney,

only with difficulty. Equicola himself wished to find the middle path between excessive praise and the desire not to compromise the truth, and was fully aware of the problems facing him:

> La historia l'è actione veramente signorile et ogni altra (exceptione la poetica et cose sacre; con pace sia detto) haver non so che del servile, exposta ad altrui rechiesta et bisogno.[5]

He could not avoid paying homage to certain members of the Gonzaga clan in the *Chronica*:

> Pur in render gratie a questa inclyta cità dove con tua gratia per liberalità de la tua Magnificentissima consorte, donna Isabella de Este, commodamente vivo mi. Altro modo per satisfare a tanto obligo non me occore che scrivere.
>
> (*Chronica*, f. A3r)

That Equicola's ambition at that time was limited may be seen in the affirmation of his attachment to the *Marchesana* who could during the period of his employment as tutor provide Equicola with some material comforts but not with power. He was happy to exercise himself in the humanist discipline of writing history, to involve himself in questions of methodology and generally to give rein to his passion for learning. He combined this with the desire to acknowledge his debt to the Gonzagas and it was fortunate that the composition of the *Chronica* hinged upon an analysis of works already written so that it could be put together quickly:

> A mi il cui sangue anchora è in vigore et la età integra basta che la celerità me commende, reducendo in ordine quanto da diversi et varii scrittori mi parerà raccogliere et quello con verità exporre.[6]

1982, pp. 79-95 and id., «Storiografia come propaganda: Il caso dei *commentarii* rinascimentali», *Società e Storia*, 22 (1983) 909-18.

[5]   *Chronica*, f. A3r. Equicola emphasizes a further aspect of historiography:

> La historia da tutti universalmente commendata, con piacere se scrive et con delectatione si lege. Quivi varii eventi di Fortuna, tardi consegli, maturo exeguir, fugace opportunità, preveder subito, repentino assalire si vedono. Indi de la vivida Virtù la forza et exempi (che molto più che le parole moveno) imparamo.

In this first preface Equicola details the joy («piacere») of writing history: the results of this enthusiasm enable the reader to assimilate the lessons of history more easily. The excitement of history, as described here by Equicola, contrasts with the cold utilitarianism associated with the latter part of the work.

[6]   *Chronica*, f. A3v. Digression is a constant feature of Equicola's work and has been just as constantly attacked by his critics. The first digresssion appears on the very first page of the book. Equicola's immense, chaotic knowledge is continually breaking down the frameworks he sets up to organize it. A digression is summoned up often by an etymological reflex, a desire to explain the origin of a word or custom, as in the first instance, brief though it is:

> Erangli consegate stanze da habitare et campi da coltivare, dond'el nome Colonia è derivato (f. A5r).

There are more conspicuous examples, such as that concerning the custom of having a beard.

The method that Equicola claimed to follow is not only applicable to the *Chronica di Mantua*, indeed, it underlies most of his written works. The *Libro de natura de amore* is perhaps the clearest example of this method since it involves the impressively organized collection of a vast number of texts, examples and quotations rounded off with suitable conclusions, drawn by Equicola from the material. He did not regard his own contribution to be in any way the essential factor: he thought it sufficient to present his material in an orderly manner. However, Equicola did add his comments when he considered it necessary in both the *Libro* and the *Chronica*.[7]

It was not the first time that Equicola had tried his hand at historical works. He had already written, as we have seen, the *Genealogia de li signori da Este* and another work, now lost, in which he discussed Alfonso d'Este, the Duke of Ferrara, amongst others.[8] The similarities between the *Chronica* and the *Genealogia* are not hard to find. The fact that he bestowed upon the latter composition and the *Chronica* the identical title of «commentarii», suggests more than chance. The methodology of the *Genealogia* is also identical to that of the work on Mantua, since the latter is really no more than a disguised genealogical history of the Gonzagas, each of its sections acquiring its unity from the head of the Gonzaga family at the time in question.[9] The *Genealogia* on the other hand had been composed with the view to providing a strong theoretical basis (in the vernacular) for the family politics that Isabella d'Este had been developing in those years. The two works concerned with Estense family history may be considered as partly repaying the debt of gratitude he felt he owed Alfonso and Ippolito d'Este. The *Genealogia* was also the kind of work likely to appeal to Isabella d'Este (if she did not suggest the idea in the first place), especially when she was desperately seeking to entrench herself as a figure of some importance in the politics of the Italian peninsula. To be a member of a family which had a long history and could claim kinship with a number of other ruling families, and having this set down

---

[7] In the *Libro* he does choose, for example, a definition of love which appeals to him more than the others he has given:

> Et perché altrimenti diffinisce il physico, altrimenti il dialectico, altrimenti lo oratore, el poeta, noi alcune opinioni prima potremo, poi con breve et dilucida diffinitione come spero, la natura d'amore comprehenderemo (*Libro*, f. 77ᵛ).

If the second part of this twofold process often remains unrealized or not fully carried through, Equicola nonetheless shows an awareness of the various solutions to the same problem even if he himself is not always prepared to commit himself to one particular answer.

[8] See pp. 158-59 of the present volume.

[9] This is not strictly true with the sections that deal with Mantuan history before the arrival of the Gonzagas. These early pages, however, do no more than set the scene for the triumphal procession of Mantua's leading family.

in a documented history, was both useful and prestigious. At the time of writing the *Genealogia* Isabella's place in the government of Mantua was becoming increasingly less certain and gradually she was being excluded altogether. Hence the clear need to look elsewhere if her political authority was to be maintained. Equicola was always tied up in the manoeuvring involved in Isabella's politics. His works frequently indicate Isabella's political position at a particular time, because this was enmeshed with his own situation, in an intricate relationship between personal and state politics. (Not surprisingly, it was difficult to distinguish his personal motives from those of Isabella.) His decision to write the *Chronica di Mantua* can be seen as a vital turning-point for both.

For Isabella d'Este the *Chronica*, written by her tutor then her secretary and not a secretary of her husband's, was a mark of her willingness to re-enter the Mantuan political scene and to be considered a Gonzaga, perhaps in anticipation of her husband's death. There is no doubt that both parts of the *Chronica* met with Isabella's approval. She could now boast that the family into which she was born and that into which she married had received their brightest accolade under her direction. Although this view of the matter contains an element of truth it was not the whole story.

We have to consider whether Equicola would have had any other motives for writing a work such as the *Chronica*. As far as we know it is the only work that Equicola dedicated to the Marquis, Francesco Gonzaga. Until that time, most of the works Equicola had written at Ferrara and then at Mantua were dedicated to the *Marchesa*, or if not, were composed with her in mind. In this sense, Equicola could be said to have turned in a new direction and the part dedicated to the Marquis construed as an attempt to attract his attention. Although this gesture by no means implies that a dramatic break with the *Marchesana* was pending, it does suggest that Equicola was taking stock of his situation, that he was evaluating the success he had enjoyed in the service of Isabella d'Este. He certainly had won the friendship of powerful and important people: among them a man no less than the Duke of Ferrara. But could he point directly to the material gains he had won in her service? It does not seem so. After some ten years as Isabella's tutor all he had acquired was a certain renown as a man of learning. He now found himself in the difficult position of having to live up to his reputation without possessing the necessary resources or the likelihood of obtaining them while in her service, at least in her husband's lifetime. (Equicola was well aware of the limited extent of Isabella's power vis-à-vis Francesco and his administration.) He found he could not live on scholarship alone, having grown accustomed to the good life afforded by the courts and he felt the necessity of making an impression whatever the cost. Even when he hoped to obtain a relatively modest source of income from church benefices it was better to have the support of the

Marquis who numbered more contacts than Isabella, the most notable being his brother, Cardinal Sigismondo. Equicola had first applied to Francesco for help in this matter around 1516, and from that time on did not cease to request support for his advancement in the Church. The fact remained that even with an increase of income from ecclesiastical sources Equicola was merely the tutor of the Marquis' wife and nothing more. The *Chronica* seems to indicate that he was now becoming impatient for social success of the kind that would ensure that he, «Mario Equicola di Alveto» would be recognized as equal to other courtiers who had found a quicker route to wealth and power. He wished for fame in his own right and this meant enjoying a higher social standing than that given a tutor.

*

His chance (and Isabella's) came with the death of the Marquis in 1519. The *Marchesana's* fury, contained until that moment, was unleashed against all those who had previously stood in her way. Her most important victim was Francesco Gonzaga's first secretary, Tolomeo Spagnuoli, brother of the famous poet Battista. Even the name of Gonzaga which the Marquis had granted to his most powerful minister could not protect him. In order to avoid punishment from the vengeful Isabella, the former first secretary made a timely departure from Mantua, much to her annoyance. She could now try him only in his absence, and the inevitable condemnation had merely a symbolic value, contrary to her hope of crushing him with the full weight of the law.[10] After the removal of this last vestige of Francesco Gonzaga's rule Equicola was able to write to the Duke of Ferrara:

> Tucte le parti et factioni son estinte. Ognun se vive et lassa viver li altri, le facende le fanno a chi è data la cura.[11]

In practical terms, this meant that Isabella had taken complete control of the government and, as we have seen, unburdened the administration of anyone likely to object to her takeover. The fiction of Isabella d'Este had now become a reality, the goddess-figure created by admiring poets was now well and truly enthroned:

---

[10]   On Spagnuoli see S. Davari, *Della famiglia Spagnolo*, Mantua, 1873 and E. Bolisani, «Tolomeo Spagnoli, segretario alla corte dei Gonzaga, filologo ed umanista», *Atti dell' Istituto Veneto di Scienza, Lettere ed Arti*, 118 (1959-60), pp. 11-51.

[11]   ASMO, ASE, C, Ambasciatori: Mantova, b. 2, 30 July 1519, Equicola to Alfonso d'Este.

> Sia certa Vostra Signoria che a Madama Illustrissima se riferisce il tutto et senza sua saputa et consenso non si move foglia.[12]

If Isabella had what amounts to total power then Equicola's chances of advancement correspondingly improved. Indeed, he did not have to wait very long for the first change in his status: his appointment as Isabella d'Este's secretary.[13] Equicola did not merely exchange one title for another. The office of preceptor had been an appointment which Isabella had virtually invented for her own personal benefit in the realm of culture. It is true that Equicola's role had occasionally been extended to include a certain kind of diplomatic activity carried out on Isabella's behalf without much reference to the political activity of the Marquis (and the political situation in Mantua) except indirectly. The most outstanding feature of Equicola's employment in this area was the fact that it led him outside Mantua, and indeed involved a great deal of travelling over the entire peninsula. It is important to stress that, for the most part, Equicola's diplomatic skills were called on only when something urgent arose, something that gave cause for concern. Apart from teaching the *Marchesana* he was at other times free to indulge his interests, and the time spent on those fell into a rhythm against which he conducted his everyday life: «Però è necessario che hora l'ocio al negocio, hora a l'ocio il negocio succeda» (*Libro*, f. 283ᵛ).

With his new appointment that rhythm was maintained with increasing difficulty. The element of «il negocio» was rapidly attempting to exclude «l'ocio», at least in its previous form of extended periods of freedom from diplomatic business. Now, Equicola formed part (an important part) of the administrative machinery. Instead of playing the role of a free-wheeling diplomat he was to be confined almost entirely to the chancellery, periodically called upon to write up Isabella's *copialettere*, and to transmit letters to and from Isabella and various local officials as long as the *Mantovano* came under her jurisdiction.[14]

---

[12] ASMO, ASE, C, Ambasciatori: Mantova, b. 2, 21 March 1519, Equicola to Alfonso d'Este.

[13] ASMN, AG, b. 1197, «Da le mie casette da Marina», 25 May 1519, Alfonso to Isabella d'Este:

> Con mio grandissimo piacere ho inteso, per la lettera de XXII del presente di Vostra Signoria, ch'ella habbia eletto suo secretario messer Mario nostro. E tanto più mi piace tal elettione quando più intendo che sia stata con satisfattione dell'Illustrissimo Signor Marchese et di quelli altri signori. E confido che la vostra insieme con le lor Signorie n'habbia ad essere ogni dì più contenta perché, oltra ch'esso messer Mario è dottissimo et ben accorto, egli è ancho fidelissimo et amorevolissimo homo, come tutti sapemo.

[14] Of Isabella d'Este's *copialettere* libro 37 is practically all written in Equicola's hand. To judge by the early date of Equicola's first entry, the beginning of June 1519, Isabella

Perhaps the most vital task Equicola was required to perform, at least as Isabella considered it, was that of go-between, a messenger between herself and Federico Gonzaga, her eldest son and the new Marquis:

> El pensamento fu che me era necessario un secretario il quale fosse grato al Signor Marchese. Et così heri, retrovandome con questi signori, parlai di questo, proponendone alcuni et tra li altri Mario. Al Signor Marchese primo et alli altri piacque Mario et così lo ho fatto mio secretario.[15]

Equicola was not an automatic choice. In spite of the undeniable advantages he could offer, such as his good relationship with both Isabella and Federico, he was not in an unassailable position. To begin with, he was not yet a Mantuan citizen and it was only after his appointment as secretary that he was able to take out citizenship.[16] Opposition to Equicola's appointment would have come from the major Mantuan families who would have preferred to see one of their own members holding the position. (Isabella's previous secretary belonged to the prominent Capilupi family.) But Equicola's particular qualities had allowed him to «usurp» and hence to challenge the established order of things. The personal preference of the new Marquis had persuaded the *Marchesana* to appoint a «new man».

The new man's most important task was to ensure that Isabella and Federico acted in unison; this meant, in effect, that Federico's conduct had to be approved by the *Marchesana* who also did her utmost to make sure that it was she who made any major decision. In his correspondence with Alfonso d'Este, at the very beginning of Federico's reign, Equicola constantly referred to the relations between mother and son; we might say this theme forms a leitmotif in the letters to the Duke of Ferrara: «Lo Illustrissimo persevera in obedientia et reverentia solita con la Illustrissima.»[17] Given Equicola's concern about the situation, it does not seem unreasonable to suggest that with the verb «perseverare» Equicola expressed the precarious nature of the relation-

---

regarded this as one of the secretary's principal activities. Equicola probably did not share her opinion, not that his handwriting in these pages is particularly untidy but he seems to be playing a game in order to extract some amusement from a boring activity. Instead of his usual large, scrawling handwriting he writes in a very small hand so that he doubles the amount of letters other secretaries manage to fit into a page. Although his writting may have a neat appearance in these pages, on closer examination it is almost illegible. Equicola was also responsible for writting some of Isabella's own letters, those written from 3 July 1519 to 19 December 1519 are all in his hand. When he is employed by Federico he will only be required to write those *copialettere* which are kept when the Marquis is travelling. At Mantua there were a number of secretaries available whose handwriting betters Equicola's.

[15]   Quoted in A. Luzio, *I Precettori*, p. 46n.

[16]   For the decree granting Equicola Mantuan citizenship see Luzio-Renier, *La coltura*, pp. 74-5. He was granted citizenship on 17 October 1519.

[17]   ASMN, ASE, C, Ambasciatori: Mantova, b. 2, 30 July 1519, Equicola to Alfonso d'Este.

ship between mother and son, that Federico's behaviour was demanding a super-human effort of self-control on his part which could not be maintained for long. At this time Federico was still profuse in his professions of love and obedience to his mother, even going so far as to encourage her interest in his affairs:

> Mi è molto grato che Vostra Excellentia dica sempre il parere suo in tutte le cose mie, che sono anche sue, perché sempre come ubediente figliolo el sequirò.[18]

This generous sentiment was accompanied by the feeling, which grew stronger with time, that Mantua was his to be ruled by him in his own way:

> Aspectamo che ni scriviati spesso che ne reposaremo assai sopra li avisi vostri et fundaremo sopra essi li disegni nostri et come ni haveremo ad governare.[19]

It seems that at first Equicola was used by the *Marchesana* to convince Federico that his mother was best suited to take charge of affairs of state. Although she had a legal share in the government of Mantua, it was meant to last only until Federico attained the age of twenty-two.[20] Isabella was thus confronted with two problems, trying to ensure firstly, that it was she who effectively ruled Mantua in the prescribed period, and secondly, that she would still find herself in a position of power after 1522. An essential element in this strategy was Mario Equicola, whose relationship with the young prince took on another dimension, that of counsellor and mentor:

> Io, omni matina che non manca mai, mi trovo in camera quando se resveglia et prima che se vesta, ragiona meco de le occurrentie passate del dì preterito. Tutti vanno alla nostra via perché la via nostra è di amore, di conservare il stato et di administrare Iustitia. (Equicola's letter of 30 July 1519 to Alfonso d'Este quoted above at n.17)

In this way, Federico was learning his political lessons almost from the mouth of his mother. At this early stage all seemed set fair, especially for Equicola. Francesco Soderini wrote to him by way of congratulations:

---

[18]   ASMN, AG, b. 2926, libro 260, Gonzaga, 3 September 1519, Federico Gonzaga to Isabella d'Este.

[19]   ASMN, AG, b. 2963, libro 9, Mantua, 6 May 1519, Federico Gonzaga to Guglielmo Malaspina.

[20]   Equicola provides a neat summary of Francesco Gonzaga's will:

> De lo testamento questa è la summa: Madama Illustrissima, Signor Cardinale di Gonz[aga], Signor Ioan Gonz[aga], restano tutori et governatori del novo et gentil Signor Marchese Federico secundo sino che sia in età di anni XXII.
> (ASMO, ASE, C, Ambasciatori: Mantova, b. 2, 31 March 1519, Equicola to Alfonso d'Este).

Federico was born in 1500. The other co-regents were Francesco Gonzaga's brothers, the Cardinal Sigismondo and Giovanni, a *condottiere*.

Molto ci piace che vi troviate in bona gratia de li Illustrissimi matre et figliolo. Sappiatelo cognoscere e usarlo bene... et pigliate fructo di tanti vostri periculi et fatiche.[21]

This was precisely Equicola's intention: to profit from the present harmonious situation where he was regarded as secretary to both Federico and Isabella. While this state of affairs lasted there was no need to make a definitive choice as to whose secretary he really was, and so he could avoid the serious implications of a split between mother and son. Meanwhile he could enjoy the prestige of his new position. Instead of writing to the Duke of Ferrara in his old capacity as the representative of Isabella d'Este he now reported on what the Marquis was doing or the general political situation in Mantua. Equicola found himself much closer to the sources of power and all that was associated with it:

Lo Illustrissimo Signor Marchese se retrova in San Bene[decto] con molte donne, de le quali è capitania la Illustrissima Duchessa di Urbino giovene [Eleonora Gonzaga] et Madama Laura [Bentivoglio] del Signor Ioanni [Giovanni Gonzaga]... Vostra Signoria forsi dirà che ho poco da fare per consumare il tempo in scrivere queste ciancie, sappia che non me mancano facende, ma in tanto il mio piacer scriver a Vostra Signoria parendomi esser con quella che se non dubitasse fastidirla. Se Dio me guarda la gratia di Vostra Signoria che me è carissime che per ordinario li scriveria ogni dì un foglio.[22]

What remained unchanged was Equicola's and Isabella's alliance with the Duke:

Io me recommando ad quella disideroso sopra ogni altro desio che m'habia di poter far cosa che li sia grata e un dì poter demonstrar quanto et quale servitore li so.[23]

In this first year of Federico's reign, Equicola remained (with certain important modifications) Isabella's man, but already Federico seemed to have it in his mind to buy over his mother's trusted agent.

In the July of 1519 Equicola was jubilant about Federico's concession to him of a sinecure worth a hundred and twenty ducats. His jubilation was due not so much to the office itself but to the fact that Federico gave it to him «spontaneamente».[24] Equicola's sensibility was touched: but until the young

---

[21]   ASMN, AG, b. 864, 19 September 1519, Francesco Soderini to Equicola.

[22]   ASMO, ASE, C, Ambasciatori: Mantova, b. 2, Porto, 18 September 1519, Equicola to Alfonso d'Este.

[23]   ASMO, ASE, C, Ambasciatori: Mantova, b. 2, 21 November 1519, Equicola to Alfonso d'Este.

[24]   Luzio-Renier, *La coltura*, p. 74, n. 4. The official document containing Equicola's appointment is to be found in ASMN, AG, Libro delle Patenti, n. 5 (1518-1524), Mantua, 16 July 1519, f. 378^r.

Marquis could take full control of the treasury he would not be able to be as generous to Equicola as he might have wished. Temporarily then, Equicola needed to look elsewhere if he was to consolidate his position in Mantuan society. He may indeed have preferred to find other ways to increase his wealth, a wealth which would serve as the foundation of his new social standing at court. Although the downfall of Tolomeo Spagnuoli marked Equicola's entry into Mantuan politics proper, his example was a warning to all those «new men» who did not have the support of powerful noble families. Equicola was in a position to accept offers from a number of quarters.

We have already seen Equicola's efforts to obtain an ecclesiastical office, both through the intervention of Francesco Gonzaga and cardinals friendly to the Gonzagas or to Equicola personally. The composition of the *Suasoriae* on the subject of the crusade may be seen as a different approach to the same problem. The *Suasoriae* were an attempt to win over the more literary-minded cardinals by appealing to a theme that was particularly dear to Leo X in the early years of his papacy.[25] From this point of view the *Suasoriae* achieved their goal: at the highest level the Pope himself expressed his approval of the work.[26] The Mantuan ambassador in Rome, Alessandro Gabbioneta, acted as Equicola's literary agent for this work in that he informed the secretary of the opinions expressed by eminent men of the Church on the *Suasoriae*, including Equicola's «friend» of old from Rome, Bernardino Capella:

> Messer Mario mio honorando, el reverendo Saliceto, cuius nota est eruditio, non pò satiarsi de legere le tre *Suasorie*, quas elegantissimas apellat, Capella quasi pre dulcedine lachrimat, ma dice: «Io pigliarò questo Mario un dì pe' li capelli che se doveria vergognare che ogne chivelli vega le cose sue per farle stampare.» ...Io voglio fare veddere alla Santità de Nostro Signore, secundo ve ho scritto per un'altra mia, queste vostre *Suasorie* elegantissime, poi vi avisarò. Sapeti ben dove è lo Archidiacono vostro, che cessa in lui ogni respetto in magnificar el nome vostro et che de quella prima non haveti el più amorevole fratello di me.[27]

We can see that the Archdeacon was doing his utmost to prepare the way for Equicola to attain to high church offices. However, it seems that the first move in this direction was not inspired by a concrete appreciation of the work itself but by the sympathy of an old acquaintance of his early days in Rome, Bernar-

[25] See C. Vasoli, «Temi mistici alla fine del Quattrocento» in *Studi sulla cultura del Rinascimento*, Manduria, 1968, pp. 225-6, 230, 233 n. 103.

[26] The Pope's expression of pleasure at the work is quoted by A. Luzio, *Federigo Gonzaga ostaggio*, Rome, 1887, p. 72.

[27] ASMN, AG, b. 864, Rome, 20 July 1519, Alessandro Gabbioneta to Equicola.

dino Capella. Again, it was the Archdeacon who informed Equicola of the development:

> Messer Mario mio charo, multa restant scribenda che reservo ad una altra volta, ma questo non tacerò. A me pareria che scrivestovi al Capella et talmente intertenervi cum esso che tuti facessemo opera vi renuntiasse el canonicato de San Petro aut farvi suo coadiutore perché lui è fato multo vechio et declinato asai, ita che pocho ge ne resta. Se questa cosa vi reusisse seria altra cosa che 'l Vescovato di Sora, poi ne poterestovi uscirne cum grandissimo utile vostro et non partirvi dalla servitù de Madamma Illustrissima, che quando havesse ad esser altrimenti non vi lo scriveria... Pensati che vi iuro per corpus Christi che mai me ha parlato tanto teneramente quanto ha fato questa ultima volta. A vui tuto mi dono, offero et mo so stracho et voglio andar a lecto.[28]

In his search for preferment Equicola was prepared to go to desperate lengths. The Archdeacon refers to Equicola's efforts to obtain the bishopric of Sora which, according to Gabbioneta, might have meant leaving the service of the Gonzagas. That Equicola was contemplating leaving Isabella d'Este at a time when his star was in the ascendant seems, at first sight, extraordinary. It may have been precisely because of his new post that Equicola was seeking an easier way to achieve financial security. The position of secretary carried a great burden of responsibility; and its onerous duties were not greatly rewarded. A career in the Church might have appeared more secure and more promising, financially and socially, than did the difficult and precarious one which committed him to the service of two masters.[29] The Church may have allowed him to pursue his own interests as he had done before, and may have enabled him to enjoy the best of both worlds.

At about the same time, probably with the intention of making his position more secure, Equicola embarked on somewhat intricate negotiations for the return of some of his possessions in Alvito, hoping to add to them if possible and entrusted them primarily to Jacopo Perillo and their mutual acquaintances in Naples.[30] Even before Francesco Gonzaga's death Equicola

---

[28] ASMN, AG, b. 864, Rome, 30 June 1519, Gabbioneta to Equicola. The passage quoted occurs in the post-script to the letter given by V. Cian, «Recensione a D. Gnoli», *GSLI*, 19 (1892) 155-56. Cian does not include the passage in question in his publication.

A careful examination of the *Censuali* (BAV, Capitolo di S. Pietro, Arm. 41-42, nos. 27, 28, 30, 31) did not reveal that Equicola took Capella's position. The latter's name appears for the last time in the list of payments to the canons in August 1524 but is not replaced by Equicola's (n. 31, f. 190^r, 191^v, 193^r, 194^v). Nor does the secretary's name appear in the next register (n. 32). It may be that other influences were at work which deprived Equicola of his canonicate or that he was not far from death himself when Capella died.

[29] Cf. C. Dionisotti, «Chierici e laici» in *Geografia e storia della letteratura italiana*, Turin, 1967, pp. 47-73.

[30] Isabella d'Estte had been in correspondence with Perillo since 1518:

> Anchora che de Mario Equicolo, nostro preceptor, vostre virtù più volte ni siano state repetite et la ingegno vostro per sublime lodato, al che habbiamo dato plena

had been urging negotiations for the recovery of his possessions. Perillo affirmed that he would take the matter in hand:

> De lo negocio vostro lassa lo pensiere a me et a lo Sanazaro tuo, quale certamente ti ama et venera. Et heri venne lui a trovarme per ragionare de la cosa tua.[31]

The affair progressed to the verge of a successful conclusion. We are reminded of the analogous situation in which Sigismondo Cantelmo found himself years earlier. However, Equicola was in a much stronger position since he was not asking for the restitution of an entire duchy. He had already been granted an «auctentica privilegia» in May 1518 but this document had not proved very useful and so accounts for the renewed activity by Equicola and his friends.[32] So the business remained temporarily unresolved, Equicola's pursuit of wealth and status suffering a slight set-back.[33]

*

credenza, non di meno la longa et dilettevole lettera vostra, da noi più di due volte letta, ni ha talmente confirmato quello che per el dire di Mario eravamo chiare, che siamo constrette ad tenervi nel numero de più cari et rari amici che habbiamo. (ASMN, AG, b. 2997, libro 35, «In lo nostro Diporto», 12 July 1518, Isabella d'Este to Perillo).

Equicola himself appears to have ruthlessly exploited Perillo who, in his turn, was hoping for some reward for his services. Perillo had successfully managed to carry out Equicola's wishes in the matter of the «privilegio autenticato» as well as other, less important, business («ve ho mandato la midaglia del Pontano», ASMN, AG, b. 1895, 6 May [1518], Naples, Jacobo Perillo to Equicola, f. 465^r). Perillo seems to have been desperate for Equicola's patronage but the latter was totally unsympathetic:

> ve ho scritto de una mia operetta che scrivo in vostro honore et de quessa Illustrissima nostra patrona et voi non ve site degnato respondere a nessuna di queste lettere. Perhò io non me extendo in altro se non in recordareve che io sempre serò tuo o vogliate o no (ibid.).

Perillo's pleas fell on deaf ears, for probably in the same year he wrote to Isabella d'Este directly informing her of his situation:

> ho pregato messer Mario che a conveniente tempo ragione a Vostra Illustrissima Signoria ove mi balestra la fortuna.
> (ASMN, AG, b. 1895, 16 November [1518?], Naples, f.478^r).

Equicola, in all probability, had not bothered to tell the *Marchesana* of Perillo's desperate plight («ricorro et imploro qualche aita ale miserie mie» *ibid.*).

[31]   ASMN, AG, b. 809, Naples, 31 January 1519, Perillo to Equicola. «Lo Sanazaro» should be identified with the poet Jacopo Sanazzaro.

[32]   Santoro, pp. 297-99.

[33]   ASMN, AG, b. 809, «In Pizzuolo», 28 May 1519, Perillo to Equicola:

> Maravegliomi che Vostra Signoria non me avisa se have receputo lo transunto del privilegio quale io fice fare con tutte quelle sollennitati che li dottori me consegliaro... Lo privilegio lo donai in mano de notare Antonio Branca de Alveto perché lui me lo domandò et Vostra Signoria me lo scrisse... et perché in lo privilegio

In spite of his increased duties Equicola found time for other matters. His interest in contemporary literature had not waned: the Mantuan ambassador to Venice sent him a copy of Poliziano's works;[34] he found time to read Vida's poem, the *Bombyx*, and seconded Isabella d'Este's wish to see the work in print.[35] The merits of his other activities have been questioned by his earlier

---

        vostro antiquo non si fa mencione di assenso et dice che la Palumbara rende non so che ogni anno a lo Signore de Alveto, io non lo ho voluto far comparere perché in lo privilegio che ho fatto expedire io, non lo fo soggietto di nullo annuo rendito, fortasse tacitamente ne lo levarimo... perché ce è più necessario lo assenso che'l privilegio, atteso che ogni novo Signore che fosse in Olvito et lo Signor Vicerè, anchora quando mutasse voluntà, ve la poria togliere non comparendoce lo assenso regio... Magister venne in Pizzuolo a trovarme et parlandome da parte di Vostra Signoria che volesse ottenere lo che scriviti dal Signor Marchese di Pescara... Lo officio di Teramo et di Solmone non ce è speranza perché sono officii reggii et non si ponno havere senza provisione del Re Catholico, perché lo Signor Vicerè non pò expedire come facea, atteso che in ogni minima cosa venono cento provisioni da la corte. Perhò mi ingegnarò di expedire con lo Signor Marchese sì de la remissione come de alcuno officio.

        Messer Pier Gravina è in Aversa. Subito che serò in Napoli, el che serà fra otto giorni, andarò ad Aversa et li parlarò di quel che me scrive Vostra Signoria et ve avisarò del tutto... Lo Sanazaro ve se recomanda, simelmente a messer Baldassar [Castiglione].

Besides all the problems involved in legally possessing territory in Alvito Equicola's pretensions went much further: his ambition was to be appointed to various offices in the region. He was no longer satisfied with his allotted share of wealth and favour. He wanted more, almost to prove himself worthy of greater rank than he actually had. The negotiations continued without their end ever appearing in sight. More allies were called upon to plead Equicola's case:

        Per questo voglio che le donne anchora vi favorescano. La Signora Contessa di Terranova insieme con la Signora Vicereina et altre signore domandaranno questa gratia al Signor Vicerè. Spero che a tante signore si vergognarà di negarla. Le donne son blande et pertinaci; vogliono per ogni modo vencere.

        (ASMN, AG, b. 809, Naples, 17 November 1519, Perillo to Equicola).

[34]   Finalmente, cum grandissima fatica, ho habutto l'opere dil Polliciano corette et ve le mando.

(ASMN, AG, b. 1454, Venice, 23 November 1519, Giovan Battista Malatesta to Equicola).

[35]   Luzio-Renier, *La coltura*, pp. 240-46. Other men of letters had been in contact with Equicola. Lelio Manfredi, the translator of *Tirant lo Blanc* into Italian, was in regular contact with him; Pietro Bembo announced his imminent arrival in Mantua to the «Magnifico messer Mario Equicolo quanto fratello honorando»: «Questa sera serò in Mantoa per nome di Nostro Signore, mandato da Sua Santità a quello Illustrissimo Marchese. Piacciavi farlo intendere a Sua Excellentia.» (ASMN, AG, b. 2498, Governo, 22 June 1519); Girolamo Cittadino wrote to Equicola to ask him for a copy of Castiglione's *Cortegiano* which he believed to be finished (see C. Dionisotti, «Recensione a *Un illustre nunzio pontificio*», p. 37). Grossino, the Mantuan ambassador to Milan, did not turn to Equicola for information on this matter, but to the Marquis himself who could be expected to act with more authority:

        Monsignor Delischu, che al present per tuta la corte hè dimandato Monsignor il Mersial de Fois,* me ha ditto voglia schriver in nome suo alla Signoria Vostra, pregando quella li voglia fare uno don de uno libro de queli ha conposto il

---

*   «il Mersial de Fois» is Odet de Fois known as Lautrec, Marshall of France, for whom see, *ad vocem*, *Nouvelle Biographie Générale*, 29, Paris, 1859, pp. 952-53.

interpreters, particularly Luzio. He acted as a go-between for the Marquis of Pescara and Sigismondo Cantelmo in their illicit love-affairs.[36] In both cases, Equicola acted in the same way and was regarded as the most suitable person to carry messages to the beloved, being in each case probably one of Isabella's *donzelle*. Sigismondo Cantelmo exhorted Equicola to perform his duties properly in this matter:

> Da Roma scrissi a Madama, mia matre, et a voi una littera con una inclusa alla signora B. Non so se l'habiate havuta et che cosa ne sia successo. Hora ve ne mando un'altra et ve prego a darla con bona gratia invisibilmente con qualche amorosa paroletta et non vi sia grave far tanta fatica per me che son paratissimo farne altrotanta et maggior per voi. In parte de remunerarve, per il primo adviso ve mandarò una bella elegia che mi è stata mandata da Roma.[37]

Cantelmo's passion for his Lady did not seem to abate: «ve ho scritto de molte littere sempre con una inclusa alla mia Dea.»[38] He was still suffering the consequences of his exile and the loss of his duchy. He could not accept the idea that he would never recover his lost territories; hence we find him away from Ferrara, perhaps seeking support from the Medici.[39] In spite of the changes in his material condition, he never allowed himself to forget he was a Cantelmo, and consequently seems to have been unceasingly tormented by his situation. Equicola served as a reminder of Sigismondo's father and of the fact that the Cantelmo family had one remaining loyal servant who, although he had left their immediate service, had not changed his personal feelings towards them. For Cantelmo Equicola represented one of the last points of reference in a world gone awry.[40] Similarly, Cantelmo's death was to dissipate

---

> Magnifico messer Baldesar da Castiglione ditto *Il Cortesano*, parlando di Sua Maestà mollto honoratament et de le virtù sue et conosute. Hesendove il Marchese Febus [Gonzaga] a questo ragionament, laudò la persona e il libro assai conposto per Sua Magnificencia, dil che Monsignor lo Mersial è in gran desiderio de averne uno et quanto non lo potese haver stanpato gie ne facese schriver uno. Io li dissi che non chredea fuseno stanpati.
> (ASMN, AG, b. 1646, 22 November 1520, Grossino to Federico Gonzaga).

[36]   For the Marquis of Pescara's affair see A. Luzio, «Vittoria Colonna», pp. 3-7.

[37]   ASMN, AG, b. 1107, Florence, 3 June 1519, Sigismondo Cantelmo to Equicola.

[38]   ASMN, AG, b. 1107, Florence, 18 June 1519, Sigismondo Cantelmo to Equicola.

[39]   «Io sono in Firenze et vi starò forsi questo mese tutto apresso al Reverendissimo Medici [Giulio de' Medici]» (see note 38).

[40]   Sigismondo Cantelmo congratulated Equicola on his new appointment:

> Sommamente mi ralegro della grande autorità vostra et più che vui reputiate parte del'obligo da casa mia che tanto più in ogni evento mi serete amorevole. Mi dole non essere in Milano poi che là potria, secondo dite, farvi servitio.
> (ASMN, AG, b. 1107, Florence, 27 August 1519).

any remaining feelings of feudal loyalty that may have affected Equicola's behaviour in his last years.

*

1519 was a year of great changes and high expectations. Equicola was fortunate that for him it did not end disastrously. In June 1519 he was set to fight a duel with Rinaldo Ariosto for reasons that have, so far, remained obscure. The Duke of Ferrara was particularly concerned because of the disturbance such a contest would inevitably cause in the city. Alfonso d'Este feared the worst: it appeared impossible to reconcile the two enemies «perché la lor querela è di tanta importanza»; if one killed the other the dead man's allies would have wreaked their vengeance. Although Rinaldo was a member of a powerful Ferrarese family, the Duke did not consider Equicola to be inferior to him.[41] But the Duke's prayers (and perhaps Equicola's) were answered when Rinaldo Ariosto died the following month.[42] The secretary did not feel

---

[41] Havemo da far opra che per niente messer Raynaldo Areosto e messer Mario Equicolo, nostri carissimi, vengano insieme a singular battaglia. Perché per le moltissime amicitie che hanno l'uno et l'altro, saria facile e pericolosissima cosa che per lor amore molti altri nostri gentilhomini e subditi pigliasseno materia di duello, il che non potrebbe succedere senza nostra gravezza e grandissimo danno del stato et populi nostri, oltra che, se la sorte volesse che uno de essi o tutti dui morissono nel steccato, sarebbe gravissima iactura. E perché la lor querela è di tanta importanza che'l conciliarli insieme potrebbe esser difficile et maxime così presto, a me parrebbe che, non possendoli placare in un tratto per meglio haver tempo da trattar lo accordio, vedessimo d'inducerli a prorogar il termine statuito al lor duello e che non combattesseno fin che non fusse fatta la santa impresa contra infedeli, perché ambidui potranno mostrare il lor valore in defensione e augumento di nostra fede et intertanto passarà questa lor furia e non staranno poi sì duri. Vostra Signoria sia contenta acceptare il tutto da me detto e proposto in bona parte et a buon fine et avisarmi del suo buon volere perché, essendo sì breve il termine deputato, non bisogna perdere tempo a praticare di redurre la cosa al sopradetto effetto e perché l'honore et util nostro et di molt'altri deve preponderare a quello di dui soli nostri subditi. Quando pur li sopradetti messer Raynaldo e messer Mario fussero renitenti e obstinati contra'l voler nostro, potressimo noi prima che giungesse il giorno prescripto al lor certame farli rinchiudere in parte che non potessino comparere.
(ASMN, AG, b. 1197, Ferrara, 14 June 1519, Alfonso d'Este to Federico Gonzaga).

[42] The Duke of Ferrara informed Equicola of his adversary's death on 8 July (ASMN, AG, b. 1197):

> Heri, fu sepulto il nostro messer Raynaldo Areosto, che è morto in quattro giorni dopo che è tornato da li bagni. E benché ordinariamente quelli che hanno differentie da diffinire con duello se sogliono allegrare se l'adversario more, credo che voi farete il contrario perché so che amavate lo adversario vostro.

Equicola's reply to the Duke's letter may, at first sight, appear to reject the appeal for moderation in his joy at his adversary's death, yet, his expressions of «grief» over the death of people who have been quite close to him are not very different:

> Restemo colli vivi. Ad messer Renaldo bone memorie Dio dia pace et a noi longha et leta vita.

(ASMO, ASE, C, Ambasciatori: Mantova, b. 2, 12 July 1519).

impelled to leave the courts of Mantua and Ferrara, being relieved of the burden of a duel.

In spite of these events, Equicola was not so transformed as to be unrecognizable: he was still employed by Isabella d'Este and some of his duties remained unchanged. The end of the year found him in Ferrara, apparently to report on the Duke's health — but there seems to have also been another more secret reason for his visit.[43]

In order to persuade Equicola to finish the *Chronica di Mantua* and to ensure that the latest Marquis had his part in it Federico Gonzaga offered him an incentive in the form of a valuable sinecure: the post of Castellan of Canedole and all its income.[44] The relevant decree emphasized the public nature of the work: instead of a historical study conducted according to the principles laid down by Equicola at the beginning of the *Chronica*, another side is highlighted to the exclusion of the first. It was to be, above all, a work of glorification, a monument that would endure forever.[45] From the very start of his reign Federico Gonzaga had no doubts about his own worth. The *Chronica* was not to be an almost private work like the *Genealogia* (which was initially circulated in a few manuscript copies) but a printed edition, creating the impression that it was of greater importance and as such accessible to a wider public rather than a restricted côterie. Equicola was thus granted the rare opportunity to devote himself entirely to literary matters. In practice, however, he could not (and perhaps did not want to) completely free himself from his duties as a secretary. In any case, he was not formally Federico's secretary but Isabella's although the Marquis was making every effort to win Equicola to his side. Equicola kept Federico informed of events in Mantua whenever the latter was in the *Mantovano*.[46] Although Equicola was probably

---

[43] Illustrissima et excellentissima Donna soror hon., messer Mario è venuto qui sta notte. Io lo retornirò tanto quanto mi parerà. Poi lo remetterò a Vostra Signoria et allei mi raccomando... Lo Signor Illustrissimo questa nocte è stato molto male, opine hogi è stato assai meglio... Arrivai ad hore XI di nocte; non me parse fare aprir le porte. All'alba intrai, lo signore dormia. Alle 16 hore li parlai, me fece gran festa. Subito me ordinò quel che havea da fare et con chi devea parlare per remediare al tucto. Et così feci. Le provisioni sono optime et tale che nulla se ha da temere. Solo io, el Giliolo sapemo la cosa et io so quello che ho da mandare spie et fare altro che si serrà da fare perché non se fida nè vole altri il sappia.
(ASMN, AG, b. 1895, Ferrara, 29 December 1519, Alfonso to Isabella d'Este, f. 373r).

[44] Luzio-Renier, *La coltura*, p. 75 and reproduced in Santoro, pp. 83-4.

[45] For a similar analysis of Equicola's role at Mantua in his last years, though less detailed and without reference to the development of his character, see E. Verheyen, *The Palazzo del Te in Mantua. Images of Love and Politics*, Baltimore and London, 1977, pp. 23, 34-6. However, Verheyen treats the *Chronica* as an organic whole and does not see a change of emphasis between the two prefaces.

[46] The following letter highlights this particular function of Equicola:
Ni sono così grate le lettere vostre che, anchor fussino brevissime, havemo piacere che voi ne scriviati et noi di legerle. Et però, ringra[tia]ndovi di quanto haveti

fulfilling his role as the messenger between mother and son under the *Marchesana*'s direction, Federico's enthusiasm betrayed his desire to use Equicola for his own purposes, independently of his mother:

> Havemo havuto li varoni che ni haveti mandati et vi ne ringratiamo. Et perché havemo da parlare con voi, voressimo che, con bona licentia di Madama, fuste qua dimane a noi ad ogni modo.[47]

Two days later Equicola still had not arrived:

> Volemo che diman di sera ogni modo con licentia della Illustrissima et Excellentissima Signora nostra matre observandissima, vi ritrovati a Capriana dove saremo anchor noi perché havemo bisogno parlare con voi. (25 March, see n. 47)

Equicola had indeed won a special place in the affections of the Marquis who took him under his protection:

> Voi sapeti quanto amamo et habbiamo caro messer Mario Equicola per le sue virtù et servitù verso la Illustrissima Madama nostra madre et noi. Et per questo potete comprendere quanto desideramo che le cose sue succedino felicemente, però non vi lo raccommandamo altramente.[48]

For the moment Equicola could not contemplate openly changing sides, however deeply attracted by the idea of entering the Marquis' employment. Equicola made no secret of his «bon animo» towards Federico Gonzaga, but for the time being was prepared to go no further than this. He performed his duties as Isabella's secretary, for some part of the year personally writing up the letters in her copybooks and accompanying her on a visit to Ferrara.[49] But he was absent from the company that attended Isabella d'Este on her pilgrimage to Loreto towards the end of 1520. It does not seem likely that Equicola

---

> scritto, vi exhortamo ad perseverare. Et volemo ne raccomandati alla Illustrissima Madama nostra matre honorandissima.
> (ASMN, AG, b. 2963, libro 10, Salò, 21 March 1520, Federico Gonzaga to Equicola).

[47] ASMN, AG, b. 2963, libro 10, Salò, 23 and 25 March 1520, Federico Gonzaga to Equicola. In both of these letters the Marquis addressed Equicola as «elegantissime», an indication of the attention Equicola paid to his appearance for which he would need a sizeable income.

[48] ASMN, AG, b. 2927, libro 264, 30 January 1521, Federico Gonzaga to Castiglione.

[49] It was Equicola who noted in Isabella's copybook her various trips:

> Alli XII de Magio de sabato partì la Illustrissima da Mantua per Ferrara dove si dimorò sino al II de iunio et di sabato si partì. Lune IIII de predecto mese iugno arrivò in Diporto.
> (ASMN, AG, b. 2997, libro 37).

It is certain that Equicola went with Isabella to Ferrara because the letter announcing her arrival there is written in Equicola's hand (ASMN, AG, b. 2124, Ferrara, 13 May 1520, Isabella to Federico Gonzaga). The Marquis himself wrote to Equicola in Ferrara:

> Ni è stato gratissimo havere inteso per le vostre quanto amorevolmente lo Illustrissimo Signor Duca ha accettato la nostra raccomandatione fatta per voi.
> (ASMN, AG, b. 2963, libro 11, Marmirolo, 15 May 1520, Federico Gonzaga to Equicola).

had fallen out of Isabella's favour or that his remaining in Mantua should be interpreted in a sinister light. On the contrary, it is probable that Isabella felt it necessary to leave in Mantua someone she could trust to keep her fully informed and perhaps even exert some influence over the Marquis. And at first Equicola did not disappoint her: «Mario, cum questa sola respondemo ad multe vostre et vi laudamo de la diligentia usata.»[50] But we have the impression that some important information concerning Castiglione's negotiations in Rome (to obtain the captain-generalcy of the Church for Federico Gonzaga) was being withheld:

> Ma, voressimo che in li advisi ne dati, usasti uno pocho del napolitano più che non fati, et maxime ne li advisi che viene da Roma, perché in questa cavalcata ni è stata fatta pocha copia, remettendoni uno sol capitulo de quella di messer Baldesare.[51]

It may be asserted that it would have been dangerous to send such details in writing: but Equicola appears to have been liberal enough with all kinds of information and there was a cypher system. Be that as it may, Federico did not yet want to break openly with his mother (he was not in a position to do so) yet in spite of his protestations that Isabella should be receiving all the information that came his way he seemed to prefer to emphasize those letters with a more ornamental content:

> Non havendo io altro di novo da avisare Vostra Signoria, ho commisso a messer Mario che le mandi copia d'una lettera venuta al Conte Nicola da la Corte Cesarea, continente lo aviso della coronatione del'Imperatore. Quella pigliarà spasso in legierla. Io havea ordinato che Vostra Excellentia fosse tenuta avisata di tutti li avisi che me veneno qui et che per questo fossero mostrate a Mario le lettere perché lui le scrivesse.[52]

Equicola thus seems to have become the Marquis' accomplice in his attempt to exclude Isabella d'Este from government at a moment of critical importance. If she could not be sure of her most trusted agents, then her position was difficult indeed. Unable to plug into the sources of information available to her son, Isabella d'Este was to find it impossible to hold her own

---

[50] ASMN, AG, b. 2124, Ancona, 26 October 1520, Isabella d'Este to Equicola «nostro carissimo secretario».

[51] ASMN, AG, b. 2124, Pesaro, 29 October 1520, Isabella to Equicola. Indeed, the negotiations in Rome had reached a crucial stage since a secret agreement would be signed with the Pope in December 1520. For a history of the progress of these negotiations which would end with the appointment of Federico as captain-general of the Church see G. La Rocca, «Il contributo di Baldassar Castiglione alla formazione della politica estera gonzaghesca negli ultimi anni del papato di Leone X: 1519-21 (Ricerche per una nuova prospettiva biografica)» in *Mantova e I Gonzaga*, pp. 57-64 and, taking a different line, S. Kolsky, «Castiglione's biography: The courtier and the Italian princes», *Spunti e Ricerche*, I (1985) 1-34.

[52] ASMN, AG, b. 2926, libro 263, Mantua, 4 October 1520, Federico Gonzaga to Isabella d'Este.

against a ruthless Federico Gonzaga. Once the Marquis was appointed captain-general, he thought that it did not befit his rank to share power with his mother.

Equicola was already making preparations for this eventuality. He considered the creation of a literary image for Federico his most important task of the year. He resumed his «commentarii mantuani» which had ended with the death of Francesco Gonzaga, in a different vein, that of the chronicler recording contemporary events and attitudes. Here, in the second part, he abandoned a strictly historical approach (his presentation of Francesco Gonzaga, already written, was incorporated into the new section) and this interestingly parallels a break in the traditions of the Gonzaga dynasty. Luigi Gonzaga, the founder of the dynasty, receives great praise, in the first part of the «commentarii» as a shining example of princely virtue. The sole way of retaining one's state is to rule according to a set of fixed principles:

> Il precipuo modo de fare stato perpetuo et che longamente dure è la prudentia la qual dispone et rega virilmente. Il che in città solamente si pò fare col mezo de la Iustitia la quale dia a ciaschuno quello selli deve: a boni premi et honore, a mali pena et infamia.
> (*Chronica*, f.H6ᵛ)

Throughout this account Equicola places emphasis on justice and liberty; Luigi's actions are judged by reference to the beneficial effect they had on society as a whole.[53] Francesco Gonzaga still preserves these qualities in the actual text of his life but Equicola, in the new «prohemio» wishes to stress his «gloria», a word not mentioned in connection with Luigi Gonzaga. The distance that separated Equicola from his subject both in the sense of time and of personal knowledge is eliminated in his study of Federico. In the first place, Equicola addresses Federico directly using the second person singular.[54] There is an intimacy here, present nowhere else in the *Chronica*, attested by the use of «tu» as perhaps he had done many times before in private conversation. This part of the *Chronica* has the same intention of providing a theoretical basis on which to build a future career just as Equicola had praised Isabella d'Este in the *De Mulieribus* years before. There is a difference, however, Federico was faced with a choice and needed guidance; Equicola realized the consequences should the Marquis choose wrongly:

---

[53] Equicola is clear about Luigi Gonzaga's achievements:

> Lois in renovatione de le conculate legi et che le antiche et bone consuetudini con equalità se observassero era intento qual bon patre di fameglia. (*Chronica*, f.H6ᵛ)

[54] Although Isabella d'Este has an important part to play in the section concerning her son Federico she had not received preferential treatment in the chapter devoted to her husband Francesco as one might have expected. The explanation for this may be found in the fact that Equicola was writing an «official» history of the Gonzagas into which Isabella enters but rarely, for example, during the imprisonment of her husband.

> Non senza latente utilità poeti ad Hercole giovenetto esser state doe vie proposte: l'una nel'intrare amena, florida, ampla, delectevole et piana. La fin di essa con la guida de la voluptà in precipitio conducea, porgea a soi sequaci infamia, biasmo et danno. L'altro, nel primo ingresso, apparea difficile, aspera, orida, strecta et erta. La viva virtù presto la mutava in odorifero prato di honore et gloria et laude pieno.[55]

However, Equicola was not going to allow himself the slightest doubt, at least in public, about which path Federico intended to take.[56] A virtuous Federico Gonzaga would ensure that Equicola's conscience remained untroubled and so he saw this as his principal task:

> Alla quale [honore et gloria] correre vede indefesso, potandoti esser a quella urgentissimo sperone li fideli amici, veridici domestici et modesti servidori. Tal semo reputati quale è il continuo commertio et assidua conversatione che tenemo.
> (*Chronica*, f. R/4^r-v)

Equicola was justifying his role before Federico — he had all the necessary qualities that make a good servant and good servants should be highly valued. It is clear that Equicola saw himself as a counsellor to the prince. There is no reason to believe that he wanted Isabella to have a monopoly over her son, otherwise there would be no room for him and his like:

> Dicea Diocletiano, «Il bono imperadore, chiuso in camera, ne pò da sé il vero intendere. Bisogna che a suoi domestici preste le orechie». (*Chronica*, f. R/4^v)

Equicola urged the young ruler to take up all the traditional virtues associated with the Gonzaga prince, particularly justice. He had also to learn how to be generous, especially to the deserving. It is not difficult to understand Equicola's meaning.[57] At this point the writer could not neglect to discuss Isabella d'Este's place in the new order. (He had managed to justify his own role to a certain extent although one wonders if a ruler endowed with all the virtues

---

[55] *Chronica*, f. R/4^r. As we have seen, Equicola was adept at appealing to the various sides of Federico's character. In this case, the public image of the young prince is being discussed; on other occasions, Equicola urges him to live «lieto et gioioso» and not solely «glorioso».

[56] Equicola makes the obvious choice for Federico:

> Sei, signore mio, della virtù nel camino intrato. Non ritarde tua passi in sì bel principio. Fatiga, sudore o vigilie non te revoche l'ocio dalla fama che tue virtù et fortuna ti preparano clarissima et immortale. Non te inviteno le delitie ad fruire della fugace gioventù li non durabili fructi perciochè se devono lasciare le minori voluptà per consequire le magiori. Et qual magior piacere al'homo che honore et gloria? (*Chronica*, f. R/4^r)

[57] Equicola was also listing the characteristic features of the Renaissance prince:

> Li subditi danno aiuto alla liberalità la quale in te splendidissimamente reluce. Nesciuna virtù fa l'homo più amabile che questa se colli debiti modi se usa, altrimente publico odio parturisce. Receve beneficio il Signore se a bene meriti et virtuosi dona. (*Chronica*, f. R/8^r)

would need advisors.) Equicola employs a barrage of *exempla* to indicate the importance of a son showing the proper respect to his mother:

> Salomone ne recorda et admonisce che la discontenteza dalla matre eradica li fundamenti del figliolo et del medesmo; sapientissima sententia è essere maldecto de Dio qualunque la matre exaspera.
>
> (*Chronica*, f. *2ʳ)

Equicola was asking for patience and understanding on both sides, above all on Federico's part. A thick cluster of *exempla* serve to illustrate the point that the mother must be treated respectfully.[58] As well as providing classical examples of the fate awaiting those who maltreat their mother, such as Nero, Equicola has some modern ones to enforce his point:

> Galeaz Sforca, Duca di Milano quinto, nulla la madre stimava. Fu li la vita nel fiore della sua età con ferro tolta.
>
> (*Chronica*, f. *3ʳ)

Equicola, nonetheless, looks forward to a harmonious relationship between mother and son re-using the same verb «perseverare» found in the letters, loaded with its certainty for the future:

> Et benché io sia certissimo perseverai in ogni actione virtuosa et in laudabile observantia verso tua preclarissima madre. Pur piacciate questo ch'io scrivo perché la laudata virtù cresce et a caval che ben corre non noce adgiongerli sperone.
>
> (*Chronica*, f. *3ʳ)

It is not inconceivable that Isabella herself instructed Equicola to place the section about mothers and sons in the *Chronica*. What we know of her character would lead us to suspect that this was indeed the case. We can easily imagine Isabella d'Este anxious not to lose control of her son, a possibility that had become very real to her almost as soon as Federico became marquis. In this sense, Equicola was carrying out the terms of his contract: to act on Isabella's behalf in anything concerning her son. However, it was also in Equicola's interest, at least until he could entirely depend on Federico's good-will, to maintain the peace between both camps. If both mother and son acted as patrons of Equicola, his position was doubly secure; he would not make powerful enemies and cut himself off from sources of influence. He would also not be troubled in conscience if he acted for both of them. His loyalty to Isabella would not be called into question.

---

[58] Equicola uses Biblical examples to support his case: «Tobia morendo al figliol commanda che honore la madre» (f. *2ᵛ). He describes the attitudes of Plato and Aristotle towards this question. There then follows a list of those great men who have honoured their mother: «Alexandro Severo Imperatore che ad Heliogabalo successe fu non men lodato dalla reverentia exhibita ad Mammea sua madre che da le singulari virtù che in lui reluceano» (f. *3ʳ).

Events were now moving quickly as the last part of the *Chronica* demonstrates.[59] The most important single occurrence is the appointment of Federico Gonzaga as captain-general of the Church.[60] Equicola wrote to Federico about this truly unexpected success:

> Questa non è per altro se non per possermi gloriare ne le mie *Chroniche* esser stato il primo che habia scritto ad Vostra Excellentia il suo honorato titulo et ben collocato Capitaniato.[61]

*

The *Chronica* was not his sole literary concern of this period. Girolamo Cittadino refers to a «poetica opera veramente piena di molta et varia dottrina.» Cittadino laments the fact that Bandello was unable to examine the work with him («io desiderava rivederla insieme con il Bandello nostro»). The reason for this was that Bandello was in Mantua, making it likely that Equicola discussed the work personally with him. The work in question would

---

[59] The last part of the *Chronica* is historical in so far as any chronicle is historical. It is not historical in the sense a humanist historiographer would have given to the word. In this section, Equicola describes Mantuan events in their local context, for example, the armed combat between two Cremonese citizens that took place in Mantua. Equicola reproduces the *patente* for the duel where Federico Gonzaga is seen as restoring order to a difficult situation (f. Bb3^v - Bb4^r). Equicola enters into a wealth of detail about the conditions of the combat and he describes the course of the struggle in an equally detailed manner: «Crudo spectacolo vedere doi ignudi con mortali arme in mano» (f. Bb4^v). It seems that «spectacolo» has become more important than «Iustitia» in the change of values that operated under Federico Gonzaga. Our writer did not miss an opportunity to elevate the situation on to a higher level: «Non altrimente li doi valenti homini pareano che quelli li quali in opere marmoree antiche in Roma si vedeno» (f. Bb4^{r-v}). However, Equicola did turn the incident to his own purposes; it seemed to be meant as a lesson for anyone who reads the book:

> Io non repono così ogni cosa in arbitrio et in potestà de la fortuna la quale mi pare scuto et scusa alli errori et colpe de molti. Fu virilità de Baptista, non mala fortuna de Vicenzo, toglierli la lancia.   (*Chronica*, f. Bb6^v)

Equicola seems to be speaking out to Federico, suggesting that he is in a position to take control: «ciaschuno essere artefece de la sua fortuna» (f. Bb7^r). As Federico's reign progresses it becomes increasingly unlikely that Equicola's original plan of a harmonious relationship between the Marquis and his mother will have any chance of success. On a more personal plane, Equicola places the burden on each individual to carve out his own destiny, usually seen in terms of social achievement.

[60] Federico Gonzaga's appointment is seen as the culminating achievement of the dynasty:

> Nel giorno primo di Iuglio MDXXI in consistorio di novo il fece, creò, ordinò, constituiò, disse, nominò et publicò general capitanio suo et de la prelibata Chiesa con assenso et consenso del Collegio di tutti signori cardinali con letitia di tutta la corte, et essa Roma diede segni de letitia evidentissimi.

> (*Chronica*, f. Cc6^v; Verheyen, *Palazzo del Te*, p. 17)

[61] ASMN, AG, b. 2499, Mantua, 15 December 1520, Equicola to Federico Gonzaga.

appear to be the *Institutioni al comporre in ogni sorte di rima* since the printed edition contains annotations signalled by the abbreviation BAN.[62]

Other works by Equicola were in demand: Grossino, the Mantuan ambassador to Milan, asked for two copies of the *Iter*:

> A li dì pasati schrisi a messer Statio [Gadio] me volese mandare dui libri di quelli havea conposto Vostra Magnificenza dil viazo di la Illustrissima Madama alla Bauma; me li mandò. Havendoli dati a persone literate et mollto savie, sono stato cari. Uno sechretario dil senato n'ebi uno et uno l'Agripa, sechretario dil arciveschovo di Piasenza. Il veschovo sufragano dil archipiscopato di Millano, persona mollto dotta et conose Vostra Magnificenza, ha lecto uno di questi suoi libri. Non li poteria schrivere quanto lauda l'opera sua et il suo hornato dire, di modo che mollto desidera aver uno di questi suoi libri: piacendo a quella di mandarmene, uno gie lo darò, havendo grandissima consolatione et apiacer che le virtù vostre sia[no] conosute in hogni locho.[63]

There was no doubt amongst his contemporaries that Equicola was a man of many talents, having all the qualities necessary to be highly regarded at court. These qualities were now used by Equicola to gain material preferment:

> Ce ho condutto tutti questi litterati in tua comendatione et lo nostro Sanazaro parlò con tanta eloquentia di tuoi meriti che non poria desiderare. Disse lui come non sapia in quale dottrina fusse magiore: in la mathematica, in la oratoria, in la philosophia et in la poesia. Eri singularissimo in le cose bellice, eri grande huomo.
> (Luzio-Renier, *La coltura*, p. 414, n. 2)

---

[62]   Dionisotti has shown («Girolamo Claricio», *Studi sul Boccaccio*, II, p. 296) that Bandello probably took part in the revision of the *Institutioni* and as a consequence we can identify the «poetica opera» mentioned by Cittadino as the *Institutioni*. ASMN, AG, b. 1647, Milan, 13 May 1520, Cittadino to Equicola:
> Mosso più da cupidità di imparare che da affetto di correggere, nondimeno per testimonio che la ho vista li trovarete postillate di mia mano alchune mie opinioni, cose però non di molto peso. (*Ibid*. The letter is now in A.C. Fiorato, *Bandello entre l'histoire et l'écriture*, Florence, 1979, pp. 295-96, with some discussion).

[63]   ASMN, AG, b. 1646, Milan, 15 October 1520, Grossino to Equicola. This letter is a valuable piece of external evidence for the dating of the *Iter* since it most probably refers to the printed text and not manuscripts. The conclusion that therefore must be drawn is that work was printed by 1520 at the very latest.

The same letter helps to throw more light on another problem. Equicola's name appears on the list of teachers appointed by the University of Pavia for the year 1520 (published in *Memorie e documenti per la storia dell'Università di Pavia e degli uomini più illustri che v'insegnarono*, I, Pavia, 1878, p. 169). As we have already seen, it would have been impossible for Equicola to have taught there for any extended period in the year in question. If he did in fact teach in Pavia for a couple of months no letters survive in the *Archivio Gonzaga*, as far as I have been able to ascertain, which either relate to a supposed stay in Pavia or which were written by him from Pavia or Milan in 1520. The letter moreover suggests that Equicola had not recently been in Milan nor was he intending to go there. Until further evidence comes to light about the circumstances surrounding his appointment, there is considerable doubt the nature of the appointment; if he was offered it, it would seem likely that he did not take it up.

Equicola is portrayed as having ability both in learning and warfare, the combination of both skills being a prerequisite for the successful courtier at a time of intense political crisis. As captain-general of the Church the Marquis actively promoted a militaristic culture forcing his servants to redirect their energies into areas that they had neglected, as can be seen from the example of Equicola. Up to now, Equicola had been content to loan his skills at very low interest but the moment had come when he demanded a greater return. Indeed, a correspondent of his in Naples had noticed the change:

> Io non ho havuto lettere di Vostra Signoria molto tempo è. Dubito che lo causa lo officio vostro. Si è così che lo officio ve desvia da lo scrivere a li amici et dal studio, dirò a Vostra Signoria uno hiatu quello che disse al secretario Zezone nostro, che havere molti dinari è cosa de mercanti, havere molta dottrina è cosa de savii. Il nostro Zezone non cura più di guadagnare molto et solo pone mano in le cose ardue, le altre cose guadagnevoli li dona a fare alli cancellieri, così lui ha tempo di essere con li amici et con le Muse. Et spesso spesso due hore del giorno è con lo nostro Syncero.[64]

Equicola would not be easily fooled by the argument that pursuit of wealth should be considered secondary to the pursuit of learning. He had indeed acted according to such principles when he was Isabella's tutor, but now, having launched himself on a public career, he exploited his literary interests to realize his ambitions. Equicola had been employed by Isabella in an almost private, informal capacity, and now he intended to find a place for himself at the centre of the Mantuan state. As secretary Equicola was to be the person to whom people would turn if they needed a favourable reception from the Marquis. It would in fact be quite appropriate to compare Equicola with a merchant, because not only was he effectively selling himself to the new regime but also, in attempting to improve his financial position, making himself less dependent on the caprices of the Marquis he set up a workshop in his own house for the manufacture, amongst other things, of paper.[65] Equicola did not seem to be concerned whether or not this enterprise would affect his social status; financial security was his principal aim, and he pursued titles and honours equally relentlessly. Federico Gonzaga lent his support to these activities, on occasion writing to Egidio da Viterbo, to urge his assistance in Equicola's affairs in Rome. The Marquis himself endowed Equicola with a grant of land in 1521, in this way investing the secretary with a material interest in Mantua which he had not previously enjoyed.[66] Federico knew how to

---

[64]   ASMN, AG, b. 809, Naples, 25 December 1520, Perillo to Equicola.

[65]   Luzio-Renier, *La coltura*, p. 64, n.1. Equicola was particularly active in matters concerning his house in the period 1522-3. These years correspond with Equicola's rise in power and influence, especially because of his appointment as Federico Gonzaga's secretary.

[66]   ASMN, Archivio degli Instrumenti, Registrazioni Notarili: «Investitura Illustrissimi domini Marii ab hospitale magno mantuano» (the year 1521, f. 620).

favour those whom he wished to use in his affairs and Equicola was not
adverse to this more concrete type of persuasion.

*

The first part of what proved to be a hectic year (1521) unfolded without
undue excitement or agitation. It was Equicola's intention to publish the
Libro de natura de amore in Venice: being unable to go to that city himself
(because of his commitments in Mantua), he was fortunate in that he could
use — through personal acquaintanceship and the authority of Federico Gonzaga — the services of the cultured Mantuan ambassador to Venice, Giovan
Battista Malatesta.[67] The year, then, began promisingly for Equicola, with the
Marquis further demonstrating his favour. It was hoped Equicola's *Libro*
would ensure his place in literature and, Federico's in the role of patron.

From the personal point of view all seemed well with Equicola; not only
had he won Federico's favour but also that of Alfonso d'Este. In this respect,
Equicola had become the Mantuan equivalent of Bernardino Prosperi,
Isabella d'Este's Ferrarese informant.[68] Equicola did not want to place any of
the contacts he had made with the help of Isabella d'Este in jeopardy, so he
continued to express his confidence in the Estense family as rulers:

> Lo animo, la prudentia et bona fortuna de quella sempre non solamente la tenerà
> secura, ma io so certo che recuperà il suo et lo stato augumentarà. Non so pro-
> pheta, ma in questo so più che propheta.[69]

Equicola's Roman business interests received the protection of the Marquis: ASMN, AG,
b. 2927, libro 264, f. 94ᵛ, Federico to Egidio da Viterbo:

> Reverendo messer Mario Equicola de la Illustrissima et Excellentissima Madama
> mia matre et mio per la servitù che l'ha anche a Vostra Signoria Reverendissima
> et devotione in lei, ha deliberato usare dil favor di quella in tutte le cose sue in
> Roma repromettendosi de non possere havere se non felice exito di soi negotii
> esseni indriciati et aiutati da lei. Et perché io per li meriti de la assidua et
> fidelissima servitù et per la dottrina et singulare virtute sue...

[67]   Although the *Libro* is not specifically metioned it would seem that the following letter
represents the first step towards the publication of Equicola's *magnum opus*:

> Viene lì Satyro, creato di messer Mario Equicola, nostro secretario, per la causa
> che intenderai da lui. Et perché è cosa importante ad esso messer Mario, quale
> sai quanto è amato da noi, volemo che tu operi quanto serà bisogno in tale cosa
> con quella diligentia che faresti se la fosse nostra propria, facendo parlare con
> quelle persone dotte lì di Venetia et con li librari perché se facci quanto è desiderio
> di esso messer Mario.

(ASMN, AG, b. 2125, Mantua, 11 January 1521, Federico Gonzaga to Malatesta).

[68]   See A. Piromalli, *La cultura a Ferrara al tempo di Ludovico Ariosto*, Rome, 1975,
p. 111.

[69]   ASMO, ASE, C, Ambasciatori: Mantova, b. 2, 5 February 1521, Equicola to Alfonso
d'Este.

Equicola continually protested his loyalty to the Duke in typical courtierly
fashion: telling the truth to Alfonso d'Este meant playing a game with him,
used to emphasize his supposed dependence on and debt of gratitude to the
ruler of Ferrara — a state of affairs not actually borne out by the historical
«facts»:

> Vole Vostra Signoria che li dica il vero. Ha quella facto male remandarme denari
> per li doi sciopecti perché quanto ho al mundo et haverò tutto recognosco dalli
> favori che Vostra Excellentia s'è dignata sempre farme.[70]

Equicola claims here to be Alfonso's «creato» and uses a trivial incident to
claim that *his* alliances have not changed. He realized that he would always
be a kind of servant and accepted this state of affairs with undiminished
vigour.[71] However subordinate his role may have been, Equicola considered
life at court infinitely preferable to any of the other possibilities open to him,
such as taking holy orders and entering a monastery. He accepted the responsibilities and time-consuming duties of a secretary in order to be assured of
a notable place in the social order.

Throughout this period Equicola's health was steadily declining yet in
spite of his deterioration he refused to give up his newly-won position in the
administration of the state.[72] Ferrara became a place where he could escape
for a little while to rest:

> Così Sua Signoria [Federico Gonzaga] è stata contenta et a mi ha facto gran pia-
> cere perché tra otto o X dì venerò a star con Vostra Excellentia sei o septe dì.
> Mutarò aere, cianciarò et tornerò a Mantua pieno di sanità et de letitia.[73]

---

[70] ASMO, ASE, C, Ambasciatori: Mantova, b. 2, 16 February 1521, Equicola to Alfonso
d'Este.

[71] It had always been the cornerstone of Equicola's career strategy to be the dependable
servant who did not aspire to power in his own right and this attitude is reiterated in the following letter:

> Illustrissimo signor mio, hogi, alle XVIII hore, mandai in Milano lo plico de Vos-
> tra Signoria ad messer Joan Fino. So certo li serà dato fedelmente. La supplico
> me commande che alhora satio o stracco serò de far cosa che sia in suo servitio.
> Quando me venerà in fastidio la vita, et questo non serà mai, perché mai mi farò
> frate né monacho. Basoli le mani.
> (ASMN, AG, C, Ambasciatori: Mantova, b. 2, 22 March 1521, Equicola to
> Alfonso d'Este).

[72] He seems to have been ill in 1520 since one of his correspondents wrote to him
«quando sereti reducto ne la sollita santitate, per mio contento me ne donate adviso»
(ASMN, AG, b. 636, Paris, 16 October 1520, Suardino to Equicola).

[73] ASMO, ASE, C, Ambasciatori: Mantova, b. 2, 23 May 1521, Equicola to Alfonso
d'Este. The opening of the letter explains the circumstances of this particular visit:

> Era per partirme questa sera per venir a trovare et fare reverentia ad Vostra Excel-
> lentia como summamente desydero. Mandavame lo Illustrissimo Signor Mar-
> chese. Et perché non me sento anchor tutto sano né libero del male ho impetrata
> gratia dal predecto Signor Illustrissimo che me lasse retornare alla mia un poco
> meglio.

But while Equicola returned to Mantua in good health and spirits Isabella d'Este was seriously ill: «Sera, ad una hora, arrivai in Mantua, trovai Madama Illustrissima malata de terzana la quale non dubito serà longa sanità perché se purgarà con questa occasione tutti tristi humori.»[74] Equicola now found himself reporting on the progress of Isabella's illness in the same way as he had reported Alfonso's many illnesses to Isabella: «Io, omni dì, tenerò avisata Vostra Signoria de quanto occorrerà. Così è il mio debito et così mi ha ordinato lo Signor Marchese.»[75] In a few days, the *Marchesana* felt better, much to Equicola's delight.[76]

*

With the appointment of Federico Gonzaga as captain-general of the Church, a dramatic change occurred in Mantuan politics, endorsed by the appearance in print of the *Chronica di Mantua*.[77] It may be said that this appointment led Equicola into a quagmire of uncertainties: on the one hand, he was proud to be associated with the man who controlled the military destiny of Italy and the Church; and on the other, his loyalty to Isabella and Alfonso d'Este was tested by the new situation. One imagines an Equicola doing his utmost to save a rapidly deteriorating relationship between mother and son. A major cause of tension was the growing influence of Isabella Boschetti who was beginning to take the place of Isabella d'Este in affairs of state (see E. Verheyen, *Palazzo*, pp. 19-21). The 1 July 1521 struck a fateful note for the future of Isabella d'Este as co-regent or as someone with a role to play in the government of Mantua after 1522. At first, Equicola continued to play his double game which became increasingly difficult as the relations between his masters grew worse.

Towards the end of July Federico was preparing to go to the battlefield in a campaign that included the siege of Parma.[78] In such a campaign it was important to know the position of the Duke of Ferrara. Furthermore, instead of having Alfonso d'Este as an enemy it would have been to Federico's

---

[74]   ASMO, ASE, C, Ambasciatori: Mantova, b. 2, 9 June 1521, Equicola to Alfonso d'Este. Her illness was considered very serious: «Li medici dicono che non è maraviglia, essendo stato XVI anni senza haver havuto male et che [è] ripiena». (Letter of 16 June 1521, Equicola to Alfonso d'Este).

[75]   ASMO, ASE, C, Ambasciatori: Mantova, b. 2, 12 June 1521, Equicola to Alfonso d'Este.

[76]   Equicola reports:

> Del che ho tanta allegreza io che non se potria dire. Sua Signoria ha già facto voltare le spalle al male.
> (ASMO, ASE, C, Ambasciatori: Mantova, b. 2, 17 June 1521, Equicola to «messer Obizo»).

[77]   For which see D.E. Rhodes, «Mario Equicola's *Chronica di Mantua*».

[78]   See Frizzi, IV, pp, 286-87 and L. Mazzoldi, *Mantova: La storia*, II, pp. 271-72.

advantage to win him over to his side. The choice of envoy appointed to initiate the talks fell almost naturally to Equicola. This was the first time that Equicola was used in a matter that concerned the Marquis as captain-general. It was also the first time that Equicola was involved in negotiations of prime importance for a Marquis of Mantua (either Francesco or Federico). Equicola's credibility as envoy was due not to the fact that he was important in his own right but rather derived from his long association with Alfonso d'Este — as Isabella's man. He was particularly useful in these circumstances although it is difficult to determine whether he would have had the same efficacy if he had had to deal with another ruler. In all probability, he would not have, lacking as he was in personal prestige and wealth. It seemed that everything he had and was depended upon the favour of the Gonzagas, and his presence alone would not suffice:

> Solamente vi dicemo che havemo mandato a Ferrara messer Mario, et domani mandaremo il Marchese Guilielmo Malaspina a parlare al signore nostro cognato.[79]

At most, Equicola's task was simply to convey a message from his superiors and his uses were thus strictly limited. But his effectiveness lay in his ability to «put over» the message, and in the strength of the relationship between himself and the person to whom he was conveying the information. It appears important that someone of greater rank was being sent to Ferrara immediately after Equicola's arrival there. Equicola's ability may have lain in his social grace which helped to prepare the way for «serious» negotiations. The following letter indicates the confidence Federico Gonzaga places in Equicola and its limitations. It is true that Equicola is allowed to explain the Marquis of Mantua's point of view but he is not allowed to become more than a messenger. However, there does seem to be some basis for stating that Equicola in this particular case might have been more effective than the normal ambassador:

> Per un' altra nostra ve havemo scritto come havevamo mandato a Ferrara messer Mario a parlare al Signor Duca. La prima lettera sua è stata di questo aviso, che'l predetto signore l'ha ascoltato attentissimamente et li disse che queste cose haveano seco peso et contrapeso, che li faria sopra qualche pensero et che li responderia il dì sequente; et questo fu alli XXII. Et che con la risposta che Sua Signoria li daria, mettendola lui in scritto, se ne ritornaria a noi. E così la aspettamo.[80]

---

[79]   ASMN, AG, b. 2977, libro 1, Mantua, 21 July 1521, Federico Gonzaga to Castiglione.

[80]   ASMN, AG, b. 2977, libro 1, Mantua, 24 July 1521. The following day the Marquis wrote to Castiglione that he had received a reply from Ferrara:

> Questo è quanto ha resposto al predetto messer Mario lo Signor Duca di Ferrara, il quale messer Mario per longhi discorsi comprende che, quando se trovasse modo et mezo di assicurare il Signor Duca, che ogni cosa haveria effetto perché

Equicola did not accompany the Marquis on his first campaign; he sent
words of encouragement to Federico from the safety of Mantua. He knew
what kind of praise most appealed to the captain-general new to the post:

> Alegrome con quella che quello che in grandi et vecchi capitani trovo da scrittori
> laudato in essa Vostra Signoria giovene si lauda: cavalcare il campo, vagare per
> quello, humanamente resalutar, con affabilità a sé chiamare li amici et li incogniti,
> tirarli alla sua amicitia con liberalità.[81]

He did not flinch from comparing Federico with the greatest Roman generals:
«sentendo la liberalità che Vostra Signoria usa tra soldati, intendendo la affa-
bilità, mi subviene di quel che dicono scrittori di Scipione.»[82] The secretary
seems to have been engaged in continuing his *Chronica* piece by piece in his
letters. He seeks to strengthen the Marquis' own view of himself as a great
warrior in the classical tradition. Federico, young as he was, according to
Equicola, had all the qualities of a mature captain. In this way, Equicola was
able to rationalize his allegiance to an immature, bloodthirsty tyrant whose
desire for power even exceeded that of his mother.[83] Equicola, wishing to
improve his position at court and to appease his conscience by creating an
image of Federico as a humane captain following in the footsteps of renowned
Roman generals, realized that the rewards promised to be all the greater since
the Marquis' promotion. Consequently, he lost no opportunity to impress his
importance on Federico. Equicola certainly understood what pleased the
Marquis, for example, he sent him astrological predictions, assured that they
would be welcome.[84] He continued to keep him informed of his mother's

---

> non li pare che Sua Excellentia se fidi non vedendo altra demonstratione. Questo
> ne ha ditto messer Mario.
> (ASMN, AG, b. 2977, libro 1, Mantua, 25 July 1521, Federico Gonzaga to Casti-
> glione).

[81]   ASMN, AG, b. 2500, Mantua, 11 August 1521, Equicola to Federico Gonzaga.
It is possible that Equicola accompanied the Marquis on the first part of his journey, then
returned to Mantua: «Arrivai sonnolento in Mantua, né mai, benché assai lo invitasse, volse
da mi venire il sonno: fecime dunque vestire» (ASMN, AG, b. 2500, Mantua, 4 August 1521,
Equicola to Federico Gonzaga). In the same letter Equicola reflects on the position of the servant:

> Ho lecto mole volte in molti boni auctori che l'officio di servitore è non preterire
> li commandamenti del patrone perciò che se se fa bene pare prosumtione, se se
> fa male meritamente il signore si pò lamentare.

[82]   ASMN, AG, b. 2500, 13 August 1521, Equicola to Federico Gonzaga.
[83]   Cf. S. Kolsky, «Images», p. 56.
[84]   Homi retrovati in casa questi tre iudicii de astrologi, li quali mando ad quella ad
ciò vacandoli ocio dalli gran negocii, veda et cognosca le pazie de indivinatori.
(ASMN, AG, b. 2500, Mantua, 5 September 1521, Equicola to Federico Gonzaga).
Equicola also conveyed to the Marquis the praise that well-known contemporaries bestowed on
the latter:

> Messer Pier Pomponazo vene da Bologna et me ha narrate infinite lode de Vostra
> Signoria, che se celebrano in quella città. Del che ne vivo et viverò sempre lieto

donzelle, especially Isabella Lavagnola: «Heri sera, hebi una di Vostra Excellentia et una di messer Mario che mi fece rider assai per quel caso de Isabella.»[85] Unfortunately for Equicola Federico soon felt the need of the former's active participation in the war instead of his admiration at a distance. Equicola would have to use more than words to prove his allegiance to the new dynamic regime.

At the beginning of September 1521 the Marquis asked his mother to release Equicola from her service for a short while:

> Vostra Excellentia sia contenta mandar subito a me messer Mario perché per lui voglio far intendere a quella cosa che li piacerà e che non voglio metter in scritto, ch'io subito lo remandarò indreto a Vostra Excellentia.[86]

That «subito» turned out to stretch over more than a fortnight.[87] The time-limit seems to have been extended gradually, first of all from «tri o quatro dì», in which case Isabella was only too glad to let him go, and then apparently indefinitely:

> La ringratio summamente così anchora di la libertà che la mi dà di retenire qua messer Mario quanto mi pare.[88]

In this situation, new to him, Federico was probably pleased to have by his side someone in whom he could trust. It should be remembered that Equicola had experience of military life, though admittedly the last time he had ventured on to a battlefield was in 1503. Equicola would further add a courtier's touch to the dreariness of the camp routine.

His arrival in camp did not change his mind about Federico's ability as a captain. If the comparisons to Roman generals do not reappear (he was no longer at his ease in Mantua) he still felt the same admiration for the Marquis who was holding his own amongst many famous soldiers: «et iurovi che è dili-

---

perché non è poco che in sì tenera età quella habia facto sì valido fundamento di virtù, vigilantia et animosità.
(ASMN, AG, b. 2500, 23 September 1521).

[85] ASMN, AG, b. 2125, «Ex castris felicissimis contra Parmam», 21 August 1521, Federico to Isabella d'Este.

[86] ASMN, AG, b. 2125, «Ex castris contra Parmam», 5 September 1521, Federico to Isabella d'Este.

[87] As a secretary in the Mantuan chancellery, *l'Abbate* wrote from Parma to Equicola, who by this time was in Mantua, to inform him that the situation had not changed since his departure:

Altro qua non è di novo salvvo che ogniuno sta admirativo. Et dicesi l'uno a l'altro: «Che si farà? Staremo qui o pur andaremo a Rezo», dolendosi dil tempo perduto, dil pocco honore havuto et di la grande spesa che fanno in comprare ogni cosa senza alcun guadagno et dil tempo che butteno via.
(ASMN, AG, b. 1370, «Di campo», 18 September 1521).

[88] ASMN, AG, b. 2977, libro 2, «Ex castris ad Sanctum Lazarum», 13 September 1521, Federico to Isabella d'Este.

gentissimo et vigilantissimo, et fa il prudente et animoso da vero Capitano.»[89]
For Equicola, the whole affair turned sour when it was decided not to proceed
with the attack against Parma because of the threat of being sandwiched between Lautrec and the Duke of Ferrara.[90] Equicola expressed his own and
Federico's bitter disappointment at being denied a chance of glory:

> Per infiniti respecti me retrovo in grande dolore. Quel glorioso, victorioso et
> laudato exercito, da nesciun inimico aperto, cacciato, è in manifesta fuga,
> lassando la presa Parma.[91]

From this point on, a single theme dominated his letters to Isabella d'Este,
that of his anger at the delaying tactics used by the papal army when a bold
assault would have cut short the war.[92] Meanwhile the pantomime of military
life in the camp went on:

---

[89]   ASMN, AG, b. 1370, «Dal campo contra meza Parma», 8 September 1521, Equicola
to Isabella d'Este.

[90]   L. Mazzoldi, *Mantova: La Storia*, II, p. 272.

[91]   ASMN, AG, b. 1370, «Dal campo che lassando Parma ha persa la palma», 9 september 1521, Equicola to Isabella d'Este.

[92]   For Equicola only Federico Gonzaga and the Marquis of Pescara acted in a manner
befitting their rank. At the meeting where the new strategy was decided by, amongst others,
Prospero Colonna and Francesco Guicciardini, Federico Gonzaga resolutely opposed the
change in tactics. Equicola lost no opportunity to emphasize the nobility of Federico's attitude:

> Disse lo Signor Marchese di Mantua, «Il pericolo ci è pocho, la gloria serà grande
> in la victoria, ma in lo retirare, infamia, perdita et dishonore.» Non odivano con
> bon vulto tale parole il Colonna e 'l Guicciardino; del che avedutosi il marchese,
> se remise al volere loro per havere dal Papa et essere exhortato da Medici [Cardinal
> Giulio de' Medici] che adherisse alla sententia del Signor Prospero.
> (ASMN, AG, b. 1370, 9 September 1521, Equicola to Isabella d'Este).

Federico da Bozzolo, who was with the French forces in Parma, could not believe his luck if
we are to believe Equicola's partisan interpretation of the event:

> Oltra questo, quando partemmo stava esso Signor Federico con Monsignor de le
> Scu ad una finestra. Vedendo il nostro campo in moto, maravigliandose quando
> poi ci videro voltare le spalle, se fecero mille † (i.e. croci) rengratiando Dio de
> tanto miraculo pensando loro dimandare accordo, si fugiva.
> (ASMN, AG, b. 1370, «Dal campo», 12 September 1521, Equicola to Isabella
> d'Este).

Between the Marquis and Equicola there is seemingly no difference of opinion about the right
thing to do. Both see «la gloria» as their goal: Equicola thinks of it in terms of Roman military
might, as does Federico up to a certain point, but the Marquis' vision of glory has an extra
ingredient formed by his reading tales of knightly valour and chivalry even while on campaign:

> Hippolyto [Calandra, a chancellor in the Mantuan chancery], mandane *Orlando
> Furioso*, lo *Inamoramento di Orlando* et *Morgante mazor*, advertendo che tutti
> siano di bona stampa et di lettere un poco grossette et ben legibile.
> (ASMN, AG, b. 2977, libro 4, «Ex castris», 30 October 1521, Federico Gonzaga
> to Ippolito Calandra).

However, at times, Federico's thirst for glory and his desire to make an impression caused concern in Mantua, especially because of his inexperience:

> Ni pare ben, come matre amorevole che siamo a Vostra Signoria, recordarli a non
> volere essere tanto facile ad compiacer altrui che entri in pericolo di tirarsi il foco

So andato per el campo collo Signor Illustrissimo, Signora mia, molto più honorato et admirato il vedo qui che non in Mantua. Tucti soldati, tucti capitanii li escone incontro, salutandolo et honorandolo et io al par con Sua Signoria fo lo ambasciatore de Vostra Excellentia. Ne rido, ma vo savio et non ragiono altro che de stato quando mi vedo qualche uno da bene vicino. Ha mai Vostra Signoria scontrati frati de San Domenico o di San Francesco, li quali como se vedono vicino homini o donne, subito dicono, «Deus in adiutorium meum intende», per monstrare che dicono officio? Io mi so governato ad imitatione de questi in parlare di stato.[93]

Unlike Federico Equicola was not taken in by the honours shown to him in the camp. His irony lays bare the falsity of his situation. On a superficial level, Equicola's behaviour was intended to entertain the Marquis and his description of the scene was to bring a smile to the lips of Isabella d'Este. She may not have been so happy about Equicola's insinuation that Federico was no better than himself: if Equicola was ill-equipped to speak about affairs of state, was Federico any better equipped to rule and fight battles? Federico, however, played his part to the end (he would not have regarded himself as acting a part, unlike Equicola, who seemed proud of his ability to fool people).[94] Equicola still had not found the «substance» of his role, and the play-element predominated to the exclusion of any serious adherence to the part he was called upon to take.

Serious elements did intrude, however, particularly in a clash of loyalties which he found impossible to resolve so that he finally found himself simultaneously pursuing two contradictory goals. This was evident in his continued support of the Duke of Ferrara who was a declared enemy of the Papacy.[95]

---

a casa et di questo parere medemo è il nostro Reverendissimo Monsignore [Sigismondo Gonzaga].
(ASMN, AG, b. 2964, libro 13, 4 September 1521, Isabella d'Este to Federico Gonzaga)

Isabella was not the only person to be concerned (she undoubtedly was extremely worried about the role her son was playing in exposing Ferrara and its Duke to papal aggression). Equicola, too, expressed doubts about certain aspects of the Marquis' behaviour:

Appena havemo potuto retenere lo Illustrissimo Signor Marchese che per omni modo volea cavalcare et così, ad omni minimo strepito, vol correre. Iuro ad Dio che ha bisogno di briglia più che de sperone. Et io vorrei che conoscesse chi è et quel che importa la persona sua.
(ASMN, AG, b. 1370, «Dal campo», 12 September 1521, Equicola to Isabella d'Este)

[93] ASMN, AG, b. 1370, «Dal campo», 12 September 1521, Equicola to Isabella d'Este.

[94] From Equicola's letters to Isabella d'Este we can see that the Marquis derived the greatest pleasure from his new role and so played it with the utmost seriousness; Equicola alternates between an unqualified admiration for Federico and the feeling that the Marquis is rather naive in his approach to the problems that arise out of the war.

[95] Equicola wrote to Isabella d'Este, expressing no doubts whatsoever over the explicit praise of Alfonso d'Este and his own presence in the papal camp:

In questa retirata non ho se non un piacere che tuct'el mundo lauda il Signor Marchese nostro per animosissimo, publicamente dicendosi che è savio et magna-

Though Federico may have attempted to reduce the force of the attack against the Duke, the latter nonetheless found himself in severe straits.[96] The secretary aimed to gloss over these contradictions, emphasizing the qualities of Federico and Alfonso in isolation from one another, as if it were still possible to combine support for mother and son, papal expansionism against the dynastic system.

This was not the only problem to confront Equicola. The anticipated glory did not eventuate; on the contrary, everything had become shabby, and the court no longer provided a refuge from the realities of war. Equicola acknowledged, on a rare occasion, the brutal hardships of life outside the privileged élite: «È cosa miserabile vedere le povere parmegiane con figliolini in braccio uscire fuora et andare verso Piacenza.» For Equicola, the chief effect of war was to destroy what people had struggled so hard to achieve over so many years:

> Né men pare digno de compassione vedere le robe che se vendono et quel che con tanto sudore et fatiga è stato acquistato et con tanta parcità servato è in man de soldati et vendese per minimo pretio.[97]

Equicola's attention seems to be caught by the nature of «le robe» as something transitory and ultimately not to be depended upon. Behind his observation lies a sense of what it takes to acquire material comfort and how easily war can destroy the work of years. This sentiment was probably made more acute by his experience in the *Regno*, in particular, the way in which Sigismondo Cantelmo was dispossessed of his territories. In addition to these, the

---

> nimo; li Spagnoli lo adorano. L'altro piacere che ho è che lo Signor Duca de Ferrara con lo solo suo nome ha impauriti quelli che di timore non monstravano segno alcuno. Vostra Excellentia se ne pò allegrare perché ha un figliolo lodato et un fratello temuto, l'uno et l'altro virtuoso.
> (ASMN, AG, b. 1370, «Dal campo», 12 September 1521, Equicola to Isabella d'Este).

When Equicola returned to the army he still secretly supported the Duke:

> Dolme del caso accascato alle genti del Signor Duca de Ferrara: qui se ne fa gran allegria per questi Pontificii.
> (ASMN, AG, b. 1647, «Da Gabioneta», 10 October 1521, Equicola to Isabella d'Este)

He was even more explicit in an undated letter to Isabella:

> Vostra Signoria ne stia alegra et de bona voglia che forsi la fortuna et iustitia aiutarà lo Illustrissimo Signor Duca.

The last letter indirectly indicates Equicola's position as Federico's *assistant*. He seems to be suggesting there is nothing *they* can do. It may be a way of absolving himself from feelings of guilt and betrayal.

[96]   See Frizzi, IV, pp. 287-89.

[97]   This and the preceding extract are to be found in ASMN, AG, b. 1370, Parma, 8 September 1521, Equicola to Isabella d'Este.

rigours of military life were proving too much for him, and his new duties
overturned the long-established routine of his life:

> Ne l'ocio letterario in quale, per gratia et liberalità di Vostra Excellentia, so usato
> et disusato dalli incommodi militari.   (Luzio-Renier, *La coltura*, p. 77)

Equicola's most cherished desire was to return to Mantua. In this instance,
loyalty to Isabella d'Este and personal comfort were closely linked. Equicola
had outgrown his soldier's role and preferred to fight at a distance. He was
now, it should be remembered, over fifty years old. His wish was not granted,
however, at least not immediately. Federico appreciated his presence too much
and Isabella did not want to oppose her son. Besides, Equicola provided a
constant and reliable supply of information back to Mantua:

> Se non fosse per longa pratica da mi conosciuto che Vostra Excellentia lege volen-
> tieri lettere, certo, non scriveria così spesso perché me levaria lo animo lo non
> haver che scrivere se non cose frivoli de le quali dar notitia è da homo frivolo. Pur
> io non dubito de incorrere in omni nome o de sempio o di pazo o de poco
> accorto.[98]

Equicola was not in any case physically able to withstand the discomforts
of a hard campaign. It is almost symbolic and slightly ironic that whilst
everyone else was hurriedly preparing for battle Equicola stayed in the Marquis' empty tent in order to keep it safe.[99]

A little before the end of September Equicola was back in Mantua (the last
letter written by him from the camp is dated 17th September). His stay there
was not destined to last very long, however. On 3rd October the Marquis ordered him to return to the army.[100] Vincenzo de' Preti, whom Isabella d'Este had
sent to the papal camp in order to gather information for her personally (some
might say to spy on her son), was no longer needed: « Vincentio, poiché Mario
viene in campo dove ha ad stare qualche dì, tu potrai ritornare a Mantua, et
così ritornarai.»[101] Equicola was indeed preferable to de' Preti for a number
of reasons:

[98]   ASMN, AG, b. 1370, «Dal campo», 14 September 1521, Equicola to Isabella d'Este.
[99]   Eran circa quattro hore di nocte quando se gridò alle arme, all'arme. Il signore,
subito armato, montò ad cavallo et tanto presto che fu il primo... Io quieto mi
stava nel padiglione alla guardia di quello perché omniuno era in arme.
(ASMN, AG, b. 1370, 16 September 1521, Equicola to Isabella d'Este).
[100] Messer Mario. Ni piacerà che veniati dimane a Canneto per venire in campo a noi,
perché retrovareti ivi il capitaneo Guido Vaino con la compagnia che ha ad accompagnare
alcuni denari al campo e venereti securo. Questo vi scrivemo in resposta di due vostre.
(ASMN, AG, b. 2977, libro 3, «Ex castris ad Broilum», 3 October 1521, Federico Gonzaga to
Equicola).
[101] ASMN, AG, b. 2998, libro 39, Mantua, 4 October 1521, Isabella d'Este to Vincenzo
de' Preti. Isabella had originally sent him a month previously:
Desiderosa in questi tempi de havere pienamente notitia di quanto in campo
occorre, mandamo Vicenzo de' Preti, nostro cancelliero, con comissione che ne

Et pochi potriano così ben scrivere la verità come voi per essere stato in fatto et a canto la persona del Signor Marchese nostro figliolo.[102]

Isabella was obsessed with the fear that she was not being told everything or that events were happening without her knowledge and approval; in her opinion Equicola would precisely fulfil this need:

Perché in esse [lettere] ni avisate così minutamente quanto occorse quel dì, di hora in hora, che, se fossimo stata personalmente in campo, non l'haveressimo potuto intendere più minutamente. Per il che laudamo la diligentia vostra, de la qual restamo ogni dì più satisfacta.[103]

As far as Isabella was concerned, Equicola's principal purpose was to report on the Marquis' every move, a task not very different from that he was used to, except that it now involved the two most powerful people in Mantua. Equicola must have been hopeful about not having to stay in the field for too long because he had not been given specific instructions to stay. In spite of the hardships of military life Equicola was at least pleased that the campaign was under way. He could not now complain that he did not have anything to write about:

Non solamente da giorno in giorno et da hora in hora, ma da momento in momento bisognarebe scriver ad Vostra Excellentia per dar a quella piena notitia di quanto occorre. Io di tal diligentia non mancarò quanto serà in me, pur che questa, o vogliamo dire diligentia o più presto debito, non sia causa de farne stare più in queste parti, che non vorrei, benché non posso altro volere che quel che vole Vostra Signoria. Hor su, non si perda tempo in ciancie.[104]

---

avise de omni particularità et de le factioni et del dire che si fa in questo exercito, ad ciò niuna cosa a nova intendiamo da altri de predetto exercito.
(ASMN, AG, b. 2997, libro 37, Mantua, 3 September 1521, Isabella to Giovanni Gonzaga).

[102] ASMN, AG, b. 2998, libro 39, Mantua, 10 October 1521, Isabella d'Este to Equicola.

[103] ASMN, AG, b. 2998, libro 39, 19 October 1521, Isabella d'Este to Equicola.

[104] ASMN, AG, b. 1647, «Da Rebecca», 7 October 1521, Equicola to Isabella d'Este. In another letter of the same date he refers to his rapid disillusionment with the situation and his own condition:

Heri fui d'oro, doman serò de argento, mercore de rame, giobia di piumbo, pesarò assai ma de poco pretio. Questo baste quanto al mio stare, il quale crido che serà a guerra finita.

At first he had high hopes that he would not have to remain in camp:

Sono hore XXII et so gionto in questo felicissimo campo a salvamento con tucti li denari che manda Nostro Signore.
Al Reverendissimo et Illustrissimo Signor Cardinal de' Medici, ligato, ho facto quanto Vostra Excellentia me scrive... Io Signor Marchese sta sano et bello più che mai. Subito che fui gionto me mandò da Medici... Sua Signoria me ha facte molte careze publice... Non so se ho da restare o non. Quando il saperò, ne darò notitia a Vostra Excellentia benché non so più como se possa passare.
(ASMN, AG, b. 1647, from the camp, 6 October 1521, Equicola to Isabella d'Este).

Equicola's attitude towards the war underwent some notable changes now that the army was actually fighting. He wished it to be known that he had adopted the grave attitude called for by the new situation. Equicola was swept along by the course of events; on his first visit to the camp he had not believed in the seriousness of the venture or what effect it would have on the peninsula. Now, however, frivolity had to be abandoned in the face of dramatic military operations.

Equicola did have his uses in the administration of the army: he was entrusted with certain financial matters[105] and with other less obvious tasks, amongst them the interrogation of prisoners which he said he conducted «ad mio modo».[106] He was also engaged to win over the generals of the Spanish and papal armies as allies, in particular, the Marquis of Pescara, to whom he was bound both by family ties and by the Marquis' illicit relationship with one of Isabella d'Este's *donzelle*, Delia, in which Equicola assisted. In this, he appears to have been effective; their friendship was personally satisfying to Equicola because the association with so great a general reflected well on him.[107]

Although Equicola was no longer properly speaking a soldier, he shared in all the excitement of the battle.[108] On occasion, he came closer to fighting than he had bargained for:

> In quest'hora, che sono XIIII, si è dato allarme et messer Statio [Gadio, one of the Marquis' secretaries] et io, retrovandoci a cavallo verso li reparti, corremmo verso 'l rumore et tanto avante che vedemmo cavalli li quali ci credevamo de nostri. Fommoli vicino quanto è longa la piaza de San Piero de Mantua, et certo

---

[105]   Equicola himself states that he is being used as a trusted courier: «Condussi li denari a salvamento li quali furono octanta milia ducati d'oro».
(ASMN, AG, b. 1647, 7 October 1521, Equicola to Isabella d'Este).

[106]   Sono stati pigliati doi de quelli fanti de Parma li quali ho examinati ad mio modo.
(ASMN, AG, b. 1370, «Da lo campo», 10 September 1521, Equicola to Isabella d'Este).

[107]   Equicola did not hesitate to vaunt his role in creating a network of allies around the inexperienced Federico Gonzaga:

> Illustrissima Signoria mia. Perché heri non puotetti far il debito mio in visitare lo Illustrissimo Signor Marchese de Pescara, questa matina ad una hora nanti dì, me condussi da Sua Signoria. Trovailo in lecto et tanto ragionai seco quanto se vestì. Multo lauda il Signor Marchese nostro... Veramente il Signor nostro Illustrissimo ha molti lodatori in questo exercito, ma de magior efficacia non n'è alcuno come è lo predecto Signor de Pescara. Tra me stesso ne godo.
> (ASMN, AG, b. 1647, 8 October 1521, Equicola to Isabella d'Este).

The Marquis of Pescara showed further signs of favour towards Equicola at a meal with all the captains present: «Io so stato coppero del Signor Marchese de Pescara.»
(ASMN, AG, b. 1647, 14 October 1521, Equicola to Isabella d'Este).

[108]   Io, Mario Equicola, servo de Vostra Excellentia, ad fè de real homo et vero gentilhomo, prometto et iuro ad Vostra Signoria che se li inimici veneranno ad trovarci qui che son rocti et tagliati a pezi.
(ASMN, AG, b. 1647, 12 October 1521, Equicola to Isabella d'Este).

andavamo a loro se non che ci fermmano ad vedere passare li Spagnoli. Da tutti, poi, intendemmo quelli essere stati li inimici, li quali hanno tolti molti saccomandi de nostri.[109]

Equicola did not altogether abandon his «ciancie» which, in this case, resemble a school-boy prank (one detects a childish pleasure at his escape). But in the midst of all the discomfort and military activity Equicola had something else on his mind which weighed just as heavily:

> Vostra Excellentia mi faccia gratia che mi possa transferire in Venetia per X dì ad far stampare il mio peso gravissimo, quel fastidioso *Libro de Amore*, perché, se non lo stampo questa vernata, non è più libro di questa età. In casa mia non lo posso né voglio stampare per essere ignorante lo stampatore et senza me non poter fare et la mia sorte mi ha facto Mercurio che non mi posso fermare. Però non vorria perdere il libro, e lla spesa, e 'l tempo: così se Vostra Excellentia mi concederà che vadi in Venetia, in XV dì uscirò de fastidio et pena la quale sole dare amore a chi bene ama, che sia certa Vostra Signoria che me la dà questo libro.[110]

The urgency of the matter was so great that Equicola wrote another letter to the *Marchesana* the same day:

> Et supplicarò Vostra Excellentia che me dia licentia per X dì, per posser andar a far stampare il mio *Libro de Amore* in Venetia, che altro modo né altro ordine li vedo, et se più se differisce la età non supporta che da mi se stampino quelle ciancie.

In the September of 1521 he had received the well-known reply form Trissino concerning the language of the *Libro* which indicates that the work was completed and only needed the comments of a few friends for it to be finally ready for publication.[111] The history of the composition of the *Libro* may be plotted against the background of the wars that swept the peninsula from 1494 onwards; a history as long as Equicola's adult life.[112] The *Libro* itself may be seen as a not inconsiderable attempt to come to terms with an ever changing situation, and a reaction against the political events of the time. As such it is a personal, almost secret work, one in which Equicola proposed a number

[109] ASMN, AG, b. 1647, «Da Rebecca», 8 October 1521, Equicola to Isabella d'Este.

[110] ASMN, AG, b. 1813, Ostiano, 25 October 1521, Equicola to Isabella d'Este.

[111] B. Morsolin, *Monografia d'un gentiluomo letterato nel secolo XVI*, Florence, 1894, p. 411, document 47.

[112] On the composition of the *Libro* see R. Renier, «Per la cronologia e la composizione del *Libro de natura de amore* di Mario Equicola», *GSLI*, 14 (1889) 212-33; I. Rocchi, «Per una nuova cronologia e valutazione del *Libro de natura de amore* di Mario Equicola», *GSLI*, 153 (1976) 566-85; G. Castagno, «L'autografo del *Libro de natura de amore* di Mario Equicola», *Lingua Nostra*, 23 (1962), pp. 74-77; *Idem.*, «L'autografo del *Libro de natura de amore* di Mario Equicola» in *Arte, pensiero e cultura a Mantova nel primo Rinascimento in rapporto con la Toscana e con il Veneto*, Florence, 1965, pp. 133-43; M. Pozzi, «Mario Equicola e la cultura cortigiana: appunti sulla redazione manoscritta del *Libro de natura de amore*», *Lettere Italiane*, 32 (1980), pp. 149-71.

of solutions to his own peculiar predicament.[113] It represents an almost desperate effort to provide a guide — intellectual, moral and social — for the times. In the *Libro*, Equicola, confronted with the chaos of the Italian political system, tried to rationalize the many theories current at the time. But the work far from being a mere compilation, also registers Equicola's long struggle to come to terms with court life and its values, as well as his attempt to define the sphere of action appropriate to a courtier. Equicola thought the work outmoded and that the problems with which it dealt were no longer an issue. The matter of love had been overshadowed by history so much so that the *Libro* would not be published until 1525 and even then Equicola was to be unable to supervise its publication in person. He was forced to disregard his personal anxieties in favour of an imposing public image, that of the authoritative writer glorifying Federico's military valour. The imposing blend of literature and philosophy found in the *Libro* was there almost for its own sake, the product of his scholarly bent, and developed during a period when his first priority was the education of Isabella d'Este. The *Libro* may also be seen not only in terms of an individual's struggle to understand the nature of human life but also in terms of a materialistic ambition to apply that knowledge to improve his position in the society in which he lived. The irony of Equicola's situation was that once he began reaping the rewards of success the *Libro* would be considered mere «ciancie», belonging to a past age, not quite relevant to the present. So he had to «purge» himself by publishing the work. The decision to make it public must be associated with the change of his position, a last chance to prove his worth as a man of learning before he was submerged by the business of administering a state. He emended a number of passages which, in the manuscrit, contained attacks against the catholic church. He hoped the book, when printed, would add to his prestige as a writer and a scholar. Equicola could not have known that the material of the treatise on love was far from exhausted and would enjoy a new lease of life through the sixteenth century.[114]

Equicola was meanwhile no closer to returning to Mantua and he was becoming impatient, so much so Isabella had to rebuke him for undignified behaviour.[115] It appears that Equicola was doing everything in his power to

---

[113] Cf. L. Savino, «La *Natura de Amore* di M. Equicola» in *Di alcuni trattati e trattatisti d'amore italiani della prima metà del secolo XVI*, vol. 10 of *Studi di letteratura italiana*, Naples, 1914, pp, 16, 24.

[114] For a history of the love-treatise in the Renaissance see, for example, J.C. Nelson, *Renaissance Theory of Love*, New York, 1958.

[115] Voi haveti fatto tanti lamenti, et con noi et con altri, di non haver cavalcatura per il famiglio che potevati molto bene restar di usare questa fatica perché, se voleti discorrere con la ragione, non doveti iustamente dolervi se non de voi istesso,

sabotage his chances of remaining with the army. Isabella realized the motive behind those childish pranks, but considered him to be unreasonable in view of the undeniable advantages (for her, principally) he would gain by staying with Federico:

> Poiché allo Illustrissimo Signor Marchese, nostro figliolo, piace che voi lo seguiati, non doveti haver molesto ubedire Sua Signoria, maxime essendovi un tale invito a grande favore. Credemo bene che 'l stare vostro qua vi sia de più commodo che non vi dà il stare in campo, ma li gran favori che ne reportiati tra tanti signori sono sufficienti ad non lassarvi sentire li incommodi. Et se dessignasti di haver favori et commodità insieme, parni che pensati a quello che nullo o a rarissimi se concede, sì che andati allegramente et commodative con li tempi et il volere de chi ha libertà di commmandarvi, come sapiamo sapereti saviamente fare volendo.[116]

Equicola must have been greatly perturbed on reading Isabella's letter, believing that his last hope had vanished. Undoubtedly, the *Marchesana* was not wrong in her analysis of the situation. Equicola now saw himself as the ideologue of the new regime, not an errandboy whose task was simply to deliver his master's orders. The court still provided the most congenial living conditions; whereas military life was best lived vicariously. Equicola was so upset by her letter that Isabella was forced to write another in order to reassure him.[117]

Equicola's sorry state was worsened by his ill-health, perhaps a serious attack of gout, which he did not fail to mention in his pleas to return to Mantua, and he attempted to make the most of his situation, portraying himself in a piteous light «al dolor de la gamba, che è quasi senza intermissione, se adgionge quel del'animo che è continuo, al quale imporre freno non si pò».[118] It is clear from other sources that Equicola's health was deteriorating and that camp-life was probably a contributory factor. Equicola continued to impress

---

quale haveti rimandato in qua el cavallo senza che vi sia sta' rechiesto.
(ASMN, AG, b. 2963, libro 14, Mantua, 31 October 1521, Isabella d'Este to Equicola).

[116] See note 115. With Equicola's departure from the camp Isabella d'Este found it almost impossible to obtain any information at all. She complained of this state of affairs to Stazio Gadio, one of Federico's secretaries:

> Non potemo fare che non ce maravigliamo et che anche non ce dogliamo di voi che ne tegnati così rare volte avisate de li successi del campo et de li progressi del Signor Marchese, nostro figliolo, che ognuno ha aviso in Mantua prima di noi et molto più diffusi che noi.
> (ASMN, AG, b. 2963, libro 14, Mantua, 18 November 1521).

[117] In una cosa sola non laudamo la continentia de le dette lettere vostre, dove mostrate esserve turbato per un'altra lettera che ve havemo fatta scrivere burlando et giocando con voi, come sa el secretario proprio, che il ordinassimo la detta lettera ridendo. Et ce maravigliamo pur troppo che siati fatto cussì sospettoso contra el solito et che non pigliate le parole nostre in scherzo. Ma circa questo ne accade dire altro se non replicarve che havemo burlato con voi et per tale voressimo che havesti intesa la nostra lettera.
(ASMN, AG, b. 2963, libro 14, Mantua, 3 November 1521, Isabella d'Este to Equicola)

[118] ASMN, AG, b. 2501, Canneto, 11 November 1521, Equicola to Isabella d'Este.

upon Isabella d'Este his precarious physical and mental health. There is no reason to believe that he was overly exaggerating. His language aimed at creating a suitable effect on his reader (Isabella d'Este).[119]

For Equicola, the crisis was complete: his intellectual disarray and inability to cope with the new role was matched by a breakdown in his health. He did finally return to Mantua but not as triumphantly as he no doubt had hoped, partly because the condition of his leg had worsened: «anchor non posso movere la gamba, ma spero per omni modo presto serò libero». His hopes were again dashed when he had to concede that he would not be able to walk before Christmas.[120] Nor was he cured the following year even though he was treated by one of Federico's most competent doctors, «maestro Abraham».[121]

Equicola was to find it very difficult to break away from the new routine that had been prepared for him. The Marquis was apparently unaware of the anguish he caused Equicola in ordering him to return to camp, either because Equicola had been careful not to display his unhappiness in front of Federico or because the Marquis, although knowing of it but wanting Equicola's company and the benefit of his experience, was simply indifferent to Equicola's suffering. On his part Equicola claimed that he would join the Marquis just as soon as his health permitted him:

---

[119]   Equicola makes great play of the soul-body dichotomy in order to give prominence to his mental anguish of a courtier *exilé*:

> Et benché la natura istessa ci persuada tollerare patientemente quel a che non è remedio, la natura istessa anchor ne costrenge a dolerci de li casi occorsi irrecuperabili perciò che irremediabili sono. L'animo, dunque, mio e 'l corpo si dole, l'uno per retrovarse in tenebre, l'altro per essere infermo (see note 118).

[120]   ASMN, AG, b. 2500, Mantua, 20 November 1521, Equicola to Federico Gonzaga. On the 26 November Equicola was still confident of a quick recovery: «la gamba non è sanata, sanarà presto» (ASMN, AG, b. 2500, Mantua, Equicola to the Marquis). By the beginning of December he had no reason to change his mind: «io commincio ad star meglio. Parme mille anni veder Vostra Signoria.» (ASMN, AG, b. 2500, Mantua, 6 December 1521, Equicola to the Marquis). However, the next day he seems to have suffered a relapse: «anchor non me posso sostener niente in la gamba et credo nanti natale non essere in tucto libero» (*ibid.*, 7 December).

[121]   The Marquis of Mantua appears almost callous in his indifference to Equicola's plight. Not that he does not want him to get better as soon as possible but his rationale is that «possi venirci a ritrovare». The Marquis was still with the papal forces:

> Havendo inteso per lettere di messer Mario, nostro carissimo secretario, con quanta diligente cura li medicati la gamba, ni havemo preso grande piacere sperando per la excellente virtù vostra, sì come desideramo che presto el sia resanato da voi, che 'l possi venirci a ritrovare. Et però vi pregamo ad volerlo liberare dil mal suo, come ni confidamo fareti, che da voi restaremo molto gratificati.
> (ASMN, AG, b. 2978, libro 1, Piacenza, 4 January 1522, Federico Gonzaga to «maestro Habram chirurgo»).

Né il male, né il tempo, né cosa altra me teneria ad retrovarmi subito da Vostra
Excellentia, ma solo il timore me tiene, che, essendo hormai la gamba quasi
guarita, non tornasse di novo a guastarse et seria uno dolore magior.[122]

For a while the cautious Equicola thought it best not to venture out of
Mantua. But there was no improvement in his health and he was practically
confined to bed «in questo carcere di casa mia».[123] To cheer himself up (and
to perhaps follow his master's example), he decided to renovate his house. He
also found other distractions to help him take his mind off his infirmity. As
was usual, he kept Federico informed of the latest events, providing him with
background information, as he did for example, about the recently elected
pope, Hadrian VI; he was optimistic about the new pope's favour: «Questo
pontefice facto mi par essere certo che sia molto a nostro proposito.»[124]

---

[122] ASMN, AG, b. 2503, Mantua, 29 January 1522, Equicola to the Marquis.

[123] By February Equicola was once more hopeful that his leg would improve:

So tornato da la Certosa et, per Dio gratia, molto più gagliardo che non vi andai.
Spero presto essere con quella già che lo sanare de la gamba va in aperta salute
et benché non mi possa per anchora sostenere senza bastone, non dubito che tra
pochi dì il potrò buttar via.
(ASMN, AG, b. 2503, Mantua, 16 February 1522, Equicola to the Marquis).

But, we find that in March he was confined to bed:

Io non scrivo da parte di Madama perché sto in lecto et non posso andare ad lo
mio studio et sigillare la lettera. Ma sappia che è così et domani scriverò da parte
di Sua Excellentia.
(ASMO, ASE, C, Ambasciatori: Mantova, b. 2, 15 March 1522, Equicola to
Alfonso d'Este).

[124] On the decoration of Equicola's house see A. Portioli, (*XIX Centenario) Mantova
a Vergilio*, Mantua, 1882; V. Montanari, «La casa di Mario Equicola, castellano di Canedole»,
Gazzetta di Mantova, 151, 2 June 1964, p. 3.
The precise details of the improvements are given in a decree issued by Federico Gonzaga:

Pro Mario Equicola secretario Marchionisse Mantuae. Donatio areae adiungen-
dae eius domi in Burgo Portus pro eius commoditate.
De Consensu Nostro
Federicus et cetera, Sanctae Romanae Ecclesiae Capitaneus generalis. Verisimile
est priscos mortales in silvis speluncisque primum more ferarum vitam degisse,
mox antra fodere coepisse, tecta fronde tegere de luto virgultisque loca facere,
inde furcis erectis gleba struere parietes. Tandem usus domorum ostendit inven-
tionem per consuetudinemque ad artes perventum quum in unum congessisset
metus ferocium animalium urbes aedificatae, quas magnificentiores credimus
quae magnificentioribus aedificiis structae sunt, si in iis facies grata et elegans
fuerit quae commodi et firmitatis rationem habeat sitque conveniens consensus
ex omnibus partibus ut in hominis corpore, cubito, pede, palmo, digito, caeteris-
que menbris responsus symmetros est adstique decor qui emendatus operis aspec-
tus est. Quum igitur Marius Equicola, matris nostrae Illustrissime et noster a
secretis, in suburbio Portus Lares sibi paret minutilis lateribus marmore expolito
ita ut non ad pulchritudinem tantum sed perpetuitatem erecti iudicentur, venus-
tasque ipsa non quaesita ab alio quam a necessitate et commodo videatur; quum
igitur publico decori et ornamento satis pro viribus consulat, visum est nobis adii-
cere eius commoditati eaque eum donare area quae contra, praeter viam est,

Equicola was proved right when Federico's appointment as captain-general was renewed.[125] Needless to say, his jubilation knew no bounds on hearing of his master's success which he was to record in the continuing *Chronica di Mantua*.[126] Both Federico's and Equicola's confidence in their abilities to control the Mantuan state was increasing. In order to assert himself, and to free himself from his mother's influence, Federico had to impress upon everyone that it was he who ruled. One of the ways he sought to achieve this goal was

---

lacumque qui infra est se extendit. Haec tantum includit latitudinem spatii quantum sexdecim cubita compraendunt, latitudo vero XI cubita continet ab septemtrione molendinum hospicii elemosinarii fines habet, a meridie porta qua in lacum, de quo supra diximus, exiri potest qui ex dicto loco orientem spectet solem ut occidentem strata viarum publica. In hac itaque area quam consulto eidem Mario nostro damus, concedimus, tradimus et donamus ita ut revocari nullo modo possit haec donatio posterisque suis et successoribus nihilque de iure requiri possit hoc concessum esse intelligimus, aedificia tollantur, vendantur, donentur relinquere cui libitum fuerit sui iuris esto... Datum Mantuae die XVI Iulii 1522.
(ASMN, AG, Registro dei Decreti n. 36, f. 106ʳ).
The decree makes explicit the connection between Equicola and the policy of the Marquis: «Magnificentia» most visible in the buildings that a prince constructs or in those that his supporters design. Building can be considered the first stage of the politics of magnificence (G. Pontano, *I trattati delle virtù sociali*, ed. by F. Tateo, Rome, 1965, in particular, the treatise *De Magnificentia*, pp. 85-121).
Equicola was serious indeed about decorating a house worthy of a humanist and an important court dignitary:
> Messer Mario Equicola, nostro secretario carissimo, ne fa intender come, havendo lui ricercato, per vostro mezo, di quelli nostri homini una pietra antica, che sta in la chiesa di San Lorenzo lì, per ornar una sua casa che 'l fa qui in Mantua, essi homini sono contenti, secondo li scriveti, di darcila, purché noi ne fossimo contenti per esser quello loco nostro ius patronato et se n'havesse la licentia del Vescovo di Verona. Ve dicemo che noi siamo contento, et così direti alli ditti homini, et che ne fanno gran piacere. Fati voi, dunque, opera che Messer Mario habbi la ditta pietra et che la se li mandi, pagandola lui per quello che li sarà tassato per li homini o in dinari o in una altra cosa per ornamento della chiesa. Se dimandarà la licentia al Reverendissimo Cardinale Cornaro come ad Vescovo di Verona et tenemo per certo se haverà, nondimeno, in caso che la non se potesse haver, noi promettemo et ce obligamo ad farla ritorna al loco dove l'è hora.
> (ASMN, AG, b. 2928, libro 272, Mantua, 31 July 1522, Federico Gonzaga to the *potestà* of Ostilia).

[125] Equicola's description of the new pope's achievements before he became pope is underlined by a fine sense of irony which intends to highlight the disproportion between the man and the great office:
> Hadriano è flammengo, ha studiato in Parisi in lo collegio di Sancto Augustino, diventò doctore in theologia et molte cose ha scritto in philosophia et bene le opere sue si vendono et, mo che è Papa, sono laudatissime.
> (ASMN, AG, b. 2503, Mantua, 11 January 1522, Equicola to the Marquis).

[126] See L. Mazzoldi, *Mantova: La storia*, II, p. 280.
> Veramente seria gran male se non ne restasse memoria (Federico's re-appointment as captain-general) a posteri, li quali per quelli et per molti altri testimonii cognosceranno la nostra età haver produco un giovene tale et tanto. Io farò quel che potrò, la registrarò in le *Chroniche*.
> (ASMN, AG, b. 2503, Mantua, 27 January 1522, Equicola to the Marquis).
No evidence has been discovered so far which shows that Equicola did actually extend the *Chronica* beyond 1521.

to «outdo» his mother in the areas in which she took an interest. This resulted in the construction of new *camerini* for himself, and on a yet grander scale, the construction of a new palace at Marmirolo and later, the Palazzo del Te.[127] *Magnificentia* was the keyword in the strategy, one which Equicola understood in all its implications:

> Ma esser magnifico et magnificentissimo non possono consequire se non quelli che sono in grandissime reccheze constituiti et che hanno facultà abundantissime, per ciò che la magnificentia non consiste se non in grandissime spese, le quali precipuamente loda Aristotele in edificare sumptuosamente.[128]

The secretary was burdened with administrative duties (financial matters connected with the campaign), as well as the intellectual one of lending his erudition to Federico Gonzaga.[129] By 20 March 1522 Equicola's leg had so improved that he was compelled to join the Marquis.[130] Five days later he arrived at Federico's camp in Pavia with the various items he had brought from Mantua for the Marquis.[131] In particular, a sum of money borrowed from his

---

[127]   Cf. E. Verheyen, *Palazzo*, pp. 39-41.

[128]   ASMN, AG, b. 2503, Mantua, 17 February 1522, Equicola to the Marquis. See also C.M. Brown, «Review of E. Verheyen, *Palazzo*», *The Art Bulletin*, 62 (1980), p. 162.

[129]   In a situation where he could not trust many people the Marquis found Equicola invaluable in the various financial transactions he was required to undertake: the payment of mercenaries and other officers employed by the Marquis:

> Die XXII Aprillis 1522 libre vintiuna pagati ad messer Mario Equicola per dare a uno fante spagnolo de commissione del Signor nostro. 21-0.
> (ASMN, AG, b. 410, f. 108ʳ).

Another entry indicates that these financial transactions were a regular part of Equicola's activities:

> Die 9 Aprilis 1522 libre trentadue, soldi dui, pagati ad messer Mario secretario per tanti pagati per lui ad Benedetto Moraro per comprar polver de schioppo de commissione del Signor nostro. 32-2.
> (ASMN, AG, b. 410, f. 103ᵛ).

Equicola was also involved in large-scale financial operations:

> Perché il Signor Marchese di Pescara ni ha restituito il scritto della promissa che gli facessimo per il Signor Theodoro Triultio de li quattro mila scuti che sono sta exbursati in man vostre, semo contenti che li diati a chi parerà a Sua Signoria, secundo che lei vi farà intender per sue lettere.
> (ASMN, AG, b. 2978, libro 2, Piacenza, 8 February 1522, Federico Gonzaga to Equicola. Cf. L. Mazzoldi, *Mantova: La storia*, II, p. 136).

[130]   Equicola had announced that he was feeling much better on 16 March:

> Io andarò in campo et in Milano chel Signor Marchese me scriva ch'io vada questa sera. Intenderò la voluntà di Madama Illustrissima, poi starò per meglio resanare. Hogi me son levato di lecto et me sento assai bene.
> (ASMO, ASE, C, Ambasciatori: Mantova, b. 2, 16 March 1522, Equicola to Alfonso d'Este).

The Marquis was as impatient as ever to have Equicola by his side and Equicola, on his part, did everything he could to delay his departure until finally it was impossible to postpone it any longer: «Domani parto per Pavia dove se ritrova lo Illustrissimo Signor Marchese di Mantua.» (ASMO, ASE, C, Ambasciatori: Mantova, b. 2, 20 March 1522, Equicola to Alfonso d'Este).

[131]   Equicola confirmed his arrival in a letter to Isabella d'Este:

> Illustrissima Signoria. Heri sera ad hore XXIII arrivai in Pavia con quanto mi fu

mother. The Marquis' financial position was so precarious, due to his not having received any money from Rome, he was forced to borrow from his own retainers. In this respect, Equicola was doubly useful: he could both be entrusted with the money Federico had to pay out and was himself able to lend a limited amount of money to the Marquis for the duration of the immediate crisis.[132] There is no doubt that the Marquis appreciated the secretary's value in circumstances such as these. But there were times when he was less useful: as for example the time of his arrival in Pavia, when his leg began to ache and he decided to rest in bed for two or three days. He only managed to perform one of his tasks, which was to call on the Duke of Milan in his capacity as Isabella d'Este's personal envoy.[133] Once Equicola was on his feet again, however, his duties were identical to those he had on the last occasion he came to Federico's camp: he reported to Isabella all the news he felt would interest her as well as the more weighty detailed accounts of the military situation. In his letters to her, he carefully fostered the impression of the Marquis as a great captain, even comparing him at one point to the Emperor Charles V.[134] Equicola judged that this war promised or threatened a momentous upheaval of all the Italian states and the major nations; consequently, it required a state of mind differing from that enjoyed in the calm of the Mantuan court: «Non è tempo più di ciancie» he wrote, perhaps this time with greater conviction.[135]

> consegnato in Mantua. Trovai lo Illustrissimo sano et bello con tucta la corte... Sa Vostra Signoria che la mia prescia de condurme in campo fu non solamente per obedir al Signor Marchese, ma perché in me non fosse mai notato alcuno acto dal quale se potesse comprendere nel'animo mio essere viltà et questo mi haria causato lo essere arrivato in campo poi che Francesi si fossero disscioli et disuniti da Squizari. Ma hora conosco che potea restare in Mantua anchora per XV dì; semo qui.
> (ASMN, AG, b. 1649, Pavia, 25 March 1522, Equicola to Isabella d'Este).

[132]   Adì 7 ditto (April 1522) scuti centocinquanta de oro in oro riceputi dal Magnifico messer Mario Equicola secretario imprestati al Signor nostro per lui in Pavia gratis a restituire per lo Magnifico Domino Thesaurario generale in Mantua. 727-10. (ASMN, AG, b. 410, f. 126^r). The Marquis also needed to borrow money from his mother:

> Restiamo satisfatti di quanto haveti fatto in mandarne dinari per messer Mario, il caviaro, composta et altre cose quale havemo havuto et ni sono state gratissime et maxime l'amorevole atto che ha usato la Illustrissima Signora nostra madre in prestarne li cinquecento ducati, che ben ne volemo havere obligatione a Sua Excellentia et ringratiamola.
> (ASMN, AG, b. 2978, libro 4, Pavia, 29 March 1522, the Marquis to his treasurer).

[133]   Hogi, lo [the Duke of Milan] visitarò et poi me ponerò in lecto perché 'l mio piè ha bisogno de reposo. Starò in lecto tri dì o doi. (See n. 131 for the reference to this letter.)

[134]   Lo Signor Marchese de Mantua è la sollicitudine istessa. La matina, ad bona hora, cavalca et va pigliando aere, va ad trovare Signor Antonio Leva, il quale observa il Signor Marchese, non dico como li soi, che non sanno o sanno poco honorare, ma como se fosse il Re suo catholico. Magna et subito cavalca al signor duca [of Pescara] perché la matina è un poco de tarda leva et li se sta assai in consiglio il qualo è ricchissimo de parole et povero de provisioni. (ASMN, AG, b. 1649, Pavia, 28 March 1522, Equicola to Isabella d'Este).

[135]   ASMN, AG, b. 1649, Pavia, 31 March 1522, Equicola to Isabella d'Este.

Equicola was more than ever conscious of being the reluctant soldier; when present (rather unwillingly) at certain events, like the capture of Novara by Federico Gonzaga he wrote: «ad mi più piaceria stare in Pavia che mettere la salute et victoria in questione et periculo.»[136] To him a siege was preferable to the rigours of a campaign vigorously pursued through Milanese territory.[137] He witnessed the preparations to fortify Pavia before Lautrec, as was expected, came to lay siege to the city.[138] When the possibility of a siege became more of a reality Equicola was happy to express his confidence in the Marquis' abilities. Propaganda and a fervent belief in his captain-general were fused together in a mixture of ancient and modern *exempla* to prove that victory was close at hand. It was clear that Equicola had chosen sides but wishing to avoid a break with the *Marchesana* pictured the sole reason for her existence as the glory of her son. He did not misjudge the situation, for Isabella still hoped to harness her son's prestige to her own.[139] In the midst of the feverish activity in besieged Pavia Federico, «lo nostro Principe», appeared as a great calming force skilfully organizing the defence of the city.[140] Equicola described to Isabella his role in the papal-imperial war-machine:

> Molte particularità non scrivo, si perché son cose che recercano magior ocio, si che io so occupato in dormire il dì, ché 'l Signor Illustrissimo me ha facto tanto favore che mai potrò essere tanto grato con Sua Excellentia che molto più non me li senta obligato, quando quelle poche hore che posa la nocte, me ha commandato che io veglie et scolte li infiniti avisi che vengono. Se è cosa che importe io lo

---

[136]   ASMN, AG, b. 1649, Pavia, 29 March 1522, Equicola to Isabella d'Este.

[137]   Equicola was confident that Pavia would be able to withstand a French siege; he recalled the unsuccessful sieges of Pisa, Padua and Verona, all of which took place in the not so distant past. Equicola was satisfied with the preparations that were being made:
> Ad iudicio di tucti pratichi de la guerra de nostri tempi et per cognitione de quelli che hanno lecte le cose de la antica militia, mai fu la più gagliardamente assediata terra che è stata hora Pavia, né mai fu città meglio difesa.
> (ASMN, AG, b. 1649, Pavia, 12 April 1522, Equicola to Isabella d'Este).

[138]   Lo Illustrissimo Signor Marchese attende ad reparare Pavia per più di mille respecti et falo bene et diligentemente. Tutto hogi semo stati in Castello ad quel frescho. Disposte le artegliarie et non mancato ad quanto specta alla conservatione de questa città: secureza de soldati et honor suo. Ha data grande et continua odientia a gentili homini per... hora non solamente con patientia ma con humanità et mansuetudine.
> (ASMN, AG, b. 1649, Pavia, 4 April 1522, Equicola to Isabella d'Este).

[139]   Equicola seems to be much better at praising the Marquis than restraining him:
> Mi è parso congratularme con Vostra Excellentia che sia matre de tanto figliolo che per virtù et sol per gloria nacque. (See n. 137 for the reference to this letter.)

[140]   Baste ad Vostra Excellentia essere certa che nulla factione si fa senza la persona sua, non se muta artigliaria che sua presentia non vi sia, non si repara dove inimici possono offendere che la Sua Signoria non ordine, non commande, non faccia presto exequire. Né io lo haveria creso se non lo vedesse continuo, né 'l dirria se non fosse ben vero et a tucti notissimo. Con humanità et liberalità provede alli feriti, con pietà fa sepellire li occisi che pur, como si fa, qualche uno di nostre pere.
> (ASMN, AG, b. 1649, Pavia, 12 April 1522, Equicola to Isabella d'Este.)

sveglie, se non, che proveda. Benché 'l favore sia stato grande, nondimeno io omni
cosa referisco ad Sua Excellentia o de importantia o non, donde sequita che sta
pochissimo in quiete. (For reference see n. 140.)

Here we see Equicola performing his secretarial duties to the letter. He
emphatically refused to pass beyond such a position although given the opportunity; it may be because he preferred to avoid the burden of responsibility for
decisions made (and the possibly grim consequences for any error of judgement) or because he simply did not feel it was his place to act for his master.
It can be seen by this that Equicola was not ambitious to manipulate events and
to be effectively in charge; for him the burdens of administering a state and of
obeying orders were sufficient to block his horizons. Although he made it clear
he had no intention of assuming Federico's power in the day-to-day running
of the state, Equicola's detractors could put the case another way: inept,
incompetent would be their choice of adjectives. They might refer to his lack
of initiative which in itself could have endangered the favour he enjoyed. No
doubt there is an element of this in his character but we must bear in mind that
Equicola chose to act in this manner because he realized that he did not have
anything else to offer except his service. In fact, the strength of Equicola's position lay not so much in his administrative abilities but rather in his willingness
to renounce any ambitions of power in the pure sense. This did not mean that
he did not wish for success; he did indeed want it, even longed for it, but wished
to be successful without the hardships he was now suffering. On the 17 April
Equicola was able to announce that the siege had been lifted.[141] It is not known
when Equicola returned to Mantua, but it is probable that he came back with
the Marquis who after a brief stay then left without him.

*

It is certain that from the beginning of May 1522 Equicola was still acting
in his official role as Isabella d'Este's secretary.[142] Nevertheless, Federico
made sure that Equicola did not forget that it was the Marquis who had the
power to improve his status by appointing him, on a temporary basis, castellan in place of the sick Calandra.[143] All the time Equicola was trying to consolidate his position in order to achieve a greater degree of stability and perma-
nence. The urgency of this desire led him into conflict with other

---

[141]   Alle hore octo li inimici se levorno da campo et remossero la obsidione.
(ASMN, AG, b. 1649, Pavia, 17 April 1522, Equicola to Isabella d'Este).

[142]   Isabella d'Este's letters to Giovan Battista Malatesta, Mantuan ambassador to Venice,
were certainly written in Equicola's hand from 5 May to 17 July.
(ASMN, AG, b. 2126A).

[143]   Messer Ian Iacomo Calandra è malato di febre terzana. Sino in mo mi ha il
Signore posto in suo loco.
(ASMO, ASE, C, Ambasciatori: Mantova, b. 2, 15 June 1522, Equicola to
Alfonso d'Este).

CHAPTER IV

Mantuans who resented what they considered his interference in their affairs;
one such case was Alessandro Spagnuoli who made a very specific complaint
against Equicola to both Federico and Isabella:

> Benché la felice memoria de lo Illustrissimo Signore vostro patre volse et ordinò
> che io havesse a sucedere in lo Archipresbiterato de la Chiesa mantuana,... tamen
> non è mai accaduto el caso se non al presente per la morte del vechio Arciprete
> per la quale... ho conseguito la possessione quieta et pacifica... Ma in questa mia
> consolatione... ho anche inteso che messer Mario Equicola intende de spogliarme
> del canonicato mio, qual similiter hebi canonicamente de bona voluntà et con-
> senso del predetto Signore quondam vostro genitore et per concessione apostolica
> lo posso tenere cum lo Archipresbiterato... Me pare che esso messer Mario, forsi
> male informato, me facia torto a disturbarme quello che Dio et la ragione et mei
> patroni et signori me hano concesso. Et benché lui forse habia qualche reserva,
> bisogna però che lo expecti che li benefitii vacano et quando gli recresciesse lo
> expectare, piglia lo exempio da me quale ho expectato fina a questa ultima età
> mia... et son certo che ad uno minimo cegno de Vostra Signoria, come obediente
> che lui sempre è stato, facilmente se aquietarà a quello che vole ragione.[144]

---

[144] ASMN, AG, b. 866, Rome, 4 August 1522, Alessandro Spagnuoli to Federico Gonzaga. Equicola did not easily give up his aspirations to Spagnuoli's benefice. We find him, two
years later, still plotting and hoping:

> Messer Mario ha inteso et per tutto San Petro qui se dice che Messer Alexandro
> Spagnolo stava male da morire et se crede che sia morto. Et questo spazo se fa
> ad instantia di messer Mario nostro... Dio voglia che la tardità usata per messer
> Angelo Germanello [one of the Marquis' agents in Rome] in fare spedire la con-
> firmatione di patronati non dia qualche disturbo a messer Mario al che Vostra
> Signoria voglia provedere non tanto per messer Mario che è vostro quanto per
> causa et respetto del Signore.
> (BAV, Vat. Lat. 8211, 29 April 1524, Calandra to Castiglione, f. 104r).

Equicola's negotiations with the papal bureaucracy proved to be even more wearisome than
Castiglione's with the Mantuan chancery over his pay:

> Messer Iacomo Picenardi ha la mia confirmatione del'iuspatronato mi diede il
> signor Marchese in San Pietro già che se fa la bulla. Dite da mia parte a Papa
> Clemente che me la confirme per un bel breve che habia del bono. Per tua fé, conte,
> ditelo ad Nostro Signore et più li adgiongerete che questo mi basta per adesso, ma
> quando il mio principe li harà levati tucti inimici et quelli reducti alli pedi di Sua
> Santità et venia che vorrò altro, fateme gratia, diticilo che Dio sa quanto desio la
> sua vita. Volete che ve dica quanto la desio quanto la morte di colui che sapete per
> chi voglio la confirmatione. Parlate con messer Iacovo prefato et interponete vostra
> auctorità in quanto bisognarà et da esso serete recercato.
> (BAV, Vat, Lat. 8211, 6 March 1524, Marmirolo, Equicola to Castiglione, f. 287r).

There seems to be no end in sight as Equicola himself was beginning to recognize:

> Heri io era in Marmirolo. Lo Signore ordinò al Calandra che expedisse per me
> circa lo arcipresbiterato de San Pietro et la capella de Santa Andrea in la medesma
> chiesa.[...] Resta che Nostro Signore mi faccia gratia confirmare lo Iuspatronato
> del'Illustrissimo circa questi doi beneficii che tene hora messer Alexandro
> Spagnolo. [...] Dite al papa che l'antiqua mia devotione con sua casa et il respecto
> de chi servo merita per me qualche cosa extraordinaria. Et sia certa Sua Santità
> che passati lo X° anno del suo pontificato che io harà LXIII anni come pane vito
> vorrò essere vescovo. Basali li pedi in mio nome et rengratia Sua Beatitudine che
> so certo che non me negarà tal gratia.
> (BAV, Vat. Lat. 8211, 5 May 1524, Mantua, Equicola to Castiglione, f. 291r).

Isabella d'Este would probably not have objected to Equicola's actions in this case because this particular Spagnuoli was a brother of the hated Tolomeo and he himself had been implicated in his brother's crimes (though he had managed to avoid punishment through the intercession of the pope). It can be seen from this incident that Equicola was prepared to go to any lengths in order to secure a financially independent position in Mantua. At the same time he was still pursuing the Roman benefices that the Archdeacon had said that Capella was ready to grant him.[145]

*

The following September, Equicola accompanied the Marquis to Marmirolo, where the latter was having a palace built and to other places in Mantuan territory, for the purpose of repose and recreation.[146]

But the peace of the *Mantovano* was again to be replaced by the sounds of war. Equicola was asked to join Federico at his camp near Gabioneta, but on setting out suffered an accident:

> Essendo in la piaza di Mantua nel mezo proprio et volendo dismontare, il cavallo se alzò perché il morso li fa male et retrovandomi io fora de la sella, sopra le spalle de un fameglio, cascai in terra tucto de un fascio. Ho guaste doe deta del piè dextro che molto mi dogliono.[147]

It may be unkind but quite reasonable to suggest that Equicola was happy at his departure being delayed or even that, in an act of desperation, he threw himself off his horse on purpose in order to prolong his stay in Mantua. He could not, however, postpone the inevitable indefinitely or indeed at all, though he did manage to return to Mantua fairly quickly. He was worried by the continued delays in the publication of the *Libro* and was determined that this time nothing would prevent its appearance in print.[148] His concern

---

[145]   Sigismondo Gonzaga's secretary wrote to Equicola to inform him of «il stato del'offitio suo».
(ASMN, AG, b. 866, Rome, 24 March 1522).

[146]   First of all, Federico had gone to Gonzaga whence he sent a letter to his mother written in Equicola's hand (ASMN, AG, b. 2126, 10 September 1522). Then, later in the same month, Federico wrote to his mother again using Equicola as the scribe, this time from Marmirolo: «Io sto sano et in qualche piacere di caccia» (ASMN, AG, b. 2126, 28 September 1522). In December he visited Goito with Equicola as his secretary: «Questa matina ho facta una assai bella caccia et li falconi se sono portati sopra modo benissimo» (ASMN, AG, b. 2126, 18 December 1522).

[147]   ASMN, AG, b. 2503, Mantua, 11 October 1522, Equicola to the Marquis. At least for that day he will not be able to join the Marquis: «Non verò dunque questa sera perché non me posso movere.»

[148]   Et perché 'l stampatore mio non so se vorrà perdere tanto tempo et io ho pagata la carta per lo *libro de amor* et anchora so certo che li quadrelli conducti per la

for the *Libro* temporarily took precedence over his obligations to the Marquis as if he considered it his last chance of having the work published.

*

By the following year (1523) Equicola could be considered to have been established as Federico's secretary. For the first time we find Equicola's name at the beginning of Federico Gonzaga's *copialettere*, an indication that Equicola had officially changed sides.[149] He still carried out missions for Isabella, however, which were usually intended to support the Marquis' policies. Isabella d'Este had seen the folly of opposing the Emperor and was faced with the problem of persuading her brother, the Duke of Ferrara, to change his allegiance.[150] It is not surprising that Equicola was chosen to communicate Isabella's point of view,[151] nor is there any doubt that Isabella was

___

fabrica me serano robati stando a l'aperto, se a Vostra Excellentia piacerà, impetrarò licentia dal Signore di poter tornare in Mantua poi che haremo facta la unione con Squizari et poi che Francesi seranno in fuga. Spero, alhora, me comanderà torne in casa, che prima, se ben lui volesse, non voglio io perché pareria che fugisse per paura. So nato homo et in me non si vedrà né comprenderà in nesun modo viltà.
(ASMN, AG, b. 1649, «Da Gabioneta», 12 October 1522, Equicola to Isabella d'Este).

[149]   At the beginning of the first book of «copialettere» for the year 1523 (ASMN, AG, b. 2929, libro 277) we find: «Registrum litterarum status Illustrissimi Domini nostri per Marium Equicolam secretarium MDXXIII.»

[150]   The year before, Alfonso d'Este had tried to persuade Federico to change sides and join the French. To this proposal the Marquis gave a negative response through the intermediary of Equicola:
Parlai col'Illustrissimo Signor Marchese molto a longo. Mi respose che molto rengratiamo Vostra Signoria del'amore li porta et de la cura che piglia di lui et sue cose. Poi, resolutamente, mi concluse non haver animo de mutar patrone perché non pò né vole mancare a quel che recerca l'honor suo et a quanto ha di novo promesso non solamente a Nostro Signore ma alla Cesarea Maestà, non havendo finita la conducta sua con la Chiesa, non è per servire alcuno potentato. Et però non li pare tempo che Vostra Excellentia si mova per adesso né che Madamma Illustrissima venga, per non haver ad fare per al presente altramente fructo.
(ASMO, ASE, C, Ambasciatori: Mantova, b. 2, 2 June 1522, Equicola to Alfonso d'Este).

[151]   Arrivai in lo Boschetto, dove trovai lo Illustrissimo Signor Duca che havea dormito lì la nocte. Parlai con Sua Excellentia longamente, referendoli quanto Vostra Signoria me havea dicto da dirli et così da parte di Madama Illustrissima, che tutto era d'un tenore. Primo, humanissimamente rengratiò Vostra Signoria delle offerte et del desio che tene de suo utile et honore.
(ASMN, AG, b. 1248, Ferrara, 28 July 1523, Equicola to the Marquis).
Isabella d'Este claims the mission as her own as well as Equicola's. She seems to have realized that the political situation had irrevocably changed in Italy and saw as the only sensible course a realignment of alliances on the part of her brother (that is, abandoning the traditional French alliance of the House of Este):
Se è expedito Mario, nostro secretario, a Ferrara con commissione di exponere il tutto al Signor Duca, nostro fratello. Siamo certe, considerarà bene il caso suo

acting on advice given her by Federico who took an active interest in the mission. Equicola had much to occupy him now that it was decided that the Marquis would take decisions through him.[152] Yet in spite of the increased work,

---

> et, como prudente, li farà quella deliberatione che conoscerà essere in proposito suo.
> (ASMN, AG, b. 2998, libro 42, 28 July 1523, Isabella d'Este to Grossino).

[152]   One of Equicola's most important responsibilities was the administration of the latest addition to Mantuan territory, Bozzolo, an imperial fief granted to the Marquis by Charles V because its ruler Federico da Bozzolo had fought on the side of the French in the recent campaign. Equicola had the difficult task of coordinating the consolidation of the new territories:

> Volemo che facciati intendere a tutti quelli nostri subditi che hanno decreti o privilegii de immunità o exemptioni di qualunche sorte si voglia, li debbano presentare al spectabile Mario Equicola, nostro carissimo secretario, dal quale intenderano quanto sia di nostra intentione.
> (ASMN, AG, b. 2928, libro 273, Mantua, 12 November 1522, Federico Gonzaga to «Potestati Insulae Dovarensium et vicariis Bozuli, Santi Martini et Riparoli»).

Just over a year later another chancery secretary commented that Equicola was overburdened with work and, as a consequence, Castiglione's pay was caught up in the system:

> Circa li conti di Vostra Signoria io ne lassava lo impazo a messer Mario, il quale ha anche lui troppo da fare, et è cosa fastidiosa et laboriosa lo havere a fare con questi rasonatti. Antonio da Milano havea fatto una certa pollice di ditti conti ma diceva che non era... de la corte lo assaldare le cose del soldo et certe altre cose che me sono più difficili a intendere che non seria lo Apocalipsi. Io vederò di havere quella pollice da messer Mario et ve ne manderò la copia.
> (BAV, Vat. Lat. 8211, f. 31r, 29 January 1524, Mantua, Jacopo Calandra to Castiglione).

From Calandra's brief asides, the chancery does not seem to have been very well organized:

> Li vostri conti io li sollicitarei volentieri se sapessi dove et con cui, tanta confusione vedo et lenteze in questi officiali. Pur so che messer Mario ve ha scritto che saranno fatte che me l'ha ditto.
> (BAV, Vat. Lat. 8211, f. 37r, idem., 5 February 1524).

Mantuan bureaucracy seems not to have been the paragon of order and efficiency. Personal intervention on the part of highly placed secretaries appears to have been the only way of getting things done. Both Equicola and Calandra worked within the system depending on their personal influence to sort the business out. Yet, one begins to doubt their efficacy at times which perhaps suggests that secretaries were «above» the system, closer to the ruler than to the bureaucratic organization. Equicola claimed on 1 January 1524, in a letter to Castiglione, that his arrears were ready to be collected (BAV, Vat. Lat. 8211, f. 279r). As we have seen from the above Calandra was still making excuses at the end of January and beyond. Equicola wrote:

> Lo desio che tengo che Vostra Signoria sia servita et libera è tanto che la imaginatione mia è sì fixa che vedo Vostra Signoria più bella, più sana che fosse mai et io così me alegro con quella. Li soi cuncti son facti, resta creditore di più de quactrocento ducati. Ho parlato col thesoriero: anchor me dice non so che del cuncto et questo expedito. State più sano et leto che circa questo negocio farò quanto et più che non potrò.

January did not produce any concrete results and Equicola continued to claim that progress had nevertheless been made in the matter:

> Li cuncti son facti. Bisognaria haver lo mandato del credito de Vostra Signoria. Questo procurarò et sia certa Vostra Signoria che tanto si mancarà de sollicitudine et diligentia quanto se fossero cose del'Illustrissimo. De ciò ve prego non crediate ad altro che alli effecti.
> (BAV, Vat. Lat. 8211, 31 January 1524, f. 286r).

As time passed, Equicola's promises became more hyperbolic:

> Che 'l desio che ho da servirla farà che si farà possibile lo impossibile.
> (BAV, Vat. Lat. 8211, 6 March 1524, f. 287r).

Equicola found time to return to his studies. He composed a work in praise of Venice which presumably helped him to win the title of «poet laureate» bestowed on him by the Republic.[153] Nor had he been forgotten by his literary friends; Sannazaro and Ianus Lascaris were both still in contact with him.[154]

The new routine imposed on Equicola by the change in masters and by the political situation in Italy did not give him respite that year. He was compelled to follow the Marquis to the battlefield to assist him in the defence of the gains won in the last encounter with the French who had once more crossed the Alps.[155] Equicola announced his safe arrival in Cremona in September 1523:

> Semo in Cremona. Il castello ha dati li obstagi che se in termine di XII dì non li vene succorso potente, chel darà in mano del'Illustrissimo Signor Duca di Milano... Noi stamo aspectando la opportunità, e 'l tempo che è dator solo de la gloria a chi ben lo sa usare.[156]

Although there was some confusion about the intentions of the French army, Federico decided to take Lodi,[157] and the campaign continued, leaving Equicola with no other alternative except to carry out his usual round of duties: writing to Isabella d'Este, the interrogation of prisoners and the organization of a spy network.[158] He even took on a more military role which caused him to break into self-parody:

---

[153] Santoro, pp. 299-300 (document 37); cf. Luzio-Renier, *La coltura*, p. 76 n. 1.

[154] The Duke of Atri wrote to Equicola that «al Signor Iacovo Sanazaro ho lecto la partita de la lettera vostra» (ASMN, AG, b. 809, 20 September 1523). Ianus Lascaris wrote to Equicola from Venice:

> Per tanto vi prego, messer Mario mio, per quanto amor portate ad Lascari vostro, che ve addoperati per lui in le soe occorrentie non altrimente che faresti per me. Che quanto fareti per lui, iudicarò l'habbiate fato per mi medesimo et restaròvi obligato de singulare obligatione.
> (ASMN, AG, b. 1457, 27 March 1523).

[155] L. Mazzoldi, *Mantova: La storia*, II, p. 281.

[156] ASMN, AG, b. 1651, Cremona, 16 September 1523, Equicola to Isabella d'Este.

[157] Io existimo che lo andar loro [the French] a Pavia sia perché existimano che la impresa non sia difficile et che, presa Pavia, non li è obstaculo alcuno che non habiano Piacenza, per ciò che non semo sufficienti ad vetarli il passo di Po et haranno victuaglie senza dubio abundantemente, che è et deve essere il primo pensiero de provido capitanio... Ma se non pigliano Pavia, sono in tutto perduti perché Milano et l'altre cità repigliaranno animo et spirito.
> (ASMN, AG, b. 1651, Cremona, 17 September 1523, Equicola to Isabella d'Este).
> However, Equicola's opinion was not universally shared:
> Gran dispute si fanno tra noi qual sia il fine et intento de Francesi. Alcuni dicono che non daranno più assalto havendo differito tanto... Sono molti che affirmano haver ad passar Po et extenderse verso Piacenza, Parma, Rezo et Modena et indi haver denari. Altri dice che torneranno in Francia. Io so in opinione che vogliano campegiar Milano et dar assalto et bactaglia, et chi more, mora, perché seria sciocheza se non facessero tal demostratione et aventurare il tutto in una giornata.
> (ASMN, AG, b. 1651, «Da Castel Leone», 20 September 1523, Equicola to Isabella d'Este).

[158] Equicola reveals that as on other campaigns he was involved in the interrogation of prisoners:

> Io son capitano de Spagnoli et de Lanschnech de la guardia del'Illustrissimo. O povera Spagna, o misera Germania in che man sei![159]

But Equicola was impatient to see the war over as quickly as possible; it was proving a drain on his deteriorating health which could no longer endure the rigours of a campaign: «So che Sua Signoria et io non dormimo mai nostri sonni: riposaremo in casa con victoria.»[160] His eagerness to see the campaign over (but also to see the Marquis victorious) led him into rather comical situations, indicative of a certain lack of common sense. Equicola had many times woken the Marquis in the middle of the night with news: on this occasion it was to inform him of a pro-French conspiracy within Pavia itself, the truth of which he had not checked personally, and which turned out to be a false alarm. In view of such lapses it seems difficult to believe that Federico could have been wholly satisfied with his secretary.[161]

However, if for most of the time the campaign was dogged by uncertainty and indecision, Equicola could console himself with the thought that Federico's prestige as a captain had grown enormously.[162] He was still to be found with the Marquis two months later, but the latter was himself now rather ill

---

Hogi li nostri cavalli legieri hanno corso sino alli padiglioni de francesi et hanno menati in Lodi tre pregioni et cinque cavalli. Ho interrogati uno d'essi, che più saputo mi parea.
(ASMN, AG, b. 1651, Lodi, 22 September 1523, Equicola to Isabella d'Este).

[159]   ASMN, AG, b. 1457, Pontevico, 4 October 1523, Equicola to Isabella d'Este.

[160]   When the campaign moved into the *Veneto* Federico needed to be even more vigilant:
Ho visto il Signor tre nocti non dormire et star attento et diligente in mandar succorso in Cremona, dicendo: «Se se perde, harò li inimici al ponte de Mercaria.»
(ASMN, AG, b. 1457, Pontevico, 16 October 1523, Equicola to Isabella d'Este).

[161]   Erano quatro hore di nocte quando Maffeo de Hostilia me fece intendere che me volea parlare. Ordinai che li fosse aperto, menò uno, ligato, il quale haveano pigliato per spia. Questo dicea che questa nocte li Francesi venivano ad Pavia et che li seriano date doe porte. Dissi io «*», saltai del lecto et corsi alla camera del Signore et narraili il tucto. Subito se mosse anchor Sua Signoria con quella parola «*» et se vestio. So che non volse calse calde, né regazi intorno, né camerieri et montò ad cavallo. Intertanto io havea mandato il pregione in casa del Signor Antonio [Leva], dove andò il Signore. Et primo havea provisto alle guardie et alle porte. Andò solo con la mità de le Lanschinech et con celerità rivedé et provedé al tucto, il che li ha data gran laude tra questi Spagnoli et tucti lo lodarno al cielo de animosità... Se è trovato che costui è un mezo pazo.
(ASMN, AG, b. 1651, Pavia, 31 October 1523, Equicola to Isabella d'Este).

[162]   Madama mia, gran laude reporta lo Signor Marchese haver con lo star qui, mantenuta Cremona, como tucto 'l mundo conosce.
(ASMN, AG, b. 1457, Pontevico, 4 October 1523, Equicola to Isabella d'Este).

and also seeking the first opportunity to return home.[163] At last, in mid-November Equicola was allowed to leave.[164]

*

Federico's illness ensured that for 1524 at least Equicola was freed from his military obligations. Moreover, Federico did not care to actively take up his captain-generalcy, mainly because the pope and the Florentines were reluctant to find the money for the army, which meant that he would have had the greatest difficulty in leading a successful campaign.[165] The dynamic opening of Federico Gonzaga's reign had come to a rapid close, in much the same way as his father's did, when the latter had to renounce active military service through illness and the complications of Italian politics.

For Equicola, this meant he could settle down to the serious business of improving his financial position. To this end, the Marquis intervened in Equicola's slow-moving affairs in Alvito,[166] and renewed Equicola's rights to certain sinecures: «motu proprio et animo bene deliberato, confirmamus dictum officium registri et castellaniam Caneduli». A necessary measure, we might add, in view of Equicola's poor salary as a secretary.[167] Equicola himself did not slacken in the pursuit of Church benefices, in respect of which Castiglione was doing his best: the secretary's name was heard more and more in the papal entourage.[168]

---

[163]   See L. Mazzoldi, *Mantova: La storia*, II, p. 283. At one point it appeared that Federico was cured of his ailment:

> In quest'hora scrivendo, messer Carlo de Bologna [the Mantuan treasurer] mi ha portata, con gran contento, l'urinale con urina bella et molta che ha facto il Signore senza molestia alcuna.
> (ASMN, AG, b. 1651, Pavia, 14 November 1523, Equicola to Isabella d'Este).

[164]   The letter of 14 November 1523 quoted in n. 163 is the last one we have of Equicola from Pavia.

[165]   See L. Mazzoldi, *Mantova: La storia*, II, pp. 283-84.

[166]   Le lettere de Vostra Signoria Illustrissima ho receputo in favore de Oliveto per causa del [...] messer Mario, mi sono state extremamente grate.
(ASMN, AG, b. 809, Naples, 15 April 1524, Ioan Antonio Musetula to Federico Gonzaga).

[167]   ASMN, Archivio degli Instrumenti, Registrazioni Notarili: «Decretum domini Marii Equicole» (the year 1524, f. 909). In this decree Equicola's salary as a secretary is given as nineteen Mantuan pounds a month, almost a negligible sum.

[168]   Castiglione wrote encouragingly back to the Marquis' secretary in Mantua: «Parlai al Papa un terzo d'hora di voi» (ASMN, AG, b. 868, Rome, 12 June 1524, Castiglione to Equicola). And Giovio wrote to Equicola on his growing fame in papal circles: «Voi avete deliberato di sepelirme con le vostre amorevole e galante lettere quale vi hano fatto familiarissimo al Pontifice» in P. Giovio, *Lettere*, a cura di G.G. Ferrero, I, Rome 1956, p. 109, letter 24.

Instead of going to war the Marquis together with Equicola travelled to various places in the *Mantovano* for a change of atmosphere and to enjoy a taste of the countryside. In January 1524, Federico and Equicola stayed at Marmirolo probably as part of the Marquis' treatment to aid his recovery.[169] They both made a number of other trips for the same reason, the most significant of these being an excursion out of Mantuan territory to the baths of Abano.[170] By the end of the year Federico was fit enough to undertake a journey to Rome without Equicola whose task it was to supervise affairs at Mantua during the Marquis' absence. However, Federico was unexpectedly called back to Mantua before he reached his destination.[171]

The last year of Equicola's life saw the fulfilment of a long cherished hope: the completion and publication of the *Libro de natura de amore*. From the beginning of 1525 Equicola had pressed for the negotiations that would lead to the work's publication. The Mantuan ambassador to Venice, Giovan Battista Malatesta, was entrusted with the delicate task of ensuring that the *Libro* was printed according to Equicola's precise instructions:

> Ho facto havere a messer Mario le sue observatione, quale serrà observate nel suo libro come desidera, quale si stamparà fra X dì. Et perché non resti il stampatore per il revedere oltra che fine adesso ho facto vedere il tutto, dapoi il Conte et messer Mario, da lo Excellentissimo in questa terra, messer Nicolò Delphino, ho ordinato al stampatore che mi porti ogni sera il quinterno bisogna stampare, che io insieme con il mio cancelleri operaremo ogni nostro sapere in servitio de quella, per la qual non recusariamo mettere la vita propria, et insieme con la mia consorte et il comune figliolo Federico baso le mane, offerendomili in anima et corpo.[172]

---

[169] Two of the *copialettere* (numbers 280 and 281) which cover the period 1524-25 are a record of the Marquis' excursions into the *Mantovano*, particularly to Marmirolo. They are almost completely written in Equicola's hand. The various letters show the Marquis intent on enjoying the pleasures afforded by the countryside and other relaxing activities: ·

> Perché domenica proxima da venire, che serà il primo di Magio, faremo festa in Marmirolo in honor de San Iacomo, volemo che dii ordine che ballarini et ballarine vengano al predetto loco, sì per far bella la nostra festa, sì anchora per guadagnar premii li quali si ponerano di sorte che 'l vincitore et la vincitrice non si lamentarano haver in vano spesi li passi perché essi pallii sono assai belli.
> (ASMN, AG, b. 2929, libro 281, Mantua, 26 April 1524, «Al vicario de Marmirolo et in simili forma al vicario da Goit[o] e de la Volta, et allo comessario de Capriana, de Midoli, de la Publica et Ceressari»).

[170] L. Mazzoldi, *Mantova: La storia*, II, p. 286; see also D.S. Chambers, «Federico Gonzaga ai bagni di Caldiero (1524)».

[171] In questa nostra partita per Roma, che ni partimo dimane, havemo lassato ordine qui a Mario, nostro secretario, che vi communichi tutti li avisi degni che veniranno perché il Reverendissimo et Illustrissimo Monsignor, nostro cio honorandissimo, aprirà tutte le lettere et le farà poi vedere al predetto Mario acciò che 'l ve possa mandare li avisi che vi saranno et voi li communicate a quella Illustrissima Signoria in nome nostro.
(ASMN, AG, b. 2965, libro 30, Mantua, 12 October 1524, Federico Gonzaga to Malatesta).

[172] ASMN, AG, b. 1459, Venice, 1 February 1525, Malatesta to Equicola.

It is important to underline the fact that Malatesta saw himself in the role of executor rather than that of corrector, in other words, the *Libro* was to be reproduced as accurately as possible from Equicola's final manuscript:

> Vostra Signoria stii secura sopra di me che 'l libro si stamparà con quella diligentia che lei recerca et non altrimente che sii il suo originale et per messer Mario non si preterirà ponto de sollicitudine circa quello desidera.[173]

As the work progressed Malatesta had to face problems of a more practical nature:

> Io non havea mai statuito cum il stampatore quello che se gli havesse a dare per quelle carte che l'ha bisognato restampare, perché lui et io se contentassimo remetersi circa ciò al Pincio. Heri, feci detterminare il tuto per puoter scriver resolutamente alla Signoria Vostra quello che si resta al stampatore. Finalmente, el Pincio concluse che in tuto, ultra quelli che l'ha havuto, se gli diino 17 ducati, li quali bisogneria al presente exborsarli aciò che si possa finire l'opera, intendendo ducati da 31 grossi l'uno. Io non gli lasarò manchar dinari.[174]

The *Libro* was finally published a little over a month before Equicola died. The tension that made itself so strongly felt in his last years finds its ambiguous resolution in this work. The *Libro* is announced on the title-page as the work of «Mario Equicola, secretario del'Illlustrissimo Signor Federico Gonzaga». This most public of pages displays his newly won honour and position, but once we turn over the page we find the dedication: «Mario Equicola di Alveto alla precellentissima Donna Isabella d'Este, Marchesa di Mantua». In its final form, the *Libro* represents a desperate attempt to bind together the opposing and contradictory forces that could affect an intellectual at court. It is fitting that Equicola managed to see through the publication of the work since it serves as his epitaph. He would not have much time to enjoy the fame and prestige that came from writing the *Libro*, his brief period of power was approaching its end almost before he had time to taste the fruits of his struggles.

---

[173]   ASMN, AG, b. 1459, Venice, 23 March 1525, Malatesta to Equicola.
[174]   ASMN, AG, b. 1459, Venice, 20 April 1525, Malatesta to Equicola.

CHAPTER V

The courtier's progress

Equicola must have felt that his position could only improve in the year of the capture of the King of France at the battle of Pavia in 1525. Federico Gonzaga seems to have been of the same opinion: Equicola had more than proved his willingness to serve; now he could reap the benefits. His post as Federico's secretary was secure and he was able to devote the amount of time required to supervise, admittedly at a distance, the final arrangements for the publication of the *Libro de natura de amore*. His duties as secretary, in the last year of his life, fell within the boundaries of the Mantuan chancery.

It was to Equicola that the authorities of Canneto, a village in the *Mantovano*, addressed their complaints concerning the financial burdens they were forced to bear.[1] This kind of problem was a typical part of a secretary's round of duties. Equicola could have made no complaints about this aspect of his work and fortunately for him Mantuan politics had lost some of the vigour that Federico Gonzaga injected in the first years of his reign. We have seen that

---

[1] ASMN, AG, b. 2506, Canneto, 28 June 1525, «servitori, li homini deputati al governo di Canneto» to Equicola:

> La gravissima et intolerabil spesa, quale havemmo patitto et de novo pattemo per quelli soldati et cavalli legieri quali già zorni tredici passati sonno allogiati qui a tutte nostre spese, è quella che ne induce et sforza ad scrivere et dare fastidio alla Signoria Vostra et de novo pregare in operare appresso alla Excellentia del'Illustrissimo signor nostro.

Another aspect of Equicola's work involved the movement of information and instructions in the opposite direction, that is, from the Marquis to his officials:

> Messer Mario. Ni spiace che a San Benedetto sia scoperto una casa apestata. Et dite al Collaterare et alli deputati che non mancano per provedere alla extinctione di essa et che non lassino venire qua alcuno di San Benedetto con robbe a questa festa, alla qual non volemo se facci alcuna fera. Et commendamo e voi et loro superiori a queste provisioni di havercilo avisato. Risanative.
> (ASMN, AG, b. 2966, libro 29, Gonzaga, 5 September 1524, Federico Gonzaga to Equicola).

In Federico's absence Equicola was empowered to speak on the Marquis' behalf to his council: «volemo che ne parlati al consiglio et gli dicati da nostra parte...» (ASMN, AG, b. 2966, libro 30, Concordia, 14 October 1524, Federico Gonzaga to Equicola). Equicola was also the «subscriptor» of marchional decrees in his capacity as Federico Gonzaga's secretary (for example, ASMN, AG, Libri di Decreti, n. 36-37, including decrees for the years 1524 and 1525).

nothing was able to keep the Marquis off the battlefield until illness and the harsh realities of military administration sapped his enthusiasm. The captain-general of the Church was thus absent from the battle of Pavia and he was just as surprised as everyone else at the news of the capture of François I:

> Non sapemo già qual maggior cosa, né degna di maggior admiratione prima, poi di consideratione, havesse potuto accadere che la captura del Re di Franza, cosa che li inimici proprii di Sua Maestà non è da credere che havessero sperato.[2]

Although Equicola would have shared Federico's sentiments over the dramatic outcome of the battle, he would not have experienced the slightest twinge of regret at not being there (unlike the Marquis whose fighting instincts were not easily suppressed). So, the principal cause of the secretary's discomfort in recent years had been removed. He preferred to receive news about battles rather than to participate in them.[3] It was much more pleasant to sit at home and watch one's prestige grow without running any personal risks. In this connection the pope's high opinion of his writings must have greatly pleased Equicola:

> Dopoi la mi ha ditto havere viste le orationi de Vostra Signoria, le quali li sonno molto piaciute, laudando il stile, la vivacità et le copiose sententie che vi sono dentro.[4]

The secretary must have hoped that it would only be a short while before he could add other benefices to those already in his possession.[5]

---

[2]   ASMN, AG, b. 2967, libro 32, Mantua, 26 February 1525, the Marquis to Francesco Gonzaga, ambassador in Rome. The Marquis had made his name at an earlier conflict in Pavia (in 1522) where he successfully withstood a French siege. His fame as a warrior had already been secured by the time the more celebrated battle of Pavia took place. The palace at Marmirolo was intended, in part, to glorify the Marquis' military prowess at its peak:

> Avisatine se a Marmirolo vi sono aieroni, et anchor datine aviso se haveti fatto voltare la logia di Marmirolo et, se non è a quest'hora voltata, se potesse subito comminciar a farla voltar, che la fosse in termine che sotto essa possessimo farli depinger Pavia questo inverno, che mandaressimo questo garzone di Lorenzo [Costa] col disegno per depingerla là. Sì che avisatine in che termine l'è e quando potremo mandare esso dissegno per far depinger Pavia.
> (ASMN, AG, b. 2965, libro 25, Pavia, 5 November 1523, Federico Gonzaga to his treasurer, Girolamo Arcario).

[3]   «Poor fat Equicola seems to have been most unhappy in military life» writes F. Hartt in his *Giulio Romano*, New Haven, 1958, p. 138, n. 43.

[4]   ASMN, AG, b. 869, Rome, 15 March 1525, Francesco Gonzaga to Equicola.

[5]   In the year before Equicola's death Federico Gonzaga had urged his agents in Rome to press his secretary's claims to certain important Mantuan church benefices:

> Et precipue instareti et sollicitareti con ogni studio la expeditione di la bolla de nostri iuspatronati et la confirmatione del breve di Leone, santa memoria, sopra lo archipresbiterato di Mantua et capella, come in esso breve se contiene, in persona de messer Mario, nostro secretario, che l'uno et l'altro desideramo sia expedito con ogni celerità et più presteza possibille.
> (ASMN, AG, b. 2966, libro 29, Mantua, 20 June 1524, Federico Gonzaga to Angelo Germanello).

Proceedings had begun in 1521 with the support of Isabella d'Este who wished to improve her secretary's financial position:

> Havendo io per cosa certissima lo animo de Vostra Signoria essere dispostissimo

But if Equicola imagined that he would be leading an untroubled life in the future, he was sadly mistaken. His downfall was not due to the machinations of other ambitious courtiers but the weakness of his own body, probably compounded by the unwanted experience of military life during Federico's campaigns. If Equicola had hoped that a prolonged absence from camp might improve his health, then his expectations were shattered by his rapidly deteriorating physical condition. He tried to seek medical advice from outside Mantua, an action which must impress upon us the extent of Equicola's desperation. Unfortunately, the doctor Equicola wished to tend him was unable or unwilling to leave his patients.[6] In March 1525 we find that the ailing Equicola had taken to his bed: «Messer Mario dui giorni fa sta in letto amalato di febre et fredore. Tiensi non haverà male.»[7]

His final illness began in a similar fashion: what, at first, appeared to be a simple bout of fever assumed complications. The doctors now feared for his life:

> Messer Mario già alcuni giorni è in letto amalato di febre, che prima era terzana simplice, poi se gli indoppiette, et finalmente si è ridutta in continua, di modo che da trei giorni in qua è stato male, et maxime heri, che li medici non havevano troppo sicuro il caso suo. Non di meno questa notte è megliorato alquanto.[8]

In spite of the fact that Equicola was informed of the seriousness of his condition he refused to believe that he was nearing death:

> Adesso adesso, che sono circa le XXI hora, Maestro Abraham, medico, quale è alla cura di messer Mario, è venuto qui in cancelleria e essendogli sta dimandato dil stare suo, ha ditto che 'l sta molto male et che è peggiorato, dicendo queste parole, «Io non vorei essere Imperatore et Re di Franza insieme et essere nella pelle di Messer Mario perché sta malissimo et lui non cognosce il male.»[9]

---

ad farne omni piacere possible recorro volentieri al suo patrocinio in questo caso. Lo Illustrissimo Marchese mio, ad mia requisitione, ha concessi beneficii del suo iuspatronato in la Eclesia Catedrale per trecento ducati, o primi o secundi che vacaranno, quando piacerà a lui, ducento a Mario Equicola, mio secretario, et cento ad Ioanne Maria Capilupo, mio scalco. Per il che prego Vostra Reverendissima Signoria che li piaccia impetrare dalla Vostra Santità di Nostro Signore che sia contenta confermare et far valida in omni evento di vacantia dicta concessione, nominatione et presentatione ad ambi doi li predetti per dicta summa.
(ASMN, AG, b. 2997, libro 37, Mantua, 3 February 1521, Isabella d'Este to Egidio da Viterbo).

[6]   Andai a trovare mestro Iacomo da Pietra Melaria et feci la imbasiata. E, infra molte parole, mi dise che, per essere medicho, non poteva abandonare li soi infermi.
(ASMN, AG, b. 1151, Bologna, 12 April 1525, «vostro arciguido» to Equicola)

[7]   ASMN, AG, b. 2506, Mantua, 29 March 1525, Vincenzo de' Preti to Isabella d'Este.

[8]   ASMN, AG, b. 2506, Mantua, 24 July 1525, Vincenzo de' Preti to Isabella d'Este.

[9]   See above, ASMN, AG, b. 2506, Mantua, 24 July 1525, Vincenzo de' Preti to Isabella d'Este. The Marquis received a favourable report of this doctor's treatment of Equicola's illness:

It seemed impossible to convince Equicola that his chances of survival were minimal:

> Il patre fra' Lodovico verrà ogni volta che 'l domandamo, ma aspettamo, Maestro Abramo et io, che venga l'altro medico. Lui sta pur sul suo dire che non ha male et niuno fin qui ha olsato dire il contrario, se non Mercurio che li disse heri sera che faria bene a confessarse et fare testamento et lui lo spazò per una bestia. Son certo se una persona di gravità, come è il patre fra' Lodovico, li ne parla, se reconoscerà.[10]

In these circumstances the Marquis was forced to intervene; Equicola needed to be convinced of the gravity of his situation:

> Ma esso non sentendo il male, anzi sempre dicendo che staseva bene, rispose a tutti equalmente che non [era] tempo alhora di confessarsi. Per il che, vedendosi questa sua pertinacia et conoscendosi apertamente che 'l cavalcava a staffetta, fu fatto intendere, per messer Zoan Iacomo [Calandra] castellano, il tutto all'Illustrissimo Signor nostro a Marmirolo, il giorno di San Iacomo, nel tempo che là si faceva la festa. Sua Excellentia mandette per questo caso il magnifico messer Thesoriero a Mantua a parlarli in suo nome et exhortarlo et astringerlo per quello si poteva alla confessione. Così, havendogli parlato, doppo molte parole, esso messer Mario si dispose ad far quanto voleva. Ma già se gli era ingrossata la lingua di modo che mal poteva farlo. Così, fatto venire un frate di l'ordine di Santo Augustino, fece una confessione generale, breve et di poche parole per il che ha potuto essere communicato.[11]

> Del stare di messer Mario io me reporto a quanto scrive a Vostra Excellentia Maestro Abramo, perché seria un replicare il medesimo. Lui li attende molto amorevolmente et diligentemente et non lo abandona, sapendo quanto messer Mario è grato et caro alla predetta Vostra Excellentia. Et certamente se lui campa Vostra Excellentia lo reconosca da Dio prima, poi da la cura et experientia di questo medico dottissimo et da bene quanto fosse mai altro.
> (ASMN, AG, b. 2506, Mantua, 25 July 1525, Calandra to Federico Gonzaga).

[10]   See above, ASMN, AG, b. 2506, Mantua, 25 July 1525, Calandra to Federico Gonzaga. The same day, Calandra reported Equicola's refusal to confess, adding a few interesting details to what we already know of Equicola's attitude:

> Messer Mario per un gran pezo hoggi ha dato un poco di speranza a Maestro Abramo, parendoli che l'havesse guadagnato alquanto. Ma, questa sera, l'uno et l'altro medico l'hanno trovato molto cascato de la virtù, et il cataro li abonda molto forte, donde hanno perduto ogni speranza de la vita sua et non credono che 'l possi campare molto. Bisogna havere patientia. Lui dice che 'l sta bene. Quando il patre fra' Lodovico fu hoggi alle desdotto hore a visitarlo, lui se turbò alquanto et non lo volse ascoltare, dicendo che lassasse lo impazo a lui del confessarse et che non pensasse né frate né prete havere la robba sua. Lo Magnifico Thesoriero, con dolci parole, da parte de Vostra Excellentia, ha fatto che 'l s'è disposto alla confessione et ha voluto confessarse dal confessore di esso messer Thesoriero, et così ha fatto. Del tutto m'è parso dare aviso a Vostra Excellentia, alla quale Satyro viene per dimandare l'officio di Canneto. So che la Excellentia Vostra sa che l'è bon servitore et allevo di messer Mario et quella non lo vorrà abandonare.
> (ASMN, AG, b. 2506, Mantua, 25 July 1525, Calandra to Federico Gonzaga).

[11]   ASMN, AG, b. 2506, Mantua, 27 July 1525, Vincenzo de' Preti to Isabella d'Este.

Equicola's consent to his confession may be seen as a gesture of submission to the secular authority rather than to the Church. Federico would have been worried and even embarrassed by his secretary's behaviour: anti-clericalism may have been acceptable in certain circumstances but when someone was set to refuse a Christian death, the Marquis had to be firm or his reputation as a Christian prince would suffer immeasurably.[12]

If Equicola himself was still not convinced of his imminent death, others did not doubt that he could not last much longer:

> Il caso di messer Mario è in tutto desperato et li medici fanno iudicio chel sia per penare fin a domani. La Excellentia Vostra se degnarà ordinare al magnifico messer Thesoriero in che modo se haverà a farli l'obito et quel honore che parerà a quella che si faci a un tal servitore et, se li piacerà, che se vestino qualche uno di suoi. Cesare, suo nepote, dice che ha reposto in un studiolo tutte le scritture et la cancellaria, le quali non se moveranno se non quanto ordinarà la Excellentia Vostra. Messer Mario parla poco, cioè parole che se intendano, et non se li può fare pigliare più cibo di sorte alcuna. Solamente se fa portare da un letto a un altro et levare alla scrana senza bisogno alcuno.[13]

On 27 July, Isabella d'Este, who was in Rome, was informed of Equicola's death:

> Et sempre doppoi è peggiorato. Heri a mezo giorno gli mancò la favella. Alle XXII hore gli fu racommandato l'anima et datto l'extrema untione. Doppoi ha penato sino poco inanti le II hore di notte, che passette di questa vita. Hoggi alle XXI hore se sepelirà et si prepara di fargli honorevole exequie, havendo commisso così lo Illustrissimo Signor nostro, il quale, per quanto intendo, ha dimostrato assai dispiacere di questo caso. Serà sepelito in San Petro dove haverà commodità di potere confabulare con messer Alexandro Baese.[14]

It is no exaggeration to say that Equicola received a state funeral with all the necessary pomp. In many ways, his funeral was the peak of a successful career — a clear indication of the secretary's status, though significantly, the

---

[12] It had been Federico who sent fra' Lodovico to receive Equicola's confession:

> Perché intendemo che messer Mario sta in mal termine, anchor che lui non lo conosca, non vorressimo che alle volte el mancasse senza la confessione et ordini di la Chiesa. Perhò volemo che fati venire il padre frate Ludovico dil Carmine, nostro confessore, ad visitarlo et indurlo alla confessione, peggiorando questa notte. Bene valete.
> (ASMN, AG, b. 2967, libro 34, Marmirolo, 24 July 1525, the Marquis to Calandra).

[13] ASMN, AG, b. 2506, Mantua, 26 July 1525, Calandra to Federico Gonzaga.

[14] See above, ASMN, AG, b. 2506, Mantua, 27 July 1525, Vincenzo de' Preti to Isabella d'Este. For references to Baese see L. Mazzoldi, *Mantova: La storia*, II, pp. 162, 163, 191. Equicola and Baese were on extremely good terms as can be seen from a letter written by the former to Federico Gonzaga. The secretary has had a bet with Baese over whether Pirro Gonzaga will marry «Madama Camilla. Il Baiese ha giocato meco una cena per tre compagni che per tutto 'l mese de aprile che vene serà sua moglie. Io ho dicto et dico de non».
(ASMN, AG, b. 2499, Mantua, 15 March 1520).

Marquis was not present in person at the ceremony. Isabella d'Este was given a full description of the funeral of her former tutor and secretary:

> Questa sera alle XXI hore si è sepellito messer Mario molto honorevolmente per commissione del'Illustrissimo Signor nostro. Vi erano tutte le Regule de Frati et tutte le Parochie di questa città, quale vennero di dreto via di San Petro et introrono sotto li portichi di la corte vecchia, voltando intorno la piazza per intrare in San Petro per la porta grande. Passata la Chieresia, fu levato il corpo, accompagnato da XXV scovatori inanti et altri tanti dreto. Il Conte de Pianella, messer Statio, messer Zoan Iacomo et io siamo andati appresso il cadeletto propinqui alli scovatori, fingendo di portarlo. Vi erano poi dreto il corpo Cesare, nepote di messer Mario, accompagnato dal magnifico Thesoriero in nome del'Illustrissimo Signor nostro, Mercurio dal magnifico Conte Otho, magister Cavallaro dal magnifico messer Zoan Philippo Fontana et Satiro dal magnifico messer Paris, che erano vestiti di gramaglie, fattole far per lo Illustrissimo Signor nostro, per essere servitori et allevi di messer Mario. Seguivano, poi, dreto loro, di mane in mane, molti gentilhomini et cittadini di questa città, tutti invitati a nome dil predetto Signor nostro. Così, honoratamente è sta portato in San Petro dove si è fatto una bella oratione in sua laude per maestro Nicola da Verona, maestro da scola qui in Mantua. Il corpo suo si è visto in una cassa nella capella dove è il Baptisterio, nel qual loco se gli farà honorevole sepoltura per havere così ordinato il Signor nostro Illustrissimo.[15]

*

The unfortunate consequences of Equicola's death were felt most of all by his nephew who could have expected to have considerably improved his own position but for the fact that his uncle had not made a will. Equicola's financial position left a great deal to be desired on Cesare Prudenzi's part: there was not much money and many debts to be paid off. The cost of Equicola's success and new social status had been high, especially in monetary terms:

> Dinari non se vi sono trovati, per quanto ho inteso, se non pochi de li quali, insieme con li mobili, et di la casa sua serà herede Cesare, suo nepote quale è qui, secondo intendo, per non haver fatto testamento alcuno. Lo archipresbiterato intendo [che] il Signor Illustrissimo l'ha promisso al Signor Conte Nicola [Maffei] per suo figliolo. L'officio dil Registro non è anchor datto via, né anche si

---

[15]   ASMN, AG, b. 2506, Mantua, 27 July 1525, Vincenzo de' Preti to Isabella d'Este. Battista Fiera, who was closely associated with the Mantuan court, wrote two poems «In obitu Marii Aequicolae» (f. AA3ᵛ) in his *Baptistae Fiaerae Mantuani philosophi, medici, theologi et poetae. De deo homine libri quattor. Hymni divini, dictatum de virgine matre immaculate concaepta. Coena et libellus de pestilentia, Silvae, Elegiae et Epigrammata*, Venice: In aedibus Ioannis Patavini et Venturini Roffinelli, 1537, fol. f. AA3ᵛ. For a full bibliographical description of the edition consult D.E. Rhodes, «The early editions of Baptista Fiera» in *Book Production and Letters in the Western European Renaissance. Essays in Honour of Conor Fahy*, ed. by A.L. Lepschy, J. Took, D.E. Rhodes, London, 1986, pp. 234-45; 243-44.

intende chi habbi ad succedere nelle facende in loco di esso messer Mario. Pur si crede si habbino a partire tra messer Zoan Iacomo et messer Statio.[16]

The secretary's failure to ensure a secure future for his nephew (due to his refusal to recognize the inevitability of his death) meant that Cesare Prudenzi was left nearly empty handed. Equicola had been rather haphazard in making provisions, though he had not neglected his nephew altogether. The secretary had insisted, in the early days of his last illness, that his nephew be granted Mantuan citizenship, a necessary condition if he were to be able to inherit his uncle's property in Mantua. However, after Equicola's death, doubts were raised as to whether this had in fact been done, because his uncle had not drawn attention to the matter.[17] In any case, it seemed likely that his nephew would

---

[16]   See above, 27 July 1525, Vincenzo de' Preti to Isabella d'Este. The following day Vincenzo de' Preti was able to be more precise about who benefited from Equicola's death:

> È stato verissimo quello ch'io scrissi heri a Vostra Excellentia che lo Archipresbiterato di questa città era datto al figliolo dil Conte Nicola per lo Illustrissimo Signor nostro. Et in vero è stato ben collocato con satisfactione de ogniuno per essere il conte quello da bene gentilhomo che sa Vostra Signoria Illustrissima, dal quale si spera non debba degenerare il figliolo. Hoggi, anchor, il Signor nostro Illustrissimo si è risoluto di dar l'officio dil Registro a messer Zoan Iacomo castellano, anchor che da molti altri fosse stato dimandato. Così, hoggi, è stato posto al possesso per il Magnifico Thesoriero. Né meno degnamente et meritamente è stato collocato quest'altro officio, essendo messer Zoan Iacomo persona virtuosa et molto affaticata in questa cancelleria, come è noto a Vostra Excellentia. Cossì volesse Idio si facesse dil officio dil secretariato, il quale per certo non è anchor ben stabillito in cui habbi ad essere collocato. Molti lo hanno instato per diverse vie. Non di meno si diceva la ellectione consisteva in dui principalmente, cioè messer Zoan Baptista Malatesta, oratore a Venetia, et messer Cappino. L'uno et l'altro di loro instavano gagliardamente, anchor che il Malatesta non vi fosse in persona, per essere partito de qui dui giorni nanti mancassi messer Mario per interesse del'Illustrissimo Signor nostro, ben però lassato qui persone che per lui hanno procurato gagliardamente, di modo che questa sera si è ditto per certo che il Malatesta è eletto, ma con alcune conditioni, le quali non si sa mo se egli accettarà.
> (ASMN, AG, b. 2506, Mantua, 28 July 1525, Vincenzo de' Preti to Isabella d'Este).

There was a little more delay before Equicola's most important office found a new occupant:

> È venuta la resposta da Venetia dal'ambasciatore [i.e. Malatesta] circa la cosa dil secretariato, il quale non l'ha voluto accettare. Et la causa è stata perché esso intendeva di havere anche il Registro, qual ha havuto messer Zoan Iacomo castellano... le facende restaranno in mano di messer Statio et messer Zoan Iacomo, cosa che a me piace molto et mi doleva che questo officio si collocasse in persona inexperta di questo maneggio.
> (ASMN, AG, b. 2506, Mantua, 4 August 1525, Vincenzo de' Preti to Isabella d'Este)

[17]   Calandra was under the impression that a *decreto di civiltà* needed to be drawn up in favour of Equicola's nephew:

> Il quale decreto non è stato fatto perché lui non l'ha poi ricercato più, credendo vi dovesse essere tempo assai. Se pare alla Excellentia Vostra, io lo farò a beneficio di questi suoi nepoti per la casa che l'ha in Porto e a consolatione di esso messer

be forced to sell Equicola's house in order to pay his debts. And it did not seem Cesare Prudenzi would fare any better with his uncle's church benefices, even before the latter's death:

> Quando accadesse la morte di messer Mario senza che lui facesse testamento, andaria a pericolo di perderse, anci, senza dubio, si perderia lo officio suo di Roma, et questi suoi nepoti restariano privi di quel bene che era pur sua intentione che fosse, per quanto intendo, di questo Cesare... quale è un gentil giovine et da bene. Havemo pensato, maestro Abramo et io, che la Excellentia Vostra li può fare questo bene di contentarse che se scriva una littera a messer Francesco [Gonzaga, Mantuan ambassador in Rome] che narri il caso al Papa et supplichi a Sua Santità, in nome di la Excellentia Vostra, a volere reservare il ditto officio, in caso che messer Mario manchi senza testamento, a questo suo nepote, che speramo lo farà per amore de la Excellentia Vostra, la quale farà questo bene a questo povere giovin. Et quella se degni farme dare presto resposta che, volendo che se scriva, spazarò il correro del Bugatto che venne heri sera.[18]

The Mantuan ambassador to Rome, Francesco Gonzaga, does not seem to have been very successful in his attempts to save any of Equicola's benefices and sinecures for his nephew:

> Havemo veduto quanto ne scriveti del officio per voi fatto in nome nostro con la Santità di Nostro Signore per il nepote de messer Mario circa l'officio che havea de portione de Ripa. Restamo benissimo satisfatto di l'opera vostra et assai più della benigna et amorevole resposta hauta dalla Santità di Nostro Signore, la quale non ni è manco cara come se fossimo effectualmente stato compiaciuto.

Mario in questo caso. Di questo anche la Excellentia Vostra se degnarà farme dare resposta.
(ASMN, AG, b. 2506, Mantua, 25 July 1525, Calandra to Federico Gonzaga).
One of Equicola's nephews «Caesar Prudentius Equicola de Albeto eius ex sorore nepos» (we know of only one other nephew, a Francesco Prudenzi) had been granted Mantuan citizenship on 8 April 1525 (ASMN, AG, Registro dei Decreti, libro 37, f. 111^{r-v}).
The Marquis granted his permission: «siamo anche contenti che si facci quel decreto de civilità, come ordinassimo, in questi nepoti di messer Mario, come mi scriveti» (ASMN, AG, b. 2967, libro 34, Marmirolo, 25 July 1525, Federico Gonzaga to Calandra).
The Marquis of Pescara and Vittoria Colonna took an active interest in the fate of Equicola's nephews:

> La lettera de Vostra Excellentia in recomendatione de li neputi et herede del quondam messer Mario ho vista. Et certo me ha rencrescito tanto de la mancanza sua quanto de amico che havesse, si per la servitù et affittione grande che teneva al servitio de Sua Excellentia como sua virtù. Et tucto quello beneficio che porò fare per dicte soe herede per lo respectu de le recomendatione de quella non solo in confirmali quello che ad loro iustamente compete ma del mio proprio sono per non mancarli. Et supra questo scrivo alla Marchesa mia consorte che voglia exequire tucto quelle che in quisto negotio conviene per beneficio de dicte herede.
> (Novara, 5 August 1525, the Marquis of Pescara to the Marquis of Mantua).

See also A. Luzio, «Vittoria Colonna», *Rivista Storica Mantovana*, 1 (1885) 13.
[18] See n. 17, first letter quoted. The Marquis was also happy to oblige in this case: «siamo contenti che scriviati a messer Francesco Gonzaga a Roma per l'officio di messer Mario per quel suo nepote, el possi havere a cui l'havea designato dare» (for this reference see second letter quoted in n. 17).

> Volemo che in nome nostro, occorrendovi opportunità, facciati scusa con Sua Beatitudine, dil cui volere ni acquietamo et restamo optimamente satisfatto.[19]

At the time of his death Equicola's finances were therefore in poor shape. Calandra's comments on this matter show just how serious the late secretary's lack of cash had been:

> Il predetto messer Mario havea di gran debiti per quello che vedo et maestro Abraham me dice che appareno creditori per forsi quatrocento ducati fin qui. Et pochissimi dinari vi sono et anche poca robba mobile utile.[20]

The implication of the letter is that the 400 ducats were only the tip of the iceberg and in reality Equicola owed much more. The financial predicament of those employed by the court is well known. While Castiglione was Mantuan ambassador in Rome his correspondence is replete with desperate pleas for money which Equicola kept at bay by making endless promises of payment. The illustrious Roman ambassador was by no means an isolated case; other Mantuan ambassadors suffered similar fates.[21] It might be thought that Equicola's situation would have been more favourable since his work brought him to the constant attention of either Isabella d'Este or Federico Gonzaga. He seems to have depended for his preferment almost entirely on the Gonzagas, something he tried to rectify, as we have seen, by seeking Church benefices and other honours which might bear financial fruit. For example, he sought and obtained an unspecified privilege from the Holy Roman Emperor Charles V shortly before he died, indicative of his tenacity in the search for income.[22] It may have been that after so many years in the relative obscure position of preceptor the more public office of secretary required a higher profile from its incumbent with a consequent increase in expenditure. The pressure for

---

[19]   ASMN, AG, b. 2967, libro 34, Marmirolo, 11 August 1525, the Marquis to Francesco Gonzaga.

[20]   ASMN, AG, b. 2506, Mantua, 27 July 1525, Calandra to Federico Gonzaga, f. 181^r.

[21]   For Castiglione see G. Gorni, «Il rovescio del *Cortegiano* o le lettere del Castiglione», *Paragone. Letteratura*, 30 (1979) 63-75 and S. Kolsky, «Castiglione's biography: The courtier and the Italian princes», *Spunti e Ricerche*, 1 (1985) 1-34. For more general considerations consult R. Quazza, *La diplomazia gonzaghesca*, Milan, 1942; M.A.R. de Maulde La Clavière, *La diplomatie au temps de Machiavel*, 3 vols., Paris, 1892-93; D.E. Queller, *Early Venetian Legislation on Ambassadors*, Geneva, 1966.

[22]   The following letter also demonstrates that Equicola was willing to use his authority in securing financial gain. Thus, anyone connected with Mantua was likely to be employed in this capacity:

> Signor Mario mio honorando, hoggi la Cesarea Maestà ha segnato il vostro previlegio de la donatione che a mio juditio ve piacerà. Lo farò mo sugilare e lo scoderò da la cangelaria e al mio ritorno l'haverete. S'altro posso fare a piacer vostro, lo farò volontieri.
> (ASMN, AG, b. 586, Toledo, 9 May 1525, «Capino de Capo» to Equicola, f. 231^r).

conspicuous consumption appears to have been such that the secretary had a new house built, perhaps to celebrate his definitive arrival amongst the powerful figures of Mantuan society and the signal favour of Federico Gonzaga appointing him his secretary.

Although demolished in the eighteenth century, enough details of its construction remain to show that it was the work of someone who wished to impress on people his wealth and position. Indeed, underneath the windows that looked onto the street his name «Marius Equicola» in Roman characters was engraved in marble. The house was no ordinary building. Apart from being filled with ancient artefacts its design included a small, domed observatory perhaps because of an interest in astronomy (he had no patience with astrology) or simply because it was a shape which would immediately draw attention to itself.[23] Such an unusual design would have been costly and put a strain on the new secretary's financial resources (the house was probably constructed in 1522, the year in which he became Federico Gonzaga's personal secretary).[24] The house is mentioned in a marchional decree of 1524 by which Federico Gonzaga donated to Equicola a piece of land contiguous to the secretary's dwelling. From this document we learn in the first place that the house was known by the name of «Letam», a name Equicola himself occasionally used to sign letters of a personal nature to the Marquis. It contains an explicit reference to his libertine philosophy and to his ideal of present pleasure above all else. Secondly, the document reveals the reasons for which Equicola required this donation of land: not to build an extension to his house in the normal sense but to set up two industrial workshops or small factories. The first was to be involved in the manufacture of paper and the second in small wheels to be used to polish armour and other metal implements. In return for this licence Equicola will be required to pay the Marquis in kind «cum onere tamen solvendi nobis mense quolibet rismam epistolaris carte et libras quatuor cere laborate».[25] It is not known whether Equicola started production since the decree bears the date 13 September 1523 and he was to die less than two years later. What is clear, however, is his determination to make

---

[23] See F. Amadei, *Cronaca universale della città di Mantova*, IV, Mantua, 1957, pp. 349-50.

[24] According to notary documents particularly those published in the Appendix, we find that in 1521 Equicola is described as being «illustrissimi domini domini Marchionis Mantue et illustrissime domine domine Marchionisse Mantue et cetera secretario» (Doc. 1, p. 273). Hence, the deed confirms officially Equicola's role as a go-between, not having yet come out (or made to) in favour of either «side». But by mid-1522 another notarial deed proclaims his changed position «illustrissimi domini nostri secretarius» (Doc. 5, p. 282). Thus, it would appear that in the latter half of 1522 Equicola was already officially considered the Marquis' secretary.

[25] For the details consult the Appendix, Doc. 7. p. 288.

himself economically independent or at least to offset some of his expenses. It is interesting to note that by entering into manufacturing he does not seem to share the aristocratic concern for the means by which financial security was achieved. Baldassarre Castiglione, for example, depended on the careful management of his estates by his mother for any economic support he might have needed. As a member of the feudal nobility it would have been out of the question for him to have become an entrepreneur. Equicola was not fettered by such considerations, given that it is unlikely he was of noble birth. In a way the idea of manufacturing paper was connnected to his work in the Mantuan chancery and he may have thought that he could become its supplier of paper.

The same decree represents the balance-sheet of his success in obtaining rewards from the Marquis. It contains information on the renewal of sinecures granted to him by Federico Gonzaga: the «officium Registri Mantue» and the «castellaniam Caneduli». In reality, it was not a great deal, especially if compared with the honours and wealth bestowed on Tolomeo Spagnuoli by the Marquis Francesco Gonzaga. That would explain Equicola's urgent need to diversify his sources of income. Church benefices had always been an attractive proposition if they could be obtained. We have already seen Equicola's efforts in this direction. By 1522 he appears to have had some success since a notary document refers to him as «Reverendus dominus Marius Equicola protonotarius appostolicus».[26] But probably this was not enough to cover his high living expenses as a courtier. Not only money was involved, good humour, joviality and a servile disposition were essential to his success.

*

His humanistic learning became inscribed in a set of discourses that served the power of the rulers. It cannot be said that there was any reluctance on Equicola's part to become involved in the transcription of court society using Latin letters as the key to his representation of its values and ideals. On the other hand, there was a price to be paid in terms of intellectual liberty which expressed itself principally in the choice of subject matter. It is no accident that Equicola's longest work, the *Libro de natura de amore* (most of his works, apart from the *Chronica*, are much shorter, an indication of the pressure to produce quickly in order to meet an immediate demand) was not made public until the year of his death. Antonio Tebaldeo mockingly wrote in a satire against Equicola that the work on love was carried out in secret at

---

[26] The document is published in the Appendix, Doc. 5, pp. 281-84.

home, the implication being that it was not suitable for court consumption.[27] The fact that the manuscript underwent numerous and far-reaching changes places it alongside the other major works of the period such as the *Orlando Furioso* and the *Cortegiano* for precisely this reason. Furthermore, Castiglione himself only published his *Cortegiano* after the manuscript entered the public domain. Previously it had circulated amongst very few intellectuals or patrons perhaps in the same way as the *Libro*.

The *Libro* in this respect is exceptional in Equicola's *opus*. Most of his writings were printed, usually only a short time after their composition (two works as far as we know never had a printed edition: the *Genealogia delli Signori da Este* and the problematic *Annali di Ferrara*). Right from the beginning of his career Equicola entrusted his works of humanist bent to the printed

---

[27] The resentment engendered by Tebaldeo's satires on Equicola's linguistic choices lasted far beyond the episode itself. Tebaldeo wrote a number of vicious epigrams against Equicola which reiterate his positive hatred of Equicola not only as far as the *questione della lingua* is concerned but also on other matters, such as the *Libro*. These epigrams are all to be found in the mauscript BAV, Vat. lat. 2835.

Epit. Marii Aequicole
Aequicola hac situs est. Vili scrobe funere cuius
Reddita tartareo tertia lingua cani est ut
Tartareo quarta est addita lingua cani.
(f. 212ᵛ, original numbering; f. 217ᵛ new)

De Mario
Cum magni vires Marius scripsisset amoris
Occultumque domi continuisset opus.
Indignans miseri succendit pectora cumque
Insuper occularet tecta ore mavit amor.
(f. 241ʳ, original; f. 246ʳ new)

Ad Marium
(the poem has a line straight through it)
Simea crudeli gallorum obsessa caterva
Iulia, res alium postulat ista ducem.
Es Marius, Marii est. Cymbros superare. Camillus
Qui gallos alias contudit, aptus erit.
(f. 165ᵛ original)

De Mario
Vertire qui lapidii Letheum acceperunt ictum
Excidit acteo littera quaeque viro.
Res haec credibili maior fuit hactenus. At nunc
Accepit casu vel leviore fidem.
Nam graium ponens habitum graio orbe petita
Cuncta simul Marius grammata leposcuit.
(f. 222ᵛ old; f. 227ᵛ new)

Equicola, in his turn, wrote a ferocious satire against the poet, calling his poetry «insulsa nenia» (the poem is published by F. Cavicchi, «Una vendetta dell'Equicola», *GSLI*, 37 (1901) 94-98 and by Santoro, pp. 205-207.

page. The reason may be discerned in a desire to make a mark in the court society to which he was a relatively new arrival. Equicola's works surviving in *incunabula* seem to serve as «publicity» announcing his imminent arrival on the cultural scene at Ferrara and giving a precise indication of his abilities and the possible networks to which he might contribute. These printed works allowed him to multiply his name in a way not permitted by manuscript circulation. Humanists at court might form a private élitist club but in the final analysis they had duties to perform with regard to court society as a whole as well as with regard to individual courts (the last category almost ensures that humanist literature became propaganda, establishing credentials for both courtiers and courts in the complex system of city states in the Italian peninsula). Even writings that one might have expected to remain in manuscript were published. An obvious example is *Nec Spe nec Metu*, originally intended as a birthday gift, then a decade later printed in Mantua. The decision to publish was taken because of the attacks on Equicola's language and style. Thus a private gift was made public in the wake of fierce controversy surrounding its author and was thought a useful means to turn to the counter-attack. It is the public nature of the court humanist's work which is emphasized by employing printing.

Significant is the fact that a Ferrarese printer, Lorenzo de' Rossi, produced four of Equicola's earlier works, including two *incunabula*.[28] The choice of the printer seems to indicate an adherence in the early part of his career (up to about 1510) to the local centre to which his patrons and employers, the Cantelmi, were increasingly attached. Indeed, his *Oratio de Passione Domini* was published twice, probably in the same period, once in Milan and once in Ferrara. And a work in which there appears a dedicatory letter of Equicola addressed to Giulio Cesare Cantelmo, the *Epithome Plutarchi*, was also published in Ferrara. This attachment to one city and one printer did not long survive his removal from Ferrara and although two of his subsequent works were probably printed in Mantua (*Nec Spe nec Metu, Chronica di Mantua*), his other books were printed in a variety of locations from Naples to Venice, the latter being the most obvious choice for a humanist in Equicola's position. This change in practice suggests a widening of horizons on the part of our courtier who did not any longer, especially after 1508, have to prove himself. Furthemore, his allegiance after that date was to Isabella d'Este and Mantua.

Changes occur in Equicola's intellectual outlook even before he officially entered the *Marchesana's* service. His two orations and the *De Religione*, all

---

[28] The two *incunabula* are the *De Religione* and the *Oratio de Passione Domini*. Dr. Dennis Rhodes of the British Library has identified the *De Mulieribus* and the *Pro Gallis Apologia* as being the work of the same Lorenzo de' Rossi.

printed between 1498 and 1500, stand apart from the rest of his *œuvre*. It is true that Equicola will not neglect the theme of religion in later works but the difference in its treatment is instructive. The *De Religione* can be described as a learned disquisition displaying Equicola's humanist method and the range of his knowledge. The treatise is the product of a relatively disinterested search for knowledge in its most esoteric guises. Of course, it should not be denied that the work would be judged either positively or negatively by his peers. The text itself was not free from controversy, as we have already seen, since it treated religion as a synchronic development from its earliest beginnings to the advent and «victory» of Christianity.[29] But compared to Equicola's later works on a religious theme one gets the impression of someone displaying his varied knowledge for its own sake. This changes once Equicola came in contact with the Gonzagas. An obvious example is the *Divae Osannae Andreasiae Mantuanae Oratio*, published in about 1515. Although Equicola employs here the same methodology as in the *incunabulum*, it is clear that he was writing above all for a particular purpose: the glorification of the Beata Osanna Andreasi, Isabella d'Este's personal saint. Here there can be no doubt about the author's intentions. As her tutor Equicola was perhaps the person best equipped to write a piece of learned propaganda, the principal aim of which was to ally the *Marchesana's* name with the saint's in order to increase the former's prestige. A different yet connected purpose may be discerned in his *De Bello Turcis Inferendo Suasoriae Tres*.

It is not the purpose of these remarks to reduce Equicola's works to one meaning but solely to emphasize the crucial connections between court society and its cultural production, probably more obvious in this type of organised society where the power structure bore down heavily on the intellectual without much regard for his particular circumstances.[30] At first sight the *Suasoriae* seem to express a generally held belief in the necessity of a crusade, a conviction which should have stemmed from particular Christian values. However, this is only a partial reading of the text which excludes extra-literary factors. One such consideration is Equicola's desire for Church benefices which in his view could have been assisted by a work that had the potential of being well-received in papal circles. Thus, it is also part of my argument that the possible reception of court-oriented writings had such significance

---

[29] See pp. 52-59 of the present work.

[30] For a survey of recent studies on the court with some reference to the role of intellectuals consult P. Merlin, «Il tema della corte nella storiografia italiana ed europea», *Studi storici*, 27 (1986) 203-44. The following studies may be usefully consulted: R. Romano, «L'intellettuale nella società italiana del XV e XVI secolo» in *id., Tra due crisi: L'Italia del Rinascimento*, Turin, 1971, pp. 117-136 and G. Benzoni, *Gli affanni della cultura. Intellettuali e potere nell'Italia della Controriforma e Barocca*, Milan, 1978.

that it visibly affected the shape of many treatises and similar works. The text and its reception in the court ambience are almost inseparable and are mutually influential in the formation of court literature. No discussion of these particular kinds of writing should effect a rupture between them and their social origins. In the case of the *Suasoriae* a synchronic discussion of the genre would not be out of place since Equicola's work belongs to a time-honoured tradition of humanist writing. Yet even here the diachronic intrudes and should be the object of proper investigation. The power of influence was no doubt great and the subject was seen to be worthy of the attention of humanists especially since it provided a neat way of combining classical rhetoric with Christian principles. However, the treatises were written in response to specific historical situations. In Equicola's case Leo X was anxious to create the right impression of his papacy from the very beginning, so a call to the crusade was seen as an appropriate response.

It is my contention that while under the tutelage of Giulio Cesare Cantelmo Equicola involved himself in suitably theological topics, but as soon as he became exposed to the environments of the Mantuan and Ferrarese courts he changed tack. The transition was tremendously abrupt to judge by his literary production. If 1501 saw the publication of a dedicatory letter to the Bishop of Nice (Giulio Cesare Cantelmo) in the *Epithome Plutarchi* it probably also saw the appearance of the short *De Mulieribus* or *Perigynaecon* again with a dedication to Giulio Cesare Cantelmo. However, the intellectual distance between the two pieces is dramatic: the latter represents an ideal commitment to the court societies of Mantua and Ferrara, taking up themes which were to increase in importance in the early part of the sixteenth century, if not beyond. After 1501 Equicola ensured that his writings did not look backwards to his Cantelmo past but to the present reality. If he now wrote dedicatory letters in other people's works they were no longer under the tutelage of Giulio Cesare Cantelmo since Equicola's network system had considerably expanded to include Battista Spagnuoli and his brother Tolomeo (the apparently «friendly» relationship with the latter was to deteriorate later on under the influence of Isabella d'Este).

Other works cement the relationship with his Estense connections: *Nec Spe nec Metu* is the result of Equicola trying to form a more «personal» bond with the *Marchesana* by playing on the theme of one of her enigmatic devices closely associated with her. And by the same token *De Opportunitate* seeks to explain the significance of various of Cardinal Ippolito d'Este's *imprese*. Again it is not hard to divine the alliance Equicola was seeking to create between certain features of court culture and his version of humanistic learning. In many ways it was a strange combination: the enigmatic brevity of the devices betrayed by Equicola's prolix explanations. Its advantage was that it gave the appearance of subtle and profound thought beneath the courtly wit of the *imprese*. On occasion, however, one has the distinct impression Equicola was trying too hard. His endless *exempla*, the propensity to paraphrase rare texts instead of genuine analysis might not have been welcomed by everyone. From this point of view Equicola's texts are distinguished by their unoriginality, being an amalgam of other people's works.

His *Pro Gallis Apologia*, for example, presents all the characteristics of his mode of composition: an extensive range of quotations-cum-paraphrases of an exceptional number and variety of texts concerning French history, society and *mores*. From another point of view, however, this short defence of the French nation, written in the period after the battle of Agnadello, defies to a certain degree the category into which most of Equicola's works fall. Its specificity cannot be satisfactorily «reduced» to a particular pleasure of the court although that may have been an element. The intellectual horizons of the *Apologia* are geared to a repayment of the debt he owed to French humanists; it is a coming to terms with the significance of his numerous stays in France. It would be wrong on the other hand not to state that the moment of this re-evaluation was part of a political choice, given that the French, after Agnadello, had come in for all sorts of abuse.[31] Yet at the same time, Equicola tries to defuse the situation by having Janus Lascaris as promoter of a crusade that would encourage harmony amongst the warring nations. Thus, the theme of the crusade makes an early appearance in Equicola's writings, having the function of endowing the intellectual with a religio-rhetorical mission which had important moral implications for the rulers.

The same work clarifies the writer's debt to Lefèvre d'Etaples, declaring himself to have been profoundly influenced by the humanist's teachings. Unlike the case of Lascaris it is not simply a question of public homage to a great man. On this rare occasion Equicola seems to be making a stand based on his perception of intellectual worth. And it should also be stated that Equicola stood alone amongst Italian intellectuals in remaining true to his belief in Lefèvre d'Etaples as a major, respected figure on the international humanist scene. It should be remembered that the French intellectual was being increasingly persecuted, finally being declared a heretic for his radical attitudes towards the Bible.[32] Thus Equicola shows himself here in a somewhat

---

[31]   C. Vecce has edited the *Pro Gallis Apologia*, with an introduction, which will appear in *IMU*.

[32]   Useful information on Lefèvre d'Etaples is contained in C.-H. Graf, *Essai sur la vie et les écrits de Jacques Lefèvre d'Etaples*, Strasbourg, 1842 (reprinted Geneva, 1970); F. Hahn, «Faber Stapulensis und Luther», *Zeitschrift für Kirchengeschichte*, 57 (1938) 356-432; R. Cameron, «The attack on the Biblical work of Lefèvre d'Etaples (1514-1521)», *Church History* 38 (1969) 9-29; *id.*, «The charges of Lutheranism brought against Jacques Lefèvre d'Etaples (1520-1529)», *Harvard Theological Review*, 63 (1970) 119-49; H. Heller, «The Evangelism of Lefèvre d'Etaples: 1525», *Studies in the Renaissance*, 19 (1972) 42-77.

different light: not someone frightened of expressing his views on a poten-
tially risky subject — in this respect breaking with his usual pattern of confor-
mity. The *Apologia* on this point shows Equicola's occasional willingness to
demonstrate intellectual allegiance with a humanist who had ranged against
him the power of the Church. Such a demonstration may indicate the depth
of his feeling towards the man and his doctrine. It further indicates that in the
matter of religious belief Equicola was prepared to move beyond conven-
tionality and attempt to seek solutions that were slightly irregular.

Throughout his career Equicola appears to have had links with intellectuals whose religious views were brought into question by the Church
authorities. Not only with Lefèvre d'Etaples but later on his connection with
the suffragan Bishop of Mantua, another southerner, Ambrosio Flandino,
has all the appearances of being amicable and founded on an exchange of
ideas.

France was to figure in another of his works, the extremely rare *Iter in Narbonensem Galliam*, an account written shortly after the pilgrimage undertaken by Isabella d'Este to Provence. Dedicated to Ferrante Gonzaga it pur-
ports to be a description of the highlights of the trip. Unfortunately for
modern scholars it is something of a disappointment if approached as a possible source of interesting details on Provençal society in the early sixteenth century. In their view it is an opportunity lost. Equicola was not the kind of
traveller impressed by natural beauty or by local customs. The *Iter* shows how
for him nearly everything had to be filtered through his classical *reading*, so
much so that the present is often lost in a fog of quotations from the ancient
authorities. Thus, if the work is judged as a travel diary it is a poor effort.
Those moments in which particular happenings or sights are described stand
out all the more because of their rarity. The bulk of the *Iter* serves as a vehicle
for Equicola's knowledge of those writers, both classical and contemporary
humanists, who have discussed the region.

It is noteworthy that in the crowd of contemporary luminaries Equicola
does not fail to praise Lefèvre d'Etaples. Obviously Equicola did not need to
mention him even if he was on French soil. This personal tribute makes clear
a life-long sense of gratitude felt by Isabella d'Este's tutor who still did not
baulk at the possible effects of mentioning this humanist now under attack
from all quarters. There are even references to Equicola's own works to which
the reader is asked to refer in order to clarify certain points.[33] So the celebra-

---

[33]   There is a reference to the early opuscule *De Religione*: «De demonibus in libro quem
de religione iamdudum scripsimus quia latius disputamus his nullam fieri mentionem decet»
(*Iter*, f. Az^v).

tion of Isabella d'Este's «epic» journey to Provence remains true to his intellectual origins and to the methodologies that he had developed.

The group of historical works which overlap chronologically with the *Iter* (*Genealogia, Annali, Chronica*) show an Equicola with essentially the same interests: employing his skills in unearthing facts about the past for the celebration of the rulers. The *Genealogia* and *Annali* are spare works which do not offer the wealth of esoteric detail present in the *Iter* or for that matter in the *Chronica*. The first two may have been written quickly without too much care given to their presentation. Or Equicola may have had a brief (from Isabella d'Este or other members of the family) to keep to the facts. The *Chronica* hence represents the norm in Equicola's writing with ample digressions and the use of much rare material. It bears witness to an alliance between his learning and the public imperative of the prince who could perceive the repute which would come to him from such a learned history. It is the most public of his works with direct subsidies coming from Federico Gonzaga and is an acknowledgement of Equicola's role as an unashamed propagandist of Gonzaga power.

The secretary's career did not really follow a clearly-defined linear progression. He was ready almost from the moment of his arrival in Ferrara (and Mantua) to exploit the needs of court society in order to find his own place in it. His success can be seen in his authorship of the *Chronica di Mantua*, written by someone from outside that society who had achieved a notable reputation by espousing Estense and Gonzaga ideals.

*

The works that have so far been discussed were not the only ones Equicola composed. Apart from translations, treatises now lost or perhaps never completed, Equicola expended the remainder of his intellectual energy on the *Libro de natura de amore*. One can trace the periods of most intense activity on the work partly through his correspondence and partly through other documents such as the autograph manuscript. According to the latter it was conceived and the idea first elaborated during the Italian wars of 1495-6. There has been some debate on just how much of the treatise at this stage was written in Latin — a large portion or just a few notes?

On balance it is more likely that Equicola put down a few thoughts in the form of Latin notes, given the circumstances in which he found himself. These notes might have taken roughly the same form as Castiglione's earliest ideas on the *Cortegiano*.[34] There appears to have been another burst of activity

---

[34] For the edition of the brief notes, which probably represent a first attempt at putting

a few years later around the turn of the century if his letters to Margherita Cantelmo are sufficient evidence. In these he works through various philosophical themes which are intimately related to the subject-matter of his treatise. The next major stage in the composition of the *Libro* is the redaction of the autograph manuscript which can be dated to the period 1509-11. These years represent Equicola's commencement as Isabella d'Este's tutor and coincide approximately with the imprisonment of her husband by the Venetians. It would support the view that Equicola, because of the *Marchesana's* commitments in government, was left without too much to do, otherwise it would be difficult to explain the production of such a hefty tome during those years. The basic text came in for diverse kinds of emendation — corrections of a linguistic nature, elimination of a number of passages, many notes were added either in the margins or at the bottom of pages. However, this manuscript does not represent the final draft. Before publication in 1525 major changes took place, for example, in the ordering of the individual books that make up the *Libro*, the addition of substantial sections, in particular, the second part of Book V which contains a review of love-poetry including the Provençal lyric. Perhaps in this, Equicola's interest was stimulated by his time spent in Provence and could be dated to the period post-1517. Thus, it is clear that before 1525 Equicola wrote at least another manuscript version of the *Libro* containing these wide-ranging alterations. However, other manuscripts have not come to light. Details are also scarce concerning the details of the *Libro's* reworking. His letters before the 1520s are silent about any re-elaboration of the text. This is particularly disappointing since with the return of Castiglione to Mantua in 1516 there would have been the opportunity to exchange views on subjects about which they were both writing or would write in the near future. The question of who influenced whom is almost impossible to unravel, but remembering that Castiglione started the *Cortegiano* as a treatise on women, clearly influenced by Equicola, it seems a likely hypothesis that influences worked in a two-way direction.

After the autograph the next burst of documented activity on the *Libro* occurs as late as 1521 when Equicola believed the text was ready for publication. Although there would be a further four-year delay Equicola must have been editing the *Libro*, introducing substantial alterations, in the period immediately preceding the letters of 1521. This desire to see the *Libro* printed may have been connected with the publication or the composition of the *Chronica di Mantua*, that most public of works. There could have been the wish by

---

a few ideas down on paper, later incorporated into the *Cortegiano* see G. La Rocca, «Un taccuino autografo per il *Cortegiano*», *IMU*, 23 (1980) 341-73.

wish by Equicola to present a rounded view of himself as a court intellectual, to make known his more personal, scholarly interests as well as his public duties as secretary-historian. That Equicola was interested in preparing the *Libro* for publication is indicated by the fact that its author sent a manuscript of the work to Giangiorgio Trissino who, it may be presumed, might have been more sympathetic to its linguistic view-point than Pietro Bembo (to whom surprisingly Castiglione sent a manuscript of the *Cortegiano*).[35] Thus, it is a likely hypothesis that some part of 1520 and 1521 was spent in the process of revision even though the circumstances of Equicola's life were far from tranquil, given that he was called on to follow Federico Gonzaga in his military campaigns. It is difficult to gauge how far, if at all, Equicola acted on Trissino's suggestions. They probably did not have great effect judging by the linguistic forms of the first edition. Trissino's letter seems to have served as a final seal of approval since just over a month later (hardly any time for major adjustments to be made so that one can be almost certain that Equicola stuck more or less to his linguistic guns) he was anxiously seeking leave to go to Venice and have the book printed. A year later the paper may have been bought but the *Libro* does not seem to be at this point particularly close to publication. The problems with the practical side of printing faced by authors are well illustrated by Equicola's concerns over the paper and similar matters. It was only in 1525 that the *Libro* finally appeared. Unable to go to Venice in person, Equicola, aware that printing errors and careless work in general could ruin a book's integrity as it had done in the past (*Nec Spe nec Metu* and *De Opportunitate* are obvious examples), delegated Malatesta to sort out the various problems that arose over extra payments which Equicola was anxious should not hold up production.

The *Libro de natura de amore* represents the ultimate codification of Equicola's methodology. In spite of the disparate subject-matter treated in the work, it is unified by a common approach as had been practically all his previous efforts. In fact, from his earliest texts Equicola displayed the same intellectual curiosity in the same sort of way. It should be noted at this point that Equicola was no humanist philologist — he does not continue the tradition of Quattrocento humanism. He was no editor of texts and his intellectual activity did not include the discovery of classical manuscripts. On one occasion Equicola reported to Cardinal Ippolito d'Este that apart from a «libro

[35] A discussion of Trissino's reply to Equicola is to be found in I. Rocchi, «Per una nuova cronologia», pp. 571-72. Castiglione's letter to Bembo, written three years earlier (*Lettere*, a cura di G. La Rocca, pp. 383-84) acknowledges Bembo's cultural primacy («V. Sig. è in capo di lista», p. 384).

de cavalli» he had not found much else of interest in Naples: «Altri libri ho visti, ma non vagliono et sonno de sorte che Vostra Signoria sende farria beffe.»[36] This was not the response of a dedicated humanist scholar who would have no doubt been impressed by the wealth of Neapolitan libraries and its intellectual life in general. The Royal library endowed by successive Aragonese kings is one example among many.[37] Equicola's statement is perhaps even more indicative of Ippolito d'Este's interests than his own. It shows the extent to which the values of the patron permeate the range of choices available to the courtier. It is further confirmation of Ippolito d'Este's limited intellectual range — books about one of his passionate practical interests, in this case horses, were perhaps the only ones that could meet with his approval. Equicola was capable of assuming a patron's *persona* even by denying his own desire to pursue scholarship.

If Equicola was no classical scholar — the emendation and correction of texts being foreign to him — he did not neglect to pursue or have an interest in other, more recondite languages and literatures. His scholarly endeavours brought him into contact both with early Italian lyric poetry and romance literature — French, Provençal and Spanish in particular. This displacement of the intellectual focus from classical to vernacular cultures suggest a widening of horizons on a contemporary European level perhaps due to Equicola's eclectic frame of mind desirous of new areas into which he could expand so as to mark himself off from humanists in similar positions. These relatively new interests, which only came gradually, show an appreciation of romance cultures beginning to make an impact at court, as the demand for Spanish texts in translation demonstrates.[38] Hence with Spanish literature

---

[36] This letter was published by Santoro, pp. 250-52; (252).

[37] For some brief notes and the relevant bibliography consult F. Sabatini, «La cultura a Napoli nell'età angioina» in *Storia di Napoli*, IV, tomo secondo, Florence, 1974, pp. 71-73.

[38] It is perhaps necessary to state here that if Equicola were to be regarded as a humanist he had one particularly glaring *lacuna*, namely his knowledge of Greek seems to have been superficial. It may have been such a combination of factors as a lack of interest in classical philology, basic Greek, and a heightened appreciation of the vernacular that can partially account for his interest in Italian and other romance cultures. For Equicola's Provençal manuscripts see G. Schizzerotto, *Cultura e vita civile*, pp. 5-27. A useful study of the section on Provençal poetry in the *Libro* is M.L. Meneghetti, «Dialogo, intertestualità e semantica poetica. Un esempio: Mario Equicola e la lirica provenzale» in *Il dialogo. Scambi e passaggi della parola*, a cura di G. Ferroni, Palermo, 1985, pp. 87-100; 95-100. See also G. Frasso, «Petrarca Andrea da Mantova e il canzoniere provenzale N», *IMU*, 17 (1974) 185-205; 199-202 and C. Bologna, «Tradizione testuale e fortuna dei classici italiani» in *Letteratura Italiana*, VI, Turin, 1986, pp. 445-928; 455-56 n. 12, 457, 465 n. 48, 509-11, 577. His knowledge of Spanish texts is documented by C.P. Merlino, «References to Spanish literature in Equicola's *Natura de Amore*», *Modern Philology*, 31 (1934) 337-47. An overview of the reception of Spanish

Equicola was keen to make it known that he was up-to-date and not buried in a classical past, cut off from the present.

It is important to note that Equicola did not stand alone in such interests. The figure who was perhaps closest to Equicola in time and temperament was Angelo Colocci.[39] The latter was more extreme in his eclecticism than Equicola, lacking almost completely any kind of conceptual framework. The two *litterati* are connected in a profound way by their intellectual allegiances. Colocci was regarded after Pomponio Leto's death in 1497 by the members of the Roman Academy as sharing the same outlook as themselves, shaped by their leader Leto.[40] Evidence of this continuity was the fact that the latter's house in the *Quirinale* was placed in Colocci's care. Thus, Equicola, whose debt to Leto I have already tried to establish and for which evidence exists, has a direct link with Colocci. It is probable that they knew one another personally; the acquaintanceship being made during one of Equicola's stays in Rome. Their relationship was such that it allowed Colocci to consult one of Equicola's Provençal manuscripts called by the former *Liber equicoli*.[41] However, Colocci was not subject to the same pressures to produce for the court. His situation permitted him the luxury of erudite ramblings, for the most part confined to manuscript notes, on a bewildering variety of topics. His interest in romance languages can be seen in word-lists which he drew up for Provençal, his translations from Spanish and Catalan, his transcriptions of Portuguese lyric poetry. His attempts to trace developments, which might explain present usage, for example, in poetic metre, remain at the stage of brief notes, hardly progressing any further. Equicola *was* fascinated by the archaeology of the word, seeing links between them in the form of etymologies, but he managed or was forced to set this interest in the context of the production of court literature. His methodology is plainly seen even in the *Chronica di Mantua*. His intellectual games were of the kind that might prove acceptable to the court élite. So much so that on the *first* page of the text proper of the *Chronica* we find the following digression which takes the form of an etymological discussion:

---

literature in Ferrara is to be found in the introduction to G. Bertoni, *Catalogo dei codici spagnuoli della biblioteca estense*, Erlangen, 1905.

[39] See the entry «Colocci, Angelo» in *DBI*, 27, Rome, 1982, pp. 105-111; F. Ubaldini, *Vita di Mons. Angelo Colocci*, a cura di V. Fanelli, Città del Vaticano, 1969; *Atti del convegno di studi su Angelo Colocci, Jesi, 13-14 settembre 1969*, Jesi, 1972 and V. Fanelli, *Ricerche su Angelo Colocci e sulla Roma cinquecentesca*, introduzione e note addizionali di J. Ruysschaert, Città del Vaticano, 1979.

[40] See V. Fanelli, «La fortuna di Angelo Colocci» in *id.*, *Ricerche su Angelo Colocci*, pp. 168-181; 169.

[41] Cf. G. Schizzerotto, *Cultura e vita civile*, pp. 9-20.

> Erangli [novi habitatori] consegnate stanze da habitare et campi da coltivare
> donde 'l nome Colonia è derivato. (*Chronica*, f. A5^r)

In spite of Equicola's protestations on the previous page the reader cannot help but feel the anarchy of uncontrolled knowledge which strives to break through the weak barriers of logical construction:

> Per dechiaratione di quel si ha da narrare fo alcuna digressione, non però dal pro-
> posito me allontane con imitatione de boni scrittori, in contioni non mi extendo
> né fo de ingegno ostentatione. (f. A3^v- A4^r)

The digression is the hall-mark of Equicola's writings and functions as a display of recondite details which will produce an effect of admiration in the reader, overwhelmed by the writer's knowledge. Facts of all kinds are Equicola's obsession and if they do not fit into the flow of discourse the latter will be sacrificed to this passion. However, his feeling for form was such that he needed to insert defences of his «method» in his writings. An example of his going out to meet possible criticisms occurs in the manuscript of the *Libro de natura de amore*. In this instance Equicola has offered the reader a veritable abundance of information on the significance of gold, culled in the main from classical literature. As in most cases the digression is an intellectual reflex action, here used to illustrate Equicola's discussion of the images of love and it is connected with the pages that follow in that they deal with Isabella d'Este's «aurea grotta», itself a digression meant to provide a neat example of where a classical statue of Cupid could be found.[42] At the end of this information-laden passage Equicola attempts briefly to explain his position on the manner in which he includes topics and the reasons for their inclusion:

> Siame licito, o iucundissimo lectore, alquanto in questo loco vagare né me sia
> imputato ad ignorantia de arte se in tal digresso pare disiunga et disloche le mem-
> bra della oratione perhò che non me parto tanto dal mio proposito che merite
> reprehensione. (f. 196^v)

The verb «vagare» indicates the pleasure Equicola feels in creating his own space in the work, collapsing the laws of logical discourse in order to give rein to his incessant activity of accumulating details. He does lay down certain rules of acceptability, particularly the fact that there must be perceptible links between the two levels of discourse. Equicola makes his point more finely in the printed edition of 1525 by using another passage from the manuscript of the *Libro* (f. 245^r- 246^r) which had been employed to justify an abrupt transition from the discussion on clothing to a mini-treatise on colours:

---

[42] The digression on the Cupid kept in the *Grotta* and associated material is to be found in *Libro*, MS. f. 198^r-202^v and in a slightly revised and shortened form in *Libro*, f. 73^v-74^r.

> Quella oratione fora de la proposta materia che in altro excorre, da Greci *parec-basis*, da Latini egressione. Se oportunamente in loco apto si usa, dar gratia a l'opera et delectar lo audire Greci et Latini rhetori scriveno. Il iocondo progresso di Ariadna del docto Catullo nel'Epithalamio di Thetide admirabile, le laudi de Italia et de la vita rustica in Virgilio, chi fora di tempo iudicasse? Non solamente alla poetica licentia questo si concede, ma in le concioni dove la utilità sola del cliente se deve attendere usare il vedemo. Demosthene molte volte da la causa si dilonga; M. Tullio nella laude di Sicilia diverte. Questa generation dunque de dilatarne, questo modo di ampliare, questo ordine di variar per confirmatione di nostri argumenti, purché la oratione sia coherente et consequente, et quel che naturalmente è congionto non disconvenga, non è vituperabile.
>
> (*Libro*, f. 73^{r-v}; in the 1525 edition f. 73^r is printed f. 83^r in error).

The passage presents a strongly argued case for Equicola's *modus operandi*. His deployment of *exempla* are aimed at demonstrating that precedent for this procedure can be found amongst the best Latin poets (Catullus and Virgil) and orators of the classical world (Demosthenes and Cicero). He argues then that changes in the direction of the discourse, if handled correctly, serve to strengthen its argumentation and not detract from its principal points. The writer appears to believe that the quantity of writing is a positive factor in its evaluation, providing *variatio* according to the canons of classical rhetoric. In this passage, by contrast to the other quoted previously, Equicola sets a higher value on the way discussions are carried on in a text. There seems to be a more critical reading of his own writing, although he is not prepared to give up the extension of knowledge for compact analysis. Indeed extension in space represents a salient feature of Equicola's methodology: listing of proper nouns constitutes the more generalized system that is found operating in the particular situation of the digression. The preface to the *Chronica di Mantua* is illuminating on this point:

> basta che la celerità me commende, reducendo in ordine quanto da diversi et varii scrittori mi parerà raccogliere.
>
> (f. A3^v)

Collecting and putting in order are the basic dynamics that propel Equicola's intellect — profound thinking, detailed and complex argument over a single issue are rare in his work. Documentation from a wide variety of sources (note the double adjectivisation of «diversi et varii» to stress the point) lies at the centre of his practice. The result is that his works resemble anthologies or manuals which are somewhat unpolished given his often unsystematic approach to his materials.[43]

---

[43]   An interesting example of Equicola's concern for accuracy in the *Chronica* and his recourse to «oral» forms of evidence which also betrays the power-base behind his writing is the following passage:

> Et in Brescia un'altra de Ugoni li quali portano le medesme insegne che Gonzagi portano. Retrovandomi in varii ragionamenti tra molti gentil spirti in Brescia, udii

On almost every page of the *Libro* the reader comes across listing of one
kind or another, for example, to illustrate the proverb «l'honore nutrisce
l'arti» (*Libro*, f. 53ʳ) he produces examples:

> Per honorare la virtù et incitare li altri appo li Scythi ne li solemni convivii non
> era licito prender taza a chi non havesse morto inimico. In Macedonia era lege
> chi non havea ammazato inimico publico se cingesse di capestro. Carthaginesi dal
> numero de le guerre in le quali se erano retrovati, li anelli portavano. A Romani
> donde venne lo uso di tante generationi di corone, civice, obsidionali, murali,
> navali? donde tanti militari doni, armille, haste, phalere, collane? donde le statue
> essendo quelle da dei alli homini trasferite?   (*Libro*, f. 53ʳ)

The most noticeable feature of the passage is the fact that grammatical
links such as relatives and conjunctions (a lack noted by Trissino in his letter
to Equicola on the *Libro*) are almost non-existent. It gives the impression of
having been written in a hurry, recalling his remarks in the *Chronica*, «che la
celerità me commende». The *exempla*, which follow one another in breathless
succession are phrases in apposition, providing little known details on ancient
practices. These are then followed by a series of rhetorical questions which
theoretically could continue *ad infinitum*. In fact, they continue for a further
six lines only to be replaced by another kind of anaphoric construction.[44]
Repetition functions as a means by which Equicola can give the maximum
extension to proper nouns organized in linear fashion without having to
modulate his argumentation. Not only do the *exempla* form lists but within
them there are more proper nouns placed in successive sequences; in this case
one can note the technical vocabulary, a calque of Latin military terminology,
again Equicola demonstrating his familiarity with many aspects of classical
civilisation.

> da uno di quelli dire li Gonzagi di Mantua haver la medesma origine che li Ugoni
> di Brescia. La mia memoria in questo di bona fede quanto alhora li diedi in depo-
> sito, il che in questa scrittione fidelmente ha restituito, donde io per non mancar
> de diligentia, pregai messer Ptolomeo Spaniolo di Gonzaga, como homo pieno
> di humanità, che volesse operare colli soi affini in quella cità, che quanto di tal
> cosa havessero li Ugoni ne dessero certa notitia (*Chronica*, f. G8ʳ).

It is interesting to note that the reference to Francesco Gonzaga's secretary has not been deleted
even though Isabella d'Este did her best to wreak revenge on him. It is an indication of Equicola's search for historical veracity and perhaps his lack of care in revising the text. It may also
be that Equicola was expressing a general loyalty to the Marquis' politics and a loss of confidence in Isabella d'Este's political judgement. The structure of the *Chronica* without a doubt
lends emphasis to the idea that history is made by the ruler and everything else is subordinate
to it.

[44]   The structure of the sentences that follow can be briefly summarized: «Se ama et desi-
derasi la patria sia grande... se da la sua exaltatione et imperio ne cognoscemo diminuire... Chi
spinse el prudentissimo Bruto...? Chi il severo patre C. Manlio Torquato...? ...Chi Syllano...?
...Perché fu Spurio Cassio dal patre occiso? Perché Fulvio commandò la morte del figliolo?
(*Libro*, f. 53ᵛ).

These procedures do not always lead to an uncritical acceptance of the entire *corpus* of knowledge that he collects. He sometimes takes considerable pleasure in proving his worth as an interpreter of documents. This usually takes the form of questioning other humanists' interpretations. Conspicuous examples can be found in the *Chronica* but not only there (the *Iter* and *Libro* offer some glimmers of a critical intelligence at work):

> Sin qui procede lo Aliprando. Non se maraveglie alcuno che noi di lui como fu Platina non sia[m]o stati imitatori per ciò che molte cose fabulose, molte false vi legemo. Chi è di sì poco iudicio che referisse quel che egli dal principio de[l] suo libro sino alli Bonacolsi narra in circa doa milia et cinquicento terzerti, tra le altre, raconta como Vergilio da una donna fu gabato et posto una corba et tirato sino a mezza torre. Ridiculo spectaculo del popolo romano et di Cesare Augusto! Et como in vendecta fece che non se pote haver foco se non dalle parti pudibunde de essa donna.
>
> (*Chronica*, f. 04ʳ)

The secretary presents a strong attack on Platina's acritical acceptance of Aliprandi's fanciful narrative based on popular traditions. The passage pokes fun at the absurdity of the anecdote which emphasizes the distance separating the writers — Equicola saw the ideological implications of reviving as a cultural model the Virgil-Augustus relationship in positive terms and hence needed to clear away the detritus of previous historians by pouring scorn on their findings.[45] At a later point in the *Chronica* Equicola outlines his system:

> Cito frequentemente li scrittori ad ciò se sapia che nulla fengo. Contradico ad essi scrittori per defensione de la verità.
>
> (f. *4ʳ)

Although Equicola himself recognizes that the «compendio» (*Chronica*, f. Aaʳ) lies at the heart of his discursive practices he allows himself enough space so that texts are differentiated according to whether they fit in with the secretary's ideological thematics and with his position as a courtier. The propensity to make lists, to include as much information as possible and to avoid harsh delimitations is nowhere more present than in the *Libro* where Equicola's eclecticism overrides attachments to particular philosophies in an attempt to install a harmonious totality. Thus, the image of the ship in which all the parts work together to achieve the desired goal of arriving at the final destination, is a traditional symbol employed by the writer at the very end of the *Libro* to suggest that he has made no acrimonious choices and indeed they are not necessary in his intellectual universe.[46] In this Equicola was following

---

[45]   See M.L. Doglio, «Le *Instituzioni* di Mario Equicola: dall' *Institutio principis* alla formazione del segretario», *GSLI*, 159 (1982) 505-35 and S. Kolsky, «'The good servant': Mario Equicola. Court and courtier in early sixteenth-century Italy», *The Italianist*, 6 (1986) 34-60; in particular, pp. 41-48.

[46]   The ship-image is introduced at the very end of the *Libro* in the postface to Isabella d'Este. The standard metaphor demonstrates Equicola's syncretic turn of mind and his general,

the Renaissance tendency towards syncretism, seeing nothing outlandish in reconciling Plato and Aristotle and these pagan philosophers with Christianity.

Equicola as a writer profoundly influenced by the court environment did not owe allegiance to a particular philosophical school. His allegiance was to the court society which was more interested in pleasurable activities than a rigorous philosophical treatise. Consequently, the *Libro* can be read as a reconstruction of court life built on the principle of pleasure which it defends by making it the philosophical centre of the book. On a more superficial level the *Libro* reads as an encyclopedia though, it must be stated, it is not an impartial, objective over-view of its subject-matter, love. It reconstitutes the material in a subtle way exposing it to an analysis which puts the needs of the court first. This is perhaps no better illustrated than in the fifth book (the *Libro* is divided into six) of the treatise.[47] It is in this book that Equicola lays

---

non-philosophical approach to the subjects he examines. After naming Plato, Dionysius, Aristotle and Augustine he abandons philosophers altogether: «et li remi mover m. Tullio, da historici et poeti aiutato» (*Libro*, f. 238^r; the whole passage is on f. 237^v-238^r). The *Libro* fulfills an essential function in the context of court writing: it combines a simplified guide to various philosophical systems with paraphrases of literary works, particularly poetry. Thus, philosophy, considered hard intellectual work, is tempered by the pleasurable activity of reading love-poetry and other kinds of literature.

[47] See G. Bàrberi Squarotti, «L'amante cortigiano» in his *L'onore in corte. Dal Castiglione al Tasso*, Milan, 1986, pp. 110-28, who now takes a different tack from his previous article (see bibliography) on the subject and does not stress in this more recent contribution the bourgeois nature of the courtier. Unfortunately, the author repeats the commonplaces handed down from nineteenth-century criticism concerning the *Libro*: «sostanzialmente, molto più erudita che inventiva, raccolta di citazioni ed esito di lunghe, varie, anche un poco farraginose, anche se attente, letture» (p. 112). In general the reading of the *Libro*, consisting of long quotations from the fifth book, does not add much to our understanding of Equicola's text. Bàrberi Squarotti treats the fifth book in isolation from the rest of Equicola's formulations and consequently cannot insert it into a wider context (there are passing references to Castiglione which are not developed). It is not surprising that the critic chose Book V as the object of his analysis: it bears an interesting resemblance to the *Cortegiano* and is almost self-contained. The fifth book is perhaps more accessible in these respects than the rest of the *Libro*. A crucial aspect of the *Libro* that Bàrberi Squarotti fails to take into account is the genesis of this particular book. In general terms the 1525 text represents a more coherent approach to the same themes as those found in the manuscript together with the addition of new subject-matter not previously found there. The manuscript opens in the fifth book with an invocation to love, celebrating its power in human affairs (f. 203^r-205^r). There then follows some traditional discussion on «la complexione»:

> Non essendo altro como sua definitione ne insigna che effecto il quale resulta dalle qualità deli elementi. Da questa procede amore et odio naturale. Questa ne parturisce et acquista benivolentia et lo contrario (f. 205$^{r\text{-}v}$).

Equicola describes the different types of humour which are viewed in terms of the instinctual and must be overcome by the lover who in this as in everything else to do with love must bring refinement and humanistic values:

> Così noi, o amanti, che la militia amorosa intrepidamente sequitamo, sforzemone contra 'l natural instinto et dispositione non solo de farne degni di essere reamati ma anchora che la qualità de la complexione repugne (f. 206$^{r\text{-}v}$). →

the theoretical foundations for behaviour at court. Its conclusions are not merely a re-writing of personal experiences but are mediated through a re-reading of classical and contemporary texts. In the printed edition of the *Libro* the latter are inscribed in the discourse in a more forceful manner which makes this particular book more topical. It may be stated at this point that the influence of Castiglione, as we shall see, is crucial in the refinement of the various arguments and indeed Book V, or at least its first part, focuses on the human subject in the specificity of the court and *his* relationship to love, no longer in an abstract sense, but to the lover.

The title of the first part of the fifth book *Virtù, diligentia, modi et arte di conciliarci benivolentia*, by its very explicitness reveals an Equicola ready to expand a «philosophy of opportunism» and make it available to those who may wish to exploit it at a basic level. The earlier title, *Causa del reciproco amore et benivolentia* (*Libro*, MS, f. 203ʳ) is certainly vague and does not press home the same point as the later version where the stress is placed on the conscious strategies needed to acquire «benivolentia».

The emphasis on acquisition and the will to succeed is a dominant theme of the fifth book. The humanist axiomatic of controlling one's own destiny permeates through the philosophical layers of the writing; it is perhaps because of this desire to demonstrate the relative liberty of the courtier in the matter of love that Equicola does not treat the latter's relationship with the prince. Love is perceived as an autonomous area which does not directly involve the ruler's authority. Its philosophical basis is not predetermination of any sort:

> Credemo adunque che la natura ci faccia idonei, la educatione et consuetudine ci possan redur in perfectione. Per la qual cosa ne persuademo di nostra voluntà in noi crescere virtù et augmentarsi i vitii.
>
> (*Libro*, f. 164ᵛ)

Natural disposition can be altered by one's education and environment; it is an act of the will, a conscious decision if a person chooses to be good or evil.

Even if the writer wishes to minimize these behavioural categories he does not shorten his analysis of them which continues unbroken till f. 212ʳ. Once this and the power of astrology have been disposed of: «Il savio domina alle stelle» (f. 213ʳ) the secretary turns his attention to the practical conduct of love. His practical advice is based upon courtly principles of timeliness and «perseverantia» («usate la opportunità», f. 213ᵛ). It picks up the theme of the irrational in love only to explain it away (f. 214ᵛ). Bodily signs that indicate that a person is in love are discussed at some length since they appear in the classical sources but without much conviction although the importance of body language in the court cannot be over-estimated (the section is on f. 215ʳ-221ʳ and will not find a place in the reorganized 1525 version for obvious reasons. The section is far too prolix and does seem to undermine the necessity of «arte» to win over the lover). In fact, the printed text begins at f. 221ʳ of the autograph manuscript. Other significant changes are examined in our text. It should be noted, however, that the section on colours, which in the manuscript is really a mini-treatise, is substantially reduced in the printed version.

This philosophical position explains the reason for the inclusion of certain sections which might otherwise be considered digressions. Equicola's diatribe against love potions fits into this category. For him they represent a surrender of human effort to superstition on a similar level to astrology:

> Et perché incidentemente è accascato fare mentione de amatorii veneficii voglio il mio lectore sia admonito: non recerche qui incantamenti né imagini né altra magica observatione de celesti influxi né segni con parole determinate percioché tutte son delusioni, tutte fraudi, tutte hami ad creduli, tutte reti dove si avoluppano li semplicetti.
>
> *(Libro*, f. 175ᵛ)

The writer's scorn for these practices almost knows no bounds; here the accumulation of examples serves the purpose of allowing him to display a rigorous rationality and a humorous touch by detailing those rites which are most extraordinary and ridiculous: «non è in parte alcuna utile scrivere note in dodece foglie di lauro et quelle fare mangiare con radici di oliva et di dictamo mixti con genital seme» (*Libro*, f. 176ʳ). Hence love potions are at the other end of the spectrum from Equicola's principal discussion on the power of the individual acting within a network of social relations. The text insists on this point with rhetorical excess.

The optimism of the text is not limited by considerations of the generally difficult conditions of the court. Indeed these are implicitly perceived as a stimulus to competitive behaviour. In this ethological analysis Neoplatonism has no place and maybe would be harmful to it. Beauty for the moment is equated with the natural state of things and consequently has to be refined: «Esser formoso et bello non è nostra laude como lo essere deforme non è nostro mancamento» (f. 165ʳ). It is important to note the use of «laude» in this context; the concept is reiterated several times in the course of this analysis, including a three-point break-down of what actually constitutes «laude» (f. 165ʳ). Confirmation of the self by the other is the determining force that produces the rules Equicola puts forward. It is at the limit where individual action and social regulation meet or in the text's terminology where «virtù» colludes with society to gain «laude» — the manuscript redaction was perhaps too blunt about the restrictions placed on the exercise of «virtù»: «De la virtù il primo officio è conciliarsi li animi de li homini e quelli reducere ad nostro uso» (*Libro*, MS, f. 223ᵛ). The obvious connection between «virtù» and the title of the first part of the fifth book is not made in the printed edition possibly because it *was* so reductive and basic. The aim of the lover whose social position is never really identified by Equicola (Castiglione on the other hand always emphasizes the nobility of his courtier) seems to be upward social mobility. This would suggest that love has become a male metaphor for conquest and the possibility of improving social status: «non desperemo de cosa ad homo in amore possibile. Pegiore è lasciarse cadere da soi meriti che ponerse in più alto loco che non si deve» (f. 165ʳ).

Love (in a court environment) allows *the man* to test his potential and even to break the rules of that society. Once again the manuscript is more crudely mercenary in its approach to the system. After stating that no possibilities are closed to «noi homini» (omitted in the printed text since it is a redundant expression conveying a haughty attitude towards the absent object, women) Equicola writes: «non contenti di nostra conditione et stato, ad summa dignità, ad summo honore aspiremo» (*Libro*, MS, f. 223^r). Thus, the ideological basis of love as a system of relations embedded in social interaction, part of the male-dominated order, is laid bare. It is not a theory tending towards some future harmonious relationship between parts. Instead it has its basis in a notion of conflict which must remain hidden in order to avoid possible anarchy or the open opposition of those higher up in the social hierarchy. It could well be that this fundamental conception of social behaviour met with Castiglione's consent and he transferred it more elegantly into his own work. Equicola concentrates on social action here rather than abstract thought («altro è scrivere de philosophia commentarii, altro amore tractare» [f. 165^r]). The subject-matter will concentrate on the means that are necessary to progress in the world of the court. General remarks on behaviour are not restricted to the lover but are applicable to any man wishing to make his career at court:

> sapere conversare colli homini, conciliarsi gli animi di quelli, redurli ad nostro uso, disporre loro opere, studii, et voluntà per nostri commodi.
>
> (*Libro*, f. 165^r)

Again the manuscript is even more explicit in its insistence on instrumentalizing the other for personal benefits:

> perché benché multo possa in le humane cose la fortuna, benivolentia è necessaria ad farne deventare excelsi.   (*Libro*, MS, f. 224^r)

Equicola describes the processes by which the courtier achieves his goal. Not far from the surface of the text the reader can notice the interaction with a fifteenth-century treatise by Ermolao Barbaro, *De Officio Legati* in which the concept of «benivolentia» plays a not insignificant role. This borrowing and subsequent reshaping of this key term from diplomatic language constitutes a fundamental operation on Equicola's part. It places relations *within* the court on the same level as those involving contacts *outside* the «home» court. Therefore, the writer places a premium on those particular qualities that are necessary to a successful ambassador. If the ambassador must pursue relentlessly the aims of his ruler, refining his methods of making/maintaining contact with the other, either at the human interface or surreptitiously through more cunning means, in other words, using the tactics of a spy, the lover/courtier finds himself in a similar situation. The means needed to acquire «benivolentia» are to a certain degree unethical and conflict with Christian teaching;

they may have been partially defensible in the pursuit of state politics, but used in the pursuit of personal satisfactions they become rather questionable and especially revealing of the court dynamics of inter-personal relations.

Thus, the behaviour of the courtier is conditioned by factors borrowed from another related field and which are now considered relevant to the general comportment of the courtier as well as his particular needs in pursuing a love-affair. Equicola's intention in regulating the courtier's behaviour is so that the latter can avoid «malivolentia» (*Libro*, f. 165ᵛ). The writer lists the negative aspects of behaviour that will alienate the courtier from the rest of the court and confer unwanted attention on him:

> Quelli meritamente sono superbi extimati, li quali sono difficili, ineffabili, altieri in dimandare, retrosi in respondere, in provocare rustici, con obstinatione contentiosi, cupidi d'esser honorati senza consideratione.   (*Libro*, f. 165ᵛ)

Equicola does not arrive at the complexities of Castiglione's concept of *sprezzatura* because his courtier is not in the business of impressing *men*. Indeed, there seems to be a desire for anonymity on the part of the «amatore», a desire to avoid judgement by the others.

This judgement rests on considerations of face-to-face behaviour, with speech reinstated to a primary function. For this reason conversation becomes a major object of Equicola's body of rules. Private behaviour has hardly any value in this arena of fierce competition not only for survival but for advancement and the achievement of one's goals. The point could not be made clearer by Equicola:

> Qualunque si voglia acto, modo et gesto che da superbia proceda, anchor che nulla a noi appertenga, subito havemo quello in fastidio. Et benché con noi et pochi altri il superbo humil si mostre non si diminuisce però il concepto odio.
> (*Libro*, f. 165ᵛ)

It is the surface that matters at the expense of the intimate or private expression of feelings. Throughout Equicola's discussion the subjects chosen for analysis are presented in such a way that it becomes clear that the courtier is very much a subaltern figure without power or authority invested in his person by virtue of a privileged status. References to the courtier are in terms of his capacities to perform, all of which can be regulated by prescription. There is no residue here of feudal superiority and it is this lack of concern for nobility together with the ethic of knightly valour which properly distinguishes Equicola's theoretical statements from Castiglione's. For Equicola at this point in his treatment of social interaction no essences exist in the absolute, *everything* is done for self-interest (in comparison to Castiglione Equicola is simply more extreme, more forthright in the expression of similar views: the lover has given way to the courtier as counsellor, thus lending a different tonality to the analysis).

It should be said that Equicola's focus on the courtier had become sharper
after the composition of the manuscript of the *Libro*. In the printed text we
find an additional reference to a work that must have been written in the
intervening period. Equicola describes it as a «piccolo volume» in which
«disputamo quali habiano ad essere le parti di colui, il qual di bon cortigiano
pò meritare il nome».[48] The public's reception of this work was negative,
apparently because of the writer's insistence on the public to the detriment of
private considerations. It may have been the «maledicentia de invidi» (*Libro*,
f. 166ᵛ) which caused Equicola to delay publication of the *Libro* itself; revealing the mechanisms of court society may have seemed too dangerous to other
courtiers, especially if Equicola put forward views that were unpalatable and
better left unsaid. This personal digression in the *Libro* serves an important
purpose, namely, to clarify in the flow of discourse the object of his analysis,
the courtier. This he had not done in the earlier version. In fact the manuscript
never specifically mentions the courtier by name. It could be argued that
Equicola's theoretical formulation had not reached that stage of analytical
clarity which it would have later on because he had not yet come under
Castiglione's influence. The nature of this influence is of course extremely difficult to define but in this instance Castiglione seems to have provided
Equicola with the stimulus to make him write his own version of the *Cortegiano*. On the other hand it could be cogently argued that Castiglione would
himself have been extremely interested in Equicoia's statements on amorous
behaviour and the chain that would eventually link it to Neoplatonic idealism.
Equicola can be seen to be pushing Castiglione's thought towards
Neoplatonism and to have led him to a more detailed appreciation of the practices of court society.

Equicola subsumes these practices under the general thematic of «virtù».
And it is here that the regulations prescribed by the text become more general
with respect to the manuscript. There, the lover was the central focus whereas
in the 1525 edition Equicola appears to be attempting to combine the former
aim with a new emphasis on courtierly behaviour in general. Horace is used
as a source for the latter: «Horatio in quel loco con belle admonitioni mi par
informe et instituisca un bon cortegiano» (*Libro*, f. 167ʳ). The secretary
posits a certain degree of interchangeability between the amorous necessities
of the courtier and his normal activities at court. However, Equicola is not
completely cynical in his manipulation of traditional virtues. The pre-

---

[48]   *Libro*, f. 166ᵛ. The work mentioned here is not to be confused with the anonymous
Novo corteggiano for which see S.D. Kolsky, «Did Mario Equicola write *Il novo corteggiano*?», *Aevum*, 57 (1983) 416-27.

supposition which underlies much of his discussion in the fifth book —
upward mobility — needs the semblance of respectability. Thus, the brief
panegyric on truth inserted in the section on «modestia» aims at wiping away
any sense of moral uncertainty that may have arisen from his basic premises.
Truth is praised as the highest good, reminiscent of Ficinian Neoplatonism's
emphasis on harmonious relations:

> Essa [la verità] da noi odio discaccia et como il sole col suo splendore il mundo
> illustra como l'anima dà ai corpi moto, como da docta mano toccata la lyra
> responde. Così questa le virtù illumina, inanima et dà loro concento. (f. 167ᵛ)

Truth is a metaphysical absolute replete with all those Neoplatonic attributes which guarantee its total separation from the world of the court. The higher realities will place the court in a better light: «questa conserva la benivolentia como la destruge la bugia» (*Libro*, f. 167ᵛ). The stress on illumination
strongly contrasts with the secret motives of individual courtiers intent on
overcoming their rivals. Yet the panegyric acknowledges its limitations and
indeed its irrelevance to the subject-matter of the fifth book:

> Se colla verità non possemo nel principio acquistare amore, senza dubio essa lo
> acquistato mantiene.
> (*Libro*, f. 167ᵛ)

It should be remembered that Equicola is really only concerned with how
the courtier-lover can win his desired object. Consequently it can be deduced
that truth or sincerity have no place in this area of Equicola's thought. Expediency is the crucial concept to which nearly everything bends: «se tali saremo
quali volemo essere tenuti, haremo expedita la via alla benivolentia» (*Libro*,
f. 168ʳ). This argument seems to put forward the possibility of making
essence and appearance coincide. However, the practical result of this philosophy is the diametrical opposite of the just quoted axiom:

> Multo iova in farne amare: il sapere accomodarne alli studii, actioni et exercitii
> di coloro dalli quali desyderamo essere amati.
> (*Libro*, MS, f. 227ᵛ)

The above principle finds expression in most of the practical comments as well
as in other similar axiomatics.⁴⁹ It is then the predominant cultural values

---

49   Equicola also examines the negative side of utterances such as the one we have quoted.
Anything that draws attention to the individual is to be avoided because it involves judgement
by the others concerning the lover who does not have the material means to combat such behaviour:

> Evitando arrogantia et iactantia in li quali vitii incorremo se li facti et gesti nostri
> più preclari et magnifici che non sonno colle parole facemo con avantarne di cose
> false como multi hogi vedemo in questa romana corte.   (*Libro*, MS, f. 229ᵛ)

The reference to the Roman court does not reappear in the printed text. It was the only reference
to an actual court but its negativity no doubt weighed heavily on the manuscript. Equicola

that overtly mould behaviour in Equicola's view of the court. The actual
impossibility of fusing the public and private together is made manifest by the
writer in a passage which continues directly on from the previously quoted
one:

> Laudemo in loro le parti laudabili, le vituperabili sforzemone redurle ad virtù.
> Laudemole nel publico, admoniamoli nel secreto. Habiamo di loro bona speranza
> che habiano ad devientare excellenti, il che li seria urgentissimo sperone et ad noi
> li farrà benivoli.   (*Libro*, MS, f. 227ᵛ-228ʳ)

The avoidance of conflict in public at all costs does not necessarily mean
a complete renunciation of moral values. However, the above passage was
deleted from the 1525 edition indicating a growing cynicism or an acceptance
by Equicola of the amorality of court life.

One can state that Equicola's three principal virtues — «modestia»,
«mansuetudine», and «urbanità» — fulfil a specific function in the society
that revolved around the court. Again Equicola's position offers a different
vantage-point from Castiglione's. The latter did not see the frivolous activities
of the court as an end in themselves, or if there were a danger of this happening the author of the *Cortegiano* viewed them as necessary steps to winning
the prince's attention and thereafter his confidence. Equicola instead justified
such activities on different grounds, almost for their own sake. He perceived
them as part of the rites of the court, equally important as more serious
events:

> Quello non extimarò io alli homini grato che con honestà sa et pò altri ad riso
> incitare, et in letitia la mestitia convertere, et ogni turbido pensiero dalla mente
> removere? In iudicii severità, in consegli prudentia, in magistrati gravità, in admi-
> nistratione de cose domestiche diligentia mi piace. In Amor facetie et giochi biso-
> gnano.   (*Libro*, f. 168ᵛ)

For Equicola there exists a clear division between what is serious and what
is not. And this chapter of the *Libro* deals with the rules of the game of love.
Amor represents a pleasurable activity as opposed to the serious work of state
or administration of one's own affairs. It is in Equicola's view part of a natural cycle necessary for the well-being of humankind: «perché natura non pate
continua fatiga» (*Libro*, f. 168ᵛ). In the court environment it offers the
opportunity of breaking down, if only for a moment, social barriers which
can be dissolved by laughter. The three virtues properly controlled («laudansi
coloro che ben l'usano», *Libro*, f. 168ᵛ) enhance face-to-face contact, in particular the various forms of conversation. They operate best on those

---

stands at a distance from the papal court, considering it as the worst example of improper conduct, based on principles which deny Equicola's formulations («la simulatione è quella che la
benivolentia extermina», *Libro*, MS, f. 230ʳ).

occasions when the hierarchies at court are less obvious and when they can be infiltrated — occasions such as the pleasurable gatherings of the court, playing games, dancing and so on. Love is the symbol therefore both of the potential fluidity of certain court structures and of pleasure itself:

> Sia adunque il mio amatore con tutti, et maximamente colla amata signora, humano, modesto, mansueto et urbano. (*Libro*, f. 169^r)

That Equicola is not solely concerned with amorous matters is proved by the reference to «con tutti», in other words the lover's overall behaviour. Such an interpretation is strengthened by a general statement to be found only in the printed text:

> Non proponemo hora di Xenophonte il Cyro, meno di Aristotele il Re, ma amante informamo et de virtù lo adornamo. Tali con le quali con non molta fatiga acquiste grata de la amata et de preclari homini la benivolentia se apporte. (*Libro*, f. 169^{r-v})

Equicola has made a not insignificant addition at this stage in his catalogue of the skills necessary to win favour either from the women at court *or the important men there*. This statement has the function of providing a framework for the material which will follow on the practical abilities required of the courtier-lover. In general, there has been a rearrangement of the sections with respect to the manuscript in order to render the text more coherent by presenting the lover in a manner which unifies the disparate subject-matter more clearly. It might be that Equicola was profoundly influenced by Castiglione's investigation into likely precedents for his courtier in classical literature. It would not have been a great leap for Equicola to have incorporated classical archetypes into his presentation of the lover. By their mere mention he hopes to raise quite considerably the status of a marginal figure and remove most of the stigmas attached to it. Thus, the lover intends to have an institutional status equivalent to Castiglione's courtier.

Although Equicola travels a different path from Castiglione similarities between the fifth book of the *Libro* and the *Cortegiano* are not lacking. Both try to ensure that their respective theories receive the maximum validation from classical sources so that the idea of the court itself comes out more refined and acceptable as an institution. After giving advice on the details of body movements and speech Equicola comments:

> dicoli, se errore vi è, che erro con Platone, Aristotele, M. Tullio et Quintiliano, de quali le sententie ho qui voluntieri exposte, non como ad ingenuamente educati necessarie, ma a coloro utili li quali quasi fungi in una nocte nati, de lettere nudi, tra amanti eleganti como se elegantissimi fossero, compareno.[50]

---

[50] *Libro*, f. 175^r. At this point it becomes extremely difficult to unravel the complex issue of intertextuality as it regards the *Libro* and the *Cortegiano*, although Equicola may have

Equicola is extremely open about his use of classical sources, not wishing to hide debts. His statements are meant to be authoritative for this very reason — the mention of classical writers lends a serious tone to what otherwise might have been considered a frivolous exercise.

The section on the practical skills of the courtier-lover offers much new material in comparison to the manuscript. Here undoubtedly Castiglione's approach has been adopted by Equicola. Previously the author of the *Libro* had only insisted on the importance of speech and body language, now he ventures into those areas which Castiglione considers are vital for success in the court such as dancing, musical accomplishments and even adding skills of his own («a tempo saper servire alla scena», *Libro*, f. 169ᵛ). At first sight Equicola appears to have ransacked the *Cortegiano* taking key ideological concepts and placing them in his own work, but without the same finesse. But even in these cases Equicola finds classical precedents:

> et overo como dice lo Terentiano patre, essere intento in nutrire cavalli o cani per caccia, overo gire ad philosophi, di queste cose niuna ne faceva fora di mesura, ma tutte moderatamente.⁵¹
>
> (*Libro*, f. 171ᵛ)

However, the later inclusion of this new section leads the reader to suspect that Equicola was stimulated to extend his investigation through his exposure to Castiglione's text(s). The unity of the description, its breadth of inclusion had not been present in the earlier version. Because of Equicola's diverse perspective on the court the same activities are treated in dissimilar ways. The matter of military valour is raised by Equicola only referring to jousts:

> Men me dispiaceria, anzi summamente laudaria, *se 'l suo grado et conditione il pate*, et se 'l tempo il richiede, che in militari giochi, in giostre, in torniamenti, di sé facesse prova et laude publica ne reportasse.   (*Libro*, f. 171ᵛ, my italics)

---

thought out the classical origins of his model earlier than Castiglione because of his almost total dependence on Latin sources. However, the matter is practically impossible to resolve. What is interesting to note is that Castiglione used a similar formula to the one quoted here by Equicola:

> A questi rispondo che mi contentarò aver errato con Platone, Senofonte e Marco Tullio (*Il Cortegiano*, Introduzione di A. Quodam, Milan, 1981, p. 10).

⁵¹ The notion of moderation underlies Castiglione's discourse almost at every point. Such comments as «io per me amerei che non fossero estremi in alcuna parte» (*Seconda redazione*, p. 111) are not infrequent. Equicola seems to have borrowed the image of a particular dance from Castiglione in order to stress the ideal of proper behaviour to which the courtier/lover must attain:

> benché in camera privatamente, come or noi si troviamo, penso che leccito gli sia e questo e ballare moresche e brandi; ma in pubblico non così, fuorché travestito (*Seconda redazione*, p. 93).

Equicola is equally forthright in his condemnation:

> Conviensi adunque al nostro amatore como hogi si usa de ballare la peritia né quel modo in lui dannaria, se privamente lo exercitasse, che da Mori ha preso et retene il nome (*Libro*, f. 171ᵛ).

Equicola's courtier was not necessarily noble and jousting would not be for him a normal part of the round of court activities. In fact, Equicola polemically reverses Castiglione's priorities. The former writes: «prima de lettere volemo sia ornato acciò non sia in soi ragionamenti rozo et inepto et sopra ogni altra litteratura la poetica li piaccia» (*Libro*, f. 169ᵛ).

There is some innovation compared with the obvious model Castiglione. Equicola starts from the shared premise that letters have their importance in promoting decent conversation but he goes much further than his model by transforming his courtier into a poet. Poetry indeed takes on greater significance for Equicola in the period after the completion of the autograph manuscript. Not only did he add a totally new section on poetry to Book V of the *Libro* but composed a treatise, the *Institutioni al comporre in ogni sorte di rima della lingua volgare*, stressing the superiority of poetry over other art and forms of literature.[52] Poetry is considered to be the area in which a non-noble courtier can assert himself and prove his worth by demonstrating a sure ability. It is significant that Ancient Rome provided Equicola with telling *exempla*:

> La età che dopo fu, perciò che l'honor nutrisce l'arte, gran copia de poeti produxe. Ne la mensa de imperatori admessi et da grandissimi homini honorati furono. Et sopra gli altri fu Vergilio in summa reverentia havuto, et dal senato et populo romano publicamente honorato et meritamente, perché noi credemo il poeta con forza et vigore di mente exercitarsi et a tutti altri scriptori, como più de li altri ingenioso, deversi preporre.
> (*Libro*, f. 169ᵛ)

These thoughts are close to those expressed in the *Institutioni* and would seem to indicate a common time of composition. The mention of Virgil is not casual here as in the *Institutioni* and represents the marriage of the intellectual to those who exercise power. The poet then has grandiose aspirations and expectations of court society. In the particular context of the *Libro* he is a link between the spoken and written word: a performer and a writer. Equicola may have had in mind the tremendously successful Unico Aretino as an example of a court poet much in demand.[53] Furthermore, Equicola makes another link between poetry and music (the latter is examined immediately after his encomium of the poet) which is not out of place in the context of court society where the poet often performed his or others' poetry to the accompaniment of a musical instrument. Perhaps the most significant example of the role of

---

[52]   Cf. S. Kolsky, «'The good servant'», pp. 41-42.

[53]   The most convincing account of Bernardo Accolti's poetry is to be found in A. Rossi, *Serafino Aquilano e la poesia cortigiana*, Brescia, 1980, pp. 130-32. One should also consult L. Mantovani, «Accolti, Bernardo detto l'Unico Aretino», *DBI*, Rome, 1, 1960, pp. 103-104. Still useful are E. Guarnera, *Bernardo Accolti. Saggio biografico critico*, Palermo, 1901 and F. Gavagni, *L'Unico Aretino e la corte dei duchi d'Urbino*, Arezzo, 1906.

the poet-musician at court is Serafino Aquilano. Isabella d'Este herself composed at least one poem to be set to music and in general her patronage of
this art is one of the most important aspects of her cultural influence. There
can be no doubt that she not only actively encouraged the development of
local musical talent but also the type of virtuoso skills associated with poetry
set to music.[54] Equicola appears to be delimiting the spaces available to the
intellectual at court. He stresses above all the performance aspect — the social
imperative of the writer to entertain.

Apart from this innovative emphasis Equicola closely follows
Castiglione's prescriptions as regards music and its societal implications:

> Volemo dunque che in musica lo nostro amante perito sia, non però Aristoxeno,
> summo musico, lo desideramo.   (*Libro*, f. 171ʳ)

These additions also serve to place in a more logical perspective the long
and detailed section on speech. No longer is it only loosely tied to the main
argument but now comes in the most prominent position in a list of attributes
that will render the courtier effective amongst his equals and superiors. In this
case Equicola may have suggested to Castiglione the absolute superiority of
the spoken code over the written in a courtly context. However, Castiglione
does not analyse the intimate details of performance to anywhere near the
same extent as Equicola does here. The latter first of all establishes the reason
why he is going to treat this subject-matter:

> Argumento ultra li altri ne è che multe cose bene pronuntiate hanno gratia et
> delectano et le medesme legendole non respondeno.   (*Libro*, MS, f. 238ᵛ)

Although the notion of «gratia» is not nearly as well developed in the
Libro as in the *Cortegiano* one can discern that it already signals a sense of
style desired by the court in its collective pursuit of élitism and pleasure. Such
a discussion cannot avoid entering the dispute of the *questione della lingua*.
In this matter the manuscript and the printed text are separated by the debate
on language which saw Equicola as one of the principal targets. His statement
in the manuscript contains a passing reference to affectation, to be developed
later by Castiglione. It puts the greatest stress on the validity of following
Latin example. Equicola is vague about exactly which kind of vernacular is
acceptable: «siano li vocabuli non affectati, non totalmente dal vulgo remoti.
Siano proximi al'antiquo latino quanto lo uso et gratia supporta» (*Libro*, MS,

---

[54] For a full discussion of Isabella d'Este's music patronage see W.F. Prizer, «Isabella d'Este and Lucrezia Borgia as patrons of music: The Frottola at Mantua and Ferrara», *Journal of the American Musicological Society*, 38 (1985) 1-33 and for an example of the *Marchesana's* patronage, C. Gallico, *Un libro di poesie per musica dell'epoca d'Isabella d'Este*, Mantua, 1961.

f. 239^v). The later formulation offers a radically revised version: «Il favellare sia del patrio idioma da voci più electe formato così evitarassi barbarismo che ne l'altrui lingua parlando ogni nostro dire non serà senza quello per la diversità de le pronuntie et varietà de li accenti che ciascuna regione de Italia ha proprii et nativi et difficillimi ad apprendere sì tosto.»[55] Equicola's linguistic thought has undergone an involution perhaps because of a lack of confidence in solutions which demand relearning how to speak: it is also an open attack on Tuscan as a *lingua franca* especially if it has to be spoken as well as written. It is likely that he was pointing to the obvious gap in Bembo's linguistic edifice and suggesting a polemical solution which again undermines the supremacy of any kind of Tuscan. The secretary has clearly understood the need to make a stand on the spoken language in order to promote diversity as against unity, plurality of courts as against domination by a few powerful states. However, attachment to one's dialect should not be blind and Equicola introduces a subtle proviso which effectively alters the complexion of his first, dramatic statement:

> dispongasi il mio amante quel che totalmente è diforme imbellirlo senza affectatione et quel che ruzo li pare redurlo in quel che meno inculto appara.
>
> (*Libro*, f. 173^r)

It is clear from this passage that Equicola is not advocating an uncritical use of one's dialect. Language has to be subject to the same rules as other aspects of behaviour. Furthermore, these rules are all meant to enforce the elitistic nature of the courts, separating them from the rest of society by granting them a distinct behavioural code. The court system is meant to be refined as against the mass brutality of those who have no access to it — they are characterized by the adjectives «ruzo» and «inculto». Hence dialect cannot be employed without some discrimination and *must* be «improved» whenever it fails to meet the requirements of a sophisticated court culture. Thus, Equicola perforce discusses other solutions to the problem of communication not as total solutions in his case but rather as possibilities or temptations that face the courtier. They may be considered as partial aids which might be used on an *ad hoc* basis to compensate for the «defects» of the «patrio idioma». Also Equicola in spite of his original premise does not totally disallow that the courtier may decide to choose a language other than his own. In this case there are two choices. The first, «fiorentina dicemo» and the second, although not specifically named, is none other than the *lingua cortigiana*:

> Altri serà che non ad una lingua sola, como ad fixa tramontana drizarà il curso del suo dire. Qui summo iudicio bisogna, perché in corte è necessario sia per gran spatio de tempo conversato et assuefacto et da li homini preclari che ivi da diverse

---

[55]   *Libro*, f. 172^v. Cf. *Trattati sull'ortografia del volgare 1524-1526*, a cura di B. Richardson, University of Exeter, 1984, pp. XVIII-XXII.

> parti si adunano, imparare le megliori et più eleganti dictoni. Costui se delecte
> de le parole che non siano aliene o remote dal commune uso. Fuga li novi et non
> consueti vocaboli. Piaccianoli quelli che da la latina lingua, de la vulgare italica
> matre sono deducti se quelli si usano, se sono frequentati, se sono dal publico
> admessi et se la publica consuetudine non li refuta.   (*Libro*, fs. 173r-v)

One could argue that Castiglione follows Equicola's prescriptions in a precise though independent manner. He demonstrates a propensity for a particular regional language, Lombard, instead of the impratical base of each individual dialect and amalgamates this choice into the theory of the *lingua cortigiana*, something which is implicit in Equicola's text.[56]

In accordance with the notion that the court is a *locus*, where the emphasis falls on the drama of presentation, writing becomes an extension of the spoken word and hence liable to the same courtly uses:

> però qual modo tenerà del parlare il mio amante, como è dicto di sopra, tal obser-
> varà nel scrivere.   (*Libro*. f. 174v)

The purpose of regulating speech and associated functions is, in the *Libro*, to ingratiate oneself with the beloved. The previous sections provide the necessary background information for successful affairs. The more general statements in the earlier part of the chapter are rigorously applied to the relationship between the courtier-lover and his beloved (who in Equicola's account does not acquire the status of «donna di palazzo» and is very much an object):

> Così habituato il mio giovene se sforze essere colla amata signora in obsequio dili-
> gente tanto che in servitù voluntaria se stesso constituisca et pervenga il suo ser-
> vire al desio di quella cui serve.   (*Libro*, f. 175r)

Nothing less than total dedication is required of the lover who must sacrifice his personality and work for the object of his desires: «ad suo arbitrio, in sua gloria et honore, hore et giorni dispensemo» (*Libro*, f. 175v). Equicola is unable to sustain his hymn of self-abnegation for very long before he launches into a learned digression on love potions, as we have already seen. These are dismissed as ridiculous superstition. In their place he sets rational behaviour in the form of carefully controlled parameters, first of all for the male courtier, now for the female at court. The homily to women is another addition with respect to the manuscript. It is difficult to say whether it is included because of the direct influence of the *Cortegiano* or is brought about by rethinking on Equicola's part after his early *De Mulieribus*. Indeed the role of the lost volume on the good courtier and the impossibility of assessing its debt to Castiglione may be considered crucial in the development of Equicola's thought. For whatever reasons the author of the *Libro* has decided to

---

[56]   Cf. the *Cortegiano*, pp. 8-9 where Castiglione expresses clearly his theory of conversational language.

present a more rounded picture of love at court, by introducing a series of direct warnings to the women, the text becomes more peremptory in tone compared to the guide-lines issued to the men:

> Et voi, o gratiose donne, assai vi prego che siate honeste et vergognose, che questo
> è il fior d'ogni belleza et calamita che tira a sé il ferro et induce ciascuno ad
> inamorarsi. (*Libro*, f. 177r-v)

The long apostrophe to women that begins here insists on a certain morality being observed in amorous relationships and takes as its starting-point the same value of «honestà» so cherished by Castiglione in the third book of the *Cortegiano*.[57] Equicola's advice, as Castiglione's, aims to make women receptive to the advances of courtiers, but at the same time imposing some order and limits on behaviour. Castiglione, however, is stricter in his attitude towards female behaviour than Equicola is. The latter does not reduce love to an exchange of glances: «Amar perseverantemente con modestia non fu mai nocivo né mai dispiacque» (*Libro*, f. 178r). Equicola is intent on imposing the male humanist ideal of the Golden Mean on women. They should only love one man but not with overwhelming passion:

> Notate, signore care, è la virtù collocata in mezo de doi extremi, però li soi confini
> et termini diligentemente vitare et fugire bisogna. (*Libro*, f. 178v)

Women are subject to the same rules of speech as the male lover.[58] Equicola gives substantially the same advice in this section as Castiglione concerning the woman's choice of a lover and the necessity to exercise care in determining who her lover should be.[59]

The section on women does read as a later interpolation; it is not well integrated with the preceding matter nor with that which follows. The end of the discussion is abrupt:

> Questo sia assai hora haver con le mie donne brevemente ragionato. Al'amante
> si ritorne del qual desideramo sia lo animo ornato de virtù et de habito conve-
> niente vestire il corpo se sforze. (*Libro*, f. 179v)

The reference to «le mie donne», which cannot avoid the accusation of patro-

---

[57] See, for example, the *Seconda redazione* where the need to conserve «la onestate» is compared to the precautions to keep safe «una gemma preziosa» (p. 261).

[58] Equicola ridicules affectation in women's speech especially when it means betraying one's own dialect:

> Questa con allegria raccoglie et resaluta, ma nel parlare è roza. Quell'altra sagia
> se tiene et sententiosamente parla et per parer de ingegno, toscaneza. Donde per
> haver ad mendicare parole, dalla improprietà de vocaboli distracta, altro sona il
> senso, altro le parole et così appare ridicula (*Libro*, f. 178v).

Equicola implicity puts forward rules for female speech through a series of negative statements which ironically comment upon women's linguistic behaviour at court.

[59] Cf. *Libro*, f. 179r-v and the *Cortegiano*, pp. 338-40.

nizing women, reducing as far as possible their difference, is not linked up in any logical way to the question of dress which will now occupy Equicola:

> Noi nel nostro amante mediocrità laudamo. Et che habia qualche cura del suo vestire, non però tanto delitioso che sia molle.   (*Libro*, f. 180ʳ)

The parallels with Castiglione are obvious. Both writers appreciate a certain masculine appeal in their courtiers who should consequently avoid trespassing on dress and ornament too closely associated with female stereotyped role-playing.

The discussion of what colours one should wear leads Equicola into a long and learned digression on colours in general, already present in the manuscript. It is a typical example of Equicola demonstrating the range of his erudition without an excessive regard for the logical succession of his discourse.

The end of the chapter becomes particularly disjointed and the uneven effort to render the whole more coherent seems to be hardly in evidence. The same material from the manuscript, a paraphrase of Ovid's *Ars Amatoria*, rounds off the chapter in a rather inconclusive way. It does, however, present an improvement in the arrangement of topics which was even more haphazard in the earlier version. To place the paraphrase of Ovid right at the end of the chapter does have a certain logic now that Equicola has introduced an entirely new chapter consisting of prose paraphrases of numerous poets on love — from the classical period to new contemporary Spanish lyric poetry. Equicola is above all interested in *what* these poets have to say that may interest the contemporary reader. Thus, Ovid may be considered as an introduction to this section. And these paraphrases of the *Ars Amatoria* may have encouraged the writer to extend the repertory of lyric poets since the writer follows in the second half of the fifth book his normal procedure of reporting in a rather pedestrian manner principal points of interest in a particular work. This procedure had already been exploited to the full by him in the first book of the *Libro* where he paraphrases a number of works which deal with the theme of love. No doubt Equicola's reading of provençal manuscript N was the final stimulus to help him write the new section on love poetry.

The choice of Ovid in a chapter dealing whith the actual practices of love was not at all strange. In fact, Ovid had been used as a guide to love before him by Calmeta and after him by Castiglione himself.[60] Calmeta's *Breve*

---

[60]   See V. Calmeta, *Breve compendio de Vincenzio Calmeta Collo sopra Ovidio de «Arte Amandi»* in Vincenzo Calmeta, *Prose e lettere edite e inedite*, a cura di C. Grayson, Bologna, 1959, pp. 95-117. Equicola makes extensive use of the *Ars Amatoria* in the *Libro*, paraphrasing quite long sections of it. For the sixteenth-century writer Ovid represents an open attitude to sexuality and sexual practice; real situations are implicitly opposed to Neoplatonic philosophy. Thus, Equicola ends his summary of Ovid's advice on a typical note, libertine and almost pre-Christian:

compendio is an important indication of the high esteem in wich Ovid's practical advice on love was still held. The use of Ovid's precepts perhaps also help to explain why both Equicola and Castiglione were dissatisfied with their texts when it came to writing the revisions which would be incorporated into their printed versions. It must have seemed that the writers' acknowledgement of sharing a common ideology with Ovid could be damaging to them as propagandists of the values of court society. The Latin poet's practical advice did not leave any space for more Christian moral values; instead it reinforced the impression that the court was the ultimate place for seduction, corruption and falsity («Parlando li fengi essere vero amante. Et mostrate ferito da vero, non è cosa difficile farcilo tosto credere», *Libro*, f. 186ʳ). Ovid is perhaps too open and too revealing about the actual operation of love at court: men conquering women with violence, sometimes by playing a part. Equicola paraphrases Ovid:

> Basala. Repugnarà la prima volta, ma como quella che vorrà essere vinciuta, poi il bascio farai il resto. Falli violentia et forza che quella violentia et forza li è grata.
>
> (*Libro*, f. 186ᵛ)

Such assertions do not help to create a positive image of the court, especially when those same writers urge the equality of women and the extension of Christian *mores* to court life.

The contradictions of Equicola's position — a realization on the one hand of how the court actually functions and the desire on the other for it to be different — lead him to juxtapose book V and book VI of the *Libro*. A similar process is at work in the *Cortegiano*. The dialectic of practical realism and the desire for change does not in these texts make for sweeping social reform. Instead we find that a certain deep-rooted impotence exists in the face of the social structure and both these writers seek solace in a rather ambiguous form of Neoplatonism. In Equicola's case it functions rather obviously as a safety-valve, a way out of an impasse and in Castiglione's it is a vision of something better but with indefinable connections with reality.

*

> Non dimandare de soi anni, se ha passato il fiore de la età. In questo, il nostro poeta [Ovid] colloca li amanti in lecto, ove noi li lasciaremo, desiderando ad ogni fidel et gentil amante tal successo (*Libro*, f. 187ᵛ).

It is therefore clear where Equicola's sympathies lie in the matter of sexual morality. He seems to share with Ovid the conquest mentality, conquest made possible by deceit, indicative of corrupt society, devoid of other values than those based on self-interest.

Castiglione also regards Ovid as an authority. In the *Seconda redazione* (p. 315) Castiglione makes a passing nod to the Latin poet's continuing influence on court society: «Pur se desiderate sapere più avanti in amore, andate e sì ve leggete Ovidio.»

Both these writers lived in close contact with the realities of the court. Not for them the contemplative life which would allow them the tranquillity to devote themselves to study. They were both actively involved at different levels in the political turmoil that afflicted the Italian peninsula from the French invasion of 1494 onwards. Their immediate reaction to events, to their environment and their own role in the political events of the period are recorded in the letters written by them. Equicola's letters survive in sufficient numbers to allow us to make several observations. The letter is the form of the most immediate mediation between the ruler or employer and the servant. Equicola had no intentions, as far as we can tell, of putting his letters together in a collection. Indeed, most of his correspondence bears the mark of hurried composition, of doing one's duty in the fastest time possible without too much attention paid to style or handwriting. This is particularly true of the letters written on campaign with Federico Gonzaga towards the end of his life. His reports, though sometimes detailed, give the impression (and at times quite openly) of someone who wished he was safely back in Mantua.

Thus, the majority of Equicola's surviving letters are only interesting in so far as they offer a detailed panorama of military life on a campaign and for the indirect and discontinuous information they provide on Equicola's personal attitude to war and related topics. It is obvious that Equicola was not the best of correspondents as far as the quality and interest of his information is concerned if compared with other letter-writers who knew that news was the way to a ruler's favour. Thus, for example, Sabadino degli Arienti's detailed commentary to Isabella d'Este on the Bolognese political scene was based on the sure knowledge that the *Marchesana* valued all sorts of information, especially because she did not have her own *formal* network of agents and depended on people like Arienti. Humanistic training came in useful for those who had nothing else to offer except a particular angle on political events. Apart from being a way of showing loyalty it was also helpful in the course of the turbulent changes in the political life of northern Italy during these years. It is no accident that Equicola's first letters to the Gonzagas addressed to Francesco Gonzaga, consisted of details on rapidly moving political events (see pp. 88-90).

Not all of Equicola's letters consisted of political *reportage*. Some of his earliest surviving letters, which were written to Margherita Cantelmo, contain a mixture of commentary on her husband's desperate attempts to gain recognition from the French king and of Equicola's own subversive remarks on the same events. He also added long sections of philosophical discussion reminiscent of the letters Bembo wrote to Lucrezia Borgia or to Maria Savorgnan. He might use a minor incident (described in humorous fashion) to create a mini-*novella*. Equicola's correspondence therefore records the necessities which weighed down upon the courtier — the absolute need to communicate and at the same time to be occasionally interesting and entertaining.

Equicola did not follow the career of a *Quattrocento* humanist. He was not a classical philologist in the mould of Ermolao Barbaro or Angelo Poliziano. He was very much a part of the struggle for survival fought out by the Italian states in the first decades of the sixteenth century. His belief, however, in letters and in the place of the intellectual in the political system was firm: his work denotes an acceptance of humanistic learning in the service of the ruler. He himself states this as a positive fact in the *Chronica*:

> Quanto vogliano le littere quanto negli Signori con admirabile luce resplendano quanto utile et honore seco apporteno è cosa manifesta. L. Lucullo per la cognitione che de historie havea, da puro divenne subito prudente imperadore. Ma che? De antichi exempi le carte son piene. Chi è colui di così malegno ingegno et insolente natura che non reverisca Andrea Matheo Aquavivo, duca de Adri, figliol del Conte Iulio, homo bellicosissimo? Per molti respecti è signore degno di honore, ma precipuamente per la singulare letteratura, la quale in tante mutationi del regno di Napoli, sempre il fece securo.   *(Chronica*, f. 04r)

The implication is that such a ruler will appreciate learning and its practitioners. However, it was unlikely that an intellectual would be purely employed for his learning; he had to perform useful tasks. Equicola's two principal functions, that of tutor and secretary, are indicative of the work available to the intellectual. The role of tutor was more in line with humanist leanings and the tendency of humanism to be pedagogic. In Mantua and Ferrara there was a famous tradition of humanist schoolmen. Equicola does not quite fit into this category. He was always used (by Isabella d'Este) for other tasks, usually political in nature. The role of secretary was to be increasingly the place to find intellectuals in the employment of the ruler. Simonetta in Milan is a good model for this type of humanist-secretary.[61]

In many ways Equicola is not an attractive figure. His position in relation to power can be described in the charged adjectives fawning or sycophantic. His attitude towards the politicization of letters recalls numerous intellectuals whose sole aim was to secure a respectable place in the power structure. He did not have the ability of an Aretino to be able to manipulate the system to the same extent: to use it and reject it simultaneously. Yet he is in his own right

---

[61] See G. Ianziti, «A humanist historian and his documents: Giovanni Simonetta, secretary to the Sforzas», *Renaissance Quarterly*, 34 (1981), 491-516; *id.*, «Storiografia come propaganda: il caso dei 'commentarii' rinascimentali», *Società e Storia*, 22 (1983) 909-18; *id.*, «The *Commentaries* of Giovanni Simonetta: History and Propaganda in Sforza Milan (1450-1490)» in *Altro Polo. A Volume of Italian Renaissance Studies*, ed. C. Condren and R. Pesman Cooper, University of Sydney, 1982, pp. 79-95; *id.*, *Humanist Historiography under the Sforzas: Politics and Propaganda in Fifteenth-Century Milan*, Oxford U.P., 1988.

a central figure in early sixteenth-century Italian court culture. His interpretation of that society is different from that offered by Castiglione but surprisingly their paths meet and overlap in unexpected ways. In the end they are separated by their class and status: Castiglione belonged to the feudal nobility and Equicola was an outsider without the advantage of a name.

There can be no doubt that Equicola's biography permits the historian of literature to study how intellectual systems become enmeshed in the politics of power. To be judgemental and dismiss Equicola as a slavish writer and time-serving politician does not help to define the environment in which many intellectuals worked. His biography also serves to highlight the importance of the secretary and the need to study the so-called minor figures of Italian humanism. It is worthy of note that the last full-lengh biography of Equicola was written at the beginning of this century and that no new interpretations of his live have really been attempted. It is of crucial importance to map out the career-patterns of courtiers in this period, based on detailed research, so that empty generalizations can be avoided. Equicola provides a key example of an intellectual responding to the *real* conditions of the court. This first step of providing information needs to be followed by producing critical editions of these long-forgotten and neglected works. Only then will it be possible to establish theories and frameworks of court society in early sixteenth-century Italy. It is hoped that the present biography is a step in this direction.

APPENDIX

Notary documents concerning
Mario Equicola

1. **Emptio magnifici domini Marii secretarii illustrissimi domini nostri et cetera a Vincentio de Arabustis una cum investitura prefati domini Marii ab Hospitali magno Mantue**[1]

In Christi nomine amen. Anno Domini a nativitate eiusdem millesimo quingentesimo vigesimo primo, indictione nona, die lune undecimo mensis martii, tempore serenissimo principis et domini domini Caroli divina favente clementia Romanorum regis et imperatoris ellecti. Mantue in officio Rectoris Hospitalis magni, posito in contrata Cornu, presentibus domino Raphaello filio quondam domini Ioannis Antonii de Donesmontis, factore Hospitalis, de contrata Cornu, teste noto et idoneo, qui ad delacionem mei notarii sua manu tactis scripturis ad Sancta Dei Evangelia iuravit et dixit se bene cognoscere omnes et singulos infrascriptos eius contestes et contrahentes ac de ipsis omnibus et singulis plenam habere notitiam et veram cognitionem; domino Petro Jacobo, filio quondam domini Antonii Schale, de contrata Cornu et Antonio, filio quondam Jacobi de Maneschis, muratore de contrata predicta Cornu, testibus omnibus notis et idoneis ad hec omnia et singula vocatis specialiter et rogatis. Ibi Vincentius, filius quondam magistri Luce de Arabustis, habitator in burgo Portus, jure proprio et imperpetuum (sic), in presentia, voluntate et consensu spectabilis domini Petri Jacobi de Vulpis, honorandi Rectoris Hospitalis magni Mantue, dimini (sic = domini) directi infrascripte petie terre, dedit, vendidit et traddidit magnifico domino Mario, filio quondam domini Baptiste Cazaluppi de Albeto, illustrissimi domini domini Marchionis Mantue et illustrissime domine domine Marchionisse Mantue et cetera secretario, habitatori Mantue in contrata Aquile, presenti, ementi et

---

[1] ASMN, Archivio degli Instrumenti, Registrazioni Notarili: the year 1521, f. 620[r].

acquirenti ac stipulanti et acceptanti pro se suisque heredibus, utile dominium unius petie terre hortive posite in burgo Portus suburbii Mantue, penes viam comunis in parte et iure illustrissimi domini nostri et cetera in parte a primo, menia burghi a secundo et tertio et iure dicti Hospitalis mediante regiola seu iure illustrissimi domini nostri a quarto, salvis aliis confinibus verioribus, si qui forent, et salvis semper iuribus clavice seu aque ductus labentis per clavicam deservientem fullia chartarum, tam ipsius Vincentii quam Bernardini et Ioannis Francisci eius fratrum, quibus iuribus non intendit dictus Vincentius quoquomodo preiuditium aliquod facere per presentem venditionem, ad habendum, tenendum, possidendum et quicquid dicto domino Mario eiusque heredibus deinceps de dicta petia terre placuerit faciendum, salvis semper juribus dicti Hospitalis cui annuatim solvuntur libras tres et solidos quatuor pro affictu anno singulo et hoc pro precio et finito mercato scutorum decem auri a soldis 97 pro scuto, quos scutos decem auri 97 pretii predicti dictus dominus Marius emptor in presentia dictorum testium et mei notarii infrascripti dicto Vincentio venditori, presenti et recipienti, dedit, solvit et numeravit. Que melioramenta et utile ut supra vendita dictus venditor se nomine dicti domini emptoris tenere et possidere constituit donec dictus emptor illorum tenutam et corporalem possessionem acceperit, quam accipiendi auctoritate propria et deinceps in se perpetuo retinendi eidem domino emptori licentiam omnimodam contulit atque dedit et, si quam habet, sibi plenissime confirmavit et per se suosque heredes dictus venditor dicto domino emptori presenti et ut supra stipulanti dedit, cessit, transtulit, mandavit et remisit expresse omnia et singula sua jura et actiones generis cuiuscumque, quas et que habet, habebat aut quovis modo habere poterat in dicto utili et melioramentis ac petia terre, faciens dictum dominum emptorem procuratorem suum et ponens ipsum in locum suum ut in rem propriam, ita quod a modo actionibus et iuribus quibuscumque predicta dicere, facere et exercere possit ipse dominus emptor prout et quemadmodum poterat dictus Vincentius venditor ante stipulationem presentis contractus promisitque dictus venditor per se et ut supra dicto domino emptori, presenti et ut supra stipulanti, de dicto utili et melioramentis ut supra venditis nullam unquam litem, causam vel questionem inferre nec inferenti consentire, quin imo perpetuo et legittime deffendere, auctorizare et desbrigare in iuditio et extra omnibus ipsius venditoris sumptibus et expensis tam in proprietate quam in possessione. Et predicta omnia et singula suprascripta promisa dictus venditor dicto domino emptori presenti et ut supra stipulanti perpetuo firma, rata et grata habere, tenere, attendere et observare et in aliquo non contrafacere vel venire aliqua ratione vel causa sub pena dupli pretii suprascripti solemni stipulatione promissa, qua pena soluta vel non, semel aut pluries, nihilominus presens contractus et omnia et singula in eo contenta firma maneant atque perdurent cum reffectione et restitutione omnium et singulorum damnorum interesse et expensarum litis et extra, pro quibus omnibus et singulis suprascriptis sic ut supra firmiter atendendis et plenius observandis dictus venditor obligavit et obligat omnia et singula sua bona presentia et futura iuravitque ad delacionem mei notarii infrascripti, sua manu tactis scripturis, ad Sancta Dei Evangelia predicta omnia et singula suprascripta vera esse et fuisse eaque perpetuo attendere et observare et in aliquo non contrafacere vel venire aliqua ratione vel causa sub pena et obligacione predictis ac sub vinculo et virtute huius iuramenti.

Ego Alexander, filius quondam egregii viri domini Petri Antonii de Gheziis, civis Mantue, publicus imperiali auctoritate notarius, suprascriptis omnibus et singulis presens fui et rogatus scribere publice scripsi et subscripsi.

2. Investitura domini Marii[2]

In Christi nomine amen. Anno, millesimo, indictione, die, loco, tempore et contestu suprascriptis. Ibi spectabilis dominus Petrus Jacobus Vulpes, honorandus Rector Hospitalis magni Mantue sub titulo Sancte Marie de la Corneta, per se suosque sucessores, habitis prius et receptis solidis viginti ab infrascripto domino investito loco unius paris caponum pro honorantia presentis investiture, cum quadam carta quam in suis propriis tenebat manibus, actualiter atque legittime investivit ad annos novem proximos futuros magnificum dominum Marium, filium quondam domini Baptiste Cazaluppi de Albeto, illustrissimi domini domini Marchionis Mantue et illustrissime domine domine Marchionisse Mantue secretarium, habitatorem Mantue in contrata Aquile, presentem, stipulantem et recipientem pro se suisque heredibus, de una petia terre hortive posita in burgo Portus suburbii Mantue, penes viam comunis in parte et iure illustrissimi domini nostri prelibati in parte a primo, menia burghi a secundo et tertio et iura dicti Hospitalis mediante regiola seu iuribus illustrissimi domini nostri a quarto, salvis aliis confinibus verioribus, si qui forent; cuius petie terre utile et melioramentum dictus dominus Marius de licentia prefacti domini Rectoris emit a Vincentio de Arabusiis, ut constat alio instrumento rogato per me notarium paulo ante presentem contractum, ad habendum, tenendum, possidendum, meliorandum semper et non peiorandum et quicquid dicto domino investito eiusque heredibus deinceps placuerit faciendum, una cum omnibus et singulis que infra predictos continentur confines vel alios, si qui forent veriores, accessibus, ingressibus et egressibus suis, viis usantiis et pertinentiis usque in vias publicas salvo semper iure dicti Hospitalis et ad dandum et solvendum anno singulo dicto

---

[2] ASMN, Archivio degli Instrumenti, Registrazioni Notarili: the year 1521, f. 620[r].

Hospitali libras tres et soldos quinque parvorum Mantue pro affictu et nomine affictus; quem affictum dictus dominus investitus per se suosque heredes dicto domino Rectori presenti et ut supra stipulanti dare et solvere promisit anno singulo sub pena dupli dicti afficti stipulacione promissa et sub obbligacione omnium et singulorum suorum bonorum presentium et futurorum, et possessionem dicte petie terre quam dictus dominus investitus confessus fuit habere prefactus dominus Rector eidem confirmavit, cum pacto inter ipsas partes facto quod si in fine novenii dictus dominus Rector seu eius sucessores qui pro tempore fuerint, recusaverint et voluerint reinvestire dictum dominum Marium vel eius heredes ad alium novenium pro dicto afficto, tunc et eo casu teneatur et obligatus sit dictus dominus Rector eidem investito vel eius heredibus refficere et solvere omnia eorum melioramenta que apparerent fuisse facta in dictis petiis terrarum ad laudem et extimationem bonorum virorum comuniter elligendorum; et presentem investituram et omnia et singula suprascripta promisit dictus dominus Rector per se et ut supra dicto domino investito, presenti et ut supra stipulanti, perpetuo firma, rata et grata habere, tenere, attendere et observare et in aliquo non contrafacere vel venire aliqua ratione vel causa sub obligatione omnium et singulorum dicti Hospitalis bonorum presentium et futurorum.

Ego Alexander, filius quondam egregii viri domini Petri Antonii de Gheziis, civis Mantue, publicus imperiali auctoritate notarius, suprascriptis omnibus et singulis presens fui et rogatus scribere publice scripsi et subscripsi.

3. Permutacio magnifici domini Marii secretarii illustrissimi domini nostri et cetera ab Hospitali magno Mantue[3]

In Christi nomine amen. Anno Domini a nativitate eiusdem millesimo quingentesimo vigesimo secundo, indictione decima, die merchurii quarto mensis iunii, tempore serenissimi principis domini domini Caroli divina favente clementia Romanorum regis et imperatoris ellecti, Mantue, in offitio Rectorie Hospitalis magni postita (sic) in contrata Cornu, presentibus domino Raphaelle, filio quondam Joannis Antonii de Donesmondis, factore Hospitalis, de contrata Cornu, teste noto et idoneo, qui ad delacionem mei notarii sua manu tactis scripturis ad Sancta Dei Evangelia iuravit et dixit se bene cognoscere omnes et singulos infrascriptos eius contestes et contrahentes ac de ipsis omnibus et singulis plenam habere noticiam et veram cognitionem, Ludovico, filio quondam Joannis Francisci de Turino, de contrata Cigni, et Hieronimo,

---

[3] ASMN, Archivio degli Instrumenti, Registrazioni Notarili: the year 1522, f. 629^r-629^v.

filio Joannis Francisci de Maguttis de contrata Mastini, testibus omnibus notis et idoneis ad hec omnia et singulla vocatis specialiter et rogatis. Cum sit quod alias magnificus dominus Marius, filius quondam domini Baptiste Cazaluppi, secretarius illustrissimi et excellentissimi domini domini marchionis et marchionisse Mantue et cetera, fuerit investitus a spectabile domino Rectore Hospitalis magni Mantue sub titulo Sancte Marie de la Cornetta de infrascripta petia terre hortive, posita in burgo Portus, cum honere solvendi anno singulo dicto Hospitali libras tres et soldos quatuor parvorum Mantue pro affictu, ut latius constat instrumento rogato per me notarium sub die lune undecimo mensis martii anni millesimi quingentesimi[4] primi, cumque ad suplicationem prefati magnifici domini Marii fuerit per illustres, reverendos et magnificos dominos Presidentes eidem domino Mario concessum et terminatum dictum dominum Marium posse dictam infrascriptam petiam terre liberare et affranchare dando et assignando aliam proprietatem idoneam qua comode percipi possit affictus predictus cum augumento iuxta solitis, ut latius constat eorum terminacione rogata per me notario sub die decimo octavo mensis decembris anni preteriti, registrati in libro terminationum in carta septuagesima quarta, et ideo dictus dominus Marius pro liberatione dicte petie terre obtulerit tradere et assignare infrascripto domino Rectori infrascriptam proprietatem, emptam per eum a Joanne Francisco de Arabustiis , prout constat instrumento rogato per me notarium paulo ante presentem contractum, laudatam et extimatam per venerabiles dominos Bernardinum Capram et Joannem Galeatium de la Strata, extimatores Hospitalis ad hoc deputatos, ut constat eorum extimatione in scriptis coram infrascripto domino Rectore. Ibi igitur magnificus dominus Joannes Petrus de Coneglano, honorandus Rector Hospitalis predicti in executione premissorum per se suosque successores iure proprio et in perpetuum alodium libere, expedite et sine aliqua condictione affictus vel decime aut alicuius oneris servitutis, dedit, tradidit et permutavit dicto domino Mario, presenti et acquirenti pro se suisque heredibus, directum dominium unius petie terre hortive posite in burgo Portus suburbii Mantue penes viam comunis in parte et iura illustrissimi domini nostri in parte a primo, menia burgi a secundo et tertio et iura dicti Hospitalis mediante regiola seu iure illustrissimi domini nostri a quarto, salvis aliis confinibus verioribus si qui forent, ad solvendum, tenendum et possidendum et quicquid dicto domino Mario eiusque heredibus deinceps placuerit faciendum una cum omnibus et singulis que infra predictos continentur confines vel alios, si qui forent veriores, accessibus, ingressibus et egressibus suis, viis, usantiis et pertinentiis usque in vias publicas et cum omnibus et singulis que dicta petia terra habet super se, infra seu intra se in integrum omnique iure et actione, usu seu

---

[4]   The word «vigesimi» has been omitted.

requisitione ipsius rei permutate modo aliquo spectante et pertinente et hoc in permutatione et contracambium tante partis pro indiviso utillis domini et melioramentorum unius petie terre casamentive cum domibus supra cuppatis, muratis et soleratis et cum edificio pro conficiendis cartis, positis in burgo Portus penes Bernardinum de Arabustiis pro iuribus Hospitalis ab uno latere, Antonium et fratres de Vitalibus pro iuribus Hospitalis a secundo, viam comunis a tertio et lacum a quarto, salvis aliis confinibus verioribus si qui forent quantum capiunt ducati quatuordecim in ratione librarum quinque pro ducato pro valore suprascripte petie terre liberate alias sic extimate per dictos extimatores Hospitalis, que melioramenta dictus dominus Marius per se suosque heredes iure perpetuo et in perpetuum dicto domino Rectori presenti et acquirenti, nomine dicti Hospitalis et successorum, dedit, tradidit et assignavit ad habendum, tenendum et possidendum et quicquid dicto domino Rectori eiusque successoribus in dicto Hospitali perpetuo placuerit faciendum una cum omnibus et singulis que infra predictos continentur confines vel alios si qui forent veriores, accessibus, ingressibus et egressibus suis, viis, usantiis et pertinentiis usque in vias publicas et cum omnibus et singulis que dicta melioramenta habent supra se, infra seu intra se in integrum omnique iure et actione, usu seu requisitione, ipsis rebus ut supra permutatis modo aliquo spectante et pertinente et quam petiam terre et melioramenta ut supra permutata dicti dominus Rector et dominus Marius unus ad instantiam alterius et e converso se tenere et possidere constituit donec unusquisque eorum de re sua tenutam et corporalem possessionem acceperit quam accipiendi auctoritate propria et deinceps in se perpetuo retinendi sibi ipsis ad invicem confirmarunt.

Et per se suosque successores dictus dominus Rector dicto domino Mario presenti et ut supra stipulanti nec non dictus dominus Marius per se ut supra dicto domino Rectori presenti et ut supra stipulanti, singulla singullis congrue referendo, dederunt, cesserunt, transtulerunt et mandaverunt expresse omnia eorum et cuiuslibet eorum iura et actiones generis cuiuscumque quas et que unusquisque eorum habeat et habet in rebus suis a se ut supra permutatis, constituentes sese ad invicem procuratorem et ponentes eum in eorum alterius et e contra. Itaque a modo actionibus et iuribus quibuscumque in, de et pro dictis rebus ut supra permutatis dicere, facere et exercere possint dictus dominus Rector et dictus dominus Marius prout poterant et potuissent quilibet eorum de re sua ante presentem contractum promitentesque sese ullo unquam tempore de dictis rebus a se ut supra permutatis nullam litem, causam vel questionem inferre nec inferenti consentire, quin imo unusquisque eorum rem a se ut supra permutata[m] alteri sibi vel habiturus omnino ab eis, ab omni persona, comuni, collegio et universitate legitime deffendere, auctorizare et desbrigare in iuditio et extra tam in proprietate quam in possessione. Et presentem permutationem et omnia et singulla suprascripta promiserunt dicte

partes per sese et ut supra sibi ipsis ad invicem solemniter stipulantes, interve-
nientes singulla singulis congrue refferendo perpetuo firma, rata et grata
habere, tenere, attendere et observare et in aliquo modo non contrafacere vel
venire aliqua ratione vel causa sub pena dupli valoris suprascriptarum rerum
permutatarum solemni stipulatione promissa, qua pena soluta vel non, semel
aut pluries, nihilominus presens contractus et omnia et singulla in eo contenta
firma maneant atque perdurent cum reffectione omnium et singullorum damnorum interesse et expensarum litis et extra pro quibus omnibus et singullis
suprascriptis, sic ut supra firmiter attendendis et plenius observandis dictus
dominus Rector obligavit et obligat omnia et singulla dicti Hospitalis bona,
dictus dominus Marius bona sua presentia et futura iuraveruntque ad delationem mei notarii eorum manibus tactis Scripturis ad Sancta Dei Evangelia predicta omnia et singulla suprascripta vera esse et fuisse eaque perpetuo attendere et observare et in aliquo non contrafacere vel venire, aliqua ratione vel
causa, sub pena et obligatione predictis et sub vincullo et virtute huius iuramenti.

Ego Alexander, filius quondam egregii viri domini Petri Antonii de Gheziis, civis Mantue, publicus imperiali auctoritate notarius, suprascriptis omnibus et singulis presens fui et rogatus scribere publice scripsi et subscripsi.

4. Conductio domini Joannis Francisci Scopuli et Joannis Jacobi de Calzonis a domino Mario Equicola[5]

In Christi nomine amen. Anno Domini a nativitate eiusdem millesimo
quingentesimo vigesimo primo, inditione nona, die mercurii vigesimo sexto
mensis decembris. In domo mei notarii infrascripti sita in civitate Mantue in
contrata Mastini, tempore serenissimi principis et domini domini Caroli
divina eidem favente clementia Romanorum regis, presentibus Joanne Francisco, filio quondam Jacobi de Blanchis, habitator in Portu, teste noto et idoneo, qui prius sibi delato iuramento per me notarium infrascriptum et ab eo
manu propria corporaliter tactis scripturis ad Sancta Dei Evangelia iuravit se
bene cognoscere omnes et singulos infrascriptos secum testes et contrahentes
ac de ipsis omnibus et singulis plenam et claram habere noticiam et veram
cognitionem, Joanne, filio quondam ser Francisci de Maiantis de contrata
Leopardi et domino Jacobo, filio domini Thimothei de Bertoldis de contrata
Mastini, omnibus civibus Mantue, testibus notis et idoneis ad infrascripta
omnia et singula vocatis specialiterque rogatis. Ibique magnificus dominus
Marius Equicola, secretarius marchionalis, scriptor honorandus Registri

5 ASMN, Archivio degli Instrumenti, Registrazioni Notarili: the year 1522, f. 57v.

Mantue, per se et heredes et successores suos hinc ad annos tres proxime futuros, incipiendo prima die mensis ianuarii proxime futuri, dedit, concessit et locavit egregiis viris ser Joanni Francisco, filio domini Gasparis de Scopulis, de contrata Serpe et Joanni Jacobo, filio quondam domini Joannis Baptiste de Calzonis, de contrata Bovis, notariis, civibus mantuanis, presentibus et stipulantibus ac conducentibus pro sese et heredibus suis Officium Registri Mantue, ipsi domino Mario concessum per illustrissimum et excellentissimum dominum marchionem Mantue, cum omnibus prerogativis, emolumentis prout tenebant et conducebant Joannes Franciscus de Compagnonis et Franciscus Scarpus, conductores olim ipsius Registri, ad habendum, tenendum et possidendum, uti frui et gaudendum cum omnibus prerogativis, emolumentis et iurisdictionibus ad ipsum Officium spectantibus et pertinentibus et ad dandum et solvendum pro affictu et nomine affictus primi anni dictorum trium annorum ducatos centum octuaginta sex auri et in auro largos, quos ipsi conductores per sese et heredes suos in presentia dictorum testium et mei notarii infrascripti dederunt, solverunt et exbursaverunt prefato domino Mario presenti et ad se trahenti in tot auro; et pro aliis duobus annis sequentibus ad dandum et solvendum ducatos centum nonaginta auri in ratione librarum quinque pro quolibet ducato singulo anno dictorum duorum annorum, solvendo singulo mense ratam scilicet de mense in mense et in fine cuiuslibet mensis, quem afficctum dicti conductores per sese et ut supra promiserunt et solemniter promittunt prefato domino Mario, presenti et ut supra stipulanti, dare et solvere modo et forma ut supra sub pena dupli dicti afficctus solemni stipulatione promissa cum refectione et restitutione omnium et singulorum damnorum interesse et expensarum litis et extra et sub obligatione omnium et singulorum suorum bonorum presentium et futurorum. Quod Officium Registri prefatus dominus Marius per se et ut supra promisit et promittit prefatis conductoribus presentibus et stipulantibus pro sese et ut supra manutenere, defendere, auctorizare et desbrigare durante tempore dictorum trium annorum ab omni persona, comuni, collegio et universitate ipsum Officium inquietante aut inquietare et molestare volente in iudicio et extra omnibus ipsius domini Marii propriis sumptibus et expensis. Item dictus dominus Marius per se et ut supra fecit et facit dictis conductoribus presentibus et stipulantibus pro se et ut supra finem, remissionem, quietationem, absolutionem et pactum perpetuum et inrevocabilem de ulterius aliquid non petendo nec non faciendo dictis conductoribus nec heredibus suis de et pro toto afficctu anni preteriti 1520 et anni proxime futuri 1521 quoniam de ipso anno 1520 asseruit ac dixit et confessus fuit ab ipsis integraliter fuisse solutum et satisfactum. Cassans, revocans et anullans omne instrumentum omnemque scripturam tam publicam quam privatam in quo, qua seu quibus appareret aut in futurum quomodolibet apparere posset dictos conductores fore ipsi domino Mario obligatos de et pro afficctu ipsius Officii anni presenti 1520 et anni proxime futuri 1521; et renuntiavit dictus dominus Marius exceptioni non numerate pecunie et non sic facte presentis confessionis modo et forma quibus supra speique future receptionis et ipse partes renuntiaverunt exceptioni doli mali vi metus causa omnique alii eorum iuri legum atque statutorum auxilio quibus unquam possint et valeant contra presentem venire contractum aut in aliquo sese defendere vel tueri et predicta omnia et singula suprascripta et in presenti instrumento contenta, apposita et inserta predicte partes per sese ut supra ad invicem ut supra stipulantes promiserunt et solemniter promittunt singule singulis congrue referendo perpetue et omni tempore firma, rata et grata habere, tenere, attendere et observare et in aliquo non contrafacere nec contravenire per sese vel alios eorum nominibus aliqua ratione, causa, modo vel ingenio, de jure vel de facto, sub pena dupli dicti afficti solemni stipulatione promissa totiens petenda, comittenda et cum effectu exigenda quotiens in aliquo premissorum fuerit contrafactum, non attenditum vel non observatum et ea pena soluta vel non, nihilominus presens contractus suam undique obtineat roboris firmitatem cum refectione et restitutione omnium et singulorum damnorum interesse et expensarum litis et extra et sub obligatione omnium suorum bonorum presentium et futurorum. Iuraveruntque insuper dicti contrahentes, manibus eorum propriis tactis scripturis ad delationem mei notarii infrascripti ad Sancta Dei Evangelia, suprascripta omnia et singula vera esse et fuisse eaque perpetuo attendere et observare et in aliquo non contrafacere nec contravenire sub pena et obligatione predictis ac sub vinculo et virtute presentis prestiti iuramenti.

Ego Leonellus, filius quondam nobilis viri Filippi de Marchesiis, civis Mantue, publicus imperiali auctoritate notarius, suprascriptis omnibus et singulis presens fui et rogatus scribere scripsi.

5. Prorogatio locationis facte per spectabilem dominum Marium Equicolam Iohanni Francisco Scopulo et Iohanni Iacobo de Calzonis[6]

In Christi nomine amen. Anno domini a nativitate eiusdem millesimo quingentesimo vigesimo secundo, indictione decima, die Iovis duodecimo mensis Iunii. In domo infrascripti domini sindici posita in civitate Mantue in contrata Mastini, tempore serenissimi principis et domini domini Caroli Romanorum regis et semper augusti. Presentibus Bernardino filio domini Antonii de Bonadeis notario qui, ad delationem mei notarii infrascripti, manu eius propria corporaliter tactis scripturis, ad Sancta Dei Evangelia iuravit se bene cognoscere omnes et singulos infrascriptos eius contestes et infra-

---

[6] ASMN, Archivio degli Instrumenti, Registrazioni Notarili: the year 1522, f. 1014[r].

scriptos contrahentes ac de ipsis omnibus et singulis plenam et claram habere
noticiam et veram cognitionem, spectabile domino Leonello filio quondam
spectabilis domini Phelippi de Marchesiis sindico Marchionali de dicta contrata Mastini et Ser Iohanne filio quondam domini... de Gazio[7] de dicta contrata Mastini, omnibus civibus et habitatoribus Mantue ac testibus notis et
idoneis ad infrascripta omnia et singula vocatis specialiter et rogatis. Cum sit
quod reverendus dominus Marius Equicola, protonotarius appostolicus ac
illustrissimi domini nostri secretarius, dederit et concesserit ac locaverit
Iohanni Francisco de Scopulis et Iohanni Iacobo de Calzonis notariis conducentibus, ad annos tres tunc proximos futuros et interdum elapsos, officium
registri Mantue, cum omnibus suis iurisdictionibus, ad solvendum singulo
mense dictorum trium annorum et in fine cuiuslibet mensis ducatos quindecim cum dimidio auri in ratione librarum quinque pro singulo ducato et tempore celebrationis dicti instrumenti prefatus dominus Marius habuerit et rece-
perit a prefatis Iohanne Francisco Scopulo et Iohanne Iacobo Calzono totum
et integrum affictum unius anni dictorum trium annorum et prout latius de
predictis constat publico instrumento rogato et scripto per spectabilem dominum Leonellum de Marchesiis, notarium et causidicum marchionalem, sub
die mense et millesimo in eo contentis; et ex post prefatus dominus Marius
fuerit satisfactus a dicto Iohanne Francisco Scopulo et Iohanne Iacobo Calzono pro afficto ipsius offitii registri usque, ad et per totum presentem mensem Iunii anni instantis et velit et intendat prefatus dominus Marius dictis
Iohanni Francisco Scopulo et Iohanni Francisco (sic) Calzono prorogare
ipsam locationem ipsius officii registri. Igitur prefatus dominus Marius per
se et heredes ac successores suos, sua sponte, motu proprio et animo suo deliberato, ad instantiam, peticionem et requisitionem prefatorum Iohannes
Francisci Scopuli et Iohannes Iacobi Calzoni, presentium, stipulantium et rec-
cipientium pro sese et heredibus suis, dixit et confessus fuit se fuisse et esse
integraliter solutus et satisfactus a dictis Iohanne Francisco et Iohanne Iacobo
pro affictu ipsius officii registri pro toto tempore preterito quo ipsum officium tenuerunt et ad affictum conduxerunt a prefato domino Mario usque,
ad et per totum presentem mensem junii anni instantis et sic prefatus dominus
Marius per se et heredes et successores suos dictis Iohanni Francisco et
Iohanni Iacobo, presentibus, stipulantibus et reccipientibus pro se et heredibus suis fecit et facit finem, remissionem et quietationem ac pactum perpetuum et inrevocabile de ulterius aliquid non petendo, cassans, revocans et
anullans omne instrumentum omnemque scripturam tam publicam quam privatam in quo, qua sive quibus dicti Iohannes Franciscus et Iohannes Iacobus
apparent aut quovismodo apparere possent debitores prefati domini Marii nec

---

[7]   The name is missing in the text.

non prefatus dominus Marius per se et heredes et successores suos, in executione decreti seu licentie prefato domino Mario concessi seu concesse per illustrem dominum nostrum dominem Marchionem Mantue possendi locare ipsum officium registri, in fine presentis instrumenti registrati prorogavit ipsam locationem seu de novo dedit, concessit et locavit ad annos quatuor proximos futuros, finitis dictis tribus annis qui erunt finiti, finito anno 1523, per totum mensem decembris dicti anni predictis Iohanni Francisco Scopulo et Iohanni Iacobo Calzono presentibus, stipulantibus et reccipientibus pro sese et eorum heredibus officium predictum registri Mantue cum omnibus suis iuribus, iurisdictionibus, exactionibus, prerogativis, honorantiis et emolumentis ad ipsum officium spectantibus et pertinentibus et modo et forma prout hactenus ipsi conductores ipsum officium registri tenuerunt et possiderunt ac gavisi sunt, ad habendum, tenendum et possidendum et ad dandum et solvendum anno singulo dictorum quatuor annorum, finitis prius dictis tribus annis, qui erant finiti ut supra, ducatos centum octuagenta sex auri in ratione ducatorum quindecim cum dimidio auri in ratione predicta pro quolibet mense et in fine cuiuslibet mensis et solvendo de mense in mensem in fine cuiusliet mensis ut supra. Quem quidem affictum dicti conductores per sese et eorum heredes promiserunt et solemniter promitunt dicto domino Mario, presenti, stipulanti et reccipienti pro se et heredibus suis, dare, solvere et cum effectu exbursare modo et forma quibus supra, sine aliqua exceptione iuris vel facti et sub obligatione omnium et singulorum suorum bonorum presentium et futurorum; et in presentia testium premissorum et mei notarii infrascripti prefati conductores dederunt, solverunt et cum effectu exbursaverunt prefato domino Mario presenti et ad se trahenti ducatos ducentum auri cum dimidio auri et in auro largo pro integra solutione et satisfatione affictus dicti registri de et per totum mensem Iulii anni proximi futuri 1523. Pro quibus ducatis ducentum uno cum dimidio auri et in auro ut supra prefatus dominus Marius, per se et heredes et successores suos ut supra, suprascriptis Iohanni Francisco et Iohanni Iacobo, presentibus, stipulantibus et reccipientibus ut supra, fecit et facit finem, remissionem et quietationem ac pactum perpetuum et irrevocabile de ulterius aliquid non petendo dictis Iohanni Francisco et Iohanni Iacobo de et pro dictis ducatis ducentum uno cum dimidio auri solutis ut supra, cassans, revocans et anullans omne instrumentum omnemque scripturam tam publicam quam privatam in quibus apparerent aut quovismodo apparere possent prefati conductores debitores prefati domini Marii ut supra et prefatus dominus Marius, per se et heredes ac successores suos, promisit et solemniter promitit dictis conductoribus, presentibus, stipulantibus et recipientibus pro sese et eorum heredibus, durante tempore presentis prorogationis sive locationis ipsum officium registri manutenere, defendere, auctorizare et desbrigare durante tempore dictorum quatuor annorum ab omni persona, comuni, collegio et universitate ipsum officium inquietante aut inquietare et molestare volente in iudicio et extra, omnibus ipsius domini Marii propriis sumptibus et expensis, et renunciaverunt prefatus dominus Marius exceptioni non numerate pecunie et non sic facte presentis confessionis modo et forma quibus supra speique future receptionis et ipsi omnes contrahentes exceptioni doli mali, vi metus causa actioni infactum omnique alii suo iuri legum atque statutorum auxilio quibus unquam possent contra presentem venire contractum aut in aliquo sese defendere vel tueri, et predicta omnia et singula suprascripta et in presenti instrumento contenta, apposita et inserta predicte partes per sese ut supra ad invicem ut supra stipulationem promiserunt et solemniter promitunt singula singulis congrue refferendo perpetuo et omni tempore firma, rata et grata habere, tenere, attendere, observare et in aliquo non contrafacere nec contravenire per sese vel alium seu alios eorum nominibus aliqua ratione, causa, modo vel ingenio, de iure vel de facto, sub pena duppli dicti affictus, solemni stipulatione promissa totiens petenda, comitenda et cum effectu exigenda quotiens in predictis fuerit aliqualiter contrafactum, non attenditum vel non observatum et ea pena soluta vel non, nihilominus presens contractus suam undique obtineat plenam roburis firmitatem, cum reffectione et restitutione omnium et singulorum damnorum interesse et expensarum litis et extra et sub obligatione omnium suorum bonorum presentium et futurorum; iuraveruntque insuper dicti contrahentes, manibus corporaliter tactis scripturis, ad delationem mei notarii infrascripti ad Sancta Dei Evangelia, suprascripta omnia et singula vera esse et fuisse eaque perpetuo attendere et observare et in aliquo non contrafacere nec contravenire sub pena et obligatione predictis ac sub vinculo et virtute presentis ipsius prestiti iuramenti. Tenor decreti ut supra, videlicet: Federicus II Gonzaga: ab obsessis data de consensu nostro ob cives (?) victis hostibus. Federicus Marchio Mantue, Sancte Romane Ecclesie Capitaneus Generalis. Cum domini Marii Equicole secretarii nostri carissimi visi sepius simus opera, presertim nunc in durissima obsidione Papie quam et protulimus et superavimus, visum est nobis...

Ego Hieronymus, filius quondam nobilis viri domini Galeati de Marchesiis, civis Mantue, publicus imperiali auctoritate notarius, suprascriptis omnibus et singulis presens fui et rogatus scribere scripsi et subscripsi.

6. **Emptio magnifici domini Marii Equicole, secretarii illustrissimi domini nostri, a Joane (sic) del Bel[8]**

In Christi nomine amen. Anno Domini a nativitate eiusdem millesimo quingentesimo vigesimo quarto, indictione duodecima, die veneris octavo

---

⁸   ASMN, Archivio degli Instrumenti, Registrazioni Notarili: the year 1524, f. 486ᵛ.

mensis iulii, in districtu mantuano, terre Marmiroli, super infrascripto loco, tempore serenissimi principis et domini domini Caroli divina sibi favente clementia Romanorum regis et semper augusti, presentibus spectabile arcium doctore domino Hieronimo, filio quondam spectabilis domini Francisci de Gabloneta, phisico, cive et habitatore Mantue in contrata Serpe, teste noto et idoneo, qui ad delacionem mei notarii infrascripti ad Sancta Dei Evangelia iuravit se bene cognossere omnes et singulos infrascriptos testes et contrahentes ac de ipsis omnibus et singulis plenam habere notitiam et veram cognicionem, spectabile arcium doctore domino Antonio, filio quondam...[9] de Donatis, phisicho, cive et habitatore Mantue in contrata Serpe et spectabile arcium doctore domino Joanne Antonio de Facinis de contrata...[10], omnibus civibus et fisicis illustrissimi et excellentissimi domini nostri ac Mantue, his omnibus et singulis testibus notis et idoneis ad infrascripta omnia et singula vocatis specialiter rogatis. Ibique Joannes, filius quondam Marmiroli del Bel, habitator in terra Marmiroli, per se et heredes suos, iure proprio, imperpetuum alodium, libere et expedite, hoc est sine aliqua condicione afficctus vel decime aut alicuius alterius oneris servitutis, dedit, vendidit et tradidit magnifico et generoso domino Mario, filio quondam...[11] de Equicolis, civi et habitatori Mantue ac secretario dignissimo illustrissimi ac excellentissimi domini Federici de Gonzaga marchionalis (sic) Mantue, ipsi (sic = ibi) presenti, acceptanti, ementi et acquirenti pro se et heredibus suis, unam peciam terre prative et salesive, quantacumque sit, sitam in teritorio predicto Marmiroli in contrata de conchis penes Cristoforum de Bommioribus (?) a primo, Petrum Antonium de Pisis a secundo, Hieronimum de Coradinis a tercio, viam novam palacii prefati illustrissimi domini nostri a quarto, salvis aliis confinibus verioribus si qui forent, ad habendum, tenendum et possidendum et quicquid sibi emptori suisque heredibus deinceps perpetuo placuerit faciendum, una cum omnibus et singulis que inter prefatos confines continentur vel alios, si qui forent veriores, accessibus, ingressibus et egressibus suis, viis, usantiis et pertinentiis usque in vias publicas et cum omnibus et singulis que ipsa petia terre ut supra vendita habet supra se, infra se seu intra se in integrum omnique iure, actione et usu, onere seu requisitione sibi venditori pro dicta pecia terre supra vendita modo aliquo spectante et pertinente, et hoc pro pretio et finito merchato inter ipsas partes concluso in totum librarum quinque parvorum Mantue. Quod precium dictus venditor voluntarie, sponte et expresse ac non vi, nec metu neque aliquo alio iure facti errore ductus, prout asseruit et confessus fuit, sed animo quieto et tranquillo et deliberato, ad instantiam, peticionem et requisi-

---

9   The name is missing in the text.
10 Illegible.
11 The name is missing in the text.

tionem prefati domini emptoris, ibi presentis et stipulantis pro se et heredibus suis, se habuisse et recepisse ante stipulationem presentis contractus, renuntians exceptioni doli mali, vi metus ac exceptioni receptionis dictarum librarum quinque ac omni alii suo iure legum atque statutorum auxilio. Quam petiam terre, ut supra venditam, dictus venditor et nomine dicti domini emptoris tenere et possidere constituit donec et usque quo dictus emptor evidentem tenutam et corporalem possessionem acceperit quam accipiendi sua auctoritate et deinceps in se perpetuum retinendi eidem domino emptori...[12] omnimodam contulit atque dedit et si quam habet vel habebat in ipsa sibi plenissime confirmavit, dans, cedens et concedens dictus venditor per se ut supra dicto domino emptori pro se ut supra in ipsoque mandans, trasferens ac libere remitens omnia et singula iura utriusque generis, que ipse venditor habet, habebat aut quovismodo habere poterat in ipsa re vendita, faciens et constituens ipsum dominum emptorem, ibi presentem et acceptantem, procuratorem suum in hoc revocabiliter et ponens eum in locum suum itaque a modo actionibus, iuribus, utilibus et directis ac aliis quibuscumque ipse dominus emptor de ipsa re vendita agere, dicere, facere et disponere possit et valeat prout et quemadmodum poterat et potuisset ipse venditor ante stipulationem presentis contractus promisitque dominus venditor per se ut supra eidem domino emptori, pro se ut supra stipulanti et recipienti, nullam unquam litem vel controversiam in dicta re vendita ullo tempore inferre nec inferrenti consentire, quin imo illam tam in proprietatem quam in possessionem ab omni omine (sic = homine), comuni, colegio et universitate legitime deffendere, autorizare et desbrigare et predictam rem venditam ac omnia et singula in presenti instrumento inserta et apposita perpetuo firmam, ratam et gratam ac firma, rata et grata habere, tenere, atendere et observare per se ut supra, non contrafacere vel contravenire per se vel alium seu alios aliqua ratione, cum modo vel ingenio, de iure vel de facto, sub pena dupli extimationis dicte rei vendite. Quam pena soluta vel non, nihilominus omnia et singula suprascripta firma, rata et grata maneant atque perpetuo perdurent cum refectione et restitutione omnium et singulorum damnorum interesse et expensarum litis et extra et sub obligatione omnium et singulorum bonorum presentium et futurorum iuravitque dictus venditor per se ut supra ad delacionem mei notarii infrascripti, manu eius propria tactis corporaliter scripturis, ad Sancta Dei Evangelia, prefata omnia et singula fore et esse vera eaque perpetuo et omni tempore atendere et observare et non contrafacere nec contravenire sub obligatione et virtute iuramenti sibi prestiti ut supra.

Ego Dominicus, filius quondam egregii viri domini Martini de Botallis, civis Mantue, publicus imperiali auctoritate notarius, suprascriptis omnibus et singulis presens fui et rogatus scribere publice scripsi.

---

[12]   The word «licentiam» is missing in the text.

7. **Decretum domini Marii Equicole**[12]

De consensu nostro

Federicus Marchio Mantue et cetera, Sancte Romane Ecclesie ac excellentissime Rei Publice Florentine Capitaneus Generalis. Concessimus anno superiori domino Mario Equicole, secretario nostro carissimo, ac ei donavimus libere per septem annos officium Registri Mantue cum auctoritate locandi, disponendi et illud tradendi, ea auctoritate qua nosmet ipsi possemus, cuicunque ei libuisset viro tamen sufficienti probato et bene experto iussimusque spectabili sindico nostro ut singulis annis ei responderet ex denariis condemnationum sive compositionum ducatos triginta exolvendos lectori institute, ut patet decreto nostro sub die XXI aprillis, et sex pro funalibus cereis portandis a doctoribus in oblationem in diem Ascensionis Domini; voluimusque ut quadraginta ducatos, quos tenetur solvere pro marchis, eos sibi retineret ad computum provisionis sue pro officio secretariatus, que est librarum decem et novem singulis mensibus; constituimus quoque prefatum dominum Marium castellanum nostrum Caneduli in septenium cum auctoritate substituendi quem virum idoneum sibi libuisset, ut constat decreto nostro sub die quinto maii MDXXII. Hec omnia ita rata habemus ut non modo velimus prefatum dominum Marium eis gaudere posse per dictum septenium sed etiam quamdiu vixerit. Itaque tenore presentis decreti, vigore nostri arbitrii et de plenitudine potestatis qua publice fungimur hac in civitate nostra Mantue totoque eius Marchionatu et districtu ex certaque nostri scientia, motu proprio et animo bene deliberato confirmamus dictum officium Registri et castellaniam Caneduli prefato domino Mario quoad vixerit cum eadem auctoritate locandi, disponendi, tradendi et substituendi quibus voluerit viris tamen sufficientibus expertis et probatis, mandantes spectabili sindico nostro, qui nunc est et qui in futurum erit, ut ex denariis condemnationum sive compositionum respondeat prefato domino Mario singulis annis triginta ducatos dandos lectori institute et sex pro funalibus cereis in die Ascensionis Domini portandis a doctoribus in oblationem, ut moris est. Mandantesque magnifico Thesaurario nostro presenti et futuris ut singulis annis acceptent ad computum provisionis prefati domini Marii ducatos quadraginta quos solvere teneretur pro marchis dicti officii Registri quamdiu vixerit et steterit ad salarium et provisionem nostram, aliquo in contrarium faciente non obstante. Preterea iudicium nostrum de prefato domino Mario non sine beneficio esse decernentes, donavimus alias et per presentes donamus et confirmamus donationem inter vivos sibi et suis posteris, successoribus et heredibus, spatium quod nostrum

---

[12]   ASMN, Archivio degli Instrumenti, Registrazioni Notarili: the year 1524, f. 909^r.

erat e conspectu sue domus Letam quod spectat ad lacum inferius in suburbio Portus, ei dono donum adiungimus ut possit ibidem edificare et machinis necessariis struere ea quibus papyrus confici possit et malleos parare quibus es rude, quod ramum dicitur, ex massa crassiori in formam redigatur ampliorem; concedimus insuper auctoritatem faciendi rotulas quibus ad polienda arma ferramentaque illustranda est opus cum onere tamen solvendi nobis mense quolibet rismam epistolaris carte et libras quatuor cere laborate cum primum opus erit paratum, in quorum robur et fidem presens nostrum decretum fieri et registrari iussimus nostrique maioris soliti sigilli impressione muniri. Datum Mantue XIII septembris MDXXIII. Olympus Zampus Cancellarius, ad mandatum domini, relatione magnifici domini Thesaurarii generalis pro spacio et edificio in reliquis relatione domini Caroli Bononie, subscripsit. Hieronimus Archarius, Donatus de Pretis, Hieronimus Frambertus, Comes Otho, Hieronimus Lucensis, Calandra.

Abbreviations

AG	Archivio Gonzaga
ASE	Archivio Segreto Estense
ASI	*Archivio Storico Italiano*
ASL	*Archivio Storico Lombardo*
ASMN	Archivio di Stato, Mantua
ASMO	Archivio di Stato, Modena
ASPN	*Archivio Storico per le Province Napoletane*
b.	busta
BAV	Biblioteca Apostolica Vaticana
C	Cancelleria
DBI	*Dizionario Biografico degli Italiani*
f.	folio
GSLI	*Giornale Storico della Letteratura Italiana*
GW	*Gesamtkatalog der Wiegendrucke*, Band VIII, Stuttgart, Berlin and New York, 1978
IGI	*Indice generale degli incunaboli delle biblioteche d'Italia*, II, Rome, 1948
IMU	*Italia Medioevale e Umanistica*
Libro	Mario Equicola, *Libro de natura de amore*, Venice, 1525. 4°
Libro, MS	*Libro de natura de amore*, Cod. III. 10, Biblioteca Nazionale Universitaria, Turin
Luzio-Renier, *La coltura*	A. Luzio-R. Renier, *La coltura e le relazioni letterarie d'Isabella d'Este*, Turin, 1903
Mantova e i Gonzaga	*Mantova e i Gonzaga nella civiltà del Rinascimento*, Atti del convegno organizzato dall'Accademia dei Lincei e dall'Accademia Virgiliana con la collaborazione della città di Mantova sotto l'alto patronato del presidente della Repubblica

	Italiana Giovanni Leone, Mantova 6-8 ottobre 1974, Milan, 1978
MS/MSS	Manuscript/s
Santoro	Santoro, D., *Della vita e delle opere di Mario Equicola*, Chieti, 1906
VSED	*Verzeichnis der im Deutschen Sprachbereich Erschienenen Drucke des XVI. Jahrhunderts*, Band 6, Stuttgart, 1986

A Note on the Transcription
of Italian and Latin Documents

In general, all abbreviations have been expanded, accents have been added and punctuation modernized. The orthography of the original documents has been scrupulously followed. In the Latin texts the u and the v have been distinguished.

Bibliography

A. THE LETTERS OF MARIO EQUICOLA

1. Archivio di Stato, Mantua[1]

(i) ASMN, AG, Serie D. IV, b. 283 (Cantelmi and Maloselli)

Date	Place	Addressee
Letters of 1501		
11 March 1501	Ferrara	Margherita Cantelmo
no date	no place, probably Ferrara	Margherita Cantelmo
13 March 1501	Ferrara	Margherita Cantelmo
14 March 1501	[Ferrara]	Margherita Cantelmo
15 March 1501	[Ferrara]	Margherita Cantelmo
15 March 1501	[Ferrara]	Margherita Cantelmo
17 March 1501	Ferrara	Margherita Cantelmo
18 March 1501	Ferrara	Margherita Cantelmo
19 March 1501	Ferrara	Margherita Cantelmo
19 March 1501	Ferrara	Margherita Cantelmo
20 March 1501	Ferrara	Margherita Cantelmo
20 March 1501	Ferrara	Margherita Cantelmo
20 March 1501	Ferrara	Margherita Cantelmo
21 March 1501	Ferrara	Margherita Cantelmo
23 March 1501	Ferrara	Margherita Cantelmo
25 March 1501	Ferrara	Margherita Cantelmo
5 April 1501	Ferrara	Ercole Cantelmo
6 April 1501	Ferrara	Ercole Cantelmo
6 April 1501	Ferrara	Sigismondo Cantelmo
6 April 1501	Ferrara	Margherita Cantelmo
6 April 1501	Ferrara	Margherita Cantelmo
no date	[Ferrara]	?
27 May 1501	Lyons	Margherita Cantelmo
13 June 1501	Lyons	Margherita Cantelmo
19 June 1501	Lyons	Margherita Cantelmo
24 September 1501	Lunello	Margherita Cantelmo

---

[1] See A. Luzio and P. Torelli, *L'Archivio Gonzaga di Mantova*, 2 vols, Ostiglia and Verona, 1920-22, for the arrangement of the archive. I have not included in the inventory «minute di cancelleria» because they are not personal letters of Equicola; such draft copies of official letters can be found in ASMN, AG, b. 2193 and were written most probably between 1520-21 and 1523, corresponding to Equicola's increased presence in the chancery as secretary. Square brackets indicate that the information contained in them is probably correct but is not written on the letters itself.

Date	Place	Addressee
27 September 1501	Milan	Margherita Cantelmo
1 October 1501	Pavia	Margherita Cantelmo
1 October 1501	Pavia	Margherita Cantelmo
17 October 1501	Lyons	Margherita Cantelmo
18 October 1501	Lyons	Margherita Cantelmo
18 October 1501	Lyons	Margherita Cantelmo
18 October 1501	Lyons	Gian Cristoforo Romano
19 October 1501	Lyons	Margherita Cantelmo
22 October 1501	Lyons	Margherita Cantelmo
6 November 1501	Blois	Margherita Cantelmo
6 November 1501	Blois	«Endelechia» (i.e. Margherita Cantelmo)
8 November 1501	Blois	Margherita Cantelmo
9 November 1501	Blois	Margherita Cantelmo
10 November 1501	Blois	Margherita Cantelmo
11 November 1501	Blois	Margherita Cantelmo
12 November 1501	Blois	Margherita Cantelmo
16 November 1501	Blois	Margherita Cantelmo
21 November 1501	Blois	Margherita Cantelmo
23 November 1501	Blois	Margherita Cantelmo
25 November 1501	Blois	Margherita Cantelmo
27 November 1501	Blois	Margherita Cantelmo
3 December 1501	Blois	Margherita Cantelmo
3 December 1501	Blois	Margherita Cantelmo
3 December 1501	Blois	Margherita Cantelmo
3 December 1501	Blois	Margherita Cantelmo
10 December 1501	Blois	Margherita Cantelmo
11 December 1501	Blois	Margherita Cantelmo
14 December 1501	Blois	«Endelechia»
14 December 1501	Blois	«Endelechia»
23 December 1501	Blois	«Endelechia»
23 December 1501	Blois	«Enzelechia»

Letters of 1502

Date	Place	Addressee
7 January 1502	Blois	Margherita Cantelmo
10 January 1502	Blois	Margherita Cantelmo
22(?) February 1502	Ferrara	Margherita Cantelmo
4 May 1502	Mantua	Margherita Cantelmo
4 May 1502	Mantua	Margherita Cantelmo
4 May 1502	Mantua	Margherita Cantelmo
5 May 1502	Mantua	Margherita Cantelmo
5 May 1502	Mantua	Margherita Cantelmo
6 May 1502	S. Matteo	Margherita Cantelmo
10 May 1502	Tortona	Margherita Cantelmo
13 May 1502	Carmagnola	Margherita Cantelmo
14 May 1502	Carmagnola	Margherita Cantelmo
14 May 1502	Carmagnola	Margherita Cantelmo
15 May 1502	Carmagnola	Margherita Cantelmo
15 May 1502	Carmagnola	Margherita Cantelmo
22 May 1502	Chambery [«in Ciammari»]	Margherita Cantelmo
22 May 1502	Chambery [«in Ciammari»]	Margherita Cantelmo

Date	Place	Addressee
29 May 1502	Lyons	Margherita Cantelmo
31 May 1502	Lyons	Margherita Cantelmo
1 June 1502	Lyons	Margherita Cantelmo
1 June 1502	Lyons	Margherita Cantelmo
1 June 1502	Lyons	Margherita Cantelmo
2 June 1502	Lyons	Margherita Cantelmo
5 June 1502	Tarara	Margherita Cantelmo
14 June 1502	Lyons	Margherita Cantelmo
15 June 1502	Lyons	Margherita Cantelmo
20 June 1502	Lyons	Margherita Cantelmo

b. 283 bis

Date	Place	Addressee
no date	no place	Margherita Cantelmo
13 June 1502	Lyons	Margherita Cantelmo
no date	Lyons	Margherita Cantelmo
no date	no place	Margherita Cantelmo
27 May 1502	Lyons	Margherita Cantelmo
no date	no place	Margherita Cantelmo
no date	no place	Margherita Cantelmo
no date	no place	Margherita Cantelmo
no date	no place	Margherita Cantelmo
April no year	Ferrara	Sigismondo & Margherita Cantelmi
9 (?) May no year	(?)	Margherita Cantelmo
25 November no year	Blois	Margherita Cantelmo
1 June 1502	Lyons	(?)
no date	no place	the dog Perlina

(ii) ASMN, AG, Serie E. XIX. 3 (Savoy)

b. 731

Date	Place	Addressee
16 May 1502	Carmagnola	«Morelletto in Ferrara»

(iii) ASMN, AG, Serie E. XV. 3 (France)

b. 630

Date	Place	Addressee
5 August 1505	Amboise	«Madama Antonia de Gonzaga» (i.e. Antonia del Balzo)

b. 634

Date	Place	Addressee
25 May 1517	Avignon	Federico Gonzaga
2 June 1517	Vienne	Federico Gonzaga

Date	Place	Addressee

(iv) ASMN, AG, Serie E. XXXI. 3 (Ferrara)

b. 1239

Date	Place	Addressee
17 May 1503	Ferrara	Isabella d'Este
8 June 1503	Ferrara	Marquis Francesco Gonzaga
8 June 1503	Ferrara	Marquis Francesco Gonzaga
12 June 1503	Ferrara	Marquis Francesco Gonzaga
12 June 1503	Ferrara	Marquis Francesco Gonzaga
12 June 1503	Ferrara	Marquis Francesco Gonzaga
12 June 1503	Ferrara	Marquis Francesco Gonzaga
13 June 1503	Ferrara	Marquis Francesco Gonzaga
18 June 1503	Ferrara	Marquis Francesco Gonzaga
22 June 1503	Ferrara	Marquis Francesco Gonzaga
24 June 1503	Ferrara	Marquis Francesco Gonzaga
25 June 1503	Ferrara	Marquis Francesco Gonzaga
26 June 1503	Ferrara	Marquis Francesco Gonzaga
29 June 1503	Ferrara	Marquis Francesco Gonzaga
29 June 1503	Ferrara	Marquis Francesco Gonzaga
1 July 1503	Ferrara	Marquis Francesco Gonzaga
3 July 1503	Ferrara	Marquis Francesco Gonzaga
4 July 1503	Ferrara	Marquis Francesco Gonzaga
13 July 1503	Ferrara	Marquis Francesco Gonzaga
23 July 1503	Ferrara	Marquis Francesco Gonzaga

b. 1240

Date	Place	Addressee
20 April 1505	Ferrara	Marquis Francesco Gonzaga

b. 1241

Date	Place	Addressee
16 May 1506	Ferrara	Isabella d'Este
17 August 1507	Ferrara	Isabella d'Este
18 September 1507	Ferrara	Isabella d'Este

b. 1242

Date	Place	Addressee
11 August 1508	Ferrara	Isabella d'Este
11 August 1508	Ferrara	Isabella d'Este
24 August 1508	Ferrara	Isabella d'Este
1 February 1510	Ferrara	Isabella d'Este
18 June 1510	Ferrara	Isabella d'Este
18 June 1510	Ferrara	Isabella d'Este
19 June 1510	Ferrara	Isabella d'Este
20 June 1510	Ferrara	Isabella d'Este
24? June 1510	Ferrara	Isabella d'Este

b. 1243

Date	Place	Addressee
9 October 1511	Ferrara	Isabella d'Este

Date	Place	Addressee

b. 1244

19 January 1512	Ferrara	Isabella d'Este
12 April 1512	Ferrara	Isabella d'Este
22 April 1512	Ferrara	Isabella d'Este
23 April 1512	Ferrara	Isabella d'Este
25 April 1512	Ferrara	[Isabella d'Este]
25 April 1512	Ferrara	Isabella d'Este
26 April 1512	Ferrara	Isabella d'Este
27 April 1512	Ferrara	Isabella d'Este

b. 1245

15 May 1514	Ferrara	Isabella d'Este
17 May 1514	Ferrara	Isabella d'Este
17 May 1514	Ferrara	Isabella d'Este
18 May 1514	Ferrara	Isabella d'Este
21 April 1515	Ferrara	Isabella d'Este
26 April 1515	Ferrara	Isabella d'Este
30 April 1515	Ferrara	Isabella d'Este
2 May 1515	Ferrara	Isabella d'Este
2 May 1515	Ferrara	Isabella d'Este

b. 1246

2 February 1516	Ferrara	Isabella d'Este
6 March 1516	Ferrara	Isabella d'Este
13 May 1516	Magnavacca	Isabella d'Este
15 May 1516	Magnavacca	Isabella d'Este
3 August 1516	Ferrara	Isabella d'Este
29 August 1516	Ferrara	Isabella d'Este
30 August 1516	Ferrara	Isabella d'Este
30 August 1516	Ferrara	Isabella d'Este
30 August 1516	Ferrara	Isabella d'Este
31 August 1516	Ferrara	Isabella d'Este
1 September 1516	Ferrara	Isabella d'Este
1 September 1516	Ferrara	Isabella d'Este
2 September 1516	Ferrara	Isabella d'Este
2 September 1516	Ferrara	Isabella d'Este
2 September 1516	Ferrara	Isabella d'Este
3 September 1516	Ferrara	Isabella d'Este
3 September 1516	Ferrara	Isabella d'Este
4 September 1516	Ferrara	Isabella d'Este
5 September 1516	Ferrara	Isabella d'Este
5 September 1516	Ferrara	Isabella d'Este
6 September 1516	Ferrara	Isabella d'Este
6 September 1516	Ferrara	Isabella d'Este
7 September 1516	Ferrara	Isabella d'Este
8 September 1516	Ferrara	Isabella d'Este
9 September 1516	Ferrara	Isabella d'Este
10 September 1516	Ferrara	Isabella d'Este
11 September 1516	Ferrara	Isabella d'Este

Date	Place	Addressee
12 September 1516	Ferrara	Isabella d'Este
12 September 1516	Ferrara	Isabella d'Este
12 September 1516	Ferrara	Isabella d'Este
13 September 1516	Ferrara	Isabella d'Este
13 September 1516	Ferrara	[Isabella d'Este]
15 September 1516	Ferrara	Isabella d'Este
16 September 1516	Ferrara	Isabella d'Este
16 September 1516	Ferrara	Isabella d'Este
17 September 1516	Ferrara	Isabella d'Este
17 September 1516	Ferrara	Isabella d'Este
17 September 1516	Ferrara	Isabella d'Este
18 September 1516	Ferrara	Isabella d'Este
19 + enc. 1516	Ferrara	Isabella d'Este
20 September 1516	Ferrara	Isabella d'Este
21 September 1516	Ferrara	Isabella d'Este
15 June 1518	Ferrara	Isabella d'Este
17 June 1518	Ferrara	Isabella d'Este

b. 1247

Date	Place	Addressee
26 April no year 13 May 1520 with another letter of	Ferrara	Marquis Federico Gonzaga
12 May 1520	Ferrara	Marquis Federico Gonzaga
15 May 1520	Ferrara	Marquis Federico Gonzaga
26 May 1520	Bellosguardo	Marquis Federico Gonzaga
26 May 1520	Bellosguardo	Marquis Federico Gonzaga
30 May 1522	Ferrara	Marquis Federico Gonzaga

b. 1248

Date	Place	Addressee
28 July 1523	Ferrara	Marquis Federico Gonzaga
28 July 1523	Ferrara	Marquis Federico Gonzaga

(v) ASMN, AG, Serie E. LIV. 3 (Bozzolo)

b. 1813

Date	Place	Addressee
16 November 1507	Gazzuolo	Isabella d'Este
5 August 1518	Bozzolo	Isabella d'Este
9 October 1521	Gabbioneta	Isabella d'Este
15 October 1521	Gabbioneta	Isabella d'Este
15 October 1521	Gabbioneta	Isabella d'Este
16 October 1521	Gabbioneta	Isabella d'Este
16 October 1521	Gabbioneta	Isabella d'Este
16 October 1521	Gabbioneta	Isabella d'Este
19 October 1521	Ostiano	Isabella d'Este
20 October 1521	Ostiano	Isabella d'Este
21 October 1521	Ostiano	Isabella d'Este

Date	Place	Addressee
21 October 1521	Ostiano	Isabella d'Este
22 October 1521	Ostiano	Isabella d'Este
22 October 1521	Ostiano	Isabella d'Este
22 October 1521	Ostiano	Isabella d'Este
22 October 1521	Ostiano	Isabella d'Este
22 October 1521	Ostiano	Paolo Giovio
23 October 1521	Ostiano	Isabella d'Este
23 October 1521	Ostiano	Isabella d'Este
23 October 1521	Ostiano	Isabella d'Este
23 October 1521	Ostiano	Isabella d'Este
23 October 1521	Ostiano	Isabella d'Este
24 October 1521	Ostiano	Isabella d'Este
24 October 1521	Ostiano	Isabella d'Este
25 October 1521	Ostiano	Isabella d'Este
25 October 1521	Ostiano	Isabella d'Este
no date	Ostiano	Isabella d'Este
25 October 1521	Ostiano	Isabella d'Este
26 October 1521	Ostiano	Isabella d'Este
26 October 1521	Ostiano	[Isabella d'Este]
26 October 1521	Ostiano	Isabella d'Este
27 October 1521	Ostiano	Isabella d'Este
28 October 1521	Ostiano	Isabella d'Este
28 October 1521	Ostiano	Isabella d'Este
28 October 1521	Ostiano	Isabella d'Este
29 October 1521	Ostiano	Isabella d'Este
29 October 1521	Ostiano	Isabella d'Este
30 October 1521	Ostiano	Isabella d'Este
30 October 1521	Ostiano	Isabella d'Este
30 October 1521	Ostiano	Isabella d'Este
31 October 1521	Ostiano	Isabella d'Este
31 October 1521	Ostiano	Isabella d'Este
1 November 1521	Ostiano	Isabella d'Este
1 November 1521	Ostiano	Isabella d'Este
1 November 1521	Ostiano	Isabella d'Este
6 November 1521	Ostiano	Isabella d'Este
no date	[Ostiano]	[Isabella d'Este]
no date	[Ostiano]	[Isabella d'Este]

(vi) ASMN, AG, Serie E. XLV. 3 (Venice and the Veneto)

b. 1444

| 13 October 1510 | Chioggia | no addressee |

b. 1447

| 14 October 1513 | Verona | Isabella d'Este |
| 14 October 1513 + *postscriptum* | Verona | Isabella d'Este |

Date	Place	Addressee
b. 1448		
18 September 1514	Arquà	Isabella d'Este
19 March 1515	Lonato	Federico Gonzaga
23 March 1515	Salò	Federico Gonzaga
27 March 1515	Sirmione	Federico Gonzaga
28 March 1515	Sirmione	Federico Gonzaga
b. 1457		
24 September 1523	Pontevico	no addressee
25 September 1523	Pontevico	Isabella d'Este
25 September 1523	Pontevico	Isabella d'Este
25 September 1523	Pontevico	Isabella d'Este
26 September 1523	Pontevico	Isabella d'Este
26 September 1523	Pontevico	Isabella d'Este
26 September 1523	Pontevico	Isabella d'Este
27 September 1523	Pontevico	Isabella d'Este
27 September 1523	Pontevico	Isabella d'Este
28 September 1523	Pontevico	Isabella d'Este
28 September 1523	Pontevico	Jacobo Calandra
28 September 1523	Pontevico	no addressee
28 September 1523	Pontevico	Isabella d'Este
28 September 1523	Pontevico	Isabella d'Este
29 September 1523	Pontevico	Isabella d'Este
29 september 1523	Pontevico	Isabella d'Este
30 September 1523	Pontevico	Isabella d'Este
1 October 1523	Pontevico	Jacobo Calandra
2 October 1523	Pontevico	Isabella d'Este
3 October 1523	Pontevico	Cavalier Landriano
3 October 1523	Pontevico	Isabella d'Este
3 October 1523	Pontevico	no addressee
4 October 1523	Pontevico	Jacobo Calandra
4 October 1523	Pontevico	Isabella d'Este
5 October 1523	Pontevico	Jacobo Calandra
5 October 1523	Pontevico	no addressee
5 October 1523	Pontevico	Isabella d'Este
5 October 1523	Pontevico	Isabella d'Este
6 October 1523	Pontevico	Isabella d'Este
6 October 1523	Pontevico	Isabella d'Este
6 October 1523	Pontevico	no addressee
6 October 1523	Pontevico	Jacobo Calandra
7 October 1523	Pontevico	Isabella d'Este
7 October 1523	Pontevico	Isabella d'Este
8 October 1523	Pontevico	Isabella d'Este
13 October 1523	Cremona	Jacobo Calandra
15 October 1523	Pontevico	Isabella d'Este
15 October 1523	Pontevico	Isabella d'Este
15 October 1523	Pontevico	Isabella d'Este
16 October 1523	Pontevico	no addressee
16 October 1523	Pontevico	Jacobo Calandra
16 October 1523	Pontevico	Isabella d'Este
17 October 1523	Pontevico	Isabella d'Este

BIBLIOGRAPHY   299

Date	Place	Addressee
17 October 1523	Pontevico	Isabella d'Este
17 October 1523	Pontevico	Jacobo Calandra
18 October 1523	Pontevico	Isabella d'Este
18 October 1523	Pontevico	Jacobo Calandra
20 October 1523	Pontevico	Isabella d'Este
20 October 1523	Pontevico	Jacobo Calandra
21 October 1523	Pontevico	Isabella d'Este
23 October 1523	Orzinovi	Jacobo Calandra
23 October 1523	Orzinovi	Isabella d'Este
24 October 1523	Orzinovi	Jacobo Calandra
24 October 1523	Orzinovi	Isabella d'Este
26 October 1523	Orzinovi	Isabella d'Este
27 October [1523]	Cremona	Isabella d'Este
31 July 1524	Caldiero	Joan Battista Abbatino

b. 1458

8 August 1524	Abano	a Joan Battista Abate
14 August 1524	Abano	a Joan Battista Abate

(vii)   ASMN, AG, Serie E. XXX. 3 (Bologna)

b. 1147

26 April 1511	Bologna	Isabella d'Este

(viii)   ASMN, AG, Serie E. XXVI. 3 (Urbino and Pesaro)

b. 1077

28 June 1512	Fossombrone	Isabella d'Este

(ix)   ASMN, AG, Serie E. XXV. 3 (Rome)

b. 860

27 June 1512	Pesaro	Isabella d'Este
5 July 1512	Rome	Isabella d'Este
5 July 1512	Rome	Isabella d'Este
8 July 1512	Rome	Isabella d'Este
9 July 1512	Rome	Isabella d'Este
12 July 1512	Rome	Isabella d'Este
13 July 1512	Rome	Isabella d'Este
13 July 1512	Rome	Isabella d'Este
15 July 1512	Rome	Isabella d'Este

b. 861

18 March 1513	Rome	no addressee, probably Isabella d'Este

Date	Place	Addressee
21 March 1513	Rome	no addressee, probably Isabella d'Este
23 March 1513	Rome	Isabella d'Este
24 March 1513	Rome	Isabella d'Este
27 March 1513	Rome	Isabella d'Este
27 March 1513	Rome	Isabella d'Este
28 March 1513	Rome	Isabella d'Este
5 April 1513	Rome	Isabella d'Este
6 April 1513	Rome	Isabella d'Este
8 April 1513	Rome	Isabella d'Este
10 April 1513	Rome	Isabella d'Este
11 April 1513	Rome	Isabella d'Este
11 April 1513	Rome	Isabella d'Este
11 April 1513	Rome	[Isabella d'Este]
13 April 1513	Rome	Isabella d'Este
16 April 1513	Rome	Isabella d'Este
17 April 1513	Rome	Isabella d'Este
20 April 1513	Rome	Isabella d'Este
21 April 1513	Rome	Isabella d'Este

b. 863

12 January 1515	Rome	Federico Gonzaga
27 January 1515	Rome	Federico Gonzaga
8 February 1515	Rome	Federico Gonzaga
25 December 1515	Rome	Federico Gonzaga

(x) ASMN, AG, Serie E. XLI. 1 (Correspondence to Isabella d'Este)

b. 1894

30 March 1513	Rome	[Isabella d'Este]

b. 1895

30 December 1519	Ferrara	Isabella d'Este
undated	no information but written by Equicola	
undated	no information but written by Equicola	
undated	no information but written by Equicola	

b. 1898

23 October 1521	Ostiano	Isabella d'Este
23 October 1521	Ostiano	Isabella d'Este
26 October 1521	Ostiano	Isabella d'Este
3 November 1521	Volongo	Isabella d'Este
5 October 1521	Caneto	Isabella d'Este

Date	Place	Addressee

b. 1902

6 February 1522	La Certosa	Isabella d'Este
2 March 1522	Mantua	Federico Gonzaga
26 July 1522	Bozzolo	Isabella d'Este
27 July 1522	Bozzolo	Isabella d'Este

(xi) ASMN, AG, Serie E. XXIV. 3 (Naples and Sicily)

b. 809

8 December 1514	Naples	Federico Gonzaga
17 March 1516	Naples	Isabella d'Este
31 March 1516	Naples	Isabella d'Este

(xii) ASMN, AG, Serie E. XLIX. 3 (Milan)

b. 1640

12 June 1514	Cremona	Federico Gonzaga
18 June 1514	Cremona	Federico Gonzaga
18 June 1514	Cremona	Federico Gonzaga
24 June 1514	Pavia	Federico Gonzaga
27 July 1514	Milan	Federico Gonzaga
31 July 1514	Milan	Federico Gonzaga
11 August 1514	Milan	Federico Gonzaga
17 August 1514	Milan	Federico Gonzaga
29 August 1514	Milan	Federico Gonzaga
4 September 1514	Milan	Federico Gonzaga
13 September 1514	Magenta	Jacobo Calandra
19 September 1514	«Belriguardo» (Bellosguardo)	Isabella d'Este

b. 1647

6 October 1521	Rebecco	Isabella d'Este
6 October 1521	Rebecco	Isabella d'Este
6 October 1521	Rebecco	Isabella d'Este
6 October 1521	Rebecco	Isabella d'Este
6 October 1521	Rebecco	Isabella d'Este
7 October 1521	Rebecco	Isabella d'Este
7 October 1521	Rebecco	[Isabella d'Este]
7 October 1521	Rebecco	Isabella d'Este
7 October 1521	Rebecco	Isabella d'Este
7 October 1521	Rebecco	Isabella d'Este
7 October 1521	Rebecco	Isabella d'Este

Date	Place	Addressee
7 October 1521	Rebecco	Isabella d'Este
8 October 1521	Rebecco	Isabella d'Este
8 October 1521	Rebecco	Isabella d'Este
8 October 1521	Rebecco	Isabella d'Este
8 October 1521	Rebecco	Isabella d'Este
8 October 1521	Rebecco	Isabella d'Este
8 October 1521	Rebecco	Isabella d'Este
8 October 1521	Rebecco	Isabella d'Este
9 October 1521	Gabbioneta	Isabella d'Este
9 October 1521	Gabbioneta	Isabella d'Este
10 October 1521	Gabbioneta	Isabella d'Este
10 October 1521	Gabbioneta	Isabella d'Este
10 October 1521	Gabbioneta	Isabella d'Este
no date	[Gabbioneta]	Isabella d'Este
10 October 1521	Gabbioneta	Isabella d'Este
10 October 1521	Gabbioneta	Isabella d'Este
11 October 1521	Gabbioneta	Isabella d'Este
11 October 1521	Gabbioneta	Isabella d'Este
11 October 1521	Gabbioneta	Isabella d'Este
11 October 1521	Gabbioneta	Isabella d'Este
12 October 1521	Gabbioneta	Isabella d'Este
13 October 1521	Gabbioneta	Isabella d'Este
13 October 1521	Gabbioneta	Isabella d'Este
13 October 1521	Gabbioneta	Isabella d'Este
14 October 1521	Gabbioneta	Isabella d'Este
14 October 1521	Gabbioneta	Isabella d'Este
15 October 1521	Gabbioneta	Isabella d'Este
15 October 1521	Gabbioneta	Isabella d'Este
17 October 1521	Gabbioneta	Isabella d'Este
17 October 1521	Gabbioneta	Isabella d'Este
17 October 1521	Gabbioneta	Isabella d'Este
17 October 1521	Gabbioneta	Isabella d'Este
17 October 1521	Gabbioneta	Isabella d'Este
18 October 1521	Gabbioneta	Isabella d'Este

b. 1649

Date	Place	Addressee
23 March 1522	Parma	Isabella d'Este
25 March 1522	Pavia	Isabella d'Este
25 March 1522	Pavia	Isabella d'Este
25 March 1522	Pavia	Isabella d'Este
25 March 1522	Pavia	Isabella d'Este
26 March 1522	Pavia	[Isabella d'Este]
26 March 1522	Pavia	Isabella d'Este
26 March 1522	Pavia	Isabella d'Este
28 March 1522	Pavia	[Isabella d'Este]
28 March 1522	Pavia	Isabella d'Este
28 March 1522	Pavia	Isabella d'Este
28 March 1522	Pavia	Isabella d'Este
29 March 1522	Pavia	Isabella d'Este
30 March 1522	Gambalo	Isabella d'Este
31 March 1522	Pavia	Isabella d'Este

Date	Place	Addressee
1 April 1522	Pavia	Isabella d'Este
1 April 1522	Pavia	Isabella d'Este
2 April 1522	Pavia	Isabella d'Este
2 April 1522	Pavia	Isabella d'Este
2 April 1522	Pavia	Isabella d'Este
3 April 1522	Pavia	Isabella d'Este
3 April 1522	Pavia	Jacobo Calandra
4 April 1522	Pavia	Isabella d'Este
4 April 1522	Pavia	[Isabella d'Este]
5 April 1522	Pavia	Isabella d'Este
6 April 1522	Pavia	Isabella d'Este
6 April 1522	Pavia	Isabella d'Este
6 April 1522	Pavia	Isabella d'Este
7 April 1522	Pavia	Isabella d'Este
8 April 1522	Pavia	Isabella d'Este
8 April 1522	Pavia	[Isabella d'Este]
9 April 1522	Pavia	Isabella d'Este
10 April 1522	Pavia	Isabella d'Este
12 April 1522	Pavia	Isabella d'Este
12 April 1522	Pavia	Isabella d'Este
12 April 1522	Pavia	Isabella d'Este
14 April 1522	Pavia	Isabella d'Este
15 April 1522	Pavia	Isabella d'Este
15 April 1522	Pavia	Isabella d'Este
17 April 1522	Pavia	Isabella d'Este
17 April 1522	Pavia	[Isabella d'Este]
17 April 1522	Pavia	Isabella d'Este
18 April 1522	Pavia	Isabella d'Este
18 April 1522	Pavia	Isabella d'Este
21 April 1522	Pavia	Isabella d'Este
21 April 1522	Pavia	Isabella d'Este
no date	Pavia (?)	Isabella d'Este
12 October 1522	Gabbioneta	Isabella d'Este
13 October 1522	Gabbioneta	Isabella d'Este
15 October 1522	Gabbioneta	Isabella d'Este
19 October 1522	Camp of the *Lega*	Isabella d'Este

b. 1651

Date	Place	Addressee
16 September 1523	Cremona	Isabella d'Este
17 September 1523	Cremona	Isabella d'Este
17 September 1523	Cremona	Isabella d'Este
17 September 1523	Cremona	Isabella d'Este
18 September 1523	Cremona	Isabella d'Este
18 September 1523	Cremona	Isabella d'Este
19 September 1523	Castel Leone	Isabella d'Este
20 September 1523	Castel Leone	Isabella d'Este
20 September 1523	Castelforte	Isabella d'Este
21 September 1523	Lodi	Isabella d'Este
21 September 1523	Lodi	Isabella d'Este
22 September 1523	Lodi	Isabella d'Este
22 September 1523	Lodi	Isabella d'Este

Date	Place	Addressee
22 September 1523	Lodi	no addressee
23 September 1523	Castel Leone	no addressee
23 September 1523	Castel Leone	no addressee
1 October 1523	Grogno	Jacobo Calandra
9 October 1523	Cremona	Isabella d'Este
10 October 1523	Cremona	Isabella d'Este
10 October 1523	Cremona	Jacobo Calandra
11 October 1523	Cremona	Isabella d'Este
12 October 1523	Cremona	Jacobo Calandra
12 October 1523	Cremona	Isabella d'Este
12 October 1523	Cremona	Jacobo Calandra
13 October 1523	Cremona	Isabella d'Este
31 October 1523	Pavia	Jacobo Calandra
31 October 1523	Pavia	Isabella d'Este
1 November 1523	Pavia	no addressee
1 November 1523	Pavia	Isabella d'Este
3 November 1523	Pavia	Jacobo Calandra
3 November 1523	Pavia	Isabella d'Este
5 November 1523	Pavia	Jacobo Calandra
5 November 1523	Pavia	Isabella d'Este
7 November 1523	Pavia	Jacobo Calandra
7 November 1523	Pavia .	Isabella d'Este
7 November 1523	Pavia	Isabella d'Este
7 November 1523	Pavia	Jacobo Calandra
8 November 1523	Pavia	Isabella d'Este
9 November 1523	Pavia	Jacobo Calandra
9 November 1523	Pavia	Isabella d'Este
8 & 10 Nov. 1523	Pavia	[Isabella d'Este]
10 November 1523	Pavia	Isabella d'Este
11 November 1523	Pavia	Isabella d'Este
12 November 1523	Pavia	Isabella d'Este
13 November 1523	Pavia	Jacobo Calandra
13 November 1523	Pavia	Isabella d'Este
14 November 1523	Pavia	Jacobo Calandra
14 November 1523	Pavia	Isabella d'Este
15 November 1523	Pavia	Isabella d'Este
15 November 1523	Pavia	Isabella d'Este
16 November 1523	Pavia	Isabella d'Este
16 November 1523	Pavia	Isabella d'Este
16 November 1523	Pavia	Isabella d'Este

(xiii) ASMN, AG, Serie E. XLI. 3 (Parma and Piacenza)

b. 1370

8 September 1521	the army quarters (near Parma)	Isabella d'Este
9 September 1521	the army quarters (near Parma)	Isabella d'Este
9 September 1521	the army quarters (near Parma)	[Isabella d'Este]
10 September 1521	the army quarters (near Parma)	Isabella d'Este
10 September 1521	the army quarters (near Parma)	Isabella d'Este
10 September 1521	the army quarters (near Parma)	Isabella d'Este

Date	Place	Addressee
10 September 1521	the army quarters (near Parma)	Isabella d'Este
10 September 1521	no place	Isabella d'Este
10 September 1521	the army quarters (near Parma)	Isabella d'Este
10 September 1521	the army quarters (near Parma)	Isabella d'Este
10 September 1521	the army quarters (near Parma)	Isabella d'Este
11 September 1521	the army quarters (near Parma)	Isabella d'Este
11 September 1521	the army quarters (near Parma)	Isabella d'Este
11 September 1521	the army quarters (near Parma)	Isabella d'Este
11 September 1521	the army quarters (near Parma)	Isabella d'Este
12 September 1521	the army quarters (near Parma)	Isabella d'Este
12 September 1521	the army quarters (near Parma)	Isabella d'Este
12 September 1521	the army quarters (near Parma)	Isabella d'Este
12 September 1521	the army quarters (near Parma)	Isabella d'Este
12 September 1521	the army quarters (near Parma)	Isabella d'Este
12 September 1521	the army quarters (near Parma)	Isabella d'Este
12 September 1521	the army quarters (near Parma)	Isabella d'Este
13 September 1521	the army quarters (near Parma)	Isabella d'Este
13 September 1521	the army quarters (near Parma)	Isabella d'Este
13 September 1521	the army quarters (near Parma)	Isabella d'Este
13 September 1521	the army quarters (near Parma)	Isabella d'Este
14 September 1521	the army quarters (near Parma)	Isabella d'Este
14 September 1521	the army quarters (near Parma)	Isabella d'Este
14 September 1521	the army quarters (near Parma)	Isabella d'Este
14 September 1521	the army quarters (near Parma)	Isabella d'Este
14 September 1521	the army quarters (near Parma)	Isabella d'Este
14 September 1521	the army quarters (near Parma)	Isabella d'Este
15 September 1521	the army quarters (near Parma)	Isabella d'Este
15 September 1521	the army quarters (near Parma)	Isabella d'Este
15 September 1521	the army quarters (near Parma)	Isabella d'Este
15 September 1521	the army quarters (near Parma)	Isabella d'Este
15 September 1521	the army quarters (near Parma)	Isabella d'Este
15 September 1521	the army quarters (near Parma)	Isabella d'Este
15 September 1521	the army quarters (near Parma)	Isabella d'Este
16 September 1521	the army quarters (near Parma)	Isabella d'Este
16 September 1521	the army quarters (near Parma)	Isabella d'Este
16 September 1521	the army quarters (near Parma)	Isabella d'Este
16 September 1521	the army quarters (near Parma)	Isabella d'Este
16 September 1521	the army quarters (near Parma)	Isabella d'Este
16 September 1521	the army quarters (near Parma)	Isabella d'Este
17 September 1521	the army quarters (near Parma)	Isabella d'Este
17 September 1521	the army quarters (near Parma)	Isabella d'Este
17 September 1521	the army quarters (near Parma)	Isabella d'Este
17 September 1521	the army quarters (near Parma)	Isabella d'Este

Date	Place	Addressee

(xiv) ASMN, AG, Serie E. XXXII. 3 (Modena and Reggio)

b. 1291

22 March 1522	Reggio	Isabella d'Este
22 March 1522	Reggio	Isabella d'Este

(xv) ASMN, AG, Serie E. XX. 2 (Monferrato)

b. 746

28 April 1517	Casale	Federico Gonzaga
1 May 1517	Trino	Federico Gonzaga
2 May 1517	Martengo	Federico Gonzaga

(xvi) ASMN, AG, «Raccolta d'Autografi»

b. 8

26 May 1520	Belriguardo	Marquis Federico Gonzaga
15 May 1523	Mantua	«Sindico»

(xvii) ASMN, AG, Serie F. II. 8 («Mantova e Paesi»)

b. 2480

18 October 1510	Sermide	Isabella d'Este
28 October 1510	Sermide	Isabella d'Este
28 October 1510	Sermide	Isabella d'Este

b. 2489

5 June 1514	Caneto (he is writing on behalf of an unidentified «Francesca»)	Federico Gonzaga
7 June 1514 with another letter of 5 June 1514	Caneto	Federico Gonzaga
27 June 1514	Mantua	[Isabella d'Este]
27 June 1514	Mantua	Isabella d'Este
9 July 1514	Mantua	Isabella d'Este

b. 2491

6 December 1515	Mantua	Federico Gonzaga
12 December 1515	Mantua	Federico Gonzaga
12 December 1515	Mantua	Federico Gonzaga

Date	Place	Addressee
17 December 1515	Mantua	Federico Gonzaga
22 December 1515	Mantua	Federico Gonzaga

b. 2492

13 May 1515	S. Benedetto Po	Isabella d'Este
14 May 1515	S. Benedetto Po	Isabella d'Este

b. 2494

3 January 1516	Mantua	Federico Gonzaga
14 January 1516	Mantua	Federico Gonzaga
29 January 1516	Mantua	Federico Gonzaga
29 January 1516	Mantua	Federico Gonzaga
14 February 1516	Mantua	Federico Gonzaga
28 February 1516	Mantua	Federico Gonzaga

b. 2495

5 March 1516	Sermide	Isabella d'Este

b. 2496

16 September 1517	Mantua	Isabella d'Este
18 September 1517	Mantua	Isabella d'Este
22 September 1517	Mantua	Isabella d'Este
23 September 1517	Mantua	Isabella d'Este
30 September 1517	Mantua	Isabella d'Este
22 April 1517	Redondesco	Federico Gonzaga
10 May 1517	Talardo	Federico Gonzaga

b. 2497

30 March 1518	S. Benedetto Po	Isabella d'Este
5 May 1518	Mantua	Isabella d'Este

b. 2498

3 November 1519	Mantua	Marquis Federico Gonzaga
4 November 1519	Mantua	Marquis Federico Gonzaga
4 November 1519	Mantua	Marquis Federico Gonzaga
4 November 1519	Mantua	Marquis Federico Gonzaga
4 November 1519	Mantua	Marquis Federico Gonzaga
5 November 1519	Mantua	Marquis Federico Gonzaga

Date	Place	Addressee

b. 2499

29 February 1520	Mantua	Marquis Federico Gonzaga
29 February 1520	Mantua	Marquis Federico Gonzaga
1 March 1520	Mantua	Marquis Federico Gonzaga
1 March 1520	Mantua	Marquis Federico Gonzaga
3 March 1520	Mantua	Marquis Federico Gonzaga
4 March 1520	Mantua	Marquis Federico Gonzaga
12 March 1520	Mantua	Marquis Federico Gonzaga
13 March 1520	Mantua	Marquis Federico Gonzaga
15 March 1520	Mantua	Stazio Gadio
15 March 1520	Mantua	Marquis Federico Gonzaga
15 March 1520	Mantua	Marquis Federico Gonzaga
16 March 1520	Mantua	Marquis Federico Gonzaga
17 March 1520	Mantua	Marquis Federico Gonzaga
18 March 1520	Mantua	Marquis Federico Gonzaga
19 March 1520	Mantua	Marquis Federico Gonzaga
20 March 1520	Mantua	Marquis Federico Gonzaga
22 March 1520	Mantua	Marquis Federico Gonzaga
23 March 1520	Mantua	Marquis Federico Gonzaga
24 March 1520	Mantua	Marquis Federico Gonzaga
26 June 1520	Diporto	Marquis Federico Gonzaga
20 July 1520	Mantua	Marquis Federico Gonzaga
7 November 1520	Mantua	Marquis Federico Gonzaga
12 November 1520	Mantua	Marquis Federico Gonzaga
16 November 1520	Mantua	Marquis Federico Gonzaga
11 December 1520	Mantua	Marquis Federico Gonzaga
15 December 1520	Mantua	Marquis Federico Gonzaga
16 December 1520	Mantua	Marquis Federico Gonzaga

b. 2500

6 July 1521	Mantua	(minute for the Pope)
4 August 1521	Mantua	Marquis Federico Gonzaga
5 August 1521	Mantua	Marquis Federico Gonzaga
7 August 1521	Mantua	Marquis Federico Gonzaga
7 August 1521	Mantua	Marquis Federico Gonzaga
9 August 1521	Mantua	[Marquis Federico Gonzaga]
10 August 1521	Mantua	Marquis Federico Gonzaga
11 August 1521	Mantua	Marquis Federico Gonzaga
12 August 1521	Mantua	Marquis Federico Gonzaga
13 August 1521	Mantua	Marquis Federico Gonzaga
15 August 1521	Mantua	Marquis Federico Gonzaga
15 August 1521	Mantua	Marquis Federico Gonzaga
20 August 1521	Mantua	Marquis Federico Gonzaga
21 August 1521	Mantua	Marquis Federico Gonzaga
22 August 1521	Mantua	Marquis Federico Gonzaga
22 August 1521	Mantua	Marquis Federico Gonzaga
22 August 1521	Mantua	Marquis Federico Gonzaga
24 August 1521	Mantua	Marquis Federico Gonzaga
25 August 1521	Mantua	Marquis Federico Gonzaga

Date	Place	Addressee
25 August 1521	Mantua	Marquis Federico Gonzaga
27 August 1521	Mantua	Marquis Federico Gonzaga
28 August 1521	Mantua	Marquis Federico Gonzaga
28 August 1521	Mantua	Marquis Federico Gonzaga
5 September 1521	Mantua	Marquis Federico Gonzaga
23 September 1521	Mantua	Marquis Federico Gonzaga
24 September 1521	Mantua	Marquis Federico Gonzaga
26 September 1521	Mantua	Marquis Federico Gonzaga
28 September 1521	Mantua	Marquis Federico Gonzaga
2 October 1521	Mantua	Marquis Federico Gonzaga
5 October 1521	Caneto	Isabella d'Este
5 October 1521	Caneto	Isabella d'Este
5 October 1521	Caneto	Isabella d'Este
5 October 1521	Caneto	Isabella d'Este
5 October 1521	Caneto	Isabella d'Este
5 October 1521	«Mantua, Cane»	Isabella d'Este
20 November 1521	Mantua	Marquis Federico Gonzaga
22 November 1521	Mantua	Marquis Federico Gonzaga
26 November 1521	Mantua	Marquis Federico Gonzaga
6 December 1521	Mantua	Marquis Federico Gonzaga
7 December 1521	Mantua	Marquis Federico Gonzaga
11 December 1521	Mantua	Marquis Federico Gonzaga
14 December 1521	Mantua	Marquis Federico Gonzaga
21 December 1521	Mantua	Marquis Federico Gonzaga

b. 2501

Date	Place	Addressee
29 October 1521	Ostiano	Isabella d'Este
11 November 1521	Caneto	Isabella d'Este
13 November 1521	Caneto	Isabella d'Este
14 November 1521	Caneto	Isabella d'Este

b. 2502

Date	Place	Addressee
20 August 1522	S. Benedetto	Isabella d'Este
21 August 1522	S. Benedetto	Isabella d'Este
22 August 1522	S. Benedetto	[Isabella d'Este]
23 August 1522	S. Benedetto	Isabella d'Este
10 September 1522	Gonzaga	Jacobo Calandra
30 September 1522	Marmirolo	Isabella d'Este
8 October 1522	Marmirolo	Isabella d'Este
21 October 1522	Goito	Jacobo Calandra
27 October 1522	Goito	Isabella d'Este

b. 2503

Date	Place	Addressee
11 January 1522	Mantua	Marquis Federico Gonzaga
11 January 1522	Mantua	Marquis Federico Gonzaga
13 January 1522	Mantua	Marquis Federico Gonzaga
16 January 1522	Mantua	[Marquis Federico Gonzaga]

Date	Place	Addressee
17 January 1522	Mantua	Marquis Federico Gonzaga
18 January 1522	Mantua	Marquis Federico Gonzaga
23 January 1522	Mantua	Marquis Federico Gonzaga
27 January 1522	Mantua	Marquis Federico Gonzaga
29 January 1522	Mantua	Marquis Federico Gonzaga
29 January 1522	Mantua	Marquis Federico Gonzaga[2]
29 January 1522	Mantua	Marquis Federico Gonzaga
30 January 1522	Mantua	[Marquis Federico Gonzaga]
3 February 1522	Mantua	Marquis Federico Gonzaga
10 February 1522	La Certosa	Marquis Federico Gonzaga
12 February 1522	La Certosa	Marquis Federico Gonzaga
16 February 1522	Mantua	Marquis Federico Gonzaga
17 February 1522	Mantua	Marquis Federico Gonzaga
19 February 1522	Mantua	Marquis Federico Gonzaga
23 February 1522	Mantua	Marquis Federico Gonzaga
23 February 1522	Mantua	Marquis Federico Gonzaga
24 February 1522	Mantua	Marquis Federico Gonzaga
25 February 1522	Mantua	Marquis Federico Gonzaga
26 February 1522	Mantua	Marquis Federico Gonzaga
26 February 1522	Mantua	Marquis Federico Gonzaga
4 March 1522	Mantua	Marquis Federico Gonzaga
9 March 1522	Mantua	[Marquis Federico Gonzaga]
9 March 1522	Mantua	Marquis Federico Gonzaga
11 March 1522	Mantua	Marquis Federico Gonzaga
16 March 1522	Mantua	Marquis Federico Gonzaga
18 March 1522	Mantua	Marquis Federico Gonzaga
18 March 1522	Mantua	Marquis Federico Gonzaga
18 March 1522	Mantua	Marquis Federico Gonzaga
9 August 1522	Mantua	Marquis Federico Gonzaga
12 August 1522	Mantua	Marquis Federico Gonzaga
1 October 1522	Mantua	Marquis Federico Gonzaga
11 October 1522	Mantua	Marquis Federico Gonzaga
11 October 1522	Mantua	Marquis Federico Gonzaga
1 November 1522	Mantua	Isabella d'Este
25 December 1522	Mantua	Marquis Federico Gonzaga
25 December 1522	Mantua	Marquis Federico Gonzaga
26 December 1522	Mantua	[Marquis Federico Gonzaga]
26 December 1522	Mantua	Marquis Federico Gonzaga
27 December 1522	Mantua	Marquis Federico Gonzaga
28 December 1522	Mantua	Marquis Federico Gonzaga
no date	Mantua	[Marquis Federico Gonzaga]
30 December 1522	Mantua	Marquis Federico Gonzaga
31 December 1522	Mantua	Marquis Federico Gonzaga

b. 2504

29 no month 1523	Mantua	Marquis Federico Gonzaga
27 November 1523	Marmirolo	Abbatino G. Battista

---

[2] This letter is signed «Letam», a reference to Equicola's philosophy of pleasure.

Date	Place	Addressee
7 December 1523	Mantua	Abbatino G. Battista
9 December 1523	Marmirolo	Abbatino G. Battista

b. 2505

31 July 1524	Caldiero	Abbatino G. Battista
4 August 1524	Mantua	Marquis Federico Gonzaga
7 September 1524	Mantua	Marquis Federico Gonzaga
14 October 1524	Mantua	Marquis Federico Gonzaga
16 October 1524	Mantua	Marquis Federico Gonzaga
18 October 1524	Mantua	Marquis Federico Gonzaga
20 October 1524	Mantua	Isabella d'Este
23 November 1524	Mantua	no addressee

b. 2506

11 May 1525	Mantua	Marquis Federico Gonzaga
25 May 1525	Mantua	«Commissario di Bozolo»
22 July 1525	Marmirolo	«Commissario di Bozolo»

2. Archivio di Stato, Modena

(i) ASMO, ASE, C, Archivi per materia:

Letterati, b. 18

6 July 1513	Mantua	Cardinal Ippolito d'Este
4 April 1515	Mantua	Cardinal Ippolito d'Este

(ii) ASMO, ASE, C, Ambasciatori: Mantova

b. 1

15 November 1507	Gazzuolo	Cardinal Ippolito d'Este
11 March 1508	Mantua	Cardinal Ippolito d'Este
28 April 1508	Mantua	Cardinal Ippolito d'Este
9 May 1508	Mantua	Cardinal Ippolito d'Este
13 May 1508	Mantua	Cardinal Ippolito d'Este
27 May 1508	Mantua	Cardinal Ippolito d'Este
18 July 1508	Capriana	Cardinal Ippolito d'Este
24 January 1512	Mantua	Cardinal Ippolito d'Este
30 January 1512	Mantua	Cardinal Ippolito d'Este
10 February 1512	Mantua	Cardinal Ippolito d'Este
10 February 1512	Mantua	Cardinal Ippolito d'Este
11 February 1512	Mantua	Cardinal Ippolito d'Este
13 February 1512	Mantua	Cardinal Ippolito d'Este
14 February 1512	Mantua	Cardinal Ippolito d'Este

Date	Place	Addressee
15 February 1512	Mantua	Cardinal Ippolito d'Este
20 February 1512	Mantua	Cardinal Ippolito d'Este

b. 2

Date	Place	Addressee
10 June [1518-22?]	Mantua	Alfonso d'Este, Duke of Ferrara
[1521?]	[Mantua?]	[Duke of Ferrara]
[20 January? ?]	Mantua	Duke of Ferrara
6 [?]	Mantua	Duke of Ferrara
8 December 1521	no place	[Coglia?]
no date	no place	[Duke of Ferrara?]
no date	no place	[Duke of Ferrara?]
14 April 1518	Mantua	Duke of Ferrara
15 May 1518	Mantua	Duke of Ferrara
17 May 1518	Mantua	Jo. Francesco Calcagno
3 January 1519	Mantua	Duke of Ferrara
2 March 1519	Mantua	Duke of Ferrara
31 March 1519	Mantua	Duke of Ferrara
8 June 1519	Diporto	Duke of Ferrara
6 July 1519	Diporto	Duke of Ferrara
8 July 1519	Mantua	Duke of Ferrara
12 July 1519	Mantua	Duke of Ferrara
17 July 1519	Diporto	Duke of Ferrara
21 July 1519	Diporto	Duke of Ferrara
21 July 1519	Mantua	Duke of Ferrara
22 July 1519	Mantua	Duke of Ferrara
30 July 1519	Mantua	Duke of Ferrara
30 July 1519	Mantua	Duke of Ferrara
31 July 1519	Mantua	Duke of Ferrara
[5?] August 1519	Diporto	Duke of Ferrara
7 August 1519	Diporto	Duke of Ferrara
27 August [1519?]	Mantua	Duke of Ferrara
2 September 1519	Mantua	Duke of Ferrara
4 September 1519	Mantua	Duke of Ferrara
10 September 1519	Diporto	Duke of Ferrara
18 September 1519	Diporto	Duke of Ferrara
21 September 1519	Diporto	Duke of Ferrara
25 September 1519	Mantua	Duke of Ferrara
28 September 1519	Diporto	Duke of Ferrara
1 October 1519	Mantua	Duke of Ferrara
5 October 1519	Mantua	Bernardino di Prosperi
10 October 1519	Mantua	Duke of Ferrara
21 October 1519	Mantua	Duke of Ferrara
5 November 1519	Mantua	Duke of Ferrara
10 November 1519	Mantua	Duke of Ferrara
17 November 1519	Mantua	Duke of Ferrara
21 November 1519	Mantua	Duke of Ferrara
24 November 1519	Mantua	Duke of Ferrara
2 December 1519	Mantua	Duke of Ferrara
5 December 1519	Mantua	Duke of Ferrara

Date	Place	Addressee
9 December 1519	Mantua	Duke of Ferrara
9 December 1519	Mantua	Duke of Ferrara
11 December 1519	Mantua	Duke of Ferrara
[1519?]	no place	Duke of Ferrara
no date	no place	[Duke of Ferrara]
4 January 1520	Mantua	Duke of Ferrara
4 January 1520	Mantua	Duke of Ferrara
5 January 1520	Mantua	Duke of Ferrara
9 January 1520	Mantua	Duke of Ferrara
10 January 1520	Mantua	Duke of Ferrara
13 January 1520	Mantua	Duke of Ferrara
13 January 1520	Mantua	Duke of Ferrara
16 January 1520	Mantua	Duke of Ferrara
20 January 1520	Mantua	Duke of Ferrara
31 January 1520	Mantua	Duke of Ferrara
9 February 1520	Mantua	Duke of Ferrara
12 February 1520	Mantua	Duke of Ferrara
28 February 1520	Mantua	Duke of Ferrara
6 April 1520	Mantua	Cardinal Ippolito d'Este
8 April 1520	Mantua	Duke of Ferrara
10 June 1520	Mantua	Duke of Ferrara
11 June 1520	Mantua	Duke of Ferrara
18 June 1520	Diporto	Duke of Ferrara
28 June 1520	Mantua	Duke of Ferrara
15 July 1520	Mantua	Duke of Ferrara
25 September 1520	Mantua	Duke of Ferrara
11 October 1520	Diporto	«messer Obizo»
3 January 1521	Mantua	«messer Obizo»
6 January 1521	Mantua	Duke of Ferrara
11 January 1521	Mantua	«messer Obizo»
5 February 1521	Mantua	Duke of Ferrara
11 February 1521	Mantua	«messer Obizo»
13 February 1521	Mantua	Duke of Ferrara
14 February 1521	Mantua	«messer Obizo»
16 February 1521	Mantua	Duke of Ferrara
24 February 1521	Mantua	«messer Obizo»
24 February 1521	Mantua	Duke of Ferrara
26 February 1521	Mantua	Duke of Ferrara
28 February 1521	Mantua	«messer Obizo»
6 March 1521	Mantua	«messer Obizo»
7 March 1521	Mantua	«messer Obizo»
22 March 1521	Mantua	Duke of Ferrara
23 May 1521	Mantua	Duke of Ferrara
28 May 1521	Mantua	Duke of Ferrara
28 May 1521	Mantua	«messer Obizo»
9 June 1521	Mantua	Duke of Ferrara
10 June 1521	Mantua	Duke of Ferrara
12 June 1521	Mantua	Duke of Ferrara
14 June 1521	Mantua	Duke of Ferrara
15 June 1521	Mantua	Duke of Ferrara
16 June 1521	Mantua	Duke of Ferrara
17 June 1521	Mantua	«messer Obizo»
17 June 1521	Mantua	Duke of Ferrara

Date	Place	Addressee
18 June 1521	Mantua	Duke of Ferrara
20 June 1521	Mantua	«messer Obizo»
22 June 1521	Mantua	«messer Obizo»
22 June 1521	Mantua	Duke of Ferrara
22 June 1521	Mantua	Duke of Ferrara
23 June 1521	Mantua	Duke of Ferrara
25 June 1521	Mantua	Duke of Ferrara
2 July 1521	Mantua	Duke of Ferrara
8 July 1521	Mantua	Duke of Ferrara
9 July 1521	Mantua	[Duke of Ferrara]
10 July 1521	Mantua	Duke of Ferrara
11 July 1521	Mantua	Duke of Ferrara
13 July 1521	Mantua	Duke of Ferrara
17 July 1521	Mantua	Duke of Ferrara
25 July 1521	Mantua	Duke of Ferrara
27 July 1521	Mantua	Duke of Ferrara
27 July 1521	Mantua	[Duke of Ferrara]
28 July 1521	Mantua	Duke of Ferrara
10 August 1521	Mantua	Duke of Ferrara
18 August 1521	Mantua	Bernardino di Prosperi
18 August 1521	Mantua	«messer Obizo»
18 August 1521	Army quarters	Isabella d'Este
28 September 1521	Mantua	Duke of Ferrara
October 1521	Mantua	Duke of Ferrara
5 December 1521	Mantua	Duke of Ferrara
14 December 1521	Mantua	Duke of Ferrara
24 December 1521	Mantua	Duke of Ferrara
2 January 1522	Mantua	Duke of Ferrara
12 January 1522	Mantua	«messer Obizo»
17 January 1522	Mantua	Duke of Ferrara
17 January 1522	Mantua	Duke of Ferrara
24 January 1522	Mantua	Duke of Ferrara
26 January 1522	Mantua	Duke of Ferrara
25 February 1522	Mantua	Duke of Ferrara
9 March 1522	Mantua	Duke of Ferrara
12 March 1522	Mantua	Duke of Ferrara
15 March 1522	Mantua	Duke of Ferrara
15 March 1522	Mantua	Duke of Ferrara
15 March no year	Mantua	[Duke of Ferrara]
15 March 1522	Mantua	«messer Obizo»
16 March 1522	Mantua	Duke of Ferrara
18 March 1522	Mantua	Duke of Ferrara
20 March 1522	Mantua	Duke of Ferrara
20 March 1522	Mantua	Duke of Ferrara
18 [April?] 1522	Mantua	Duke of Ferrara
30 April 1522	Mantua	Duke of Ferrara
2 May 1522	Mantua	Duke of Ferrara
11 May 1522	Mantua	[Duke of Ferrara]
14? May 1522	[in Castris]	no addressee[2]
16 May	Mantua	Duke of Ferrara
22 May 1522	Mantua	Duke of Ferrara
28 May 1522	Mantua	Duke of Ferrara
28 May 1522	Mantua	«messer Obizo»

Date	Place	Addressee
2 June 1522	Mantua	Duke of Ferrara
2 June 1522	Mantua	Duke of Ferrara
5 June 1522	Mantua	Duke of Ferrara
6 June 1522	Mantua	Duke of Ferrara
7 June 1522	Mantua	Duke of Ferrara
9 June 1522	Mantua	Duke of Ferrara
15 June 1522	Mantua	Duke of Ferrara
15 June 1522	Mantua	Duke of Ferrara
17 June 1522	Mantua	Duke of Ferrara
19 June 1522	Mantua	Duke of Ferrara
20 June 1522	Mantua	Duke of Ferrara
7? June 1522	Mantua	Duke of Ferrara
20 June 1522	Mantua	Duke of Ferrara
24 June 1522	Mantua	«messer Obizo»
24 June 1522	Mantua	Duke of Ferrara
3 July 1522	Mantua	Duke of Ferrara
3 July 1522	Mantua	Duke of Ferrara
4 July 1522	Mantua	Duke of Ferrara
5 July 1522	Mantua	Duke of Ferrara
6 July 1522?	Mantua	[Duke of Ferrara]
13 July 1522	Mantua	[Duke of Ferrara]
17 July 1522	Mantua	Duke of Ferrara
20 July 1522	Mantua	Duke of Ferrara
14 September 1522	Gonzaga	Duke of Ferrara
30 September 1522	Marmirolo	Duke of Ferrara
16 December 1522	Mantua	Duke of Ferrara
no date	no place	Duke of Ferrara

(iii) ASMO, ASE, C, Ambasciatori: Francia

b. 4

Date	Place	Addressee
6 October 1505	Blois	Cardinal Ippolito d'Este
12 October 1505	«in corte» (Blois)	Cardinal Ippolito d'Este
9 November 1505	Blois	Cardinal Ippolito d'Este
9 November 1505	Blois	Cardinal Ippolito d'Este
12 November 1505	Blois	Cardinal Ippolito d'Este
4 December 1505	Blois	Cardinal Ippolito d'Este
4 December [1505]	Blois	Cardinal Ippolito d'Este
9 January 1506	Blois	[Cardinal Ippolito d'Este]
no date	[Blois]	[Cardinal Ippolito d'Este]

---

[2]   This is a copy of a document made by Equicola providing details of a pact between Prospero Colonna and the Marquis of Saluzzo. It was probably inserted in a letter to the Duke of Ferrara.

Date	Place	Addressee

(iv) ASMO, ASE, C, Ambasciatori: Milano

b.20

| 24 May 1507 | Milan | Sigismondo d'Este |

b. 21

17 July 1514	Milan	Cardinal Ippolito d'Este
27 July 1514	Milan	Cardinal Ippolito d'Este
8 August 1514	Milan	Cardinal Ippolito d'Este
21 August [1514]	[Milan]	[Cardinal Ippolito d'Este]
22 August 1514	Milan	Cardinal Ippolito d'Este
23 August 1514	Milan	Cardinal Ippolito d'Este
16 September 1514	Pavia	Cardinal Ippolito d'Este
16 September 1514	Parma	Cardinal Ippolito d'Este

b. 24

[9? April? 1522?]	[Pavia?]	[Isabella d'Este]
12 April 1522	Pavia	[Isabella d'Este]
14 April 1522	Pavia	[Isabella d'Este]
15 April 1522	Pavia	[Isabella d'Este]
15 April 1522	[Pavia]	[Isabella d'Este]
17 April 1522	Pavia	[Isabella d'Este]
18 April 1522	Pavia	[Isabella d'Este]

(v) ASMO, ASE, C, Ambasciatori: Napoli

b. 8

10 December 1506	Naples	Cardinal Ippolito d'Este
10 December 1506	Naples	Cardinal Ippolito d'Este
24 December 1506	Naples	Cardinal Ippolito d'Este
25 March [1507]	Naples	Cardinal Ippolito d'Este
29 November 1514	Fundi	Cardinal Ippolito d'Este
2 December 1514	Capua	Bernardo Bibbiena
2 December 1514	Capua	Cardinal Ippolito d'Este
13 December 1514	Naples	[Duke of Ferrara]
14 December 1514	Naples	Duke of Ferrara

Date	Place	Addressee

3. Biblioteca Estense, Modena

MSS Italiani, Alpha G, 1, 16 (It. 834)

12 October 1505	Blois	Cardinal Ippolito d'Este
1 November 1505	Blois	Cardinal Ippolito d'Este

MSS Italiani, Beta I, 3, 1 (It. 1827)

15 June 1510	Mantua	Aldo Manuzio

[Copy of BAV, Vat. lat. 4105; for details of this and other copies see E. Pastorello, *L'epistolario manuziano. Inventario cronologico-analitico 1483-1597*, Venice-Rome, 1957, pp. 33, 253.]

4. Biblioteca Apostolica Vaticana

(i) Vat. lat. 8211 (Letters to Baldassare Castiglione[i])

Date	Place	Fol. No.
15 December 1523	Mantua	278
1 January 1524	Mantua	279
12 January 1524	Mantua	280
23 January 1524	Mantua	281
23 February 1524	Mantua	282-283
23 February 1524	Mantua	284
29 February 1524	Marmirolo	285
29 February 1524	Mantua	286
6 March 1524	Marmirolo	287
1 April 1524	Mantua	288
25 April 1524	Mantua	289bis-290
28 April 1524	Mantua	189 (mistake: should read 289)
1 May 1524	Marmirolo	291
5 May 1524	Mantua	292
7 May 1524	Mantua	293
22 June 1524	Mantua	294
22 June 1524	Mantua	295
26 July 1524	Caldiero	296
21 August 1524	Mantua	297
29 December 1524	Mantua	298

(ii) Vat. lat. 8213

28 April 1524	Mantua	(To) Pope Clement VII

(probably enclosed with a letter, now lost, to Castiglione. A copy of this letter is to be found in Vat. lat. 9065, f. 210[r])

---

[i] In the same manuscript there are two letters (3 May 1521, f. 433, and 28 May 1521, f. 435) from Isabella d'Este to Castiglione written in Equicola's hand.

Date	Place	Addressee

(iii) Vat. lat. 4104

10 March 1510   Mantua   Aldo Manuzio

(iv) Vat. lat. 4105

15 June 1510   Mantua   Aldo Manuzio

(for further bibliographical details consult Pastorello, p. 33).

B. EQUICOLA'S MANUSCRIPT WORKS

1. *De Religione* (XVI cent.).
    BAV, Vat. lat. 5121.

2. (i) *D. Isabellae Estensis Mantuae Principis Iter in Narbonensem Galliam* (XIX cent.).
         Biblioteca Comunale, Mantua, MSS Negri 1252.

    (ii) *Gallorum Apologia*, (XVI cent.).
         Bibliotheek der Rijksuniversiteit, Leiden, BPL 183.

3. *Ristretto della Storia di Mantova* (XVI cent.).
    Biblioteca Nazionale Braidense, Milan, A DX 41.

4. (i)   *Genealogia delli Signori da Este composta da Mario Equicola di Alveto nelli 1516 del mese di octobre* (XVI cent.).
          Biblioteca Estense, Modena, Alpha F. 3. 11 (Ital. 162).
          The work is dedicated to Alfonso d'Este's eldest son, the future Duke of Ferrara, Ercole II. The manuscript continues, in the same hand, beyond the death of Alfonso d'Este (there is indeed a reference to the death of Alfonsino on 18 August 1547). Cf. Santoro, p. 152 no. III.

    (ii) *Genealogia de Signori da Este* (XVI cent.).
          Biblioteca Estense, Modena, Alpha W. 6. 28 (Ital. 265).
          «Finisce *lo Estense* composto da Mario Equicolo et scritto da mi Fra Paulo de' Clerici veronese carmelitano de osservantia. A dì XXII di febraro MDXXXVIII».
          No additions have been made to Equicola's text. Cf. Santoro, p. 152 no. I.

    (iii) *Genealogia de Signori da Este Prencipi in Ferrara composta da Mario Equicola di Alveto. MDXVI del mese di ottobre intitolata «l'Estense»* (XVI cent.).
          Biblioteca Estense, Modena, Alpha G. 8. 29 (Ital. 731).
          «Scritto in due dì nella medesima mala maniera di ortographia in che era scritto per non partirsi dalla antiquità» (f. 432^r old numeration; f. 53^r pencil).
          The scribe was Giraldi Cintio who transcribed the text, without making any additions, between 26 and 28 July 1554. Cf. Santoro, p. 152 no. II.

    (iv) *Genealogia delli Signori Estensi, Prencipi in Ferrara con breve trattato de loro preclari gesti, composta da Mario Equicolo de Alveto dell'anno MDXVI* (XVI cent.).
          Biblioteca Estense, Modena, Alpha P. 4. 19 (Ital. 482).
          The MS ends with the section on Alfonso d'Este at the battle of Ravenna.

    (v)   *Genealogia* (XVI cent.).
          Biblioteca Estense, Modena, Alpha F. 3. 3. (Ital. 410). Cf. Santoro, pp. 152-53 no. IV.

    (vi) (a) *Compendio di Mario Equicola in ordine alla casa da Este* (XVI cent.).
          (b) *Genealogia delli Signori Prencipi in Ferrara* Incomplete (XVI cent.).

(c) *Compendio* (XVI cent.).
ASMO, Archivi per Materie: letterati, b. 18.

(vii) *Genealogia delli Signori da Este* (XVI cent.).
BAV, Vat. lat. 13506.
Copied by Gabriele di Ferrari in 1527.

(viii) There are late copies of the *Genealogia* in the following libraries:
(a) Biblioteca Comunale Ariostea, Classe II. n. 349 (XVII cent.).
Genealogia delli Signori Estensi. The text continues until the year 1609.
(b) Biblioteca Municipale, Reggio Emilia (XVIII cent.).
Genealogia de' Signori Estensi.
(c) Biblioteca Romana Sarti, Rome, A. 43 (XVII cent.).
Genealogia delli Signori Estensi.
(d) BAV, G. VI. 168 (XVII cent.).
Genealogia delli Signori Estensi.

5. (i) *Annali della Città di Ferrara raccolto da Mario Equicolo di Alveto* (XVII cent.).
Biblioteca Comunale Ariostea, Ferrara, Classe II n. 355.
The work continues to the year 1582.

   (ii) *Cronaca ferrrarese* (1477-1557) (XVI cent.),
Biblioteca Comunale, Forlì, MSS Piancastelli I/46 (formely Cod. 384).

6. The dedicatory letter to Isabella d'Este in Demetrio Mosca's translation of Philostratus' *Imagines* (*Icone*) (XVI cent.).
Bibliothèque Nationale, Paris, Ital. 7757$^{3.3}$ (formerly Colbert 5198). Another sixteenth-century copy of this MS is to be found in Cambridge University Library (Add. 6007). For some discussion of this text see my «Further corrections and additions to the bibliography of Mario Equicola», *Aevum* 62 (1988) 310-11.

7. (i) *Libro de natura de amore* (autograph) (XVI cent.).
Biblioteca Nazionale Universitaria, Turin, Cod. N. III. 10.

   (ii) Spanish translation of *Libro* to be found in Biblioteca Nacional, Madrid (9095 [Aa64]) (XVI cent.).

C. EQUICOLA'S PRINTED WORKS

1. (i) *De Religione Libellus — Oratio dicta Papiae* [Ferrara: Lorenzo de' Rossi, not before 1498.] 4° (IGI 3710) (GW 9373).

   (ii) *Libellus in quo tractatur unde antiquorum latria et vera Catholica Religio incrementum sumpserint* [i.e. *De Religione Libellus*].
[Munich: Adam Berg, 1584] 4° (VSED E1853).

   (iii) *Oratio de laudibus trium philosophiae facultatum et legum Pontificiarum ac Caesarearum praestantia, cum paraenesis ad LL. studiosos* [i.e. *Oratio dicta Papiae*].
[Munich: Adam Berg, 1585] 4° (VSED E1854).

2. (i) *De Passione Domini Oratio.*
[Ferrara: Lorenzo de' Rossi, after 29 March 1499] 4° (IGI 3708) (GW 9371).

   (ii) *De Passione Domini Oratio.*
[Pavia: Giovanni Andrea de Bosco, Michele and Bernardino Garaldi, after 29 March 1499] 8° (IGI 3709) (GW 9372).

3. *De Mulieribus.*
[Ferrara: Lorenzo de' Rossi, after 8 May 1501] 4°.

4. *De Opportunitate.*
[Naples: Giovanni Antonio de Caneto, 11 February 1507] 4°.

5. *Pro Gallis Apologia. Iano Lascari.*
[Ferrara: Lorenzo de' Rossi, end of June — beginning of August 1509] 4°.

6.   *Ad Invictissimum Principem D. Maximilianum Sforciam Ducem Mediolani M. Equicoli viri doctissimi de Liberatione Italie Epistola.*
           [Rome: Marcellus Silber, 1513] 4°.

7.   *Marii Equicoli Olivetani Nec Spe Nec Metu. Dialogus ad Iulianum Medicem.*
           [Mantua: Francesco Bruschi, 27 November 1513] 4°.

8.   *Marii Equicoli in conservatione (sic) Divae Osanne Andreasiae Mantuanae Oratio ad D. Isabellam Estensem Mantuae Principem.*
           [c. 1515] 4°.

9.   *Marii Aequicolae de Bello Turcis inferendo Suasoria Prima/Secunda/Tertia.*
           [Rome? not before June 1519] 4°.

10.   (i)   *Chronica di Mantua.*
           [Mantua? after 10 July 1521] 4°.

      (ii)   *Dell'Istoria di Mantova libri cinque scritta in commentari... Riformata secondo l'uso moderno di scrivere istorie per Benedetto Osanna Mantovano.*
           [Mantua: Francesco Osanna, 1607] 4°.

     (iii)   Facsimile edition of (ii), Bologna: Forni, 1968.

     (iv)   *Dell'Istoria di Mantova libri cinque.*
           [Mantua: Francesco Osanna, 1608] 4°.

      (v)   *Dell'Istoria di Mantova libri cinque.*
           [Mantua: Francesco Osanna, 1610] 4°.

     (vi)   *Dell'Istoria di Mantova libri cinque.*
           [Mantua: Francesco Osanna, 1616] 4°.

11.   (i)   *Libro de natura de amore.*
           [Venice: Lorenzo Lorio da Portes, 1525] 4°.

      (ii)   *Libro di natura d'amore di Mario Equicola novamente stampato con somma diligentia corretto.*
           [Venice: Gregorio de' Gregorii, 1526] 8°.

     (iii)   *Libro di natura d'amore.*
           [Venice: Gioanniantonio & Fratelli de Sabbio, 1526] 8°.

     (iv)   *Libri di natura d'amore nuovamente stampato et... corretto.*
           [Venice: Francesco di Alessandro Bindoni & Maffeo Pasini compagni, 1531] 8°.

      (v)   *Libro di natura d'amore.*
           [Venice: Bindoni & Pasini, 1536] 8°.

     (vi)   *Libro di natura d'amore.*
           [Venice: Pietro di Nicolini da Sabbio, May 1536] 8°.

    (vii)   *Libro di natura d'amore. Ristampato e corretto da L. Dolce.*
           [Venice: G. Giolito de' Ferrari, 1554] 12°.

    (viii)   *Di natura d'amore. Di nuovo ricorretto et con somma diligentia riformato per Thomaso Porcacchi.*
           [Venice: G. Giolito de' Ferrari, 1561] 8°.

     (ix)   *Di natura d'amore.*
           [Venice: G. Giolito de' Ferrari, 1562] 8°.

      (x)   *Di natura d'amore.*
           [Venice: G. Giolito de' Ferrari, 1563] 8°.

     (xi)   *Di natura d'amore.*
           [Venice: G.B. Ugolino, 1583] 12°.

     (xii)   *Di natura d'amore.*
           [Venice: G.B. Bonfadino, 1587] 12°.

    (xiii)   *Di natura d'amore.*
           [Venice: G.B. Bonfadino, 1607] 12°.

   (xiv)   *Di natura d'amore.*
[Venice: L. Spineda, 1626] 12°.

   (xv)   *La Natura d'Amore. Primo libro*,
a cura di N. Bonifazi, Urbino: Argalia, 1983[1].

12.   (i)   *Institutioni di Mario Equicola al comporre in ogni sorte di rima della lingua volgare.*
[Milan (no printer's name), 1541] 4°.

   (ii)   *Introduttione di Mario Equicola al comporre in ogni sorte di rima della lingua volgare.*
[Venice: S. Boudogna, 1555] 4°.

13.   Translations of Equicola's works.

   (i)   *Pro Gallis Apologia*:
Apologie de Mario Equicola ou contre les medisantz de la nation françoise par Michel Roté.
[Paris: V. Sertenas, 1550] 8°.

   (ii)   *Les six livres... de la nature d'amour tant humain que divin... mis en françoys par Gabriel Chappuys.*
[Paris: J. Housé, 1584] 8°.

   (iii)   *Les six livres* etc.
[Paris: J. Housé, 1589] 12°.

   (iv)   *Les six livres* etc.
[Lyons: Veyrat, 1597] 12°.

14.   Prefatory Epistles etc. in

   (i)   *Epithome Plutarchi.*
[Ferrara: Laurentium de Valentia (Lorenzo de' Rossi), 1501] 4°.
now published in G. Resta, *Le epitomi di Plutarco nel Quattrocento*, Padua, 1962, pp. 78-79.

   (ii)   E.F. Rice Jr. *The Prefatory Epistles of Jacques Lefèvre d'Etaples and Related Texts*, New York and London, 1972, pp. 126-28, 130-31.

   (iii)   *Fratris Baptistae Mantuani Carmelitae Theologi ad Ptolemeum Fratrem Epistola Contra Calumniatores.* The epistle follows this work and serves as a general introduction to *Ptolomei Spagnuoli Apologia contra detrahentes operibus fratris Baptistae Mantuani.*
[Lyons: B. Lescuyer, 1516] Fol.
«Marius Aequicolus Ioan. Iacobo Bardellonio salutem» (fs. Cc3ʳ-Cc3ᵛ).

   (iv)   Ambrosius Flandinus, *Quadragesimalium Concionum Liber.*
[Venice, 1523] 4°.
«Marius Equicola amplissimo patri et Illustrissimo domino Sigismundo Gonzage Mantuano Cardinali Salutem» (f. bb4ᵛ).

15.   Undated work.
Iter in Narbonensem Galliam 4°.
[See p. 194 of the present work for dating: 1519-20 would be the most probable date].

16.   Inscription at the Spa of Giunone di Caldiero (Verona) for which see Santoro p. 207 and D.S. Chambers, «Federico Gonzaga ai bagni di Caldiero (1524)»*.

---

   [1] Sections of the *Libro* have been published separately. See, for example, P. Barocchi (editor), *Scritti d'arte del Cinquecento*, II, Milan-Naples, 1973, pp. 1613-1627 (vol. 1 contained a part of the *Institutioni*, pp. 259-60). S. Matton's edition of Diacceto's *De Pulchro Libri III* has the section on the Florentine philosopher found in the *Libro*, pp. 379-83.

   * *Civiltà Mantovana*, n.s., 4 (1984) 45-61.

C. WORKS OF UNCERTAIN OR DOUBTFUL ATTRIBUTION

1. *Novo corteggiano de vita cauta e morale.*
    [Venice? 1530?] 4°.
    This work is definitely not written by Equicola. See S. D. Kolsky, «Did Mario
    Equicola write *Il Novo Corteggiano?*» *Aevum*, 57 (1983) 416-27 and P. Cherchi,
    «Ritocchi al canone di Mario Equicola con atetesi del *Novo Corteggiano*», *Studi
    di Filologia Italiana*, 44 (1986) 209-222; 213-222.

2. *Epistola in Sex Linguis.*
    [Bologna: Benedictus Hectoris, after 21 November 1512] 4°.
    This is a work written *against* Equicola for which see C. Dionisotti, *Gli umanisti
    e il volgare fra Quattro e cinquecento*, pp. 112-30.[2]

---

[2] There are also a number of lost works to which Equicola himself alludes. A translation for Cardinal Ippolito d'Este is alluded to in a letter of 11 March 1508 (ASMO, ASE, C,
Ambasciatori: Mantova, b. 1):

> Ho comenzato ad fare vulgare il libro de messer Petri Monte. Credo che piacerà
> ad Vostra Signoria Illustrissima la quale supplico se digne commandarme et sia
> certa che anchora non habia scripto, ho facto optimo officio et farrò de conti-
> nuo.

In all likelihood, the translation was never completed. Equicola refers to a work on the Latin
language in item 14 (iii):

> Nos enim de ortu linguae latinae et ut altera facta sit ut in hanc quam vulgo loqui-
> mur veteris umbram paulatim longa oratione disputamus (f. Cc3^r).

The probable date of composition of this lost work would be the period 1507-8.
Equicola is known as a Latin poet for which some evidence does exist, particularly in the form
of poems inserted into printed works. These are published by Santoro. There are undoubtedly
other poems by Equicola scattered in manuscript miscellanies. One such poem is noted by P.O.
Kristeller, *Iter Italicum*, IV, p. 437. I have been unable to see this ode with a prose preface
to Federico Gonzaga.

Select Bibliography

Ady, C.M., «The invasions of Italy» in *The New Cambridge Modern History*, ed. by G.R. Potter, vol. 1, Cambridge, 1957, pp. 343-67.

Altamura, A., *L'umanesimo nel mezzogiorno d'Italia*, Florence, 1941.

Amadei, F., *Cronaca universale della città di Mantova*, I, II, Mantua, 1954, 1955.

Anderson, P., *Lineages of the Absolutist State*, London, 1974.

Andres, G., *Catalogo dei codici manoscritti della famiglia Capilupi di Mantova*, Mantua, 1797.

Antonelli, G., *Indice dei manoscritti della civica biblioteca di Ferrara*, Ferrara, 1884.

Ariosto, L., *Lettere*, a cura di A. Stella, Milan, 1965.

Ascari T., «Cantelmo, Sigismondo», *DBI*, 18, pp. 277-79.
— «Cantelmo, Francesco», *DBI*, 18, p. 264.
— «Capilupi, Benedetto», *DBI*, 18, pp. 528-30.

Asor Rosa A. (editor), *Letteratura Italiana*, Turin, 1982-.

Aurigemma, M., *Lirica, poemi e trattati civili del Cinquecento*, Rome-Bari, 1973.
— «Il gusto letterario di Mario Equicola nella prima parte del *De natura de amore* in *Studi di letteratura e di storia in memoria di Antonio Di Pietro*, Milan, 1977, pp. 86-106.
— «L'umanista Mario Equicola di Alvito» in *L'umanesimo in Ciociaria e Domizio Palladio Sorano*, Sora, 1979, pp. 39-59.

Bacchelli, R., *La congiura di Don Giulio d'Este*, 2 vols, Milan, 1931.

Bagolini, G., Ferretti, L., *La Beata Osanna Andreasi da Mantova, terziaria domenicana (1449-1505)*, Florence, 1905.

Ballistreri, G., «Capella, Bernardino», *DBI*, 18, pp. 468-70.

Bandello, M., *Tutte le opere*, a cura di F. Flora, 2 vols, Verona, 1952.

Baratto, M., «La vie culturelle en Italie au début du XVIe siècle: L'intellectuel et le prince», *Chroniques Italiennes*, 10 (1987) 37-66.

Barbaro, E., *De coelibatu, De officio legati*, a cura di V. Branca, Florence, 1969.

Bárberi Squarotti, G., «L'amore in corte: il trattato dell'Equicola», *Critica Letteraria*, 35 (1982) 211-24.
— *L'onore in corte. Dal Castiglione al Tasso*, Milan, 1986.

Barberis, W., «Uomini di corte nel Cinquecento tra il primato della famiglia e il governo dello Stato» in *Storia d'Italia. Annali 4. Intellettuali e potere*, Turin, 1981, pp. 855-94.

Barocchi, P., *Scritti d'arte del Cinquecento*, vols 1-2, Milan-Naples, 1971-73.

Becker, P.A., *Christophe de Longueil. Sein Leben und sein Briefwechsel*, Bonn and Leipzig, 1924.

Bedouelle, G., *Lefèvre d'Etaples et l'intelligence des écritures*, Geneva, 1976.

Bellonci, M., *Lucrezia Borgia*, Milan, 1960.

Belluzzi, A., and W. Capezzali, *Il palazzo dei lucidi inganni, Palazzo Te a Mantova*, Florence, 1976.

Bembo, P. (editor), *De Virgilii Culice et Terentii Fabulis Liber*, [Venice, 1530] 4°.

Benedetto, L. F., «Il *Roman de la Rose* e la letteratura italiana», *Beihefte zur Zeitschrift für Romanische Philologie*, 21 (1910), 191-95.

Bergamaschi, D., *Storia di Gazolo e suo marchesato*, Casalmaggiore, 1883.

Bertoni, G., *La biblioteca estense e la cultura ferrarese ai tempi del Duca Ercole I*, Turin, 1903.
— «Nota su Mario Equicolo bibliofilo e cortigiano», *GSLI*, 66 (1915) 281-83.
— *L'«Orlando Furioso» e la Rinascenza a Ferrara»*, Modena, 1919.

Bettinelli, S., *Delle lettere e delle arti mantovane*, a cura di L. Pescasio, Mantua, 1973.

Bianchedi, M. (ed.) *La figura e l'opera di Alessandro Luzio*, San Severino Marche, 1957.

Bianco Di San Secondo, E. *Baldassarre Castiglione nella vita e negli scritti*, Verona, 1941.

Bietenholz, P.G., Deutscher, T.B. (editors), *Contemporaries of Erasmus. A Biographical Register of the Renaissance and Reformation*, 2 vols, Toronto U.P., 1985.

Bigi, E., «Barbaro, Ermolao», *DBI*, 6, pp. 96-99.

Biondo, F., *Roma Triumphans*, [Brescia: Bartholomaeus Vercellenses, 1482]. Fol.

Boase, R., *The Origin and Meaning of Courtly Love*, Manchester, 1977.
— *The Troubadour Revival*, London and Boston, 1978.

Bolisani, E., «Tolomeo Spagnoli segretario alla corte dei Gonzaga filologo ed umanista», *Atti dell'Istituto veneto di scienze, lettere ed arti*, 118 (1959-1960) 11-51.

Bonora, E. (editor), *Accademia Virgiliana di Mantova. Convegno di studio su Baldassarre Castiglione nel quinto centenario della nascita, Mantova, 7-8 ottobre 1978. Atti*, Mantua, 1980.

Bonora, E., *Critica e letteratura nel Cinquecento*, Turin, 1964.

Bosio, V., *Francesco II Gonzaga marchese di Mantova*, Turin, 1938.

Brenzoni, R., *Fra Giovanni Giocondo Veronese. Verona 1435 — Roma 1515*, Florence, 1960.
— «Fra Giocondo», *Studi storici veronesi*, 14 (1964) 75-83.

Bridgman, N., *La vie musicale au Quattrocento*, Paris, 1964.

Brinton, S., *The Gonzaga. Lords of Mantua*, London, 1927.

Brown, C.M., «Comus dieu des fêtes... Allégories de Mantegna et de Costa pour le studiolo d'Isabella d'Este-Gonzague», *Revue du Louvre*, XIX, 1, 1969, pp. 31-38.
— with the collaboration of A.M. Lorenzoni, *Isabella d'Este and Lorenzo da Pavia. Documents for the History of Art and Culture in Renaissance Mantua*, Geneva, 1982.
— with the collaboration of A.M. Lorenzoni, «The Grotta of Isabella d'Este», *Gazette des Beaux-Arts*, Part I, 89 (1977) 155-71; Part II, 91 (1978) 72-82.
— Review of E. Verheyen, *The Palazzo del Te in Mantua*, *The Art Bulletin*, 62 (March 1980), no. 1, pp. 162-65.

Bullock, W.L., «A Cinquecento meaning of the word Romanzo», *PMLA*, 46 (1931) 441-49.

Burke, P., *Tradition and Innovation in Renaissance Italy. A Sociological Approach*, London, 1974.

Calcagnini, C., *Opera aliquot*, ed. A.M. Brasavola, [Basle: H. Frobenius & N. Episcopius, 1544.] Fol.

Calmeta, V., *Prose e lettere edite e inedite*, a cura di C. Grayson, Bologna, 1959.

Carbonara, C., *Il secolo XV*, Milan, 1943.

Carlini, L., *Girolamo Verità. Filosofo e poeta veronese del secolo XVI*, Verona, 1905.

Carpi, P., «Giulio Romano ai servigi di Federico II Gonzaga», *Atti e Memorie dell'Accademia Virgiliana di Mantova*, n.s., 11-13 (1918-20) 35-150.

Cartwright, J., *Beatrice d'Este, Duchess of Milan, 1475-1497. A Study of the Renaissance*, London, 1899.
— *Isabella d'Este, Marchioness of Mantua, 1474-1539. A Study of the Renaissance*, 2 vols, London, 1903.
— *Baldassare Castiglione. The Perfect Courtier, his Life and Letters, 1478-1529*, 2 vols, London, 1908.

Castagna, R., *Un Viceré per Eleonora Brognina alla corte di Isabella d'Este Gonzaga*, Mantua, 1982.

Castagno, G., «L'autografo del *Libro de natura de amore* di Mario Equicola», *Lingua nostra*, 23 (1962) 74-77.
— «L'autografo del *Libro de natura de amore* di Mario Equicola» in *Arte, pensiero e cultura a Mantova nel primo Rinascimento in rapporto con la Toscana e con il Veneto*, Florence, 1965, pp. 133-43.

Castiglione, B., *Il libro del cortegiano*, a cura di V. Cian, Florence, 1947.
— *La seconda redazione del «Cortegiano»*, per cura di G. Ghinassi, Florence, 1968.
— *Le lettere*, a cura di G. La Rocca, I, Milan, 1978.

Castrucci, G.P.M., *Descrittione del Ducato d'Alvito nel Regno di Napoli in Campagna Felice*, [Naples: C. Cavallo, 1686] 8°.

Catalano, M., *Vita di Ludovico Ariosto*, 2 vols, Geneva, 1931.

Cavicchi, F., «Una vendetta dell' Equicola», *GSLI*, 37 (1901) 94-98.

Cessi, R., «La cattura del Marchese Francesco Gonzaga di Mantova e le prime trattative per la sua liberazione», *Nuovo Archivio Veneto*, 25 (1913) 144-76.

Chambers, D.S., «The economic predicament of Renaissance cardinals» in *Studies in Modern and Renaissance History*, III, ed. W.M. Bowsky, Lincoln, Nebraska, 1966, pp. 289-313.
— «Federico Gonzaga ai bagni di Caldiero (1524)», *Civiltà Mantovana*, n.s., 4 (1984) 45-61.

Cherchi, P., «Ritocchi al canone di Mario Equicola con atetesi del *Novo corteggiano*», *Studi di Filologia Italiana*, 44 (1986) 209-22.

Chiappini, L., *Eleonora d'Aragona, prima duchessa di Ferrara*, Rovigo, 1956.
— *Gli Estensi*, Varese, 1967.

Cian, V., *Un decennio della vita di M. Pietro Bembo*, Turin, 1885.
— «Una baruffa letteraria alla corte di Mantova. L'Equicola e il Tebaldeo», *GSLI*, 8 (1886) 387-98.
— «Recensione a D. Gnoli, *Un giudizio di lesa romanità sotto Leone X* ecc.», *GSLI*, 19 (1892) 151-58.
— *Una giostra mantovana nel carnevale del 1520*, Turin, 1893.
— *Un illustre nunzio pontificio del Rinascimento: Baldassar Castiglione*, Città del Vaticano, 1951.
— «Pietro Bembo e Isabella d'Este Gonzaga», *GSLI*, 9 (1887) 81-136.
— «Recensione a F. Nitti, *Leone X e la sua politica* ecc», *GSLI*, 21 (1893) 416-21.

Nozze Cian-Sappa-Flandinet 23 ottobre 1893 (Al prof. Vittorio Cian per festeggiare le sue nozze... offrono gli amici O. Bacci, E. Bellorini, I. Carini ecc.), Bergamo, 1894.

Ciapponi, L.A., «Appunti per una biografia di Giovanni Giocondo da Verona», *IMU*, 4 (1961) 131-58.

Clough, C.H., (editor), *Cultural Aspects of the Italian Renaissance*, Manchester and New York, 1976.
— «Niccolò Machiavelli's political assumptions and objectives», *Bulletin of the John Rylands Library*, 53 (1970-71) 30-74.
— «The library of the Gonzaga at Mantua», *Librarium*, 15 (1972) 50-63.

Coccia, E., *Le edizioni delle opere del Mantovano*, Rome, 1960.

Cochrane, E., *Historians and Historiography in the Italian Renaissance*, Chicago and London, 1981.

Collenuccio, P., *Opere*, a cura di A. Saviotti, 2 vols, Bari, 1929.

Coniglio, G., «La politica di Francesco Gonzaga nell'opera di un immigrato meridionale: Iacopo Probo d'Atri», *ASL*, serie nona, I, (Anno 88), 1961, pp. 131-67.
— *I Gonzaga*, Milan, 1967.

Cortese, P., *De Cardinalatu*, in Castro Cortesio, 1510. Fol.
— *De Hominibus Doctis Dialogus*, a cura di M.T. Graziosi, Rome, 1973.

Cosenza, M.E., *Biographical and Bibliographical Dictionary of the Italian Humanists and of the World of Classical Scholarship in Italy, 1300-1800*, Boston, 1962.

Cottafavi, C., «Palazzo ducale di Mantova — I Gabinetti di Isabella d'Este — vicende, discussioni, restauri», *Bollettino d'arte*, 28 (1934) 228-40.

Crane, T.F., *Italian Social Customs of the Sixteenth Century and their Influence on the Literature of Europe*, New Haven, 1920 and 1971.

Croce, B., *Isabella del Balzo in un inedito poema sincrono*, Naples, 1897.

D'Amico, J.F., *Renaissance Humanism in Papal Rome*, Baltimore and London, 1983.

Dannenfeldt, K.H., «Egypt and Egyptian antiquities in the Renaissance», *Studies in the Renaissance*, 6 (1959) 7-27.

D'Arco, C., «Notizie di Isabella estense», *ASI*, Appendice II, Florence, 1845, pp. 205-326.

Davari, S., *Della famiglia Spagnuolo*, Mantua, 1873.
— *Notizie storiche intorno allo studio pubblico ed ai maestri del secolo XV e XVI che tennero scuola in Mantova*, Mantua, 1876.
— *I palazzi dei Gonzaga in Marmirolo*, Mantua, 1890 and 1974.
— *Federico Gonzaga e la famiglia Paleologa del Montferrato*, Genoa, 1891.

Debenedetti, S., *Gli studi provenzali in Italia nel Cinquecento*, Turin, 1911.

De Frede, C., *Studenti e uomini di leggi a Napoli nel Rinascimento. Contributo alla storia della borghesia intellettuale nel mezzogiorno*, Naples, 1957.

De Lollis, C., «Ricerche intorno a canzonieri provenzali di eruditi italiani del secolo XVI», *Romania*, 18 (1889) 453-68.

De Maddalena, A., *Le finanze del ducato di Mantova all'epoca di Guglielmo Gonzaga*, Milan, 1961.

De Montera P., *L'humaniste napolitain Girolamo Carbone et ses poésies inédites*, Naples, 1935.

De Nolhac, P., *La bibliothèque de Fulvio Orsini*, Paris, 1887 (reprinted Paris, 1976).

De Piacenza Di Nardò, R., *Opere (cod. per. F27)*, a cura di M. Marti, Lecce, 1977.

De Robertis, D., «La composizione del *De natura de amore* e i canzonieri antichi maneggiati da Mario Equicola», *Studi di Filologia Italiana*, 17 (1959) 189-220
— «Cammelli, Antonio, detto il Pistoia», *DBI*, 17, pp. 277-86.

Diacceto, F., *De pulchro libri III*, edidit S. Matton, Pisa, 1986.
— *Panegirico* (i.e. the *Panegirico allo Amore*), Rome: L. Vicentino, 1526. 4°.
— *I tre libri d'amore*, [Venice: G. Giolito de' Ferrari, 1561]. 8°.
— *Opera omnia*, [Basle: H. Petri & P. Pernam, 1563]. Fol.

Dickens, A.G. (ed.), *The Courts of Europe. Politics, Patronage and Royalty 1400-1800*, London, 1977.

Di Fazio, R., «Su alcune questioni riguardanti Mario Equicola di Alvito» in *L'umanesimo in Cicociaria*, Sora, 1979, pp. 131-33.

Di Napoli, G., *Lorenzo Valla: Filosofia e religione nell'umanesimo italiano*, Rome, 1971.

Dionisotti, C., «Recensione a *Un illustre nunzio pontificio*», *GSLI*, 129 (1952) 31-57.
— «'Lavinia venit litora': Polemica virgiliana di M. Filetico», *IMU*, 1 (1958) 283-315.
— «Appunti su Leone Ebreo», *IMU*, 2 (1959) 409-28.
— «Niccolò Liburnio e la letteratura cortigiana», *Lettere Italiane*, 14 (1962) 33-58.
— «Girolamo Claricio» in *Studi sul Boccaccio*, II, Florence, 1964, pp. 291-341.
— *Geografia e storia della letteratura italiana*, Turin, 1967.
— *Gli umanisti e il volgare fra Quattro e Cinquecento*, Florence, 1968.
— *Europe in Sixteenth-Century Italian Literature*, Oxford, 1971.
— *Machiavellerie*, Turin, 1980.

Doglio, M.L., «Le *Instituzioni* di Mario Equicola: Dall'*Institutio Prinicipis* alla formazione del segretario», *GSLI*, 159 (1982) 505-35.

Donesmondi, I., *Dell'istoria ecclesiastica di Mantova*, 2 vols, Mantua, 1612-16.

Dovizi, B., *Epistolario*, a cura di G. L. Moncallero, 2 vols, Florence, 1955-1965.

Elam, C., *Studioli and Renaissance Court Patronage*, unpublished M.A. report, Courtauld Institute, London, 1970.

Elwert, W.T., «Pietro Bembo e la vita letteraria del suo tempo» in *Storia della civiltà veneziana*, ed. V. Branca, II, Florence, 1979, pp. 281-307.

Ermini, G. (ed.), *Ordini et offitii alla corte del serenissimo Signor Duca d'Urbino*, Urbino, 1932.

Eubel, C., *Hierarchia Catholica Medii Aevi*, 4 vols, Monasterii, 1898-1935.

Faccioli, E., *Mantova: Le lettere*, II, Verona, 1962.

Fahy, C.F., *The Intellectual Status of Women in Italy in the Later Sixteenth Century* (unpublished Ph.D. dissertation, University of Manchester, 1954).

— «Three early Renaissance treatises on women», *Italian studies*, 11 (1956) 30-55.

— «The *De Mulieribus Admirandis* of Antonio Cornazzano», *La Bibliofilia*, 62 (1960) 144-74.

Fantaguzzi, G., *Caos. Cronache cesenati del sec. XV*, a cura del dott. D. Bazzocchi, Cesena, 1915.

Faraglia, N.F., «La casa dei conti Cantelmo in Popoli e il suo arredamento secondo un inventario del 1494», *Rassegna Abruzzese di Storia ed Arte*, 4 (1900) 3-33.

Fasano Guarini, E., «Modellistica e ricerca storica. Alcuni recenti studi sulle corti padane del Rinascimento», *Rivista di Letteratura Italiana*, 1 (1983) 605-34.

Fatini, G., *Bibliografia della critica ariostea (1510-1956)*, Florence, 1958.

Fava, D., *La biblioteca estense nel suo sviluppo storico*, Modena, 1925.

Fenlon, I., *Music and Patronage in Sixteenth-Century Mantua*, I, Cambridge, 1980.

Feola, R., «Cantelmo, Pietro Giampaolo», *DBI*, 18, pp. 272-74.

Festugière, R., *La philosophie de l'amour de Marsile Ficin*, Paris, 1941.

Ficino, M., *Opera Omnia*, [Basle: *Ex Officina Henrici Petrina* 1576]. Fol.

Fiera, B., *De Iusticia Pingenda*, ed. J. Wardrop, London, 1957.

Filangieri, R., «Una congiura di baroni nel castello d'Isola in vista di una seconda spedizione di Carlo VIII (5 Agosto 1496)», *ASPN*, n.s., anno 28, 1945, pp. 109-33.

Fiorato, A.C., *Bandello entre l'histoire et l'écriture*, Florence, 1979.

Firenzuola, A., *Opere*, ed. A. Seroni, Florence, 1958.

Fitch Lytle, G., Orgel, S. (editors), *Patronage in the Renaissance*, Princeton, 1981.

Flandinus, A., *De Animorum Immortalitate*, Mantua, 1519. Fol.

— *Quadragesimalium concionum liber*, Venice, 1523.

Floriani, P., *Bembo e Castiglione. Studi sul classicismo del Cinquecento*, Rome, 1976.

— «La 'questione della lingua' e il 'dialogo' di P. Valeriano», *GSLI*, 155 (1978) 321-45.

— «I personaggi del *Cortegiano*», *GSLI*, 156 (1979) 161-78.

— *I gentiluomini letterati*, Naples, 1981.

Frasso, G., «Petrarca, Andrea da Mantova e il canzoniere provenzale N», *IMU*, 17 (1974) 187-205.

Frizzi, G., *Memorie per la storia di Ferrara*, 5 vols, Ferrara, 1847-50.

Fubini, R., «Biondo, Flavio», *DBI*, 10, pp. 536-59.

Gams, P.B., *Series Episcoporum Ecclesiae Catholicae*, Ratisbonae, 1873-86.

Garin, E., *La disputa delle arti nel Quattrocento*, Florence, 1947.

Gasparini, G., «L'*Anteros* di Battista Fregoso», *GSLI*, 162 (1985) 225-49.

Gavagni, F., *L'unico Aretino*, Arezzo, 1906.

Ghinassi, G., «Arienti, Giovanni Sabadino degli», *DBI*, 4, pp. 154-56.

Giovio, P., *Illustrium Virorum Vitae*, Florence, 1551. Fol.

— *Lettere*, a cura di G.G. Ferrero, I, Rome, 1956.

Giustiniani, V.R., «Sulle traduzioni latine delle *Vite* di Plutarco nel Quattrocento», *Rinascimento*, 1 (1961) 3-62.

Gnoli, D., *La Roma di Leone X*, Milan, 1938.

— *Un giudizio di Lesa Romanità sotto Leone X*, Rome, 1891.

Goffman, E., *The Presentation of Self in Everyday Life*, New York, 1959.

Gorni, G., «Il rovescio del *Cortegiano* o le lettere del Castiglione», *Paragone. Letteratura*, 30, 354 (1979) 63-75.

Guarnera, E., *Bernardo Accolti. Saggio biografico-critico con appendice di documenti inediti*, Palermo, 1901.

Guidalotti, D., *Tyrocinio de le cose vulgari*, [Bologna: C. di Bazaleri, 1504]. 4°

Guidi, J., «Baldassar Castiglione et le pouvoir politique: du gentilhomme de la cour au nonce pontifical» in *Les écrivains et le pouvoir en Italie à l'époque de la Renaissance*, (première série), ed. A. Rochon, Paris, 1973, pp. 243-78.

— «De l'amour courtois à l'amour sacré: la condition de la femme dans l'œuvre de B. Castiglione» in *Images de la femme dans la littérature italienne de la Renaissance. Préjugés misogynes et aspirations nouvelles*, Paris, 1980, pp. 9-80.

— «L'Espagne dans la vie et dans l'œuvre de B. Castiglione: de l'équilibre franco-hispanique au choix impérial» in *Présence et influence de l'Espagne dans la culture italienne de la Renaissance*, Paris, 1978, pp. 113-202.

Gundersheimer, W., *Ferrara: The style of a Renaissance Despotism*, Princeton, 1972.

Halecki, O., «The defense of Europe in the Renaissance», in *Didascaliae. Studies in Honor of Anselm M. Albareda*, ed. S. Prete, New York, 1961, pp. 121-46.

Hay, D., «The Renaissance cardinals: Church, state, culture», *Synthesis*, 3 (1976) 35-46.

Hayez, M., «Cantelmo, Restaino», *DBI*, 18, pp. 274-75.

Heller, A., *Renaissance Man*, transl. by R.E. Allen, London and Boston, 1978.

Holzknecht, K.J., *Literary Patronage in the Middle Ages*, Philadelphia, 1923.

Houghton Jr., W.E., «The English virtuoso in the seventeenth century», *Journal of the History of Ideas*, 3 (1942) 51-72; 190-219.

Hutton, J., *The Greek Anthology in Italy to the Year 1800*, New York, 1935.

Hyde, T., *The Poetic Theology of Love. Cupid in Medieval and Renaissance Literature*, Delaware U.P., 1986.

Intra, G.B., «Degli storici e dei cronisti mantovani», *ASL*, 5 (1878) 403-28.

Iverson, E., *The Myth of Egypt and its Hieroglyphs in the European Tradition*, Copenhagen, 1961.

Kent, F.W., *Household and Lineage in Renaissance Florence*, Princeton, 1977.

Kent, F.W. and Simons, P., with Eade, J.C. (eds.), *Patronage, Art and Society in Renaissance Italy*, Oxford, 1987.

Knös, B., *Janus Lascaris: Un ambassadeur de l'hellénisme*, Upsala and Paris, 1945.

Koenigsberger, H.G., «Republics and courts in Italian and European culture in the sixteenth and seventeenth centuries», *Past and Present*, 83 (1979) 32-56.

Kolsky, S., «Italo Svevo and Mario Equicola: A strange encounter», *MLN*, 102 (1987) 128-40.

— «Culture and politics in Renaissance Rome: Marco Antonio Altieri's Roman weddings», *Renaissance Quarterly*, 40 (1987) 49-90.

— «'The good servant': Mario Equicola. Court and courtier in early sixteenth-century Italy», *The Italianist*, 6 (1986) 34-60.

— «Castiglione's biography: The courtier and the Italian princes», *Spunti e Ricerche*, I (1985) 1-34.

— «Did Mario Equicola write *Il Novo corteggiano*?», *Aevum*, 57 (1983) 416-27.

— «Further corrections and additions to the bibliography of Mario Equicola», *Aevum*, 62 (1988) 310-15.

Kolsky, S., «Theorizing Pleasure in the Renaissance», *Spunti e Ricerche*, 4-5 (1988-1989) 33-49.
— «An unnoticed description of Isabella d'Este's *Grotta*», *Journal of the Warburg and Courtauld Institutes*, 52 (1989) 232-35.
— «Women through men's eyes: the third book of *Il Cortegiano*», in *The Shared Horizon. Melbourne Essays in Italian Language and Literature in Memory of Colin McCormick*, ed. T. O'Neill, Dublin, 1990, pp. 41-91.

Kristeller, P.O., *The Philosophy of Marsilio Ficino*, New York, 1943.
— *Studies in Renaissance Thought and Letters*, Rome, 1956.
— *Iter Italicum*, London and Leiden, 3 vols, 1963-87.

Landino, C., *Formulario de epistole vulgare missive e responsive e altri fiori de ornati parlamenti*, [Bologna: *Angelo di Rugierii*, 1485] 4°.

Larner, J., «Europe of the Courts», (Review article), *The Journal of Modern History* 55 (1983) 669-81.

La Rocca, G., «Un taccuino autografo per il *Cortegiano*», *IMU*, 23 (1980) 341-73.
— «Reperti castiglionei. Due ignoti autografi letterari in lingua latina», *Gazzetta di Mantova*, 11 May 1979, p. 3.

Lauts, J., *Isabella d'Este, 1474-1539*, translated into French by G. Welsch, Paris, 1956.

Lazari, V., «Della zecca di Sora e delle monete di Piergiampaolo Cantelmi», *ASI*, n.s., 3 (1856), dispensa seconda, pp. 221-25.

Lazzari, A., *Un enciclopedico del secolo XVI: Celio Calcagnini*, Ferrara, 1938.

Lee, E., *Sixtus IV and Men of Letters*, Rome, 1978.

Le Goff, J., *Les intellectuels au moyen âge*, Paris, 1957.

Lemay, R., «The fly against the elephant: Flandinus against Pomponazzi on fate» in *Philosophy and Humanism*, ed. E.P. Mahoney, Leiden, 1976, pp. 70-99.

Leto, P., *De Romanorum Magistratibus, Sacerdotiis, Iurisperitis et Legibus ad M. Pantagathum Libellus*, (1490?) 4°.
— *Togatorum in Lingua Latina Facile Principis*, Paris (1505) 4°.
— *Francisci Philelphi Elegantes et Familiares Epistolae Pomponii Laeti ad Amicos Epistolae Aliquot Tersissimae. Eiusdem Vita Sabellico Autore* (1502) 4°.

Liebenwein, W., *Studiolo*, Berlin, 1977.

Lightbown, R., *Mantegna*, Oxford, 1986.

Litta, P., *Famiglie celebri italiane*, Milan, 1819-

Lorenzoni, A.M., «La vita e le vicende matrimoniali di Margherita Gonzaga, figlia naturale del marchese Francesco II», *Civiltà mantovana*, Anno XI, 63-4 (1977) 173-219.

Lowry, M., *The World of Aldus Manutius. Business and Scholarship in Renaissance Venice*, Oxford, 1979.

Luzio, A., «I preliminari della lega di Cambray concordati a Milano ed a Mantova», *ASL*, ser. IV, 16 (1911) 245-310.
— *Fabrizio Maramaldo. Nuovi documenti*, Ancona, 1883.
— «Vittoria Colonna», *Rivista Storica Mantovana*, I, 1885, pp. 1-52.
— «Federico Gonzaga ostaggio alla corte di Giulio II», *Archivio della Reale Società Romana di Storia Patria*, 9 (1886) 509-82.
— *I precettori di Isabella d'Este. Appunti e documenti*, Ancona, 1887.
— *La galleria dei Gonzaga venduta all'Inghilterra nel 1627-1628*, Milan, 1913.
— «Isabella d'Este e la corta sforzesca», *ASL*, 15 (1901) 145-76.
— «Isabella d'Este ne' primordi del papato di Leone X e il suo viaggio a Roma nel 1514-1515», *ASL*, 6 (1906) 99-180; 454-89.
— «Isabella d'Este e Leone X dal Congresso di Bologna alla presa di Milano (1515-1521)», *ASI*, 40 (1907) 18-97; 44 (1909) 72-128; 45 (1910) 245-302.
— «Isabella d'Este e il sacco di Roma», *ASL*, 10 (1908) 5-107, 361-425.
— «La reggenza d'Isabella d'Este durante la prigionia del marito (1509-1510), *ASL*, 44 (1910) 5-104.

Luzio, A., «Isabella d'Este di fronte a Giulio II negli ultimi tre anni del suo pontificato», *ASL*, 17 (1912) 245-334; 18 (1913) 55-144; 393-456.
— *Isabella d'Este e i Borgia*, Milan, 1915.
— *L'archivio Gonzaga di Mantova. La corrispondenza familiare, amministrativa e diplomatica dei Gonzaga*, vol. 2, Verona, 1922.
Luzio, A. and R. Renier, «Gara di viaggi fra due celebri dame del Rinascimento», *Intermezzo*, 1890.
— «I Filelfo e l'umanismo alla corte dei Gonzaga», *GSLI*, 16 (1890) 119-217.
— *Mantova e Urbino*, Turin, 1893.
— *La coltura e le relazioni letterarie d'Isabella d'Este*, Turin, 1903.
Maclean, I., *The Renaissance Notion of Women*, Cambridge, 1980.
Mantova e i Gonzaga nella civiltà del Rinascimento, Milan, 1978.
Marani, E., and Perina C., *Mantova: Le arti*, II, Verona, 1961.
Marani, E., «Una monografia sullo 'Studiolo' di Isabella d'Este», *Atti e Memorie dell'Accademia Virgiliana di Mantova*, n.s., 40 (1972) 113-135.
Marcel, R., *Marsile Ficin (1433-1499)*, Paris, 1958.
Marek, G.R., *The Bed and the Throne. The Life of Isabella d'Este*, New York and Toronto, 1976.
Marchetti, V., De Ferrari, A, Mutini, C., «Calcagnini, Celio», *DBI*, 16, pp. 492-8.
Marsand, A., *I manoscritti italiani della regia biblioteca parigina*, II, Paris, 1838.
Marti, M., «Tre studi su Rogeri de Piacenza di Nardò» in *Nuovi contributi dal certo al vero*, Ravenna, 1980, pp. 123-91.
Martindale, A., «The patronage of Isabella d'Este at Mantua», *Apollo*, 79 (March 1964) 183-91.
Martines, L., *Power and Imagination. City States in Renaissance Italy*, London, 1980.
Marzola, M., *Per la storia della chiesa ferrarese nel secolo XVI (1497-1510)*, I, Turin, 1976.
Mattingly, G., *Renaissance Diplomacy*, London, 1955.
Mayer, E., *Un opusculo dedicato a Beatrice d'Aragona, regina d'Ungheria*, Rome, 1937.
Mazzacurati, G., *Conflitti di culture nel Cinquecento*, Naples, 1977.
— *Misure del classicismo rinascimentale*, Naples, 1967.
— «Pietro Bembo» in *Storia della cultura veneta*, ed. G. Arnaldi and M. Pastore Stocchi, 3/II, Vicenza, 1980, pp. 1-59
— *Il Rinascimento dei moderni. La crisi culturale del XVI secolo e la negazione delle origini*, Bologna, 1985.
Mazzatinti, G., *Inventario dei manoscritti italiani delle biblioteche di Francia*, I, Rome, 1886.
Mazzoldi, L., *Mantova: La storia*, II, Verona, 1961.
Medici, G. de', Duca di Nemours, *Poesie*, a cura e con uno studio di G. Fatini, Florence, 1939.
Memorie e documenti per la storia dell'Università di Pavia e degli uomini più illustri che v' insegnarono, I, Pavia, 1878.
Meneghetti, M.L., «Dialogo, intertestualità e semantica poetica. Un esempio: Mario Equicola e la lirica provenzale» in *Il dialogo. Scambi e passaggi della parola*, a cura di G. Ferroni, Palermo, 1985, pp. 87-100.
Mengaldo, P.V., «Appunti su Vincenzo Calmeta e la teoria cortigiana», *Rassegna della Letteratura Italiana*, 64 (1960) 446-69.
Mercati, G., *Ultimi contributi alla storia degli umanisti*, Città del Vaticano, 1939.
Merlino, C.P., «Boccaccio in the works of Mario Equicola», *Italica*, 12 (1935), 142-45.
— *The French studies of Mario Equicola (1470-1525)*, California U.P., 1929.
— «Mario Equicola's knowledge of Dante», *PMLA*, 37 (1933) 642-47.
— «References to Spanish literature in Equicola's *Natura d'amore*», *Modern Philology*, 31 (1934) 337-47.

Migliorini, B., *The Italian Language*, abridged, recast and revised by T.G. Griffith, London, 1984.

Minieri Riccio, C., *Biografie degli Accademici Alfonsini detti poi Pontaniani dal 1442 al 1543*, Naples, 1881 [reprinted by Forni, Bologna, 1969].

— *Memorie storiche degli scrittori nati nel regno di Napoli*, Naples, 1844.

Miscellanea linguistica in onore di Graziadio Ascoli, Turin, 1901.

Monarca, G., *Agostino Nifo*, Latina, 1975.

Moncallero, G.L., *Il cardinal Bernardo Dovizi da Bibbiena, umanista e diplomatico 1470-1520*, Florence, 1953.

— «La politica di Leone X e di Francesco I nella progettata crociata contro i Turchi e nella lotta per la successione imperiale», *Rinascimento*, 8 (1957) 61-109.

Montanari, V., «La casa di Mario Equicola Castellano di Canedole», *Gazzetta di Mantova*, n. 151, 2 June, 1964, p. 3.

Morsolin, B., *Giangiorgio Trissino. Monografia d'un gentiluomo letterato nel secolo XVI*, Florence, 1894.

Moutsopoulos, E., *La musique dans l'œuvre de Platon*, Paris, 1959.

Mozzarelli, C., «Lo stato gonzaghesco. Mantova dal 1382 al 1707» in *Storia d'Italia*, diretta da G. Galasso, vol. 17, Turin, 1979, pp. 357-495.

Negri, P., «Le missioni di Pandolfo Collenuccio a Papa Alessandro VI (1494-1498)», *Archivio della Reale Società Romana di Storia Patria*, 33 (1910) 333-439.

Nelson, J.C., *Renaissance Theory of Love*, New York, 1958.

Neri, F., *Letteratura e leggende*, Turin, 1951.

Neri Pozza, (Editor), *Convegno di studi su Giangiorgio Trissino (Vicenza 31 marzo-1 aprile 1979)*, Vicenza, 1980.

Nicodemo, L., *Addizioni copiose alla Biblioteca napoletana del dottor Niccolò Toppi*, [Naples, Salvator Castaldo, 1683]. Fol.

Nitti, F., *Leone X e la sua politica*, Florence, 1892.

Nogara, B., *Scritti inediti e rari di Biondo Flavio*, Rome, 1927.

Ossola, C. (Editor), *La corte e il «Cortegiano»*, I, *La scena del testo*, Rome, 1980.

Orlando, S., «L'ideologia umanistica negli *Apologi* di P. Collenuccio» in *Civiltà dell'umanesimo*, a cura di G. Tarugi, Florence, 1972, pp. 225-40.

Palesa, A., *Dante: Raccolta*, Trieste, 1865.

Panofsky, E., *Studies in Iconology*, New York, 1967.

Pansa, G., «Francesco De Aristotile di Sulmona rettore dello studio di Padova ed i personaggi illustri della sua prosapia», *Rassegna Abruzzese di Storia ed Arte*, 4 (1900) 127-40.

Papagno, G., Quondam, A. (Editors), *La corte e lo spazio: Ferrara estense*, I, Rome, 1982.

Papaleoni, G., «Il codice ashburnhamiano-laurenziano delle poesie di Nicolò D'Arco», *Archivio Trentino*, 5 (1886) 219-50.

Paparelli, G., *Feritas Humanitas Divinitas*, Florence, 1960.

— «Umanesimo e paraumanesimo napoletano: Diomede Carafa precursore del Machiavelli e del Castiglione» in *Civiltà dell'umanesimo*, a cura di G. Tarugi, Florence, 1972, pp. 241-62.

Paratore, E., «Beroaldo, Filippo, Junior», *DBI*, 9, pp. 384-88.

Pardi, G., *Titoli dottorali conferiti dallo studio di Ferrara nei secoli XV e XVI*, Lucca, 1900.

— *Lo studio di Ferrara nei secoli XV e XVI*, Ferrara, 1903.

Paschini, P., «Una famiglia di curiali nella Roma del Quattrocento: I Cortesi», *Rivista di Storia della Chiesa in Italia*, Anno XI, 1957, pp. 1-43.

— «Una famiglia di curiali: I Maffei di Volterra», *Rivista di Storia della Chiesa in Italia*, 7 (1953) 337-76.

Pasquazi, S., *Umanesimo ferrarese*, Rome, 1955.
— *Rinascimento ferrarese*, Caltanissetta-Rome, 1957.
— *Poeti estensi del Rinascimento*, Florence, 1966.

Passerini, L., *Genealogia e storia della famiglia Rucellai*, Florence, 1861.

Pastore, R., «Carbone, Girolamo», *DBI*, 19, pp. 695-98.

Patterson Meyer, E., *First Lady of the Renaissance. A Biography of Isabella d'Este*, Boston-Toronto, 1970.

Pecci, B., *L'umanesimo e la «Cioceria»*, Trani, 1912.

Pedìo, T., *Napoli e Spagna nella prima metà del Cinquecento*, Bari, 1971.

Pedrazzoli, A., «La Marchesa Isabella d'Este Gonzaga a diporto sul lago di Garda colla sua corte», *ASL*, serie seconda, Anno 17, 7 (1890).

Pélissier, L.G., «Prêt et perte de manuscrits de la bibliothèque de Louis XII», *Revue des bibliothèques*, 3 (1893) 361-62.
— «Dépêches des ambassadeurs de Ferrare» etc., *Revue des bibliothèques*, 8 (1898) 239-45.

Percopo, E., Review of D. Santoro, *Della vita*, etc. in *Rassegna Critica della Letteratura Italiana*, 12 (1907) 224-27.

Pescasio, L., «Un enigma dell'editoria mantovana del Cinquecento. L'edizione del 1521 della *Chronica di Mantua* di Mario Equicola d'Alveto», *Gazzetta di Mantova*, n. 61, 4 March 1971, p. 3.
— «Il dialogo *Nec spe nec metu* di Mario Equicola», *Gazzetta di Mantova*, n. 121, 6 May 1971, p. 3.
— «La prima orazione ufficiale per la beata Osanna Andreasi», *Gazzetta di Mantova*, n. 142, 27 May 1971, p. 3.
— «Il viaggio d'Isabella d'Este attraverso la Provenza con Mario Equicola», *Gazzetta di Mantova*, n. 356, 30 December 1973, p. 3.
— *L'arte della stampa a Mantova nei secoli XV-XVI-XVII*, Mantua, 1971.
— *Parnaso mantovano*, 4 vols, Mantua, 1969-1972.
— «Per un ritratto di Isabella d'Este», *Gazzetta di Mantova*, n. 279, 8 October, 1961, p. 3.

Petrucci, F., «Per un'edizione critica dei memoriali di Diomede Carafa. Problemi e metodo», *ASPN*, quarta serie, Anno XV, 1977.

Pieri, P., *Il Rinascimento e la crisi militare italiana*, Turin, 1952.
— «La guerra franco-spagnuola nel Mezzogiorno (1502-1503)», *ASPN*, Anno 33, 1952, pp. 21-69.
— *La battaglia del Garigliano del 1503*, Rome, 1938.

Piromalli, A., *La cultura a Ferrara al tempo di Ludovico Ariosto*, Florence, 1953, (second edition, Rome, 1975).

Plautus cum Correctione et Interpretatione Hermolai, Merulae, Politiani et Beroaldi, (1500?). Fol.

Pontano, G., *I trattati delle virtù sociali*, edited and translated by F. Tateo, Rome, 1965.

Porro, G., «Pianta delle spese per l'Università di Pavia nel 1498», *ASL*, ser. 1, 5 (1878) 507-16.

Portioli, A., *Mantova a Vergilio (XIX Centenario)*, Mantua, 1882.

Pozzi, M., «Mario Equicola e la cultura cortigiana: appunti sulla redazione manoscritta del *Libro de natura de amore*», *Lettere italiane*, Anno 32, n. 2, April-June 1980, pp. 149-71.

Pranzelòres, A., «Niccolò D'Arco. Studio biografico con alcune note sulla scuola lirica latina del Trentino nel sec. XV e XVI», *Annuario degli Studenti Trentini*, 7 (1901) 3-118.

Praz, M. *Studies in Seventeenth Century Imagery*, 2 vols, London, 1939-1947.

Prete, S., «Humanism in fifteenth century Ferrara», *Thought*, 43 (Winter 1968) 573-85.

Prizer, W.F., Review of L. Lockwood, *Music in Renaissance Ferrara, 1400-1505*, *Journal of the American Musicological Society*, 40 (1987) 95-105.
— «Isabella d'Este and Lucrezia Borgia as patrons of music: The frottola at Mantua and Ferrara», *Journal of the American Musicological Society*, 38 (1985) 1-33.

Prodi, P., *Diplomazia del Cinquecento. Istituzioni e prassi*, Bologna, 1963.

Prosperi, A., (Editor), *La corte e il «Cortegiano»*, II, *Un modello europeo*, Rome, 1980.

Quazza, R., *La diplomazia gonzaghesca*, Milan, 1942.

Raimondi, E., *Codro e l'umanesimo a Bologna*, Bologna, 1950.
— *Politica e commedia. Dal Beroaldo al Machiavelli*, Bologna, 1972.

Rajna, P., «Per chi studia l'Equicola», *GSLI*, 67 (1916) 360-75.

Renier, R., «Per la cronologia e la composizione del *Libro de natura de amore* di Mario Equicola», *GSLI*, 14 (1889) 212-33.
— «Qualche documento di Publio Fausto Andrelini», *GSLI*, 19 (1892) 185-93.

Resta, G., *Le epitomi di Plutarco nel Quattrocento*, Padua, 1962.

Rhodes, D.E., «The early editions of Baptista Fiera» in *Book Production and Letters in the Western European Renaissance. Essays in Honour of Conor Fahy*, edited by A.L. Lepschy, J. Took, D.E. Rhodes, London, 1986, pp. 234-45.
— «A book from the Gonzaga library at Mantua», *Journal of the Warburg and Courtauld Institutes*, 17 (1954) 377-79.
— «A bibliography of Mantua, II, 1507-1521», *La bibliofilia*, Anno 58, dispensa 3, 1956, pp. 161-75.
— «Mario Equicola's *Chronica di Mantua*», *Gutenberg Jahrbuch* 1957, pp. 137-41, now in his *Studies in Early Italian Printing*, London, 1982, pp. 153-57.
— «Notes on Aurelio Pincio», *IMU*, 16 (1973) 403-408.

Rice Jr., E.F., «The humanist idea of Christian Antiquity: Lefèvre d'Etaples and his circle» in *French Humanism 1470-1600*, ed. W.L. Gundersheimer, London, 1969, pp. 163-80.
— «Humanist Aristotelianism in France. Jacques Lefèvre d'Etaples and his circle» in *Humanism in France at the End of the Middle Ages and in the Early Renaissance*, ed. A.H.T. Levi, Manchester and New York, 1970, pp. 132-49.
— (ed.) *The Prefatory Epistles of Jacques Lefèvre d'Etaples and Related Texts*, New York and London, 1972.

Richardson, B. (ed.), *Trattati sull'ortografia del volgare 1524-1526*, University of Exeter, 1984.

Rill, G., *Storia dei Conti D'Arco 1487-1614*, Rome, 1982.

Robb, N.A., *Neoplatonism of the Italian Renaissance*, London, 1935 and 1968.

Robertson, G., *Giovanni Bellini*, Oxford, 1968.

Rocchi, I., «Per una nuova cronologia e valutazione del *Libro de natura de amore* di Mario Equicola», *GSLI*, 153 (1976) 566-85.

Romano, R., «L'intellettuale nella società italiana del XV e XVI secolo» in *Tra due crisi: l'Italia del Rinascimento*, Turin, 1971, pp. 117-36.

Rosi, M., *Scienza d'amore. Idealismo e vita pratica nei trattati amorosi del '500*, Milan, 1904.

Sabbadini, R., *Storia del Ciceronianismo e di altre questioni letterarie nell'età della Rinascenza*, Turin, 1885.
— «Una satira contro Battista Pio», *GSLI*, 27 (1896) 185-86.

Saitta, G., *Marsilio Ficino e la filosofia dell'umanesimo*, Bologna, 1954.
— *Il pensiero italiano nell'umanesimo e nel rinascimento*, II, Florence, 1961 (second edition).

Sansovino, F., *Del secretario*, [Venice, *Altobello Salicato*, 1588] 8°.

Santagata, M., *La lirica aragonese. Studi sulla poesia napoletana del secondo quattrocento*, Padua, 1979.

Santoro, D., «Appunti su Mario Equicola», *GSLI*, 15 (1890) 402-13.
— *Della vita e delle opere di Mario Equicola*, Chieti, 1906.
— *Il viaggio d'Isabella d'Este in Provenza*, Naples, 1913.

Santoro, M., *Tristano Caracciolo e la cultura napoletana*, Naples, 1957.

Savino, L., *Di alcuni trattati e trattatisti d'amore italiani della prima metà del secolo XVI*, (vol. 10 of *Studi di letteratura italiana*, under the general editorship of E. Percopo), Naples, 1914.
— «Un precedente del *Cortegiano*», *Rassegna Critica della Letteratura Italiana*, 15 (1910) 102-22.
Savioli, G., «Dal convegno su Mario Equicola in Alvito», *Comune di Ferrara. Bollettino di notizie da archivi e biblioteche*, 2 (1980) 129-30.
Saviotti, A., *Pandolfo Collenuccio umanista pesarese del secolo XV*, Pisa, 1888.
Schizzerotto, G., *Cultura e vita civile a Mantova fra '300 e '500*, Florence, 1977.
Signorelli, G., *Il Cardinale Egidio da Viterbo (1469-1532)*, Florence, 1929.
Simar, T., *Christophe de Longueil, humaniste 1488-1522*, Université de Louvain, 1911.
Simone, F., «Fonti e testimonianze mantovane sulla civiltà francese del Rinascimento», *GSLI*, 154 (1977) 1-44.
Spagnuoli, B., *Primus (secundus, tertius) operum B. Mantuani tomus*, [Paris: *Praelo Ascensiano*, 1513]. Fol.
Spitzer, L., *Classical and Christian Ideas of World Harmony*, Baltimore, 1963.
Stadter, P.A., *Plutarch's Historical Methods: An Analysis of the «Mulierum Virtutes»*, Cambridge Mass., 1965.
Stäuble, A., «L'inno all'amore nel quarto libro del *Cortegiano*», *GSLI*, 162 (1985) 481-519.
— *La commedia umanistica del Quattrocento*, Florence, 1968.
Stephens, J.N., *The Fall of the Florentine Republic 1512-1530*, Oxford, 1983.
Storia di Milano, VII, Milan, 1956.
Storia di Napoli, IV, Florence, 1974.
Strozzi, T.V., and Strozzi, E. *Strozii poetae pater et filius* (their poems ed. by A.P. Manutius), [Venice: *In aedibus Aldi et Andreae Asculani Soceri*, 1513] 8°.
Sulpizio, G., *De Componendis et Ornandis Epistolis ad Philippum Gentilem Pallavicinum Patritium Genuensem Opusculum*, (Venice?, 1488?) 4°.
Summonte, G.A., *Dell'historia della città e regno di Napoli*, III, Naples, 1640.
Tenenti, A., *Il senso della morte e l'amore della vita nel rinascimento (Francia e Italia)*, Turin, 1957.
Tiraboschi, G., *Storia della letteratura italiana*, vol. 7, Florence, 1812.
Toppi, N., *Biblioteca napoletana et apparato a gli huomini illustri in lettere di Napoli e del Regno*, [Naples: Antonio Bulifon, 1678]. Fol.
Torre, A., Della, *Storia dell'accademia platonica di Firenze*, Florence, 1902.
— *Paolo Marsi da Pescina. Contributo alla storia dell'accademia pomponiana*, Rocca San Casciano, 1903.
Tournoy-Thoen, G., «La laurea poetica del 1484 all'accademia romana», *Bulletin de l'Institut Historique Belge de Rome*, 42 (1972) 211-35.
Trabalza, C., *La critica letteraria nel Rinascimento*, Milan, 1915.
Trissino, G.G., *Tutte le opere di Giovan Giorgio Trissino, gentiluomo vicentino non più raccolte* (ed. by the Marquis S. Maffei), 2 tom., Verona, 1729. Fol.
Ubaldini, F., *Vita di Mons. Angelo Colocci*, a cura di V. Fanelli, Città del Vaticano, 1969.
Valenti, F., «Note storiche sulla cancelleria degli Estensi a Ferrara dalle origini alla metà del secolo XVI», *Bollettino dell'Archivio Paleografico Italiano*, nuova serie, 2 (1956).
Valeriano, P., *De Litteratorum Infelicitate*, ed. Dom. Egerton Brydges, Geneva, 1821.
Vallese, G., *Studi di umanesimo*, Naples, 1972.
Vasoli, C., *Studi sulla cultura del Rinascimento*, Manduria, 1968.
— *La cultura delle corti*, Bologna, 1980.
Veblen, T., *The Theory of the Leisure Class*, London, 1924.

Venturi, A., «Gian Cristoforo Romano», *Archivio Storico dell'Arte*, 1 (1888) 49-59, 107-18, 148-58.

Verheyen, E., *The Paintings in the Studiolo of Isabella d'Este at Mantua*, New York, 1971.
— *The Palazzo del Te in Mantua*, Baltimore and London, 1977.

Verheyen, E., «Eros et Anteros. *L'éducation de Cupidon* et la prétendue *Antiope* du Corrège», *Gazette des Beaux Arts*, 65 (1965), 321-40.

Vial, S.C., «Equicola's *Di Natura* as a source of Montaigne's *Essais*», *Comparative Literature*, 15 (1963) 311-20.
— «Equicola and the School of Lyons», *Comparative Literature*, 12 (1960) 19-32.
— «Mario Equicola in the opinion of his contemporaries», *Italica*, 34 (1957) 202-21.

Vincenti, P., *Historia della famiglia Cantelma*, Naples, 1604.

Vitale, M., *La questione della lingua*, Palermo, 1971.
— «L'origine dei volgari romanzi e le ricerche linguistiche durante il secolo XVI», *ACME*, 6 (1953) 175-205.

Viviani, C., (Editor), *Intellettuali e potere. Storia d'Italia. Annali*, vol. 4, Turin, 1981.

Walker, D.P., *The Ancient Theology*, London, 1972.
— *Studies in Musical Science in the Late Renaissance*, Leiden, 1978.

Walker, J., *Bellini and Titian at Ferrara*, London, 1956.

Weber, M., *Essays in Sociology*, translated and edited by H.H. Gerth and C. Wright Mills, London, 1948.

Weinberg, B., *A History of Literary Criticism in the Italian Renaissance*, 2 vols., Chicago, 1961.

Weise, G., *L'ideale eroico del Rinascimento e le sue premesse umanistiche*, Naples, 1961.

Weiss, R., «Lineamenti per una storia degli studi antiquari in Italia dal dodicesimo secolo al sacco di Roma nel 1527», *Rinascimento*, 9 (1958), pp. 141-201.
— «In obitu Ursini Lanfredini. A footnote to the literary history of Rome under Pope Innocent VIII», *IMU*, 2 (1959) 353-66.
— «Augurelli, Giovanni Aurelio», *DBI*, 4, pp. 578-81.
— *The Renaissance Discovery of Classical Antiquity*, Oxford, 1969.

Wind, E., *Bellini's Feast of the Gods. A Study in Venetian Humanism*, Cambridge, Mass., 1948.

Woodhouse, J.R., *Baldesar Castiglione. A Reassessment of «The Courtier»*, Edinbugh, 1978.

Yates, F.A., *Giordano Bruno and the Hermetic Tradition*, London, 1977.

Zabughin, V., «L'insegnamento universitario di Pomponio Leto», *Rivista d'Italia*, 9 (1906) 215-44.
— *Giulio Pomponio Leto. Saggio critico*, 2 t., Rome, 1909 and Grottaferrata, 1910.

Zaccaria, V., «La fortuna del *De Mulieribus Claris* del Boccaccio nel secolo XV: Giovanni Sabbadino degli Arienti, Iacopo Filippo Foresti e le loro biografie femminili (1490-1497) » in *Il Boccaccio nelle culture e letterature nazionali*, a cura di F. Mazzoni, Florence, 1978, pp. 519-45.

Zambrini, F., *La defensione delle donne d'autore anonimo. Scrittura del secolo XV, ora pubblicata a cura di Francesco Zambrini*, Bologna, 1876.

Zapperi, R., «Calandra, Giovanni Giacomo», *DBI*, 16, pp. 427-31.

Zarri, G., «Pietà e profezia alle corti padane: le pie consigliere dei principi» in *Il Rinascimento nelle corti padane*, con una premessa di P. Rossi, Bari, 1977.

Zonta, G., *Trattati d'amore del Cinquecento*, Bari, 1912.

Index

Accolti, Bernardo (Unico Aretino), 108, 263.
Acquaviva, Andrea Matteo, Duke of Atri, 271.
Alexander VI, Pope, 82, 166.
Alexander the Great, 169.
Aliprandi, Bonamente, 252.
Andreasi, Beata Osanna, 103, 148, 150-152, 154, 240.
Aragona d', Don Cesare, 105.
Aragona d', Eleonora, 67-68.
Aragona d', Don Ferrante, 154.
Aragona d', Federico I, King of Naples, 48, 49, 84.
Aragona d', Ferrante, I, King of Naples, 26, 49.
Aragona d', Giovanna, 149.
Aragona d', Luigi, Cardinal, 128, 134.
Aretino, Pietro, 271.
Arienti, Sabadino degli, 67, 270.
Ariosto, Lodovico, 18.
   Orlando Furioso, 238.
Ariosto, Rinaldo, 186.
Aristotle, 73, 92, 99, 214, 253, 261.
Aristoxenus, 264.
Atri d', Iacopo, Count of Pianella, 69-70, 89, 232.
Augustus Caesar (Gaius Julius Octavianus), 101, 252.
Aura, Isabella d'Este's pet dog, 121.
Avalos d', Ferdinando, Marquis of Pescara, 14, 19-20, 185, 207.

Baese, Alessandro, 231.
Baldo, Antonio Augusto, 36.
Balzo del, Antonia, 25, 102.
Balzo del, Caterina, 49.
Balzo del, Isabella, wife of Federico d'Aragona, 25, 48-49, 50, 102.
Bandello, F. Matteo, 171, 193.
Barbara of Brandenburg, Marchioness of Mantua, 68.
Barbaro, Ermolao, 34-35, 92, 256, 271.
Becichemo, Marino, 171.
Bembo, Pietro, 17, 138, 246, 265, 270.
Bentivoglio, Annibale, 114.
Bentivoglio, Laura, 180.

Bentivoglios, the (family), 113, 114.
Bibbiena, Bernardo, 135, 160.
Biondo, Flavio, 54-55, 57, 163, 166.
Boccaccio, Giovanni, 73.
Bonaventura, Mario, 70.
Borgia, Jofré, Prince of Squillace, 82.
Borgia, Lucrezia, 69, 108, 125, 270.
Boschetti, Isabella, 146, 198.
Brogna [Brognina], Eleonora, 70, 136-137.

Caccialupi, the (family), 22.
Caccialupi, Battista, 22.
Caccialupi, Mario [Mario Equicola], 20, 22, 23.
Caesar, Julius, 140.
Calandra, Jacopo, 95, 96, 97, 121, 171, 217, 230, 232, 233, 234, 235.
Calcagnini, the (family), 81.
Calmeta, Vincenzo, 268-269.
Cantelmos, the (family), 18, 19, 20, 21, 23, 25-26, 40, 46, 47, 48, 50, 59, 60, 62, 63, 64, 67, 77, 78, 82, 83, 85, 86, 89, 92, 101, 108, 185, 239, 241.
Cantelmo, Cornelia, 75-76.
Cantelmo, Ercole, 60, 77, 101.
Cantelmo, Ferrante, 20, 48-50.
Cantelmo, Giulio Cesare, 21, 26, 41, 42, 50, 51-52, 56, 61, 64, 77, 82, 90, 239, 241.
Cantelmo, Margherita, wife of Sigismondo, 60, 64-65, 66-67, 69, 70, 72, 74, 75, 76, 77, 79-80, 81, 82, 83, 90, 93, 102, 106, 108, 245, 270.
Cantelmo, Pietro Giampaolo, 18, 19, 20, 21, 23, 25-26, 27, 38, 42, 46, 47, 48, 49, 52, 56, 61, 62, 109, 185.
Cantelmo, Restaino, Count of Popoli, 84.
Cantelmo, Sigismondo, son of Pietro Giampaolo, 20, 21, 43, 48, 50, 60, 61, 62, 63, 64, 66, 77, 78, 80-84, 85, 86, 87, 88, 90-91, 92, 101, 102, 107-108, 109, 113, 157, 183, 185-186, 204, 270.
Capella, Bernardino, 27-28, 29-30, 38, 41, 85, 181-182, 219.
Cappello, Francesco, 117.
Capilupi, Benedetto (Isabella d'Este's secretary), 118, 178.

Carafa, Diomede, 68.
Cardona, Ramos [Raimondo], Viceroy of Naples, 136-137, 143.
Castiglione, Aloisa, 237.
Castiglione, Baldesar/Baldassare, author of *Il Libro del cortegiano*, 13, 14, 16, 18, 75, 76, 88, 116, 127, 152, 224, 235, 237, 238, 244, 245, 246, 254, 255, 256, 257, 258, 260, 261, 262-263, 264, 266, 267, 268, 269, 271, 272.
Caterina, da Ferrara (one of the *donzelle*), 162.
Castrucci, G.P.M., 18, 21.
Catullus, 250.
Ceresara, Paride da, 59.
Charles V, Holy Roman Emperor, 168, 215, 220, 235.
Charles VIII, King of France, 20, 46, 48.
Chigi, Agostino, 126.
Cicero, Marcus Tullius, 18, 55, 60, 99, 139-140, 250, 261.
Citrarius, interlocutor of *De Opportunitate*, 99, 100, 101.
Cittadino, Girolamo, 193.
Clement VII, Pope, 224, 228, 234, 235.
Collenuccio, Pandolfo, 59, 141.
Colocci, Angelo, 248.
Colonna, Fabrizio, 125, 127, 128.
Colonna, Prospero, 137.
Colonna, Vittoria, 14.
Cornazzano, Antonio, 67.
Cortese, Paolo, 34-36, 45, 140.
Costa, Lorenzo, 105.
Cyrus, 167.

Da Bologna, Carlo, Mantuan treasurer, 230, 231, 232.
Da Fermo, Ludovico, 118.
Delia, one of Isabella d'Este's ladies-in-waiting, 14, 19, 207.
Delfino, Nicolò, 225.
Demosthenes, 250.
Diacceto, Francesco, 43, 44.
Diocletian, Roman emperor, 191.
Dovizi, Bernardo, da Bibbiena, 135, 160.

Egidio da Viterbo, 195.
Equicola, Mario, his works —
    Ad Invictissimum Principem... Epistola, 136.
    Annali di Ferrara, 174, 238, 244.
    Chronica di Mantua, 24, 39, 161, 165, 171-176, 187, 190-193, 200, 213, 237, 239, 244, 245, 248-249, 250, 251, 252, 271.

De Bello Turcis Inferendo Suasoriae, 110, 165-169, 181, 240-241.
De Mulieribus or *Perigynaecon*, 39-40, 42, 67, 69, 70-76, 88, 190, 241, 266.
De Opportunitate, 90, 97-101, 241, 246.
De Passione Domini Oratio, 51-52, 56, 59, 239.
De Religione Libellus, 51, 52, 53-55, 56, 57, 59, 239-240.
Divae Osannae Andresiae Mantuanae Oratio, 150, 152, 154, 240.
Epistola in Sex Linguis, 138.
Epithome Plutarchi, 41-42, 239.
Genealogia de li signori da Este, 39, 158-159, 174-175, 187, 238, 244.
Institutioni al comporre in ogni sorte di rima, 193-194, 263.
Iter in Narbonensem Galliam, 162-164, 194, 243-244, 252.
Libro de natura de amore, 15, 18, 24, 29, 42, 44, 46, 96, 112, 141, 142, 146-147, 174, 196, 208-209, 219-220, 225-226, 227, 237, 238, 244-246, 249-252, 253-269.
Nec Spe Nec Metu, 93-97, 100, 130, 139-141, 239, 241, 246.
Oratio dicta Papiae, 55-59.
Pro Gallis Apologia, 109-110, 166, 242-243.
Este, Estensi (ruling family of Ferrara), 39, 67, 101, 108, 113, 117, 135, 148, 159, 160, 174, 196, 241, 244.
Este d', Alfonso, Duke of Ferrara, 83, 84, 111, 113, 114, 119, 120, 121, 122, 123, 124, 125, 126, 127, 129, 130, 131, 132, 134, 135, 148, 150, 154, 155, 157, 158, 167, 174, 175, 176, 178, 180, 186, 187, 196-198, 199, 202, 203-204, 220.
Este d', Beatrice, eldest sister of Isabella d'Este, 131.
Este d', Ercole I, Duke of Ferrara, 48, 59, 66, 68, 81, 90, 91, 113, 159.
Este d', Ferrante, 129.
Este d', Giulio, 91, 111, 129.
Este d', Ippolito, Cardinal, 50-51, 52, 60, 86, 90-91, 92, 93, 97, 98, 99, 100, 101, 112, 113, 119, 123, 125, 157, 174, 241, 246-247.
Este d', Isabella, Marchioness of Mantua, m. Francesco Gonzaga, 13, 14, 18, 19, 30, 42, 59, 65, 67, 68, 69-70, 74-75, 76, 79, 86-88, 93-94, 97, 100, 101, 102, 103-107, 108, 109, 110-112, 113-116, 117, 118, 119, 121, 122, 123, 124, 125, 126, 127, 128, 129, 130, 131, 132-135, 136, 137, 138, 139, 141, 142-146, 147-150, 151, 152, 154, 155, 156, 157-158, 160, 161-162, 163-164, 173, 174, 175, 176-

177, 178, 179, 180, 182, 184, 187, 188-190, 191, 192, 195, 196, 198, 199, 200, 201, 202, 203, 205, 206, 207, 208, 209, 210, 211, 213, 214, 215, 216, 217, 218, 219, 220-221, 222, 226, 231, 232, 235, 239, 240, 241, 243-244, 245, 249, 264, 270, 271.

Este d', Lucrezia, wife of Annibale Bentivoglio, 114.

Eustathius, 105.

Farnese, Alessandro, interlocutor in *De Hominibus Doctis*, 36.

Ferdinand II, the Catholic, King of Spain, 97, 137, 154.

Ficino, Marsilio, 43-44, 45, 75, 92, 259.

Filelfo, Francesco, 36.

Flandino, Ambrosio, 243.

Folenghino, 130.

Fontana, Giovan Filippo, 232.

Foresti, Jacopo Filippo, 67.

Foschi, Tommaso, Bishop of Comacchio, 141.

Fra Lodovico, 230.

François I, King of France, 153, 168, 227, 228.

Gabbioneta, Alessandro, 27-28, 29, 41, 143, 148, 152, 181-182, 219.

Gadio [Gadius], Stazio, 95, 96, 97, 129, 194, 207, 232, 233.

Galen, 99.

Galilei, Galileo, 15.

Giocondo, Giovanni, da Verona, Fra, 63.

Gogio, Bartolomeo, 67.

Gonzagas (ruling House of Mantua), 39, 113, 146, 152, 161, 172, 173, 174, 181, 182, 190, 199, 235, 240, 244, 270.

Gonzaga, Alvise, 118.

Gonzaga, Eleonora, Duchess of Urbino, 108, 180.

Gonzaga, Elisabetta, Duchess of Urbino, 70, 108.

Gonzaga, Ercole, 2nd son of Isabella and Francesco, 116, 168.

Gonzaga, Federico, eldest son of Isabella d'Este and Francesco and successor to Francesco, 24, 112, 121, 128, 129, 141, 142, 144, 145-146, 147, 149, 153, 161, 162, 164, 167, 171, 172, 178, 179, 180, 181, 187-190, 191-192, 193, 195, 196, 197, 198, 199, 200-204, 205, 206, 210, 211, 212, 213, 214, 215, 216, 217, 218, 219, 220-221, 222, 223, 224, 225, 226, 227, 228, 229, 230, 231, 232, 234, 235, 236, 237, 244, 246, 270.

Gonzaga, Ferrante, 243.

Gonzaga, Francesco, Marquis of Mantua, 68, 69, 88-90, 91, 110, 112, 114, 115-116, 117, 118, 119, 126-127, 130, 132, 133, 134, 135

137-139, 143, 144, 148, 160, 161, 164, 167, 169, 171, 172, 175, 176, 177, 181, 183, 190, 199, 218, 224, 237, 245, 270.

Gonzaga, Francesco (Mantuan ambassador in Rome), 234.

Gonzaga, Giovanni, 180.

Gonzaga, Ippolita, 121.

Gonzaga, Luigi (founder of the dynasty), 190.

Gonzaga, Ludovico, Bishop of Mantua, 120.

Gonzaga, Ludovico, Marquis of Mantua, 68.

Gonzaga, Margherita, illegitimate daughter of Francesco, 126.

Gonzaga, Sigismondo, Cardinal and brother of Francesco, 176.

Gritti, Andrea, 117.

Grossino (Mantuan ambassador in Milan), 194.

Hadrian VI, Pope, 212.

Hannibal, 169.

Henry VIII, King of England, 168.

Hercules, 191.

Hermes Trismegistus, 57, 73.

Horace [Quintus Horatius Flaccus], 258.

Iaceto, Francesco (see Diacceto, F.).

Inghirami, Tommaso [known as Phaedra], 39.

Innocent VIII, Pope, 166.

Innocenza (one of the *donzelle*), 162.

Isabetta (one of the *donzelle*), 142.

Joan, Pope, 73-74.

Joshua, 167.

Juliana, Bernardino Capella's mother, 27-28, 29, 30.

Julius II, Pope, 117, 119, 125, 126, 127, 129, 130, 132, 134.

Landino, Cristoforo, 37.

Lascaris, Janus, 63, 92, 109-110, 222, 242.

Lautrec, 202, 216.

Lavagnola, Isabella (one of Isabella d'Este's ladies-in-waiting), 138, 142, 145, 146, 149, 201.

Lavinia (?), 21.

Lefèvre d'Etaples, Jacques, 91-92, 242-243.

Leo X (Giovanni de' Medici), Pope, 134, 135, 136, 148, 160, 165, 167, 181, 241.

Leto, Pomponio, 23, 29, 30-32, 34-35, 37-38, 39-40, 42, 69, 248.

Livia (one of the *donzelle*), 142.

Livy [Titus Livius], 23.

Longueil, Christophe, 29-30.

Louis XII, King of France, 62, 63, 66, 80, 82, 83, 84, 270.

Lucia (one of the *donzelle*), 142.
Lucullus, Lucius Licinius, 271.
Luzio, Alessandro, 13, 14, 15, 19, 185.

Machiavelli, Niccolò, 17, 136.
Maestro Abraham, doctor to Federico Gonzaga, 211, 229, 230, 234, 235.
Maffei, Count Nicola, 232.
Maffei, Raffaele, 34-35, 39, 163.
Malaspina, Guglielmo, 199.
Malatesta, Giovan Battista, 184, 196, 225-226, 246.
Malegnono da, Giovanni Antonio, suffragan archbishop of Milan 194.
Manuel I, King of Portugal, 168.
Marquis of Pescara, see Avalos d', Ferdinando.
Martin V, Pope, 28.
Mauro, Cesare, 98, 99.
Maximilian I, Holy Roman Emperor, 113, 148.
Medici, the, 132, 134, 136, 185.
Medici de', Alfonsina, 73.
Medici, Giovanni, see Leo X, Pope.
Medici de', Giuliano, 125, 130, 148.
Medici de', Lorenzo, Duke of Urbino, 73.
Mercurio (one of Equicola's servants), 230.
Monteolivetanus, Hieronymus, 151.
Moses, 73.

Negri, Francesco, see Niger, Pescennius Franciscus.
Nero [Lucius Domitius Ahenobarbus], Roman Emperor, 192.
Nicola da Verona, 232.
Nifo, Agostino, 98.
Niger, Pescennius Franciscus, 59.
Nonius Marcellus, 32.

Orsini, the (family), 85.
Otto, Count, 232.
Ovid [Publius Ovidius Naso], 140, 268-269.

Paleologa, Maria, 162.
Pallavicino, Antonio, 156.
Papirius Fragellanus, L., 18.
Pascal, Blaise, 34.
Pedoca, Tortorina (one of the *donzelle*) 142.
Perillo, Jacopo, 183.
Perlina, Margherita Cantelmo's pet dog, 66.
Petrarch, Francesco, 74.
Phaedra, see Inghirami, Tomaso.
Piacenza, Rogeri de, 48-49 (*Lo Balzino*).
Pico della Mirandola, Giovanni, 92.
Pincio, Jano, 226.
Pio, Battista, 51, 59, 104.

Platina (Bartolomeo Scacchi), 252.
Plato, 40, 58, 73, 92, 253, 261.
Plautus, 32, 35.
Pliny the Elder [Gaius Plinius Secundus], 172.
Plutarch, 70, (241).
Poliziano, Angelo, 140, 184, 271.
Pontano, Giovanni, 98.
Pope Joan, see Joan, Pope.
Preti de', Vincenzo, 162, 205.
Probus, Marcus Valerius, 30.
Prosperi, Bernardino, 196.
Prudenzi (family of Equicola's mother), 21.
Prudenzi, Cesare (Equicola's nephew), 231, 232-233, 234.
Pythagoras, 40, 58.

Quintilian, 261.

Renier, Ridolfo, 13, 17.
Riario, Raffaele, 38.
Ripa, Luca, 59.
Rossi, Lorenzo de' (Ferrarese printer), 239.
Rozone, Costanza, 70.
Rozone, 136.
Rucellai, Giovanni, 43.
Rucellai, Palla, 43.

Sannazaro (Sanazaro), Jacopo, 25, 63, 153, 183, 194, 195, 222.
Sanseverino, Antonello, Prince of Salerno, 48, 49.
Santoro, Domenico, 15, 16, 19, 20.
Sardi de', Gentile, 81.
Savorgnan, Maria, 270.
Scalona, Battista, 117.
Scipio Africanus Major, 200.
Scacchi Bartolomeo, see Platina.
Serafino Aquilano, 264.
Sforzas, the (Dukes of Milan), 113, 136.
Sforza, Galeazzo, 192.
Sforza, Ludovico, Duke of Milan, 51, 62.
Sforza, Massimiliano, Duke of Milan, 130, 131, 132-133, 136, 144-145, 149, 215, 222.
Silvestri, Francesco, da Ferrara, 103, 151.
Simonetta, Giovanni, 271.
Sixtus IV, Pope, 166.
Socrates, 58.
Soderini, Cardinal Francesco, 38, 45, 62, 63, 80, 134, 143-144, 179.
Solomon, 192.
Spagnuoli, Alessandro, 218-219.
Spagnuoli, Battista, 53, 59, 95, 97, 176, 241.
Spagnuoli, Tolomeo, Battista's brother, 160, 176, 181, 219, 237, 241.
Spinola, Giuliano, 134.

Strozzi, Agostino, 67, 70-74.
Strozzi, Ercole, 104.
Sulpizio, Giovanni (Verulano), 37-38.

Tebaldeo, Antonio, 94, 137-139, 141, 142, 153, 237.
Tebaldi, Tebaldo, 81.
Terence [Publius Terentius Afer], 140.
Theodosius I, 140.
Tiberti, Dario, 41.
Trissino, Giangiorgio, 208, 246, 251.
Trivigiano, Andrea, 117.

Uberti, Francesco, 41.
Unico Aretino, see Accolti, Bernardo.

Valerio, Carlo, 117.
Valerio, Giovanfrancesco, 117.
Valerius Soranus, Quintus, 18.
Valla, Lorenzo, 32.
Varro, Marcus Terentius, 32, 99.
Vectius Marsus, Quintus, 18.
Vida, Marco Girolamo, 184.
Vigilio, Francesco, 121.
Virgil [Publius Vergilius Maro], 23, 250, 252, 263.
Vitruvius [Marcus Vitruvius Pollio], 38.
Voscus, Antonius, 23.

Xenophon, 261.